SERMONS ON 2 SAMUEL

SERMONS ON 2 SAMUEL

CHAPTERS 1–13

John Calvin

Translated by Douglas Kelly
[*Reformed Theological Seminary,*
Jackson, Mississippi, USA]

THE BANNER OF TRUTH TRUST

THE BANNER OF TRUTH TRUST
3 Murrayfield Road, Edinburgh EH12 6EL
PO Box 621, Carlisle, Pennsylvania 17013, USA
*

First published 1992
ISBN 0 85151 578 9
*

Typeset at The Spartan Press Limited, Lymington, Hants
Printed in Great Britain by
St Edmundsbury Press Limited, Bury St Edmunds, Suffolk
and bound by Hunter & Foulis Limited, Edinburgh

Contents

THIS TRANSLATION
IS DEDICATED
WITH LOVE AND APPRECIATION TO
DOUGLAS F. KELLY II
MY FIRST-BORN

His testimony and his law
in Isr'el he did place,
And charg'd our fathers it to show
to their succeeding race;
That so the race which was to come
might well them learn and know;
And sons unborn, who should arise,
might to their sons them show . . .

PSALM 78:5–6
(SCOTTISH METRICAL VERSION)

Introduction

This is the first of a two-volume translation of the sermons of John Calvin on 2 Samuel. Included in this volume are forty-three sermons, approximately half of Calvin's 2 Samuel series. These sermons should be of particular interest to biblical expositors, since Calvin wrote no commentaries on the books of 1 and 2 Samuel.

Although John Calvin is most generally renowned as a theologian, biblical commentator and ecclesiastical statesman, there can be little doubt that his work as a preacher took as much, or even more, of his time, and was at least as influential as these other activities. When he first came to Geneva in 1536, his earliest official title was 'Reader in Holy Scripture'; he later became 'Pastor and Doctor in the Church'.

We are not certain how often Calvin preached or precisely what books of Scripture he may have expounded during his first Genevan stay. After his banishment by the Town Council of Geneva, he became pastor of the French Church in Strasbourg from 1538 to 1541, when he was recalled to be chief pastor in Geneva. At Strasbourg, Calvin lectured or preached nearly every day, and preached twice on Sundays. Among many other duties there, he preached through Romans, John's Gospel and 1 Corinthians.

After his return to Geneva in 1541, Calvin resumed his expository preaching by continuing from the verse following the one that he had preached on before his banishment in 1538 – the better to show the nature of his ministry as a mere servant of the Word of God written. From 1541 until his death in 1564, Calvin preached effectively and voluminously, apparently considering the pulpit as the heart of his ministry.

Upon his return, he seems to have preached twice on Sundays and once on every Monday, Wednesday and Friday. Then, in the words of T. H. L. Parker:

> In the autumn of 1542 some who appreciated his preaching urged him to preach more frequently, 'which I have already commenced and shall endeavour to do until the others have become more acceptable to the people'. But this proved too heavy a burden and after two months the council released him from preaching more than once a Sunday. In October 1549, however, sermons were ordered for every day of alternate weeks as well as twice on Sundays.
>
> His custom was to expound the Old Testament on weekdays, the New on Sundays, although sometimes he gave up Sunday afternoons to Psalms. We have little evidence as to what books he expounded or even what individual sermons he preached before 1549. Certainly he was preaching through Hebrews until August 1549, and it would therefore seem that he began that book in 1548. At some time probably between 1546 and 1548 he was expounding on Sunday afternoons the metricized psalms in the service book. Since he did not preach on Romans, St. John's Gospel, Philippians, Colossians and the Catholic epistles after 1549, we may conjecture that he preached on them earlier.[1]

It is much easier for us to trace the details of Calvin's preaching after 1549, for in that year the French emigrants to Geneva hired an able professional scribe, Denis Raguenier (who developed a system of shorthand), to take down, transcribe and bind in sets all of Calvin's sermons (usually around six thousand words in length). We refer again to Parker:

> And so we can trace him preaching on Sundays with one hundred and eighty-nine sermons on the Acts between 1549 and 1554, a shorter series on some of the Pauline letters between 1554 and 1558, and the sixty-five on the harmony of the gospels between 1559 and 1564. During this time the weekdays saw series on Jeremiah and Lamentations (up to 1550), on the minor prophets and Daniel (1550–52), the hundred and seventy-four on Ezekiel (1552–54), the one hundred and fifty-nine on Job (1554–55), the two hundred on Deuteronomy (1555–56), the three hundred and forty two on Isaiah (1556–59), one hundred and twenty-three on Genesis (1559–61), a short set on

[1]T. H. L. Parker, *John Calvin* (Lion Publishing: Berkhamstead, Herts., 1975), pp. 108, 109.

Judges (1561), one hundred and seven on 1 Samuel and eighty-seven on 2 Samuel (1561–63) and a set on 1 Kings (1563–64).[1]

By the time Calvin preached the 2 Samuel series (1562–63), which we have translated here, Denis Raguenier had already died (in 1560 or 1561), and a group of four different scribes took down the 2 Samuel sermons.[2] During this series Calvin followed the custom of preaching on the Old Testament on weekdays (including Saturdays). This 2 Samuel series goes straight through the text of 2 Samuel and consists of eighty-seven sermons (768 pages in the printed *Supplementa Calviniana* edition of H. Rückert). These sermons were preserved in the original French of Calvin, whereas the sermons on 1 Samuel (like the vast majority of his extant sermons) were translated into Latin before they were printed, and the French originals were thrown away.

The late Professor Rodolphe Peter has estimated that John Calvin preached some 4,000 sermons in his lifetime, and of these we possess nearly 1,500. Bernard Gagnebin explains how the majority of the manuscripts of Calvin's sermons were carelessly sold (by weight – for the mere value of the paper) by the library of Geneva in 1805.[3] Perhaps it was felt that what mattered was Calvin's commentaries, not the sermons, and in addition, the sermon manuscripts were not transcribed by Calvin himself and were difficult to read. At any rate, in 1823 some theological students of the French Monod family found several volumes of these sermon manuscripts (less than half of them), and returned them to their home in the Library of Geneva.

[1]Ibid., p. 109.

[2]Bernard Gagnebin, *L'Histoire des Manuscripts des Sermons de Calvin*, in *Supplementa Calviniana*, vol. 2, *Sermons sur le livre d'Esaie*, chs 13–29 publiés par Georges A. Barrois (Neukirchen Kreis Moers: Neukirchener Verlag, 1961), p.xviii. See also *Supplementa Calviniana, Vol. 1. Johannes Calvin, Predigten über das 2. Buch Samuelis. In der Ursprache nach der Genfer Handschrift herausgegeben von Hanns Rückert* (Buchhandlung des Erziehungsvereins Neukirchen Kreis Moers, 1936), pp. xxviff.

[3]Bernard Gagnebin, op. cit., pp. xiv–xxviii. See also the account in T. H. L. Parker, *Supplementa Calviniana: An Account of the Manuscripts of Calvin's Sermons Now in Course of Preparation* (London: The Tyndale Press, 1962).

These 2 Samuel sermons were not printed in the great *Corpus Reformatorum* (published at Brunswick from 1863 to 1897 by Baum, Cunitz and Reuss). They remained in their difficult-to-decipher, handwritten form in the library at Geneva until well into this century.

This is how matters stood until in 1936 Professor Hanns Rückert of Tübingen published the first *Lieferung* of his edition of the Series on 2 Samuel. The war interrupted publication, but Professor Rückert took up the task again after 1945 and had the satisfaction of bringing it to an end in 1961.[1]

Since that time (and especially since 1961), the *Supplementa Calviniana* have printed (in addition to the eighty-seven sermons on 2 Samuel), sixty-six on Isaiah 13–29, twenty-eight on Micah 1–7, twenty-five on Jeremiah 14–18 and two on Lamentations. Eight more volumes are planned in the *Supplementa Calviniana* series, to contain at least 370 more sermons (on Psalms, Easter, Pentecost, the Passion, 1 Corinthians, Acts, Ezekiel, Isaiah and Joshua). Most of Calvin's other sermons are found in the *Opera Calvini* of the *Corpus Reformatorum* (especially in volumes 8, 23, 25–29, 32–35, 41, 46, 54).

The vast majority of these sermons, which played such a large part in transforming much of northern Europe, have yet to be translated out of their original French and Latin into English. Some of these sermons, of course, have been available in English translation for centuries, such as those on Ephesians, 1 and 2 Timothy, Titus and Deuteronomy, which have happily been reprinted by the Banner of Truth Trust in Edinburgh in recent years.

Nearly forty years ago, Leroy Nixon translated three volumes of forty-seven selected sermons of Calvin from Job, Isaiah 53, the Gospels and Acts (published by Baker Book House, Grand Rapids). T. H. L. Parker retranslated these sermons on Isaiah 53 in 1956, and in his introduction very truly stated that: 'Nixon is usually so over-literal that it sometimes leads him into misinterpretation and nearly always makes the style creak'.[2]

[1] Parker, op. cit., p. 11.

[2] T. H. L. Parker trans., *Sermons on Isaiah's Prophecy of the Death and Passion of Christ* (London: James Clarke & Co., 1956), pp. 17–18.

In the late 1970s, Professor Benjamin Farley of Erskine College in South Carolina retranslated Calvin's sermons on *The Law of God* (also published by Baker Book House). In 1990 Blair Reynolds published in English translation two more volumes of previously untranslated Calvin sermons: *Sermons on Micah by Jean Calvin* (comprising twenty-eight sermons) and *Sermons on Jeremiah by Jean Calvin* (comprising the twenty-five extant sermons on this prophecy, from chapter 14 of Jeremiah to chapter 18). Both volumes were published in the series: *Texts and Studies in Religion* by the Edwin Mellen Press (Lewiston, N.Y. and Lampeter, Wales). The former is volume 47 of the series and the latter is volume 46.

In his *Oracles of God* T. H. L. Parker lists the early English translations of several of Calvin's selected sermons (generally, available only in good libraries).[1] So, although the situation is improving, most of Calvin's sermons are still not available to us in contemporary English.

I began this translation from the original French some twelve years ago with the encouragement of the late Professor Ford Lewis Battles, then of Calvin Theological Seminary in Grand Rapids, and of Professor John H. Leith of Union Theological Seminary in Virginia. I finished it approximately eight or nine years ago, but with the help of my good wife and many others, have revised it three or four times since then. Throughout, my desire has been constant: first of all to be absolutely faithful to what Calvin actually said, and secondly to turn it into as normal and non-stilted, 'non-translationese' English as is consistent with strict fidelity to the original text. When faced with the choice of either being literally correct but awkward, or on the other hand, attractive but only loosely connected to the original text, I have consistently chosen the former, although not without struggling as hard as I could to 'make the crooked straight and the rough places plain'. Others will have to judge how successful I have been.

It may be asked why the sermons on 2 Samuel have been selected first, rather than those on 1 Samuel (which, of course,

[1]T. H. L. Parker, *The Oracles of God* (London & Redhill: Lutterworth Press, 1947), pp. 169, 170.

were preached earlier). The reason is strictly personal: I preferred to work with French rather than Latin. In 1982, however, I did translate one of the 1 Samuel sermons from Latin into English, which was then published.[1]

It is sincerely hoped that this first translation into English of the first half of Calvin's *Sermons on 2 Samuel* will not only be of historical interest to Reformation scholars but far more that it will enrich the life of the contemporary pulpit and pew by giving access to one of the very finest expository and applicatory models of faithful and fruitful handling of an Old Testament book – one that preachers have not always found so easy to preach through with profit to their people.

A careful reading of Calvin on 2 Samuel may well set the preacher's heart aglow with passion to communicate the truth of the triumphant grace of the covenant-keeping God to sinful men and women whom he calls to himself in order to turn them into his instruments of spiritual transformation for their own generation and for those to come. Perhaps above all else, these sermons can communicate a serene, trusting spirit to steady the hearts and move forward the feet of those who feel most keenly their own weakness and the frailty of the Church in face of the most rampant evils of the day.

To all who are ever tempted to draw back and give up the fight against the fearsome forces that the New Testament ultimately identifies as 'the world, the flesh and the devil', Calvin's 2 Samuel sermons bring strong, healing words of counsel. He abounds in such relevant words as the following:

What would happen if the wicked – and even the devil, who is their father – could do something by themselves without the express permission of God? What would our condition be like? Here we are surrounded by so many thieves and all sorts of people just seeking to devour us . . . If, therefore, the devil were not held in control, and all the wicked were not governed by the counsel and the secret and incomprehensible power of God, where would we be? Thus, let us realise that whenever the wicked are in control over us, and trouble us, although

[1] 'Calvin's XXXIX Sermon on First Samuel (1 Samuel 8:11–22)', in *Calvin Studies: Papers Presented at a Colloquium on Calvin Studies at Davidson College Presbyterian Church and Davidson College* (Davidson, North Carolina, March 19–20, 1982), pp. 66–77.

they do it unjustly, God is still in charge of it, and we must return to that fact. For we will never know how to profit from it, although we endure it, unless we hold to this principle. That is, though the wicked are pursuing their disordered lusts, yet God is guiding them nevertheless . . . God does not fail to exercise his justice in such a way that the evil is turned into good. That is to say, as far as he is concerned, he knows how to use evil beyond our thoughts, so that he converts it into good – that is, to a good end – in such a way that he will not only always remain just, but we shall have occasion, all the time of our life, to glorify him everywhere, in every way.[1]

Ultimately these sermons of Calvin will strengthen our flagging spirits to the renewed thrill of obedience because they force us to contemplate the 'admirable providence of God', not as a dark, impersonal activity, but in the loving face of the Lord Jesus Christ:

In our Lord Jesus Christ 'are hidden all the treasures of wisdom', so that we may come to him.

Thus, since the fullness of the Spirit of wisdom and understanding rests upon him, let us not doubt that he possesses it totally so that he can distribute it to us in the measure that he knows is useful for us . . . and we will be satisfied – particularly when, in all humility, we ask only to be disciples of God and our Lord Jesus Christ. Let us ask that he would give us sufficient guidance that we may never fall short in any duty.[2]

In a word, painstakingly careful and fair as he is to the historical context of the reigns of the judges and early kings of Israel, Calvin can never keep you long in the presence of Saul and Abner, Samuel and Jonathan, David and Bathsheba, Nathan and Solomon without introducing you to Another. If you will read these sermons prayerfully, Calvin will take your hand and place it in the hands of the One whose Word and Spirit were already preparing his Old Testament saints to reach forward to him who held them and holds us:

Therefore, let us learn to follow the voice of this eternal Shepherd, that is, our Lord Jesus Christ. Let us learn to put ourselves entirely in his hand and under his leading and let us be submissive to him so that he might enjoy us. It is certain that 'we will want nothing' (Psa. 23:1)

[1]Sermon 36, pp. 547–8.
[2]Sermon 4, p. 32.

that he will provide us with everything that he knows we need for our salvation.[1]

It is appropriate here for me to acknowledge the deep debt I owe to so many who have helped me one way or another for more than a decade with this project. My wife, Caroline, has done more than anyone else to help me work through, rework, and then rework again, the English phraseology of this long translation. Many others have made helpful suggestions in this process: the late S. M. Houghton of the Banner of Truth Trust, Professor Sinclair B. Ferguson of Westminster Seminary, Robert Lucas of Greenwood, Mississippi, and his mother Mrs John Fair Lucas, and my cousin Cary L. McLeod of North Carolina. Dr Ross MacKenzie, then Professor in Union Seminary, Richmond, generously took time with me to work through various translation problems when I first started. Mr Steve Wilburn of New York also gave me helpful critique in the early stages of my work. Dr Michael Brown and Mr James A. Atkins, both of Dillon, South Carolina, read over some of the translated sermons for style and comprehensibility.

Mrs Maude Rogers and her daughter Linda, of Marion, South Carolina, did the original typing of the manuscript, which was paid for by a generous grant from Dr R. J. Rushdoony of Chalcedon Foundation. Later, Mrs Rosemary Finnie of Southampton retyped the emended edition, and most recently, Dr Richard S. Alderson of London has diligently worked over the entire material, much to its improvement. I thank them all.

In the early days of this project, the Session of the First Presbyterian Church of Dillon, South Carolina, on several occasions allowed me time off to work on it, and I am ever grateful to them and to the congregation we served together. I did part of the work in the Presbyterian Historical Foundation of Montreat, North Carolina, whose staff always made my stay pleasant. The late Mrs Fred J. Hay and Dr and Mrs John Akers opened their Montreat homes to me and my family over and over again through the summers and Januaries when I

[1]Sermon 12, p. 178.

pursued much of this translation work in the beauty of the Appalachian Mountains.

My wife and I did considerable revision work during the summers of 1985 and 1986 when I was teaching on the staff of the Presbyterian Theological College of Melbourne in Australia. Professor Alan Harman was of constant help to us there, as was Dr Sally Hare, in whose happy home all seven of us stayed. Mrs Anne Neill and Mrs Philippa Thorne frequently baby-sat for us during those summers to set us free to revise these translations, with which we were somehow never satisfied. Our gratitude to these and other Christian friends in Victoria is deep and lasting.

Dr Luder Whitlock, President of the Reformed Theological Seminary in Jackson, has been of great encouragement in this work, as have many of his fine staff. The Rev Iain Murray, Editor of the Banner of Truth, has gently and skilfully guided me in many helpful ways over the last five or six years. Mr Peter De Klerk, formerly librarian of the Calvin Theological Seminary, kindly copied out hundreds of pages of *Supplementa Calviniana* for me and mailed them to my Dillon manse. He has done much to further Calvin studies across the world.

Many others have given me encouragement or rendered valuable assistance. Indeed, if I were to list only those whom I *know* to have faithfully prayed for matters relating to the project their names would fill several pages. But perhaps such names are best left where they are properly recorded: in the account books above.

I close this introduction with thankfulness to the Lord for his enabling and for the incomparable friends whom he has given me.

Douglas F. Kelly
Jackson, Mississippi.

I

*On Facing Affliction and Divine Judgement**

It came to pass after the death of Saul, that after David returned from destroying the Amalekites, he stayed two days in Ziklag. On the third day, a man arrived from the army of Saul with his clothes torn and dirt upon his head. Coming up to David he bowed himself to the ground and feigned reverence . . . (2 Sam. 1:1–16).

There was only one way for David to be able to relax his guard and that was for him to know that Saul was dead. For it was while Saul was alive that David had first been banished from the land of Israel. After that, his life was in continual peril, so he lived in a nation where he was not welcome. He was suspect there, and from one day to the next could be sought out and accused if anyone wished to catch him and his people. He was, thus, in a miserable and perplexing situation and would be a fugitive until God removed Saul from the world. Yet when this did happen, David began mourning, and the death of Saul was harder for him to bear than his own death. This was not because of Saul himself, but because of the consequences. For the people of God were so disastrously defeated that it seemed as though the worship of God would be abolished. It is quite certain that the well-being of the Church was more precious to David than his own life. So when it seemed that God wished to give him relief, it was then, in fact, that he became even more distressed. Thus, we can see how God exercised him in all sorts of conditions, which provides an example for us.

*Saturday, May 23, 1562.

Let us remember this at times when the Lord multiplies our sadness. For we may be expecting him to reassure us. Indeed, he may give us the opportunity to feel his grace, and yet at the same time we may have the opposite experience of being angered and frustrated. Since this has already happened to David, we will by no means find it a new experience. So when God does not put an end to our distress and anxieties, we will not complain at all. In fact, when he withdraws one perplexity from us, he sends something else on us from which we were desperately fleeing! Thus, our faith and our patience have to be tried in various conditions. Let us humble ourselves, and submit ourselves to what God knows to be just and expedient. Above all, let us benefit from the example of David, so that we will not be dismayed when we experience what God was doing in him.

The text says, 'On the third day, having returned from the destruction of the Amalekites', news was brought to David of the death of Saul (2 Sam. 1:1–4). The victory that he had won was intended to cause him to give thanks and praise to God. We have seen[1] how he did not keep the booty, but sent it to his friends in the country of Judah who had helped him in his troubles (1 Sam. 30:26). This was a great opportunity for David to praise God for prospering him. But suddenly, here was a message which turned his joy into sorrow. With these things in mind, let us contemplate how easily our life can change. Any time God blesses us, let us be prepared also to accept the reverse, that is, all the afflictions with which he wants to test us. Even pagans have been well able to demonstrate this lesson, and have lived by it: namely, that a man should never fail to remember that a hundred different situations with a thousand sorts of annoyances and distresses can happen to us. That is how our joys are often tempered, as if we were pouring water in our wine. We see, for instance, that those who drink too much come to grief, even though God gave them what they wanted. They enjoy themselves to the point of getting drunk, like a man who has found good wine, and does

[1] A reference to Calvin's earlier sermons on 1 Samuel.

not drink it moderately nor merely for his health, but over-indulges to such an extent that he is out of his senses. It is the same with people who enjoy themselves too much when they are prospering. That is the reason God chastises them, and why he sends them affliction when they abuse his grace in this way.

What, then, are we to do? When we think that we are besieged by infinite dangers, as I have mentioned, and feel that even if we have escaped from one affliction, there are a thousand others which may smother us, and that an infinite number of things may happen to us, here is how we can control ourselves. Let us not fail to give God thanks for his blessings to us, even when we feel like expressing our fears. Let us not allow our spirits to wander aimlessly about, but rather let us be prepared ahead of time for any afflictions which God may send us. That will help us to bear them all the more patiently when they come.

That is what we must learn from the example which is given to us here. David had recovered his wives. After that, he won a great quantity of spoil from his enemies, and everyone who was in his company made themselves rich in one day. Well, two days had been spent in this business. But the third day brought them news of the defeat of the people of Israel (2 Sam. 1:2). Thus, when God has given us cause to rejoice – whether for a day or a month – let us learn to accept any trial which he chooses to test us. And let us carefully note the example that we have of Job, who said, 'If we receive good from the hand of the Lord, then why should we not also receive evil from him?' (Job 2:10). By saying this, Job teaches us not to think that because God blesses us and treats us kindly at one time, he is therefore always obliged to do so. Instead, let us realise that God moves us from one side to the other so that we cannot relax and fall asleep in our dullness and stupidity. For we need to be continually tried, because our senses are too attached to this world; and we wish to make our own paradise on earth as though there were no blessedness greater than that! That is why God subjects us to so many changes, and causes us to be cast from one side to the other and thrown about hither and thither, so to speak. Let us think carefully about this.

Now it is stated that a 'young Amalekite came before them, with clothes torn and dirt thrown on his head' (2 Sam. 1:2). When David asked him, 'Where have you come from?' he answered that he was an Amalekite, of the nation which David had defeated earlier, but that he had been reared among the people of Israel, and had followed Saul's army. He said that he had 'happened by chance' to go where Saul was lying half dead. Saul had commanded him to deliver the *coup de grâce*, so that he would not fall into the hands of his enemies. Then, in order to please David, the Amalekite presented to him 'the crown which he took from Saul, and his bracelets' (2 Sam. 1:10). (Bracelets were fashionable ornaments in that country at that time.)

Now the young man's story seemed very likely, and it was confirmed when he presented Saul's crown and bracelets to David. These insignia proved that Saul was dead, but they did not prove that the young man had killed him. Indeed, it is more likely that he lied, that he was boasting of something that was not true. This is how we take the words of David: 'Your blood be upon you, in that you have testified that you have killed the anointed of the Lord' (2 Sam. 1:16). David would not have chosen to express it like this if he had not perceived that his boasting was false. That is why David said that his blood would be on his own head. But it is not necessary to worry ourselves a great deal on this point; it is enough for us to remember the principle.

The reference to the young man whose garments were torn was intended to show the custom common in that country. Whenever people were in mourning or had some terrible experience, they tore their clothes. That would be a bit excessive among us, but each nation has its customs, and the Eastern countries were more inclined to ostentatious ceremonies than we are. We would not consider this kind of thing praiseworthy today. If we were to tear our clothes in pieces and take ourselves by the hair and tear out our beards like the pagans do, it would be wicked and would certainly be an unnatural way to treat ourselves. Yet one does see some nations which carry on such a fanfare! They seem totally unable to demonstrate their affection except by some melodramatic sign. And that was the common custom then.

Moreover, 'to throw dust on the head' (2 Sam. 1:2) had another reason besides that one. It was a sign of humility. When people were affected by a genuine apprehension of the wrath of God, they immediately confessed their offences and threw dust on their heads. This bore witness that they were not fit to live in the world, that the earth ought to open to swallow them up and that they judged themselves deserving of death. All this was involved in their confession, and that is what this ceremony signified. It was approved by God. Even the holy fathers used it for a good purpose. Hence, this young man was doing what he had seen, but there was more pretence on his part, because he was a foreigner without fear of God and without religion. He thus went through the motions of repentance without having a single drop of it. We see this pretence still carried on by the papacy on 'Ash Wednesday', as they call it, when they put ashes on their foreheads in order to show that they are nothing but dust. They want to appear to carry out their duty faithfully in this matter, but in fact they are pitting themselves against God and despising him. Thus, they do the very opposite of what the sign portrays, which is how it was with this young Amalekite. David then interrogated him, and his reply resulted in his own well-deserved condemnation (2 Sam. 1:13–16).

We must consider here precisely why David should have grieved over the death of Saul, for it would seem, at first sight, that he should not have been grieved so much since this was the only way he had of saving his life. Moreover, he had seen how totally incorrigible Saul had been every time he had tried to counsel him. He had always found him disloyal and so cruel that he had reached a state of rebellion from which it was impossible to reclaim him (1 Sam. 19; 20; 24; 26). Granted that there was no hope for Saul, it surely seems that David ought to have let him be – considering that God had obliterated him from this world – and ought to have rejoiced in the death of the one who was preventing the establishment of what God had ordained. We have seen earlier how often David could have killed him, but how he refrained out of reverence for God's anointing of Saul. The result was that David was more concerned to preserve Saul than his own life (1 Sam. 24:7; 26:9ff.). Now we can understand why David's weeping was not in the least insincere. For he considered not only the evil side of Saul – his desperate rage, driving him to murder the innocent – but he also recognised that he was king, elected and chosen by God as head of the people, and placed in the seat that God had consecrated. Thus, he could not hate the evil in him without at the same time honouring the favours God had bestowed on him.

We really must remember this. For instance, when we become indignant against someone, we very often fail to take account of all the favours which God has given to the one whom we hate, as though those favours were beneath contempt. Even when we must hate and detest a person's evil side, we must not be so carried away with the violence of our feelings that we are utterly unable to accept the good, for then we have lost our perception and discernment. On the contrary, we must honour the Lord for everything that comes from him. This is what we are to remember from David.

David certainly knew that Saul was a desperate man. Nonetheless, God had chosen him to reign over his people, and had anointed him for that purpose. What is more, David knew that he would offend the Lord, and would commit a sacrilege if he ignored this grace which God had put in Saul. That is why he mourned over his death. Perhaps he also recognised the vengeance of God, for we can clearly see that vengeance in what happened later. David was not thinking only of Saul's temporal death, but he was looking further. He considered how God finally had to use his arm to rout Saul, and yet the Lord had previously chosen this very one to be king. Indeed, all the punishments which God sends on the sinful should be instructive for us, so that we can learn, as the saying goes, 'at someone else's expense'.

It is easy for us to say, 'This is the hand of God. This is a just punishment.' But in reality, these statements can be evidence of a terrible pride in us which we are displaying towards those whom we hate. However, when the Lord executes his judgements on our enemies, we do have occasion to think of ourselves. On the one hand, we can rejoice insofar as he demonstrates how he cares for our safety by punishing those who are against us, and who mock us. Yet he does not want us to be so presumptuous in our rejoicing that we fail to consider our own sins, and thus displease him. Thus on the other hand, when those of us whom God has spared consider the matter more carefully, we ought also to tremble before his majesty, knowing that we, too, are as deserving of punishment and grief as those whom he punishes.

David experienced both feelings. We can see in so many passages how he rejoiced when God put his hand on his enemies; when he destroyed their plans, when he wiped the smiles off their faces, and when he threw them in the depth of the abyss (e.g. Psa. 124). When his enemies had been defeated like this, David composed a song of praise to the Lord out of these experiences. Nevertheless, he grieved for Saul, who was the worst of his enemies. He wept, he tore his clothes. On the other hand, his sorrow shows us how well he controlled his feelings, by realising that God had had pity upon him. He thus made God his shield and, trusting in divine protection, waged war against those who opposed him and troubled him unjustly. But that is not to say that he rejoiced in such a way that he failed to bow his head and humble himself or to realise how necessary it was for him to continue fearing God, so that the same thing should not happen to him.

This is what we must recall whenever God unleashes his severity on people who have worked with unjust cruelty against us and against the children of God. We are to remember that he is showing himself to be our Father in this. He is opposed to all the trouble and harm that such men cause us. It is as if he were declaring that he experiences everything in common with us and that he is taking our battles upon himself. As Scripture says, when he has adopted us for his people, he will be 'the enemy of our enemies' (Exod. 23:22). That is one point. But on the other hand, we must keep in mind St Paul's exhortation to us, that when God punishes unbelievers, it is not inappropriate for us to tremble ourselves (Rom. 11:21ff.). Why? To remind us not to be envious of their condition so that we will not be conformed to their iniquities, and hence God will not have to unleash the same severity against us.

Furthermore, the passage includes the statement that David also wept 'because of Jonathan, because of all the people of God, because of Israel which had been defeated' (2 Sam. 1:12). We have shown why David wept over the death of Saul. But he had a different reason for weeping over Jonathan, for David clearly knew that Jonathan had not spared his own life to be his loyal friend, as we will discuss later. And so David had been deprived of the greatest blessing he could possibly have hoped for next to the royal crown, and that was the friendship of Jonathan. For he could have spared Jonathan's life as a recompense to show that he was not ungrateful for all the benefits he had received from him. Now he saw that Jonathan was dead, and was in anguish at seeing the people defeated – for David was, in the first place, a member of the people. But more than that, he had already been ordained head over them (1 Sam. 16:1–13), although he did not rule them yet. But humanly speaking, even while he was banished far from his country, he naturally had a paternal care for those whom God had committed to him, and for whose protection he was responsible, since God's decree that he was to be head of the people was immutable.

Thus David had double cause for weeping and grieving over the people. As we said earlier, the temptation was for him to give up, and die of a broken heart, for it had been expected that God would give him possession of the kingdom. Now he saw everything desolate, the towns abandoned, and the people fleeing hither and thither like poor wandering lambs. Their enemies, however, were rejoicing in triumph. We know how once the wicked have shed innocent blood, that increases their appetite, and they are like drunkards who are always thirsty – the more they drink, the more they want! So it is with those who have once tasted human blood – they always want to continue in their cruelty.

David recognised these things, so there is no doubt that he was in terrible anguish, even as a mere member of the people whom God had elected – people who had received the promise of his presence and favour, and to whom it had been said, 'I will live in the midst of you, and cause my presence to be your fortress' (see Exod. 29:45; Lev. 26:11; Joel 4:16–17.). On the one hand, God reassures his people in order to give them a sense of peace, and yet at the same time he seems to mock them, so that his care of them seems useless. That is a sore temptation indeed. Yet David, above all, had this special promise that the crown was reserved for him. When he saw the people over whom he was to reign so terribly afflicted and deprived of everything, it was easy for him to despair. Thus, it was inevitable that he should weep and sigh and dissolve into tears of regret.

But David still kept himself under control. Scripture says that in order to show us that he turned himself towards God he fasted in addition to mourning (2 Sam. 1:12). We see here that, strictly speaking, fasting includes prayers. Such praying bears clear witness to repentance. Unbelievers can very well cry and carry on, and can easily shed many tears if God touches them seriously. But not only do they resent their condition in secret, they also pull out their beards, and tear out their hair, disdaining the very presence of God. They vomit out blasphemies against him, as though they were creatures who had no sense at all. But the children of God will not act senselessly when they are touched by some evil; they will not be like blocks of wood. They may very well weep and groan, but the point is that they look to God and condemn themselves so that he may show them mercy.

That is what David's behaviour demonstrates to us. How distraught he was – apparently almost to the point of excess – yet he fasted in order to show that he had not gone overboard in his grief. Thus, he was thinking, 'This is the hand of God which is upon the people, and consequently upon us' (because he and his band were members of the Church). So when he fasted, he was humbling himself before God, and was not putting on an act, as hypocrites like to do. He then confessed his sins, for he recognised that there was no other way to appease the wrath of God so that he might have mercy upon the remainder of the people.

Here again, we must notice that whenever God afflicts us or his whole Church, he is giving us an opportunity. Indeed, he does call on us to weep and grieve, but we are not to grieve without considering the cause of our sadness, nor are our cries to be the brayings and screechings of wild animals! Rather, everything is to be directed towards God. That is, we are to be aware that we must glorify him, even when he whips us severely with heavy strokes. So even when he seems intent on breaking us in pieces, we must not fail to confess that he is a just Judge. And since we gain nothing by being stiff-necked against him and stubbornly hardening ourselves, let us learn to humble ourselves truly. That means that we not only confess that he is just, but that we actually live for him. Humility implies this attitude, and is necessarily joined to faith. Thus, we will not act like unbelievers who feign the appearance of sanctity but inwardly are filled with pride. They maintain an inflated estimation of themselves as long as they avoid facing God. Therefore, let us willingly humble ourselves in the hope that God will have mercy on us, and restore us to his fatherly kindness.

We really do need this admonition, for we can see how God is afflicting this poor world today. Even people who are strangers to us are still related to us, because we are all made in the image of God, and have a common nature which should be a mutual bond of love and brotherhood. Then there is a far closer union between ourselves and the suffering believers who are scattered here and there in all churches which God has chastened on every side. Indeed, we see troubles everywhere: we see fires burning; we hear that the throats of poor innocent people have been cut; that they have been subjected to mockery and contempt, and that they are being led to the slaughter. We see the enemies of truth ready to annihilate everything, and we do not know what God is intending to do. Nevertheless, see how his sword is unsheathed. The fire, as I have said, is kindled and we do not know how far it will burn.

Let us thus allow ourselves to be genuinely touched by

mourning, anxiety and grief so that we will not be careless, hardened, or unfeeling over what our poor brothers are going through. Instead, let us have the kind of compassion towards them which members of the same body owe to one another. On the other hand, let us not give way to despair, like those who become so grieved and full of lamentation that they refuse the remedy of consolation in God. Rather, let us confess our sins, knowing that our Saviour has not ceased to pour out his blessings upon us, even though we have sinned. Then, in the midst of our sorrows, let us recognise all our offences so that he may show himself merciful to us, as he always has done to those who clearly take refuge in him. That is how we can benefit from this teaching.

Now when the text says that the young Amalekite 'presented the crown and bracelets of Saul to David', it is certain that he had despoiled the body of Saul (2 Sam. 1:10). We are not told whether or not he actually killed him. In any case, what we see here is the judgement of God on the person of Saul. When this young man, who was descended from the Amalekite race, came to tear off the royal ornaments and the crown from his head, Saul had to beg someone who was his enemy to kill him, since he was unable to do so himself (2 Sam. 1:9). Saul, in desperation, had thrown himself on his sword in order to kill himself, but then he was not able to achieve it by himself and, as I have said, he had to beg his enemies to help him to do so. Since he had wickedly persecuted David, who was chosen and elected by God to succeed him, there was a very good reason why he should not simply die one death, but that he should actually die two or three times, as it were.

Now let us assume that all this man did was despoil him, which is very likely the case, as we have already noted. This, again, was a just punishment which God sent Saul in accordance with his sin. Why? We have seen that he committed his first transgression when God sent him to destroy the Amalekites (1 Sam. 15). He was not supposed to spare anything, yet he preserved the king in order to show him off. He even kept the cattle and the better furnishings. He was not content merely with sparing the people but, as I have said, he also wanted to keep the cattle – either out of avarice or ambition, or for some other reason. He had been told that if he had disobeyed God's command, evil would rebound on him, and that condemnation would fall on his head (1 Sam. 12:15; cf. 1 Sam. 15:23, 26). Then he was shown by the prophet Samuel that obedience is better than all the sacrifices in the world; and to obey God's voice is far better than the fat of sheep (1 Sam. 15:22). So he had clearly rebelled in this matter.

Here, then, was Saul's sin. He wished to be more merciful than God, and did not execute the vengeance which God had commanded him – namely, to make war against the Amalekites until they were rooted out of the world, as God demanded (Exod. 17:14, 16; Deut. 25:19). Thus, it was God who hated Amalek, and Saul was the executor to administer this judgement. But he refused to carry out his duty. So we see how, after Saul's death, God sent a man of this very nation, who snatched the crown and royal ornaments from his body, so that he was left in even greater ignominy.

Notice how God often 'pays the wages' of those who have offended him, although neither they nor others are aware of what he is doing. When some affliction strikes us out of the blue and we cannot understand why, it should be a warning for us to start seriously examining ourselves. Assuming that we all understand our duty in the various conditions of life, we must pursue the matter and ask, 'What have I done in the light of my obligations? In this point I find myself guilty, and when I carefully examine my life, I find rottenness and an infinite number of offences.' Now that is how we should always be examining ourselves. We are given this example of Saul as an admonition, especially when God punishes us in some strange and unusual way which we cannot understand. For there was no-one who perceived with the human eye that God was punishing Saul now for not fully executing vengeance upon Amalek, but instead pardoning them, which he had no right to do. Thus we should recognise what happened to Saul, so that we can be even more on guard ourselves.

We can see, however, how this Amalekite pretended to grieve, and yet was nothing but an insincere flatterer. When he came to present Saul's crown to David, he thought that he would be welcomed and even rewarded! It would not have been out of place for him to come and inform David that his enemy had been defeated, and that now was the time when God called him to possess the kingdom. He could even have presented him with the crown, as if he had been sent by God to say, 'Come now and take the place of Saul'. This is how you would assume that he should have recognised this great blessing. But this wretched person thought that he would surely gratify David and be gloriously received by him, yet we see that his vanity cost him very dearly. Thus, let us learn not to put ourselves forward, hoping to please men, for when we do this, God will cast us down all the more quickly. It is quite true that those who ingratiate themselves by sinful means often get their own way. God permits them to get ahead, to be held in respect, to get rich. This is amazing to watch. However, after they have been elevated, it takes only one fall to break their neck.

We see how many people struggle desperately to climb up to a position of dignity and grandeur, sparing neither their substance nor their lives to attain honour or fame, and acquire wealth. Well, they can do what they want, but God will mock their efforts, and 'cast them down like crayfish', as the saying goes. We can easily see this kind of thing happening, and scarcely one man out of ten can be found who does not come to total ruin. That applies to all those who are striving after and pouring their lives out for this kind of advancement. This is graphically illustrated when the text states that the man who wished to ingratiate himself with David by boasting of having killed Saul received his just deserts and was put to death as a murderer instead of gaining favour.

However, we also notice that God puts down the arrogance of people who exalt themselves for no reason and, indeed, against what is actually true! For when we are led by a haughty spirit to speak of our own virtue because we wish to be highly esteemed, we are partaking of a vice that God cannot stand. God cannot put up with it. So then, what is the outcome when we wish to hold on to what does not exist, and be admired on the basis of lies and what we have imagined? Let us learn, first, never to attribute to ourselves more than belongs to us, and furthermore let us never preach our own virtue! If God has worked through us and we have accomplished something praiseworthy, let us never cease to be covered with humility and modesty.

Now to return to the text. When David had the Amalekite killed (we cannot at this time go into the matter of what he said), he was clearly 'condemned by his own testimony' (2 Sam. 1:16). Certainly, if we pay attention to what he did, he was justly punished. As for the rest of the matter, David had no respect for that nation. He had come from defeating the Amalekites. He already knew that they were condemned by God and that they were a reprobate nation. Thus, it was just as though God had said that David had a sword in his hand to cut down everything and leave nothing of all their villainy and corruption in the world. David was aware of that, and hence he acted more severely than he would have done towards an Israelite. Nevertheless, he indicated the reason, for he said, 'How have you dared to touch the Lord's anointed?' (2 Sam. 1:14). Here David wanted to establish a precedent so that no-one would ever undertake more than was legitimate for him – especially in the matter of public authority, which is a sacred thing. For Saul was king, and members of the populace owed him subjection. Someone who has the audacity to kill the one whom God has ordained immediately beneath himself to have the privileged position of serving as God's own officer and lieutenant – someone who kills a king like that, certainly cannot be tolerated for one moment.

So here is a point that we must particularly notice. David showed that since Saul was the anointed of the Lord, it was not legitimate to attempt anything against him until his hour should come, as we have stated above. Now it is true that today there is no physical anointing, because the custom of applying oil to ordain kings, princes, and those who wish to ape them is no longer in practice. But nevertheless, 'all power', as St Paul shows us, 'is of God' (Rom. 13:1). There is no principality in this world which is not ordained by him. No matter how much those who reign are enemies of the truth, no matter how tyrannical and cruel they are, an individual does not have the right to punish them. Why not? Because God is the one who has to take his sword in his hand. Let us understand, then, from this never to touch the authority that God has established and sanctioned in his name. Rather, let us patiently endure the shame, injuries, cruelties, and extortions of those who rule, until God has remedied the matter in a way that is unknown to us. Let us realise that it is his business to uphold those who are unjustly oppressed.

Now let us prostrate ourselves before the majesty of our good God, recognising the infinite faults of which we are guilty, praying that it will please him to make us feel them more and more, so that we may ask him to pardon them. And may we recognise ourselves as we truly are, in order to compel ourselves to reform by correcting all the vices which are still in us, and to submit ourselves to his holy will, so that we may not cease blessing him in our afflictions. Thus, may we recognise our offences and, at the same time, may we ever taste the fatherly love he shows us, so that we invoke his name and call upon him until he shows us signs of his favour, after we have felt his wrath. May he show his grace not only to us, but also to all the people and nations of the earth . . .

2

*David's Response to the Philistine Victory**

David lamented with this lamentation over Saul and over Jonathan his son. He ordained that the children of Judah should learn to use the bow, even as it is written in the Book of the Law. The excellence of Israel has been slain on the high places; how are the mighty fallen, publish it not in the places of Gath, announce it not in the regions of Askelon, for fear that the daughters of the Philistines rejoice, and that the daughters of the uncircumcised triumph . . . (2 Sam. 1:17–27).

We have already begun to see that even though Saul had cruelly persecuted him, that did not keep David from weeping and mourning his death. Thus David showed that he did not have a vengeful spirit, and also that he had more concern and felt more deeply for the public good than for himself. David showed this by ordering the death of the man who brought the message that he had struck the final blow in Saul's death. Now since we have dealt with this earlier, we need not search closely to know whether or not it was true. It is enough for us to know that the sentence that David pronounced on him was based on the testimony that he himself gave as his own judge, and that he was condemned by his own mouth (2 Sam. 1:16). We all remember how this messenger from Amalek boasted that he had killed Saul, even though it was not true; but that is not important enough to make us investigate the matter. It is enough to observe that David had demonstrated that he was not Saul's enemy, even though he had had

*Monday, June 1, 1562.

the opportunity to harm him along with the other men who had been pursued by Saul for such a long time. Yet notice how he kept on doing him kindnesses and, as we have shown earlier, he was not found guilty of any crime. So much for the first point.

Now for the second point. David's zeal for the public good and the safety of the people made him forget Saul's personal failings. Both these points are important, for there is a terrible corruption in vengeance, which is so deeply rooted in men that they think it is a virtue. They are proud of it and almost overcome by it. If someone has offended us, we never let it slip our memory; we always resent it. If something bad happens to our enemies, it makes us rejoice, and when we have the chance to injure them and pay them back for their evil, it is very difficult for us to keep from doing so.

We see, then, that this is a very common vice to which all men are inclined and in which far too many indulge. How carefully, therefore, should we notice what is revealed here about David. For when we are shown that we should not be vindictive, we always come up with the excuse that we are not made of iron or steel, and that patience is quite contrary and repugnant to our nature; that it is impossible for us not to be hurt and thus motivated to harm our enemies. That may be so, but was not David a man subject to similar passions as ourselves? How, then, was he able to overcome the urge to take vengeance, since he too could have given so many good reasons? It is certain that he did not give way to his excessive passions, but chose to fight against them all the way, because the Spirit of God worked in him.

Hence, let us learn to resist those emotions which incite us to evil. No matter how strongly we may be able to protest that those whom we hate and whom we wish to injure have assailed us without cause, and no matter how many excuses we can bring up, such as that we only sought peace and friendship, but that they would not allow us to be friends – let us not fail to keep ourselves strictly under control. When we are tempted to do evil, let us ask the Lord that it would please him to govern us by his Spirit, which is the Spirit of clemency, so that we will be purged of any bitterness or malice, and thus be able to practise what he says; 'Love your enemies and do good to them that persecute you, and pray God for those that curse you' (Matt. 5:44; Luke 6:27–28).

Now this is so very repugnant to our natural inclinations that the papists have been so shameless as to measure the commands of God by what they find in themselves. Hence they say this is only a 'counsel'. Since it is too difficult, they deemed it would be too rigorous as a straight command for everyone! This, certainly, is dreadful blasphemy. It shows how far they are from reaching the goal of suppressing all feelings of vengeance, but that is not the way we are to act. We are not to obscure the commands of God in order to excuse ourselves. On the contrary, knowing very well that all vengeance is condemned by God, we must loathe it. And then, whenever we are tempted to give way, let us learn to run to God, who controlled his servant David and bestowed on him the grace of being able to stamp on those violent passions which could have moved him to hatred and bitterness towards Saul. This is the first point.

Secondly, let us learn from David's example to seek the common good of those with whom we live, particularly since God grants us the grace of being his Church. Since he presides over us and dwells among us, and his name is honoured, let us seek, I say, to maintain and preserve peace in the community, so that our personal profit and loss holds no influence over us when it is a question of the public good. Thus people should not just look after themselves. Of course, if we say that this is very difficult, that is true; but David shows us the way. Insofar as he was a frail man like ourselves and did not lack feelings, he was in the same natural condition that we are in; nevertheless he put first things first rather than his own personal concerns! They were nothing compared to the salvation and preservation of the Church. That is why he mourned over Saul. This will seem strange at first glance, but it is certain that his burning zeal for the good of the Church over which God had placed him as head made him forget everything else. So he fought against himself and submitted himself to the will of God in order to proclaim Saul's good characteristics, for his death made him indignant.

As for the rest, there is no doubt that the lamentation recorded here was made to be published all over the country – so everyone would realise that David was not cut off from the people of Israel, and would take him as a faithful member, recognising that he had always pursued the welfare and safety of the people, and was still seeking that goal.

That is why it says that he ordained 'that the children of Judah should learn to use the bow' (2 Sam. 1:18). This has been explained in various ways. No-one thinks that it means that they did not use the bow previously, for we can see that they did. Others have made one suggestion or another. However, it is easy to recall that David had composed this lamentation so that it would be spread all over the land. It was especially to encourage the children of Judah to practise shooting with the bow and to engage in military exercises so as not to lose courage after such a terrible defeat. The point is that this lamentation was linked with David's exhortation to the people always to be valiant. In other words, this is a sentence that is cut short. It says that David composed this lamentation over Saul, and commanded people to teach the children of Judah to draw the bow. Here we have two things which, at first glance, do not agree. He seems to be comparing apples with oranges, as they say. But here we are shown that David had the same goal when he bore such solemn witness in his mourning over Saul and Jonathan, as when he urged those of his nation to take courage and not despair or be too stunned by this defeat which had overthrown them.

The text then adds that this was 'written in the Book of the Law', which no-one takes to be the life of the patriarchs or the books of Moses. Probably, there were many other books with fuller histories of these events, all of which would surely be useful for us today. Why then has God allowed such teaching to be lost, since it could have given us good instruction? Well, look at our laziness, and we will not be surprised! Look at the books which do remain and which are the most essential to us, for they relate events in a brief, concise fashion. Matters are not drawn out at length, with the result that we do not have to occupy ourselves a great deal with them. Thus, it seems that God wishes to trace with his finger, as it were, how he chooses to govern his Church for all time. As for the prophets, we do see terribly obscure sentences scattered throughout their books, but we do not worry about it. The words are, thus, to be explained by details which we draw from other scriptural language. This is just as important as finding some lost book. This shows us how inexcusable is our laziness in not applying ourselves to the study of these matters so that the content of Scripture would be thoroughly familiar to us.

Yet we seem to think we have done enough if we have just read a tenth of the Scriptures in our whole life! Seeing, then, how cold and listless we are in the study of the doctrine of God, we should not find it strange that he has removed many things which otherwise would have been useful to us, and that he has left us only what is necessary for our salvation. Anyway, we can easily gather that this lamentation of David was more fully stated and understood, and that there was a longer quotation of it elsewhere.

It is sufficient for us to know that after David heard of the death of Saul, he sent this throughout the nation in order to rescue them from the trauma which had overtaken them, and to keep them from being conquered because they were scattered. For their enemies could have used the opportunity to press home their victory with further success and so completely destroy the poor Church of God. David, of course, was aware of that. So in order to help the people understand the situation better, he sent them a hymn of lamentation – for if he had not done something, they could have been seriously alienated from him. For who would ever have judged these to have been his feelings? We are so used to 'measuring others by our own yardstick', as we say.

Well then, here was David, who had been thrown down and banished by Saul's cruelty. He had wandered throughout the countryside among dangerous animals, in deserts and caves, and finally had been forced to flee to the country of the Philistines, the enemies of God. They were men who, for sheer pleasure, kept their swords drawn to kill anyone they could.

They had already caused terrible butchery. The king and his sons were devoured by it (1 Sam. 31:2, 6).

Now when David had fled from the country of Judah, everyone assumed that he would never return, for the king of the Philistines had given him a village, as we have seen (1 Sam. 27:5–6). After David had seen such a calamity strike his people, and their enemies excited by blood, no-one would ever have imagined that he would ever have rejoined the people of God at a time when they were so sorely afflicted that they seemed to have been rejected and abandoned by everyone. Moreover, since he had been received so kindly by the Philistine king Achis, no-one would have thought that he would risk his neck or have the courage to rebuild the Church of God. Rather, they could have conjectured that the opposite might easily have happened, since he had fought valiantly for such a long time for the people whom he had defended so many times against the Philistines. And yet they had not recognised what he had done for them as much as they should have (1 Sam. 17; 18; 19; 23 *passim*).

The Philistine victory could have given David a good excuse to live among the uncircumcised, where he would have had some rest. He could easily have said, 'Look at the people of Israel receiving the wages of their ingratitude – which they fully deserve! God has avenged the trouble and injuries that they unjustly caused me.' Now that could have been the way David felt, so that it was quite necessary for him to be touched to the quick by the Spirit of God so that he would willingly employ himself in his service as well as for the common good. He thus showed his true feelings, so that one could not hold him suspect nor think of him as a rebel, for he proclaimed the opposite in his hymn.

To summarise, we can see now how the two things fit together: why David composed this lamentation over Saul, and also commanded that all over the country the children of Judah should learn to use the bow – in other words learn to practise and prepare for war. Then whatever evil might occur, they would never fail to resist their enemies, knowing that God would be their Protector. That is what we must remember as the main lesson.

Here is another point worthy of observation. David put himself forward in order to gain access to the opportunity to serve the common good of the people, however much it would be a risk to himself and expose him to so many troubles, as we will see later. Whenever we are able to plead the excuse that the means are not at hand, we are glad to retire far away from the action of the battle in order to avoid any annoyance or trouble.

Let us suppose that it is our desire to expose ourselves to this or that difficulty, but the moment we see some obstacle, we say, 'I would very much like to do this, but it would put me into a dangerous situation. There are such obstacles here that I cannot do it.' We think that these excuses will permit us to wash our hands of the matter, and that the whole world should absolve us! If we continue to do nothing and do not even try to see if we can do what God commands, we will easily be convicted. But we still do not fail to search for some kind of hiding place where we can avoid our duty! That is common human nature – which is all the more reason why we should observe what it says here about David. Even though he had the best will in the world to be used for the people of God, it certainly seemed that the door had been closed to him. Why? Because he was held to be the enemy of the true religion. The people distrusted him and hated him because of the ill will that Saul bore to him. That is how he could have excused himself before men and said, 'Whatever may happen, I cannot possibly be used for the salvation of this people, who have always resisted me. And I know that I will not be welcome, no matter how much I may offer myself.'

So David had all these fine excuses, but that did not keep him from going to the people to encourage them to constancy and steadfastness. Furthermore, another possibility could have occurred to him: that he would not have been immediately received. They could also have accused him of dishonesty, saying, 'Oh, he is only putting on an act and making fun of us'. Nevertheless, he went to his friends to show that no matter how much he had been unjustly afflicted and his life sought after, and no matter how much the people had offended him, nonetheless he would never cease to be as friendly towards them as his own brothers.

He showed this by the affection that he bore to Saul. It could have been said that hatred had been ended by death. This can be seen even among pagans and unbelievers, so that when you see that the person you hated is dead, then all the ill will that you bore to him is effaced. But David had a different feeling, as we have already stated. Here he shows us that he had not changed in commitment or courage since the death of Saul. Rather, he declared that although Saul had been wrong to be his enemy, still he was not failing to carry out his duty to him. When David prayed to God and bore this testimony, it was not with any pretence or merely outward appearance, but with the kind of true affection which he felt for his brothers. Even before that, he had always sought Saul's welfare, no matter how much Saul molested him or was cruel to him. Even though Saul unleashed all his vengeance against him, David continued (I say) with the same affection that he demonstrated in this lamentation. Even though Saul had been like a lion with his mouth open to tear David in shreds, or like a bear with his paw ready to break him apart, in spite of it all, David grieved for him after his death. He still honoured him as his king, and desired to do him good as far as he could.

Let us come now to the substance of the hymn, 'The Excellence of Israel has fallen and been killed on the high places. How are the mighty fallen!' (2 Sam. 1:19). These words in David's song may make him seem very admirable, but if they literally indicate his true attitude, we can conclude from his own viewpoint that his emotions were out of control. We see here, as though in a mirror, a man showing excessive grief, with complete lack of self-control. This teaches us that even though our grieving and our tears are for a good purpose and proceed from a good source, evil will still always be mixed in among our virtues. There will always be so many shadows and vices in our virtues that their existence should break down all our pride. So we will not boast, but will recognise that God will always find something amiss in everything that we do. No matter how blameless men may consider us to be, we will not fail to be condemned by God if he chooses to be strict. But actually, he supports us when we come to him without pretence, and he does not take into account the infirmities which are mixed in all parts of our life, for it pleases him to bury them.

This is what we must notice, then, in this lamentation of David's. For if he had been in complete control of himself, he would certainly not have employed the hyperbole that he has used here. Rather, he would have humbled himself before God, and exhorted the people to repentance. Then after that, he would have made public prayers and encouraged them. But here he has produced the kind of lamentation which makes him look like someone who is lost! He is not able to contain himself and is, as it were, 'dragging his wings'. It seems he even wishes to drown in his passion, and make the people miserable as well.

This should warn us that when we mourn, we must still keep in mind the Church of God, so that we only mourn with the kind of good and holy zeal that God can approve. Yet often, if we are not on our guard, we are thrown into disorder, and our emotions carry us all over the place so that we do not keep to the straight and narrow path. We experience this all too often. For instance, when some dreadful calamity happens in the Church, it is a good sign if we are moved by zeal, for it is written that 'the zeal of the house of God' ought to 'eat us up' (Psa. 69:9; John 2:17). However, we may experience emotions that are so violent that they become excessive. Only with great difficulty will we be able to keep from gnashing our teeth and complaining against God. 'How could this possibly have happened?' we cry. 'How could God allow such terrible ruin, and allow his Church to be exposed as prey? And how could a good cause be beaten down like this?'

That is how we act, and we see the same thing in David, for he clearly recognised that God had chosen to punish Saul and all the people. Now why should God allow the wicked to get the upper hand? Is it possible that his people could be abandoned, and led to the slaughter? Thus, we see that this emotion which stirred him up was, indeed, excessive. Let us realise that we are similar. If such an excellent man, a true servant of God endowed with such rare and unusual virtues, was subject to this vice, how much more must we be on our guard! Now, we may weep because of our true affection for God's name, and our desire for him to be glorified, served and honoured as he deserves, so that poor believers might be upheld. But even though we hold all these principles, when some adversity strikes us, it is still necessary to realise that we may utterly abandon ourselves and not hold on unless God sustains us. We must meditate beforehand, so that we will not give way to an inordinate grief which can toss us about all over the place. This is a point which we must carefully observe.

David addressed the words 'The Excellence of Israel!' to Saul – although they could be said of the land. It would have been better for him to cry out, and then address himself to the land afterwards. We know that when we mourn, we do not use sentences which flow with a continuous train of thought. Rather, we blurt out something in broken phrases. We mix in 'woes' with what we want to say. For every word that is properly pronounced, there is immediately a sigh that nearly strangles us, and thus we are not able to say what we wanted to say. That is what we see in this hymn. David cried out, 'The Excellence of Israel!', speaking of Saul. And then he said, speaking of the land, 'They have been killed on the high places'. In other words, in a prominent place, as though someone had shamelessly built a scaffold so that it could not be hidden, placing it on a high mountain so that the spectacle could be clearly seen by everyone. When David thus called his enemy 'excellence, nobility and desire', he used words that applied to Israel, just as he did when he praised Saul, attributing to him at the same time the praise of virtue and prowess. In this, he showed that he always prized the virtues which he recognised in Saul, no matter how full Saul had been of malice, rage, and stubbornness, just as though he was a wild animal.

Saul must have been devil-possessed, since he persecuted David like that when David was innocent. Now this is what we have to observe. Although David saw that Saul was a man controlled by a satanic fury, like some desperate maniac, and that he was a rebel against God to the point of wanting to destroy what God had established, yet he did not fail to contemplate the virtues and favours which God had granted him. This fact should be carefully observed, for it only takes a small vice to blind our eyes, so that all the virtues that God has put in a man are distorted. For instance, if a man is excellent at many things, if he serves the Church of God, and exhibits many exquisite qualities – in short, if he is worthy of being highly esteemed and honoured – and yet has some little vice, that can be enough to disgust us so much that the good that the Lord has granted him is quite obscured. This is especially true when we are bearing a little envy or ill will. Then it takes nothing to make us blindfold our eyes to keep us from perceiving the grace of God which is so evident in him.

All the more, then, should we strive to follow David's example, because he could easily have used the corruption of Saul as an excuse to despise him, and say, 'Even if Saul had been an angel of God, he still resisted God's inviolable decree. Then he became worse than an unbeliever, in that he was an enchanter and sorcerer – so he deserves no honour.' David could have said that, and it was true with regard to Saul. But it was necessary for David to pay attention to something else – as it also is for us. Even if our enemies are the most wicked in the world, God still does not want his grace to be overlooked. Thus, even when we can say, 'This person received grace from God but abused it terribly', and can legitimately plead this to be true, we must still value what came from God. For when we stamp underfoot and disdain the favours of God, we are not merely offending a mortal creature, but rather our ingratitude is against God himself.

Moreover, let us be aware that those who thus efface the memory of their enemies' virtues do a great wrong. Why? Because God gives us an opportunity to praise and esteem him when he bestows these favours on men, for they always serve some purpose, whatever it may be. I say that whatever wickedness there is in men, God clearly knows how to draw out the good that he has placed in them and use it for the welfare of his people. Indeed, no matter how much they may abuse it, we must still always contemplate the good, so that we will commit ourselves to it. We must be alert to discern the favours which

God has given to this person or that – even though they also have vices – so that we will be encouraged to do well. When we see that some people abuse and misuse the grace of God which they have received, we should be particularly willing to be instructed by it, as this is useful for us. Now it is true that they are committing a sacrilege – and God will hold us responsible when we misuse his Spirit in our vocation. He will hold us responsible for all that he declared for our salvation, and which we abuse to our own ruin and perdition.

We must gather this kind of instruction from the good which we see in our enemies, and then apply it to our own advantage. Indeed, if we do blot it out, it is just as though we do not deign to subject ourselves to obedience to God, or that we pretend that the malice in men can hide and bury the good. So let us strive to follow the example of David and prize the favours of God wherever they are found. However much we are bitten and infected with venom, so that we feel bitterness of heart against our enemies, let us still begin to recognise the good that God has put in those whom we hate, so that we can retrieve ourselves and correct our bitterness.

David would not have let this word out of his mouth if he had not recognised: 'It is God who elevated Saul, whatever he was, and who am I to contradict God, since he chose him to be the first king of his people? Since this is the case, I must submit myself to God, and honour whom he honours. For if I do not honour Saul, it will be as though I am purposely dishonouring God, and ultimately opposing what he has pronounced. Furthermore, I know that his kingdom is sacred. Saul received the anointing which bore witness to that. God took Saul by his hand, sending him the prophet Samuel, who marked him on earth with this anointing, which is an image of the grace of the Holy Spirit.'

Thus, David recognised all these things and thought, 'Since God elevated Saul to such dignity, that is reason enough for me to honour him'. That is how greatly he esteemed the grace of God in a man who was so perverse. Therefore, we must learn when we are angry and bitter against our enemies, to think, nonetheless, that if God has honoured them, then he must wish us to close our eyes and discern nothing. Thus, we can temper our passion, just like putting water into wine when it is too strong. This, in short, is what we must remember from this verse.

Now we have already stated that David's exaggeration here was evidence of his excessive and uncontrolled grief. Let us remember, therefore, when we have times of sadness, always to take hold of ourselves and think, 'Alas, if this is what God has shown me, whatever it may be, I must fully submit to him. And if things go totally against me, let me submissively drink all the bitterness in the cup.' If we do this, it will be a way of showing our obedience. Let us always think of that. Very often some excessive expression escapes our lips. Very well, when that happens to us, let us pray to God to strengthen us in our weakness. This is not to indulge in self-flattery and pardon ourselves, like some people who, under the shadow of human weakness, give themselves permission to do everything, and then expect everyone to tolerate them! All that is needed is this word 'weakness' to make us believe that we deserve absolution! That is what the papists do. Let us not flatter ourselves in this way. Rather, let us accuse ourselves and recognise the evil that is in us. Let us reprimand ourselves as much as possible, and continue to hope that God will at last have pity on us, and not judge us any more severely than he did his servant David.

Now notice how David spoke of 'the High Places of Judah' (2 Sam. 1:19). There is no doubt that he considered that God had willed to shame his people far more than if Saul had been killed in private. For if someone had killed him in some obscure, unknown place, very well, that would have been shameful, but the memory would soon have faded. However, when it was right there in the presence of everyone, it would not be noticed even by someone who happened to be passing by. Rather, it was as though Saul had been lifted up on a mountain, so that it would be widely known – 'Saul is dead'. So David had a good reason for putting these words first. It was as though he were saying that God had built a scaffold in order to humiliate his people to such a degree that they would recognise their offence every time this defeat came to mind. Now by this, we are taught that if, when God afflicts us, it pleases him to make our punishments publicly known and exposed to view, it is intended to confound us all the more. If God sends us some secret punishment, very well, it shows us that we have offended him and that we must benefit from this correction. But on the other hand, if God deals with us with direct force and exposes our afflictions to the sight of men so that we are embarrassed, we may then know that he is doubling the punishment because we have been too late in turning to him. Let us really benefit from this – when he publicly shows the punishments he is sending us – and let it be an opportunity to humble ourselves even more.

It says, 'Publish it not in Gath, make it not known in the places of Askelon, so the daughters of the Philistines will not rejoice, and the daughters of the uncircumcised will not triumph' (2 Sam. 1:20). Here again, one feels his emotion to have been excessive. For David was wanting this calamity to be silenced, and not spoken of, for fear that the enemies of God would have the opportunity to triumph over it. Gath, as we have seen, was one of the chief cities of the Philistines, and Askelon was also a famous city. It was just as if he said, 'May no-one speak of this in the land of our enemies, and above all in the populous towns. Let it not even be mentioned so that this history will be unknown.'

Well, he was talking, then, like someone who was very overwrought. But at least his desire was not unreasonable, because it did arise from a sound principle. Why? Because he knew that the Philistines would mock not only the people of Israel, but most especially the religion that God had given them. Then his name would be blasphemed along with his Law. That is why he used this word 'uncircumcised', for it would be just like saying today, 'Unbelievers, Turks and the like . . .'. Thus, David was motivated by the honour of God, and hence he was deeply distressed and grieved to see that the name of God would be mocked and that the infidels would 'vomit out' their blasphemies against him. They would say that the hope that Israel had in their God was only a silly fable, and that they had gloried in his protection quite in vain. He thus saw that the name of God would be torn apart, the true religion would be shamelessly mocked, and people would trample the Law and the prophets underfoot.

These things deeply distressed him, and not without good reason, for when God afflicts us through our enemies, we must think more of the shame that is reflected on him than on all the evil that we personally experience. Why? Because David and the other faithful servants of God always placed the honour of his holy name first when they prayed for his help against their enemies. David is a good and faithful exponent of this for us in another passage where he prayed that it would please God to maintain his honour. 'Is it necessary, O Lord,' he asked, 'that the unbelievers should say, "Where is their God?" and must the wicked rise against you and reproach your poor faithful ones whom you have abandoned? How long, O Lord, will you allow your truth to be blasphemed by these evil, perverse people and shall they mock your strength as if you were not able to help us in time of need?' (Psa. 79:10; 94:3ff.). When David made use of this sort of prayer, he was warning the people not to spread the news of the death of Saul and Jonathan to the Philistines, so that the daughters of people who were profane, those who despised God and who were enemies of his Church, would not rejoice over it by triumphing and openly despising God, as we have said.

That, in short, is what we should draw from this passage. Thus, no matter when God afflicts us, as soon as we have become aware of any evil touching us, let us also consider that when the wicked and the enemies of the truth of God rise against him and spew out their venom against his majesty, it should cause anguish and despair to arise within us. That will show the extent of our affection and zeal for the honour of God when it is trampled down. May the reproaches that are cast on him fall on us, as it says in Psalm 69 (v. 9), so that we will make every endeavour to undo the effects of any scandal. And if our Lord permits his name to be blasphemed because of us, may it cause us to be even more distressed at our vices. When we see the reproach directed against him, let us accept it as though it were made against us, and even be willing to accept more. Let us always, I say, hold his honour in such high esteem that we will dissolve in tears whenever we see it despised, without any regard for our own personal reputation.

Now let us prostrate ourselves before his majesty, recognising our faults, praying that he may be pleased to make us feel them so deeply that we will call on him to pardon them, and also that we will want to correct them, driving ourselves to be increasingly stripped of them, and be clothed in his righteousness, so that we may be able truly to conform ourselves to his will . . .

3

*Calmness in All Circumstances**

O mountains of Gilboa, let neither rain nor dew come upon you; let there be no fields of offering: for there the shield of the mighty has been cast away; the shield of Saul, as though he had not been anointed by God . . . (2 Sam. 1:21–27).

What we read at the beginning confirms what we began explaining yesterday, namely, that every human passion tends to vice, whenever they become excessive and are not held in check as they should be. For although it was certainly proper for David to have wept over the death of Saul because of the defeat which had occurred, nevertheless he should not have condemned and cursed the place where it happened. Thus, when David asked that 'neither rain nor dew should ever descend on the mountain of Gilboa' because Saul had been killed there, we can clearly see that he was utterly carried away and distraught in his grief. There is no doubt that God was offended, for we cannot curse his creation like this without committing a kind of blasphemy, even when it appears to have done us some sort of harm. If a man died while gathering grapes or the harvest, and someone then, because of his death, hated those things which after all have been ordained for the common welfare, such a person would be criticised. We would say that they were driven by some sort of furious passion. Undoubtedly, this is an extremely common vice, and yet that does not justify it.

Thus, we see that David's mourning over Saul was excessive.

*Tuesday, June 2, 1562.

Let that instruct us to keep ourselves under control when we feel inclined to anger and despair over something. No matter what happens, we are to remember that we are under a rule which requires us not to be carried away. What reason is there for becoming so attached to part of God's creation that we then curse a mountain or a city or large town? Now if David lost control over what started as a reasonable grief, arising out of his zeal and concern for the Church of God, then how much easier it is for us to fall into a similar fault. We must pray to God all the more to temper us by his Spirit and keep us so closely that if we are pushed at times by powerful feelings, he will apply the remedy, whch will correct the evil before we are swallowed up by it.

Well, it is very likely that David did not actually want to curse a mountain so that it would produce no fruit, as though it had previously been fertile. Rather, he was taking into consideration its actual nature, which God had already put there, so that it was as if he had said, 'Mountain of Gilboa, you deserve to be barren and produce no fruit'. In fact this mountain was already barren. So it is as though David said, 'God has already imprinted a mark on it, which shows that some kind of evil would have to happen in that place, and thus it is as though God has already destined this place to warn of a calamity which was coming. Hence, because of this coming calamity, the place had to remain as a desert, because all the men of the country would be lost and the heritage of God made desolate.' This is what David meant. Now his curse would have been evidence of even greater vice if this mountain had been good pasture, or if people had gathered wheat or other grain from it, or if there had been some beautiful vineyard planted on it. But since it had been an uninhabited place which appeared deformed, what David was intending to say was that God had already given a premonition of this evil which would take place on it.

When David spoke of the 'fields of offering' or of the first-fruits, he was referring to the custom of the Law (1 Sam. 1:21). He could well have said that there were no arable fields on it which produced great quantities of wheat or other fruit.

But his statement was fields of first-fruits or offerings, which referred to the fact that it was not proper to eat the wheat until one had first honoured God, and confessed that one had received from him what the earth had produced (Lev. 23:14). David thus had in mind this aspect of the Law. Now although we do not have the same ceremony today, the truth of it still remains – that is, when we take our nourishment from the good things that God gives us, we need to recognise that we live by his pure liberality, and that even what we eat is to be dedicated to him. In this way, we will be doing what St Paul says we are to do – to glorify the name of God even in eating and drinking (1 Cor. 10:31), which means that we lift our eyes up to him and receive food from his hand as though he were the Father that feeds us. But anyway, as I have said, David went beyond what was proper when he placed a curse on the mountain of Gilboa.

Next, David felt that 'the shield of the mighty had been thrown down', namely, 'the shield of Saul, as though he had not been anointed with oil' (2 Sam. 1:21). This has been explained by some as referring to those who used to anoint their shields with oil when they went to war, so that when they were assailed by their enemies, they would not be captured, because the oil would make their enemies slip this way or that. But that does not really apply here, because the oil of which he is speaking refers to the kingdom of Saul. It is the same as saying that Saul's shield had been thrown down maliciously, as though he were not privileged above others, and as though God had not accepted him as king and head of the people. For although death is common to all of us and may happen like this to us, yet it is particularly shocking if God sends an ignominious death to someone whom he had previously elevated to dignity and high honour. It is true that the human condition is general. Everyone is subject to heat and cold, to hunger and thirst and many other needs, to illness and, finally, death. Yet it causes horror like some hideous spectacle if some great prince, who has been banished, winds up begging and cannot find either bread or water. Why? Because if a man has been elevated by God to a place of high degree, the honour which he previously possessed causes the evil and adversity to shine more vividly.

That is why David expressed his grief here that the shield of Saul, which was supposed to have been a sign of his prowess and virtue, had been thrown down. For when a man was far off, he always placed his shield in front so that it would be seen. When someone wanted to indicate that there had been a victory, he used the shield as a sign. Or if someone wanted to show that men had died valiantly, he used it also, as if to say, 'How firm you stayed behind it!' Even the mothers in some countries used a similar language and symbolism towards their children when they went to war, to show them how brave they must be, urging them, 'Bring back your shield (dead or alive)'. Thus, the shields of Saul and of Jonathan were spoken of here to express the fact that their death was ignominious. This raises the question: How could this have happened? For Saul was chosen by God to govern the people, and had been anointed by the hand of the prophet. Thus, it was God who had elevated him above the common rank of men; he had ordained him as his lieutenant and officer. It was certainly a situation which could cause great astonishment when the glory of God had shone for a time in a man, and then he was trodden underfoot so that his dignity was turned into shame and embarrassment.

That is what David wanted to express. We can gather a valuable principle from this – that we should be touched with sadness when the favours of God are cast down, for we ought to honour them everywhere they are seen, as has been stated in this context. Therefore, we ought to be deeply affected and cut to the quick when we see the destruction of those marks – meant for glory – which God has placed in men and in all creatures, for to the degree that they are destroyed, the glory of God is diminished. When that happens, we must experience his wrath, for he does not spare those who have been ennobled through a generous bestowal of his gifts. Whenever we see God unleashing his anger against those who seemed to be chosen by him for public leadership, so that those very people are ruined, confounded, and destroyed, we have every reason to 'lower our eyes' and realise that it is the wrath of God – so that we may humble ourselves under his mighty hand and plod along much more carefully. That is what we must learn, then, from this reference that David made to the anointing of Saul. We should be horrified at the end he met, exposed to such disgrace and all the shameful abuse of his enemies.

We read that the 'arrow of Jonathan had never turned back, and the sword of Saul had never returned empty' (2 Sam. 1:22), and was never employed without success, without his killing his enemies. Now it is true that shedding human blood is a terrible thing in itself, and that we are supposed to detest it thoroughly. For we know that men are created in the image of God, and when his image is violated, the very hairs of their head witness against us. But the malice of man is such that it will actually often be legitimate to shed blood and even for many to be killed. How so? When we wage a just war to defeat enemies who have taken up arms wickedly and unreasonably. God wishes to be glorified when he gives us this kind of victory.

Then God also wants his vengeance to be known, by punishing those who deserved it. That is why Saul and Jonathan were praised for having killed their enemies, and for having spared nothing; that the bow of one of them had never turned back; that he had not broken up his troops. For the text is clearly speaking here of war. Since Jonathan had defeated his enemies, it was necessary for him to be praised for it. Why? As I have said, if men were what they ought to be, it is quite certain that shedding a drop of blood should horrify us. The Philistines were enemies of true religion and they were so swollen with pride against the Church of God that they wanted to ruin it. Their insatiable avarice drove them on so much that they wanted to gobble up and swallow down everything in their uncontrollable greed. That is why it was necessary for the blade of Saul to be employed in the name of God, and likewise for the bow of Jonathan to be drawn, for they were officers of God to execute his vengeance.

Thus, when we praise the prowess of those who have been valiant in war, who have routed and defeated the enemies of God, let us learn that when men behave like cats and dogs in this way, it is because they have become like brutes, no longer considering the image of God engraved in us. In short, they no longer recognise themselves in their neighbour, as though looking in a mirror. So let us, in this case, recognise that when God withdraws his grace from those who are unworthy of it, he is intending to reprove everyone. When God punishes them (as mentioned above) by abandoning them in such a condition that they get themselves chained up like wild boars, and seek their own ruin and perdition, let us recognise it as the judgement of God. If this were not true, how could magistrates continue to hold a position of honour when they have to send malefactors to death, if it were not that God had delegated his authority to them? In the same way, anyone who justifies the sinful is just as guilty before God as if he had condemned the innocent. The same principle is true of legitimate wars.

But we must look out a hundred times and more before engaging in combat, to see whether God is calling us or not; whether we have been sent by him; and whether he really is authorising and advising us in this cause which we are undertaking. When that is known for sure and approved ahead of time, then whoever is the most valiant is certainly the one who will be the minister of God in this situation.

It is quite true that the Scriptures, in order to keep us from desiring to commit murder, always describe it by using a word which signifies 'to defile oneself'. We can see this when it is stated that the most valiant followers of David, even though they did well, were still described as having defiled themselves in the death of so many people. Now that is not to say that the Spirit of God condemned them, but it is stated to make us react in horror to the shedding of blood, to urge us to seek true peace and concord, avoiding any occasion for brawling or strife, so that no murder or killing will be committed among us. Anyway, the text has every reason to say, in praise of Saul and Jonathan, that they were strong to attack their enemies and did not spare them when necessity called, and even constrained them to do so.

It then says afterwards that 'Saul and Jonathan were dear and lovable in their lives, and were not separated in their death' (2 Sam. 1:23). Now here David recalled the sort of things that would move men to compassion and, at the same time, could sweeten their sadness when there was need for consolation.

That is why it says that Saul was not separated from Jonathan, his son, in death, just as they had loved one another in their life, as a way of praising the union which God gave them, and of showing that he maintained it as an indissoluble bond. It is, of course, true that their union was not so holy that Saul for his part did not violate it. For we have seen that he was ready to kill his son – so much so, that if he had not fled and hidden himself, Saul would not have spared him (1 Sam. 20). That was because Jonathan had maintained the innocence of David in the hope of appeasing the anger – or, rather, fury – of his father. But David here paid no attention to that, for he buried Saul's offences and recognised him as the one whom God had ordained as head over his people. Now he repressed everything that would have shown Saul to be ignoble, and explained to us the reason why. For he wished to show how grieved he was over the evil which had happened to his people, so that they would realise that he was not careless about the outrages and injuries that they had suffered. That, then, was his intention and that is why he did not wish to mention Saul's offences. Thus, we are not surprised when he said there was harmony in life and death between Saul and Jonathan.

Now beyond that, it is however very likely that they were separated in the condition of their souls. Saul was to the very end a rebel against God; he despised him like someone who is incorrigible. Not only did he persecute the innocent, but wishing to reverse the decree of God, he committed a most wicked act. He went like a wretched magician or enchanter to ask counsel of a witch (1 Sam. 28). That was the most desperate act of all. What about Jonathan? Although he should have succeeded to the royal crown, it was taken away from him. When he saw that God did not favour his succession, he humbled himself and gave up any honour connected to this royal dignity. He managed his affairs modestly like a commoner. In short, he submitted himself to David from the time he was first under attack until the end. He considered the whole matter in the light of the promise that God had given. Thus, there is no doubt that Jonathan was very different spiritually from his father. And yet it is enough that their external condition was similar, and so David was mentioning in this hymn only those things which were apparent to men.

Still, we must move on to consider the commendable goal that David was pursuing. He wanted to show his love for the state of the Church and for political stability. That was why he was lamenting in this hymn and teaching everyone through it, so that they would remember to maintain what God had established. It was, indeed, a singular blessing that Saul had provided leadership to guide and uphold the people, and that he had served as a wall to defend the common peace. That was all David was thinking of and that was why he drew attention to such a union between the father and the son. It is as though he were declaring that even though he had been called by God to succeed to the kingdom, nevertheless, he had not been an enemy of Saul's house, and that he would even have wished that the succession had been from father to son – as he demonstrated more specifically later (2 Sam. 4:9–10).

Furthermore, he turned his attention to all the women of the country, saying, 'Daughters of Judah, mourn over Saul, who clothed you with beautiful and precious garments, who even gave you excellent ornaments, and put gold on your clothing' (2 Sam. 1:24). In this, he did not mean to say that Saul had been so generous as literally to give away expensive and exquisite dresses, chains of gold and other adornments! Rather, this referred to the fact that the people had experienced prosperity for a long time. Now when there is peace in a country and no revolution, we know that everyone gets richer, that is to say, those who work and are good managers of their resources. For there will always be people who are dissolute and debauched, and just wasteful consumers. They are utter spendthrifts; they devour everything they can get their hands on. However, the majority grow wealthier when there is no war, for then there will be no tax or tribute imposed on them, so everyone will be free to take care of his own business and amass goods in doing so. That is what was meant when this passage said that the daughters of Judah had good reason to mourn, in that they had been sumptuously dressed in the time of Saul. Thus, David was summarising and including the whole community, but he chose the women rather than the men, since he wanted to speak of clothing.

Now we know that this is an ambition that motivates women much more than men! Although there are many men who will presume to ask to be elevated in status, yet if you compare them to women, you will find them to be very modest and under control! In other words, women are stirred up by this passion to be well dressed and attractive, and are envious of their neighbour if she appears to be better dressed, complaining 'Oh, she has a beautiful coat of such and such material. And this other person has a fancy collar made in a particular fashion; she wears it every day and not just on holiday! Then there is someone else who has such a well-made dress but who does not have my social standing! Now do I not deserve as much as the rest of them?'

This kind of corruption has existed from the beginning of time. In fact, one can see this in the prophet Isaiah, who gathered all the baggage and useless objects which women have in their dressers and cabinets to deck themselves out (Isa. 3:16ff.) when he said that God would chastise them and destroy their garments so that their private parts would be uncovered (those are his own words), and that they would be shamed as a punishment for their arrogance (Isa. 47:2ff.). We see that this is a very common vice, and only with great difficulty will you find one woman out of a hundred who is able to maintain her balance here. Here, then, David was wanting to express the idea that where there is great abundance of goods and riches, women will always desire to show themselves off ostentatiously, and be so decked out that there will be gold glittering all over them!

Well, it certainly seems that this should be taken as humour, but we must note that when Scripture speaks of riches, it mentions the abuse without approving it. This would be rather obscure if it were not illuminated by examples. When it speaks of the blessing which God would give to the line of Judah, it says that his 'eyes will be red with wine, and his teeth white with milk' (Gen. 49:12). By that, it signifies that he would give an inheritance to this line that would be so fertile with wine that their eyes would turn red and be inflamed because of drink. They would have such rich pastures that milk would fill them up like babies who have plenty to suck when their nurses have an abundance of milk. Thus it is said that the line of Judah would drink milk because of the abundance of pasturage, so much so that their teeth will be white. Does all this mean that God would permit this line to gorge itself and have its eyes rolled back by drinking, or to abuse milk with such intemperance that it would have to be vomited or disgorged again like pigs? Certainly that was not what the expression meant! But as I have said, it is a common custom in Scripture to take even the abuses to show how generous God is – that he gives to men not only what is useful and necessary, but that he also sends them superabundance, and much more than they need. Nevertheless, men will not fail to come under condemnation if they do not come to show that attitude of which St Paul speaks – namely, that they understand what it is to be rich, and how to use wealth responsibly and without ostentation (1 Tim. 6:7–8).

Now when it stated here that the women had been sumptuously dressed under the reign of Saul, it was not intended (as I have said) to praise their covetousness or foolish ambition. For we have already pointed out the passage of Isaiah, where it shows that God will not tolerate such outrageous desires. He will cause such violent change in their lives that everyone who seeks to be so arrogant and over-dainty will have to be made into a shameful spectacle, and people will look at them with embarrassment.

In summary, David wished to declare that under the kingdom of Saul, not only was everyone able to live in comfort, but that there had been a superabundance. He illustrated this prosperity by referring to numerous people who go much too far – especially women – as this vice of desiring only to primp and preen is more deeply rooted in that sex. This statement is similar to what you might say of a prince who maintains his subjects in peace and harmony, and who is fair and knows how to handle his neighbours effectively. This prince is like the good earth which fattens cattle with its increase. In other words, he makes it possible for his people to turn their teeth white on milk.

Since he does not plunder them by extortion, he gives them the opportunity to banquet and dance, and enjoy their leisure. You may say these things. That does not mean, however, that dancing is approved. It does not mean that gluttony is praised, nor that you are supposed to abuse the good gifts of God. This is not to say that fertility is despised for all that, but all in all, he was wanting to signify that Saul's subjects had experienced prosperous times.

Now by this we are taught, in the first place, that when God shows himself to be so generous as to pour out his favours upon us so abundantly, we must remember to put ourselves under voluntary restraint. When we are able to live well, I say, when it pleases God to give it, when there are beautiful grape and wheat harvests, let us bless the Lord for having provided our food. And yet when we have bread and wine and such abundance that it appears we could afford to waste it, let us remember to keep ourselves in check voluntarily. Let us not fail to use it as we should, properly and very responsibly, not heaping it up greedily. Rather, let us use it to provide us with sustenance so that we will be able to busy ourselves in the service of God and in helping our neighbours. After a man has become rich, he is well advised to regulate himself carefully and keep himself under the Law, for it is certain that God is testing him. When he gives us goods in abundance, it is to examine us to see if we will be responsible and maintain true modesty. For when there is a famine, people are forced to live modestly. And when a man is poor, he does not have the leisure to think of acting ostentatiously. But when we have the wherewithal and the opportunity, it shows that we know what it is to obey God, when in spite of the temptation to abuse it, we do not fail to use the goods which God has put in our hands in accordance with his will.

Let us, therefore, deliberately follow a course of self-restraint when God gives us more than we need to eat and drink. When he gives us good things, let us not fail to keep ourselves within proper limits. Let us remember that someone who is rich should be generous. God commands him to help those who are in hard circumstances and serious need, and that is what he should do. Nevertheless, let him enjoy his possessions, and use them in such a way that God will always be recognised as their source. Even though he is rich, let him not bring glory to himself. For here are the two vices in which we indulge. Some people simply wish to show themselves off when God has given them something, thereby forgetting God and blowing their own trumpet! Yet Scripture says that riches should not make us lift ourselves up, or consider the blessings of God to be nothing, but that we are always to be humble. There are other people who exhibit a different vice. They are not given over to pride and luxurious living, but act like pigs in the trough! Let us, therefore, be careful with regard to both of these risks. This is one concern.

There is still another principle to be taken from this passage – namely, it is praiseworthy for a good prince to relieve his subjects' poverty. This must be carefully noted, for it is very rare. Today, princes do nothing but seize everything they can for themselves, and then they support those ravening wolves who never have enough to satisfy their appetite. For when someone comes to court, instead of serving his prince, he tries to make himself important. One man will preen his feathers to try to be included among the brave; another will look for debauchery; someone else will aim to be a cook, and others jockey for this or that position. They will not be satisfied with remaining at a low level, but, by using others, one man will acquire some lordship or the rights to a rental income of 15,000 francs; another will get 20,000; another, 30,000; another, 50,000; the sum must keep increasing in the attempt to win great titles and great honours! But at whose expense? It is the poor people who are skinned alive, and are eaten up and taken advantage of from all sides. But nevertheless, they must keep their mouths politely closed when 'my lord' speaks, so that is how this rabble of princes can be left in shock after they have despoiled their wretched subjects to cater to their own extravagant life-style.

That is why I have said that this doctrine must be carefully observed, particularly so that people may recognise the virtue of a king or prince who keeps his subjects in comfort. Then they can grow richer as they run their households, and each one can have enough for himself and his descendants. When, I say, a prince maintains these conditions, he will be valued far more highly than if he enriches twenty or so people who behave like famished wolves, eager to suck the blood of the poor and even break their bones with their teeth and tear them apart piece by piece with their paws! That is what we are to remember from the praise which David gave to Saul here.

Now it says, 'How are the mighty fallen!' (2 Sam. 1:25). Concerning this phrase, we must bear in mind that we discussed yesterday the fact that David was so carried away with his grief that his spirit was not calmly prepared to recognise the judgement of God, and then declare and make confession of the sins of the people so as to ask pardon for them. Now this song is not given to us as an example of a perfect product, but David's goal in it, as I have stated, was to encourage the people. That is evidence of how stunned they were, as though it was a strange thing that God had permitted such valiant men to be defeated by their enemies.

But above all, David missed Jonathan and said, 'I am anguished over you, my brother Jonathan', for there was nothing which surpassed 'the love which I had for you' (2 Sam. 1:26). It was a 'marvellous' love, he says, 'passing the love of women'. This shows that David was not ungrateful to Jonathan after his death, for he declared that if he had lived, he would have kept the promise which he made to him. As we have seen, they had made a covenant on the condition that Jonathan would voluntarily give up his royal succession, and at the same time David had promised to be his loyal friend (1 Sam. 20:11ff., 42; 23:17–18). Now if Jonathan had lived, David declared here that he would never have been false to his promise. And he was still concerned about it after his death, as he declared in the other passage.

Some people take this 'love of women' to mean the love that mothers have for their children, for we know that their love is much more tender than that of men, whose love is more hidden. Others take it to mean the love that wives have for their husbands. But we can see from what is said in another passage of Scripture that this love is taken to mean the kind of love found in marriage between husband and wife; love that is mutual. When Daniel mentions the Romans, he shows how they would be a brutal and cruel nation, which did not know the love of women or the duty of marriage (Dan. 11:37). Now our Lord wished for human kindness to be shown particularly in this sphere, namely, in the kindness and consideration which husband and wife owe each other. Indeed, the basis of marriage is that we must love one another. For just as God has loved his own from the greatest to the smallest, he wants us to be members of one body.

The common nature which we men share is a God-given privilege, and if we observe how this nature is maintained, we find that it is by means of marriage. For since the husband will be one with his wife, from that will come children. Then the lines will extend themselves, so much so that they will separate from one country to another, and will multiply themselves so that towns will be produced and large towns, and finally the whole world will be inhabited by this means! Therefore, the expression 'love of women' indicates something as valuable as this love and union in marriage. That is why David says, as we have seen above, that he loved Jonathan even more than that type of love. Nevertheless, there was such chastity involved that if he loved Jonathan above his wife, it was a love that was absolutely pure, in accordance with the character of God. For we have seen above that this love was founded in God and according to his Word, and that his name had been invoked as a solemn dedication. All in all, David showed here that his love for Jonathan was very remarkable and that was why he experienced such great distress over his death.

It is true that David's expression of his emotion was too vehement and, as we have explained, it was not right for him to have sunk as he did into the depths of sorrow. Although it was not perfect, still the basis of his emotion was good. However, let us note that the children of God are not insensitive, that they are saddened by the death of their neighbours and friends, and that they especially feel more regret, bitterness and pain over the loss of those whom God has bound very closely to them.

This will happen to the children of God, but the point is for us to realise that we must control our feelings and hold ourselves captive in submission to God. Thus, when it is said that we are supposed to accept the death of our relatives and friends patiently, it does not mean that we do not feel it at all or that we are like blocks of wood, for God does not take our nature away from us. But even when we are sad, we must not fail to continue to bless his name and accept his will, not only as just and right, but also as good and salutary for us. We are to accept willingly what he sends us, so that on the one hand we are sad, but on the other hand we do not fail to bring ourselves to bless God deliberately – of our own accord and not because of external constraint. When at last we do calm down, after having lost proper control of our emotions, we can greatly sweeten our sadness by remembering that nothing can hinder us from going to God. That is what we must keep in mind.

In conclusion, David says again, 'How are the mighty and strong fallen, and the munitions of war perished!' (2 Sam. 1:27). When we understand what David meant, we see that he was frightened by the effect this calamity could have on the people, so he wanted to encourage all those whom God had left to take heart and not leave the battle. Rather, he was concerned for them to be gathered together, so that the name of Israel would remain strong, and true religion and the service of God would function as formerly. He was concerned that the wicked should not triumph over truth by defying the Law of God, stamping underfoot what he ordained, and making fun of the promises which God had given to the line of Abraham. That, in short, was what David meant. He did not want to leave the people scattered and lost, but rather to urge them to be encouraged after their time of despair. They would thus strengthen themselves in God, and be able to fight on valiantly, and so give thanks to God for the victory that he would give them over their enemies.

Now let us prostrate ourselves before the majesty of our good God, recognising how many faults there are of which we are guilty, praying that he would make us feel them so much that the punishments that he sends us may be of real value to us, and that we may never cease following him and submitting ourselves to him, however grievous the afflictions he may send us. In the end, let us learn how to govern ourselves in such a manner that he may rule over us, and have complete mastery and superiority. And may we not only be governed by the written laws, but may we have such obedience to his Word that it may cause us to conform ourselves entirely to it . . .

4

*Guidance to Hebron**

Now it came to pass that David took counsel of God, saying: Shall I go up to one of the towns of Judah? The Lord said to him: Go up. Again David said: Where shall I go up? He said: to Hebron. David then went there with his two wives; Ahinoam the Jezreelite, and Abigail, the wife of Nabal . . . (2 Sam. 2:1–7).

After the death of Saul, the time had come for David to be given possession of the kingdom as he had been promised. Well, what was the state of the kingdom at that time? Everything was ruined in Israel; there was only confusion. The poor people were so troubled that they were expecting the enemy to come and exterminate everyone who was left.

It was a terrible trial for David to be outside Israel at this time. He was among enemies in the Philistine town of Ziklag (1 Sam. 27:6–7). He could not move from there without being pursued, for not surprisingly the enemies of Israel were always suspicious of him, especially after the recent death of Saul (1 Sam. 29:4). Moreover, since their great victory over Saul, it would have cost them practically nothing to have killed David and his little company. There were only six hundred men with him (1 Sam. 30:9), and they were more like slaves than soldiers. The Philistines had defeated nearly all Israel, which they could not have done without a large army. It is true that David with his men had defeated the Amalekites (1 Sam. 30:17), but that

*Wednesday, June 3, 1562.

was nothing compared to this Philistine victory. Thus, we find David more perplexed than ever.

Saul had cruelly chased David from pillar to post, until at last he found refuge in the land of his enemies. After such a brave fight, you would have thought that David had more than earned the crown, but that is not what happened. Thus, God tried him all the way, so that he could serve as an example for us today. When God seems to enjoy afflicting us and testing us over and over again, we should be willing to accept blows as long as he pleases to give them. Let us not give up in mid-stream.

Now it is stated that 'David took counsel of God' (2 Sam. 2:1) and received the reply that he could go up to the country of Judah. God even told him the precise town: Hebron. Here we must note that David did not enter battle without good preparation. He would undertake absolutely no enterprise unless he was continually guided by the will of God. It had to be proven to him that it was the right way. We have already seen this several times, but it is a doctrine that cannot too often be repeated. That is why it is mentioned so often in the Holy Scripture. Let us by no means think that it is a waste of time for us to study most carefully how David plodded on in such humility, how he never moved a finger, so to speak, or lifted a foot to go one way or the other, unless God guided him with the infallible testimony of his Word.

The true way to distinguish brave from foolhardy action is just this: to ascertain the will of God. Here we might have a man who does not in the least hesitate risking his life for a cause, and thinks nothing of all that could happen to him in the course of duty. He might be praised as brave and magnanimous. Now another man who does nothing without good counsel might, in fact, be called rash by people joking that he is presumptuous and foolhardy. Why? Because the world does not discern as it should. Or we might have another man who is very prudent, who does not go to the firing line. Another man is hare-brained and does not know what he is doing. Yet having made all these observations, we still have not come to the main point or principle. For where does prudence come from, if God does not give it by his Spirit? Let us be especially careful not to undertake anything, unless duty requires it, and then let us keep within bounds without going off at a tangent.

Let me illustrate this principle to make it easier to understand. One sees many worldly people who are advised and urged to take counsel, to manage their affairs carefully, to avoid dangers. But they miss the main principle – they have neither justice nor equity in mind. When the typical unbeliever, for instance, wages war, he does use a certain type of prudence: 'I must camp here; I must occupy such and such a town; we must resist our enemy by such and such a means'. Although praiseworthy as far as it goes, this sort of prudence is employed by the most perverse people in the world. But true prudence, as I have said, lies in considering why we are doing this. Before we commit ourselves, we must know that a particular course of action is the will of God, and that he approves what we are doing.

Such insight does not come from the brain of men. We must turn to God, so that he will declare his will to us when it is hidden and obscure, and that is done in two ways. First, we must come to Holy Scripture, where God tells us what is to be done. In the second place, just as certainly as the blind cannot see even at high noon, so all the doctrine and insight of Scripture will be useless to us unless God blesses it by his Holy Spirit. Indeed, we will become much more confused every day, especially when we know in general what is good, but are unable to decide what particular course of action is to be chosen.

Hence, we must follow what Scripture says to us: that since God has the Spirit of wisdom and understanding, we must come to him and ask him to take our hand and guide and lead us as he knows to be best for us (cf. Jas. 1:5 and Isa. 11:2). And we are not to do this on one occasion only, but throughout our whole life.

David was well taught in the Law of God. He had the gift of prophecy. When he was anointed king, God very richly endowed him with graces and virtues which were appropriate and essential for that position. Nevertheless, he asked God what to do. David did this, as we have stated elsewhere, by means of the ephod, which was part of the priestly garments

(1 Sam. 23:9; 30:7). Anyway, David clearly knew that it is not enough to have heard what the will of God is in general, but that he had to know specifically which way to turn in his own life. For instance, when we have to take a trip, it is easy to know what general direction we want to go. Very well, we have all experienced this several times. Yet often, we come to a particular crossroads and do not know whether to turn right or left. Thus, we will be unexpectedly halted.

As I said before, we know the general direction very well, and we have gone that way previously without much trouble. On this occasion, however, we may not have the address with us, or a companion to guide us. So it is with the guidance of our Lord. Even when we have been clearly taught by his Word what is good and right, we still need God to give us understanding of his will that, being enlightened by his Spirit, we will understand what he has said to us in his Word. But that is not all. For we can be undecided about several things, and after much consideration still not have found the solution. In that case, we must call on the Lord, and turn to him.

Let us learn from this passage that all our life we are to have God as our Guide, and his Word as the unquestionable standard of right and wrong. So, to know God's guidance, let us be aware that we must diligently read and have our ears wide open from morning until evening to the exposition of Holy Scripture. Unless God gives us his Scripture, we will still be confused, as experience teaches us.

There are many who will return from the sermon much more ignorant than they came, because they are only interested in ceremony and come out of duty. They even bring books with them to make a good show. But they only mutter without any understanding, and derive no profit from the Word of God, because they have not applied their spirit to it. On the contrary, we must humble ourselves before God, recognising not only the weakness and insensitivity of our spirits, but also that we are totally ignorant – indeed, that we are nothing but poor brute beasts, unless God gives us reason and intelligence. That is what we must pray God to give us.

Further, the better we know his Word, the better we can

advise those who ask us. For each day someone may come to us with a difficult case, full of confusing contradictions which tie us in knots, so that finally we do not know which way to turn. To function properly, we must learn to call on God every day, to return to him, and diligently seek his will, as we see David did. Even with all the evidence that God had ordained him king, still he dared not attempt to take possession of the crown, nor move his foot from the town where he was, even though he was in the land of his enemies. But he came to ask God to speak to him and tell him what to do.

Of course, as I said before, we no longer have the priestly ephod, which was formerly used, but instead of the symbol, we have the actual truth. For the one who offered sacrifice formerly was only a symbol or picture of our Lord Jesus Christ. Today we have all we need, because not only has God shown us by the Gospel what is good and useful, but also in our Lord Jesus Christ 'are hidden all the treasures of wisdom' (Col. 2:3), so that we may come to him.

Thus, since the fullness of the Spirit of wisdom and understanding rests upon him, let us not doubt that he possesses it totally, so that he can distribute it to us in the measure that he knows is useful for us. Let us come, then, to that source, and drink from it all we need, and we will be satisfied – particularly when, in all humility, we ask only to be disciples of God and of our Lord Jesus Christ. Let us ask that he would give us sufficient guidance that we may never fall short in any duty. And let us realise that all of our life we have a long way to travel and that often the paths are very tortuous; that there are even mountains, rivers, stones, thorns, and ditches. In sum, when there is no way out nor clear path, at that point God will faithfully guide us by our Lord Jesus Christ, his Son, insofar as we allow ourselves to be taught by him.

When we do not look to him, we will take many wrong steps. Why? Because all those who turn away from the right path do it either from carelessness or from foolhardiness and rebellion. Some have too high an opinion of their wisdom and trot around like fools, often falling, so that one breaks his legs, another an arm, and finally all break their necks. All such people can expect a downfall. To avoid the wages of ignorance, they must call on the Lord.

Others are even worse, for they preach marvellous things to such a degree that they seem to be great doctors, and then undertake their enterprises without consulting the will of God! In their rebellion and audacity, they think that all their ideas must be carried out, and therefore they do not condescend to seek the Lord's counsel. Why? Because they have already decided not to submit themselves to what he has ordained and, above all, because they are enraged by their wicked desires.

So let us carefully observe what Scripture says here. Even though David clearly knew that God had constituted him king and that Saul had trespassed, even though the time was ripe for him to enjoy the crown, nevertheless he asked God to tell him what he should do. Why? Because although he was on the way, he still knew that he could err seriously if God did not guide him. Let us learn through all of life to go to the Lord, especially when we are facing an important decision. Let us find out what is to be done, and let us not be so self-assured that we fail to pray God to show us what is useful and expedient. For without that, as I have said, we might make many false steps; we might even fall – or what is worse, we might go astray so seriously that we no longer know the way of salvation. And that is why people with the right attitude, who refuse to be governed by their base desires, are scorned by presumptuous and arrogant men.

When the text says that God replied to David that he should go to the country of Judaea, it teaches us that we have only ourselves to blame if we do not accept good advice. For Scripture says that we 'are to knock on the door, and it will be opened to us; that we are to seek and we shall find; that we are to ask and it will be given to us' (Matt. 7:7). David certainly had this promise engraved in his heart, but it had not been stated in its fullness, as we have it today. Instead, he had the ceremony of seeking God's will by means of the priestly ephod.

Now we have far more than that. Our Lord Jesus Christ came down here below to fulfil his promise to his disciples that he would no longer call them his servants, but his friends (John 15:15). This means that he has come so close to us that we can learn all we need to know like good pupils. This will prevent wild thoughts, and the brainstorms that lead to reckless behaviour.

When, therefore, we clothe ourselves in humility, it is certain that God will respond to our need. Are we lacking in wisdom? St James says there is the 'Father of lights' (Jas. 1:17), who is ready and able to help us in our weakness and needs. Thus, let us go to him. Above all, when we need wisdom, let us realise that God reserves the right to give it, and not be so foolish as to attribute it to ourselves. Instead, let us worship him for such an excellent gift. This should persuade us that if we ask God to give us the Spirit of understanding which he knows we need, then we can be assured that he will respond if we are ready to subject ourselves to his Word. Thus, we will find him ready and inclined to grant our requests, and we will never be frustrated for having waited to make our requests to him.

Notice that even after we have received the first instruction, he gives us a second message. For the text states here that David, not content with being told that he could go, asked further, 'Where and in what town?' and he was shown Hebron. This teaches us that God will be favourable and kind to us not only once, but even after he has granted our requests, he will continue to receive our prayers.

Let us, then, boldly run to him and continue doing so (Heb. 4:16) and we will find that we have in him a faithful guide all our life. He will not just put us on the right road and then leave us there in suspense, but he will always be with us. You could compare him to a guardian of little children, standing behind them in order to say, 'Go this way'. Thus God has his eye on us, even when we do not see him. That is the main thing that we must remember from this passage.

Next, Scripture adds that 'the men of Judah came and anointed him king' (2 Sam. 2:4). Note that this was only one tribe, for there were eleven other tribes who had not committed themselves to David. Here is a new trial, especially since Abner took sides against him and set up Ishbosheth, the son of Saul, as a rival king (2 Sam. 2:8). As I have said, God had at last elevated David to the royal throne and all the people (of Judah) submitted to him. But it was only a single tribe. God does not seem here to carry out or fulfil his Word, because the people of Israel are one body. God so united them, by calling them his inheritance (Exod. 34:9; Deut. 32:9; Psa. 33:12; Isa. 19:25, etc.) that he clearly shows that they should have only true concord and union. Also, he compares the people may times to a woman to whom he is married (Hos. 1:2). When David sees that the people are thus torn in pieces, and that he has only one tribe – even though it was the most noble – what could he think but that what he had been promised by the mouth of Samuel was a vain and frivolous hope, and that God seemed to want to mock him?

Now that shows us, as I have already mentioned, that we must never cease to let ourselves be examined and proved by many temptations – indeed, by an infinite number when it pleases God. Let us always be ready to fight new battles as they are sent to us. And when God has examined us in one way, let us not think that we are finished but let us come to offer ourselves to him, so that he may peaceably master us without any resistance. Insofar as we lack that strength, let us ask him to fortify us, for it is certain that David would have failed a hundred times if he had not been sustained. Thus, let us learn to lean on God and on his truth if we wish truly to persevere in well-doing. We do not ask to be strengthened in order to remain lazy and grow idle in slothfulness, but to work more than ever. If, for instance, a man who must take a trip arrives at a lodging and rests a while, he does not plan to stay there three days, but he will leave immediately after his meal, and will continue his journey. If he arrives late and stays for the night, he will always have half an eye open, ready to leave us soon as morning comes.

So, when we have undergone some temptation, when we have been afflicted in some way, let us persevere in the right path, however it pleases God to arrange it. And let us pray that he will sustain us in all our needs. So much, then, for the point that David was anointed only by the tribe of Judah.

Now a question might be raised here: how could the men of Judah dare anoint David, given that this would efface the original anointing, or declare it insufficient? And how could

David allow it? For when Samuel came to him, David knew that he was the organ and instrument of the hand of God (1 Sam. 16:1–13). Though David had received that anointing, he then seems not to be content with it, and despises the authority of God and of his prophet by receiving this new anointing by the people.

We must note that that anointing was not like baptism, for we are baptised only once, and if we return for a second baptism, this is in effect wishing to negate the true baptism which was ordained by God. But anointing was different. For when Samuel came to David, it was to assure him that God had chosen and kept him. So when the people anointed David, they were not implying that what Samuel did was ineffective, or that it was not powerful enough to accomplish anything. Rather, it is as though they were replying 'Amen', and ratifying what had been done. We should understand, therefore, that David is not elected king here by the desire of men, but that he received approbation because God authorised it, and thus men agree with it.

In fact, it was a miracle of God that the tribe of Judah so quickly went over to David. It is true that necessity constrained them, for they saw themselves exposed as prey; they were like a little flock of lambs in the throat of wolves. The Philistines were ready to swallow and gobble them up entirely. Nevertheless, the tribe of Judah, in order to obey and please their king, had previously not ceased to pursue David as his enemy. He was like a poor fugitive, and dared not show himself in the company of men. He was not even safe among the caves of the mountains in the midst of wild beasts. This same tribe of Judah had rejected David as a rotten member and banished him from favour and friendship. We can surely see, in the complaint that he made to God, what extreme anguish he was experiencing. Neither father nor mother knows me, he said (Psa. 27:10). Actually, his father and mother did, indeed, come to find him. Still, he was not recognised for a while and dared not show his face, or put himself in any eminent position. So when, in one moment, these people changed their minds, we know that God caused them to do so.

Let us plainly see, then, that the anointing which David received from the men of Judah was not an attempt to do something new. It was not to add anything more to the anointing of Samuel – as though it did not possess enough virtue or assurance. Rather, it was a confirmation of what he had done. It is true that the people did add to the anointing by Samuel, but they did not mean to say, 'The prophet only did half of the work, and we must finish it so that final perfection will come from us'. This is not what they meant; they rather were saying, 'God anointed David, and we cannot resist it. Indeed, we have already resisted it too much. God could easily punish us for our ingratitude and deprive us of such a blessing. But now, since he is pleased for this anointing to take effect, let us come together and proclaim what God has pronounced. Let us vow of our own accord. Since Samuel was his herald, let us assemble here to give our consent, and to conform to what he once decreed himself.' This is what the people meant to do.

We must note in this passage that God holds the hearts of men in his hand (Prov. 21:1), and turns and controls them as it pleases him, in order to carry out his will. This is a most necessary doctrine, for in this world we see many gainsayers who can trouble us until we feel that there is no way that we can reach our goal. Therefore, in order to dissolve all fears, we must hold the principle that God governs the courage of men. It certainly seems that these presumptuous people, in their pride, can go from one place to another; that they can plod on as they wish; that they can do their will. Yes, but at the same time God is holding them with an unseen bridle, so that in the midst of their undertakings they remain in the place where God has shut them up. Even in spite of their rage, he constrains them to obey him and carry out what he wishes to happen.

Therefore, when we see many things contrary to our salvation, and especially when we have enemies who work and seek only to ruin us, let us come to this point – that God holds their hearts, and when it pleases him, he can turn them in the opposite direction of their original intention. Hence, instead of making us fall, as they had hoped, they will advance us. It is necessary, I say, that we gather this principle from the present story, which says that the men of Judah came to anoint David. Those who formerly were his enemies would never have come over to his side unless God had caused them to. Therefore, everything is governed by his strict counsel.

However, the text says that when 'David heard that the men of Jabesh-gilead had buried Saul, he sent to them messengers' (2 Sam. 2:4–6) to approve what they did, and to show that he held them in high regard and, indeed, that this had moved him to love them all the more. He hoped that this would end all quarrels and all suspicions that they might have had concerning him, since he needed their support. For David well knew that it was the will of God that he had been constituted king over all the people. Thus, he had to study as much as possible how to reunite the people, so that they could be preserved in the future. Now if there had been a split, he could not have fulfilled his duty. Indeed, if a division had come from him, he would have been blamed and reproached for it – as has already been mentioned, and will be explained more fully later. So it was David's responsibility to remedy all ill will, bitterness and contention, and take great pains to get rid of all those things.

Further, his communication to the inhabitants of Jabesh, who (as we have seen) had taken the body of Saul and buried it (1 Sam. 31:11–13), was meant to show his kindness. Now one could have thought that David would have been angry with them for taking down Saul's body, because he ought to have been pleased, from a purely personal and worldly point of view, to let Saul's body continue hanging on the wall where the Philistines had nailed him (1 Sam. 31:10). Unlike David, those who are not led by the Spirit of God will always rejoice when some ill comes to their enemies, and will not wish them decently buried. Well then, David declared that if anyone thought he hated Saul, they were mistaken. For that reason, he notified the inhabitants of Jabesh of the friendly affection he had towards Saul, and that what they had done pleased him and was as acceptable to him as if they had done it for David himself.

We must always remember what we have just said, that David rose above this vice which is rooted in our nature. Thus, we must fight valiantly when we are annoyed with our enemies and have the desire for vengeance. Let us learn to conquer all our passions and to hold them captive, no matter how hard it is. This will not be done without a fight, for all our feelings go in the wrong direction, and since we are all given to self-love, we wish to battle those who have hurt us. But let us learn from the example of David to reject such wicked corruption and attempt always to do good to our enemies, to those who both hate us and persecute us (Matt. 5:44). That is one point.

Let us attempt also, as far as we can, to make peace whenever there is discord and bitterness; for it only takes a small spark to start a great fire. Therefore, when we do not apply our minds to eliminating the contentions, quarrels and troubles which can take root between people, it is certain that a fire will inevitably be started which cannot be put out. Therefore, let us endeavour, as far as we can, to conduct ourselves peacefully, and force ourselves to bring harmony and love between those who have occasion to quarrel; since men are only too inclined in themselves to cause trouble.

David says, 'You are blessed of God', and 'May the Lord grant you mercy and truth' (2 Sam. 2:5, 6), to show that all good things that men do will be returned to them by God, and that one must judge in the light of that. Since we are perverse, we often want to remember vices instead of virtues, which is why people bury what God approves. That is another point. However, let us learn from the example of David always to look to God and to keep this sentence engraved on our hearts: Those who have sown good seed will reap the fruit of it (see 2 Cor. 9:6; Psa. 126:6).

We must make ourselves remember this lesson well when we see that the world is so perverse that it often returns evil for good, and even that God – in order to prove his faithful ones – permits them to receive only evil after they have tried to do good. The prophet Isaiah teaches a similar lesson when he wants to show the arrogance of those who judge the poor afflicted believers – 'Say and learn this conclusion: There must be restitution for the righteous' (Isa. 3:10). It is as if he said, 'If you foolishly believe that what God has permitted in this world will be permanent, leave your blasphemies and realise that those who have done well will not perish. For God is a faithful rewarder of those who persevere in well doing' (Heb. 11:6; Rom. 2). That is why, after enduring many a combat, David says that the righteous will never perish and will have the fruit of his labour (Psa. 37:17, 25, 28; 112:6), and after having tested him in various circumstances, 'God will not allow them to fall and break a bone' (Psa. 34:20). Rather, he will discover in the end that God has been favourable to him, and has neither deceived him nor tricked him; but that he has always had his eye on those who have been guaranteed his help. Now this is what we should remember from this passage, where David promises Jabesh God's blessing by saying that since their deed is good and praiseworthy, and since their humanity exemplifies virtue, God will bless them.

Then he adds his prayer and says, 'May the Lord grant you mercy and truth'. This way of speaking is common in Holy Scripture, so we must pay careful attention to it. For here are two words which include all that we could desire from and ask of God. First is his mercy, and then his truth. Now this word 'mercy' means that God cannot love us or consider us agreeable except out of his pure goodness and grace. For who are we? What dignity can we plead before him? Therefore, the love that God has for us comes from this source of his mercy. Having pity on our frailty, he receives us in mercy. Well, this statement is intended to show that all the gifts and graces which we receive each day are so much fruit given to us by the hand of God. In brief, under this word 'mercy', all the paternal love which he has for us is comprehended. That is one point.

Now then, how is the happiness of men, and of all that they can wish, made possible unless God is favourable to them – unless he makes them prosper and shows them his liberality face to face? And where will we find assurance unless we know his faithfulness – that is, that he is constant in his promises – and also that he makes us taste and feel that everything that he promises to us is certain and infallible? For when someone speaks to us of his mercy, we will only be able to conceive of a confused fantasy unless we have actually known that he, indeed, wants to be our father. Therefore, unless God speaks to testify to us that he chooses us for his children and that he wishes to undertake the responsibility for our salvation, it is certain that we will always be unstable, and tortured with many doubts and worries.

For this reason, express mention is made of the truth of God, so that we might be assured of his mercy when we come to seek the certitude which is given and offered to us by his Word and by virtue of his Spirit, by which we feel and experience it to be true. His promises are not only for one day, but he tells us that what he has begun he will complete (Phil. 1:6). Thus, when we have grasped and understood this point, let us realise that he will not repent; that he is not mutable like men, but that he will, as I have said, complete his work.

Now that is what this 'truth' refers to. Let us therefore learn, when we are addressing ourselves to God, to fix our eyes and all our senses first of all on his gracious goodness. And then let us be aware that this faithfulness is not interrupted, but that he will so persevere that we will reach the full realisation of all the good things that we are to hope for. He will love us, I say, 'unto the end' (John 13:1), and will guide our path through this life, so that we will be victorious in combat and will pass through all difficulties.

Let us put this truth into practice, especially when we see the Church so afflicted, and that there are so many threats and burning fires. Let us realise that God will destroy all that men have undertaken themselves. He is well able to put out their fires or to use them for their own ruin. When, I say, we see so many troubles, when everything seems about to be lost, let us go back to this truth of God which is stated here.

Above all, let us learn to be constant and ever aspire to the kingdom of God by his promises. These may thus assure us that he will never fail to make the reign of our Lord Jesus Christ fruitful for our salvation and for the whole Church, in spite of every hindrance and all the resistance of a world fighting against it as hard as it can today. This promise is the basis on which we must always rest, for the earthly reign is a token in which we must contemplate the reign of our Lord Jesus Christ and the salvation of his Church to the end of the world.

Now let us prostrate ourselves before the majesty of our good God, recognising all our faults, praying to him that he may touch us with such repentance; that groaning over and confessing our sins, we may be displeased with them; and that we may be confused in ourselves and may seek in him all that is lacking in us. May this not only serve to abolish our past offences, but may it renew us in such fashion that, being clothed with this righteousness, we may glorify him in all our life and words and deeds and thoughts. Thus, let us all say, Almighty God, heavenly Father . . .

5

*The Dreadful 'Game' of War**

Now Abner, son of Ner, captain of Saul's army took Ishbosheth, son of Saul, and made him go to Mahanaim, and made him king over Gilead and Asshur and Jezreel, and over Ephraim and Benjamin and over all Israel . . . (2 Sam. 2:8–17).

We see here how the ambition and desire to rule is blind, for after the people of Israel were defeated, as mentioned above, no-one should have desired to rule over them. Nevertheless, a contention arose among them which would cause a greater disaster than before.

Here is a body without a head, and enemies whom victory has made bold are near. Nevertheless, since Abner, who was captain under Saul, feared that he might become less important and lose the position that he held previously, brought forward the son of Saul to be king. Well, this was, as I have already said, about to cause a greater division among the people. For with so many outside enemies, the twelve tribes of Israel were ready to break up and, indeed, the tribe of Judah was alone over against the eleven others. Even if the Philistines had not touched them, they could easily have destroyed themselves.

These happenings warn us to conduct ourselves with such modesty that we will not seek to be too great. For if this wretched desire dominates us, it is certain that we shall pay no attention to right or fairness or anything else. Abner should have thought that, even though the kingdom belonged to the sons of Saul, there was no other way to save the people unless

*Thursday, June 4, 1562.

David became leader. He should have concluded that it was a foolish undertaking to set Ishbosheth on the throne with but few people under his rule, for he could have had his throat cut. However, having a good reputation, he trusted in his own strength. But he was thus exposing the people to butchery, and did not recognise that the Philistines would be all the more incited to pursue their victory when they saw such a division and civil war within Israel. That is one point.

We have here a mirror to show us how pride and haughtiness is a mortal plague which is bound to dissipate the Church of God, of which the reign of David was a type. We see the present state of the Church reflected in the war. Abner put on a good appearance, claiming to fight for possession of the kingdom which was once for all established; thus implying that the tribe of Judah wished to introduce innovations and to resist God. Therefore Abner, on his part, could claim that he was maintaining the law, which even in his day was of ancient date. David and his followers were accused of causing a revolution, of attempting to take the seat of authority and of spreading sedition among an impoverished people. In the same way today, the papists claim antiquity and establishment and custom when they want to exalt themselves. And, indeed, they make our cause odious by charging us with introducing novelties and changing the character of the Church. In this way, they wish to make us guilty of all the evil which has happened during the last forty years, and which grows and increases more and more.

We must stand firm against such wicked accusations. At first glance, it would seem that we are left without excuse, and that our enemies could win their case out of hand if their claims were true. But we are shown here that such false accusations are nothing new. We cannot doubt – and they also will be constrained to confess – that the cause of David was approved by God, that it was just and good. It is also true that Abner was a rebel guilty of mutiny, and that Saul's kingdom, which he wished to maintain, was a bastard, for God had undoubtedly chosen David to succeed Saul (2 Sam. 3:9–10, 18). Since, then, by the very confession of our enemies, the cause of Abner was a bad one, let us despise all their calumnies. And let not the weak be worried and distressed if they are told that we are trying to bring in novelties, and that the papists still maintain the established order of things and ancient customs.

But let us be certain that there was no novelty on the part of David, for he did not push himself forward into the kingdom, but was called to it by God. Therefore, we can reply and protest in good conscience that we have not the least intention of changing anything in God's Church, and that we are not causing trouble in it. Instead, our hearts are set on him whose perpetual reign has been ordained by God his Father, and this promise belongs far more to Christ than to David. And as long as there is a sun and a moon in the sky, there will be testimonies that his sovereign empire is permanent and inviolable (Psa. 72:5). All the more, therefore, do we seek that all men give homage to our Lord Jesus Christ, that he be recognised as sovereign Saviour, and that all should bow the knee to him (Phil. 2:10). Our following of Christ proves that we are in no sense guilty of any novelty. On the contrary, we want the judgement which God himself has pronounced and published to be carried out and to be retained in all its rigour. Thus, no matter what superficial covering the papists claim on their side – that they retain the ancient ecclesiastical structure; that traditional procedure favours them; that the order of their Church has been confirmed through long ages; that everyone has consented to their position; and that they have the majority of men on their side – all of that is nothing in the eyes of God. Indeed, what they must do is become companions of Abner, since in contempt of God they wish to retain abuses and corruptions which are made manifest and rejected by Holy Scripture. Furthermore, their great numbers are like a mass of wandering beasts which have no regard for the unction which God has given to his only Son. This is what we must note.

Nevertheless, it is a lamentable thing that those who are joined together, who bear the name of God, and claim to be of him, should be ready to tear themselves in pieces. Although such a scandal exists, it should not astonish us. Having come from the time of David, it is necessary that these former things be fulfilled today in the person of our Lord Jesus Christ. For we have to make a comparison between the earthly reign which is spoken of here and the spiritual reign which was manifested at the coming of our Lord Jesus Christ. Therefore, although those who have been baptised in his name may take up arms against one another, still we must not be appalled, as are many who do not know which way to turn. Amidst conflicting opinions, they do not know what to believe.

That is how it happens that many lower themselves to the level of brute beasts, reject all consciousness of God (Rom. 1:18), and stamp underfoot the clarity of the Gospel in order to extinguish it. This is their sole excuse, that in the light of the troubles and disintegration which one sees in the world, it is best to give up everything.

Next, we take note of the fact that the members of the tribe of Judah were approved by God in that they ratified his unction and received as king him who was given to them from on high. If those who accepted David, a mortal creature, in the name of God are thus approved, what will be done to us if we ignore our Lord Jesus Christ, who is the life and salvation of the world, when we fail to recognise that majesty which has been given to him by God his Father? He bears that 'name which is above every name' (Phil. 2:9), as St Paul says.

Therefore, however much we deplore the contentions and debates which exist today among those who are called Christians, we must be sure to take sides with the true party, so that we may be prepared, in every case, to maintain that which God has constituted. And if we are assailed, let us fight valiantly for him, maintaining his empire against all those who rise up against him.

With these things in mind, we must strengthen ourselves today and arm ourselves with invincible virtue when we are called to battle for the truth of God against the idolatries and superstitions of the papist; indeed, against all idolatries and falsehoods by which the truth of God has been corrupted. Now that is one point.

Should it also happen, however, as experience shows us, that some of the unenlightened ones who are in the Church do not cease to love foolish ambition, it should not surprise us too much. It is true that it is a crime against truth and against nature for people to pour evil upon evil on someone who is already afflicted. Well, that is how it was in the time of Abner, and again today one can see it happening afresh.

When the Church is faced with enemies, when she is assailed on every side and greatly endangered, in brief, when it appears that at any hour all may be lost, still there will be those who want to elevate themselves, to seek to be honoured, and to take advantage of the situation. That is detestable, but since it has been so from the beginning, let us rise above it and do our best to correct the evil as much as possible. And let us see to it that we ourselves are never turned from the truth.

It must also be noted that David's trial was all the more grievous because it lasted so long; for we are told that he reigned in Hebron for seven and a half years (2 Sam. 2:11). It might have been expected that God would have given him rest after the death of Saul. But even though he was accepted as king by his own tribe, still he saw the Church dismembered. He saw that the people were not one body and, whereas they should have had one head, he found them sadly divided. The eleven tribes wholly misjudged the situation. They followed evil advice, and went against the line indicated by God. A year went by, then two or three more. Even after seven years, the divorce still remained. Civil war set in among the people, and it seemed that David would never obtain the kingdom for which he was waiting.

By these events, we are admonished not merely to be patient for a day or a year, but to hold on to the very end. Let us realise, I say, that we must prepare ourselves to sustain many temptations and battles, and to resist evil. Even though God sends trial after trial and it appears that they will never end, we must never lose courage.

For where is our repose? We will not find it in this world. We do, indeed, find some relaxation here – God sustains us in our weakness and does not want us to be without periods of quiet in the midst of the battles. But be that as it may, it would be self-deception to let ourselves think that we should be at our ease here below, and that we should escape all vexation and every trial which has been ordained to prove our faith.

It is not so. We must patiently endure all temptations and resist them when it pleases God to test us. If we are frail and our trials seem interminable, let us cast our eyes on the example of David. We must realise that what is written of him pertains to us, in that we are members of our Lord Jesus Christ of whom he was a type.

Furthermore, we must note well what St Paul says, that 'all things work together for good' for the children of God (Rom. 8:28). It will make us feel the love that he has for us much more when we are tested all the way, and seem to be falling backwards rather than advancing. When, instead of being raised up, we seem to be cast into a deep abyss, God's help at such a time confirms much more the trust we ought to have in his fatherly love and care. And then, also, it is a situation which gives God opportunity to continue his mercy towards us. Let us take note of what Jeremiah tells us: 'I remember you,' says the Lord, 'from the [deeds of] kindness of your youth, when you followed me in the desert' in hideous and horrible places (Jer. 2:2). Our Lord here compares himself to a young man who has taken a young woman, whom he has promised never to abandon, and who is ready to endure both heat and cold and hunger and thirst and all other wants; and to experience many pains and troubles. Therefore, when we follow God, when each one of us adheres to him in our life's work and remains firm in obedience, although he tosses us about with miseries, anguish, burdens, worries, and torments – that will certainly make us feel his grace all the more. It will also make him show himself even more merciful to us.

Thus, when God chastises us for our offences, he will still feel and be moved by compassion, especially when we conduct ourselves patiently and persevere in following him, since we are joined and united by the sacred bond of spiritual marriage which he has made with us. That is what we must remember about the times that are spoken of here – that is, the seven and a half years when David reigned in Hebron.

Now the trial is growing worse, as if a fire were starting to burn up everything. The passage says that the army of Abner or of Ishbosheth, son of Saul, had emerged 'from one side of the well of Gibeon', and that of David 'from the other' (2 Sam. 2:13). Here is a spectacle which is very sad, but one which shows the true state of those who think too highly of themselves, as did the people of Israel. For they were the only people in the world that God had chosen and adopted for his heritage. The promises of salvation and all its benefits were exclusively theirs. Scripture says that there was nowhere else among all the heathen nations where God manifested his will as he did in Israel (Deut. 4:7–8, 32–40).

Moses, indeed, says that God, having all the world in his hand, placed his everlasting name on this people which he chose for his service. And yet, in another passage, he remonstrates with them that it was not for their greatness nor for their nobility and dignity that God chose them above all others, but only because he took pleasure in their fathers (Deut. 4:37). This showed the excellence and the prerogative which that people had when it pleased God to choose them, as though they were more worthy than others, and when he showed himself so familiar to them as to give them his help and make them feel it in their time of need. Indeed, he declared that he was their gracious Father, and he proved it by his promises. Here, then, was God, who had spread his treasures among this people whom he adopted as his children. Here then, I say, were the people, who were armed against one another. Though supposed to be united as a single body, as I have already said, they engaged in deeds of cruelty. They were ready to exterminate themselves from the world without even a second thought. Is not that a most hideous and detestable thing? Must we not say that the devil has possession of them, at least in part?

By definition, one would have said that the tribe of Judah and the eleven other tribes were all one. And yet the tribe of Judah alone is here seen to be maintaining the cause of God. Thus, when we see contention between those who bear the same name, and that the majority is enraged against the minority so as to ruin them, let us remember that it so happened in ancient times to David. Be that as it may, we still lament as we see those who bear the mark of Christianity engaged against those who seek only their salvation – yes, against the name of that very power by which they claim to be the people and the Church. Let us lament, I say, such a calamity, and yet let us never fail to maintain the cause of God, come what may.

So much, then, for this point where Scripture says that the two armies came, the one from one side of the well of Gibeon, and the other from the opposite side. Now here are all those who claim to be in favour of the Church. They are fighting against one another. It is not a question here of fighting against foreign enemies. On the contrary, they are waging a deadly war among themselves to exterminate from the world the memory of the very name of Abraham – to abolish the Law of God and the pure religion.

The Scripture tells us that it was Abner, captain for Ishbosheth, who started the battle, while Joab led the troops of David (2 Sam. 2:14). Now there is not the least doubt that this resulted from the pride and presumption of Abner, who, being the stronger, went forward and mocked David for wanting to be king, since he was followed by one tribe only, whereas Abner's master was followed by eleven. We see this same thing today when the papists vomit out their boastings. They reproach us for having only a handful of people, while they have an infinite number on their side. They say, 'Where are the kings and princes who belong to your small party and will maintain it? Where are the great cities and countries? Where are the people of authority, and where are the great prelates who instruct you against us?' In a word, they are in such pre-eminence that their sole work is to stamp us under their feet and spit in our faces. Thus, they certainly advance against us in the manner of Abner.

Furthermore, they resemble too much Abner's presumption and recklessness in that they rejoice in shedding human blood. It ought to horrify us when Abner says, 'Now then, let the young men play' (2 Sam. 2:14). But play what game? The game of killing one another, so that no-one will be spared but all will be included. In this, I say, Abner in his pride and presumption shows us his cruelty. Well, we say the same thing today of the enemies of the Gospel, for we see how their pride causes them to rejoice in shedding innocent blood. When it was a matter of burning [at the stake], did any one of them have the least scruple? People have, indeed, had pity on thieves, highway robbers, murderers, whoremongers and all other malefactors, but it seems that everyone has been so enraged against the poor Christians that when they burn them, they do it, so to speak, with extra large bonfires; and everyone who comes to watch it triumphs over it, rejoicing with hearty laughter. Thus, we see that they have kept their eyes closed.

Again today, when their rage is similarly inflamed, we see that they spare nothing; that they are as much like Abner as if they were his bosom friends. It is only a matter of playing a game. Indeed, it is certain that if God had not often held them in check, they would without difficulty have wiped towns and cities off the map. And how has this poor place here remained until now? It is certain that they have conspired a hundred thousand times to destroy it, and not to leave one stone on another. And he who became noted for his cruelty would have been considered the finest, the most charitable and solid of men. And who prevented them? They were not held back by any feeling of humanity from carrying out their malice, but God prevented it, as it were, in spite of the gnashing of their teeth (Psa. 112:10).

Thus, we see that it has always been a game, as I have said, to shed human blood and to get drunk on it. It has even been worse to see poor people dragged to death for the testimony and confession of the Word of God. Well, when we see that happen, let us close our eyes and pray to God that he would make us feel, and would show us in effect, that our lives are precious to him, as he says in the 116th Psalm: 'Precious in the sight of the Lord is the death of his saints' (Psa. 116:15). If, therefore, the iniquitous and wicked play their games and pastimes, employing such cruelty that human blood is poured out like the blood of cattle and sheep at the slaughterhouse, let us pray to God that, as he has begun, he will continue still to hold back these wretched ones – who are thus inflamed and indeed possessed by demons – from destroying their fellow-men and becoming drunk on innocent blood. That is one point.

Furthermore, if the servants of God, that is to say, those who uphold his Word, are sometimes badly advised, evil then is doubled, as we see here in Joab. He upheld a good cause. He was David's captain. In brief, he was one of the leaders of the Church. Thus, he had to conduct himself in the fear of God, and keep himself from murder. It is true that he could not flee from battle, and yet he was too thoughtless when he said, 'Very well, let them play' (2 Sam. 2:14), and treated as a game what he should have detested. Now it is a pathetic sight when poor people kill one another in this way. Joab was motivated here by ambition, for he did not want to let Abner get the better of him, and thus let him be puffed up with pride. Hence, he agrees to this game, which ought to have been abhorrent to him. Let us, therefore, note that when swords are unsheathed, and when men are armed to enter into battle, not all will conduct themselves as could be hoped. Much excess will result. Thus, let us detest as much as possible these wars and combats which arise because of religion.

It is true, as I have already said, that we cannot avoid them, for God intends to prove us by them. Hence we are constrained to fight, but let it be in spite of ourselves. And moreover, when we are involved, we must be very careful to pray to God that he will govern the hearts of his own – for today we see once again that in the army marshalled under the name of Jesus Christ and of the Gospel, there are many rascals among the troops. Some of them are there to strip and pillage, and others to commit outrages; some to satisfy their appetite for vengeance; others to murder no matter how; and still others for publicity. Hence, let us learn to pray to God that he will not allow the armies which have been gathered in his name to be blackened, either by our wicked affections, or by the desire for vengeance, or by any such thing. And if the enemies of the truth seek only to bathe themselves in blood, let us for our part try to spare it, as much as we can. And if they make a game out of killing, let us always keep in mind that it is a detestable thing to ruin and efface the image of God which is in his creatures, since all men are created in his image. Now this is what we must remember from this passage, where it says that Joab agreed with Abner, saying, 'Let the young men play'.

And yet we see how these miserable people came as helpless beasts to stab themselves – for Scripture says that 'they killed one another' (2 Sam. 2:16). It is true that this was considered memorable, so much so that the place became renowned and was called 'the field of the strong, or of the brave men', as though it was desired to celebrate their praises after their death. But that does not mean that their 'game' was praised by God, for they came there rashly. How much more must we keep ourselves strictly under control when we see that our enemies are exasperating us as much as they can in order to make us quarrel! Let us in no way be eager seekers of vainglory or of high position. Rather, let us humble ourselves, and although we see our enemies so addicted to evil, let us not be ashamed to seek their good as far as we can.

However, that will not prevent us from resorting to arms when it is necessary. In that case we will do all that necessity requires. But be that as it may, let no evil proceed from us, and let us never seek to shed human blood, except to maintain the cause of God when it is necessary. That, then, is another point which we take from the death of the twenty-four who killed one another, which is spoken of here.

But still God had pity on his own, and it says that 'Abner was defeated' (2 Sam. 2:17) with his army. Scripture describes 'the battle' as a 'very hard' one – on the one hand, to show us that God was afflicting his people as a punishment and yet, on the other, showing us in their victory that he still recognised his own and watched over them to show them mercy and maintain their cause. Now this admonishes us that no victory in a civil war is desirable. We ought not, I say, to have victory over domestic enemies. Why? Because the Church of God will, to that degree, be reduced in number; much blood will be shed. It is much better to seek peace and to do everything we possibly can for Christ to reign without entering into combat. That is one point.

But be that as it may, this shows us that God finally will not allow his own to be oppressed for ever. Although for a time they endure oppression, he will at last relieve them, and will elevate them so that they will be able with ease to ruin and stamp underfoot those who were previously persecuting them.

The battle was hard from the side of David. It was horrible in that some of David's men were cut in pieces, and that others of them killed men in Abner's army. But still Abner was defeated and overthrown, despite the great multitude that followed him. Thereby let us learn today, as far as possible, to hold ourselves back, so that battles will not be cruel, and blood will not flow without good and just cause.

We should always bear in mind this principal consideration – it will sweeten our sadness – that God gave the victory to Joab, David's captain. Hence, let us hope that today he will act in a similar manner. When he gives us a victory, let us realise that it is a sign of his favour to us, and let us learn to glory in him, and thus to follow the route he has shown us. For when we go thus on our way, we may say that we have received a manifest blessing from God. Let us, therefore, hope that God will overcome our enemies and when sometimes he gives us a good beginning, let us be aware that it proceeds from him, and let us give him the praise that he deserves. Thus, being clothed in humility, we may say that we are ever his, come what may. Let us not make it an occasion to rejoice in ourselves when it pleases God to make us feel his blessing.

Now, for the rest, let us note this circumstance, that Abner, having been so bold as to start the war, was defeated with his army, and the single tribe of Judah was victorious. Let us notice then, in the first place, that if it is our enemies who start a war, we can protest both before God and before men that we have in no way sought quarrels or fights with them and that we only ask to live in friendship and concord with others. It is our enemies who have been enraged against the children of God and even against the name of our Lord Jesus Christ. This is because, enraged by demonic audacity, they have developed brutal hatred, and they have persecuted us incessantly – as in fact they would have done again and again unless God had prevented it by what he has ordained. I say, then, that the whole war has been caused by them; their malice and rebellion made them strike out against God. Let us wait in true faith for him to care for and prosper our cause; not only because it is good, but also because we did not take up arms through recklessness and presumption, but because we had to resist them. Necessity constrained us.

Now for the rest of the matter, let not the great multitude of our enemies overawe us, since we see here a single tribe defeating eleven. If, therefore, the papists have many armies and are helped on every side, if they have impressive equipment and go forward as though the wind were in their sails, let us not talk only of them. At all times, let us not fail to hope in him who gives victories, and there is no doubt that we shall obtain them – for as good King Jehoshaphat says, it is not by a great multitude of men and of horses that God shows his strength (2 Chron. 20:6, 12, 15ff.). It is just as easy for him to give victory to three or four men as to a hundred thousand. Therefore, let us not fail to have good courage. Let us trust God to maintain his cause, however much stronger than ourselves his adversaries may seem in the eyes of the world. Moreover, when God gives us strength and it seems that we are well fortified, that is not to make us eager in our desire to throw ourselves into the firing line, confiding in our strength. Rather, let us rise above our passions and always keep our eyes on our Captain and Protector by whom we are guided. Let us be careful, I say, not to indulge in vainglory and to confide in it, but let us ever rest on the Lord. Let us call on him to be pleased to govern us. If he has strengthened us, may he temper our zeal and keep us from throwing ourselves into excessive cruelty. Instead, may he give us grace to use our zeal modestly. And may we ever look straight in front of us, so that we will not proceed foolishly, and be ruined. But may we never take a step unless the way is shown to us by him!

So much, then, for this point concerning the victory which was given to Joab and his men. Now it is not that the tribe of Judah was better than the others, but rather that it held fast to what God had ordained for it and followed the leader whom God had chosen. Today we have our Lord Jesus Christ, who is not a type, as was David, but who has all perfection of virtue in himself, under whose protection we live in true assurance. He saves us from the hand of our enemies, and indeed leads us even to eternal life when we follow him as we should. Let us always carry our weapons, both spiritual and temporal, for the glory of his name. And when we have thus valiantly done battle, let us not doubt that he will give us cause to rejoice in his goodness.

Now let us prostrate ourselves before the majesty of our good God, recognising the infinite faults of which we are guilty, praying to him that he may more and more cause us to feel them, and that this may serve to lead us into a true repentance and to strip us utterly of our carnal affections, so that we are clothed with his righteousness. May we be patient in all our adversities, peaceable and modest with one another; yet may we on our part be courageous when fighting for him is at stake. And above all, let us take up spiritual arms to battle against Satan and against all iniquity (Eph. 6:11–12; 2 Cor. 10:3–5). And let us not doubt that he will assist and strengthen us more and more when we request this of him with sincere affection, until he brings all our battles to an end and calls us to his eternal rest. And may he not only grant us this grace . . .

6

*Disunity and War**

Now Zeruiah had three sons, Joab and Abishai and Asahel. Asahel was as light of foot as a roe or a wild goat. And Asahel pursued Abner and turned not to the right hand or to the left but followed only Abner. Abner looked behind him, and said: Are you not Asahel? And he said: I am. And Abner said to him: Turn aside one way or the other and lay hold of one of these young men and take his armour . . . (2 Sam. 2:18–32).

Scripture tells this story, here, to explain why we see such a wicked act committed later by Joab against Abner. This passage describes how Abner killed Joab's brother. Here are the details. The young man Asahel, being light and agile, was pursuing Abner. Abner did not want to kill him, but this young man kept on following until he did turn round and kill him. That is the first point. Afterwards they talked about the details of the defeat and the retreat of the two armies.

The first detail that we must notice concerning the death of Asahel is that he was 'swift in running'. This is intended to show that those who have some strong point always presume on it more than they should. That is what caused the death of Asahel. He trusted too much in his own agility. He pushed himself in running, and he thought it was great to have pursued and caught up with his enemy. He gave no thought to their encounter, and felt that he was valiant enough to fight Abner. He thought that he had done enough by merely stopping him, but was foolishly deceiving himself. Let us learn therefore, from

*Friday, June 5, 1562.

this example, that when God gives us some strength, we are to be so temperate that we will in no way abuse it.

Moreover, when Abner told Asahel to go back and seek someone else, he was speaking out of pride and mockery, as though he were saying, 'Follow someone who is your equal. How dare you come after me!' There is no doubt that Abner disdained encountering this young man, seeing that he was giddy-headed and unimportant and was simply driven by this foolish glory which he wanted to display – namely, how fast he was. This is one point.

However, it is possible to see that Abner had hopes of gaining promotion, and that he wished to show that he was well disposed towards the house of Saul. It is true that he had not usurped the crown, but he had put Ishbosheth on the throne. Nevertheless, there were always two motives in his actions. He thought that if something bad were to happen, he might be appointed himself. That could not be done without betraying his master, but that is the way with such people. We have already seen that he could have been led only by a deliberate malice, in that he was not ignorant of the promise and unction given to David. Therefore, he was resisting God by wanting to name a successor to the crown instead of the one whom God had ordained. He was not really seeking the well-being of the house of Saul, since he wanted to be looked up to and to rule. For however much Ishbosheth had the name and title of king, it was Abner who had all the power and who was using Ishbosheth as a figure-head. In short, he cared only for himself, just as worldly people always tend to do (however they may cover it up), for each one is addicted to himself. That, I say, is what motivated Abner when he divided the people and made of them two bodies, so to speak.

Then Abner said, 'How could I dare look in the face of your brother, Joab?' Now why should he care about that? He was Joab's mortal enemy, so he should have been seeking his destruction instead. Yes, but then we are shown that when he saw himself conquered, he was prepared to make peace with the house of David and gain their favour. Abner was willing to desert his master, and he finally did so.

Let us learn, therefore, that when men do not have a good foundation, they will involve themselves in all sorts of iniquity and will go from bad to worse. However much they may protest their innocence, they still continue adding sin to sin, until they go so far that God puts a bridle on them. Now that should teach us not to do anything against our conscience. For when we begin to do some evil, even though we think it will all be over soon and will not last long, yet we are voluntarily throwing ourselves into the snares of the devil, and God will pay us the wages that we have earned. One evil will cause another and we will spin a long thread. It will be like a chain which has many links, in that offences will attach themselves endlessly one to another. Therefore, let us learn to keep ourselves strictly under the control of the fear of God, so that we may never permit ourselves to start some evil, and then go on and do still worse.

Furthermore, let us recognise that among all other virtues, well-rounded balance should recommend itself to us. Abner was praiseworthy in many things. However, we see that he was disloyal, so that all his excellence was contaminated and was nothing less than rotten! For we also know that when God regulates our life, he renews us so that in no way will we be double-minded. There will be no pretence in us. We will conduct ourselves with such a degree of integrity that even in our dealing with the children of this world, whatever malice, disloyalty and fraud there may be, still we will not fail to be always straightforward. Our simplicity will be united to a prudence which is both good and right, but is without any cunning (Matt. 10:16).

Moreover, when we see that Asahel was killed, we must note, on the one hand, that when swords are unsheathed there will be no more freedom, and even those who wish to keep from evil-doing will not be able to do so. However perverse and rebellious against God Abner may have been, he still wished to spare Asahel. But in the heat of battle, he could not, for Asahel would have overtaken him. All the more should we avoid going so far, seeing how war brings so much confusion.

But on the other hand, let us notice also that the excessive boldness of Asahel was the cause of his death, as we have already said, for he was over-confident in the lightness and swiftness which had been given to him. And there is not the slightest doubt that he desired to be seen, and wanted to do a memorable deed in getting his enemy. Well, it cost him very dearly. Hence, let us learn to be brave according to rule, and not according to rashness. So much, then, for this particular story.

Now for this act one cannot condemn Abner. Since there was a war going on and since Asahel attacked him and refused to turn from him in spite of warnings to the contrary, what else could Abner have done? Even if he had not been such a great enemy, what he did would still have been excusable. We will see that soon afterwards Joab took vengeance on him by treason and trickery (2 Sam. 3:27). But that will be discussed in its place. Scripture briefly mentions it here to show us the reason for which this story is included.

Now to show that this young man, Asahel, was well known, it says that 'when they came to the place where he had fallen dead, everyone stopped'. That was a sign that he was held in higher esteem than all the others, for there were several others dead – indeed, nineteen – and yet they were ignored while everyone stopped at Asahel. We must also carefully note that Joab took such vengeance for the death of Asahel because he considered him so well favoured, since people had loved and esteemed his brother. But that did not justify him before God, as will be stated more fully in the proper place. But we see here that one man will often carry away more than a hundred or a thousand, for all stopped at Asahel, and the sight frightened them. After a great defeat, people are not astonished, and yet when they see a single man dead, everyone is shocked. Battles are often broken up and an army put to flight by the death of a captain or a leader, for it will seem that everything is lost and scattered when there is no-one in command. Therefore, even though Asahel gained a great reputation, he thus hindered the army of Joab – so much so that it turned the tide for the enemy and worked to their advantage. So instead of David's men winning, in the end they were vanquished.

Now let us come to what Scripture adds concerning this

defeat. It says, in the first place, that Abner exhorted Joab to stop. 'How long', he said, 'will the sword devour? Do you not know that there will be bitterness in the end? Why do you not call back the people from following their brothers?' Here Abner changed his language. Formerly, it had been a game to him to make men kill each other. Now the game pleased him no longer, since it could only get worse. Hence, he began to exhort Joab to pursue it no more, in that it would be a great cruelty for brothers to kill each other in this way.

Now in the first place, we see how God broke down the foolish arrogance which puffed Abner up when he said: 'Let our people come out and enjoy themselves' (2 Sam. 2:14). He joked about shedding human blood; it was all mockery to him. But now he knows that the outcome was not what he had imagined. Let us learn, thus, that God will punish any pride that strengthens our cruel passions so that we have no pity on men, but expose them to butchery like calves or sheep. That is an enormous vice to which we must give serious consideration. I speak to those who have power of some sort, for one sees how earthly princes only rejoice when they fill the fields with dead bodies. There will be many poor widows and orphans as victims of their greed. That, to them, is only a pastime; it is of no more concern than wiping their mouths. Well, since God has declared a manifest judgement on them, they will in no way escape giving an account for such cruelty.

Yet let us notice, in the second place, this example of Abner. He was now no longer speaking with his customary haughtiness and pride, saying: 'Let them play', or: 'Let them enjoy themselves', but instead: 'How long will the sword keep devouring?' He was horrified, it seems, on seeing these murders, and yet he had derived joy and entertainment from it. He changed, however, only because he saw that this pursuit affected him and was harmful to him.

That, therefore, is why the cruel make a pretence of being moved and touched with compassion when they fail to get what they desired and sought for. We often see that those who have been the most addicted to tyranny and cruelty become religious hypocrites and use beautiful rhetoric when they realise that they can do nothing more. If necessary, they are ready to seek peace. When they have the upper hand, it is certain that they do not care how much confusion they cause. But when they see that their designs have been frustrated, they begin to preach peace and concord, and want to make people believe that they are doing this out of pity. But such hypocrisy is too hard to maintain, and the shamelessness of such people is soon seen when they lose their tempers and revert to their previous desire to kill and wipe out everything. But even in doing that, they will put on a good appearance of wishing to set right what has been wrongly done. It is obvious, I say, that they are completely without shame.

We should learn from this example, for such things do happen, as in fact we have seen. This kind of experience is only too frequent. It is particularly clear when Abner says, 'How long will everyone pursue his brother?' For in fact, it was a horrible spectacle to see the children of Abraham fighting with those to whom they were united and who were called by God to be his heritage. They should have been joined, therefore, in the unfeigned union which is spoken of in the Psalm (Psa. 133); they should have 'dwelt together in holy and cheerful brotherhood' before God, 'which is like the ointment that anointed Aaron which flowed down upon his garments, and like the dew that fell on the hill of Hermon' in the plain. They should have been united in this way, and such a union would have been God's principal blessing on them. But when they killed each other like dogs and cats, was it not as though they wanted to throw God out of the country, so to speak! For they went against everything that God had established among them.

Well, while on the surface Abner's statement was holy indeed, his motive was insincere; for it was he who had started everyone in this tumult and fury, as Joab later reproached him. But he added a threat: 'Do you not know that there will be bitterness at the end?' – as if he were saying that when it was to his advantage, he could still repent and, at the same time, cause them to be so desperately angry that they could not control themselves. That is what Abner was really saying: 'Now you are pursuing me . . . but be careful, for if you keep on and you get paid back equally or doubly, all the people will be exterminated. There will be only a very small number left of either you or our people.'

That, in brief, is how Abner remonstrated with Joab, saying that if he did not compromise and put a stop to his pursuit, the rest of Abner's army might return. Then if no other solution had been found, there would be a greater defeat than ever. All of this is certainly true, but we can see that Abner was acting like a sly fox when he saw that he could no longer exercise his cruelty, realising that he was vanquished.

For such a result would not have mattered to Abner. If he could have won the victory, he would gladly have destroyed the entire tribe of Judah. Brotherly love would hardly have affected him in that case. But now look at the holy man seeking the union of the people! He foresees dangers, true enough; but as we have said, this is an example to make us wary of those who have neither principle nor law. But though we are warned about such situations, let us always listen to reason. For while we have no faith in what they say, that still does not mean we must attack head-on without good counsel, even though it is not legitimate to accept everything they say. We must always listen to reason and truth as proceeding from God (no matter what its source), even though we do not respect wicked speakers, such as teachers and doctors.

Now for the rest of the matter, it says that Joab replied to Abner that had it not been for him, there would have been no pursuit, and that it would be morning before everyone had returned from the pursuit. Joab meant that Abner had started it, and that the swords were unsheathed by his advice and command and that the killing came from that. Indeed, he shows that he detested the accusation that Abner was making. In sum, Joab condemned his adversary and excused himself – and rightly so.

Joab's speech is as though he were calling God as witness, so that Abner would be all the more convicted. Now we know that hypocrites always have new subterfuges. One thing that we can never do is win them over, for truth does not matter to them. They will argue to the very end, and will still have some kind of reply. That is why Joab swears 'by the living God' that if Abner had not first started it, everyone would have gone away and would have ceased pursuing their brethren.

Now from this response, we must gather that when we are accused by the wicked who have caused some evil, we may protest that the evil displeased us and that we did not seek it. We may add that we did not start it. We must, I say, state this protest, but it can be stated before God. For what have we gained when we have washed our hands before men and have made them believe that we are innocent, and yet our conscience condemns us both before God and his angels? Let us, therefore, look within ourselves when we have reason to protest our integrity, to purge ourselves from slander directed at us, and to rid ourselves of defamation of character. Let us do this as in the presence of God, and let him be our Witness, our Judge and Defender. Now that is what we must remember from this passage.

Furthermore, let us note also that we have to use preventive medicine to avoid evil. For once we have begun, it will not be easy to stop. That is why Joab says that 'in the morning', if Abner had not begun, his brothers would have stopped killing one another. When he says, 'in the morning', he means that he did not start it. Therefore, as far as we can, let us prevent all contentions, for where the fire is lit it is difficult to put out. So as much as we can, let us resist starting anything, and when the devil tries to incite us to contentions and debates, let us be prepared ahead of time not to give him an opening. For when he gets in, it is very hard to run him out. We must also remember that point from this passage concerning the protestations of Joab.

The text then says that it was discovered that there were 'three hundred dead men on the side of Abner' (2 Sam. 2:31), and 'sixty from David's band' (2 Sam. 2:30).[1] Earlier, it was stated that the battle was hard and grievous. Now this does not seem to agree with that. For one would not consider it a

[1] *Supplementa Calviana*, p. 49, suggests that the meaning is: 'that there were three hundred and sixty men dead on Abner's side, and twenty from the band of David'. There is an obvious error in the copyist's text.

great defeat if three hundred men on one side and sixty on the other were dead; and on the other hand, that there were only twenty. This seems to be a contradiction. But it shows even more how horrified we should be over the shed blood of the faithful and of those who are joined to us in the name of God. In general, one cannot kill a man without the image of God being violated. And that is why Scripture says that a man, being created in the image of God, cannot be killed without the offence being against God himself (Gen. 9:6), who has stamped his image in our nature. It is a crime also because everyone should see himself in his neighbour. We are worse than savage beasts when we are thus burning to destroy one another. And there is, in particular, a sacred bond among those who claim to be the people of God – as it was formerly among the whole family of Abraham, so it is today in the Church. That is why, even though there were only 380 men killed among all who were defeated, it is still said that the battle was hard.

That is for our instruction. Thus when we see that in Christendom people are tearing one another apart; let us realise that this is being taken into account by God, and even if men harden themselves, God does not change his mind. We have already seen battles for such a long time. There is no end to them. And even apart from battles, we have seen how many people have been killed by wars. This has not been the case merely in one place and in a single army, but it has gone on among princes who claim to be Christians and Catholics – and yet they are killing an infinite number of people. And then the war has swept through one country like a storm. One sees poor people dead among the bushes, and others who are left have to endure hunger and thirst, and heat and cold, and many deprivations – to such a degree that if you cut their throat, you would do them a favour. For they are suffering and will die ten times, so to speak, before death strikes the final blow.

Now that is nothing to us, because we have become too used to it. But be that as it may, the whole affair will be brought to account before God. For what is written here, that battles are grievous and hard even when only a small number of people die, is a strong and truthful description when we consider that the ones involved are those who claim the name of God and profess to be his people and Church.

Not only is it unbelievers who attack one another in a diabolical rage, but also the adherents of Christianity are thus embittered against one another. Notice the extremity of the situation, that the bond (as I have said) of our union consists in the call that God has given to us to be his people, and yet we come to the point of breaking and dismembering it. Well, under the shadow of the name of God, under the shadow of the pure religion which ought to keep us united in one body, under the shadow of our Lord Jesus Christ who is our Head, if we are in strife and contentions, what will be the outcome?

There is a double war in the Church because of religion, for often it is the case that swords are not unsheathed, and yet they manage to have a battle. Indeed, if there are heresies and errors, it is legitimate to kill one another, for poison, when it is widespread, does far more evil than the sword. Now this is one kind of mortal combat. When people are banded against one another in sects and when there are heresies in the Church, eventually they reach the point of action with swords. After people have waged verbal debates and have grown even more stubborn so that they exercise less restraint, it becomes necessary to resort to arms.

Well, be that as it may, these things must still happen. As St Paul says, 'It is necessary that there be heresies' (1 Cor. 11:19), so that all who are solid and have true zeal might be approved by God. He thereby gives them a mark by which people can recognise that there was no hypocrisy when they declared themselves to be Christians. It is also necessary that, from time to time, there be controversies and debates, even to the point of killing one another, as we see in the statement of St Paul when he says that he will carry on amid seditions (2 Cor. 6:5). When he speaks of debates and strife, he holds that up as a mirror to us of the universal condition of all Christians. He says that he was not able to avoid seditions and quarrels. Now that is a terrible word, and we should detest it – and not without cause. Even so, it was still necessary that St Paul, who was of a docile and patient spirit, should experience it. Why? Because the devil never ceases to incite and inflame all his followers to do battle; so much so that the Gospel cannot be preached without fires being started, without troubles, battles, wars and many calamities among those who claim to be the very people of God, as was the case in olden days.

Let us not be astonished, therefore, if this takes place in our own times. For however horrible a thing it is to hear that only three hundred faithful men are dead and that they bear the name of God, still we must not conclude that Joab did wrong in fighting against Abner and his army. It is true that he did wrong when he consented to this ridiculous game, but still it was right for him to take up arms. And why? Because the fight was good and just and approved by God. It would have been by no means proper for David to give up his right to the crown and to fail to go forward when God had given him his hand. Now then, are we to condemn those who fight not merely under a mortal man, but for the truth of God, for his service, for the pure religion, for the kingdom of our Lord Jesus Christ?

Therefore, let us note well when there are wars inside the Church, that even if the matter is wrong in itself, still that does not mean that one should confuse judgement by considering both parties in the same class or as wrapped up together in the same bundle. That would be a failure to discern properly. And even when there are two opposing camps in the Church, if one is opposing the truth of God in order to overthrow it and the other holds to the good so that it may always follow what is commanded, it is certain that whoever is neutral will be disloyal and a traitor. For we are not to follow a compromising course, as when we see one side fight for the name of God, and indeed for the cause of our salvation, and yet fold our arms. Nor are we to be in the position of knowing how to use our tongue to speak evil and yet not daring to utter a word to maintain the honour of God. So today there are many who would like to be neutral in the midst of all these troubles. They think: 'Very well, I do not want to be involved on one side or the other. I will wait and see who is going to be the strongest and is more likely to win.' So it is a matter (for believers) of becoming as deeply involved as possible. Therefore, far be it from us to condemn those who follow the right party. So much, then, for this exhortation.

Nonetheless, let us try to carry on peaceably as far as we can and to pursue brotherhood as far as possible. For the love of Joab is shown here to be worthy of praise, when he had compassion on his unfortunate brethren. Even though those people in history, with the exception of the tribe of Judah, were his enemies, he nevertheless treated them kindly, keeping in mind the fact that God had chosen them to be his heritage along with the others. When he took that into consideration, he was moved with pity for them. Therefore, even when we do battle for the cause of God, we should still seek reconciliation when it is genuine and necessary, but not hollow reconciliations. For it would be much better for everything to be lost than to act falsely in any way, so that the service of God, above all, might be carried out in integrity, as befits pure religion. This is better even than sparing the lives of men – and, indeed, the whole world. When things are going against us, still we must put first the service of God so that its integrity is untarnished and not reduced in the least.

But when we see miserable folk scattered, let us not fail to pray to the Lord that he will be pleased to build up his flock; in other words, that he would pour his Spirit out upon those today who are given over to evil and who nevertheless belong to him according to his secret decree and are eventually to serve him along with us. Let us pray that they will be made ready for this sacred union with us, and be dedicated to the name of his Son, our Lord Jesus Christ; that they will be joint soldiers with us in his defence, and that in this way human blood will be spared. Now that is what we must remember from this story of the killing of 380 men who were destroyed from the family of Israel. That is why it was called a great and grievous defeat, because they were descendants of the line of Abraham, and because God had given them the mark of his adoption.

Well, finally it states that Joab returned to David, and Abner went to Gibeon, to Ishbosheth, whom he called and had ordained to be his master. Now this shows us that Abner admitted that he was beaten. For when he retreated with a much larger army than Joab, slinking away like a dog with his tail between his legs, that, I say, is a confession which shows how much he realised that he was defeated. But even so, he still did not return to or subject himself to David. He always used retreat as the means to go forward even more. Hence, we see that hypocrites, even when they are humiliated, come back with pride, stubbornly malicious. Thus, they will not change under any conditions, in spite of any good appearance they may put on, as long as this rancour is eating them up.

Now the wicked can certainly tremble, and do so especially when God pursues them. For that matter, even if they have no enemies here below, their own shadow can frighten them. At such times, they see how God is pressing in on them and thus do not know which way to turn. And yet does that mean they will return to the right way? Not at all. But they are always there in their holes and caves, full of treason. When they remain hidden, it is to cover up their venom, to do this and that according to their own desires and wicked intentions, and to cause fires which afterwards will declare and demonstrate their presence. Now that is how all those behave once they have joined themselves together against God. And even when they are overcome by force, that does not mean that they will remain peaceable, or that they will want to submit themselves, or lay down their arms. Indeed, they will do worse than ever if they can.

Concerning Joab, it was a praiseworthy thing that he returned to Hebron with David. He wanted to see if there was any way that David could reign, as God had decreed. It showed that he had no regard to the matter of personal benefit or profit in who should reign, but he was concerned with the mutual benefit of the whole people – that they would not be harmed. That is why Joab is to be praised.

Therefore, let us note that however much the wicked never cease to be enemies of God, still if we seek the reign of our Lord Jesus Christ – that everyone should be given over to his obedience – God will bless it. For we cannot exterminate all the wicked from this world. It is impossible and, indeed, what would it accomplish? Then let us attempt to reform all those who are not totally incorrigible, and at the same time leave the others to the judgement of God. For all punishments cannot be given now. It is true that those who are in charge of justice ought to punish those living in their land and country. Nevertheless, when one has done all one's duty, one must realise that there will be the wicked who remain among the good, so that the Church of God will always have to fight, either with weapons or with verbal disputations.

Let us, therefore, endeavour as far as possible to put far away from us all that could corrupt us, and let us concentrate all our thoughts and energy on our Lord Jesus Christ, having his authority. Let our aim be that everyone should do him homage and recognise him as sovereign, that everyone should submit to him. While we confess to deserving eternal death, nevertheless, we should not be so horrified by it that we despair and flee from his presence. Rather, in true repentance, we can avoid the dangers to which we have been exposed, and instead embrace his mercy as he is pleased to offer it to us by his Word. Now it is certain that we would be traitors if we did not fight both for his name and for our salvation with those whom he has taken under his banner, as I have already said. But I am speaking now in general, that we should flee conflicts as far as possible, and follow the example of Joab, which is set before us here. Even so, we have no other refuge than our king, the Son of the living God, for whom we should hold back nothing, whether it be goods or our lives and everything that God has given us.

Now we must carefully note this point, that Joab came to Hebron to have fellowship with David. Well, the papists and enemies of God would certainly like to make peace with us in such a way that they would then be able to ruin us, so that we would no longer know what it means to be on David's side, nor what the pure religion is. That is what they are attempting. We must withstand such malice in all cases and, above all, have no agreement or understanding with them. We must not listen to them nor even regard their practices, as far as consenting to them is concerned. But when we have made a judgement concerning them, in accordance with what the Word of God teaches us, let us make use of this judgement as we have been taught. In that way we will always hold fast to our Lord Jesus, our Captain and our Head. That is to say, let us hold on to the doctrine of his Gospel, that he may govern with all authority, and exercise his sovereign authority over his Church, so as to maintain it and that he may govern us by his Word.

When we have done that, I say, if there are some who wish to perish, then let them perish. But be that as it may, at least let us not perish because of our own cowardice. Instead, let us embrace God's promises so that we can be firmly grounded on them. And when we see that we will be attacked from every side and that he will find no way by which to rescue us, when it seems that heaven and earth are against us, nevertheless, let us be assured of our good cause, let us bravely follow David – not the one who was a temporal king, but our Lord Jesus Christ, the sovereign King. He has taken us under his protection and to him all power is given by God his Father (Matt. 28:18), with the result that when we are his obedient people, as the Psalms say, he will distribute to us our necessary and sufficient portion (Psa. 81:14ff.; 85:9ff.; 110). He will do this even as we place our neck beneath his yoke, in order to say, 'Here am I, O Lord!' every time and always when he calls us to his service.

Now let us prostrate ourselves before the majesty of our good God, recognising all our faults, praying that he will make us feel them so much that it will cause us more and more to be displeased with ourselves. Let us pray that, in our afflictions and in all our battles, he will give us an invincible constancy, so that we may walk the narrow path according to his Word, and rest totally on him, making no compromise with the wicked when we are aware of their cruelty and craft. At the same time, may we have pity on them without deviating from what is taught us by our Lord. Thus may we always be at his disposal and totally dedicated to his glory, so that we will never deviate or turn from our vocation, in any way. And may he show this grace not only to us . . .

7

*Abner's Face of Brass**

There was long war between the house of Saul and the house of David. But David advanced and grew stronger, and the house of Saul grew weaker. Unto David were born six sons in Hebron: his first-born was Amnon, of Ahinoam, the Jezreelitess . . . (2 Sam. 3:1–11).

The first thing that is said here confirms the doctrine which we dealt with yesterday. That is, that David was agitated by grievous temptations. Even though God had given him control over that part of the kingdom which consisted of one tribe, still he could have been tempted to give it all up, since he saw that it caused rebellion among the people, and division into opposing camps. These things could result in tremendous difficulties and contentions.

We know that peace should be dear and precious to us, and the most acceptable sacrifice to God is when we are united in order to honour him with one heart and one voice. But when we are banded against one another and have no union or concord between us, the door will be closed to us so that we will not be able to present ourselves to God or have any access to him. In brief, the reign of Jesus Christ is called the kingdom of peace (Rom. 14:17). Therefore, David, who was not seeking his own personal profit but was seeking for God to be honoured and for the people to be God-fearing, could have thought this several times: 'My kingdom is cursed by God, because I see the people torn into pieces. Would it not be better for me to withdraw so

*Saturday, June 6, 1562.

that there can be union?' Yet he remained constant, because he had to follow the calling of God. He did not put himself forward, as we have seen, but since God had called him, he had to obey and accept the charge, and battle on to the very end – just as he did.

Nevertheless, although his virtue is lauded here, on the other hand we are shown that he did not keep God in mind in all his conduct (2 Sam. 3:2–5). For it is stated that he abandoned and forgot his true position most seriously, in that he had several wives – although he was not ignorant of the Law of God. Since he already had one wife, it was as though his marriage was violated and broken by this plurality of women. For as was shown earlier, God did not create two women for one man, but a man must be the husband of one wife only. Here is the sentence which God pronounced on the matter: 'It is not good for a man to be alone, let us make a helper suitable for him' (Gen. 2:18). He does not say, 'Let us make him two or three women', but simply one. Thus it is a direct overturning of the ordinance of God and the institution of marriage when a man takes several wives.

Moreover, David committed a double sin, for in addition to the common law which speaks to everyone, it is stated particularly that the king should not take several wives (Deut. 17:17). Now that prohibition is even stricter on kings, because kings tend to allow themselves more licence, either when they are flattered or when no-one dares to contradict them. Hence, they may think that they are not bound by the rules that control the common herd. That is why God pronounced this law.

David, on the one hand, abused marriage by taking several wives, which was, as I have said, against the Law of God, and was an overturning of his decree, which should have been kept inviolable. And on the other hand, he further forgot his own position most seriously, in that he had not yet come to the kingdom; he had only one tribe, and yet we see how he made merry and let himself go. When he went against the ordinance of God, he should, instead, have been applying himself to meditation on the Law in order to govern himself by it – but he did nothing. These are most serious and inexcusable offences.

Now this is shown to us so that we will know that although David was chosen by God and had been declared to be 'a man after God's own heart' (1 Sam. 13:14), still he did not cease to be a poor sinner who had need of mercy, as we all have. Thus he confessed, 'Do not enter into judgement, O Lord, with your servant, for who can stand before your judgement?' (Psa. 143:2). Then, not without cause, he cried, 'Who can understand his own sins?' (Psa. 19:12). He well knew that there were still secret sins to which he might be blind, and thus he asks God's pardon for them. And after doing that, he goes to the very womb of his mother to confess his iniquities and admit his sorry state, as though he were saying that he was totally steeped in evil (Psa. 51:5). He had outstanding virtues but, nevertheless, he saw how ungrateful he had been to God. He even published his sins in this word: 'You have revealed your secrets to me' (Psa. 51:6 paraphrase), as though he had said, 'I am much more wicked than everyone else, because although you have chosen me king, you have made me a prophet to teach others. Although I have known your secrets, and am not ignorant of what I ought to do, nevertheless I have forgotten my position, and cannot excuse myself.'

Now we see here two things: on the one hand, that David stumbled badly and, on the other, his repentance. As for his fall, let us learn to keep ourselves on guard, for we are no better off than David. And if such an evil happened to him, it can happen to us ten times more easily if we experience the same provocation. How much more, then, do we need to increase in the fear of God than he! For such an excellent man teaches us to watch ourselves all the more closely and not to let ourselves escape, for we are so terribly weak and know that we will be even more addicted to our evil desires if we are not kept in the hand of God. That, in brief, is how we are taught to behave ourselves in private, and to take heed to our steps, so that we will not deviate and turn from the right path. We are also to be careful of a downfall such as happened to David.

Indeed, the point is not that he merely took two or three women, for he already had two when he began reigning in Hebron – Abigail the Carmelite, and Ahinoam the Jezreelitess

(2 Sam. 2:2). It is also stated above that he took a daughter of Talmai, king of Geshur (2 Sam. 3:3). It is likely that he did this in order to make an alliance and strengthen himself. He did not do it out of intemperance, but saw that he needed to gain friends. But be that as it may, he is still not to be excused for it. For if he was not excused for one iniquity, how could he be excused for increasing iniquities, especially since the law is expressly laid down for kings? He deserved, therefore, the chastisement of God. Hence, there is not the least excuse for David – no matter what circumstances one may allege. Indeed, after the third wife he takes the fourth, and fifth, and even the sixth – and finally he wants Michal back (1 Sam. 25:44; 2 Sam. 3:13).

Now when the last wife is mentioned, many think it refers to Michal. It is true that Michal is mentioned here, but this is only a conjecture. It is far more likely that it was someone else, and thus one can see that he had as many as seven wives when he recalled the one who had been given to another man, as will be discussed later. There, then, was David, like a dissolute and thoroughly immoral man.

We must note, over and over again, that this sin is condemned by God – not as a minor weakness, but as an intolerable crime. It is true that the sentence had not yet been pronounced by the prophet Malachi. But still, it should have been engraved on all hearts, for he charges the Jews that their sacrifices were not acceptable to God, 'For the altar of the Lord,' he says, 'has been polluted with the tears of your wives who come there to weep and cry out' (Mal. 2:13ff.). In other words, when a man had several wives, it meant that they were oppressed and tormented with anguish.

Now we have shown that divorce would be more tolerable than polygamy – that is, than a plurality of wives (Mal. 2:16). For he says, 'If your wife does not please you, then leave her; but why must you torment and make her sad because of jealousy, since people are only too inclined towards jealousy?' It is certain that divorce is detestable in itself, because it falsifies the promise of God and the sanctity of marriage. If a man contradicts himself by his own word, he will immediately be considered untrustworthy. But if he vows to uphold something and, nonetheless, breaks his vow, he is even more culpable. If he falsifies his authentic signature, it is an intolerable evil. Now marriage is more important than any of that – so much so that he who breaks it must be punished by God. It is as though he were making God a liar, for he must consider God to be just that.

Therefore, whoever wishes to overthrow God's order is a treacherous impostor and perjurer, and shows himself even to be in contempt of God's majesty. And yet, as we have said, such confusion would be more pleasing to him than polygamy. Thus he charges the Jews: 'And why', he says, 'do you not see how God planned it from the beginning? Did he not have enough sense and strength to make several wives for Adam? But, nevertheless, he gave him only one. Therefore, when you go against monogamy, are you not overturning the entire order of nature?' (see Mal. 2:15).

Well, that is enough on the offence of David. Yet let us be sure not to use David as an excuse to cover our sins. Instead, let his repentance touch us to the quick, so that we will detest the evil which came to him, even as he detested it. For we have already shown how he not only asked pardon, but knew that he was more guilty than others because of the degree of honour and authority entrusted to him – in addition to the fact that God had given him the gift of prophecy. All the more, then, should we be careful to watch over ourselves soberly, so that everyone will live in marriage without having two or three wives – especially since there are some outlandish people who would like to return to that practice. And, furthermore, let us note very carefully that today, in addition to what has been explained from the Law, we are to hold most strictly to the rule: 'let every man have his own wife' (1 Cor. 7:2) – in order to avoid incontinence – and 'let every wife have her own husband'. He joins the two together. He does not say, 'You may take a second or third wife when you get divorced; but you shall be married to one wife only'. Hence, let us seek chastity, and for everyone to be contented with the party that God has given him.

For the rest of the matter, we see that in addition to the fact that David felt his sin and confessed it, God did not fail to chastise him. And do we consider ourselves to be more privileged than he? Even if he did have several wives, still we see that he had a deep repentance: 'I am like a cursed man, and more guilty than all the others' – and thereby he begs pardon for it.

Nevertheless, we see how it seemed for a time that God was so displeased with him that his benediction had been changed into malediction, both on him and on his posterity. It seemed that God had made him sterile, for during seven and a half years no wife had been able to bear him a single child. We see, thus, how God chastised him in this area. But that is not the main thing, for here is his son Amnon, who committed incest with his sister (2 Sam. 13), and then left her to be dishonoured and debauched. Now that is what polygamy is worth. After that, his second son, Absalom, who wanted to take vengeance for the shame that was done to his sister, actually killed Amnon. And after having killed him, we see that he even persecuted his father, and pursued him even to death, as far as he could (2 Sam. 15). What terrible punishments on so excellent a person!

What shall we say about ourselves? If God did not spare David, whom he had chosen and confirmed with the crown, should we not tremble when we think of these things? Let us, therefore, observe carefully and weigh the repentance of David, that we may humble ourselves before God for all our offences. And let us refuse to please ourselves, so that we will not be so rash as to follow our foolish desires and get ourselves into an abyss of sins. Yet such punishments do us double service; for we are not to think that we will escape the hand of God when we have provoked him to wrath, seeing that David was treated so roughly. Furthermore, we can follow his example of repentance when God has chastised us with his rods. Even when he beats us hard, let us not fail to be patient and to bow our head without murmuring, since David has shown us the way. That, in sum, is what we must remember from the beginning of this chapter.

Now there is a second point, where it says that Abner sent word to David (2 Sam. 3:12). It is true that the house of David was growing and getting stronger, and that the house of Saul was falling into decay. Well, that was certainly intended to relieve David particularly, for since God is faithful, he did not want him to be pressed beyond measure. For although he may test his sons by various trials, still he knows their frame and spares their infirmity and sweetens their sadness (Psa. 103:14). So although David was reigning only in Hebron, he had reason to thank the Lord and to take courage, and not to be vexed that he had only the one tribe of Judah, while all the others were his enemies. For he knew that this was an introduction to lead him on to the fulfilment of the promise. Of course, it was only little by little, but still God showed him in this way that he wanted to give him a taste of his goodness. When God put a division between Ishbosheth and Abner (2 Sam. 3:7), he was already showing David that he intended finally to abase the house of Saul, as indeed happened. And so we must learn from the example of David that when God does not allow us all at once to enjoy the good for which we had hoped, we should be satisfied to be given a little foretaste by him.

It is true that men desire all their appetites to be satisfied, as those who are hungry want to be filled with good food, without noticing whether or not it is profitable. But our Lord, knowing well our necessity and disease, gives us, as it were, a little piece of bread to strengthen our heart, and that should satisfy us until the time comes when he knows it is appropriate to feed us fully. For, in fact, we would not be able to endure his blessings if they came suddenly in all their fullness. We are like sick people who, when they start getting back their appetites, want to be stuffed full. But this should not be allowed, because it would spoil everything – their stomach is so weak that it could not bear such a large quantity of food. Equally, we would be in danger of being blinded by too much sudden prosperity. That is why God keeps himself from granting all our wishes – he would not otherwise have to be parsimonious towards us. When it appears to us that he is being parsimonious, the reason is that he knows that it is good for us to be kept in check. Let us learn from the example of David that when God gives us some little sign of his grace, we are to remain calm and to wait until the time comes when he will be more generous to us. So much, then, for this point.

But above all, we must put this principle into practice in regard to the kingdom of Jesus Christ, for we will not see it flourish as we wish, nor will it reach perfection all at once. God chooses to take care of it under the appearance of weakness, so that it will manifest neither pomp nor splendour before men. Now that angers many people, because they want God to employ his strength in a clearly visible way. However, it pleases God for the kingdom of his Son to rise and increase and be maintained in a humble way – with an appearance of weakness, as we have already said. Now if we think that that is strange, let us notice what the text says here about David, that even though the house of Saul was falling into decay, still David did not have undisputed control over all Israel.

When we see that our Lord causes his Church to grow by degrees – when he brings various ones to obedience to the faith; when the devil is thrown back and superstitions start being reversed and are no longer in vogue with the whole wretched world – then these changes ought to make us earnestly desire for God to be adored by everyone without a single contradiction. Nevertheless, we cannot wait for him to accomplish his work, for we have our own anxieties which motivate and drive us, and we seek to advance his work by our own recipes for success, or rather by our inconsiderate zeal. We should certainly have zeal, as I have said, but even so, we are not to be impatient. We must especially take his promises into consideration and await their fulfilment, for it is his part to know the opportune time.

However, here we see that Abner left Ishbosheth, whom he had made king, and went over to David (2 Sam. 3:6ff.). This is the greatest blow that befell the house of Saul, for it is expressly stated that Abner maintained Ishbosheth (2 Sam. 2:8) and that this poor man reigned only by total dependence upon the one who had him ordained king by the eleven tribes. Well, that should not have puffed up Abner with pride. For even assuming, for the sake of argument, that he did it out of sincere affection and virtue – which he did not, for this wicked rebel against God actually confessed it himself (2 Sam. 3:8–10) – still, Ishbosheth was king, and it is certain that Abner was subject to him. Indeed, he had made himself a subject. He was only his captain.

Yet Abner behaved in such a way that the king whom he had enthroned by his ambition and audacity was nothing to him but a fool to be used. He certainly treated him shamefully and showed him no respect. On the contrary, he poured out venom when he saw that Ishbosheth wanted to take some of his royal authority.

Here is the story. Saul had a concubine, whom Abner took. Now it is true that Abner was Saul's uncle, but even so he had no right to pretend to be king over all. At the very least, he should have received permission from the one who was his superior – namely, Ishbosheth – if he wanted this concubine as his wife. Thus, he despised the very one whom he himself had set up as king, and to whom he had pledged fidelity and obedience.

Then Ishbosheth complains to him and remonstrates with him for the evil that he had done. There was no great injury here, no criminal accusation or threats. It is simply stated that Ishbosheth remonstrated with him that he should not have taken his father's concubine. Now here the Jews have imagined (for they are ready to fabricate lies on the least pretext) that it was not proper for the widow (or concubine) of a deceased king to be remarried to a private person, no matter how great a lord he was. This is an unsubstantiated trifle. Nevertheless, Ishbosheth did have reason to complain to Abner, because he had done it without his seal and consent, for at least he should have asked his permission, as I have said. He could scarcely doubt that Abner, by this action, wanted to take vengeance on him and had shown enmity towards him so that he could get the crown himself. Also, he wanted to try his patience so that he could ridicule him, and later seize the opportunity to take over the throne and cast him out. When he thus despised his person by this incest and is gently rebuked for it, he takes it as a great injury. Well now, what is a king to do, who cannot judge justly without his subject seeking to make the king and everything else subject to himself?

Even so, Ishbosheth made a very modest complaint about the matter, but Abner became utterly furious with him – 'What, am I a dog?' (2 Sam. 3:8). Some explain it as though he were saying, 'Am I a guard dog, since I have acquired for you the kingdom over eleven tribes and since I have resisted David and his followers?' In other words, they take 'dog' to mean 'guard dog' by similitude. But that does not fit.

But be that as it may, Abner is boasting here, on the one hand, of the services that he has given to the house of Saul, and is showing that the king owes him everything that he has and was wrong to notice the offence that he had committed in contempt of his king. That is one point. Secondly, he makes light of his fault as a mere game. Thus it did not merit being spoken of, nor a single word being said about it. That is the second point. The third point is more grievous: namely, he threatens to return the kingdom to David according to the promise that had been made to him. Indeed, he swears that just as the Lord has spoken, he will fulfil this promise, and David will be established king over all Israel.

Now as regards the first point, here is Abner boasting about the service that he has given to the house of Saul. It is true that Ishbosheth should have realised that he ruled only by his help. But still, Abner was a subject of the king, and that should not have kept him from having to discharge his duty. Although one can do all sorts of marvellous things for the benefit and profit of one's superior, nevertheless, one must always pay attention to one's duty, because God wishes to be honoured by kings and princes and, in turn, wishes us to be obedient to them. Therefore, since Abner had put Ishbosheth on the royal throne, and if he wanted to keep him there, why did he not show him any respect? If he actually desired to have this woman, why did he not marry her without treating her as a whore? He had no excuse for doing so, and yet we see that he took great offence when he was reproached for his behaviour. Indeed, how readily those who have no fear of God will complain of being afflicted, when one is actually working as much as possible for their welfare and attempting to bring them back to the right path.

Abner said, then, that he was not like a dog (or a guard dog – take your choice), or that he was not like a scoundrel or a beast. So he said. But is it a matter of being either a scoundrel or a beast when the king has reproached him for having dishonoured the name and memory of his father? When the king dares to open his mouth to utter such a word, is it because Abner is like a beast? Now that is an example of how the proud cannot stand any rebuke whatsoever – those, I say, who are not governed by the Spirit of God. If you accuse one of them of his cruelties, another of his whoredoms, another of his evil doings, another of his envies, another of his murders, another of his wicked conspiracies – with intense indignation they will get on their high horse (as the saying goes) and thunder out, 'To whom do you think you are talking? How dare you? You have the nerve to come to me, as if I were a scoundrel or mere trash!' Then one simply shows them the real facts in order to calm them down, but nevertheless, they think that they have been done a terrible wrong and been seriously injured. They foam with rage over it and would love to trample us under their feet and to spit in our faces.

This should make us learn all the more to be modest, so that we will be able to take the rebukes that we are given and profit from them. So when modesty is deeply imprinted in our minds, and someone does accuse us of our faults, even though it cuts us painfully, still we will bear it patiently. When someone does rebuke us, as we have seen, we have all the more reason not to become contentious. For this will be only to 'kick against the pricks', as if we wished to be considered so sacred that nothing could touch us, as though it were a threat to defile us. So much, then, for this first point on the vanity of Abner.

We must also note (all of this will be dealt with in more detail later) that Abner was proud of himself, and of having been an outlaw and a rebel against God – I call a spade a spade. Indeed, he confessed it indirectly, and as good as says so in another way. But when he said, 'I have supported you against the house of Judah and against David' (2 Sam. 3:8 paraphrase), it is as if he were saying, 'I have been opposed to God in all pride and arrogance: I have been a rebel against him; I have been wicked and his enemy to please you; I have committed sacrilege, treachery, and disloyalty to his majesty to elevate you. And now are you dropping me?'

We see here how the wicked always cut their own throat by their vanity. For when they want to prove how much one is obliged to them, they do not do it by mentioning their virtue, but by mentioning how much they have sold out their conscience – how they have been thieves, whoremongers, perjurers, and have committed the most enormous crimes that one can think of. To please their own relative, friend, or companion, they are not in the least embarrassed to throw all of it up to them as though it were a gracious gift. If a wicked person is in a position of legal authority, he will sell out justice, and will have no second thoughts about it. He who is called on to give testimony will perjure himself without the least difficulty. Another will spend his time running a whore-house; another will help his companion steal or kill this person here or that person there. Now when some contention arises between them, what they will do in order to make their complaints more effective is to vomit everything out of their belly. What they have done together, I say, will no longer be hidden. And how? 'Have I not rescued you from peril? And what were you without me? Are you not obligated to me for everything you have? Did I not turn your mistake into success by my brilliant plot? Have I not served you in such and such a way? Have I not hurt my conscience out of love to you?' Such are their usual reproaches. Such remarks reflect Abner's speech like a mirror.

Nevertheless, we see Abner's hypocrisy when he says, 'And today you accuse me of sin with a woman', as if it were some great crime, and Ishbosheth had no more respect for him than for a dog. He says this, hoping to excuse his fault and make it so minor that no attention will be paid to it. For when he says 'sin with a woman', he is speaking disdainfully – 'Now that is some evil! It must be talked about. And yet it does not amount to a hill of beans, as it were.' That is what Abner meant.

Well, he had to act like a brazen-faced whore, for he had taken the concubine of a king, and whether he wanted her as his wife or as a whore, he should not have done it without the approval of the one who was supposed to have all authority over him. And for it to be called a very small fault which was not worth even mentioning – now where could this have led to? I say that Abner must have had a face of brass to talk like that. But that is the way with all hypocrites. When they have committed the most villainous crimes in the world, they merely wipe their mouths. They do not want it even mentioned.

One sees this attitude in our common language. There will never be a criminal who is not half absolved as soon as you listen to his excuses. Now here is a murderer. He will always have a good excuse: 'Anger made me do it; I was so preoccupied at that moment that I didn't know where I was. I did not want to do it, and am worried about it.' In brief, there will always be some good excuse for him to show why his evil deed is not so grievous as people say. Someone who steals wood will claim that he had to, and then will say that someone else caused him to be immoral. Whores have still more subterfuges. They do not have enough strength to keep their flesh under control; they have been so infected with this terrible desire that they are not able to abstain. It is the same way with all of the others. For they never wish to go inside themselves for self-examination. Instead, they will always try to lessen their offences and want to shrug off all sorts of crimes.

In sum, one sees that men who are abandoned to evil will always be found innocent, and will be guilty of nothing if one chooses to believe them. So we must remember all the more what we are shown here. For the Holy Spirit sets Abner before us, so that we may be ashamed of such impudence and not be so rash as to pretend that wicked deeds are merely venial sins, when actually they are as enormous as Abner's. When we act in this way, we will only aggravate our sins all the more. So that is what we must remember when it says, 'Sin with a woman? That is no big thing!' – just as whores and pimps always want to make their profession a good one, and to excuse their moral filth. When we see that and, on the other hand, the Holy Spirit shows us what is involved, let us learn to detest such wicked deeds and enormous sins. Hence, if we are tempted, let us begin to examine the matter so that we will be disgusted with it. And we will be cut to the quick, I say, with such repentance that we will be aware of the perils and dangers of our position, and will mourn over and groan about our past sins. Let us do this not to be approved by men only, but to be received by God as a sweet-smelling savour. So much, then, for the second point.

The third point shows Abner's rebellion against God and his king, which is the most terrible thing of all. He swears, 'May God do such and such to me' (2 Sam. 3:9), which is a customary form in Scripture, as if he were saying, 'May God punish me not only in one way, but in two or three, until he exterminates me'. But there is also here a particular emphasis, as though men would show that they are careless when they say 'such and such' in order to prove that they will think about it two or three times before making such a protestation. But we will speak in more detail about that later.

Let us come to the main point. Abner threatens to take the crown from Ishbosheth. Why? Because 'the throne will be established' in the house of David (2 Sam. 3:9ff.), as it was promised to him. But what have you done up to now, you wicked man? You knew that God had established David over the kingdom, and with whom have you been siding until now? Have you not fought against God? Now what has fighting against him won you? You cannot excuse yourself; for if you confess that God elected David to rule over his people, how have you dared to attempt resisting his decree?

Now we see how the iniquitous cut their own throats and pluck out their own eyes in such a way that they conduct their own trial. Hence, even if there be no other witness, judge or plaintiff, yet they condemn themselves from their own mouths, as though they were being forced by torture to speak.

God pronounced that David would be king – and you, wretched person, have done battle with him, as if you wanted to be the stronger! You have been a devil, in order to overturn the truth of God, and turn it into a lie. You have acted as if you were saying, 'God promised that David would be established king over Israel; but if I oppose it, it will not happen'. You have vomited out such blasphemies, and have said in effect, 'I will abolish this promise, and it will have no effect; nothing will come from all this, unless I will it and work it out'. Now that is how this abominable villain, Abner, knew that God was his Judge, and yet shamelessly continued on his own way – which would without fail be uncovered, although it had been hidden up to this point. For no matter how much he might claim that he had no other desire in carrying out his duty than to uphold the house of Saul, still the results of his behaviour prove the contrary. He was motivated by nothing but ambition and pride. And however much he may have wanted people to consider him qualified, in fact, his malice and stupidity were completely uncovered. It is clear that he was fighting directly against God.

Thus, when we see that God reproves his enemies and those who despise his majesty, let us fear becoming like them, since the Holy Scripture so frequently warns us against this. Let us also learn to submit ourselves to God, and to pray that he will never allow us to become so stupid and wish for such a high position that we become blinded by it; and so by our pride and arrogance, our sins become so increased that they totally swallow us. May he never permit it, so that in the end we do not turn into brutes with no discretion, and do not prostitute ourselves in shame and disgrace before God and man, as St Paul mentions in the first chapter of Romans (Rom. 1:18ff.). So much for that point.

Now for the rest, here is Abner, who wants to become a preacher. One would say that he is a prophet. How? 'Here is the throne which God has promised to David; he has received the sign of this sacred unction from God's prophet. Oh, these things must be accomplished!' Indeed, one would say that Abner has become an angel – but the truth is that he is no better whatsoever. For he is a rebel against God, and everything he does is for vengeance alone – as we shall soon see when he revolts against the king, his master, and changes sides so that David will be received by all the people.

Now that, in sum, shows us again what hypocrites are. For they will frequently imitate good and holy persons on specific occasions, but one must always be careful of their malice and place absolutely no trust in them. For we often see that after a life of dissolution and utter wickedness, they will pretend to be touched with repentance. After they have done all the evil that they could, and their intentions have been frustrated and fortune has turned against them, as they say – then they will imitate the faithful believers, and will come forward to accuse others who have been their companions in wickedness. They say, 'Such and such things have happened to me, and I have lived the worst possible life up to this point. But from now on I want to live right. We have conspired at this and that against you, and if it had been possible, we would have exterminated all of you. But now I repent of it and am most grieved over it.' In other words, here they are – half angels! But why? All of that is nothing but hypocrisy, which Scripture illustrates for us in the person of Abner.

It is true that God can easily convert those whom he pleases, and we must refrain from judging precisely who these may be. If it pleases him to grant mercy to the worst sinners in the world, then very well – let us receive them. But still let us be prudent and know how to discern whether those who have been so perverse want to make a good show, or whether they are sincere. Let us consider what has caused their action, and whether they have the 'root of the matter'. Let us be diligent to examine them. When we see that their affections have changed, that they are continuing in the service of God, are keeping themselves from past follies, and are in faithful fellowship with their neighbours without reproach, let us embrace them as our brothers. On the other hand, someone who is insincere can certainly manage to cover his moral corruption for a while, but in the end the Law of God and his service will examine him in such a way that he will have to spit out his venom and his hypocrisy will be known. We have an example of this in Abner.

Now for the rest of the matter. Let us learn to serve God voluntarily, since we are his and since we ought to subject everything that concerns us to his will. Let us be ready to follow him everywhere he may call us, and let us endeavour to make ourselves useful to our neighbour, without on the other hand doing less in the service of God. That is what we must do, and not protest hypocritically, as did Abner: 'Well, what God has decreed will be accomplished; it does not depend on me, for his will overrules mine'. Nevertheless, he is mocking God and his prince.

It is certain that such insolence cannot be tolerated by God. He cannot be fooled like men, for he is the one who searches their hearts. Now here is Abner, who protests that he is helping David take possession of the crown, as though God had never been offended by this kingdom of Ishbosheth, which he had not willed. Abner swears, 'As God has promised it, so I will do'. What does he mean? 'Everything that pleases me, God will do, insofar as it pleases me.' He demonstrates, thereforc, a diabolical audacity, by presuming that God can only consent to his will, and that God must consult and agree with him. It is as though he were saying that even if he should attempt to resist him, David would still remain behind.

Now that is how Abner preens himself more than ever, and abandons himself to pride and arrogance, as we have seen. All the more, then, must we learn to humble ourselves before God and to recognise that even if we were hardened towards him in the extreme, it would not stop him from accomplishing his works. So let us be careful not to reach such an extremity. From the example of this poor wretched soul, let us learn to detest our vices and to come boldly to God to tell him in truth that we are asking of him only to conform us to his will. This being done, we cannot doubt that he will reign in us, and at the last will show us, indeed, that he accepts us for his own.

Now let us bow down before the majesty of our good God, recognising the infinite faults of which we are guilty and praying that he will make us so to feel them that we will genuinely repent by asking pardon of him in true humility. Let us seek to be received under the shadow of his wings, that we might be maintained and kept safe by him, and that we will be patient in all our adversities, knowing that all the good that we receive comes from his hand, and still hoping that at the end he will show himself full of pity for us, and that we will experience the fruit of his mercy for our salvation. And may he not only bestow this grace upon us, but upon all people and nations of the earth . . .

8

*Abner's Moral Crime**

Abner thus sent messengers to David on his behalf, saying: Whose is the land? Make an alliance with me, and my hand will be with you to bring about all Israel to you. And he said: Well, I will make an alliance with you, and yet I will require one thing from you: It is that you will not see my face, unless first you bring with you Michal, the daughter of Saul, when you come to see my face. Then David sent messengers to Ishbosheth, son of Saul, saying: Return me my wife Michal . . . (2 Sam. 3:12–27).

The old proverb says that motive is the judge of everything men do. In fact, a thing can be considered a great virtue, and yet it may be a moral crime, even as there are deeds that one can condemn, which nevertheless are excusable when the motive was not evil. Now it is true that men are often mistaken in their intention, as those who imagine that they are serving God when they invent and dream this and that in their brain. Therefore, it is not said that when a man imagines he is doing good, his work will be approved before God. But the proverb is true in that a work is never worthy of praise if the motive is not right. We have an example of that in what is recounted here of Abner.

For he pretends to give David possession of the kingdom which was promised him by God. Now that seems to be a praiseworthy deed, for since God ordained it, is he not to be considered the servant of God when he is working for this goal? On the other hand, as has often been shown, this kingdom of

*Monday, June 15, 1562.

David was a type of the grace which God wished to pour out on his Church in becoming its Redeemer in the person of his only begotten Son. Therefore, when Abner comes forward to do all this, what could one say about him except that he is acting in the most virtuous manner in the world? Nevertheless, he does not cease being wicked and a traitor, for he does not really wish to serve God, but wants vengeance against his king, because he cannot stand having been rebuked for his whoredom. Well, that is how what is good in appearance and has a beautiful lustre before men cannot fail to be condemned before God.

We see the same in Judas, for when he betrayed our Lord Jesus Christ, he did not want to procure the salvation of the human race. But nevertheless, this was the means. Now on the one hand, there is the Son of God, who was delivered up to be a sacrifice, so that we might be reconciled to God his Father. And who was it that delivered him up? God declares that it was he, as it says, 'God so loved the world' (John 3:16) that 'he spared not his only son but delivered him to death for us' (Rom. 8:32). On the other hand, here is our Lord Jesus Christ, who presents himself and gives his own self up. When it says that God exposed his only Son to death, let us contemplate his inestimable mercy in this action. Our Lord Jesus Christ also showed us the singular love that he had for us when he offered himself and had no regard for his own person, but chose to suffer the pains that we deserved. Well, it certainly seemed that Judas had served God in purity and was conformed to his will, for God had decreed that our Lord Jesus Christ should suffer death and passion. Judas carried it out, indeed, but for what reason? What was his intention, and what were his feelings?

Therefore, let us learn to walk the right path before God – because everything that we can do, however valued before men, will be nothing but refuse and dung when we have to come before this eternal Judge, who knows the hearts and searches them, as Scripture says (Psa. 7:9; 139:23; 1 Kings 8:39). Often men judge us as though we were angels, and yet God condemns us. But when our malice cannot be hidden from the judgement of men, then they will not fail to condemn us, even though we thought that we had done well. The pagans were well able to say, for instance, that such a person could actually kill his father, yet often not be guilty before God. For if he did it while imagining that he was helping him, even though there was fault in his error, still he had a pure and true affection in that he wanted to help his father, and one could not condemn him for having been the occasion of his death. Another could be like a doctor to heal his father, and often people would condemn him as a murderer, because his intention was wicked. So the pagans certainly had this imprinted in their nature, and their common sense led them to it. How much more should we learn lessons, since Scripture exhorts us so often to simplicity and straightforwardness, and tells us that we must walk as before God, having our eyes fixed on him, and on the other hand admonishes us that he is not interested in a beautiful outward appearance, which seems good to mortal men who judge by outward appearance, but that he searches down to the depths of the heart and sees our affections and thoughts (1 Sam. 16:7). How much more should we learn not to put on false appearances in order to be approved, while we are still going on an oblique course in the opposite direction.

For it happens every day that some man does good things either for the public welfare or for some particular good. Who drives him to do it? On the one hand, he is driven by ambition. One sees ambition in deeds of great prowess – such as saving a country – and often these ambitious men will not be greatly esteemed. They did it only because they wanted to become well known, and to outdo someone in whose shadow they thought they were hidden. That is what forced them to do well. So after a careful look, one will find many persons whom one would have judged to be good by their deeds who nevertheless are full of dishonesty. And what they have done was only to harm this one or that one out of wicked vengeance, for they regarded only their own ambition, and were driven by their pride, which led them to do it. Now it is true that what is good in itself is always to be accepted, but that is not to say that the person will be approved and that one should consider as virtuous what proceeded from their wicked and perverse affection. That is what we must remember from this deed of Abner, when he wanted to give David possession of the kingdom. Although he seemed to want to serve God, still his intention was false and he only sought to take vengeance on his king by his perversity.

Now concerning Abner's vengeance, we have seen earlier that it was most iniquitous. For Ishbosheth had not forgotten him, and even though he had mildly rebuked him, he had not condemned him to death – which he could have done as king. Rather, he was content with telling him that he had committed a villainous and detestable crime. He did not cause him to be put in prison; he did not condemn him to death. As I have said, he only pointed out his fault. If, therefore, one word so enraged him, must we not say that his courage was motivated by malice and rebellion?

So for this cause, it says that he 'sent on his behalf' (2 Sam. 3:12). The Hebrew word signifies 'under him', and yet none of his men revealed that he sent word in secret. It is quite certain that he was despising his king, and was doubtlessly acting as a traitor and disloyal subject towards him, for if he could have taken over the kingdom, he would have tried it, rather than becoming subject to David. Therefore, this word is added on purpose to signify that Abner was excusing himself in saying that God had ordained it. But nevertheless, he was falsely attempting to ruin the one whom he had established and to whom he had solemnly sworn. He tried to ruin Ishbosheth by joining himself to David, but, nonetheless, he was still guilty of treason and shamefulness.

Yet we see how the faithful, such as David, are often perplexed when they are constrained to co-operate with people who are worthless. David was not fooled by Abner, for he well understood that he was coming to him in order to do evil. Formerly, he had been hardened in the extreme, so who had caused him to change so suddenly? David therefore knew that Abner was fickle and unreliable. He saw the real reason, namely, that Abner, because of his pride, had revolted against the one whom he himself had set on the royal throne. David knew all these things but, nevertheless, he says, 'This is a good move', and agrees (at first sight) that he will make an alliance with Abner. We see, therefore, that we cannot always avoid being surrounded by the wicked. It is true that we should flee from them, as far as possible, and have no dealings with them, as the Psalms say (Psa. 1:1; 26:5). For we cannot touch their dirty hair without being blackened. The best thing for us to do, then, is always to stay away from these who hold God in contempt, since we will be infected by their company if we have private fellowship with them, and will also be totally corrupted.

Therefore, if David had been able, he would certainly have rejected Abner, but he was afraid of tempting God. He saw his own difficulties. He also saw that much blood could be shed, that eleven tribes still remained obedient to Ishbosheth and that the people of God would be torn in pieces like a dismembered body. David considered all those things, and came to an agreement with Abner as a solution to the problem. We cannot excuse him for all this, but still we see that he was constrained and forced to do it for obvious reasons. We cannot condemn him, as though he had committed some great offence, for this would be rash and presumptuous on our part. Well then, this example should urgently warn us to pray the Lord to deliver us from similar trials, and that we would not be pushed by urgent necessity to yoke ourselves with the wicked, whose company we ought to flee.

Further, we see here that David always maintained some love for Michal, his wife, who had been snatched from him to be given to Phaltiel, the son of Laish (1 Sam. 25:44; 2 Sam. 3:13). Therefore, he replied to Abner that he would never receive him until he first returned his wife, Michal, to him. It had been a long time since she had been taken from him – indeed, long enough to have effaced all the love that he formerly had for her. For even though a man once loved his wife, still if she is given to another and she consents and lives with him, it would cause him so to disdain her that his love for her would not only be effaced, but turned into bitterness – when a man saw that his wife had thus left him and had allowed herself to be joined to another. When he sees that, I say, he is certain to be angry with her and to reject her completely, and have no desire to hear her speak. But we see the opposite in David, for even though Michal had been handed over to Phaltiel, he still had this affection which he had previously felt for her – no matter how little she cared for him nor how much she was devoted to her second husband. For it is said that Phaltiel followed her, weeping and lamenting, until he was strictly commanded to return, unless he wanted to die (2 Sam. 3:16). He would have followed her to Hebron, which was very likely if Abner had not prevented him – and this would have caused trouble there. We see, thus, the love that he had for her, and it is likely that the affection was mutual. Hence, we can judge that David had the opportunity to reject her. But he loved her nonetheless, although at last he saw clearly that he was at fault in his extreme and excessive passion. For later, it says that Michal was so puffed up with pride for the house of her father Saul that she made fun of David – when he followed the ark of God, to show his devotion and zeal by dancing – and that she considered him a fool and mocked him (2 Sam. 6:16, 20). Well, by this we see that even the most perfect have overwhelming emotions, and cannot contain their joy, so that they always go to excess.

Furthermore, it is likely that David was considering his own reputation when he wanted to recover his wife. For it was a disgrace to him that his wife had been snatched away from him, and that another was enjoying her. He was the king of Judah, and being in such a shameful condition did not help his dignity. Therefore, it seems that he considered how not to give anyone cause to despise him. But be that as it may, we still see how intense was the love he had for Michal.

Now it says that he 'sent to Ishbosheth' (2 Sam. 3:14). In this, we see that Ishbosheth was willing to agree with David, and to admit that he was king in Hebron. From that, we may remember that it was always well known that God had chosen David, and wanted him to be leader of his people. Nevertheless, Ishbosheth wanted to retain the rest of the people, and did not want to submit to David and do him homage. Thus, he is motivated by two contrary feelings. On the one hand, Ishbosheth did not accuse David of being a rebel; he did not call him to trial for having snatched away one part of his country and subjects. And these considerations could have been added, for Judah was the leading tribe in all Israel, and David was king over it.

Well, Ishbosheth did not want any quarrel with him over that, and even sent his sister to him – that is how much he honoured him. He was content for him to remain king, as I have said already. From that, we can judge that he knew well that David would have to reign, since it was the good pleasure of God. Now his feeling about this was good as far as it went. But nevertheless, why did Ishbosheth, on the other hand, remain attached and as it were tied to his throne, and why did he not resign and leave the place for David? He could not, because he did not want to humble himself before him. Thus, it was haughtiness which kept him back. He was born in the house of a king, and remained successor to the crown, he thought. Now that is how, on one side, he resisted God but on the other, was faithful to him.

Now this shows us that we ought not to obey God only partially. When we are double-minded, we cannot steer a straight course. So even though we put on a good appearance, and seem to place ourselves under obedience to him, yet when God wants us to march forward, instead of agreeing with him, we will seek to go backwards. In brief, he who makes that kind of show of obeying God will always be infected with rebellion. Now we must pay serious attention to this, in order to be displeased with it and to strip ourselves of it.

Insofar as this is a humane deed which is spoken of here, it should in fact have induced David to love Ishbosheth and to come to some kind of agreement. And why did he not do so? Well, he did not have the liberty to do so, because it was necessary that what God had ordained should be accomplished. Therefore, however much Ishbosheth might attempt to win favour with David, still it would not give David any reason to give up the best of what was rightfully his, because in so doing he would have broken the promise of God. Here is a point to be noted well, which we must always bear in mind. Whenever we are dealing with men, let us give up our own rights absolutely, so that God might ever retain all of his.

Today we have an example of it in these differences and

troubles involved in religion. Let us assume that our enemies only ask to negotiate with us, and that they are prepared to dive and swim between two seas to accommodate us in every way. Let us assume that they are acting most humanely. For our part, it is certain that we must do the very same, but only if it does not have to be done at the expense of God's truth. Here let us notice carefully that whenever men treat us kindly, we must give them credit for it, insofar as we rob God of none of his rights, and that we do not trade at his expense (as we have already said).

That is why David is not to be criticised when Ishbosheth attempted to become his friend. In so doing, Ishbosheth repaired the relationship which he had formerly broken with his sister, in order to say: 'Let us be friends from now on, and let each one reign and keep for himself what he already has'. However much Ishbosheth forces himself to agree with David, so that they might be good friends and have an alliance between them, still for all that, David cedes nothing to him which had been assigned to David by the authority of God. That is because he does not hold the kingdom from men, but he knows that the will of God is that he should have it, and hence he concludes that the downfall of Ishbosheth is irrevocable. So much, then, for this point.

One could be surprised, granted that Ishbosheth had been so willing to accord to David what he asked of him. And why was it not recognised by David? That is where one could begin wondering. But as I have said, the reply is easy – that David has regard to what is proper and necessary for him. For he did not negotiate in the least for the kingdom to remain with Ishbosheth, and yet he would have given it up one hundred times in one day if God had wanted him to do so, as he had already shown by experience. But insofar as it was not for him to exchange anything that God had decreed, that is why he agrees in part with Ishbosheth. And thus in sum, although numerous troubles may parade before our eyes to tempt us to loosen the bridle here and there, nevertheless, let us always march on the path to which God calls us, and let us agree with men – insofar as it will not cause us to go astray or to backslide from God, and to turn our backs on him.

Let us now come to what is added, namely, that David received Abner when he came to him (2 Sam. 3:20). In the first place, we see that David had the reputation, even among his enemies, of fidelity and integrity, so that one could trust him – for 'Abner came to Hebron'. And how large a company did he bring? Only 'twenty men'. That is nothing compared with the host of David. So if David had wanted to beat him down, could he have resisted it? For he was enclosed in a city, and thus one could easily have cut his throat. We see, therefore (in sum), that when he comes to put himself in the hands of David, he does so out of respect for David's fidelity. And by that we are admonished so to live among men that they will be able to trust us, and we will reap the fruit of our integrity. Otherwise, one might say that whoever acts like a lamb will be eaten by the wolf, so he must howl with the wolves. We see the contrary, that is, when we walk straightforwardly and fairly, we will do wrong to no-one. We will always loyally keep our promises, and this will cause all pride and arrogance of our enemies to be broken, and they will be constrained to come to us peaceably. The trust that they will have in our fidelity will be the reason why they will more easily appeal to us to live in peace.

For where do so many wicked acts, which one sees among men, come from, except from the fact that people distrust one another; so much so that they cannot come to an agreement for any promise which they make? And if we insist on living in a perverse manner, it is certain that we will never approach one another for reconciliation. Let us notice, then, that there is nothing better than to conduct ourselves in integrity and simplicity. Not that our simplicity should be foolish, for we ought to have a true prudence mingled with it. But when we are well balanced, we will not be double-minded, but will show that we only seek to do good. People will then be able to recognise that we are motivated by a spirit of gentleness, which will help to appease our enemies and make them approach us, and will purge all hearts of ill will, in such a way that it will turn them into friends.

However, we must also note how God relieved his servant

David, without his even having thought of it, as the Psalm says. God will procure the salvation of his own 'even when they sleep' (Psa. 127:2). For David did not solicit Abner, but Abner sent messengers to him of his own accord (2 Sam. 3:12). David did not turn him from the love of Ishbosheth; he did not make him rich promises as a reward; he did not even think of all that. But nevertheless, as he sleeps, God watches over him, and disposes and ordains things in such a way that Abner sends to supplicate and ask that they be friends, and strives to do this by putting him in possession of the kingdom. Let us carefully note that when we follow everywhere that God calls us and everywhere that he commands us, then he will make everything turn out well for us. And we are not to be too wise, like unbelievers who insist on long explanations; instead, let us simply accept everything which appears to occur for our benefit. But be that as it may, let us draw this conclusion, that God will make all our enterprises prosper when our intention is right, and that we are to expect nothing outside of his will. Well, that is the point we are to note here.

As for Abner, we see here again his hypocrisy, when he preaches, as though he were a prophet, that David ought to be king – since God had sworn to him, and he had even declared to him by his prophet that the people ought to be kept under his protection, and that it was an irrevocable event (2 Sam. 3:18). If Samuel had been resurrected, he would not have known how to talk any better than Abner! And yet he is led to do this by treachery and wickedness, as one can recognise. For he is revolting against his master, the king, to whom he was obligated by solemn oath. Hence, we see how hypocrites transform themselves and put an attractive cover on their iniquities. But that does nothing to lessen their offences before God; indeed, they are even further from being excused and absolved from them. It is true that they will still make believe that they are pardoned for their offences. There is no doubt that Abner washes his hands and takes refuge in this excuse: 'It is true that now I am revolting against my king, but up until now I have been foolish and shy. It has been presumptuous of me to impede the course of David's kingdom, since it is ordained of

God. Thus, it is now necessary that I return to the right path.' Here is Abner, who thinks that he has found grounds to be excused. But be that as it may, when one examines him to the very bottom, one sees that he was always motivated by vengeance, and that if Ishbosheth had allowed him total licence, as he asked, if he had left him in his whoredom and, in brief, if he had reigned under the name of another, then it is certain that he would always have remained a rebel against David.

Well then, in the first place, let us note that we must carefully be on our guard when we have attractive excuses to show that all we are doing is good and just, and that there are no wicked motives mixed with them. For just as a little leaven can make a great mass of dough ferment (1 Cor. 5:6; Gal. 5:9), so only a twisted or oblique motive is needed to deprave and pervert everything that would be the best in the world. Therefore, let us note that, before God, all the affections of hypocrites will gain nothing; all that they satisfy is men. For there are many who would approve Abner. For instance, experience shows that the Israelites forgot past history: although they had always been faithful to Ishbosheth, they suddenly went along with Abner and clung to him, since they thought that his shift of position was based on virtue. That is how he tricks men under this attractive covering that 'God had sworn to David'. Though it is true, he nevertheless always remains wicked and perverse. The reason? Because he is not motivated by a true zeal and affection, but only by his vengeance. Because if he could have occupied the throne, there is no doubt that he would have revolted more than ever against David, and would have made open war to fight against God.

Well in sum, when we see these beautiful words of Abner, let us note that all those who have the Word of God in their mouth do not necessarily have true religion. Here is Abner, who brings forward the authority of God: 'since God has sworn, who is it who will go against him?' And then he adds the promise that God wants to save his people by the hand of David. Now here is the whole sum of our life, namely, that we endeavour to place ourselves under the teaching of God and that we come to humble ourselves under his sovereign majesty and acquiesce in his good will. That is one point. And then that we embrace his promises when he testifies that he will be our Saviour. Let that delight us, and let us recognise that all our good, our happiness and our rest lie in his mercy. Well, these two things are contained in Abner's harangue. Concerning the first point, it is God who has promised the kingdom to David; therefore, one must come over to his side. And then for the second point, God has said that he will save his people. If, therefore, we begin to resist these things, it will be in contempt of him, rejecting what he has ordained, and all of his graces. It is necessary, therefore, that we accept David as king – he is God's minister.

Now when we see that hypocrites speak in this way and imitate the prophets, when it seems in fact that they are like angels descended from heaven, let us learn to speak from the heart, as Scripture says, 'I have believed, therefore I shall speak' (Psa. 116:10; 2 Cor. 4:13). Let there be, I say, a living root (of piety) in our hearts, which makes us tremble before the majesty of God when it is time for us to take a stand. Not as unbelievers who have no hope, but rather let us fear to offend him, whether in our deeds, our words, or our thoughts. And we are shown the reason for our trembling: it is that we should add faith and trust to his promises (Heb. 4:2). Then let us open our mouths, once our heart is in the right place. Nevertheless, let there be no going backwards, like many who will say that it is necessary to obey God, but only for this or that occasion. There will be some particular concern which will motivate them, rather than a pure and whole resolution. What, therefore, is necessary? If we want to have God for our Father, let us ascribe to him the right which is his. And how will we do this? By saying one thing and doing another? Take these of whom I have been speaking. They will properly say that it is necessary to submit oneself to God, but their submission is selective. As long as they fear some present punishment which frightens them, they will obey. And yet they will give way in another area, and it will scarcely bother them that they irritate God in the extreme, as soon as they are no longer afraid.

As for the promises of God, even the wicked certainly want to have their refuge in him and in his mercy when they can do nothing else. If some evil is causing them anguish, they will say, 'Alas, and where would I have any recourse if God did not have mercy upon me?' Now that is a blast of hot air! Rather, let them have obedience to God so rooted in their hearts that they will want to be subject to him and to have confidence in his promises – but they will have none of it. Let us, thus, be careful not to emulate them, but let us continue to the very end in his service and obedience, and rest in his pure goodness, thus causing ourselves to testify to what he has given us. So much, therefore, for this beautiful harangue that Abner made!

Nevertheless, we see that God made good use of this. The truth is that, as for Abner, he receives double condemnation from it, for he is condemned by his own mouth when he says, 'God has sworn to David'. O wicked man! Why, therefore, have you fought against him until now? What did you mean by the whole war that you have conducted for the space of two years? You have even persecuted David, whom you knew to be innocent. But again, after the death of Saul, when you saw that David ought to reign, why is it that you introduced Ishbosheth, his son, to the crown, who did not have the right of succession? When you have taken a good look at yourself, will you not discover a manifest rebellion, which you are trying to cover? But again, Abner has spoken against his own motivation, however much it was intended to soften the hearts of his hearers, so that they would make them pliable and obey David (2 Sam. 3:19). Those hearers, of course, were the tribe of Benjamin, for whom it was a great honour that there was a ruler over all Israel who was descended from their tribe. That consideration should have made them more fiercely opposed than anyone else, when they saw the succession to the crown returning to the tribe of Judah. Nevertheless, they are softened. Abner wins them.

That is how God will often put to good use the words of hypocrites and wicked persons. We see how the Gospel is often advanced by their activity and by the malice of those who have no proper affection for it, but who are full of ambition. That was already the case in the time of Paul, and we see it practised everywhere today (Phil. 1:15). Paul says that there are those who have preached the Gospel out of a certain malice, in order to build up the fire against him, and yet others have not failed to submit – that is, their hearers. Some of these miserable creatures did this for their own profit, to advance themselves and have authority and credit, and others did it to falsify pure doctrine. Well, he says that it is all the same thing to him, as long as God is glorified. Thus, we see again today that there are many who will do marvels, it seems. Be that as it may, it is not because they have a true affection to advance the honour of God, to edify his Church, and to procure the salvation of the faithful – not at all. Nevertheless, their labour will not be in vain. Here is how God uses such hypocrites, as he used Abner, who was worth nothing. And yet the men of Israel were moved to profess obedience to David by his remonstrance, although it came out of a wicked mouth.

Indeed, even though he who speaks is not what he ought to be, still we must always receive the truth of God which is pronounced by his mouth. And God's honour will not be diminished in the least by this, because his truth does not consist in the virtue of men, but in the fact that it comes from him alone, and it is made to shine among men, even by those who are unworthy of it. Hence, when those who preach the Word of God do not govern themselves as they should, but manifest a contradiction between their life and their doctrine, let us not fail to accept in all reverence what they bring forward from God. For it is not reasonable that we pay attention only to the evil that we see, so as to tarnish his Word and his honour. This is what we must remember, therefore, from the remonstrance which Abner makes here.

Now by the action of Joab, we see how difficult it is to mortify annoyances and troubles which have existed for a time, even among those who have been in some degree of honour. Here is Joab, who has been David's captain. Well, Abner was his opposing captain. Here, therefore, is Joab, who for a long time has nursed a mortal hatred against Abner, so that he can in no way come to terms with him, even though David has kindly received him. He continues to nurse all the more this wicked feeling engraved in his heart. But there is no doubt that the main reason was this ambition and envy which he had against Abner. For he sees that he is a valiant man, and had also proved it, when he brought the eleven tribes under his control in the name of Ishbosheth. He sees that he had authority with the people to bring them back to David and accept him as king, and how the people would have been against David for a long time if he had not taken them and reconciled them with him. It seemed, therefore, to Joab that this would be an occasion to bring him back to the king, his master, and that Abner would very likely by this means be able to be promoted to his position. Because of our lack of time, we will have to expound the death of Abner later.

Now let us prostrate ourselves before the majesty of our good God, recognising all our faults, beseeching him to make us so sensible of them as to become dissatisfied with ourselves, and that we, recognising also that we are full of every sort of evil desire, may have the wherewithal to fight against these desires every moment of our lives, so that nothing may hinder us from placing ourselves in obedience to God and his service. And may we learn so to commit ourselves to him that we seek only to conform ourselves to his will, and that we may not turn from it either to the right or to the left. But may we expect from it all our prosperity and the happy issue of our undertakings, when we have followed his holy calling. Let him bestow his grace not only on us, but on all people and nations of the earth . . .

9

*The Infamous Murder of Abner**

Joab then went out from David and sent messengers to Abner, and brought him again from the well of Sirah, without David knowing it. When Abner was returned to Hebron, Joab took him aside in the middle of the gate to speak privately to him, and smote him there under the fifth rib, and he died for the blood of Asahel his brother . . . (2 Sam. 3:26–39).

We saw yesterday what motive Joab had in killing Abner – that he was led by envy in that he feared that Abner would reach a higher degree of honour, and that he would no longer be David's enemy. Thus, we saw that the honours of this world always carry people away with ambitions; that envy makes it very difficult for those who are there to maintain themselves in such modesty that they do no evil in the midst of grandeur, for there will always be some jealousy. And that is how the devil always seeks to spoil the gifts of God and make them odious. For there is nothing more useful than to have, as governors, people of authority and pre-eminence. Because without that, our condition would be worse than that of brute beasts. For the lions, bears and tigers get along together in the forests, but it is impossible for men to live together if there is not some leader to keep them in check. Otherwise, they would eat one another up.

Well, it is God who ordains superiority and chooses that there be some to rule. If there are kings, it is necessary that there be such and such a number of officers; it is necessary that

*Tuesday, June 16, 1562.

they have their council, and even in all republics it is necessary that they have several leaders. And then there has to be a certain company of people, for a single person is not able to have enough virtue and magnanimity to govern alone. Rather, we need the counsel of others in order to contemplate the paternal care that God has for us. The devil, therefore, wants to pollute it, and mingles jealousies in it, which cause contentions to break out later. He who is envious of another will have the greatest difficulty in keeping out of some kind of trouble or quarrel with him. So much more do those who are elevated in honour and dignity have need to pray God to give them the grace so to control themselves. Then everyone will recognise that they have a spirit of gentleness which does not seek more than their office allows. And even that they be as 'little babes weaned from the breast' (Psa. 131:2), to use David's image, protesting that 'he has not been puffed up with pride, and that his spirit is not given over to haughtiness'. That is one point.

But we all, in general, need also to pray God to remove this plague and to purge it from the world and especially from his Church. For it is certain that ambition is the most mortal evil that can possibly happen to the Church of God, when everyone wants to advance himself and wants to be seen by others. And hence (as I have said) let us learn to pray God to give a gracious spirit to all those to whom he has extended his hand to place them thus in some dignity, so that they may conduct their business in all modesty and seek nothing else than to carry out their duty without any contention and without bearing any envy towards one another.

Moreover, Joab's courage was tinged with vengeance and impelled by a wicked, envious motivation. For he wished 'to avenge the death of his brother Asahel'. Well, if there had been a drop of reason and humanity in him, he ought to have stopped himself from committing such cruelty. How did Asahel his brother die? Abner did not take him by treason, but he killed him in battle (2 Sam. 2:17ff.). He did not seek to kill him as someone often may seek out his enemy, so greatly desiring him that he will spare many others to reach that particular one. Abner did the very contrary. He was pained to have to harm him; he even begged him to go back, but Asahel by his obstinacy forced Abner to kill him. When, therefore, Joab had considered the truth about Abner, he most certainly should have suppressed this ill will which he bore towards him. Because that which is done in a war ought not to incite perpetual hatred, as it would in time of peace. One can see those who have been enemies in war; one has been taken prisoner; the other has killed the father, the other the brother; and yet they will not fail to be friends afterwards. And why? Because the war causes all that. Well, one must say that the courage of Joab was inflamed beyond measure and, on the other hand, that Abner had wanted to spare Asahel his brother insofar as that was possible, as has been said.

Now in this we see that when God does not correct the felony of men, they are so addicted to evil that they cannot be kept in bounds, so that no other consideration will restrain them. Even though Joab had people of good counsel around him who could have remonstrated with him, still he kept on bearing this grudge against Abner. Well, when ill will lodges for a long time in the heart of man, Satan will take possession of it, as St Paul says (Eph. 4:26–27). Let us take seriously, then, the warning that he gives us, namely, that the sun set not upon our wrath, so that the devil may not possess us in order to carry us away into all evil. And again, if we have for a long time nourished some evil feelings, let them be buried and put underfoot. For if someone asks us if we wish to be slaves of Satan, everyone would be horrified, and yet there is no-one who does not throw himself voluntarily into this miserable and wretched servitude. We ought all the more to be taught to drown our readiness to commit every felony and all malice and ill will, so that whenever we have occasion to hate someone, it will be beaten down. And furthermore, let us not close our eyes to all reason and fairness, and let us not harden ourselves against what might be pointed out to us, or against that which we might think of ourselves, without anyone saying a word. There will not be anyone among us who does not detest Joab's action. It is a detestable act; everyone will so judge it. But nevertheless, there will not be anyone who does not follow him, unless God takes care of the matter, and governs us by his Holy Spirit.

However, we see also that Joab showed himself to be so wicked towards men, for God wanted to uncover his dishonesty. Here is how those who wish to be considered strong and brave will fall into dishonour – indeed, in the view of everyone – so that even the little children would be able to condemn them when they have abused either their credit, or counsel, or virtues, or prowess which God has put in them. There is no doubt that Joab was an excellent choice when David appointed him as his captain general. He knew that there were things in him worthy of such a position and, on the other hand, that he had carried out his responsibility so well that he was renowned. He wanted to keep this reputation for himself; it seemed to him that it would be a dishonour for the death of his brother not to be avenged. There, as I have said, pride was involved, and from it proceeded the envy which he bore towards Abner. But be that as it may, the fact is that he wanted to prove that he was a valiant and noble man; that is what he sought. Well, God caused him to be dishonoured, just as if he had been on a scaffold, in order to be shamed in front of everyone. For how did he proceed to maintain his reputation? 'He sent messengers to Abner, who had already departed from David.' This is one point.

When Abner returned, he had to speak to him again amicably, to see if he had good will towards him or not. For when one party has forgotten some past bitterness, it is certain that the evil will increase in the other who wants to pursue the quarrel. It is necessary, therefore, before continuing it, to enquire diligently whether men's attitudes have changed.

For example, if there is a man whom I hold as suspect (I speak, naturally, in the manner of men), it will seem to me that I shall have all the more occasion to do evil, and that I will be all the more excused. But on the contrary, when I see a man conduct himself in integrity, and even though I had formerly conceived some evil against him, or I had done him some sort of harm, yet he trusts me and does not suspect any evil, it ought to break my heart when I see that he thus comes to speak privately to me. Well, here is the dishonesty of Joab, who is all the more detestable, for he sees Abner turning round at his message, and then calls 'to speak to him in secret'. Abner goes to him, for he considers him a friend, since he is reconciled with the king. He never thinks that the servant would dare to undertake anything so wicked, and on the other hand, it seems to him that Joab represented David. Well, Joab called him in secret to kill him treacherously under the cloak of friendship and Abner did not protect himself, given the fact that he considered Joab loyal. In all of that, it is not as though Joab had totally blinded himself to his duty, as though he was possessed of no honour, and as though he despised all the men on earth and wished to be esteemed a wicked traitor and disloyal in the presence of all, is it?

It is certain that Joab did not speak in this way, and clearly had no desire for such a reputation. But as I have said, here is the way God knows how to pay the wages of those who do not fear him. Those who wish to exalt themselves he abases, and uncovers their crime by force. When they wish to advance themselves, he throws them back. Hence, let us take this for an example and let us live in such honesty with one another that as more trust is placed in us, we will be the more careful not to engage in trickery or dissimulation. And especially if we are held as suspect, let us endeavour, insofar as we are able, to prove that it is wrong, so that our enemies, being convinced by experience, may recognise that we are not what they thought, that they will change their disposition towards us, and that this will be a means of reconciliation. Here again, therefore, is what we have to remember.

Well, it is true, it seems, that Joab is half excused, since it is stated that he killed Abner 'because of the blood of his brother, Asahel'. Nevertheless, the Spirit of God wanted to present to us here, as in a mirror, that this act proceeded from wicked motives, as we have said. Let us learn from this. For it is certain that Joab is set before us here as a wicked and perverse man, and the Spirit of God afterwards condemns him by the mouth of David, as we shall see. Nevertheless, the death of Asahel is spoken of. Why? It is so that we will know how envy leads to many excesses. Now here, therefore, is Asahel alone, killed by the hand of Abner. Well, Joab ought to have borne patiently what had happened; he ought to have forgotten all this bitterness which he bore to Abner, who only asked to be reconciled with him. He does not do so, but perseveres in his malevolence, as though he were continually holding a burning fire. That is how, therefore, he is more and more hardened to evil. For the devil fans and illumines this enmity which he bears towards Abner, and renews it more and more.

This is what the Spirit of God wants us to consider from what has happened here; namely, that Joab has been blinded, and his hatred, at the very least, has served as a bandage to hide his eyes from evil, so that he would not recognise the evil that he committed. And then, that man employed a villainous and detestable treachery; he troubled the whole kingdom. So far as he could, he prevented David from having peace and all the people from being brought together under their leader, who was ordained for the salvation of the Church. Thus, when we see this hatred, which has been carried for a long time – and that it has borne such wicked fruits – we ought to let it teach us not to entertain and nourish ourselves with flatterers, nor with vices which can lead us to crimes which will be even greater and more enormous. Let us fear (I say) lest vengeance so cover our eyes that they be turned to all cruelty. We can do nothing then but think that everything is legitimate for us.

For he who plans to avenge himself is willing to do anything. He will take occasion to do all that he conceives to be for his profit, under the excuse of having been offended, as we see Joab did. It is certain that if he had not borne envy towards Abner, he would have ignored the death of his brother. But what he feared was being demoted, and that Abner would occupy his position – that is why he goes to excess. Thus, as I have said, when we have our eyes closed so as not to discern between white and black, God will put us in such shameful circumstances that we will be odious to the whole world. Well, it is true that we ought not to fear so much the judgement of men as him before whom we must render an account of our whole life. But however imperfect we may be, still out of fear of God we ought to avoid the judgement of men. And that again ought to serve as a bridle for us, to restrain our wicked and extravagant passions when we see how God has thus willed that Joab should be dishonoured and condemned by the common people. And not only that – he was condemned by the very mouth of the king, and would be imprinted with this mark for ever as a murderer, traitor, and disloyal.

Well now, since we see why Scripture states that Abner was killed because of the death of Asahel, let us come to what is said about David. When he heard of the death of Abner, he protested that he was 'innocent of it, both he and his kingdom', and prayed to God that the evil would return 'upon the head of Joab and on all his family, and that never would they fail to have those with an issue', and others 'leprous' (which is a different thing from ugliness, for leprosy is a disease which is unknown today), others 'who beg their bread', others 'killed by the sword', and others 'involved in violence'. These are the plagues with which God was accustomed to punishing sinners and iniquitous persons, as we know that the plague, war, and famine are the three principal rods of God. Well, instead of the plague here, there are illnesses and then, in addition, deaths.

David's protestation is meant to serve as an effective testimony before men. For he could easily have turned to God and protested his innocence, but he wanted it to be published, and also he needed this to be done. It is true that in such and such a way he turned to God, for the prayer that he prayed proved it well. If he had had his eyes and senses fixed only on men, he would not have asked God for the evil to return upon the head of Joab. Here, therefore, David intended to present himself before God as before his judge, and desired that his case should be known and decided there, and then that men should be witnesses of it. And this is what we ought to do. In the first place, let us keep our consciences pure and clean, so that we are able to walk with our heads up, to present ourselves before the judgement seat of God. Now, it is true that this cannot be done, as if we were righteous in everything and at everything and were like little angels! But I mean that we must live in such a way with our neighbours that not only will we be able to have men for our witnesses – so that we will be able to say that no-one can reproach us with anything and that we cannot be convicted – but that God will always be our first witness.

In fact, when David said that he was innocent, it is certain that he was, because he well knew that God would not leave such a crime unpunished. That is why he published this curse against Joab, his captain. And then he had in mind his kingdom, for he thought not only of himself as a private person, but he knew to what God had called him, namely, for the salvation of his people and of his Church. That is why, then, he included those who had been committed to him, and all his subjects. He included them with himself, as though he were saying that it was not only for his person that he was worried, but for all those for whom he ought to be a protector, since God had ordained him as their leader. In sum, we see that it was not only himself that he had in mind. We see also why he did it, that it was not for his person alone but for all the people.

Here, therefore, is where we ought to follow David when it comes to maintaining our innocence. For we should have reference not only to mortal creatures as in the too common fashion, but should always come to be examined before God in the first place. And we should not do so in the manner of hypocrites, who take the name of God in vain, and are the boldest to protest – so much that one would say there is nothing but righteousness among them. Instead, let us always walk in the truth of God. And in fact, this is the main consideration which we can bring forward. For it can happen, as we see only too frequently, that we have been innocent of the evil which we have been charged with, and yet men are blind to it. We see good people often being defamed, with everyone spitting in their face and slinging mud at them, yet nevertheless God is their good witness that it is wrong for them to be persecuted like this.

Now that is why I have said that we must carefully observe this rule, that we might be able to present ourselves before God when there is some crime attributed to us, or of which we are accused. Let us be able to say, 'There is God, who is my guarantee'. As we see also that the prophet had his refuge there, when he was torn in pieces, and when men were so iniquitous to him that everyone was inventing slanders against him (Isa. 50:6ff.). 'Well, I have my guarantee in heaven', he said, and despised men. St Paul says as much: 'I bring the case to the Lord' (1 Cor. 4:4). What we often see happening – especially when it is a matter of the cause of our Lord Jesus Christ – is that men will always find things to say against us, and we will be defamed because of him. Each one will mock us. There will be neither small nor great who do not criticise us. What must we do, then? There is only one remedy. We must run to God, and call on him for our witness and for our judge, and that he will be sufficient for us when we are judged by iniquitous and perverse people.

Well, nevertheless, we must have the good testimony of our innocence when we come thus before the Lord. We must not do like many people who say, 'God knows it, and I call him as witness of it' – and yet their iniquity is quite manifest. When, therefore, we come before the Lord and we ask him to be our Judge and to declare what we are and that our cause is very clear, at the same time may we be able also to request that he examine us and enquire of us, and look into the situation. Well, the hypocrites will often speak in this very way. But their shamelessness is seen at the same time. Let us be careful not to do this, but let us present ourselves to God so that he will search us, as it says in the Psalm, 'Lord, you have searched my reins' (Psa. 26:2), that is, my most secret thoughts. And then let us ask that men see the facts and that the whole enquiry be made on the facts, so that the whole truth will be known. That, in sum, is what we must remember for one point.

It remains to be known why we ought to desire men to be witnesses of our integrity. Well, the point is not, as we have been accustomed to think, that we are so delicate that we cannot suffer any injury! We wish to keep our honour to the end, without considering the basic question. But let us pay attention to the real question, so that we might be able to say that people cannot use us for a bad example and that, above all, we seek that God may in no way be blasphemed. Now that is what concerned David. For he knew that the death of Abner would be odious, and that people would say, 'Now here are wicked and wretched dealings'. How? A king called a man, gave him his word and showed him friendship, even inviting him to sit at his table to drink and eat with him. And yet he had him treacherously killed, and he is not fit to live. He is so far from deserving to control the kingdom that he ought in fact to be exterminated from the world. And then, what about this tribe of Judah, which has yielded itself to a tyrant who pledged faith to Abner, and then betrayed him – how, then, shall we submit ourselves to a man who has not the least religion?

David knew the scandal which could have arisen, that it would have caused horrible dissension and that many would have revolted, and the others would have been like men torn to pieces. He considered all of that. Therefore, in order to avoid such a scandal, he made a protestation of his innocence and of all the people's innocence. This is what St Paul says, that we must seek the good, both before God and before men, that living with a good and pure conscience, we may not give occasion to the wicked and malign to open their mouths to criticise our failings (1 Cor. 10:32–33). Instead, we live so that our deeds will be known, and all will know that in fact we have earnestly striven to serve God in all fear and reverence, and have dealt with men in integrity and fairness. That, therefore, is the goal towards which this protestation of David leads.

Well, one sees that kings are constrained to put up with many things which displease them, inasmuch as they will not always be able to punish evil with the required virtue and generosity of spirit. We see this problem in David, who was such an excellent man yet who, nevertheless, first pleaded his 'lack of ability' (2 Sam. 3:39). It is as if he were saying, 'I have scarcely been constituted king' (I do not speak of this unction which David received by the prophet; but he says, 'I have scarcely been accepted as king'), 'and here I am again like a bud on a tender shoot. I have only one tribe which follows me.' There are 'the sons of Zeruiah' who lift themselves up, as if he were saying, 'They undertake things which will cause the people to rise up against me. Everyone will hate me and I will not be able to resist.' Well, we see, therefore, how the evil displeased him, but nevertheless that he dared not punish it. And hence we know (as I have said) that princes often attempt to bring order everywhere, but they are unable fully to establish it. Also we know, on the other hand, that even those who have shown a firm constancy that is marvellous will often be so weakened in some deed that they will not dare to move a finger to execute the duty of their office.

It is certain that what David claimed, he did not want to do: 'When I become king, when I have been placed in possession of the crown, I will throw out the detractors. I will chase them far away, and all people who are addicted to pillaging and stealing will have no acquaintance with me.' Now that is what David promised God before he was king, as Psalm 101 says. Well, there is no doubt that this was without hypocrisy and that his words came from the heart. Yes, but he did not reach such perfection that he was able to carry out his will. And God by this means wanted to humble him, by showing him that he did not have enough constancy to keep him from failing at the last. Hence, may the great of this world, that is kings and emperors, learn to pray God to give them such a strong spirit that they will not put up with evil. For it is certain that of all that is committed, they must render an account. Every private person merits punishment for what he commits, but those who have the sword in their hand and the rod of justice – those (I say) are guilty of acting illegally when they allow evil to go unpunished. In that case, they will be accomplices with the authors of evil, insofar as they have tolerated them. Well then, that is one point.

We see that David failed in this area. It is true that he indeed wanted to chastise such an enormous crime, but he dared not. Nevertheless, it was his responsibility to remedy it, and someone could have reproached him: 'Since you are king and have dominion over your servants, why is it that you do not chastise the malefactors?' David could (I say) have been reproached for that. Therefore, in all and by all, we are taught to regard the duty of our office, and that each one is faithfully to carry out his duty, without regard to this or that. For even when we have thoroughly condemned evil with our mouths, that will not be enough to excuse us before God. It is hardly necessary that we make a general rule to follow up what is said here of David, that he did not punish him who was under his power.

As to what some have thought, that the curses which David pronounced (2 Sam. 3:29) returned on his successors, that is a foolish, mistaken idea. David prayed God to send on Joab a discharge of blood – and that came to his own successor, namely Rehoboam. He prayed that he would send him leprosy – and that happened to Uzziah (2 Kings 15:5). Afterwards, he prayed that he would send him dearth – and that happened to Jehoiakim, the king (2 Kings 24:15ff.). And then he prayed that he would live with the sword – and that happened to Asa his successor, who was impotent (1 Kings 15:16). Well, as we have said, such are the people who desire subtleties and think that they have all wisdom enclosed in their brain. But let us be content to know that David was not a hypocrite when he uttered these curses.

Nevertheless, one simply cannot absolve David altogether, inasmuch as he must have thought of the position in which God had placed him, and in what degree of honour he had put him, and what his charge was – to punish crimes and not to tolerate such an evil deed. And indeed, he bore the punishment of it in this mourning that he engaged in. There is no doubt that he was caught up in great distress in making such lamentation over Abner, for he commanded Joab, the murderer, 'to rend his garments and to wear sackcloth on his back and to weep and make lamentation' (2 Sam. 3:31–32). That is one point.

Well, should he not rather have had Joab put in prison and have carried out justice, than command him to put on sackcloth, and come there as a traitor and villain, so that everyone could point him out with their finger, and so that he could be placed in dishonour, and be held guilty for such wicked disloyalty? How is it that David (I say) let him off so cheaply? But we see that if he spared him on the one hand, still he did show by mouth and speech that he was inexcusable before God. And since David so detested his crime, Joab was therefore held in derision by all the people: 'Is Abner dead as a fool dies?' (2 Sam. 3:33–34). As if he were saying, 'He did not die in war, for he could have defended himself, but he died at the hands of the wicked'. Here, therefore, was Joab, who was put in disgrace. And this was not in a secret chamber, nor in a cupboard, but before everyone, so that he would be known as a despicable man in front of everyone. Well, in that we see that David seemed to be half dead, and that the poor man was half stunned in himself, since he did not have the virtue and constancy to punish Joab as he deserved.

Thus, let us note well when we see such an example, and when we have liberty and power to punish evil, that we demonstrate in actual effect the fruit of our good conscience. We cannot do that without having recourse to him who has all power in his hand. Again, let us have true zeal, for if we do not have the virtue to carry out what we know to be our duty, we will always find little details in the matter which will give us occasion to seek subterfuges. For we will have our thoughts attached to this and to that in order to excuse ourselves, and will thus be drawn back from our duty, so that our corruption will be uncovered both before God and before men. Here, therefore, is the punishment of those who are not sufficiently constant to carry out their duty, even though they may have some genuinely true motivation. And what will it be with those who deliberately pay no attention to doing justice, and who even hide evil? If the good and those who detest vices are condemned for having spared the wicked, what will it be with those who not only have hidden evil, but who also have helped others perpetuate it, and given them opportunity to start it?

So much, then, for this point, where we see that David was so anguished and did not know which way to turn when it was a matter of purging himself of the death of Abner. He showed his grief even more when he declared that he 'would eat nothing until sunset' (2 Sam. 3:35). It is true that that was a little thing, but still he needed it to be that way. For he would have been dishonoured for ever and the disgrace would have remained after his death, if God had not given him the grace to purge himself from it. Whatever affection, therefore, he may have had towards Joab, still he did not fail to defame him and to pronounce his condemnation before everyone, in order to show that he preferred the honour of God above all the men on earth.

And this is demonstrated even better by his refusal to drink and to eat. Should he be exhorted to do so, he said he would in no wise do it, and confirmed his promise with a solemn oath.

It is true that this action could be considered utterly trivial, but it was an act of great importance, so that the kingdom of our Lord Jesus Christ would be purged of such evil and infamy. And so it is written also that God has made the true facts prevail, which 'all have known' (2 Sam. 3:36). It was not only the tribe of Judah (which was aligned in obedience to David) but also 'all Israel knew' that he was not guilty of the death of Abner, and had in no way consented to it (2 Sam. 3:37). So this is how God caused what was done out of true zeal to prevail, in order to remove the scandal which could otherwise have arisen. Well, it is true that, on the one hand, God justly punished Abner and also, on the other hand, that by his marvellous wisdom God thus prevented the kingdom from coming into the hand of David by such means, and by a traitor who had revolted against his king. But anyway, that in no way absolves Joab, for God was looking further.

Well, we cannot at present explain the details of this whole matter which we have just opened up. It will have to be explained another time. Nevertheless, let us be aware that if today God allows there to be some in his Church who are to put a mark of shame on the reign of our Lord Jesus Christ, still we must rise above such scandal. The kingdom of David was not condemned, even though Joab, who was its captain, had committed such a villainous act. Sometimes we see people elevated in honour, who are even pillars of the faith, yet in whom there may be much to be criticised, and who do not live as they should. Then let us recognise that God wants to humble us for all that, and that it ought not to prevent us from obeying our Lord Jesus Christ, and from always adhering to his majesty.

It is true that many would very much like to be excused under the shadow of that. For they claim: 'Since Joab was in the company of David, why do you condemn those who do the same thing? Yes, and if today there are perverts who cause scandals in the Church and who are yet capable of serving the republic, must one be rigorous with them all the way?' Well, if one concedes this, it is certain that God will chastise such indifference. But whenever someone sees that they are not able to establish total order, let us groan before God, and pray him to cleanse and purge his church of scandals. And when we have done all that we can, and have prayed God to give us patience, if things cannot be brought to such perfection as could be wished, nevertheless, let us not cover up the evil deliberately – as we see David doing, since he retained Joab as captain. He still did not want to approve him, but he preferred rather to tolerate part of the shame than to say that white is black (Isa. 5:20). For we know that the prophet says to all those who desire to obscure the Word of God, who say good is evil and evil is good, that they can only expect a horrible curse on their heads (Isa. 29:15). And in another passage, that there are many who are exasperated and who, under the cloak of their authority, want to be reputed good people and do not want the memory of their iniquities to be known, even though their deeds have been seen by all.

Well, here is David, who is not ashamed to confess his captain's evil. He even constrains him to come and mourn over Abner's corpse. In this, we are taught that if there are people who make a profession of Christianity and yet behave badly and cause scandals, we are not to excuse them but to condemn them outright. We are to protest that their deeds displease us and, at the very least, we are not to consent to what they do. And if we are not able to remedy it at the first attempt, let us maintain this modest determination to try, little by little, to correct the wrong as much as we can – and yet be patient when we see that there will be things which cannot be corrected so soon. And let us pray God to equip and arm us with an invincible constancy, and never to permit us to countenance deeds done by the wicked and by those who despise his majesty.

Let us recognise all our faults and poverty before our God, and beseech him that it may please him to receive us in mercy, seeing how we are far too unworthy of it; and that when we have been received as his children, he may govern us by his Holy Spirit. Thus, may he so draw us back from evil that we may show that we and evil are true enemies indeed, and that our only desire is that he may be honoured above all, and that his righteousness may be preserved in its entirety. And also that he may give us such constancy – seeing the confusion in his Church today – that we do not stop praying him that it may please him so to rule his own by his only Son, our Lord Jesus Christ, that we may be a faithful people for him. May we thus voluntarily put ourselves under his Word with one accord. And may he bestow this grace not only upon us, but upon all people and nations of the earth . . .

10

*Lessons from Ishbosheth's Death**

When the son of Saul heard that Abner had been killed in Hebron, his hands were weakened, and all Israel was terrified. Well, the son of Saul had two men who were captains of bands. The name of one was Baanah, and the name of the other was Rechab, son of Rimmon . . . (2 Sam. 4:1–12).

We saw yesterday the dirge which David composed lamenting the death of Abner, and the grief that he experienced. We showed yesterday the end and intention of this: namely, since this murder could have been turned into a great scandal, David did not want such a great evil to be imputed to him. For the name of God had been blasphemed by this occasion, and it could have prevented him from reigning – seeing how he had been ordained by God for the salvation of all the people. But nevertheless, even though Joab and Abishai his brother may have been declared wicked, as indeed they deserved, still God used them to reach his goal and to carry out his marvellous counsel, which was to elevate David to the kingdom, but not by a method which would have brought some blame and an element of shame.

If Abner had actually succeeded in what he attempted (2 Sam. 3:21), as he could easily have done had he lived – for everything was already disposed in his favour, especially since he had caused the eleven tribes of Israel to revolt and had withdrawn them from obedience to Ishbosheth – people could have said, 'David has been made king; but by what means and

*Wednesday, June 17, 1562.

in what way? By a traitor, who broke faith with his king, and a hundred times with the people. Now is that not some way to take rule, well ordered by God!' People would have mocked him for it, and would have said that David had usurped the crown by tyranny, so much so that people would have detested him and his sceptre. Well, he was a type of our Lord Jesus Christ and his kingdom. It would not, therefore, have been appropriate for him to have been blamed in this way. And that is why God so worked it out for Abner to die. This would not have happened if God had not wanted to give David possession of the eleven tribes, or wanted people to know that he had conducted the whole affair so that the praise would be given to him. From that, one can conclude that David did not reign because of men, but that God was the Author of it, as if he had taken him by the hand, and had set him on the royal throne.

We see, therefore, how God has a secret method which is incomprehensible to us, to bring all his works to completion. In this, he uses the wicked and employs them in whatever way pleases him – not that they are to be excused. For Joab could not have alleged – nor Abishai his brother – that they had accomplished the will of God, for their intention was to avenge themselves. There was pride and envy in their motivation, all wrapped together. Hence, they despised God in their wicked counsel. And yet God turned everything that they did in the opposite direction of what they intended, and by this means achieved his goal: that although David should not reign by the machinations of Abner, still Israel would understand that, in spite of what Joab had done, they must be under obedience to David, as we shall see.

Furthermore, God also punished Abner, although he did not use ordinary methods, as the saying goes. He did not want his trial to be arranged for him, as he deserved. He was spared at this point. And yet his guilt deserved death, indeed a hundred times over, since he had resisted the decree of God, had done all that he could to keep David from reigning and had turned the people from obeying him. He was a murderer and even a traitor. Therefore, he well deserved being brought to trial. Moreover, Joab and Abishai were contravening the will of their king. It would not have mattered to them if David were considered thoroughly infamous and if people were waging war with him worse than ever. Well, God allowed it. But be that as it may, still he did not escape the punishment that he deserved. He was put to death. Here again, therefore, is God, who executes his just judgement by means of Joab, who was called wicked by David (2 Sam. 3:34).

So we see how God has a secret bridle to guide and lead men. It is true that he deals in a different manner with his own than he does with unbelievers. For by his Holy Spirit he touches our hearts, which we come to offer him with an open spirit, because he forms our hearts for that purpose. He moulds them, and whereas they were once stone (Ezek. 11:19; 36:26), he makes them pliable and soft, so that they are fully prepared to obey him. And that is how the faithful obey God with an honest affection. The wicked greatly desire to rebel against him and to fight against his will, as far as they can. They even force themselves to do so. Nevertheless, God constrains them, in spite of themselves, to serve his providence. And so it is with Satan, their chief. For the devil is enraged with a desire to reverse everything that God has ordained, as far as he possibly can. His machinations are for this alone. But nevertheless, it is necessary that everything he attempts be accomplished by the counsel of God. Therefore, we see (as I have said) that when there are many troubles in the world, when murders are committed, when there are wars and everything is in confusion, it is not that God is asleep in heaven. For however men may do battle in this way, he knows why he gives them free rein. He wants to punish their sins and the sins of others, and prove the patience of his children, showing them that their rest is not here below. So when we see such confusions, let us be aware that all is governed by the incomprehensible providence of God, so that he will guide the things which are ordained to the end that he has determined within himself. Now this is what we have to remember, in summary, and this is what is confirmed to us by the following text.

It says, on the one hand, that 'the hands of Ishbosheth were weakened when he heard of the death of Abner, and that all

Israel was terrified' (2 Sam. 4:1). As for Ishbosheth, we see that he had no royal virtue in him. And if he had been the most valiant man in the world, he would have had no foundation for his reign. It is true that, from the time of Abner, he was as though he were drunk, and paid no attention to himself. But God woke him up now in such a way that he saw himself deprived of help. That is how his hands were weakened. Now when hands are spoken of, more is intended, in that hands are instruments for doing what men have decided to do. When it says 'strong hand', it means the whole strength of men. When it says 'weak hand', it means stripped of all help. Here, in sum, is Ishbosheth, who was deprived of all strength when Abner died. Even if he had lived for some time, not only would he have been weakened, but he would have been completely dead. For if he could not reign without the help of this man, what would it have been like if he had gone against him? Therefore, we have to remember that God, as it were, awakened him, so that he knew that henceforth he must give up the crown which he had wrongly usurped, and which he had held by force, namely, by resisting the will of God.

Well, it will happen from time to time that people will be profane and abandon themselves, without any restraint, to every sort of evil, because they think that they are allowed to do everything. They glory in this and no longer have any fear. They spit fire out of their mouth (as it is said); they have their triumphs. But when God removes the grounds of all their presumption, you will see them totally lost, as weak as water. One then sees that their presumption was only a drunkenness in which they were asleep. Now that is what we have to consider in Ishbosheth.

It is true that when God removes the help that he has placed in our hand, we will have good reason to be stunned. For we are not insensitive, nor are we to despise the means that he has given us. Thus, when he removes from us people who are useful for the government of the public, it cuts us to the quick, for otherwise we would be more stupid than brute beasts. But nevertheless, if we do not fail always to trust in God, we will request him to supply us with others, or to take care of us by his own power. If it pleases him for us to be stripped of the help of men, we will ask him to supply everything. So that is how we will be weakened when God disarms us and removes all our provisions, and even when those who have served us turn against us. But it is not for us to remain in that situation, fainting at it all. For our weakness will rouse us and lead us to turn to God, as has already been shown us.

Well, it was thus with Ishbosheth and with those like him, for this poor man could not call on God, because he had no other refuge than Abner, and trusted everything to him. Hence, let us note, since God thus awakens those who are drunk in their vainglory and presumption, that we are not to place our trust in men. Let us help ourselves and use those whom it pleases God to give us, but let us realise that they are testimonies and pledges of God's goodness and of the paternal care that he has for us, and that we must always look above them. So when we have people who, we recognise, are helpful to us, let us be aware that they are like the hands of God, so that we will definitely sense that he wants to be our Father. Then when he removes from us what he has given us, this attitude will cause us always to look to him. So let us learn also to be so grounded on a good conscience that we will expect nothing except from the good will of God.

So when we live on this basis, even when we become very weak again, when we are all but dead, there will certainly always be something to revive us. Nevertheless, let us not doubt, when we see the enemies of our Lord Jesus Christ in power, that it will take nothing to make them broken people, who will not know which way to turn. And why? Because they do not have God on their side; they cannot call upon him. When, therefore, a man is taken away from them, that is how their hope is lost and their salvation totally annihilated. So let us learn to consider this lesson well, and when God thus strips us of human forces, let us not fail, as I have said, to place our reliance upon him. Even when it seems that all forces are our enemies, let us wait in patience, so that he who has the strength will show that he is indeed our Protector. God will well know how to find these enemies in the midst of their evil triumphs.

And then, let us pray God also that he will be pleased to abase them, so much so that they may recognise, to their confusion, that they have been dealing with him. May they recognise that all that they have been doing will vanish into smoke and that, since they have been so insane as to fight against him who has all power, they must remain broken and destroyed.

It is said, on the other hand, that 'Israel was terrified' (2 Sam. 4:1). And that is because it was necessary for God to lead them by force, as it were, to David. It was a thing that everyone clearly knew, as if someone had sounded the trumpet through all the land, that David had been promised the kingdom. And yet here, making a profession of serving God, are eleven tribes, all circumcised, who resist what has been pronounced by the mouth of Samuel, and ratified by unction. Samuel had been held to be a prophet of God and as an angel from heaven (1 Sam. 16). Well, he had pronounced that the will of God was that David should reign. The men who held Samuel to be holy and the one under whom they were aligned, did not in the least want to obey him now. Because of this, David was rejected. Since the people were so obstinate, they would certainly have created all the difficulties in the world to keep from following David if God had not, so to speak, dragged them by the hair. Here is also why it was necessary that Ishbosheth should be removed from them. For although he may not have been a man of strength, and may have had in him nothing worthy of a king, still they were as attached to him as to an idol, and would always have returned to him. Because of this obstinate stupidity, they would never have accepted better counsel. Well, it was therefore necessary that this idol should be removed from them.

Furthermore, if there had still been someone else in the house of Saul, they would have made him king. No matter how useless it would have been, they would not have failed to accept him. There was only one single 'child of Jonathan', and he was from seven to eight years of age, for he was only 'five years old when his father died'. Moreover, he was 'lame, because his nurse had dropped him', and had broken his legs. So here is a poor lame body, so much so that he is denied the crown. Well, we are told all of this so that we may contemplate what profane persons will not consider: that God has governed in such a way that the crown has had to be placed in the hands of David. And why? Because Israel had so abused itself that it had taken more and more steps to distance itself from David, in that they had, as it were, become stupefied and drunk with this house of Saul. And that is why God removed Ishbosheth from them, so that they would be constrained to honour David. For all the time that Ishbosheth lived, there was nothing but confusion, and they even rejected the yoke of our Lord, not wanting to submit to the one whom he had chosen and elected to rule over them. That, therefore, is what we have to remember from this text.

This tale will seem to us nothing but tiresome history. We could read a hundred times that Ishbosheth was killed by traitors and that Mephibosheth was crippled, having had his legs broken. Very well, what we are told shows us that the house of Saul had been defeated. But the intention of the Spirit of God is to represent for us, as in a tableau and in a living picture, what we will never understand with our natural reason and sense: namely, that God overcame the children of Israel in such a way that they had to submit to David.

This is an example of what God does in us when it pleases him to call us into subjection to our Lord Jesus Christ. For we would never be inclined to it, as our natural bent is quite the reverse, and we are intractable. Not only are we slack, slow and as cold as ice when our Lord calls us to give honour to his Son, but we are always like savage and ferocious beasts; we only kick against the pricks (Acts 9:5). In brief, we are, so to speak, completely enraged – which keeps us from becoming submissive. It is necessary, therefore, for God to remove the occasions which could prevent and retard us from submission, and he must immediately handle the situation. For even if all of those things which seem scandalous to us – that is to say, those things which prevent us from coming to our Lord Jesus Christ – if they were all removed from us, yet we have in ourselves and on the inside something still worse. That is, we are addicted to evil and always hate both our Lord Jesus Christ and his doctrine.

Be that as it may, when God wants to call us to faith, he must not only touch us, so as to live in our hearts by his Holy Spirit, and remould, remake and re-create us new creatures, but he must also cut short all opportunities that we could take to be remiss, or to wander here and there, or to hold back so that we can live to ourselves when we have the chance. We see this only too clearly if everyone examines only himself, for it is only necessary for a fly to pass in front of our eyes, as the saying goes, to make us completely turn round.

When it comes to following God, one will be kept back by his riches, another by some vain excuse, another will have his wife, another his children, another his father (see Luke 14:18ff.). In brief, there will never be anyone who does not always find excuses and subterfuges to keep from submitting himself in obedience to God. Thus it is necessary that our Lord should remove all hindrances from us. For example, when there is a path which is full of briers and thorns, we will not be able to walk down it, unless they are cleared away. Or when there are trees so thick that one cannot walk any further, because one cannot get one's head through; they also must be cut down. Thus, God watches over us. And yet, if from time to time he strips us of that of which we are fond, if he removes this from one, and that from another, let us recognise that he does it so that we may be better able to approach him, and that we may come to him in full liberty. We have (I say) to consider this in the present record, where we see that the kingdom of our Lord Jesus Christ will never be established, since men are so corrupt and perverse, unless God constrains them to come by force. For it is certain that this which is written of the kingdom of David will have its accomplishment and full effect in our Lord Jesus Christ and in the whole course of his reign.

Well, when it says that God removed the whole race of Saul, leaving Mephibosheth (who was deformed in his body), and had removed Ishbosheth (who was reigning), and that the people were like a body without a head, and totally lost, and that necessity constrained them to come to their senses, let us recognise what I have said. That is, there is such a perversity in men that they will never be disposed to obey God and our Lord Jesus Christ (freely), if he does not force them to do so and if he does not break their neck. He must at the very least bend them, so that they can resist no longer. For if we have something with which to amuse ourselves in this world, we will never be able to seek God with a right affection. We only need rattles like little children, and there we are in ecstasy over them! And yet God says, 'Come, come!' But we are deaf and stupid, and all the exhortations that he gives us do not at all touch us. It is, therefore, necessary that he remove all that thus abuses and tricks us, and all these vain flatterers and allurements, so that we will be disposed to come to him.

That is why it is said by the prophet Hosea that he leads his Church through the desert because of her rebellion. 'You are as a dissolute woman', he says. 'O Israel, you have turned from me as a whore from her husband. I see well that I shall never prevail with you, unless I lead you through the desert and make you fast, and make you endure both hunger and thirst, so that you will be constrained to come to me and renounce all your lusts.' If God thus dealt with these people whom he had elected, let us realise that we still need it today. Hence, when we see that God is using violent means, and that we are stripped of what we need, let us realise that it is because we have taken the opportunity of deserting him, and have given place to our lusts and made idols of them. And he sees clearly that he cannot win us, except by force. Let us recognise our perversity, therefore, and let us humble ourselves and sigh and groan, so that it may please God to purge us of all our lusts, so that we might follow him without any contradiction.

Now that again is what we have to remember on this point when it says that Israel was stunned, that its king was removed from it, and finally that it could find no more of this race of Saul, nor anyone who could reign. Hence, it was constrained to follow David. We see, therefore, that it is not enough that God had given the rebels one blow on the head. They will indeed be stupefied, but still it will not be enough to make them come to account. When he has struck them the second time, still they will not be biddable until he has dealt with them in such a manner that they do not know which way to turn, and then they will be constrained to follow him. Hence, when God doubles the blows in chastising us, like someone who keeps beating an ass, let us realise that it is not without cause. For not only are we as stubborn as asses, but we are like wild and crazy people, carried away by our passions to resist God. And then we play games and do not fail to do somersaults to avoid him, until he has beaten us down!

Well, the description which is here given of the death of Ishbosheth is to be noted. It says that 'two of his captains came to him and cut off his head, even while he was sleeping, that is during the heat of the day' (2 Sam. 4:5, 7). Now the custom of those times was different from ours today, for the ancients in this Eastern country were not accustomed to dining at midday, which was when they slept. For they got up with the sun in the summer, and stayed awake in winter until the sun had risen, so that they took part of their sleep in the middle of the day. And thus it is stated that Ishbosheth, being on his couch, had his throat cut by these two brigands – who, nevertheless, were his captains.

Well, we have here reason to contemplate the judgements of God. Even though it was a despicable act, that those who were officers of the king should come and cut off his head, still it was a just ordinance of God, inasmuch as Ishbosheth was reigning contrary to his will. And why is it that his subjects had been faithful to him, seeing that he did not want to submit to David, who was God's lieutenant and deputy? He knew that God had put David on the royal throne – indeed, as his lieutenant and officer – but Ishbosheth desired to receive the perpetual inheritance of the crown, under the excuse that Saul his father had reigned. But God did not want it to be this way. He established Saul for a time, but then afterwards he retained for himself the authority to appoint a king. Here, therefore, was Ishbosheth usurping the authority of God, who had sovereign rule over this people and, as much as was in him, he wanted to reverse this decree. When he thus resisted God, did he deserve to find faith and loyalty among his subjects? For he could not have them in his service and devotion unless he fought (as I have said) against God. Therefore, the subjects of Ishbosheth had to be wicked in order to serve him. And why? Whenever there is a tyranny, and whenever people want to do all that they can to maintain it, are not those who adhere to such tyrants like them when they maintain a wicked cause?

Here are the enemies of God who fortify themselves today with arms. What excuse will a man make who comes to join them, seeing that they are a rebellious people both against God and against their prince? One will certainly say: 'Well, I would like them to be exterminated from the world. What I am doing is not by force. I can do nothing else.' Another will say: 'I have been a servant of their house for a long time, and they have rewarded me well. If I depart, I will be stripped of all my goods.' Another: 'I can do nothing else as my duty, and I will be defamed, but God knows my heart'. Another will say: 'Well, I shall see what it is like. If I do not find it good, I will give it up.' Indeed, but the fact is that they are wrapping themselves up in the iniquity of those who are blatantly provoking the wrath of God. For when they, for all practical purposes, give themselves over to the enemies of God, who are maintaining such an unjust struggle, it is certain that these also are declaring themselves to be his enemies, whatever they may pretend, and however they pretend to believe that this is not their intention. Since they hold their masters to be persons with wicked consciences, they also have to make themselves like them, and so cannot more effectively bring condemnation on themselves. Since they know them to be tricksters, how can they dare be at rest under them? For it is certain that, as they do not spare the majesty of God from being trampled underfoot as much as they possibly can, so much less will they be spared if their evil masters are able to do them in.

Hence, we must note (in sum) that those who seek the favour of the world in order to be upheld in reputation, have to fight against God when they help his enemies. They must await similar wages as those which were paid to Ishbosheth – that those who have been their accomplices and companions cut off their heads. And as there is mutual friendship between them, there will also have to be war and horrible confusion in the midst of those against them – so much so that the great ones who use those playing on both sides will at last be betrayed by them. Hence, those (I say) will finally cut their throats, without others stopping them.

When this history is recited to us, let us learn that in order to be under the protection of our God, we must be content with the grace that he gives us. May each one remain satisfied and at peace in his station and condition. When, therefore, we call upon God in this way, it is certain that he will take care of us, whether sleeping or waking. For if we sleep, it is said that 'he that keeps Israel never sleeps' (Psa. 121:4), and when we are awake, God will be even more awake. And when there are troubles and fires burning all over the world, which only seek to devour us, he will be well able to secure us, and be to us an impregnable fortress. When we are thus able, in good conscience, to put ourselves in the hands of God in life and in death, it is certain that we shall always be preserved. Well, it is true that even his own will suffer in this world. But we know that our true life is not here below. We must look far beyond this world. But be that as it may, when God wishes us to be afflicted, he will cause his angels to camp about us for our defence (Psa. 34:7), and whatever the wicked may try, they will be able to do nothing. And when he has permitted them to have power over our lives, we will die happy.

Furthermore, let us not envy the wicked, who have their own reign in this world, and who rejoice in their prosperity, and then stop at that (Psa. 37:1). For they will finally have to cut their own throats, or their flatterers and allies will do it. God shows his just judgement in this. Often he does not want his enemies to be punished in another way, so that it will be necessary, as I have said, that those in whom they have trusted, or those with whom they live, cut their throats and are their ruination. Such people (I say) will be executors of the just judgement of God against them.

Well, if such a punishment happened to Ishbosheth, what will it be with those who are much worse? Although Ishbosheth may have been condemned and convicted of having been a rebel against God, and having been allied and joined to the wicked who were like him, nevertheless, he still had some excuses. These were such as: he had not made himself king by his own power, and he did not originate the usurpation of what in no way belonged to him, but rather he had succeeded his father as his legitimate heir, and then he was encouraged by Abner. He had all these excuses. Be that as it may, still God punished him, because he had undertaken this with a wicked conscience. Well, what will it be (I say) with those who desire notoriously to despise God, and would like to topple God down, so to speak, from his seat, in order to stamp him underfoot, and to cover his majesty with shame? What confusion has been appointed for them?

In reading these acounts, let us always be moved to come to God, and to pray to him that again today it would please him to continue his grace towards his poor Church. For we see the dissension among those who call themselves Christians, just as in the time of David, when all had circumcision, which was both the sign of brotherhood and also the seal that God had given, showing that he considered them his children. Well, in spite of the circumcision, they are like dogs and cats, and the confusion is so great that it seems everything must perish and be destroyed. Moreover, David is the weakest, humanly speaking. He has only one tribe and his adversary has eleven. But nevertheless, God has abundantly provided for everything. And now, when we see that the iniquitous and wicked are exercising cruelty and tyranny in his Church, that there is war between those who ought to be joined in a fraternal union, let us realise that this is to prove the patience of his faithful ones and the constancy of his own. And we must not, because of that, be disgusted with the Gospel. Afterwards, when we see no way out, and it appears that evil must always conquer, let us pray God to grant us his grace today. For he does not want this story to be preached to us without our feeling the effect of it. That is, that we may perceive the power of his arm to do battle for us when it appears that we must be crushed, lest by our unbelief we prevent his grace. And let us see, when our adversaries despise our weakness, that God will mock them and will scatter their forces. He will break their hearts, their arms and their legs, so much so that their greatest consolation will be in weeping and gnashing their teeth.

When God does not cause us to understand at first glance, let us realise that it is for our good, and that we are not better than David, who was not put in possession of his kingdom by the desire of men. Therefore, let us fight virtuously against all the scandals which we see today, and let us learn to look to God and to study him. May we let this instruction, which is written here, prevail. As St Paul says, it is written so that we might exercise patience and have grounds to find our joy and our rest in God (Rom. 15:4). But nevertheless, let us always take refuge in praying to him. It is not enough to bite on the bit when one is oppressed, and pretend not to be grieved. Rather, it is necessary that we find that all that we suffer for his honour is so agreeable that prayer will still serve as a remedy for us. Well, he afflicts us only to prick us when we are too sleepy to come to him. However, he does not strike us inconsiderately to crush us, but rather he shows his kindness to us in the midst of our afflictions. And yet, when we see that the wicked are in power, may it not cause us to lose courage or weaken us internally. But with the weapons of faith, let us pray our gracious God that the help which he gave to David and his followers be granted to us today, so that we will have grounds to glorify his holy name. And may the people who come after us, as a new people, preach the praises of our God to the end of the world.

Now let us prostrate ourselves before the majesty of our good God, recognising the infinite faults of which we are guilty, beseeching him that it may please him to bury them in such a way that he may still fully draw us back to himself. And however much we are like poor, ferocious beasts, may he nevertheless tame us and make us return to the right way, in order to hear the voice of our Pastor. And indeed, if it pleases him to break us in by violence, may he give us a peaceable and meek spirit, in order to receive his corrections until we are wholly disposed to his service. Thus, let us all say: Almighty God, heavenly Father . . .

11

*God's Judgement on Murderers**

The sons of Rimmon the Beerothite, Rechab and Baanah, went and came in the heat of the day to the house of Ishbosheth, who lay on a bed at noon. And behold Rechab and Baanah his brother entered into the house, as though to fetch wheat, and smote him under the fifth rib and fled . . . (2 Sam. 4:5–12).

Yesterday we dealt with the death of Ishbosheth. Now we have to see what happened afterwards. The text repeats twice that he was sleeping on his bed, that is, well inside his house, and that the murderers entered in order to show our need to place our life in the hands and protection of God. For if a king had his throat cut, even though he was hidden and had retired to a secret place, what can we expect when we have to come and go? It is very necessary, therefore, that we realise that our life is hanging by a thread unless God sustains it, and that it will be exposed to all winds, as they say, unless he spares us, and unless we are hidden under the shadow of his wings, as the Scripture mentions.

Moreover, the text says that they came to David and brought him the head of Ishbosheth, saying to him, 'There is the head of your enemy, who sought your life. Well, the Lord has avenged you today of the whole race of Saul.' They annoyed him, in the first place, by saying that Ishbosheth was his enemy, and then they made it even worse by implying that Ishbosheth had been very eager to kill David. Well, all of this talk was simply to win themselves favour. Nevertheless, they falsely used the name of

*Thursday, June 18, 1562.

God, as though God were their companion – which is typical of the way in which the wicked are not ashamed to bandy about the name of God. For these men had no reason to kill their king. They did it out of spite. They were traitors and perverse. In brief, they were fully condemned, and had made their own judgement. Nevertheless, they did not fail to use God's name as a shield. But as I have said, this is common with hypocrites, who, in order to cover their dishonesty, think that God should lend them his name. Indeed, they borrow it so boldly that by it they intend to claim: 'God has done this or that', as though he were their companion and associated in their crime.

We see, for instance, how Sennacherib talked when he came to besiege Jerusalem (2 Kings 18:19–25). For at least his lieutenant Rabshakeh stated, 'Do not think that God must help you, for he has sent me here'. Well, it is possible that he was definitely aware that God wanted to chastise his own, and that he and his master were like rods to correct this people. But who is it that incited them to wage war? Did they not manifestly despise God when the enemy said, 'I shall put my camp on the side of the north' (see Isa. 14:13), as if God were reproaching Sennacherib for his audacity in imagining that God had no remedy with which to help his people? Well then, here is Sennacherib, who is notoriously fighting against God, and still his lieutenant does not fail to boast that God has sent him there. That is how the wicked always falsify the name of God, and harden themselves, in order to give themselves licence to do all the more evil – as if God must excuse them, or as though he were constrained to take part of their guilt on himself. When we see that, let us not be surprised, seeing that it has always been this way.

Moreover, let us learn never to abuse the name of God (Exod. 20:7). And may he effectively remind us of this threat, which is in the Law, that we will not remain unpunished when we are guilty of such profanation and sacrilege. For God wants his name to retain its integrity. There is good reason for that also. Thus, to handle the name of God for our own desires, to use it to paint over or to practise our iniquities, is to falsify it. That is why we must watch ourselves carefully that when we speak of God, it may be with all reverence; that we attribute nothing to him unless it is consonant with his majesty and in which he may be glorified, as he is worthy. That is what we have to remember from this point.

It is true that God wants to avenge David of Ishbosheth, who was usurping the kingdom against all rights. But it was not for Rechab and Baanah to speak in this way, because they were joined with those who troubled the people and who were retaining the largest part of the kingdom by violence. They had taken part in this and had done it against God. Therefore, they ought to have kept their mouths shut. For if the good and faithful were persuaded that it was right to give praise to God and to recognise that finally his promise had been brought into effect, no matter how greatly the faithful would have chanted God's praise with open mouths, still the wicked would have been excluded from it. Yet these people speak of it the most boldly.

On this matter, we must note what is written in Psalm 50: 'You who run with adulterers, with thieves and with robbers, do you wish still to speak of me in boasting; will you say that you are one of my servants and of my Church?' Well, God cannot tolerate such corruption, for if we pretend to be his people, we must 'depart from all iniquity' as St Paul exhorts us in 2 Tim. 2:19. Now that is how we shall have the privilege of calling upon the name of God. We must abstain from evil and dedicate ourselves to his service in all purity of soul and of body. If, on the contrary, we are dissolute people, and join ourselves to adulterers, murderers, the proud, to drunkards and to thieves, and then want to usurp the name of God and make claim to the title of the Church, it is certain that we will be doing him an intolerable injury. This also is what we must note on this passage.

It says afterwards that 'David replied to them: As the Lord lives, when a man came to bring me news of the death of Saul, thinking that he had certainly gratified me, well, he received his wages; for his reward I took him and had him killed. And now, how shall I pardon you, who are much more wicked, who have killed the innocent in his bed?' Hence, he thereby commands them to kill them. Well, they are disappointed in their expectations, and yet we have here a memorable example of the constancy of David. For we see how he persevered in always acting loyally towards Saul. No matter how many times he had been provoked to anger against him, on whom, humanly speaking, he could have avenged himself time and again, he still refused to do so.

Well, these men gave David homage and said, 'God has avenged my lord the king'. Yet formerly, they were mortal enemies and had wanted to exterminate him from the world, so far were they from recognising him as head and superior. But that is how the wicked change with every wind. In brief, when they speak in this way, it is either in pretence, or because they always have in mind their own profit and advantage. They do not have regard to what is legitimate and for what God has commanded in the matter. It makes no difference to them, but they do have in mind their own profit or loss. And on that point, either they are as proud as lions or they act like cowering chickens. First, they will exhibit an overweening pride, and then they will offer nothing but flattery, which they will pour out like slaves. Hence, when we see such inconsistency, let us learn to walk in the fear of God and by no means to vary or falter either for this or for that, for we are only too changeable in ourselves. We see how light our spirits are and, above all, we are inconsistent in doing good; so much so that we need to be held with a double bridle. What will happen, therefore, when we go along with things which are presented to us? For the devil does not cease to put before our eyes things which draw us away. He will only endeavour to make us stumble over this or that, especially if we desire single-mindedly to persevere in well-doing. For Satan is opposed to God, to his will, and to all that he commands us.

Now this is clearly demonstrated to us in the example of David. When he mentions what he had done formerly, he means to show that he did not intend to discharge his duty with one blow, in order afterwards to give himself liberty to forget all about it by doing the very opposite. He says, 'I have killed him who boasted of having put Saul to death, and thus I must continue'. By this, he signifies that he did not execute justice by 'a flash in the pan', but always wanted to maintain an equitable rule and a consistent measure. This is a passage which is well worthy of notice. For we see that when even those who do have some zeal in carrying out their duty happen to be in a position to mete out justice, they will often deal very rigorously. They say, 'This man must be punished'. They will be well able to pursue a case through to the end. But then, afterwards, they will want to accommodate themselves, little by little, with each one, and 'sit on the fence'. 'Very well, this poor man has made a mistake and does merit punishment but, after all, no-one is perfect. The evil is not so bad as they say.' And so, although they have justly punished a crime of that sort some time before, now they forget all about it. Someone else, who has done the same thing, will be exempted, or at the very least he will be treated very gently. Thus he will not persevere in doing his duty.

But when one is thus punished and the other is pardoned, there is not the least doubt that those judiciary authorities who act in this way will have it put to their account on the last day, and they will have to answer for it before their sovereign Judge. For 'there is no acceptance of persons with God' (Rom. 2:11). He judges righteously. When they have punished one malefactor and spared another, they must face the fact that they will have it no better themselves before God. And in this also they show that they have no love for justice. That is why I have said that we must note what David mentions here: 'I have killed', he says, 'him who boasted of having done a wicked act, and now shall I not require the blood of the righteous at your hands?' So much, then, for one point.

Well, it is not only those in a position of justice who have to receive instruction from this passage, but each one of us as well. For if God has given us the grace to have behaved virtuously in any area, it should incite us all the more to be determined not to change, and not to turn away from the right path. And we should note all the more that everyone excuses himself and makes himself believe, when he has served God for a time, that he should be exempted and given special privileges. There are very few who remain in the centre of the path. And yet we think that God should pardon us and ought not to pursue us, to remind us that we should always attempt to execute our duty. We would like to compromise with him. 'Well, when I have done it once, must I not have some relief?' But what relief? Merely the right to do evil.

One can see some of those who will do marvellously for a time, and will think of themselves as little angels. But later they will begin to wander and go off the course in such a way that one would say that they are totally out of relationship with God. Seeing, therefore, that we are so weak and giddy-headed as to want ourselves exempted from the Law, we must remember, all the more, the lesson which is given to us here – namely, that when we have taken great pains to employ ourselves in the service of God, what we have done in the past may serve to prick us and urge us to persevere more and more. For instance, when God has granted someone grace to confess his name openly, he must watch that such grace may never be buried. Or suppose someone says, 'God's mark is on me, for I have been in danger of my life'. Then they should add, 'Well, I must go even further. Because that has happened to me, I will not cease to pray him to give me grace that I will not spoil his good work, but that I may be all the more given to living rightly and setting a good example for all.'

That is what St Paul says, that those who have lived chastely and in sobriety should be all the more careful, and be more ashamed to go over to adultery, overeating, and other vices (Rom. 6:12–14; 13:13). And why? Because God has thus far led me and governed me, and must I now spoil the gifts of his Spirit which I have received? Since my living beyond reproach up to this point has glorified God, how could I now let my life bring dishonour to his name? Now that is how we should profit from this doctrine, where David declares: 'He who has already exercised justice against him who boasted of having killed Saul, must not now be inconsistent or contrary to himself, but must vigorously go forward with such constancy that he proves that his action was not motivated by a zeal which was only "a flash in the pan", as they say'. Instead, he did it with a calm and collected spirit, from the depths of his heart, which brought forth good fruit not only for a day, but continually.

Nevertheless, we must carefully consider here the words which he uses. First, he 'swears', and then he adds to his oath the fact that 'God has preserved him from all afflictions'. Well, in this oath he takes the name of God in order to bind himself, so that there need be no further wrangling. It is true that we must not swear frivolously. For the glory of God is so precious that we must not lightly take his name and play with it like a ball. Oaths ought, therefore, to be made in sobriety. But when necessity requires it, God permits us to use his name as a pledge. Here, therefore, David wants to bind himself, so that there may be no further discussion and so that no-one can dampen his courage – as someone could have remonstrated with him: 'These people here deserve being spared, and if you do not want to recompense them, at least run them off. For since they are bringing the head of your enemy, what can one say, except that you cannot tolerate those who seek your profit and have true affection for you?'

That is how David could have been tempted to pardon these two wicked murderers. For that reason, he places the name of God here as a bar, so that he may be held back, and so that no-one can come to alter his convictions at all, and to show that it is a salutary thing for him to carry out his duty directly. He therefore takes the name of God, since he wants to do a deed that is just and good. He swears in this way like a preface, to get people's attention. People would not have noticed so clearly the continuity with his former action if David had not protested that it was in the name of God. Therefore, this also served as a warning to all those who were on the scene and who then heard it talked about. Even today we should be cut to the quick when we hear that David was motivated in this way and that he took the name of God to show how determined he was to execute justice.

But this word is still worthy of being studied, namely, 'The Lord who has delivered my soul from all affliction'. David signifies by these words that since God has shown him the grace of having cared for him and for his salvation, he will not allow himself to profit from a wicked deed. And why? Because he wants to receive everything from the good will of God. Well, if he had derived some profit from these two murderers, it would have been an approval of their deed. If David had done such a thing, he would have renounced the grace of God, and would have manifested terrible ingratitude to him. And why? Because God had preserved him till then and if he had drawn back from his duty, he would have manifested distrust in God, as if God did not have the means to sustain him to the end – and so he had to use murderers to take care of his own life.

This would be obscure, unless it had already been applied to general practice. If, after one of us has felt that God has had mercy on him, and that he has not failed him in time of need, he then abandons himself to evil out of distrust – does this not do injury to God? For instance, a poor man may have lived simply, but still God has always provided him with nourishment; he has escaped from many troubles. Then there may arise some occasion on which he is tempted to evil. If he employs stealing and dishonesty, if he gives himself to unjust gain under the excuse that he fears a dearth in the future, is he not trampling underfoot the goods which he has received from God? Is it not as though he were saying: 'God has helped me up to this point, but I do not know if he will always want to do as he has been accustomed to, or not. Be that as it may, I prefer to leave God out.' Now that is a most wicked lack of fidelity. We may know that God has nourished us for ten or thirty years or more, that he has given us his hand in many necessities, and that he has always cared for us more than a father. And yet, with the excuse that we do not know that he wants to do as we desire, we turn our back on him and seek better help and conditions with Satan. Now is that not an utterly enormous blindness?

Well, that is why David says: 'The Lord has delivered me from all affliction' – as if he were saying: 'Has the time come for me to start using evil deeds to avenge myself on my enemies, or to assure myself? For God has kept me in his protection and has showed, in effect, that I ought to rest in him. Well now, if I consent to this murder, it would be as if God were not strong enough for my salvation, and as if I would be better off with the devil.' For he who consents to evil certainly makes acquaintance with the devil, and by this means abandons God.

Let us, therefore, hold tightly on to this doctrine, as it is very useful for us. Whenever we are tempted to evil, under the excuse of saving our life, under the excuse of ridding ourselves of some worry or anguish, or of having some remedy for our troubles, let us think: 'Has not God taken care of us up till now? When we have called upon him, has he frustrated us? And have we not experienced his goodness to us? Since, therefore, we have known him to be so merciful to us, and he has gone beyond the affection of our earthly fathers for us, and we have been saved by his hand so many times, should we now abandon him?' Now that is why we should commit to memory the good things which God has done for us in the past, so that we may be all the more confirmed in our actions, in order to keep ourselves in his fear, and to attempt nothing unless it pleases him. That, in sum, is what David wanted to teach by his example, in saying that the Lord kept him back from affliction.

Still, he is not content with saying that God had helped him on one occasion, but he recounts how many good things he has experienced, so that he does not doubt that if he were to fall into a thousand dangers, God would be sufficient to uphold him and guarantee his safety. That is what should be recalled by this word 'in all affliction'. For it was not for one day, nor for a single space of time, that God had shown himself favourable to David and employed his virtue to uphold him. But rather, he had proved him in many situations. Although he might have fallen as much as seven times a day, he had been, as it were, relieved endlessly and unceasingly. God thus showed himself so kind to him; also, by faith, David was attached to him like glue, so as never to depart from him. It is as if he were saying that no danger should incite him to evil, since God had shown him, in effect, that he ought to wait on him and take refuge in him. So much, then, for this word.

Now he adds: 'If I had not spared those, shall I not now require the blood of these wicked ones? For you have killed the innocent in his bed, and in his house.' Well, it could be asked here how David justified Ishbosheth, who had gone against the command of God, for the kingdom which he usurped was governed by tyranny. On what basis, then, is he called innocent? Rather, David is referring to those who committed the murder. He is said to be innocent in relationship to them. And in fact, God will punish those who have committed murders, just as though the slain person were innocent. Yet what will happen is that the punishment will be double when God, on the one hand, wanted to kill someone and yet, on the other hand, the murderers who did it will still not be excusable. We have already seen that when the sons of Eli were killed in battle, God wanted to kill them (1 Sam. 4:11). That very word is expressed in the text.

Now were the Philistines absolved before God because of that? Certainly not. For we must always consider the intention of him who does every deed. Well, the Philistines wanted to exterminate the people of God, indeed the very memory of his name if they could. They had, therefore, shed as much innocent blood as they could and that is why David reproaches these two brothers for having killed the innocent. They had recognised him as their king, they had been nourished and maintained at his expense and wages. They had taken an oath of loyalty to him. What right did they have, therefore, to come to kill him and to cut his throat? They could not have alleged: 'We have punished him because he deserved it'. Who gave them this commission? And since they had nothing against Ishbosheth by which they could condemn him, and since he was their king, it was their duty to put up with him. Therefore, it is not that Ishbosheth is here also loved before God – as if David were approving his usurping the royal crown – but David is taking the perspective of those to whom he is speaking. Let us, therefore, learn not to be judges of those who have committed no offence against us. And when we have committed some evil, it might seem appropriate to claim: 'He to whom we did wrong has done wrong to others; he deserves these wages'. All of that (I say) will in no way serve as an excuse for us.

For we must pay attention to what God commands us, namely, to do injury to no-one, nor commit any outrage or extortion – nor to think that we can wash our hands of evil by claiming that we have carried out the command of God. Yet this will get us nowhere, for all the reasons that we may plead will only serve to cover us with a wet sack, as they say! That is how David understood Ishbosheth to be innocent. For what he proposed we must accept as a sentence of the Holy Spirit, of whom David was the instrument, to declare to us that when we are motivated by some wicked feeling towards our enemies, their blood will be required and demanded of us, as if it were totally pure and innocent, inasmuch as it is not for us to wreak vengeance. Now this is what we must remember about this point.

Then Rechab and Baanah aggravated their crime even more in that they killed Ishbosheth 'in his house and on his bed'. It is universally true that everywhere murders are committed, they must certainly be brought to account, for they are detestable before God and will finally be judged. But the murder is even more punishable when there is such thievery connected with it. 'Every man's home is his castle', as the old proverb has it. If a man is assailed while he is in his house, it is certain that the deed is much more villainous and detestable. And in fact, a murder will be unforgivable when one man comes to attack another in his own house. If he had been inflamed with anger in the street, it would have been more of an excuse; but it is inexcusable when someone is in his house, and what is more, in his bed, asleep and half dead, with neither arm nor leg to help himself – and thereupon someone comes to cut his throat! That is how, therefore, their cruelty is much greater and utterly excessive. And this is what David wanted to say, that not only had these two killed an innocent man, but they had also done it in his house and in his bed. Indeed, the judges should always pay attention to such circumstances, for two deeds could be similar in appearance, and yet one would be much more grievous and wicked than the other. If a judge has no prudence to discern the case, he can confuse many things. Thus we should keep these circumstances in mind: namely, if a man was so desperately rash that he seemed like someone possessed by the devil, if he was held back neither by zeal nor by fear, if he despised all fidelity, and if he was out of control, like a savage beast – when (I say) these things are known, it is certain that the crime is all the more inexcusable. So much, then, on this matter.

Well, in general we must note that God wants to spare human blood, and that murderers are such an abomination to him that we ought never to tolerate them, and allow them to go unpunished (Gen. 9:6). It is no small thing that man has been created and formed in the image of God. If there had only been this common nature, as Isaiah says that each one is our flesh, still even that should have kept us under control (Isa. 9:19; 58:7). But when we contemplate this image of God in a man, and then we go on to shed human blood, must it not clearly be said that in such cruelty there is a contempt of God and a pride and rebellion which says that it does not bother us to offend him? It is, therefore, not without cause that God holds murder in abomination, that he wants human blood to be spared, and that if it is shed, he will avenge it. That is one point.

Now this lesson applies not only to those who have the sword of justice in their hand to punish evil-doers, but it is also addressed to us, that each one may learn to abstain from all injury and vengeance towards his neighbours. We certainly ought not to have to be controlled by the fear of just punishment; that would scarcely be a virtue. But let us realise that God thus detests murders, that he holds them in horror, and this consideration should conform us to his will. Now in the eyes of God, these are also types of murders which we commit: extortions, detractions and similar things. That is why we ought to be taught to remain humble, to live in peace and fraternity with all men. And he even goes further, for he says: 'He who hates his neighbour in his heart, has already murdered' (1 John 3:15) – that is, even though no-one has perceived it and it is hidden from the world. Therefore, let us learn to keep ourselves unspotted from all bitterness and extortion, and let us have fellowship with one another without any harm. That is what we have to remember.

When David says 'that he will require the blood', he speaks as a royal person, for it is not for each individual to punish murders and other evil doings. We should certainly see that crimes are punished and that those who have done wrong are dealt with, but God has willed that there be police in this world. So let us carefully note that David had the sword of justice when he made such an execution. And it is to keep anyone from going beyond the scope of his responsibility that it is said: 'Here are the two wicked people, I will punish them'. Now if we act in this way, we could well double the evil; but God will bring us to account for all that we do, no matter how much zeal we may have. Let us, therefore, learn so to hate evil that we will let the police deal with those they should, and that we will pay attention to what God calls us to do, and to what our degree of responsibility is. And let each one (I say) be content with his own position.

But let those who are placed on the seat of justice also carefully consider that if there is some injustice which remains unpunished by their default and negligence, God will require the blood at their hands, and they shall have to give account for those whom they have spared. Now that is how all magistrates and those who have charge of justice truly execute their office, without regard to everything that could turn them aside. When it is a matter of punishing evil-doers, let them always have the eyes of their understanding fixed on him who established them in this degree and dignity of honour, and continually uphold his honour and glory.

Well, finally it says that 'David commanded that one kill' these two brothers. It is also said that he 'cut off their hands', and then that 'they were hanged over the pool' of Hebron, so that they were exposed to the full view of everyone, and that 'the head of Ishbosheth was buried in Hebron'. Well, it is true that someone might say: 'When the feet and hands of those people have been cut off, what does it matter to them if they are hanged after their death? It will cause them neither heat nor cold!' But this was for an example, for if one executes justice in secret, it is as though one were ashamed of it. Now that in itself is an evil. And on the other hand, punishments and chastisements would be useless if one chastises malefactors in this secret way. Public punishment serves, therefore, first of all to correct evil, inasmuch as it is displeasing to God, and to purge the land of it. It is thus like an acceptable sacrifice to God when evil-doers are put out of the world. Even if one chastises evil-doers and it does not cause their death, it should serve for repentance and also, even in death, malefactors should feel the offences which they have committed, otherwise they would never have thought of them, but would have been hardened.

Well, there is a place provided for public punishment so that the people might assemble there to recognise their own faults, to have an example and to be incited to pray God to control us. So that is how justice must be exercised – that is, in public, since we are so lustful that when we are left for some time without the application of justice, everyone goes out of bounds. Even the best will become unbridled and corrupt, and at the end there will be such horrible confusion that nothing can be worse. If for only half a year, a magistrate abstained from punishing crime, he would not be able to control the people, for there would be such brutality that we would no longer know how to discern between good and evil. Therefore, punishments should be meted out, as by the virtue and authority of God. And people should realise that it is he who has commanded it, so that he might be glorified when those who hold in contempt his Law and his justice thus receive their wages. Then the country will be more and more purged of evil, so that everyone may have an example and instruction. Now that is why it is clearly said that the two murderers' feet and hands were cut off and then that they were hanged over the pool of Hebron in a busy place, so that everyone would know that the judgement of God had been carried out.

On the other hand, when the burial of the head of Ishbosheth is spoken of, it is to show that David did not want to avenge himself, however much reason he had, humanly speaking, for doing so. He could have shown his vindication everywhere. It often happens that when someone has the opportunity to rejoice over the head of his enemy, he causes it to be carried on the end of a pike or a lance, and triumphs over it, glorifying himself in the rage and fury that he has executed. Well, David abstained from all these things and had it buried, to show his humanity.

Furthermore, as for the burial, there is no need to deal with it now, for enough has been said about it above, where we explained that it was the custom from all antiquity to show that the human body was placed as a deposit in the earth, to be rendered account of when it pleases God to call it. Human bodies are placed there (I say) in safe keeping, in hope of the resurrection which shall occur on the return of his Son, our Lord Jesus Christ. And then we shall appear before his judgement seat, to be clothed in holiness and immortality, to be crowned with the crown of righteousness, and to rejoice in his eternal glory.

Now let us prostrate ourselves before the majesty of our good God, recognising the great poverty and many faults of which we are guilty. Let us pray that it may please him to be merciful to us; not only to bury our sins, but also so to reform us by his Holy Spirit that we may more and more learn to forsake ourselves, to detest all iniquity and to hold it in horror, and to have such a zeal that we may persevere until the end in his service and obedience, in order to glorify his name more and more. May he not only bestow this grace upon us, but upon all peoples and nations of the world . . .

12

*All the Tribes Submit to David's Yoke**

Hence all the tribes of Israel came to David at Hebron saying: Here we are your bones and flesh. Also formerly, when Saul was king over us, you led out and brought in Israel . . . (2 Sam. 5:1–5).

We have seen above how God tested the patience of David from the time that he began to fulfil his promise to him. Certainly, it gave him some relief and softened his grief when he was constituted king over the tribe of Judah, but it seemed that God only granted him the fifth part of the territory that he had promised him, for though he was to be leader of the whole progeny of Abraham, yet he had only one tribe. He was far from possessing what he expected, and yet Saul was dead and the kingdom was practically ruined. But still God held him in suspense, which was (as we have said) to prove his faith. This should serve as an example and instruction to us, so that if God delays fulfilling his promises to us, we will not lose courage, but will persevere to the end. For God knew when it was the right time to do what he had determined, and he never prolongs it any more than is useful for us.

Now it is said that 'all the tribes of Israel came to him'. There is no doubt that he had done all his duty to reduce the people to union and harmony; it was also his office. But be that as it may, we see here a voluntary desire – that the people of their own will should come to him without a battle. David did not put his

*Monday, June 29, 1562.

forces in the field; he was in Hebron, as though he were content with the little portion that God had given him, when they came to seek him. And that is how God holds the hearts of men in his hand, to mould them and 'turn them where he pleases', as Solomon says (Prov. 21:1). Therefore, when Scripture says here that the tribes of Israel came to do homage to David, it shows that God did not want this division to last for ever, but that after David had waited in apparent weakness, the thing was put in his hand, without his earning it or worrying about it. Hence, having experienced such grace of God, he then says that the faithful will prosper 'while they are asleep' (Psa. 127:2). This does not mean they are not to work at their vocation, nor that God does not hold them responsible. But nevertheless, if he grants them this grace, when they think they are far removed from what they desire, before they have even thought of it, God makes them enjoy more than they could have hoped or thought. That is how God showed his care when all the tribes of Israel came to Hebron.

Well, it says that they recognised that 'they were the bones and flesh of David', and even that they were obliged to him, inasmuch as 'he had governed them well under the reign of Saul'. Thirdly, they recognised that 'God had ordained him to be their head and king'. And hence, they confessed that they must submit themselves to him and give him homage. Well, here is everything that David could have asked of them, without God sending them a prophet, or even an angel from heaven. Here, in sum, is what it took to induce them to place themselves under obedience to David. There are these three points: fraternity and parentage, and then there is their recognition of the goods which they had received from him. There is, above all, the decree that God had made, for this was inviolable. Since God wanted David to rule, it was necessary that this be done, no matter how much the world might contradict and resist it.

Well, who is it that speaks? It is those who had not only refused to obey David, but who had persecuted him for such a long time, and who had held him in abomination. They had taken him for an enemy of the peace, a traitor and rebel to his king. In brief, there was no criminal who was so detested as David. Even after the trespass of Saul, they remained obstinately malicious, and always sought a way not to submit to David's yoke. Until God constrained them to come to their senses, they always held back. Even though Ishbosheth was scarcely competent to reign, still they preferred to have him for their leader than to accept David. And after his trespass, still they remained as though they were asleep for a while, and looked here and there, always wanting to find an excuse not to obey this decree of God, of which they were always witnesses and heralds.

This shows us that when men are preoccupied with wicked desires, they lose all reason and their judgement is perverse and confused. In fact, if we were not hindered by evil affections, we would always be able to judge equitably and rightly. It is true that we are full of ignorance and error, but be that as it may, that which hinders us from judging as we should is only our pure malice. Even if we do not recognise it today, it is certain that, on the last day, what men thus judge wrongly and perversely by making themselves believe that white is black and vice versa, will be made manifest. Now, bad judgement is so rooted in hardness of spirit that it influences men's passions, turns them aside and dazzles them, so they are not able to follow what is good, but give themselves over to unbridled living so that they wander like poor beasts.

We see this even in the teaching of the Gospel. For however much this may be a singular gift of faith, and we may not understand with our natural sense (as St Paul says) the marvellous secrets of God which are adored by angels, still, if one looks closely at why the great majority reject the doctrine of salvation, one will discover that men willingly choose the darkness (1 Cor. 2:7; Eph. 3:10; Heb. 11:6; 1 Pet. 1:12). And why? Because they are given to evil, as our Lord Jesus Christ explains (John 3:19). He does not simply say that men do not understand the truth of God because they are poor blind souls, but he adds that they are rendered inexcusable because they flee the light, since they want to do evil. Hence, a thief or some other wicked person who may want to commit a crime will not want to do it in the light of midday, but will seek some secret place. So it is with unbelievers. For since they do not want to give themselves to good, and cannot put themselves in the service of God, that is, they do not want to do so – this is why they deliberately blind themselves, shut their eyes, and close their ears, so they will not see and will not hear.

Well, this can be recognised in every aspect of human life. It is true that the majority will always claim: we are not clerics; we have not been to school. In brief, those who do not want to use their reason or to understand the truth of God will always take this shield of ignorance as an excuse. But be that as it may, when someone comes to the poorest idiot, and if he explains a fact to him and he is not preoccupied, he will know more or less what to say, even in his condition. Well, if someone speaks to a man whose case involves profit or loss, that man would prove unreceptive. Instead of being as he was formerly – master or doctor, capable of good judgement – he cannot even follow or receive the reasons that are explained to him, even if (so to speak) one chews up the pieces for him and he has only to swallow them. That is how we are: I must say that we are terribly ignorant. Yet the fact that we judge badly, and are not able to discern between white and black, does not come from a weakness in judgement and in knowledge; it comes from our evil passions (Rom. 1:18–32). These cause us to be intractable and to be unable to understand what otherwise would be familiar and known to us.

We have a beautiful illustration of that in this passage. Here are the elders of Israel, who know best of all how to preach that they should humble themselves under the rule of David. And why did they not know it formerly? What school have they attended since then? Who has taught them? They recognise what they already knew, but they were hindered by their hatred for David, because of this wicked ambition which inflamed their pride. This was because they wanted to keep the house of Saul and remain loyal to it. It seemed to them that since he had been elected as their king, his possession ought to remain inviolable, especially since God had not previously given them such a distinguished position (of having their relative as king).

Now that is how they wanted to fight against God, and thus they avoided thinking about the things that they were now saying. And why? Because of these evil affections, which were like bandages over their eyes. The matter was quite clear, but a blind person sees nothing at midday. Let us learn, therefore, that as often and as far as we want to judge properly, we must strip ourselves of all our passions. Even when it involves some definite fact, let us continue to hold ourselves suspect, until we have learned deliberately to despise all that can affect either our own gain or loss, or which could turn us away from judging as we should. That is the direction, therefore, in which we must begin.

Now this rule must be carefully observed when it comes to the doctrine of our salvation. For why is it that we profit so poorly when every day our ears are besieged with the Word of God, if it is not that we are retarded by our carnal lusts, which are repugnant to God? And that is how we blind ourselves. All the more, then, since God gives us this honour and blessing of being called to himself, must we labour not to be held back by our passions, but to resist everything that could turn us away from his obedience or keep us from being peaceably submitted to his will. That, in sum, is what we must remember.

The text also says: 'We are your bones and flesh'. With these words, all the elders of Israel wanted to be reconciled to David, as though they were saying: 'Let us forget all the enmities which have existed until now between us, for we are still relatives'. That is how those who have forgotten all benevolence will always find reasons from which to profit, when it comes to forgetting the offences which they have committed. If David had pleaded the same thing, he could have protested a hundred thousand times that he was their brother and of their kindred. It would not have moved them in the least, for without hesitation they would have replied that he had alienated himself from them, and had cut himself off as a rotten member. Well, when they brought forward this kinship, they wanted it to be received as an infallible reason. But that is the manner of those who do not walk in righteousness. They bring up everything which is to their advantage, and their hypocrisy also so blinds them that they think that they must always have won the case. Well, all the more must we pay careful heed to ourselves, so that we might go by a fair and equitable rule, that we might not use a double standard and measure. Rather, when we offer some rule to others, let us at the same time accept it mutually. Or when it is offered to us, let us not expect others to hear us, and yet at the same time shut our ears to what someone wants to say to us, as we see Israel did. This is one point.

Here is the second point, namely, that they recognise that they are obligated to David in that he had guided and governed them during the very reign of Saul. Well, they were speaking as their natural sense led them, which illustrates what I have already said, that when we are not stupefied by our wicked desires, it is because God has still given us some reason with which to discern. Yet we are not able to attain such knowledge by ourselves, especially when it comes to the doctrine of the Gospel, which is held in admiration by the angels of heaven. It is true that we do not understand it by ourselves, as St Paul says, 'it will always be foolish to us, until we are illumined from on high and the Holy Spirit is our inner Master' (1 Cor. 2:6ff.). But with regard to what concerns human life, we will always be convinced that we have enough reason to understand what is just and right, and the opposite; but it is only our malice which causes this confusion by which we are not able to judge as we should. In brief, 'the light shines in the darkness' (John 1:5). However much we are poor blind souls because of original sin, still God does not fail to cause some beams to shine, so that we are inexcusable. And this is what St Paul says in the second chapter of Romans, that we have the Law written in our hearts. He says that even if there were no Scripture, and it were not preached to us, we would learn from pagans who had never heard God spoken of. They (says St Paul) still have the Law engraved on their heart. Yet they cannot obtain salvation, but will be convicted, so that they can by no means be exempted from condemnation, under the pretence that they knew nothing and heard nothing about their salvation. It will be necessary for the conscience of such a person to be a record for him, as though he had a hundred thousand cases stated against him.

Let us consider this seriously when it says that those of Israel knew well that they were obliged to David, and that they should not refuse to submit to his yoke. Indeed, they recognised this when God led them by force, removing from them all the reasons that they had for following the house of Saul. What will it be when we are called before the throne of God and all our thoughts are discovered, so that there will be no hypocrisy under which we can hide? Indeed, it will even be necessary that each one's life be so opened, as though one were reading and publishing a legal case. Now this warns us not to wait for God to convict us on the Last Day, but to prepare ourselves early. And if, for a time, we happen to forget our duty and wander, let us realise this and let us practise what the Psalm says: 'Sons of men, enter into righteousness; realise what it is' (Psa. 4:2–5 paraphrase). For David rests his case there, as in the hands of his enemies, and there is no doubt that he was heard and that God at the end led all those who had been his former enemies to make honourable amends and to accept the shame of having been rebels against all equity. Therefore, he says: 'Sons of men, hear and realise', as if he were saying: 'The fact that you persecute me so cruelly is not from true zeal because of anything I did to you. It is from nothing else except that you are stopping your ears and not wanting to hear in order to discern. You would not like to examine the case. In brief, you are attempting to pervert all reason, and be savage beasts, as though God had given you no intelligence.'

Well, that is shown in what we see now, that when God has kept them restrained, and they have not been able to pull this way or that way to seek their accustomed hiding places, then they have had to condemn themselves with their own mouths and have recognised that, truly, they have been well governed by David during the reign of Saul, and that their ingratitude alone prevented them from accepting him as their king in accordance with the decree of God. So much, then, for the second point.

Well, the principal fact in what we have dealt with is that they recognised that God had promised the crown and royal sceptre to David. So, what a rebellion this was when they wanted to oppress David and cause this promise to be annulled! Must they not have been possessed by a demonic rage? God has spoken, and mortal men dare oppose his decree and irrevocable decision! Here are creatures who are only dust and ashes, yet who want to exalt themselves and, filled with pride, to say: 'That which God has decreed will not be done'. And by what authority and virtue? Simply because those of Israel wanted to do so. When we see that they were thus blinded, let us fear, for we are no better than they. If God spares us so that we do not fight against him, to our ultimate confusion and ruin, here is a monstrous thing which ought to make us pull our hair out. We see here that those who claim to be the people of God, who have been circumcised, as we today are baptised, who have the law and the sacrifices, and who have, in fact, been chosen as the heritage of the Lord and as his Church (there was no other people then in the world who knew God or the true religion) – we see that these knew that David ought to reign and that God had so decreed it. Nevertheless, they resisted and could not tolerate it, and even dared to contradict his majesty not only with their mouths, but also with all kinds of actual violence. Well, since that happened to them, let us fear lest today we fall into such a rage through our wicked affections. Let us learn (I say) to submit peaceably to all that we know is agreeable to God. Let us seek his will diligently, in the first place, and then having known it, let us accept it without murmuring.

And above all, when it comes to the kingdom of our Lord Jesus Christ as our guide, let us be careful not to be like those of Israel. It is true that it is better late than never, when it is a matter of submitting to him. But still, we must labour to advance ourselves, so that (I say) we may be prompt in humbling ourselves under the mastery and reign of our Lord Jesus Christ, knowing that God his Father has given him all power and sovereign rule (Matt. 28:18). That is clearly proclaimed in the second Psalm: 'I will declare that decree', says our Lord Jesus Christ (Psa. 2:7). And in fact he announces it by the ministers of his Word. Since that is the way it is, let us learn to master all our wicked lusts, which make us like savage beasts, and do not allow us to be unhesitatingly docile and obedient. And on the opposite side, we have a problem in that we foolishly dislike and regret things that we recognise to be good and right. It annoys us to go along with what is good, for it brings us loss and was not chosen by us. Well, as soon as we know what pleases God, and as soon as his will is quite clear to us, we must break with all our rebellions, and push ourselves with such force that we are captive to his will; indeed, willingly so. It is our entirely malign and perverse nature which makes us corrupt everything. That is why we will not be moved to obey God fully – without force and violence. But nevertheless, we must use force and we must always fight against ourselves, so that we ask nothing but to submit ourselves to everything that our Lord shows us to be good and equitable.

So much then (I say) for this point where the children of Israel recognised that they had clearly understood that God had decreed that David should reign. They had not at all submitted to it; they were very late in coming now. Well, it is true that they were received – but, nevertheless, let us fear. For if we so abuse his patience, it will have to cost us very dearly in the end. We will howl, but the door will be closed to us. Hence, let us seriously consider what is preached to us by the prophet Isaiah (Isa. 48:9; 65:12; 66:4). It is that when God calls us, we must respond to him, and we must know what is 'the acceptable time', and the 'time of our salvation', when the Gospel is preached to us, so that as soon as we know this grace which God grants us, we will be inclined to receive it and adhere to it.

And moreover, under this word 'pastor', the office of a good king is expressed to us in this reign of David; namely, that he must care for his subjects as a shepherd for his flock. Now two things are required of a shepherd. The first is that he provide his animals with good pasture, and then that he keep them safe from all thieves and wolves and trouble. Now that (I say) is what princes must do. If they think that they will render an account to God for the charge that is committed to them, they must see to it that their subjects live in peace and that they are maintained; and then, in the second place, that they defend them against all troubles. How far from that are those who call themselves pastors but who ask for nothing but the wool – and are not even content with that. They must fleece their poor subjects; they cut their throats to suck up their blood.

One sees today that princes have neither regard nor consideration for their duty, which is to keep their subjects in good pasture. They are supposed to care for them but, on the contrary, they are like lions. Puffed up with pride, they think the world is created for them alone, and hence they have no scruples about swallowing up and eating the substance of poor people. And after they have thus consumed their poor subjects, ambition also pushes them to wage war. It does not matter to them that people burn and kill, and that the earth is full of orphans and widows. And why? Because they are princes, they say, and have power to do this. Indeed, but as the psalmist says, 'God is seated in the midst of them and has ordained them with this charge for which they must give account' (Psa. 47:8–9). And they will be judged like the very smallest. For 'this world will pass' with its 'fashion' (1 Cor. 7:31). But those who hold a slightly higher rank and dominion over the people must carefully note this – that they are pastors. That was known even by the pagans, for when they spoke of kings and princes, they called them pastors, as their writings demonstrate. And who taught them such language? God, who imprinted it in their hearts, so as to render inexcusable those who employ tyranny. So much, therefore, for this point.

Furthermore, let us note that David was established as a pastor of the Church, insofar as he was a type of our Lord Jesus Christ. Now let us act as his sheep by being submissive to him, so that he who has been given to us as pastor by God his Father may fulfil his office to us, as he especially declares in the tenth chapter of St John. Therefore, let us learn to follow the voice of this eternal Shepherd, that is, our Lord Jesus Christ. Let us learn to put ourselves entirely in his hand and under his leading, and let us be submissive to him, so that he might enjoy us. It is certain that 'we will want nothing' (Psa. 23:1), that he will provide us with everything that he knows we need for our salvation. He will defend us when we voluntarily submit ourselves to his protection, so that we will be assured that we will not perish. As he says himself, none will perish of those given him by God his Father, and he will employ his strength to guard from all danger those who are under his hand (John 6:39; 17:12). So much, therefore, for this word which is given here.

Well, it says afterwards that 'David made an alliance before the Lord with the elders of Israel'. This shows us that there is a mutual duty between a prince and his subjects. Since, therefore, subjects must bear the yoke which is imposed on them, and voluntarily render homage to God in the person of their superiors – because whoever resists this higher authority (as St Paul says) resists God – by the same token, princes and those who have dominion and high rank must concern themselves with what involves the public good, and the peaceable condition of their subjects. These authorities (I say) must realise that God obliged them to do this when he established them in such honourable dignity. And they must be prompt and diligent faithfully to carry out the charge which is committed to them. For this covenant which David makes is a solemn oath. By it, he pledges that he will not be tyrannical towards the people, and that his reign will be for the common welfare. So much, then, for one point.

Well, it says that this alliance was made in the presence of God, to show that David carried it out without pretence, and this word is not written without reason. It is true that all oaths will be brought into account before God, but people do not always make them as though God were present. For they actually make fun of them, and those who have thus sworn, afterwards merely shrug their shoulders,[1] and are not in the least concerned at being perjurers. Even today, the ceremony is still kept, so that not only those who are in a public position, but kings and emperors take an oath, which seems remarkable. But how will they carry it out, who on the very same day would have liked to reverse everything that they have promised? And not only do they take complete licence in regard to God, but they harden themselves; they have absolutely no shame before men. For even small children can discern their dishonesty, so that

[1]Literally: 'wipe their mouths'.

no-one will know what became of their oath, but that makes no difference to them. Hence, let us note here that the integrity of David is not only brought before us for instruction, but that all those who have to swear, especially those who may be in a position of legal authority, are to recognise that the oath ought to be inviolable, and that they are to take it as in the presence of God.

Then we must draw a general rule from that. It is this. However much we may think that we are absolved from promises which we have ratified in the name of God, we will have to know that in the end God is annoyed when we have taken his name in vain, and that such a sacrilege will not remain unpunished. Yes, it is true that this matter has been dealt with earlier, so of course I have briefly touched on it. But still it is a matter which is well worthy of being stated again.

The text says that David was 'anointed king over all Israel', and then the term is inserted that he 'reigned seven years and a half in Hebron over Judah', and 'thirty-three years over all Israel', and that the time of his reign was 'forty years'. Well, the anointing which is here spoken of was not intended to abolish that which had been given by Samuel (1 Sam. 16:13) (as we have mentioned earlier). Mention has been made that the tribe of Judah had anointed David, that is, in Hebron (2 Sam. 2:4). Now it is reiterated that there was a general anointing by the elders of Israel. If someone asks how they dared attempt to anoint him who had already been anointed with the authority of God and by his express command, the reply is easy. They by no means wanted to derogate from what had been done by the prophet Samuel. Rather, they only gave the approbation of their obedience. Now it is not up to us today to give validity to the ordinances of God, as a letter is inspected and approved by legal authorities. It is not (I say) for us to authenticate what God has decreed, or what proceeds from him. For who are we? To do this would make it seem that the truth of God depends on our fantasy; and if it were received on this basis, then people would consider that it had proceeded from the will of men. So when everyone would like to be on an equal footing with God, this would be like mixing heaven with earth. Hence, let us note that it is not for us to authorise what God has once decreed. But we can very well give approval to it by obedience. And that is how this anointing should be understood. That is, the elders of Israel did not want to efface this mark which had been given by Samuel, but they testified their consent to it, as if they had responded 'amen' to what God had already declared.

This is well worthy of being noted. For we see with what impudence the papists have come forth when they dare to spit out their blasphemy that the Word of God has no authority, except by the approval of the Roman Church, and then that the Church has determined what testimonies and Scriptures are to be received. 'This is what we must believe and hold to', they say, 'or otherwise there will be no certainty in our belief.' Now there is no more detestable blasphemy than this. And how have they dared thus to mock God, and have forgotten who they are? Because they have not held to this principle which I have just demonstrated. Their attitude testifies that we are puffing ourselves up with too much pride, and exalting ourselves against heaven, as though we were devils incarnate when we wish to attribute to ourselves the power of determining truth: 'Here is what is good and pleases me, and it is thus acceptable insofar as I give my consent to it.' The papists, therefore, have never demonstrated a more diabolical pride.

Hence, when we add our approval to that which God has once pronounced, let us say with all humility that all wisdom and right is in God, so that we adore all that proceeds from him. Furthermore, let us learn by the example of these men to hold as valid all that God has ordained. It is true that those of Israel did it too late. But (as I have said) we must go forward in all the immediacy of faith, to align ourselves with all that God has ordained. But let us do so with harmony and melody, so that we receive everything that he has decreed and demonstrate its reality by the obedience of our faith. So much, therefore, for this matter of anointing which is spoken of here.

Well, finally the phrase is added: the 'forty years' that David reigned. But in fact, his rule for seven and a half years was partial. This is to remind us of what has been mentioned, namely, that when God wanted to establish the reign of David, it was not all of a sudden perfectly completed. It is true that we see the persecutions which he suffered, and how far he was removed at that time from the crown and royal dignity, for he was driven from the society of men. Now he is a fugitive and vagabond amid the deserts and caverns in the midst of savage beasts. Now he is banished from the country of Judah and constrained to dwell amongst idolaters. So that was his situation for a long period of time. So when God wanted to exalt him, his kingdom was still very small, lasting for seven and a half years.

This is written for us. For in the first place, however much we realise that God reigns, yet our Lord Jesus Christ is hidden in him, and his reign is even hidden in this world. It does not shine with lustre, but is despised; indeed, rejected by the great majority. Hence, let us not find it strange that our Lord Jesus Christ, however much he is established King by God his Father, does not yet have the authority that he merits among men.

Moreover, there are today no definite boundaries that can be assigned to us. We see that the kingdom of our Lord Jesus Christ is small, as there is only a little handful of people who have submitted to him. Here there may be a town which has received the Gospel, and then there may be a great country where idolatry reigns. When, therefore, we see that the kingdom of Jesus Christ is small and despised by the world, let us turn our eyes to this illustration which is given to us here, and let us wait for the extension which God knows, but which is hidden from us. Let us wait (I say) in patience until his kingdom be established in perfection, and God gathers in those who are dispersed, and restores what is broken down, and puts in order what is confused.

So David's case is an illustration of how we must practise this doctrine. It is said that not only was he tormented for a long time before reigning, but also, even when God gave him his hand, that he reigned only over one tribe for seven and a half years in Hebron, and the rest of the people did not want to agree with and submit to him. Furthermore, however long the time seems to us, still God will uphold us in patience, as we keep our passions under control. But the problem is that we wish to be advanced immediately; we want to see the kingdom flourish in this world, and to experience only joy and sweetness. Indeed, but yet we do not consider why God often does not permit the kingdom of Jesus Christ to flourish more perfectly. It is so that we will not lull ourselves to sleep, as we are only too inclined to do. For if the Church were at peace and people received the Gospel without contradictions, and if there were no kings or princes who did not voluntarily align themselves with it, we would be immoderately sunk in our own ease, and Jesus Christ would reign by our opinion and not by his virtue. God thus wants the kingdom of Jesus Christ to exist in the midst of his enemies, as Psalm 110 says, so that we may be kept in close control.

And for the rest, let us learn that there is a good which is incomparably more excellent than that of David. For however much he was a type and image of our Lord Jesus Christ, still he had an earthly and inferior reign. Thus, the kingdom of our Lord Jesus Christ must be totally spiritual and eternal. Hence, let us not find it strange that the kingdom is so small now and not taken into account, and that it is even openly opposed, and seemingly will never be advanced. Let us not find it strange, but let us realise that this is for the best. And yet, be that as it may, let us not fail to pray God that he will advance it and make it increase, and that everyone will work in it and strive for it. And let us be governed by him in such a way that he will always be glorified in us by life and by death.

Now let us prostrate ourselves before the majesty of our God, recognising the infinite faults of which we are guilty, praying him to make us so feel them as to draw us to a true repentance. And thus more and more may we be stripped of the lusts of the flesh, so as to be reclothed in his righteousness, in order that we may serve and honour him in such a way that when we have offered both body and soul in homage to this great King who has been set over us, we may be assured of attaining the kingdom which he has obtained for us. And may he bestow this grace not only on us, but on all people . . .

13

*David's Dealings with the Jebusites and Hiram**

Then the king and his men went to Jerusalem to the Jebusites, who inhabited the land, who spoke to David saying: You will not enter here, unless you remove the blind and lame. For they thought that David could not enter there. But David took the fortress of Zion, which is the City of David . . . (2 Sam. 5:6–12).

Here is something very strange. In the midst of the land of Judaea, the Jebusites, whom God had long ago condemned, were still living – in the very city which was to be the royal seat of God, where his temple was to be built. Hence, we see what the other passage says, how laziness kept the people from acting virtuously to win the country which God had given them for a heritage. If you want to know why the Jebusites had come there, it was certainly because the people had been lax in executing what God had commanded them (Deut. 20:16ff.; Josh. 15:63; Judg. 1:21). That is also how the people of God were rewarded – that the unbelievers, who were mixed with them, were like briars pricking them on all sides (Num. 33:55). They were like thorns sticking in their eyes. How did it happen that these people corrupted themselves so often in idolatry and debauchery from the pure worship of God, if not because of opportunities given them by their neighbours? It is impossible for people to converse privately together without picking up wicked customs, and without being infected by the examples that they see with their own eyes. Well, here are unbelievers among the people of God. Therefore, their contagion naturally

*Tuesday, June 30, 1562.

spread further and their superstitions were followed, so much so that this land, which God had dedicated to his honour, became full of pollutions.

Well, as for the people of Israel, they thoroughly deserved it, for God had expressly ordained the extermination of all the ancient inhabitants of that country. They had no right to dispute whether or not to pardon them, for it is not for mortal creatures to change anything of the sentence of God. Moreover, we have shown that this condemnation was not cruel, however severe it may have appeared. For God had already put up with the Jebusites for a long time – some four hundred years. However perverse they were at the beginning, nevertheless they had been spared because their iniquities had not come to their fullness, as Moses says (Gen. 15:16). So that is why all these people of Canaan fully deserved to be destroyed, and their memory abolished. But since the reason was not known by men, it was enough that God had commanded it. The children of Israel paid no attention to this sentence, partly because of their faithlessness, and partly because of their laziness and ingratitude combined. They manifested (I say) faithlessness, for if they had rested on the promise of God when they had the sword in their hand, they would certainly not have doubted that he would have given them the promised victory. When, therefore, they feared their enemies and fell back, it was a sign that they did not add faith to what God had said to them (Heb. 4:2). Ingratitude made them lazy, for it is faith that gives us courage and defends our very life and body and our souls. On the contrary, we will have our legs and arms broken, and we will be totally useless if we do not embrace the promises of God so as to rely upon them. Then we will be like a body without a soul.

Well, ingratitude was also involved in this situation, for the people still did not enjoy the good that was offered to them. And to whom must the blame be imputed? Now here is this land of Judaea, of which God said to Abraham, 'I will give it to your seed after you' (Gen. 17:8). And yet here it is, occupied by unbelievers. Has God broken his promise? Certainly not. But the people were kept from the possession of their heritage because of their malice. Well, in addition to his condemnation of them for having despised him, there is another dishonour. God wanted to be glorified in that country – and yet the seat that he had chosen on which to build his temple was inhabited by profane people. What a nasty situation it was! It seems that they had conspired deliberately to keep the kingdom of God from running its course.

Here is an example which should be carefully noted. It says that even in the time of David, Jerusalem was occupied by the Jebusites – that is, by the enemies of God. (We shall later carefully discuss the reason for this, which we have already touched on.) Hence, let us keep learning this doctrine of the need to purge the Church of God as thoroughly as we can. We must pull up every bad weed if we do not want them to grow and take over in such a way that they will spoil everything, and we cannot remedy the situation at the end. Why is it that the wicked often arise and take over, so that they pervert all righteousness and honesty and fly the banner of total licence? It is because the wicked have not been punished in space and time, and because they have not been held in check by a short bridle: this is why people have suffered evil and have not progressed as they should have.

We see again in our experience today what is written in this passage. That is, that if one is not so strict as one should be in punishing evil, it will take such root that it will be very difficult to pull it up later. So let us all punish evil as swiftly as we can. When we see that this happened in the time of David, let us note carefully that when our Lord has given us the grace to come to him, we should be all the more diligent to root out all scandals. When David began to reign, it was as if God had prepared his seat, for David was only his lieutenant and officer. He thus showed that he wanted the people to be reunited, and that he would be their shepherd. Well, the Jebusites were driven out of this fortress of Zion which they held. All the more, then, should we be vigilant and exercise justice, in order to remove all pollutions from the land in which God wants to reign, and to cleanse it from all filthiness when it pleases God to declare himself our King. He is there, as it were, with his hand stretched out to say, 'Come to me and I will come to you' (Prov. 1:23–24). There, again, is a point which is eminently worthy of being noted.

Well, it says that 'David and all Israel came to exterminate the Jebusites'. There is no doubt that David could have felt tempted regarding his decision to fight such a war, for the people could have murmured against him, in that they were accustomed to tolerating the Jebusites at arm's length. That policy was costing them nothing. They considered them neighbours, and hence they could have picked a quarrel, since David was starting wars without any pressing need. They could have said, 'This man has come to lead us into deeper trouble. We have other enemies on the outside, and now here on the inside we have started a fire which cannot be put out. It would have been far better for him never to have reigned over us.' David could certainly have been held back and turned aside by that fear, but God gave him strength to sustain the endeavour. Hence, let those in authority recognise that there will be perils which will be a menace to them, or some difficulty, which ought not to freeze them with fear from executing what they recognise to be their duty. If there are complaints thrown against them, let them not fail, for all that, to go where God calls them. Everyone in his private life should do the same, for we would never move a finger if we waited until things were easy to handle, and there were no resistance or objections. But God wants to prove the zeal and desire which we have to obey him. When what he commands us is difficult, and we cannot do it without a fight, then God is testing our zeal to follow him everywhere he calls us. So much, then, for one point.

Yet we must note what is said, that all Israel came with David, for this would not have happened if God had not given them the will to do so. As I have said, to start this war was a troublesome matter, and then it was a question of fighting in the centre of the country – and for what cause? To drive out the Jebusites. Well, the people could have claimed that they had put up with them, that they were their neighbours, and that it would have been better to tolerate them than to make a change which would cause such trouble and confusion everywhere.

Therefore, the people could have fallen back. But it says that all followed David because God helped him. Therefore, let each one do his duty, and let us not look at one another and say, 'Wherever the majority goes, I will follow'. But let us heed God, and when he has given the Word, let us conclude that it must be so; that he will always give us sufficient help; and that those who have previously angered and molested us will be our companions and diligent in lending us a hand. God will so bend their will that we will be united in one accord. Now that is what we must hope from God, that those who have been against us, or who could be against us, will be our companions. Let us not notice at all who is going on, but let each one in his own place do what is his duty. Above all, those who have the leadership and the superiority over others should observe this rule, which is to put duty first and to do all they know that God has ordained them to do, and then it is certain that they will be followed. Even though, at the beginning, they may have doubted that it would be so, God will make them prosper, as we see it stated that all Israel followed David.

It is amazing that the people had been so stupid not to be stirred until this time to see that the Jebusites held their seat in so eminent a place, the centre of the country. It is true that God had not yet declared that he wanted to have his temple there and it was not yet written that God had preferred Zion above all the dwellings of Jacob (Psa. 87:2). But nevertheless, it was a rather notable location, and it had even been ennobled by the consideration that Melchizedek had had his seat there – thus Zion had been blessed (Gen. 14:18). Hence, the people were so dull that they did not think: 'Here am I, deprived of a portion of the land which God has given me, and indeed in the very centre of it' – and in this we see that the promises of God did not have great authority to move them.

Now if we are not totally stupefied when the things which God has promised us fail us, it should touch us – not to embitter us, not to inflame us with impatience, but to look into ourselves and to know that it is only our sins which keep us from fully enjoying all the goods for which we may hope and wish. Therefore, if the people of God had done some good reasoning within themselves, they should have thought: 'Here are the ancient inhabitants of the land, who have their banner unfurled to win victories and mock the promise of God. It was said to our father Abraham: "This land will belong to your seed" (Gen. 15:18). Well, we see the contrary. We are kept out and they remain.' The people should have examined themselves in this way. When they were not thinking about it, it was a sign that they were dull, as I said.

Well, this should help us a great deal today, since every time we compare the promises of God with our actual state, and consider how far we come short, and how much we lack of what God has declared to us, it should cause us to think of our sins. They are like bars which keep us from reaching the goods which were all prepared for us. Let us groan over this. We have every reason enough to do so in every direction we turn. For when we consider the general condition of the Church, we will see that it is stated that the inheritance of the world has been given to our Lord Jesus Christ: 'Ask of me, and I will make you king over the east and the west. Distant kings and cities will come, and each will bring you gifts, and will give homage to you' (cf. Psa. 2:8; 68:29ff.; 72:8; Isa. 49:7, 22–23). There will even be, in addition to that, rebels who have been his enemies, who will come to submit to our Lord Jesus Christ. Hence, if we had the fulfilment of these promises, there would be a unity of faith everywhere. There would be only one brotherhood among us. There would be only one mouth, so to speak, and one heart to glorify God.

But we see so many disputes that whenever a small number worships God, others will obviously despise them, and then we see how pure religion is torn in pieces. We see how those who call themselves Christians are enemies of God. We even see persecutions which are directed against the poor faithful. And what is the cause of all this? It is true that, at first glance, we could be troubled, thinking that God had frustrated us in our hope. But we must go beyond this and realise that this benediction of God, which is certain and infallible for us, has been removed, because we are, by our vices, preventing the kingdom of our Lord Jesus Christ from advancing. It is the same with the rest. For if we have enemies who annoy and trouble us, it is certain that God is punishing us for not having done our duty. Whenever someone is afflicted with poverty and illness, let him look to the promises of God, that he 'will be guardian of the bones of his faithful ones, and not one of them will be broken' (Psa. 34:20). The good will be afflicted, but those who fear God will in no way despair of his help. Well, we see that some experience dearth, others continue in despair. Let us realise, therefore, that we have kept God from fulfilling what he declared with his mouth, for he has great wealth, and he will not be miserly to us when we call on him in confidence. Let us thus learn to consider how far we are, in fact, removed from the promises of God, so that we might examine ourselves and ask pardon for our faults – and, nevertheless, take courage to seek what he offers us, so that we might obtain it and enjoy it.

Well, it says that the Jebusites were confident of their city fortress, and made fun of David, saying: 'You will not come in until you remove the lame and blind'. Because this passage is a bit obscure, the Jews invented fables, as they are only too bold to do. For since they are wicked dogs, it does not bother them to invent all sorts of things which are pure mockeries of God. Therefore, they imagined that there were statues there, of which one was blind and the other lame. One represented Isaac, who in his old age could not see a mite (Gen. 27:1). The other represented Jacob, who was lame in one hip after the angel of God had struck him (Gen. 32:25–26). This, they said, was a memorial that the Jebusites should remain there because of the covenant which had been made between Abraham and Abimelech, and ratified by Jacob (Gen. 21:22ff.). Well, as I have said, these are just so many blasphemies against the Word of God.

Instead, one generally understands this passage as if the Jebusites were saying: 'Even if there were nothing here but lame and blind people, still they would be sufficient to defend themselves. Hence, you had better retreat.' But still this is rather strained, and one clearly sees that these words do not imply that they expect him to drive out the lame and blind who were in the city.

The true sense of the passage is much more natural and easy.

This should be taken as mockery of the people of David, or an expression – as we might say: 'You are nothing but a pack of dogs, and do you think you will conquer us?' One can, therefore, easily explain this as applying to the army of David, as if the Jebusites were saying: 'And who are you, and who are your people, if not lame and blind like tree trunks?' That is how they spoke in mockery against the people of David. If we do not take it in this way, still it would be much more apt than saying: 'There are nothing but lame and blind men in the army of David'.

When all is carefully considered, it is the same as if someone were saying: 'You would have to exterminate even the women and little children'. When, therefore, they speak of lame and blind, it is the same as if they were saying: 'Even if only the most wretched were here, you would never take this place; everything would have to be wiped out'. Since, therefore, the place is so secure, and all are fully resolved to hold on to it, they may say: 'Even if there should be one man standing, though the very invalids who are lying on their beds should get up, even to the biggest coward, even to the old folk and little children – even if all the others had been exterminated – still we will never surrender the place, and you will never enjoy the possession of it'. When people have such determination, they can easily say: 'Well, everything would have to be destroyed, down to the lame and blind'. Now that is a sufficient exposition, without searching for a frivolous conjecture.

It is true that David afterwards says that he 'will smite these lame and blind, who are hated by his soul'. He calls them all this. But that is because they had reproached him that he would have to get rid of even the lame and blind. 'Very well, I will show you', he says, 'that neither lame nor blind will escape me, for I will consider all of you to be such, and you will pass under the edge of the sword.'

That, in sum, is what we have to remember from this passage. The point is that the place was so strong that it gave courage to the Jebusites not only to resist, but to despise David by such defiance. Well, it happens regularly that those who may think that they are very secure become puffed up with pride and glorify themselves. Their pride is the reason why they will irritate their enemies all the more. Let us learn, therefore, that when the despisers of God become so proud that they show contempt by their mockeries, God surely knows how to master them at the right time. Even their pride, by which they are inflated, will be the cause of humbling them, for while they imagine they are provoking men, they are actually provoking God. Well, that is one point.

Let us note, however, that when God gives us weapons and fortresses, it is not to elevate us in pride. Rather, let us behave in all modesty. Let us use what God gives us, and yet let us realise that all our strength will be nothing unless he causes it to prevail. That will serve to give us what reassurance we need. And yet we will not look down our noses at everyone in contempt. For when there is such haughtiness, it is certain that God will not tolerate it – inasmuch as it comes from men putting their confidence in the earthly means that they have, which effectively obscures the power of God. Hence, when we hear this word about the Jebusites, let us note that it is brought before us so that we might know what was their end. It was that this mockery cost them very dearly. Let us learn that when God gives us some advantage against our enemies, we are not to rest upon it. And we are not to jump on wild horses so that we will have our necks broken because of our pride.

Moreover, let us also hope that when our enemies are thus lifted up in pride, God will indeed choose to subdue them, and after they have been contemptuous and wagged their tongues, they will all be appalled, and everything will be turned to their confusion. That is why we have this quotation about how the Jebusites defied David.

Well, it says that he promised a reward to whoever would go in first and reach the gutters. We are not told in this passage who it was, and it is not even stated what David promised. But we can supply this lack here from the First Book of Chronicles, where it says that David promised the one who first entered the fortress that he would make him captain of his army; and it was Joab who won the prize (1 Chron. 11:6). Not that he had not already been captain for a long time, but he was confirmed in his position (cf. 2 Sam. 2:13). That, in sum, is what we have to note in regard to the taking of the city of Zion, which was called Salem, and afterwards Jerusalem.

Well, it is added that 'David went on increasing and growing stronger', since God was with him. This is not added without reason, but so that we may know that this victory was given to him by God, and was not acquired by his own strength. He put duty first; he worked faithfully. He was not eaten up with vanity, nor held back by any worldly consideration. It is true that all that is to be prized; but still, these are the favours of God. The whole thing would have amounted to nothing if this campaign had not been brought to a good issue by the goodness of God. Therefore, in order that praise should not be withheld from God, it says that David went on increasing and growing stronger because God was with him. If it had simply been stated that David went on increasing and growing in strength, one would say that it was good fortune, or that he was a king worthy of being honoured, that he had certainly advanced himself by his prowess, and that he surely knew how to govern his people by his prudence, for he was very virtuous, having defeated his enemies so many times.

Now that is how we often describe good fortune, or canonise men. Well, since David attributed the praise to God for all the good which came to him, this is why we should take him as an example for ourselves. He would have had no prosperity unless God had taken his part. In sum, it is the same as if he had declared that the favour of God and his goodness, and the fatherly love which God had for David, was the cause of all that had happened to him. That is, he had been promoted by this means, had been confirmed in his kingdom, and had even brought the whole country back to obedience to him. He had, indeed, driven away his enemies, and extended his boundaries very far.

Here we must note, in the first place, that inasmuch as the kingdom of David was a type of our Lord Jesus Christ, which is the state of the Church, it was not enough that God, in one swoop, should establish the kingdom of his Son. Rather, he had to cause it to grow and multiply day by day, which is quite necessary. For when God had given some sign of advancing his Church and making it fruitful, it seems that all has been won, and that only laughter awaits us – and we, like foolish people, despise this grace which is so necessary. It is the same as if we no longer had the least need of God, and were carrying in our pocket everything that we could wish. It says that God must build his Church, give it foundations and direct it (cf. Eph. 2:20). On the other hand, he must maintain it, and not only that, but he must make it grow and increase. For the reign of our Lord Jesus Christ will never be perfect in this world. Far from it. First, there will always be afflictions and contradictions, and secondly, there will be much hypocrisy and internal enemies who, under the pretence of making a profession of faith, will only cause scandals to keep our Lord Jesus Christ from reigning. Even the faithful will be full of many weaknesses and imperfections. Hence, it means nothing for the reign of Jesus Christ to be set up once in our midst unless it is maintained. For, because we are so fragile without his help, all will fall down like water if not fortified from on high.

Then in the second place, we must increase and this kingdom must keep growing, that is, in numbers. Hence, those who have despised the doctrine of the Gospel, and have been open enemies of God, must be held in check, in order to give place to it. And the hypocrites must be known, or at least held back in such a way that they cannot do harm. Also, he must augment the gracious influence of his Spirit in those whom he has already renewed. In brief, he must bless us in such a way that the kingdom of Jesus Christ will increase. From whence will it come? We must always remind ourselves of this word: 'God must do it'. For if it were a question of conforming ourselves to him by our own action, far from doing so, we would discover ourselves to be utterly weak; it would only take a blow to knock us down. Well, the devil strikes a hundred thousand times a day. We would thus be thrown back every minute if God did not sustain us with his hand. Then it is not a matter of our having persevered by ourselves in serving God; rather, we must be renewed every day because we still carry so many remnants of our wicked lusts that it is pathetic. All the more, therefore, must we note that if God did not continually take care of us, even though the kingdom of our Lord Jesus Christ had once been set up, still it would have immediately fallen down.

It should incite us to prayer and intercession when it says that God was with David. And why? Because that is where growth and increase come from. Let us notice, in the first place, how much the Church in general needs to be increased, for the number of believers is very small. Indeed, there are many who are being butchered in the mouths of wolves. We see our poor brothers killed and slashed. We see raving wolves who spare them not, and it ought to make our hair stand on end. We see so many countries which are still peacefully in the possession of the devil and of antichrist. When, therefore, we see that the reign of our Lord Jesus Christ is only over a small handful of people here and there – one could even say that the state of the Church is in disarray and that it would take practically nothing to reduce it to destruction and ruin – we have good reason to pray God that he will be pleased to increase and advance us. Moreover, even when we see that some are preaching and publishing the Word of God in several places without contradiction, and that great and small want to obey it, let us realise that we are still very far from seeing it advance as it should. Our very life misleads us, for we have so many vices that turn us aside from following our leader that it almost seems that we are turning our back on him, rather than approaching him. All the more, therefore, should we pray God that his reign might increase, that he will watch over it and keep his hand upon it, since the power to do so is not in us.

Well, as this, on the one hand, should serve to exhort us to pray to God, so on the other hand, it can confirm us in the confidence that we can be glorified in God, as we seek the advancement of his kingdom, even as we pray for it every day. We say, 'Your kingdom come'. Well, if we say it without hypocrisy, it is certain that we will be heard and this prayer will not fall to the ground. For if God manifested his power towards this earthly king (that is, David), let us not doubt in the least that our Lord Jesus Christ, who has a fuller and more excellent dignity, will cause us to grow and multiply in feeling and actual experience, insofar as we seek nothing but the kingdom of God (Matt. 6:33). What is written here of the kingdom of David should also be applied to all the faithful and to the members of the Church, since we need to be strengthened by it. For instance, someone may be prevented from eating with his family; another will be perplexed and in want. In such cases, then, let us run to God, praying him to cause us to advance, that is, in everything that is useful and profitable for us. So much, then, for this word.

Now an example is added as a confirmation, namely, that Hiram, 'king of Tyre, sent messengers to David' with presents ('cedar wood', to build) and craftsmen ('as many masons as carpenters to build his palace'). Well, when the text adds that God was with David, there is no doubt that this was a testimony of the goodness of God – for King Hiram, who was a miserable pagan, was led to seek friendship, and to act in such a liberal way towards David. But yet, we see that David could not resist abusing this grace. This should serve as very useful instruction for us, to make us accept all the favours of God which he offers us by the hand of pagans, without becoming corrupted, as happened to David. Although they gave him a present of many cedars, it was not right for him to acquiesce in the will of a pagan to make an alliance. He should have been content with the fact that God had granted him his favour and immutable goodness, and should always have hoped for the same, insofar as he behaved faithfully in his vocation. Well, he obeyed (the pagan), and joined with King Hiram in order to advance himself. Yes, but he should have considered using this inestimable gift which God gave him, and not have usurped what was not permitted him.

Let us note carefully, then, that when it pleases God to let us enjoy a friendly relationship with unbelievers, we ought to be friends to them in such a way that no prejudice will be caused to God and his Church because of them. We should most carefully consider this point, for often when one makes an alliance with people who are unworthy, one gives them many concessions. Well, if it is only a question of our own loss, let us overlook it, and then all these concessions will be approved by God when we have given up our own rights. But people are not satisfied merely with that. Often God is betrayed when one concedes many things which are against his honour and do harm to his Church. And then we have to give way to this, and that, which is no great sacrifice, in order to win friendship. Yes indeed, but God is still offended by the procedure, and these concessions are often made at the expense of his Church. This is how, therefore, we are to receive gifts and favours from God.

It is the case, moreover, that when profane people have some friendship for us, and we receive some goods from their hands, God by this declares that he is our Father, caring for us as his children. When it says that King Hiram sent to David, this is not merely a fact of history, but one must add the text which says that God was with David and made him increase. Hence, it is the same as saying that King Hiram sent gifts to him because he was moved to – not because he was liberal within himself, but because God led him to do so by his Spirit, on account of the fact that he was with David, and wanted to show him that he was the author of his reign and that he also maintained him (Phil. 1:6). This confirmed that what God had begun he would continue, and would indeed bring the work to perfection. So much, then, for this point.

In sum, all the goods which we receive from creatures proceed from the hand of God. That is one point. Secondly, when those who are not united with us in faith show us some kindness, let us realise that it is because God is merciful to us and has led them to do so. Thirdly, let us not refuse all friendship with those who are not yet led into obedience to God. For 'we would have to leave this world' (1 Cor. 5:10) if we wanted to be separated from all those who do not know what the true religion is. But in the fourth place, let us note that the honour of God must always be put first. That is, we must not become surrounded by pagan people in such a way that we fall away from God. And we must be careful not to become familiar with them to the prejudice of our salvation, and to the prejudice of what concerns his honour and service. Hence, may his Church not be harmed, but may we so know how to moderate natural feelings that we will be careful of those who are separated from us in the faith of the Gospel. May we thus remain enclosed in the fear of our Lord, and may we be careful to maintain his Church to the end, and to see that his worship remains pure.

Finally, it is added that 'David knew that God made him prosper in his reign and that truly he had established him'. This knowledge could be considered strange, as though David had not known, until then, that God had blessed him and that he held everything by his aid and help. If this were how we interpreted the phrase, it would follow that he would have had no true vocation, nor certain foundation, but that he had only been rash when he advanced himself, and had done it in presumption and arrogance. In addition to all of this, such an attitude would have manifested ingratitude. Many times God had delivered him from the grave, and did he not already know it? Afterwards, when he began to reign in Hebron, he was already able to feel the grace of God. But what is spoken of here is a knowledge which does not remove what we have already taken for granted. It is true that the matter could not have been realised at that hour. But to sum up for today, let us realise that when David knew that God had established him, it was not that he had forgotten the first benefits which he had received from him. Rather, he confesses by this that God is continuing to make him prosper. Hence, let us learn that when the graces of God are added one to another, it should be a sure testimony to us, to confirm us in the fatherly love he has for us, so that we will have reason to give him thanks, and strengthen ourselves in him with such trust that we will constantly persevere in our vocation until we arrive at the goal we are seeking.

Now let us prostrate ourselves before the majesty of our good God, in recognition of the many faults of which we are guilty, praying him that it will please him to make us feel them more and more, and that we may ascribe to him all the praise for our prosperity. May we give him homage for all the goods which we have received from his hand, that is, dedicating ourselves totally to him and glorifying him not only in word, but in all our deeds. And may he bestow his grace not only upon us, but upon all people and nations of the earth . . .

14

*David's Polygamy**

And David took more concubines and wives out of Jerusalem, after he had returned from Hebron, and more sons and daughters were born to him . . . (2 Sam. 5:13–21).

Yesterday we began saying how God lets himself be known more and more by his faithful people, so much so that their knowledge of him after only a year or two seems nothing in comparison with the value of the knowledge which is given to them later. When God has helped us in time of need, it is a testimony which should surely convince us that he has mercy on all those who take refuge in him. Well, we may only taste a little drop of the goodness and strength of God, but if he increases it and demonstrates his care for us in an even more excellent manner, then we will be more and more assured by it. Hence, we will recognise what we already knew well, but with much greater certainty. We will have such assurance that we will no longer feel the least worry, but have an experience which will remove all our scruples and doubts.

Now that is how this passage states that 'David knew that God had established him king' (2 Sam. 5:12). Even formerly, this matter had not been hidden from him, otherwise (as we have shown) he would have been lacking any foundation or certainty. In that case, all of his undertakings would have been foolish and rash. Indeed, his anointing by Samuel was sufficient to show him that God had chosen him (1 Sam. 16:13).

*Wednesday, July 1, 1562.

Well, when he went through many difficulties, these facts served as frequent assurances to him. Finally, he was king in Hebron (2 Sam. 2:3–4), and although it was only over one tribe, it was not accomplished without the amazing power of God (2 Sam. 5:6ff.). Now it is added that when he became king peaceably over all the twelve tribes, and the people were reunited, then he knew that God had constituted him king and, above all, he knew it when God gave him courage to drive out the Jebusites.

Let us, therefore, learn so to profit from all the favours which God bestows upon us that we may always benefit from knowing him. Let us aspire to greater strength and certainty, which he may give us from his power and goodness and everything else which can serve to establish our trust in him. And so let us invoke him in full assurance and seek also to walk with such faithfulness everywhere he calls us that we will never doubt that he always has his hand raised and stretched out to aid us.

Indeed, these degrees of assurance are certainly well known in the faith. For once we have recognised even the smallest spark of the knowledge of God when he speaks to us through his Word, it will be sufficient to lead us to him. There is, therefore, a general knowledge which is found in all the faithful, even in those who are the simplest and smallest. I do not mean those idiots who say one word: 'I am a Christian'; but I mean those who have received the faith. Those (I say), however simple and stupid they may be, will not fail to know their salvation, as the prophet Jeremiah says, 'All will know me from the greatest to the smallest' (Jer. 31:34). The prophet Isaiah also says, 'All will be taught by God' (Isa. 54:13). Here, therefore, is knowledge which faith shows us sufficiently clearly, even faith which is still very weak. But when God instructs us with even more familiarity in his school, and we have clearer instructions than we had previously heard; when we see that one passage of Scripture is confirmed by another, it serves to reassure our conscience all the more. That is, not that we were totally ignorant of everything before, but rather that what we have learned afterwards assures us more and more of the truth of God – such as when it says that the disciples of our Lord Jesus

Christ knew after his resurrection what Scripture said (Luke 24:26–27, 32, 45). Did they know nothing before that (John 20:9)? It is quite certain that they had some foundation, but their understanding was still rather limited. Therefore, when God opened their eyes, they had their experience adjusted to what they had grasped concerning the doctrine of salvation, that is, now their understanding reached greater perfection.

Well then, as we see every day what is shown to us, or according to what we have understood thus far, let us always march forward and let us advance in the knowledge of God. However, let us also note that experience and practice increase our knowledge, which we will not have from simply reading the Word of God. For example, when God tells us that he wants to be our Father, we receive it and do not doubt that he will make us feel the reality. However, we have only the mere doctrine, and we must add faith to what God proposes, while all may be hidden from us (Heb. 4:2). For 'faith', says the Apostle, 'is the vision of things invisible' (Heb. 11:1). And St Paul says, 'If our faith were in visible things, it would no longer be hope' (Rom. 8:24). Therefore, whenever God has spoken to us, we ought to be persuaded and resolved that his Word is infallible truth. Nevertheless, we may not have experienced how he wants to help us, how he cares for us and is our Father, in order to keep us safe. We may not have felt it. Well, if he sends us afflictions and then, after we have called on him, he shows his mercy towards us, and the outcome proves that our resting on his promises was not in vain, this is how God confirms our knowledge in actual experience. David, therefore, already knew that God had established him king over his people. But still he had not experienced it as thoroughly as when what had been told him was actually done, and was seen by his very eyes.

In sum, let us remember from this passage to believe purely and simply in the Word of God, although what it promises us seems unbelievable. For as St Paul says in another passage: we must 'hope against hope', having followed 'our Father Abraham', who 'regarded not his own body, which was as good as rotten with age, nor the womb of Sarah, which was closed' (Rom. 4:16–21). He hoped in the promise of God, and put his confidence in it. And why? Because, knowing that this promise came from him who had all power to accomplish it, he rose above the merely human level, to add his faith to all that God had promised (Heb. 4:2). And that is how we should do it every time someone sets before us the Word of God. Nevertheless, the good things which we receive from his hand must serve to assure us of the knowledge which we have felt rather distantly. That, in sum, is what we should get from this example set before us here.

Well, it says that David knew to what end 'God had exalted his reign, because of his people Israel' (2 Sam. 5:12). Here, again, is an illustration from David, who rose above all that men can receive from their common sense. He could easily have felt that God was causing him to prosper, by putting forth his power to maintain him over the kingdom. But to know the intention of God and to what end he was doing it takes far more prudence. Well, it says that it was because of his people Israel. So David knew the reason why he was reigning. It was not for his personal profit, but for the common salvation of all. This is well worth noting, for we always need to recall this word: that it is not enough for us to recognise the blessings of God, but we must always *use* them properly. How? When God has brought us back from some illness, when he has saved us from some danger, we must realise that it is done so that we might thank him and honour his name. Moreover, let us realise that we must apply it all to his service. We must also consider the special gifts which God gives us. In sum, let us learn that whenever God shows himself merciful towards his Church or towards each member of the body, it is so that we will call on him and recognise him as the author of every good, and then give ourselves to his service and dedicate all that we have to it.

On the other hand, when I see that God has set me apart for some service, I must think that it is not because of me that he has prolonged my life, but because he wants to use me in the service of his Church. That is why, therefore, he does not allow me to die, nor expose me to the hand of my enemies. This is the prudence which we should manifest whenever God favours us. Let us realise that these blessings are not to be useless, but let us always think: 'It is God who has preserved me so many times. I must, therefore, show that I am aware of this.' That is why David showed himself to be so generous – as he confessed. 'God has established me king.' In other words, he did not show off his dignity, as if to say, 'God has poured out his treasure here upon me', as though God were attached to his person! Rather, he took a longer look! 'Why did he elect and choose me? It was not for my person, but for the profit of his Church, that I might duly execute my charge, and peaceably maintain his people.' All of these things show us how David made the most of the favours of God, and that he acted very prudently. First, he was careful to attribute nothing to himself, but rather to remember that God had used his power for him. On the other hand, it encouraged him to carry out his duty with the greatest zeal and affection.

But it happened afterwards that 'he took women' (2 Sam. 5:13) in addition to those that he had brought from Hebron. Well, he had already offended God most seriously, for in taking a second wife, he had already despised the Law of God, so that he was not content with taking three or four more. Now he was not content with taking a dozen, but eighteen! Here one sees how his virtues were mixed with his vices – which should certainly be condemned – and, above all, that this taking many wives is a corruption of marriage, which God has chosen to consecrate in his name. All promises ought to be kept and held among men, but this one is inviolable among all the others – that a man is joined to his spouse. It is not without cause that Scripture has said, 'Man shall leave his father and mother in order to be one and united with his wife' (Gen. 2:24; Matt. 19:5; Eph. 5:31), to show that this union is holier than all the others, and also that it is an indissoluble link. Well, when David took the second wife, it is the same as if he were reversing the order of nature. Scripture says, 'It is not good for a man to be alone, let us make a helper suitable for him' (Gen. 2:18). It does not say, 'Let us make him three or four or twelve or eighteen helpmeets'! Well, when David took two wives and then added such a number, it shows us that he let himself go totally out of bounds.

Furthermore, we must also note that when one has begun to

go astray from the right path, one sins without measure, and one always goes from bad to worse. If David had conformed himself to the order of marriage, he would have had his wife, Abigail, and lived chastely with her. When he took the second one, he disobeyed God, and it made him even bolder. For if we are kept under control, it is certain that temptations will not be so great as when we are acting like wild horses! But after we have taken the liberty of offending God, the devil intoxicates us, and the goodness which we have abused puts us to sleep and hardens our conscience even more. And it will not stop there, but always go from bad to worse. That is just how it is.

Therefore, let us learn to be careful not to become debauched. For indeed, if we fail to take preventive measures, it is certain that we will immediately be caught up in such violence that we will no longer be able to restrain ourselves. One sees how a sick person who departs from following medical regulations will very seriously hurt himself, and thus suffer more. If he drinks immoderately, for instance, then he will despise nature, and it will no longer be a question of glutting himself, but of bursting wide open (so to speak)! If he eats rotten meat, he will go from one intemperance to another! So it is with this. If we do not accept the corrections which are given to us for our spiritual healing, we are simply lifting ourselves up presumptuously. And little by little, when we have relaxed our control, we will be dazzled by our vices. We will wander from one side to the other; we will roam about, as though our lust encloses us in an abyss.

We see this process in David, who was such an excellent servant of God, and gifted with holiness and virtue. How much more should we be on our guard, for if God permitted him to fall so disastrously, will he spare us? Let us note carefully that having a number of wives is so damnable that God wanted to punish David's self-indulgence, so that he would be an example for us. Far be it from us, therefore, to use this as an excuse, as do many hedonists when they want to misbehave! As though they were mocking God, they will bring up David, to say that he committed adultery, having had several wives. Then they will bring up Noah, to say that he was drunken. Afterwards, they will help themselves from St Peter, to say that he renounced Jesus Christ! Let us rather look at how many chastisements David underwent for the faults he committed. And let us humble ourselves, and be all the more vigilant when we hear that God did not pardon a man whom he had elected far above all others. If this was done in the green wood, what will it be with the dry (Luke 23:31)? Will it not burn even more?

We must also note another circumstance. David did not actually forget God all at once, but it was a slow process (as they say). For David was exposed for a long time after he committed adultery with Bathsheba (by whom he had Solomon) – not the first year nor the second, but afterwards, while he was a king at peace (2 Sam. 11). Therefore, this evil was all the greater, because he continued in it without restraining himself, but kept on acting like a man asleep in his vices. When a man has no remorse for some sin for a whole month, he is stupefied. But if he continues for a whole year (2 Sam. 12:24), it appears that he has been totally perverted (Pss. 32;51). Well, David did not continue one year nor two, but already had several wives in Hebron. Then, too, since he had reigned for a long space of time, and especially when he became old, he should have watched himself more carefully. But the more he flattered himself, the more God permitted him to be, as it were, alienated from his own sense, and his memory to be totally buried. He would have remained like a stupid and incorrigible man if God had not put his hand on him.

There is no doubt, also, that the adultery which he committed with Bathsheba was a just punishment for the licence that he took in abusing the institution of marriage. He had not ravished anyone else's wife previously, because when he took back Michal, although she was married to another, still she was his legitimate wife (2 Sam. 3:13). As for the others, he always went through the superficial formalities of marriage, and did not take someone else's wife. But nevertheless, when he corrupted the order of God, and made a villainous and profane confusion of it, it caused him to become permanently blind, and in the end he became a traitor and murderer in order to commit adultery, which was an even greater evil.

Therefore, when we see these things and gather them together, let us feel the deepest concern and fear. In the first place, let us realise that it is profane and sacrilegious to have a number of wives, since it repudiates the primal institution of marriage. That is one point. Then let us be aware that we must anticipate the wiles of Satan and not wallow in our mire, so that we will not be plunged to such depths of condemnation that we have no more concern or grief, but instead are totally hardened. Further, let us realise that we must not so abuse the example of the saints as to say, 'Now here is one who did this, hence I will be permitted to follow him'. But we must make neither rule nor law, unless it is approved by the Word of God. This is a point which is very worthy of being noted. We see, for instance, how the papists are scattered across the fields, instead of keeping to the narrow way – and, pretending that they are apes, mimic everything that the saints have done! Now we know only too well from the example of David that men can divert us from the right path, unless we compare all they do with the Word of God. Then we will follow carefully what God has approved and confirmed in the way that he has intended. Here, then, is one point.

It is true that God did not fail to bless David in giving him offspring (2 Sam. 5:13–16). Even if he had not had such a number of wives, he would not have failed to have children. We have seen above that the children which he had in Hebron were not so numerous that he could not have had them by one wife. Each of his wives had only one child (2 Sam. 3:2–5), and one wife could have had twelve – indeed, even up to twenty-five. When it says that David had six wives and six children in Hebron, although it was a sign of the grace of God, still it was also a mark and sign of shame in that now he had a veritable 'heap' of wives, and yet did not have a comparable number of children! This is sufficient to show that the grace of God was not fully reflected in his experience. Therefore, when we see it, let us realise, on the one hand, that God chose to put up with it – but also, on the other hand, that he did not allow him enough to cause him to rejoice too much, as would have been the case if he had had a greater number of offspring.

It is likely that David sought to have children so that the crown would not be taken away. But there is no doubt, also, that he was motivated by his evil lusts and by pride and pomp. Beyond the fact that he committed adultery for its own sake, there was the customary attitude of princes that they ought to be privileged to do wrong above everyone else. They want to be as far above the rank of human beings as is possible for them, and then to show their importance and have allies on every side. Thus, it is likely that David was motivated by all of these considerations. Well, although one can always come up with plenty of excuses, nevertheless one must not do evil that good may come (Rom. 3:8). David is to be totally condemned in every way, but especially because he relaxed control over his wicked and perverse pleasures. Then he is condemned on account of vanity and presumption, because of which he extended his wings too far and took off in the air, not knowing his limits. So God (as we have said) tolerated him, in that he did give him offspring, but that is not to say that he approved him.

Well, we have mentioned that if he had not had so many wives, he nevertheless would have been able to have children with a true brotherly feeling for one another. But there was incest there! One of his sons violated his own sister and thought nothing of it; another was a murderer, and another wanted to usurp the crown. Thus, here was the house of David, full of scandal (2 Sam. 16:21–22). And finally, he was driven from the kingdom by his own son, who pursued him even to death. And his wives, by whom he glorified himself, had to be shut up. David had to go into a bedroom to commit adultery, but here was his own son sleeping with them. In what way? Did *he* hide himself? By no means! Rather, he built a platform in an eminent place, and there committed his villainy in the presence of all the people and of the sun itself. Well, this was such a detestable and enormous crime that it ought to make our hair stand on end every time we read this story! For this detestable villain was not content with separating himself from his father, but in despising him, he despised God and all his works – as if he were saying, 'And what do I have to do with my father? That old man has abandoned himself to pleasure, and is he worthy of being king? Well, I want to show that it belongs to me, and that he cannot keep me from enjoying the crown. And far from my being afraid of it, in the very place where he has been honoured I will put him to public disgrace and shame.' All of these things are God's chastisement of David, so how can we now proclaim his prowess and righteousness? Nevertheless, God did not fail to have pity on him when he gave him offspring, that is, of the marriage with Bathsheba – which was founded on the murder of Uriah, who had been so faithful to him.

This warns us that however much God puts up with us as his children, and however long he may abstain from chastising us as we deserve, and even though he turns our faults to the good, still we are not to become proud about it and pleased by it. For instance: someone may have done some foolish deed. Very well, God may pardon him for that action, and the outcome may even be happy. But if he continues, and concludes: 'Oh, I have got along well', is this not to abuse God's patience? Therefore, when we see that David prospered – though not in everything and in every way, but that he prospered in these illicit marriages – let us realise that if God dealt with him humanely and tolerated him, it was not intended to elevate him to greater licence. This warns us that when we have been given some privilege, if we misuse it, we must not fail to recognise what we have committed, and to be displeased about it. And beyond that, let us realise that we would have fallen into disgrace if he had not had mercy on us. Well that, again, is what we are to remember from this account of the children that David had by his numerous wives.

Now there is another point, 'that the Philistines knowing that David had been anointed king of Israel, came and spread their army, and established themselves in the valley of Rephaim (2 Sam. 5:17–19). When David heard it, he entered the fortress and yet had his refuge in God. He 'enquired of him' (2 Sam. 5:19) whether to pursue them or not, and what would be the outcome, and 'God promised' (2 Sam. 5:19) to give him victory. Even though David had often been tested when the Philistines came against him, they still surprised him. Yet God had clearly shown his singular concern for his Church in that the Philistines had not moved from their position sooner. It is true that the simple story does not teach us this, but when we read what is contained in Scripture, we find that there are common laws which show how he governs his Church, and that he does not watch over it just as he does over the whole human race, but as our Father. Since he is more protective over it, he is always there, with his hand extended to help his Church. That is why it says that 'a hair will not fall from our head' (Luke 21:18) without his having permitted and ordained it.

This can be clearly seen in what we have just noted: that the Philistines, who had won everything by the death of Saul, had been held back. Why did they not pursue their victory? Because it is certain that God kept them in check. Moreover, when they saw that the people were demoralised, that the eleven tribes had such hatred for David that they wanted him to be exterminated, that David also had to be on guard among his own people and that he desired (but did not have) the means to secure the kingdom of Israel – when the Philistines saw all this, did they not have a good opportunity totally to overrun them? Surely they could have said, 'Here are the people, torn in pieces. They are at war among themselves. There are two kings who cannot agree. In brief, there is nothing but breakdown; why do we wait?'

Well, if the Philistines had come to attack David then, it would have been while he was only a little company, so to speak, when he had only one tribe. Furthermore, it would have been most difficult for those of Judah to dare to budge from their houses, because they would have been attacked by their own brothers. If they had come into Israel, some would have been banded against their own people. The Philistines, however, remained there, and did not see this advantage. And why? Because God had covered their eyes. He did not prevent them from being quite perverse – they did not change their nature. Therefore, when they did not use the opportunity which was put in their hand and did not take advantage of it, it shows us that they were stupefied, in that God held them back. Instead, they came to attack David when he was peaceably established as king, and had six times more strength than he had formerly.

Indeed, if he lost an army now, he could recover another one.

We see, then, how God has placed here before our eyes a mirror of his admirable providence, which he uses when he thus traps the enemies of his Church. We see that he does not tempt his children beyond measure, but that he afflicts and tries them according to their capacity (1 Cor. 10:13). This is not written for David, nor for those of his time. It is for our use and instruction. God certainly did all that is quoted here for the salvation of his people at that time, but to whom is the Holy Scripture addressed? It is not for the dead. It is for us, therefore. Let us, hence, learn to rest in God when we see that we are assailed by so many enemies who surround us on every hand, since God will not permit them to arise at a time when we are too weak. Even if they do so sometimes, God will take care of it in another way. It should satisfy us to hold this principle, that God keeps the minds and hearts of his creatures in his hand (Prov. 21:1). Their minds are kept in control, as though God puts fog before their eyes so that they do not see a single thing at midday. Their hearts and courage are kept in control so that they have no means to carry out what they have desired.

Well, when we come to realise this, let us then learn to maintain ourselves by this powerful doctrine: that God blinds the iniquitous, and changes their courage (Isa. 19:14). The devil intoxicates them, as it says in Scripture (2 Cor. 4:4), so that they are lulled to sleep when we need them to be, and then when they want to devour us, God will allow their plans to be frustrated. But it is not the case that we do not need always to be on our guard, for it should encourage us all the more to pray to God, who holds the remedies for our salvation.

There are many who are overwhelmed with shock when they see their enemies' trappings, when they learn of their tricks and crafty devices. And there is so much treachery that it is amazing; whatever way we turn, we always have to suffer. Here is such a garrison; they are supplied with such captains, oh, it is certain that we will never be able to escape from them! That is why Scripture shows us the proper way to get ourselves out of such a trial. That is to realise that God will confound the wise in their craftiness (1 Cor. 1:25–28), and well knows how to neutralise and confound all their tricks. Therefore, let us realise that our enemies are blinded by God while we are exposed to death. When (I say) our Lord wants to test us, he will give us faith with the means to resist, so that the outcome of our afflictions may be always happy and blessed when we leave our case in his hands.

In fact, what is written here concerning David has been experienced by us again and again in our own times. So often we have been so oppressed that it certainly seemed that we would never be able to escape. For our enemies are found to be so strong and of such determination that they could gobble us up a hundred thousand times with one grain of salt, as the saying goes. And what distress the Church of God finds itself in from time to time! The number was very small and yet who kept back the wicked from using what was in their hands? I shall take only one example, which will be sufficient for us. During the time that tyranny ruled the kingdom of France, only a word was needed for the enemies of the Church of God and of his truth to have won all. But nevertheless, it did not come into their mind to do what could have abolished the Church of God and its worship. And I may say that twenty years ago, nearly thirty, I was in such distressing circumstances that I would almost have preferred to have been dead, and remove all this anguish from my sight. At the least, I would have desired to have had my tongue cut out, so as never to say a word. Yet when the enemies of the truth are determined to abolish it (as I have said), they cannot find the means to do so, for it would have taken only a word of confession by me to have stamped out the whole doctrine of our salvation. If they had been sought out, one by one, among all the people, it is certain that the true believers would have been recognised, and the wicked, by this means, would have been able to exterminate them. Oh, but that never came into their thoughts! And who prevented that? God blinded their eyes and made them like stupid brutes. Yet since this certainly entered their imagination, and God opened their eyes to realise all these things, so that they could not plead ignorance as the cause, it is clear that he thus kept his own secure.

Of course, the enemies of the Church did not fail to harden themselves in their stubbornness and seek to make up for lost time when it was already too late. At least, they understood enough to consider their options: 'We ought to do such and such; oh, but it is too late! Oh, that we had done it in time! How great it would have been! Would we now be in this trouble?' But after they had ruminated over all their theories, they could do nothing but remain confused in the end. Hence, let us recognise that God has preserved us so many times in amazing ways while we could see nothing going on. The very graves were open to swallow us like a net; the dead were near enough to make us descend into the tomb. We did not see through the situation, but God watched over us, and covered the eyes of our enemies so they would not realise the means that they had to trap us. He did not give them the desire to use their trickery and crafty devices. Therefore, we have not only to read this event in history in order to understand the discourse, but also to profit from it ourselves when we compare with it all the experiences that God has given us of his liberality. Now that is how we must draw correct doctrine from this passage.

Moreover, when David saw the great strength of his enemies, it was not the case that he was not in great trouble and anguish. He may even have been quite stunned. But it turned out well – that is, he prepared himself to resist them. And how? He had his recourse in God, and God gave him counsel (2 Sam. 5:19). Therefore today, when God permits his and our enemies to attempt to ruin us, armed on every side and with a great abundance of weapons and munitions, let us run to God, praying him to hear us, that we may experience help such as he gave to his servant David. Hence, we may profit by his example, and it is certain that what is said of him in this place will be accomplished in us – indeed in an even more excellent way, since God prefers this spiritual kingdom of our Lord Jesus Christ (under whom we are) to its ancient type. Hence, let us not doubt that God, however much he may arm our enemies to prove our constancy and humility, will give us power to resist them, and that he will provide all that we lack, and give us his hand. In brief, let us not doubt that, in everything and in every way, he will undergird us in such a manner that even our enemies and all their deeds will turn to good and to salvation (Rom. 8:28). Only let us endeavour to glorify him, and to strengthen ourselves more and more in his promises, knowing that in him alone we will find all our victories. And finally, let us not doubt that the heritage that he has promised us in heaven above will be reserved for us, after we have valiantly done battle here below.

Now let us prostrate ourselves before his majesty, recognising our faults, praying him that he may make us so to feel them that, being grieved by them, we might return to him in true repentance. Hence, may we walk according to his holy calling, so that it will not occur to us to forget and wander from the right path. But rather, when we have forsaken it, may he call us back by his means, so that we will never depart from it. Let us all, therefore, say: Almighty God, heavenly Father . . .

15

*God Glorified in David's Victory**

Again the Philistines came and spread themselves in the Valley of Rephaim and David asked counsel of the Lord, but he said: Do not go up, but turn behind them over against the mulberry trees . . . (2 Sam. 5:22–25).

We saw yesterday how God vitiates his enemies' judgement so that when they have the thing that they want to do easily within their grasp, he causes them to miss their opportunity – and then when they seek it, they do not find it. In the same way, God preserves his Church. He covers the eyes of the wicked so that they cannot benefit from what is offered them. Furthermore, we must note here that God casts down his enemies so that they end up seeking their own perdition. The Philistines could have remained in their stronghold, and then David would neither have sought nor troubled them, but they took up arms and threw themselves against him. God had determined to give him memorable victories, as we shall later see.

Now if David had begun the war, people would have considered him ungrateful, because the Philistines had received him in their country in his time of affliction, and had kindly provided somewhere for him to live there. People would have said that it was a bad way to repay such kindness. David, therefore, was under the kind of obligation that meant that he could not start a war against the Philistines, that is, unless it came from their side. This is where God knew how to dispose

*Thursday, July 2, 1562.

his works with absolute precision. So here were the Philistines, coming to start a war, and David, whether he wanted to or not, compelled to defeat them. And that was a situation which made him go further, as we shall see presently. This is the second point to remember: that after God has held back our enemies and has, as it were, lulled them to sleep so that they see nothing at all and know even less, similarly, he can move them to battle when he wishes, so that they spread out on the field and rush hither and thither without knowing why! But it is God who wants to lead them to their end.

Since this is so, let us learn to run to God when we see that we are hated and threatened, and that there are many people whose sole desire is to injure and totally destroy us. Then on the one hand, let us hope that God will not permit them to raise their hands to smite us, or execute the evil which their wicked will concocts against us. On the other, when things are easy and simple for them, let us pray that God will not permit them to carry out their intentions, any more than the Philistines did towards David. In the end, whenever it may please God to afflict us, it is in fact those who stand against him who will be the ones who are really confounded, and all their efforts will return on their own heads. The nets that they have spread will catch them – as is often said, the ditch which they have dug is for their own ruin, and they themselves will have to fall into it (Psa. 7:16; 9:16; 35:8; Prov. 26:27; 28:10). These sentences are often reiterated in Scripture, with the specific purpose that we might have more confidence in them. Let us use this present story to our advantage. When we see that the Philistines rose up in this way, it is as if God had put the sword in the hand of David and said, 'March forward and join battle now' – which he could not have done if he had not been given the opportunity.

Moreover, we can see here what the other passage says, namely, that the wicked man will be afraid for no reason (Psa. 53:5), that he will tremble when he hears the leaves of a tree stir (Lev. 26:36). Indeed, his very shadow will frighten him. It says that 'the Philistines marched to war, because David had been anointed king' (2 Sam. 5:17). This should not have excited them so much. David had been their guest, and now that he was king, he would have refrained from causing them any trouble – so why did they come to attack him? Often the wicked (as I have already mentioned) remain uneasy and their shadow scares them. But it was David's very nobility that forced open their eyes, for it is above all when the wicked see some gift of God that they become absolutely enraged. Here God shows that it was he who was persecuting them, for it was just the time when everyone in the world would have let them alone!

Well, this warns us that when we are hated by the wicked because God has given some grace to us, we should wait patiently. It is true that we should use the gifts of God for the welfare and benefit of others, but there are many who cannot stand seeing virtue, for they are so filled with venom against God that the moment they perceive some sign of his presence, they become like madmen. Hence, the enemies of God are like someone who is out of his mind, who sees the sun and wants to fight against it; or like a man with eye trouble, who cannot stand brightness! Similarly, God's enemies become violent and furious – without knowing why – as soon as they see the gifts and favours of his Spirit in believers. Well, let us get used to it, because we serve God, and even though we know that it has always been this way, let us pray that it may still please him to pour out upon us his good gifts. That, therefore, is what we must remember when we see that the kingdom of David so shocked and threatened the Philistines that it caused them to start a war.

Since the Davidic kingdom was a type of the kingdom of our Lord Jesus Christ, let us not find it strange if the world joins battle when Jesus Christ reigns in the midst of us. It is true, when you ask the reason why, that you will get no explanation other than that it is like fire and water: that the justice and kingdom of our Lord Jesus Christ, and the doctrine and order which can reform the world on the one hand, and the iniquity which is amongst unbelievers on the other hand [are opposed like these two basic elements]. For under pressure from Satan, they inevitably raise their fists against God and attempt to reverse all law and order. That is how they join battle. For instance, when we see thunder and lightning in the air, it is because the fire cannot tolerate the water and the cold resists the heat. Thus, the world will feel very threatened, since the wicked cannot tolerate the throne of our Lord Jesus Christ being established, since it might reform the world.

Nevertheless, we must notice that however strong David felt against the Philistines, still he did not trust in his own strength, but turned to God and asked him if he should go against them; that is, if he should actually join battle (2 Sam. 5:19). For these words 'go up' signify that. One can gather this from the thread of the text, because it is added that, in the second campaign, God said to him, 'You shall not go up, but you shall go behind them', as another way of saying 'do not put yourself in front' but 'circle behind them', which is the opposite (2 Sam. 5:23). Otherwise, it would seem strange when it says: 'Shall I go up against the Philistines?' (2 Sam. 5:19). For where were they? In the valley of Rephaim. 'To go up' in a valley would hardly make sense! We see, therefore, what the question of David really was. He knew for certain that he was king, that he could protect the people, and resist any enemies who came to make war on him without just cause. But he was uncertain of the means and the results, and that is why he took counsel of the Lord. As we said earlier, he had the privilege, which we do not have today, of interrogating God by means of the ephod.

Even so, we should apply this example to our own situation, for though we do not have the special revelation that was given at that time, God still declares that he always has available the Spirit of wisdom to guide us, and by it calls us to himself. Thus, when we do not know which way to turn and are in real perplexity, we must come straight to him, and pray to him to hear us and show us what is expedient for us. Even if today this particular benefit of God making himself known by revelation and through the prophets is no longer in the Church, our condition is none the worse for that. Instead, we have some compensation, as we said in the other passage, so that we ought not to be envious of the ancient fathers for how God assisted them. For although a hen leads her chicks when they are little, one must not be surprised when their mother no longer covers them, and no longer hides them beneath her wings after they become able to provide for themselves. It is the same with children whom you get up and put to bed! When they have become men, it would be unnatural if they still wanted to be treated in the same way! Hence, the reason that our Lord gave special revelations to the ancient fathers was to strengthen their weakness, for they were like little children. Our Lord Jesus Christ has appeared to us with the clarity of the Gospel which we now have. They did not have the fullness of such promises as we experience today. Our Lord had not yet used his mighty power in the same way that he has today. There were still obscure shadows then. Hence, it was necessary that the kinds of help that he gave should have been appropriate to that situation.

But though that is true, we do have the very thing that we wish for – that is, as we turn to God, we will always be governed by him; he will show us the roads which we must follow; he will give us his hand when we are straying. In brief, we will have wisdom and prudence as we need it. For although we do not have this sacerdotal system, we do have our Lord Jesus Christ, who is the truth of all these types, and by turning to him we will find that it is with good reason that the prophet Isaiah says that 'the Spirit of God will rest upon him; that is, the spirit of understanding, the spirit of judgement, and of discretion and of all virtue' (Isa. 11:2). All in all, when God sends adversities which hinder us, so that looking all around, we can see no way out, and do not even know which way to turn, it does not mean that he has failed us. Rather, let us seek him, knowing what our need is. Let us come (I say) to the remedy, and we will always have guidance, as David had. Through all our afflictions and distresses, we will always experience that he has not forgotten us. Now that is one point.

Furthermore, we must note that David was strengthened through this assurance that since God has spoken, the thing was done. Therefore, the more strongly he held to the promise of God, the better did he march forward without faltering (2 Sam. 5:20). This point certainly deserves attention, for that is how he was continually able to see through the audacity and recklessness of men. When we follow God and have assurance of his goodness and his strength, we will not act presumptuously during those times when we have to pass under a cloud. Let us live, then, as God has commanded, and all will go well. But if ever we want to lift a finger on the basis of our own desires, without any reference to the will of God by which he teaches us what is good and right, we will simply end up doing something foolish, and everything will be upside down and back to front because of our utter presumption. Now that is how he tests David: we are to be strengthened by faith to seek God (Isa. 35:3) when he calls us to obedient action.

Notice how the apostle to the Hebrews applies this passage from the prophet Isaiah to this doctrine (Heb. 12:12–13). For the prophet says to all those who preach the Gospel, 'Confirm trembling hands, and strengthen feeble knees'. The Apostle says that when we receive the doctrine of God in faith, it is the same as if we were drawing strength where formerly we were wavering and even paralysed, as though our arms and legs had been broken, and we were unable to move ourselves. If we have received the Word of God, it will give us such strength, I say, that we will be swift to apply ourselves to everything that God commands us. Now that is what this episode teaches us about David's immediate reaction to his dilemma.

Well, it finally says that after he went down, he won the victory, as he had been promised. Here we see that those who follow God and wait on him will not be frustrated for having waited. We do not have definite promises for this and that, but in general we know that God will always show himself as a Father towards us whenever we place our hope in him. That is why St Paul says that religion and true piety and fear of God give us his promises not only for the life to come, but for this present life (1 Tim. 4:8). When we possess these promises, let us not doubt that God will rise above everything that we could hope, insofar as we honour him by holding what he has declared to us by his Word to be certain and infallible.

It says that 'the Philistines left there their idols' (2 Sam. 5:21), from which we must remember that unbelievers will always abandon their devotions when they are in extremity.

There is no doubt that they had brought their idols so as to have the favour of God against David. We see again today that the idolaters carry their crosses and relics and shirts, which have touched no telling what shrine! Well, it has always been this way, and even unbelievers, not knowing that God is present or near to them unless they have visible signs, are always attached to them, just as today we see the same thing amongst the papists. Here, therefore, were the Philistines bringing their idols to the temple, to indicate that God would be gracious to them, and that they would fight under their banner. So much for that hope, for when they were defeated, they abandoned their idols and fled! That is what their devotion was like: nothing but a puff of wind with no endurance. It is true to say that unbelievers hold on to their foolish devotions only too obstinately. This venom can never be drawn out of them. But when God seriously afflicts them, then they do not know how to maintain their opinions with the same pride. We see this here just as though it were in a painting! Here were the Philistines, who thought that they had won everything by having carried out their idols to drive David back. Undoubtedly, they were boasting over it, as if they had already conquered their enemies. But with all this haughtiness and stubbornness, when the hand of God smote them, they would renounce their idols! Not that they did not retain in their hearts the errors in which they had been steeped, as well as their false fantasies, but yet their devotion became so cold that they threw away their gods! That is how it is, therefore, with all unbelievers.

For our part, we should learn that it is when we are afflicted that God wants to be especially honoured by us, for that is the opportune time to run to him. Therefore, instead of being like idolaters who pay no attention to their imaginary gods when they are deriving no profit from them, let us learn to glorify our God in the midst of all our miseries. When it pleases him to send us such extreme temptations that we know that they are for our sins, let us run to him more than ever; let us magnify his virtue and wait with patience, knowing that it is his office to lift up his own from the grave. That is another point which we must remember here.

Moreover, we see how little value there is in the false confidence of all the enemies of God. They may well lift themselves up as they wish, yet their pride and presumption will always come back upon them with devastating effect. Thus, as Scripture says, they will just find sadness and torment in all that they desire for their life and salvation (see Isa. 8:22). That is why idols are often said to be pain and tribulation in Scripture, for this is what God pays as wages to all those wretched unbelievers who transfer his honour to dead and insensible creatures, so that in the very place where they sought to rejoice, they will have to find the hell in which they will be buried (1 Sam. 15:23; Isa. 41:29; 66:3; Amos 5:5). Let us not be surprised to see the wicked inflated with pride like this. Instead, let us realise that God will use it all to bring about their downfall, and right where they would like to build and reach up to heaven (see Gen. 11:4), God will throw all their works down on to their heads, and cast them into the depths of hell.

As for this word in the verse which says that 'David and his men took the idols' (2 Sam. 5:21), we know that he did not do it to protect them or use them, but rather to get rid of them. That is why this word can also be used for 'burning', as some take it. In fact, from other passages of Scripture we can see that this usage of the word signifies 'to inflame', so that we could very properly explain it here to mean that David burned the idols. Anyhow, even if we do not accept this interpretation, the text says that he removed them from the midst, that is, that both he and his people destroyed them. Well, this teaches us that when God grants us victory over our enemies, we are to remove anything that they may have which could infect or contaminate us. It is quite certain that all their superstition and related customs are so infected with corruption that they pollute the land and dishonour God. Therefore, Scripture praises David's zeal to us here, in that he removed the pagan idols and did not want the land to be further polluted by them, for they were an intolerable abomination. The main reason Scripture points out this zeal of David as being such a wonderful virtue is to show that it did not come from him, but from God.

Well, his people are mentioned as well, to show that they

agreed with him in doing this. In what sense? It was insofar as they were led, for if David had not started, he would not have had such moral fibre in his army.

Hence, in the first place, we must note that we should not simply mock idols, but that we are to hate them so vehemently that we become unable to tolerate them. Let us practise what is written in Psalm 16, where David shows how he removed the idols of the Philistines. For there he says, 'Evil upon evil will fall upon those who worship strange gods. Well, as for me,' he says, 'I hate them so much that even their names will not be in my mouth' (Psa. 16:4). Just as David procured the honour of God, so we must detest any idolatry, and we must do so in the same way as he did, knowing that there is a sense in which our eyes are almost soiled when we turn them towards such filth and pollution. It is quite true that it is not for us to purge the land of idols. That must come from the authorities – though, in fact, there are many people who go about it lightly, without knowing how. It must not surprise us if God sometimes lowers their reputation when they throw themselves beyond the pale in this way. However, when we do have the means, and God gives us the liberty to do so, we must try as far as we can to scrape away all these infections and putrid sores, and eradicate their memory.

It says that David started, and his people followed him. From that we should learn that whoever is in authority must set an example to all the rest. In fact, when a man who knows how to guide others wants to be 'just one of the troops', he will not be excused if he says, 'The others have done no worse than I'. That may be so, but it is another reason that God wants you to show the way to others. Hence, let everyone take his vocation seriously, as well as the position to which he has been ordained, and when he has some position of leadership or responsibility over others, let him show them the right path, and march forward, hoping that God will strengthen the others when he carries out his duty. Then, insofar as each of us has received the gifts of the Spirit, we should apply them, so that we always employ the full measure which God has given to us to be used. Let us, at least, do our duty with them. Now that is the reason that some people go ahead of others to show the way, since God does not bestow his graces equally, and everyone will not have the same degree. In summary, this is what we must remember from this passage.

Scripture then adds that 'the name' was called 'Baal-Perazim, since God defeated his enemies there, and made them go down like water' (2 Sam. 5:20). However hard David may have fought, he still recognised that the victory was given to him by God. As he says in another passage, 'It is not by my arm nor by my sword, but in the name of God that I shall overcome my enemies' (Psa. 44:6–7). Well, he stated this in general of all the victories which he had won. Not that he did not conduct himself more bravely than all the kings and princes of today. But did he do it all? He concluded that his arm and his sword did nothing, and that God assisted him by his strength. Thus, he did the same thing in this passage. First, he said, 'It is the Lord who has defeated my enemies', and then once again he praises God's grace to him here even more, adding, 'Yes, he made them flow down like water before me'. Therefore, when we have faithfully carried out the particular responsibility to which God has called us, let us always be careful to recognise that we hold everything from him, and that all the means which we have used would amount to nothing unless he made them prosper. In brief, all the praises which men are quite used to usurping to themselves are reserved for him, and we would be nothing except in him. It is true that we can easily glorify ourselves, but the crucial principle here is that we should reject any glory which we could claim for ourselves, so that we might know, instead, what it is to glorify ourselves in God. Now that is one point.

Well, when David praised the victory in this way, it was because he clearly understood that it was humanly impossible for his enemies to have thrown themselves down like this, if God had not been watching over it and had not moved his hand. Now here is the reason why we obscure the favours of God or bury them altogether. Our problem is that we fail to recognise the seriousness of the dangers that we have been in, and yet, at the same time, we over-emphasise our solutions, which were in fact nothing. David, on the contrary, did not presume on his own strength, and he also knew that his enemies had an arrogant desire to ruin the whole country, and that he and his army would have been driven back if God had not taken care of him. Now that is what caused the collapse in which God made his enemies go down like water.

Again, David was not content with having given thanks to God for this great outcome, but he wanted there to be a perpetual memorial for time to come. That is why the name 'Baal-Perazim' was given to that place, because God, as we have already seen, showed himself master over those whom he broke and ruined, making them fall down like water. This warns us not only to recognise, personally and in private, the goodness of God in all the help that we have received from him, or to acknowledge it and praise him just for one day, but also to see to it, as far as we can, that his praises are celebrated from age to age, and that those who come after our time will be strengthened and receive instruction from what we have known and felt. That, therefore, is what we must remember when it says that David wanted the place to be made a memorial for time to come, so that people would know that God had assisted him against his enemies.

Well, then it adds that 'the Philistines again came and camped in the valley of Rephaim', as before, 'and then David inquired of God'. He was told 'that he should not go up', that is, that he should not place himself in front, but that he should go round behind them and wait until God signalled him 'from the top of the trees, in which there would be some wind', and that 'then he should spring on them' and immediately they would be defeated (2 Sam. 5:22–24). In this account, we have first to note that when God has given us one victory against our enemies, it does not mean that we will be relieved of enemies for the rest of our life, or exempt from annoyances and troubles. For we are involved in a war against Satan, who never ceases doing evil, governing and driving the wicked, so that when we have escaped one time, we must prepare for the second and third, and as many times as it pleases God to try us. Therefore, let us not be like those who rejoice when God has helped them once, thinking that it is done and that it will never happen again! On the contrary, when we have experienced the help of God, let us expect that he will still cause us many other conflicts. Let us hope in him, not finding it strange if the enemies of God do everything they can to overthrow us. Sometimes, when they seem to have been subdued, they start again, for the devil whips them up into such a fury that their machinations actually turn out to their own perdition. Hence, no matter how often we see that God wants to try us in various ways, we should realise that God has shown us the way. We must conform ourselves to him, as David had to in the second raid by the Philistines, where it says that they spread out as before.

Even if David had started the war, one would still have said that this second raid was an absolutely desperate measure. For David was content with having defeated and overturned them, and yet they came to renew the war! This admonishes us that the more our enemies go beyond bounds and become totally unreasonable, the more God will punish their excess. Therefore, let us not be surprised when we see them enraged against us, for it is a sign that God wants to lead them to perdition. Just as he dealt with the Philistines, he will also do the same towards those who are our enemies.

Nevertheless, we see how David continued to run to God. We may see some people sufficiently affected on one occasion that when God calls them to himself, they come. What is incredible is that they are ardent in their devotion one minute – and they do not remember it the next. This is why David's perseverance is set before us here. For he did not seek the will of God just once, he did it again. This is why it has been confirmed that those who seek God find him, and that the hope of the faithful will never be confounded. Now that shows us how the grace that David had received earlier acted like a thorn, spurring him more and more to praise God, seek him, and find his total refuge in him.

We could find God's response to David rather strange when he says, 'Do not go up, but go away, as though defeated, and hide yourself, and await them there, for you are not to budge or move at all, until I give you the signal'. What was the need for all that? Why did God not accomplish his work? Why did he not allow David to pursue the Philistines, and why was there now more difficulty than there was in the first defeat? One could use this response to argue against God. Indeed, if men choose to give way to their wild imagination, as they often do so presumptuously, it is certain that they will always raise an argument against God! We also may easily have set our tongues wagging, ready to contradict him. We will always deceitfully dispute with God in our own minds. But insofar as we have genuine wisdom, let us learn to recognise that everything that God has done is good, even when the reason is not at all clear to us.

It is true that there was some reason why God commanded David to go around behind his enemies and not to attack them directly. For our faith must be proved in various ways, and if David had always conquered his enemies in one way, he would not have been aware of the help of God as keenly as he was. His name would not have been as glorified as it was when people saw how he scattered his enemies in so many different ways. Moreover, there was another benefit in David's recognising that God could smite his enemies both in the back and in the front. He could punish them now one way, and now another, and cleverly surprise them. In other words, when one means fails us, God has more than a million in his hand, and that is what David recognised. Let us carefully recognise that when God uses different methods which we cannot understand with our own minds, we must humble ourselves and adore his wisdom. When he is hidden from us and we cannot see the reason why, still we must turn everything over to him and accept as good everything that he declares to be in his will. That is how 'the foolishness of God will overcome all the wisdom of the world' (1 Cor. 1:25). Well, he calls it folly, not that it actually is in reality but, rather, that is the common opinion of it. When we cannot discover why God does thus and so, there is such arrogance in our nature that we want to be his judges and boldly condemn him! That is the context in which St Paul speaks of the 'foolishness of God'. Some do believe that that is what it is, but it overcomes all wisdom, for after men have tried all sorts of trickery in an attempt to find some way to contradict God, they can only remain confounded. Well then, that is one point – that God takes care of his people in such a strange way that we cannot understand why he should be using this approach. But when God's way seems foolish to us, let us learn to receive with deep sobriety and reverence what we know has proceeded from him.

Moreover, when there is some variation in his works, let us remember that St Paul says that the wisdom of God takes many forms, and that the purpose of this is to keep us in the dark (Eph. 3:9). However, if there is some variation in his works, it is for our good and benefit. We have already shown that if the Philistines had been conquered in the same way, so that David had immediately beaten them down, people would certainly have said that he defeated them because they were already intimidated, for he naturally had more courage after his first victory. That is how men always mask, as far as they can, God's power and moral superiority, so that it will not be recognised as it should be. And that is why he commanded David to begin by rushing down on his enemies. Indeed, although the Philistines had been conquered in the previous campaign and Saul was already dead, God still wanted to test the obedience of David when he sent him to join battle with his enemies, who could have overwhelmed him. But instead of attacking them head-on, God told David to do quite the reverse, for after his victory, God wanted him to look like a coward and appear to seek out his enemies secretly. That was particularly to test his humility and modesty.

Hence, let us note carefully that when God does not want to arm us to defeat our enemies openly, it is to know whether we will obey him, making us march by long, circuitous routes, just like David, with nothing to do but drag our feet sluggishly! Notice here the reason for this difference of method when it says that even after David had won such an excellent victory, God sent him in secret so that he would act as though he did not dare look at his enemies, until God finally led them to their ruin. Of course, we also see that God wanted to be glorified in this second victory, so that it would not be attributed to men. He wanted to show, by using alternative means, that he has many ways, incomprehensible to us, to defeat our enemies in absolutely every time of need. Thus, if we are stripped of human help, we are not to doubt that his divine help, which is infinite, will be employed in our favour. Let us not doubt that we will obtain victory through him when everything, high and low, when the heavens and the earth (I say) combine to ruin us. All of them, with all their scheming, will not prevail in the end.

Now let us bow down before his majesty, recognising all the faults of which we are guilty, and praying him that he may bury them so deep, that we may become so truly displeased with them that we do not continue in them. And may he so reclothe us with his power that we will walk in pure obedience wherever he calls us, that with true courage we will march under his banner to resist our enemies, that is, our spiritual enemies, and that we will not cease to fight valiantly until he has given us the final victory, calling us into his eternal rest. May he bestow this grace not only upon us, but upon all peoples and nations of the earth . . .

16

*The True Worship of God**

Again David assembled all the chosen men of Israel, thirty thousand. Thus David arose and went, and all the people who were with him of the men of Judah, to bring up the ark of God, of which the name is called: the name of the Lord of hosts who dwells between the Cherubim upon it . . . (2 Sam. 6:1–7).

We are told here that when David realised that his kingdom was at peace, he turned his attention to restoring the integrity of the worship of God. In the time of Saul, as we gather from the First Book of Chronicles, there had been a great falling away so that the ark of God was practically forgotten and despised (1 Chron. 13:3). When he saw that he could not prosper unless the Lord was worshipped in purity, he recognised that God had made and established him as king for that very purpose. David assembled 30,000 men, as we read here (2 Sam. 6:1). Apparently, we have a discrepancy here from the other passage, where we read that he assembled all Israel from Egypt to the other end of the land, which reached to the Euphrates (1 Chron. 13:5). If he had literally assembled all Israel, the number would have been infinite. But the Scripture is simply using everyday language. When one gathers people together from all over a country, one can say that the whole country is assembled. But there it is speaking of his deliberations with his captains and officers (1 Chron. 13:1). Here it simply says that he gathered everyone together.

The way that he assembled them is specified in the other

*Friday, July 3, 1562.

passage, where he enquired of them whether it would not be good to bring back the ark of God from where it was. When the matter was concluded, we read that he published it throughout the whole country and assembled the people. In other words, no city or town failed to send several people – perhaps five or ten to represent the population. These were the chosen ones, the cream of the crop. So in that sense, the whole country was assembled into a great company which acted in the name of all. That is how we harmonise what on the surface seems contradictory.

We must keep in mind what we saw above, that the ark of God had been in a borrowed place in the house of Abinadab (1 Sam. 7:1) since its return by the Philistines, who had captured it. In explaining that unbelievers could not have had the ark except by permission of God, we have mentioned the passage from the Psalms, where God subjected his name to similar contempt in order to punish the iniquities of the people and make them more ashamed (Psa. 78:61). So the men of Kirjath-jearim received the ark and took it to Gibeon, where it was lodged in the house of Abinadab.

Now the ark was in a place to which it had not yet been assigned. Moreover, we can gather that it was seriously profaned. We are clearly told that people were not seeking God in the time of Saul (1 Chron. 13:3). Of course, there were always some faithful people (1 Sam. 14:19); indeed, Saul took the priest with him when he went to battle (1 Sam. 14:36). Although there was an outward appearance of religion, it was very coldly and grudgingly performed. We must realise that it takes far more than making a formal profession and merely declaring that we are God's people and want to serve him. When we hear what was pronounced by the Spirit of God, it should encourage us to seek him voluntarily, and not in such a cold manner.

If someone had asked all the people in the time of Saul, 'Do you not want to seek God?,' each one would have replied, 'Yes, this is my intention'. But so what? God disdained their talk, and declared that they were despising and rejecting him, and in fact denying him. Why? Because they had no zeal and no pure and true affection for him. Let us, therefore, be careful not to seek God half-way. On the contrary, let us earnestly seek his face, driving ourselves forward as we realise that he is the mainspring of our whole life, upon whom we must concentrate all our thoughts and study in order to be pleasing to him.

It is true that David was not given further information concerning where God wanted to be worshipped (1 Chron. 21:18; 2 Chron. 3:1). We will see later that when Mount Zion was finally chosen, these words of the Psalms were fulfilled: 'I rejoiced with those who said to me: Let us go and worship God in this holy mountain, Jerusalem will be his dwelling, and Zion will be the place of his habitation; then God shall have a lasting abode' (Psa. 122:1; 99:9; 76:2; 1 Kings 8:13). It was not for mortal men to assign him a place. Moses had said, 'When the Lord your God has shown you where his name is to be called upon, and where you are to come and worship and sacrifice' (Deut. 12:11). So we see, then, that God reserved to himself the authority to declare where they should come solemnly to worship him.

David presumed to remove the ark from the house of Abinadab to another place, without being specifically commanded to do so, because he expected God to do what he had announced through Moses. He wanted the ark to be lodged in the centre of the country – away from the remote location where it had been left by the people when the Philistines were forced to return it, after God's hand grievously afflicted them. Because the ark was in a corner, it could scarcely be honoured as it deserved and the people who opposed it had an excuse for not coming to the solemn feasts, as the law commanded. That, in turn, caused religion to grow cold, in addition to the fact that men were far from devoted to it. That is why David brought back the ark: so that it would be in a place where people could come more easily, and so that everyone could more readily do their duty. For men seek nothing but excuses to draw further away from God, as we see too frequently. When things are not easy, we think that we can 'wash our hands of the matter'. We pretend that we would like to do it, but lack the opportunity. That is why David wanted to remove every obstacle, so that those already too careless could not say that the ark of God was in any out-of-the-way place too far to reach.

We must gather from this that insofar as we see the same kind of laziness in ourselves, along with a lack of inclination to worship God and an absence of convenient means of worship, then we will never profit from worship as we should. Why is it that the Church chooses the hours which are the most appropriate, a definite place to assemble, and a bell to ring, with all these matters carefully arranged? It is because we humans have practically no desire to give ourselves to God unless we are first drawn to do so. Therefore, on the one hand let us note how feeble we are when we ought to be stirring ourselves to honour God, and then let us use every available means to move ourselves to break through this coldness and laziness to which we are so strongly inclined. That, in sum, is what we must remember from this passage.

Now it says that 'the ark carried his name: the eternal God dwells between the cherubim' (2 Sam. 6:2). Some explain it: where on the ark the name of God was revealed. In fact, the passage in Chronicles cannot be taken otherwise (1 Chron. 13:6). But because this word is repeated here – 'The name (of the eternal), the name of God' – undoubtedly the Holy Spirit wanted to state this honourable title so as to emphasise that this ark was a definite sign and seal of the presence of God. Indeed, Scripture speaks in this way all the way through. Psalm 24 says: 'Lift up your heads, great gates, so that the Lord of Hosts may enter in' (Psa. 24:7). David addressed the same words to the temple, as if he were saying: 'Here is God who wants to make his entry'. Therefore, his majesty must be known even to the doors, that they may be lifted up in order to receive such grandeur. It is certain that this was nothing but an ark, but it was named, as I have said, 'the Living God'. And why? Because the promise was given, and Scripture often says: 'You shall come before the face of God' (1 Chron. 16:11; Psa. 100:1); and then: 'Lord, according as you have commanded your people, I have ever sought thy face, and will yet seek it' (Psa. 27:8). And what was this face of God? It was this ark in which the Law was placed (1 Kings 8:9; Heb. 9:4).

In order to understand better what this means, let us note in the first place that the majesty and glory of God are incomprehensible. Not only do we not see God with our eyes, since he is of a spiritual essence, but when we apply all our senses to know him, we will certainly be dazzled a hundred times over, before we can even approach him. For we are too crude and weak. We can only crawl upon the earth, while 'the heaven of heavens cannot contain him' (1 Kings 8:27), as the other passage says. So when we want to approach God, it is certain that we will not be able to and that he is totally inaccessible to us. Therefore, he must come down to us when we cannot reach up to him. And how does he come down? It is not that he changes his place as far as his essence is concerned, but he must make himself known in a familiar manner. So when he conforms himself to our smallness, he does it only insofar as he abases himself. Not that there is change in him, but his coming down refers to our capacity.

Therefore, consider how God, who from all times has had pity on the crude capacities of men, has for that very reason come down to them, since they could not reach up to him. How has he come down? He has done so in the fashion of men, as if to say: 'Here am I, and when you come through these means, it is the same as if I were manifest to you and you were seeing me with the naked eye' – that is what the ark meant. It was a means by which God made himself known to the people so they would be without excuse and could not say: 'We do not know which way to begin when we ought to pray to God and honour him. We do not know how he will be our Protector, and how we will feel his help.' On the contrary, the ark was a standing witness that God wanted to dwell in the midst of the people.

Notice that there was absolutely no idol or representation of God in it, because that would have served to hold the people in superstition; rather, the Law was enclosed in this box. This shows us that God declares himself only in his Word. So when we want to have a living image of him, we must not forge idols, of stone or wood or any other material, but we must know him in his Word. If we fall away from his Word, we wander astray; we will be like vagabonds – indeed, like straying beasts.

When God says that he wants to show his face, it is eminently reasonable for us to believe that, because he placed his Law in the ark – the two tables which he had written with his own power, without human help (Exod. 31:18; Deut. 10:4–5). This is what we must remember.

Again, it is not enough to state that God must not be represented by statues and paintings, but this declaration ought to make the people reach above the heavens. Indeed, we see how the Jews were reproved in their superstitions for thinking that they could keep God contained (1 Kings 8:27; Acts 17:24). Solomon, in dedicating the temple, clearly told them that they could not enclose God in any particular habitation, by saying: 'The heavens cannot contain God', and 'he cannot dwell in a place made by the hand of man'. Whenever the Jews glorified themselves by saying: 'The temple of the Lord, the temple of the Lord' (Jer. 7:4), they wanted to keep God almost as their prisoner. That is why Isaiah cries with a loud voice: 'And what place do you think to build for me? For the earth is only my footstool, and my seat is above the heavens, and do you think to make me a house here?' (Isa. 66:1). 'Do you come to seek me in a superstitious manner so that you can say that I am with you?' This shows how the Jews abused this familiarity which God had granted them.

Thus, we must note that when God declares himself to us, we must not cling to any earthly thing, but must elevate our senses above the world, and lift ourselves up by faith to his eternal glory. In sum, God comes down to us so that then we might go up to him. That is why the sacraments are compared to the steps of a ladder. For as I have said, if we want to go up there, alas, we do not have wings; we are so small that we cannot make it. God, therefore, must come down to seek us. But when he has come down, it is not to make us dull-witted; it is not to make us imagine that he is like us. Rather, it is so that we might go up little by little, by degrees, as we climb up a ladder one rung at the time. The sacraments are like this, and the ark was like a sacrament – at least in principle. The people had to be moved to seek God in a very tangible manner.

When Scripture says that God was between the cherubim,

that did not make the ark into an idol. For the cherubim had their faces hidden, and their wings covered the ark (Exod. 25:20) to show that God was invisible in his essence, and that even the angels adored him in all humility, and that there was a shadow so obscure over the ark that making God a mouth or nose or anything else terrestrial was totally out of the question. So much, then, for the ark.

Now let us apply this to ourselves, for we are no more competent than the Jews. Yet we need God to make himself small, so that we can have access to him, otherwise we would be completely shut out. However, he does not make himself so small because he wants his glory to be lessened, but rather he does this out of goodness to lift us up to admire his glory and to adore him with the reverence that he deserves.

When we have access to the preached Word, God speaks in a common and ordinary fashion to us. It is an illustration of his condescension. Hence, the preaching of the Gospel is like God descending to earth in order to seek us. We must not abuse this simplicity of the Word of God by disdaining it. Rather, we must receive it all the more, recognising that he indeed deigns to transfigure himself, so to speak, that we might approach him. He is not content with giving us his Word, but he adds baptism to confirm it. When we are baptised – though only a little water is used – it stands for crucifying our old man, for renewing our souls, and for being united with the angels. Baptism is performed to ensure that we inherit the eternal kingdom, to make us enjoy adoption, by which we are companions and brothers of the angels – but can a little water do that? The point, of course, is that since God has come down to us (in this symbol), we must go up to him (in faith).

It is the same way with the Lord's Supper, which the papists greatly abuse and corrupt by wanting God to be present in it, and wanting him to come down in an earthly fashion to suit their appetite. But we are shown here that he descends to us, not to stupefy or bind our senses in these low and feeble things. The papists are far too dull-witted, for under the excuse that our Lord Jesus Christ has left a testimony and a pledge of his body and blood under the bread and wine, so that men might know that truly he is the nourishment of their life, what have they done? They have turned it into an idol, as though he entered into a piece of bread and wanted to be adored there in a gross fashion, with the result that men become so bewitched with such poison that they have no longer enough discretion to discern anything. Even this is not enough for them, for under the excuse of this presence, they say he had to hide in a sacramental cup and be held captive in it as a prisoner. Furthermore, they handle the sacrament like apes and make a farce of it.

Well, when we see how very much inclined the world is to superstition, we must all the more remember the rule which I have given: namely, that when God has come down, it is not that we should remain down here, but rather that we should be lifted on high to adore him spiritually, and that we should thereby rise above the world by our faith.

Nevertheless, in order that we might know that God does not want to frustrate us, and that the signs which he gives us are not frivolous and empty baggage, like toys for little children, it says that God truly dwells between the cherubim. This does not mean that his essence is enclosed in the ark, but that he wishes to display his virtue there for the salvation of his people. Similarly, today in the waters of baptism, it is the same as if the blood of our Lord Jesus Christ poured down from heaven to water our souls and cleanse them from their uncleanness. When we have the bread and wine in the Lord's Supper, it is the same as if Jesus Christ were coming down from heaven and making himself our food, so that we could be filled with him. We must not, therefore, take these signs as visible things and figures which are to feed our spiritual senses, but are to realise that God joins his virtue and truth to them, so that the thing and the effect are joined to the figure. We must not put asunder what God has joined together. That, in sum, is what we must keep in mind from the statement that the ark of God has the name: the name of the God of hosts, dwelling between the cherubim.

In fact, that is also why David invokes him in this way: 'Lord God of Israel, who dwells between the cherubim, hear my prayer, look upon me in pity; continue no longer to afflict me as you have done' (Psa. 80:1). Now if David had not had the ark as a sign, he might have become lost in seeking God. But he knew by the Law that God wanted the ark to be a pledge of his presence. He was certain of this and assured himself that he would be heard, and that he could perceive God or communicate familiarly with God, as though he inhabited the country of Judah as his own residence.

Of course, today we have no such ark, but we do have the fulfilment of all that it implied in our Lord Jesus Christ. Even the covering of the ark was truly a type of Jesus Christ (Exod. 25:17ff.). However much one may deduce about Christ from this 'covering', it certainly means 'propitiation', in that sins are blotted out. Therefore, Jesus Christ is called our propitiator today. He is called our propitiation so that we may no longer be taken up with these ancient symbols in themselves, but rather that God may draw us to himself by using these humble signs as a help in our present weakness (see Heb. 4:16; 9:5; Rom. 3:25).

Let us, therefore, learn that every single time that we want to invoke God, if his majesty is terrible to us, or if we want to say that he is too far from us and that we cannot have access to him, even though we recognise our infirmity – still let us recall that the prophet says that he is Emmanuel, which means: God with us (Isa. 7:14). Let us also remember that our Lord Jesus Christ, who dwells in eternal glory, has left his mark upon us by baptism; that we have the knowledge of him by his Word, which assures us that he will employ his power in our lives, and that we will be filled with his own substance in the Lord's Supper. In brief, he dwells in us by faith, as St Paul says (Eph. 3:17). This is how we must follow David, making use of the humble means which are available to us – whenever we are prevented by our lack of trust from coming to God.

Further, it says that the 'ark of God was placed in a new cart' (2 Sam. 6:3). David cannot be excused for doing this, because this duty was assigned to the Kohathites, who were a portion of the tribe of Levi (Num. 4:15). They should have carried the ark; since God had ordained it this way, it should have been done in obedience to him. Why did they tamper with his requirements? This shows us what happens when people are not used to participating in the worship of God, and are total novices in it.

Here was David, who had the high priest with him and the Levites following him, who could have taught him. He had the gift of prophecy as a master and doctor in the church (1 Sam. 16:13). Nevertheless, he did not know how to carry out what was expressly stated in the Law concerning this matter. Instead, he took a new cart. What was the cause of this failure except that the people had increasingly adulterated themselves, were not accustomed to the worship of God, and were ignorant of the simple elements of it?

We have certainly seen this sort of thing, and we see it again today in the corruptions and villainies of the papacy, which are so bad that one scarcely knows which way to start restoring the true order of the Church of God. Instead, we see very little willingness among the papists to do this. There are many who will make a profession of the Gospel, but when you want to lead them to a pure rule of practice, when you do not want to tolerate a half-way religion but rather a pure and whole religion, they reply: 'We do not want any of that!'

Why? You cannot reclaim them and make them submit to the obedience of God, simply because they have been stupefied by their pollutions and nourished by their villainy. Let us be aware, then, that we are – with good reason – greatly exhorted to take thought of ourselves day and night (Matt. 26:41; Col. 4:2), and to be vigilant (1 Pet. 5:8) to know how God wants to be worshipped and served. That is why we are to apply all our powers to serve him and are to bring back to memory things which we may have too quickly forgotten. This, in sum, is what we must remember when it says that David took a new cart to carry the ark of God. The ark should have been placed, instead, on the shoulders of the Kohathites, who would have done their duty cheerfully if David had required it of them. His failure to do so showed contempt, both on his part and on the part of the people, for since they were so asleep in their religion, they were truly novices in it, which is why they did not follow the rule of the Law.

Certainly, they could have given some reason for taking a new cart – but these reasons came from imitating the Philistines and from their own ideas. But when it is a question of the service of God, it must be separated from everything which belongs to this terrestrial life. Our filthy and profane affairs must not be mingled with what is sacred. We must, when we eat and drink, says St Paul, do all in the name of God (1 Cor. 10:31). All must be blessed and sanctified by him. But nonetheless, we must clearly be separated (from merely human ideas) in the worship of God. Thus, for example, we cannot mingle our prayers and petitions with our worries, and so when we have to pray, we have to lay aside everything which is otherwise good. If we try to pray to God in the manner of unbelievers, our prayer is a pollution and sacrilege. A woman, for instance, is doing well when she does her housework, makes up her bed, cleans the house, boils the pot, and governs her children; all of this is very appropriate. But on the other hand, if like some of the papists, she half-heartedly mumbles through her devotions while she is doing these things, muttering the Lord's Prayer and seven psalms while she is working her way through the house with her mind on other matters, in effect God and the devil are thrown together. Is this not a sheer mockery of God, who wants 'to be served and worshipped in spirit and truth' (John 4:24)?

Hence, we must separate ourselves from everything which concerns our earthly welfare when we have to pray to God. Moreover, when we want to serve him in purity, if we instead think of our domestic affairs, our needs, our household, and our possessions, then we cause villainous and detestable confusion. We certainly profane the name of God by doing this.

Of course, David had a certain amount of good intention when he chose a new cart, which had not carried anything else, to carry the ark. But that by no means totally excuses him, for 'obedience is better than sacrifice', as we have seen in the First Book of Samuel (1 Sam. 15:22). Since this regulation was given by the Law, it should have been observed, but this was not done, because the people had neglected the Law for a long time.

The text adds that Abinadab walked in front of the ark and 'his sons one after the other led it' (2 Sam. 6:3). Now it could well be (as we shall see more fully) that there was some ambition involved, and that this man very much wanted to show that he had lodged the ark of God and that his house had been like the inner sanctuary. But still, he was showing reverence towards God when he and his sons conducted the ark. Indeed, we see that he did not resist the removal of the ark, as many do who are resentful against God when they lose such a privilege. Here was Abinadab, who had been like the host of God. This was a greater dignity than anything else. But they came to remove the ark, so that his house was stripped of this honour, which excelled all that is excellent in this world, for there is no royal sceptre which can be compared with the temple of God. That is the degree to which the ark had ennobled his house. If Abinadab had been annoyed when David came to remove the ark, he could simply have left the scene, to show that he was compelled by force and that he could not have resisted the king with the 30,000 men who kept him company. So it was a sign of humility and modesty when he led the ark and voluntarily ceded this privilege, which he had enjoyed for a long time. He gave visible proof that he was not sad that the ark should be put in a place where all the people could easily come to worship God, so that everyone should be encouraged to go there, and all the regions of Israel might assemble there, as was commanded in the Law (Deut. 12:2f.).

On the other hand, it says that 'David and Israel sang a hymn to God, that is with instruments' and music (2 Sam. 6:5). David assembled such a multitude that all might worship God with one accord. He well knew that God had not made himself known to him alone, but had established the whole family of Abraham. Thus, David wanted everyone to imitate him, and showed the way for there to be mutual accord, that small and great might demonstrate that they wanted to serve God. Here we see the true use of hymns: we are to encourage one another to celebrate and magnify the name of God in our hymns (Eph. 5:19–20). It would be enough for each one to pray to God in his heart, and for each one to give him thanks. This is the true worship of God: 'Call upon me in the day of your trouble' (Psa. 50:15), says the Lord, 'and then praise me when you know that I have answered'. We can surely do that from the heart, but our mouth must state ever more clearly the very concerns which cause us to pray to God. Even though everyone can still privately invoke God by themselves, we have this privilege of assembling in public in order to testify to our faith, and then to encourage others by our example. When we pray to God here in the church, and sing the psalms, it is not to show ourselves off, as hypocrites do, but to declare that we seek nothing but that God may be glorified among us. Our assembling in his name also should certainly serve as a thorn to prick us because of our laziness. That is how we are to encourage one another (Heb. 3:13), and that is why people were not to sing hymns of praise to God for only a temporary period of time, but until the end of the world. Since we are surrounded with flesh and blood, we need means such as these (to lift our spirit up to God), and thus the obligation to sing hymns of praise is common both to us and to the ancients.

There is a difference, however, concerning the instruments of music. It would be nothing but mimicry if we followed David today in singing with cymbals, flutes, tambourines and psalteries. In fact, the papists were seriously deceived in their desire to worship God with their pompous inclusion of organs, trumpets, oboes and similar instruments. That has only served to amuse the people in their vanity, and to turn them away from the true institution which God has ordained. We must, at the same time, be aware of all the privileges which we have in common with the fathers who have lived under the Law and, on the other hand, be aware of the things wherein they are separated from us. All those things which we have in common with them are lasting, and must be maintained until the end of the world. But we are not to keep observing these things which were only for the time of the Law, unless we want to make a confused mixture which confounds heaven with earth. In a word, the musical instruments were in the same class as sacrifices, candelabra, lamps and similar things. There is nothing that the papists have not turned to some use. Because there was the chandelier with the lamps (in the Old Testament), thus there had to be candles (in the church); because there was perfume then, there had to be incense now. There were ritual washings then, so there had to be holy water now. The papists, in brief, have shown themselves in every possible way to be apes without any discretion!

As I have said, we must notice that what God had instituted for the time of symbols (before the coming of our Lord Jesus Christ) must be put aside and not enforced today. It is true that God ought to be heartily praised, both by musical instruments and by mouth. But it is another matter when we conduct the worship of God in church. If we want to sing praises in the name of God, we would do much better to have psalms instead of common dissolute songs. We sing in order to give him thanks – and not in order to produce a solemn ceremony as a meritorious work that we do for God. Those who take this approach are reverting to a sort of Jewishism, as if they wanted to mingle the Law and the Gospel, and thus bury our Lord Jesus Christ. When we are told that David sang with a musical instrument, let us carefully remember that we are not to make a rule of it. Rather, we are to recognise today that we must sing the praises of God in simplicity, since the shadows of the Law are past, and since in our Lord Jesus Christ we have the truth and embodiment of all these things which were given to the ancient fathers in the time of their ignorance or smallness of faith. They did not have such revelation as we have today in the Gospel.

In sum, we see how God was adored both in truth and in type. He was adored in truth because, in giving him praises, people magnified his name and recognised that all came from him. Nevertheless, there were types joined with the reality, insofar as they were necessary at that time. Today, we certainly have some ceremony, but it is not like old times. We have it in sobriety. The pure worship of God today is called heavenly, in that it is not enclosed amid these shadows, and with a half-effect. This is the meaning of the account of their moving the ark.

The text then adds that 'Uzzah touched it and God smote him' (2 Sam. 6:6–7) because of his hastiness. But that cannot be explained today; it is reserved for tomorrow.

Let us be content with knowing that David's intention was to awaken the people, who had for a long time been asleep towards God, to seek him. He wanted to put the ark in a place appropriate and available for all the people, so as to stir them up to do all that the Law commanded. David did this, not out of superstition nor against the ordinance and command of God, but to influence the people, because the true religion had for a long time been put under foot and forgotten. In spite of that, he endeavoured to honour and treat the name of God in all reverence. Let us also be aware that when the name of the ark is spoken, the very name of the eternal God is given so that we might learn to embrace the promises of God in his sacraments. His name is given so that whenever we truly seek him with a faith that has no superstition mixed with it to hold us back, we may not doubt that we have him with us and, indeed, inside us – so that we may go to him in true affection, looking for his eternal glory.

Now let us prostrate ourselves before the majesty of our good God in recognition of our faults, praying that he may make us so to feel them as to draw us to him more and more; and to incline us to his service in such a way that we do not imitate the hypocrites, who have only forms and external ceremonies. But rather [let us act] out of a heartfelt affection. May we be so enthusiastic to sing his praises that it becomes our main pursuit. May we so profit each other that, with one accord, we proclaim that truly all our good consists and lies in him, and may that encourage us more and more to come to seek him that we may find rest. May he not only bestow this grace upon us, but upon all people and nations of the earth . . .

17

*Lessons from the Death of Uzzah**

When they came to the threshing floors of Nachon, Uzzah stretched forth his hand to the ark of the Lord and held it; for the oxen shook it. And the Lord was very angry with Uzzah, and God smote him there for his error, and he died there near the ark of God . . . (2 Sam. 6:6–12).

We have here a very strange story, that a man attempting to honour God, burning with a good and holy devotion, was punished like a criminal. Now this certainly offends our feelings. We know that the main cause of offending God is our wicked will: it is the root of all sins and of the contempt that we have for God, which makes us rebels against him, so that we cannot subject ourselves to the rule which he gives us. But on the other hand, when our desire is to glorify him, and we have no ill will in us, even if we have erred and made a mistake, still it seems that God ought not to hold it against us, especially when we do not wilfully get out of line or go beyond the rule which he gave us. Especially this would seem to be so when we are not being rash and superstitious, as if we were saying: 'This is what I find attractive, and so this is the way I will do it', but rather we do it in simplicity. It seems that this ought to be acceptable to God. Well, here was Uzzah, who was walking in front of the ark of God. He saw that it was in danger of falling, because the oxen were shaking it. He wanted to put his hands on it to hold it up. But he died there. Was being zealous that the ark of God should not be shamed a

*Saturday, July 4, 1562.

crime worthy of punishment? Well, if not, he should have remained unpunished. What is the case, then?

Let us take closer heed to ourselves here, and not be like those profane people who want to call God to account. You see many of these people who, not daring to blaspheme openly, murmur when the judgements of God do not agree with their understanding and fantasies. But let us note that the Scripture so often warns us – not without cause – that the judgements of God are a profound abyss. This should make us utterly astonished, so that we fear God and his judgements, and find good all that he does – even when we are confused over it. Let this sober attitude be ours: that is, to be totally persuaded that nothing proceeds from God which is not just and irreprehensible. If many of his works still do not agree with our appetites or our reason, let us remain his captive, and realise that it is quite necessary that God should surpass all our senses.

For what is his wisdom? It comprehends both heaven and earth, and yet cannot be perceived, because it is infinite. And what is our reason and intelligence? It is nothing but a little drop, so to speak. Therefore, it would be preposterous on our part to want to subject the judgements of God to our fantasy, and to the way we imagine it ought to be, as though we wanted to envelop heaven and earth in a little box! But the example which Scripture gives us here ought to turn us away from such attempts. For if we could have been the judge, Uzzah would certainly have been swiftly absolved. Why? Because he who does something with a good motive (says the proverb) cannot be considered bad. The intention of Uzzah was good, as far as one can judge, for it would seem that he was moved by a virtuous zeal that deserved a reward, rather than chastisement, as if he had offended God. Nevertheless, after men have squawked all that they want to, they still remain confused, and God always closes their mouths, for he clearly knows how to justify himself when he pleases, as the psalmist says (Psa. 51:4).

Let us remember, therefore, what it says here – namely, that God justly punished Uzzah, inasmuch as it was his responsibility to discern between good and evil. God's will is the sole standard of all perfection, and we cannot comprehend the reason for his admirable works because of our crudeness. The very angels of paradise are confused in looking at the glory of God, and have their faces hidden, according to the description of the prophet Ezekiel (Ezek. 1; Isa. 6:2). What shall it be with us who are only poor vessels of clay? Now that is the attitude with which we must begin to read this story, in which God so gravely punished Uzzah.

Moreover, we must gather from it that none of our devotions will be accepted by God unless they are conformed to his will. This rule ruins all the man-made inventions in the papacy's so-called worship of God, which has so much pomp and foolishness. All of that is nothing but sheer trash before God, and is in fact an abomination to him. Hence, let us hold this unmistakable rule, that if we want to worship God in accordance with our own ideas, it will simply be abuse and corruption. And so, on the contrary, we must have the testimony of his will in order to follow what he commands us, and to submit to it. Now that is how the worship which we render to God will be approved.

Well, for the second point, let us note that we must undertake nothing outside of our vocation. For what may seem to be virtue to us will be considered vice before God if we go beyond our limits. Why? Because our vocation is to prove the obedience that we render to him. We call vocation the duty to which God binds us. It is that which belongs to the office of someone in the condition and degree to which God has called them. This word 'vocation' signifies calling. Well, this calling means that men do not thrust themselves forward, and that everyone does not take his own portion and share. Rather, when God says to one: 'Do this' and to another: 'Do this', that is how each one should walk and follow him. Therefore, when we desire that God should call us, it is a sign that we must not go further than is legitimate for us. But he who does go beyond his limits is acting just as though he wanted to overrule God in the matter, and wanted to have the fruit of God's grace as defined by his own thoughts! Well, we are not to act in this way.

In the example of Uzzah, we are instructed not to attempt to go beyond the demands of our own office, nor beyond the condition or degree to which we are called by God. It is as if a private citizen wanted to take the office of magistrate or if, quite indiscriminately, he wanted to take authority – as if someone wanted to rule the house of his neighbour and of this one and that one. Such things would be utterly preposterous! If someone argues: 'It is done in good faith and with good intentions' – yes, but it is not for us to put ourselves forward in such a way. Therefore, such presumption and recklessness are displeasing to God, particularly when we prefer to do what is not our business, so that everyone takes over what is by no means given to him. In sum, let us be modest enough to pay attention to that to which God calls us, which he strictly requires from us and which belongs to our office. Let everyone openly devote himself to it, so that we will not go beyond our boundaries like wild horses.

The papists certainly corrupt this passage when they use it to prevent anyone but themselves from tampering with the rule of the Church. Indeed, it is a similar evil when we attempt to use this text to prove that God has forbidden those who are not pastors of the Church from being involved in religion. Well, it says that kings and princes are supporters of the Church. From that it follows that they ought to extend their hand so that religion might retain its purity, and the worship of God not be corrupted. We have the example of good kings who have seen to it that everyone else was reformed and united in the Church, and God has accepted them and their testimony by his Spirit, so that theirs has been an agreeable service to him. Therefore, it is false and tyrannical of those who are called pastors or prelates in the Church to use the example of Uzzah to close the door on those who want to help them maintain the honour of God for which they are responsible. Nevertheless, everyone should know his limits, and we should not let ambition ever cause us to want more than is legitimate for us. There should be no envy or emulation which says: 'And now what? If we cannot have this position and are kept from taking charge here, then you are attacking our personal authority.' Let us not act in that way, but instead let us realise: 'It is God who wants us to be governed in this way. So let everyone be content with his condition.'

Yet we see how God wanted to keep his people fearing him, and keep the worship that he had instituted in the Law preserved from all pollution, without any mixture which would make it contemptible. That is why he commanded (as we discussed yesterday) that the ark be carried by the Kohathites, who were of the house of God. Indeed, only a specified part of the tribe of Levi was commissioned to carry the ark. Anyway, here were those whom God had chosen as ministers of his sanctuary, who were to carry the ark on their shoulders. Now what if the king and all the governors of the people had claimed: 'Although we are not worthy of putting our hand on the ark, still, if we go through this devotion of humbling ourselves before it, why should we not then be allowed to do so?' Such talk would be worth nothing. For God has required that those whom he has ordained over the worship of the sanctuary and over the utensils be consecrated. We know that that office was separated from the common people.

Of course, we do not have the same situation today, for all such sacrifices were types of our Lord Jesus Christ. Now we are all called Levites, as we see by the prophets (Isa. 66:21), so that we will not carelessly misuse these examples from the Law. Today, therefore, in the person of Jesus Christ, who is the sovereign High Priest, we are Levites to him, dedicated – from the greatest to the smallest – to his service. Thus, there is no such distinction as there was in the Law (yet we must always return to this customary relationship between the types and the truth). God, therefore, wanted from that time to maintain his worship in such a way that when people approached the sanctuary, everyone would be humbled and touched with fear, and that no-one would go there frivolously.

Even though these ancient shadows have passed, we must remember that when we worship God, we ought to be touched with such a deep affection that it would serve to separate us from all the pollution of the world. May we never begin praying without practising what the Psalms say, that when we trust in the goodness of God, we will always be received (Psa. 17:7; 33:18; 147:11). Yet on the other hand, we must tremble before his majesty. Let us not come to him like hypocrites, who only twist their mouths and make fun of God and make sport of him. Let us not do that, but instead, let us be nothing in ourselves, and let us realise how great his grandeur is – not in order to be utterly overawed by it, but rather to be beneficially instructed by the present story. For we will be in serious trouble unless we contemplate God in the spirit of the psalmist: 'Lord, how terrible you are, and all your judgements!' (Psa. 47:3; 119:120). Thus, what we must remember is that God wanted his worship under the Law to be very carefully guarded. How much more today – when we have come to 'the fullness of the time' (Gal. 4:4) in which we ought to serve him 'in spirit and in truth' (John 4:24) – should we learn to walk in such a way that we will not profane his holy name. When we do speak, let us do so with the immense reverence and dignity which he merits. That (I say) is what we have to remember.

Moreover, if someone argues: 'Why did God exercise such excessive severity on Uzzah? Would it not have been sufficient merely to admonish him?', we could offer many arguments (as we have said), but God knows exactly how to silence our babbling and our rash judgements. When we haggle against and contradict his sentence and execution, we not only waste our time, but we also bring down a great load of wrath and vengeance on our heads. Let us learn, therefore, to avoid such arrogance, and to adore the judgements of God – and to realise that since Uzzah did not stay in his place, God had just cause to chastise him for his recklessness, in accordance with the text which says he was too hasty.

Now you might consider this hastiness to be commendable zeal, but in the eyes of God it was inconsiderate zeal, and merited punishment. Let us, therefore, carefully remember that the death of Uzzah was not cruelty on the part of God, but a just chastisement, for it was the duty of the Levites – and specifically the Kohathites – to be in charge of carrying the ark. Indeed, the Kohathites themselves were not to dare to open it (Num. 4:19), for it could only be opened by the High Priest. Well, if those whom God had dedicated to his obedience and service were not supposed to look in it (as we saw in First Samuel) and in fact those who acted so presumptuously were grievously punished (1 Sam. 6:19), then what should happen when a private person thrusts himself forward and recklessly touches it, as though to say: 'By my help I shall prevent the ark from falling'? In fact, both he and his party may have been ambitious, as we have seen earlier, in that they may have wanted to glorify themselves – since their house had been the lodging place of the ark of God. Well, be that as it may, still his hastiness was displeasing to God.

When it says that 'his wrath was stirred up' (2 Sam. 6:7), let us understand that God was justly angry. For God is not like mortal men, who become angry and whose passions are disordered. Rather, whenever God is annoyed, let us tremble, knowing that his justice is fair, and not like that of sinners. Thus, this single word should suffice to condemn Uzzah and to hold us captive so that we do not come to argue with God, or pose questions, or quarrel against him. That, in sum, is what we have to remember from this example.

Nevertheless, let us carefully observe that God will certainly punish the body of anyone who has done wrong, yet it will be for their profit. Be that as it may, their death will serve as an example, as it does not say that God was so angered against Uzzah that he condemned him for ever. He died there, indeed, but it is a very small and light thing to pass out of this world. When God takes us from here, it is not a judgement so grievous as we think, in that we do not understand the life eternal to which he calls us. Therefore, death could have been profitable to Uzzah, in that being thus punished, he did not fail to obtain pardon from God, and that it was even a mercy which God bestowed upon him when he took him out of this world. For even though he had been inconsiderate and had committed a punishable offence, yet God, seeing his zeal, had pity on him. Thus, he punished only his body in order that his spirit might be saved (1 Cor. 5:5), as St Paul says, for often God chastises us in the flesh in order to call us to eternal salvation. If he spares us here below, it will cost us, at the last, very dearly, but when he chastises us in this body, and even when he takes us out of this world, it is a sign of his love and of his grace, in that he knows that it is good to leave here, so that we will not be corrupted.

Nevertheless, the death of Uzzah has served as an example to instruct us. God did not at all kill him because of the ark and because of his hastiness, but because he wanted everyone to be admonished not to play lightly with his worship, but rather to engage in it with the fear commanded in his Law. It is true that he was angry with Uzzah, since he punished his offence. For we must not corrupt Scripture, which states that God condemned this action and was displeased over it. But what I mean is that he punished Uzzah and turned his punishment to his good and salvation. Yet he did it so that it might serve as a perpetual memorial to others, who might in turn give more serious thought to the appropriate way to worship God. Thus, the ark would no longer be carried about on ox carts but on the shoulders of the Levites, as the Law required. It was to be lifted up in this way so that everyone would respect this pledge of the presence of God in their worship, as we dealt with yesterday. The ark should have caused everyone to be thrilled, since God actually came down upon them, and displayed his virtue and his grace by making it his dwelling place. This was reason enough for them to be inflamed with true zeal in worshipping God, tempered with such humility that they would recognise that they were unworthy to approach him, and that there was no other way, except for the High Priest to present himself on behalf of all, so that he might make peace for everyone (Lev. 4:13–21). Even today, when we have this marvellous privilege of approaching God, we must remember still that our approach is in the name of our Lord Jesus Christ, who is our mouth to carry our prayers and requests to God, and who enables us to find grace before him. For if we came in our own names, we would be utterly confused. Therefore, we should place all our confidence in him.

It says above that 'David was filled with displeasure', and that he thought he could 'not keep the Ark of God at his home, and lodged it with Obed-Edom' (2 Sam. 6:8–10), fearing that he might receive the same punishment as Uzzah. In the first place, we see here the impatience of David, who in so many ways was excellent. For the Scripture says that he was inflamed with indignation, which is certainly a sign that he was annoyed with God. Let us pay careful attention to this word. We know that David had such a root of piety in him that if we had asked him: 'Do you want to be angry with God and to despise him?', he would have said: 'I would never do that – I would rather die'. Indeed, he would have said it without pretence. Nevertheless, when he saw that Uzzah was smitten by the hand of God, he was angry and annoyed. We cannot deny that he was annoyed with God, for the text palpably shows us that he was. Well, since David was inflamed with anger, what will it be with us, who have not profited nearly so much in the school of God?

Therefore, let us learn to watch ourselves carefully, since we run like escaped horses, our emotions at boiling point, and thus are not able fully to subject ourselves to the will of God when he takes away from us our relatives and friends. Even when we want to maintain a modest composure, still we always feel a certain inner bitterness, which makes us want to murmur if we dare. In brief, it is very difficult for us to mourn without giving way to excessive grief. Thus, it is most difficult for us to be able to mourn without losing control of ourselves and giving way to rebellious feelings. Hence, whenever we experience heightened zeal and passionate emotion, we have good reason to condemn and detest our perverse nature. As soon as God sends calamities upon us, let us immediately remember how normal it is for us to feel grieved (since we are not insensible creatures) and let us then encourage ourselves in God, knowing that he does it for our good and profit, and that he often uses this as a means to prove our patience. Even though we put up a good front and do show a certain amount of modest composure, still our emotions are always disordered, and we inevitably have a certain amount of venom against God. That is why we must subject ourselves to him, and make short shrift of our annoyances and not feed and flatter ourselves in them. So much, then, for this example of David.

Moreover, we see that even those who are disposed to the service of God always have something that holds them back, so that often for very little reason they are turned aside from the right path. What was David's problem? He sought to be in great favour with the people, to show that the greatest desire of his heart was to be a member of the Church, and to maintain the rule of the faithful. Now that was a very praiseworthy virtue, but it involved him in the scandal of seeing Uzzah die, which made him displeased and angry. Hence, let us note that even when we seem to be totally dedicated to the service of God, if something annoys us, it makes us lose control of ourselves and totally abandon our vocation. That is why we must pray to God continually that whatever sort of trial he chooses to test us will not overcome us, but rather we will overcome it. This, again, is a point which we have to remember.

It says that David 'feared' (2 Sam. 6:9) to have the ark of God brought to his house or to the city of David. He was a prophet of God and an excellent one, but now was acting like a small child. He was utterly shocked and afraid of falling into the same peril as Uzzah, which (as we have said) should serve as an example for us to be all the more dedicated to the service of God. David certainly should have been as affected as the others, to think that the ark of God had not been honoured as it should. Therefore, he ought to have thought of what God had commanded in his Law. In the same way, let us determine to submit to God's Law, and not to go beyond our bounds. Now that is what David should have remembered, and if his fear had been in line with Scripture, it would have been good and holy. But he drew a false conclusion from a good principle. For he feared God, and then was seized by anger, and he finally concluded that the ark did not have to come to him.

Well, this is an important example, for if we seriously consider the person of David and analyse his fear, we will see that he was certainly deprived of his senses for a time, and that God made him stupefied. Nevertheless, let us note that not only can it happen to us, but even more so, as this example shows us. Let us carefully note that it is not enough to have a good foundation, but we must build upon it. For as we have said, fear would have been praiseworthy in David, but he drew a false conclusion from it. So although David had a good foundation, he built a bad superstructure upon it. Nonetheless, he did well when he concluded that he was not to play with God like this, but that he must not err in the least from the Law.

Thus, let us note that in fearing God, we must maintain a balance and know where this fear should lead us. Well, where should it lead us? We will never get the point unless we first see a specific illustration of it. For instance, many who truly fear God are unnecessarily agitated with despair when they hear only certain sentences from Scripture, such as: 'God is a consuming fire' (Deut. 4:24; Heb. 12:29), and that he consumes all before him (Joel 2:3). Or they hear such statements as: 'The day of the Lord' is terrible, and 'it is not light but darkness' (Amos 5:18); and then: 'Who can dwell with a devouring fire?' (Isa. 33:14). And so many other similar passages. Now this kind of thing can make them draw back from the service of God, and say: 'What does he mean by all these things? Alas, what will happen to a poor creature like me? Since he is so severe and strict, how shall I approach him? How shall I be able to acquit myself in such a way that I shall be able to satisfy him with my performance? It is impossible for me! Even the angels could not accomplish by themselves what he commands me to do; they could not subsist one single minute before such a power and majesty. And I, who am a poor disordered creature, how can I reach such a position?'

This line of thought undoubtedly could turn many people away from serving God into the depths of fearful despair. For this reason, St Paul advises us to know the wiles of Satan so that we will not be overwhelmed by our disappointments (2 Cor. 2:7). When we only think about our sins, it certainly may serve to abase and confound us, but let us always remember how to find, in the goodness of God, the remedy to sweeten our grief, and let not our unbelief plunge us into the depths of the abyss, so that we say: 'Oh, it is impossible to approach God'. Let us not draw such a terribly wrong conclusion. We see what happened to St Peter when he saw the miracle of our Lord Jesus Christ. 'Lord,' he said, 'do not come near me, for I am only a poor sinner' (Luke 5:8). He did well to recognise himself as a sinner and to apprehend the high position of the Son of God, and then to worship him. But nevertheless, he did not have to request our Lord Jesus Christ to go away from him. For when he confessed poverty as a sinner, he should immediately have sought the means by which to obtain grace. Being in death, he ought to have sought life in our Lord Jesus Christ. He did not do so, but in his fear and apprehension he remained like someone stunned.

Therefore, when we are cut to the quick with the awareness of our sins, let us remember how to take control of ourselves so that we will not be weighed down with despair. Furthermore, when we think of the greatness, majesty and power of God, it should not make us so fearful that we are frightened into saying: 'Let us flee, for we can never approach him; let our ears be stopped in order not to hear his burning voice; and let our sense be so deadened as to take in nothing!' Of course, it would be much better for us not to draw such a conclusion. Instead, let us come to what I have already mentioned from the Psalm: 'Lord, I come to you in the multitude of your goodness, and I await your mercy, and I shall walk in your fear' (Psa. 5:7). Now here are two things which seem quite divergent, but David joins them together, as they are in fact inseparable. That is, when we come to God, let us fear, let us be stunned by his majesty, above all let us realise what we are, that we are full of nothing but rottenness and infection. However, let us not fail to taste the goodness of God; indeed, I say, to drink in this infinite number of good benefits which we receive from him. Let us, then, realise that however innumerable our needs may be, he will always continue his liberality towards us, and answer our requests. Now this is the kind of fear that we ought to have.

We see that, under the shadow of the fear of God, the world has become addicted to so many follies that pure religion has been totally bastardised. For what has been the reason for building so many chapels and making so many base flatterers, founding masses, and then employing all one's substance in this empty mockery and entertainment? What has been the reason that some have been monks or hermits, others this or that, others have vowed to make a pilgrimage, others to wear sackcloth, others frocks and capes, and a thousand other fanfares? The standard answer is always: the fear of God! Yes, but these are wicked conclusions, which men have drawn out of their own heads. Out of fear, they imagined all of these things as ways of appeasing the wrath of God. 'Alas,' they said, 'it will be good to make satisfaction to God for our sins. Very well, the satisfaction will consist of our own good works and of our merits, which each one must work out for himself. We will wear unusual habits, for we must have some sign of humility to give ourselves all the more to his service. We shall wear a frock; we shall gird ourselves with cords and wear shoes of a particular style; we shall have feasts; we shall make a distinction between meats.' Now these conclusions are utterly frivolous. Why do they behave like this? They always reply that these practices are based on the fear of God. Therefore, we must study this passage carefully, in order to learn so to dread God in his majesty that we realise how he wants to be feared, and refrain from mixing our fantasies with this fear of God, and thus build an evil superstructure upon a good foundation – as I said earlier.

Above all, let us note that David drew the wrong conclusion when he cried: 'How shall I ever be able to bring the ark of God to Zion?' For our God is so powerful that he will always find a way to accomplish what he has promised, namely, that he will deal kindly and patiently with his own, and 'will show mercy unto a thousand generations of those who dedicate themselves patiently to his law' (Deut. 7:9). David also knew how to recognise him clearly and give a very ample description of him, calling us to God so that we might come to him as members of his family. Thus, when God is terrible, as we have stated, it is not to make us frightened. For he never forgets his nature, which is to be gracious and to answer all those who call upon him (and, above all, to answer poor sinners who approach him in truth). Thus, the dreadfulness of God is not intended to shut the door of his grace on us and exclude us from his favour. This is why we see how David was confounded for a time, and how God executed a terrible judgement for our instruction.

Not realising this, David asked, 'How shall I ever lodge it in Zion?' (2 Sam. 6:9). He should not have drawn this conclusion, but rather the following: 'Since Uzzah was punished for having touched the ark of the Lord, we must be certain to follow whatever God commands us. It is not legitimate for us to change anything.' Now that conclusion would have been a good one. The ark of God would have been held in honour, and the people would have come to worship, as commanded in the Law. Let us carefully remember what I have stated, that God exercises his terrible judgements, not to frighten us away from his presence so that we attempt to flee as far as possible from him, but rather to draw us to approach him in all humility so we might willingly recognise his all-surpassing grandeur and superiority. Then, as we trust in him, we will not be like the hypocrites who presumptuously thrust themselves forward and then become frightened in their sins. On the contrary, genuine trust in God causes us to rejoice at the profound assurance that we have of being accepted by him, without ever ceasing to feel deeply ashamed for the sins that we have committed. That is what the passage means.

It goes on to say that God made fun of this foolish fear of David, for 'David lodged the ark in the house of Obed-Edom, and this man prospered and all his family' (2 Sam. 6:10–11). This prosperity gave evident testimony that God accepted the worship of Obed-Edom for having lent him his house in which to lodge his ark. In the first place, David's motive was a bad one, for if he feared to bring back the ark of God for himself, why did he charge Obed-Edom with it? Was that either right or charitable? He thought that death would draw near if God entered Zion. Well, if the ark of God would cause such trouble, did David not deserve to be paid the same wages as the person with whom he deposited the ark in hopes of avoiding the very evil which he feared would ruin the one who kept it? This shows us how one evil brings another, and how the fear that we previously discussed made him forget how to be humane and level-headed. For he should rather have said: 'Let us build a place for the ark: let the Levites carry out their duty, that each one may be employed in the service of God, and pure religion be maintained'. But he did nothing of the sort! On the contrary, not content with refusing the ark, he actually charged someone else with it, hoping, of course, that he could avoid evil by putting it on someone else.

Let us notice that when men begin to go astray, they wander everywhere. For I have already said that the simple instruction which David should have taken is that we should no longer transgress the Law, but instead hold to the way that God has shown us. David failed to consider simply opening the Book and following God's ordinance. If he had done that, he would have repaired the damage. In spite of everything, God would have been worshipped, and would have shown himself merciful to the people. Certainly, he feared God, but he failed to remember that his worship must be carried out with full integrity. He paid no attention to the fact that the damage would come not only on him, but also on his neighbours. He should have begun by encouraging all his officers, who could then have encouraged others. In fact, when we fail to honour God with an appropriate zeal and affection, it causes others to grow cold. Then little by little, such corruption develops that it causes an entire nation to become totally rotten. These things do not happen because God changes his nature, nor because he ever fails to keep his eyes on those who call upon him in truth, no matter how evil the multitude may be. Instead, let us be sure to remember that a true fear of God should cause us to reform ourselves under the rule of his Word, and then that we should join the fear of God with the love of our neighbour, for these are two inseparable things. In fact, it is impossible for us to bring honour to God when the one with whom we should be united is rejected – or at least, when we do not act towards him in as brotherly a way as we should.

Now God's punishment of David and his 'making the house of Obed-Edom to prosper' (2 Sam. 6:11) was not a rejection of David. It is true that it shamed him when God clearly demonstrated how foolish David had been for wanting to avoid the ark, as though it would bring him evil. This was how God showed him how foolish his thinking had been. Yet at the same time, it was meant to relieve his fears, for if he had remained in a stubborn frame of mind, it is certain that he would never have dared consider the ark. Still, he needed to go to the ark to obtain mercy. 'Seek my face', says the Lord, as was mentioned yesterday. David should always have turned to this pledge which had been given to him. Therefore, when he neglected it, he was drawing back from receiving the salvation which it represented, for it was also the type of Jesus Christ, as has been explained. Hence, he would have been excluded from it if he had remained in such a state, and would never have found his sure refuge in God. But when God made Obed-Edom and his family prosper, then David recognised his error, and actually realised that he had done a great injustice to God in thinking that evil would happen to him if he brought back the ark to his house and to his city. Indeed, it was a sort of blasphemy to want to change God's nature – as we have already shown. David, therefore, accepted this good and useful instruction: namely, that God had shamed him, but that it was a good and necessary discipline. Let us realise, therefore, that when God chastises us for our errors, we must use it for our advantage, and not be shocked or chagrined by it. Let us, rather, realise that God does not want us to perish if he shows us our ignorance before our very eyes.

Moreover, we see that David repented for having placed the ark of God elsewhere than in his city (2 Sam. 6:12). Nevertheless, David's understanding was not totally and immediately converted, for he was still confused about several important matters. He really based his action simply on the prosperity of Obed-Edom, as if he envied him, and wanted to bring back the ark to himself, and derive profit from it. Why did he not rather think of the promises which God had given him? It is true to say that the examples of the grace of God which we have before our eyes ought to strengthen our trust. But we must look higher, namely, to the promises of God. For we must not only focus our attention on what we see; God must speak, and we must hear him. So here was another fault in David's change of mind. He really should have said: 'Since God is always consistent with himself, I shall trust in his promises. Now he has declared what is required in his worship, and so I shall bring back the ark in accordance with his instructions and put it in a convenient place for all the people, so that none can make the excuse that it is inaccessible.' But he drew back from such appropriate action until he actually saw the fruit of this promise, which he found hard to believe. Thus, when he saw that the house of Obed-Edom prospered, he concluded: 'I must have the ark'. But why did it take so long? He failed to obtain the blessing quickly because of his lack of trust.

We see then, in all this, that when we regard the works of God without his Word, we will be blown about by every wind (Eph. 4:14); we will be reeds pushed one way and the other (Luke 7:24), with no firm foundation. Hence, let us follow this general rule, namely, that we will never benefit from all the works of God – either to fear him or to trust in him – unless his Word be added immediately. Why? Because all our senses become troubled and confused after we have seen the judgements of God. Of course, we do have some grasp of the truth, but we soon lose it, as we see in David. Because of this weakness, we draw mistaken conclusions which keep us from judging the matter properly. Let us keep on praying and seeking God's face until we obtain the spirit of discretion.

Even in times of blessing, we need this spirit of discernment. When the Lord gives us some signs of his grace and mercy, we certainly are able to experience and perceive a taste of his goodness. But that in itself is not sufficient to cause us to stop and to take in the lasting significance of it. We are so flighty that what we hear in the morning goes out of our head by the evening! We are always scatter-brained. If we consider the works of God apart from his Word, we will be totally blind as to their meaning. But since God does give believers a certain amount of perception, we are like poor people who cannot see without glasses. Well, our glasses are doctrine. Through these glasses of true doctrine, we fear God and interpret his works.

Thus, when we have the Word of God to regulate our senses towards a proper appreciation of his works, then our judgement is right. When God exercises his judgement, we will say that it is just and equitable, and we will bow our necks beneath his yoke; we will make no complaint. When he bestows his mercy, we will be ready to embrace it and place our trust in him, and be encouraged by it to call on him more boldly. Yet our fear will make us humble and our faith will always remain constant and firm. But if we, even for a while, follow the example of David, it is certain that we will think falsely and act like stupid people. Then we can abuse the favours of God, and at last remain plunged in the mire of our own foolish opinions and imaginations. We must not (I say) follow the example which David gives us in this passage of distrusting God and floundering from one side to the other. But we must follow him in that he recognised his fault, detested it, asked pardon for it, and applied himself more and more to God's service. Now that is exactly how we should act. Namely, we must so regulate our senses by the Word of God that we recognise his works, in order to adore them, and learn to serve him in all purity. Above all, we must have such great trust in his goodness that we will boldly call on him in our need, in order to obtain favour and grace in the name of our Lord Jesus Christ.

Now let us prostrate ourselves before his majesty, recognising our offences, praying him that he may make us feel them in order completely to remake us in his own image. Since we know that he wishes to be honoured by us, we are not to doubt that he will always show himself to be our Father until we at last find our refuge in him. And yet, let us not fail to recognise his greatness and majesty, but rather humble ourselves beneath them. And may the Lord make us feel our faults, not to drive us to despair, but to cause us to walk in such sobriety that our whole being will soon become totally dedicated to his service. May God grant that our dedication will not mean giving him a servile obedience which actually drives us away from him, but rather a voluntary obedience which draws us near to him. And may he grant this grace not only to us, but to all people and nations of the earth . . .

18

*Humble David and Proud Michal**

> *So David went and brought up the ark of God from the house of Obed-Edom into the city of David with joy. After those who bore the ark of God had gone six paces he sacrificed an ox and a fatling . . .* (2 Sam. 6:12–19).

We have seen what motivated David to bring home the ark, which he had placed in the house of Obed-Edom. He had changed his mind about the chastisement of Uzzah. Now he turned round. We have shown that David's response was not entirely free from sin, for even though God had exacted a severe penalty, David should not have been so shocked that he drew back from him and thought that the ark would bring him trouble. Instead, he needed to learn how to bring the ark back reverently, as he later did. But that illustrates how the faithful are not always provided with good counsel on the field, but in the end God brings them back to the path from which they have temporarily wandered. It may suddenly happen that while we are in pain and do not see clearly enough, we may suffer frivolous worries which proceed from our carelessness. Well, God wants to humble us in this way for a time, so that we may learn to return to him and be governed by his Spirit.

Now it goes on to say that 'David brought the ark with joy' (2 Sam. 6:12), especially since he had tasted the grace of God which had come to Obed-Edom. He therefore concluded that it would be profitable for him, and so he rejoiced. Indeed, it is certain that we cannot serve God without joy, even as the Psalm

*Monday, July 13, 1562.

says (Psa. 100:2). And fear ought to be joined to this joy in such a way that we do not doubt God's paternal goodness to us. For otherwise, all the service which we render him will be forced, since it also says that he approves the oblations which are offered him with an open heart (2 Cor. 9:7). It follows, therefore, that we cannot do any service for God unless it is based upon his goodness, which may give us hope for our salvation, and then cause us to rejoice in it. That is why it says: 'Serve the Lord with fear, and rejoice with reverence before him' (Psa. 2:11). After exhorting us to serve God with fear, it says that we must rejoice. In particular, at the very moment when we tremble before his majesty, we must not fail to recognise that he will be our Father and Saviour, and thus we shall rejoice.

We have mentioned that David now had the ark brought in a different way from before. He was therefore remembering what was commanded in the Law (Num. 4:15). For it says that the ark was 'carried' (2 Sam. 6:13). And by whom? It is true that the name of the Levites is not expressed here, but still it can certainly be assumed. For David had seen the example of Uzzah, who for having merely touched the ark – from what was, apparently, a very real devotion – had nevertheless been smitten by the hand of God. From that we can gather that he returned to this rule which was given (in the Law), which had been treated as though it was open to doubt, namely, that the Levites bore the ark on their shoulders, for God had indeed chosen them for that duty.

It is true that they were no better than the rest of the people. But the point is that their office did not come from their own dignity or their own virtue. It was because God had called them to it (Heb. 5:4). Therefore, the fact that they had this privilege depended only on the election of God and on his pure liberality, such as when it pleases God to call either this one or that one to such and such a charge. It is true that he will enable the one whom he calls to fulfil this position, but nevertheless, if one looks for the source and first cause of the aptitude, it will only be that God uses men as he pleases and applies them to his work. That is why St Paul, wanting to crush all presumption, says:

'Who is it who makes you different from others?' (1 Cor. 4:7). By these words, he means that if there is anything excellent in us which might possibly – or, indeed, actually – cause us to be preferred to our neighbour, still it does not come from us, and we have no reason to lift ourselves up because of it. Rather, in all humility, we should recognise the grace that God has bestowed on us. Well, enough then on this point, that the ark was carried and that it was not brought in a cart as before.

Well, it adds that 'David offered sacrifices, those whole burnt offerings called peace offerings' (2 Sam. 6:17). Now these are sacrifices of prosperity, for they were testimonies that men gave praise and thanks to God for all the goods which they had received from him. David, therefore, made this offering to God in order to procure grace. Well, we must always remember the principle that sacrifices were offered in those times in order to ratify prayers. For in fact, we cannot invoke God or give him thanks unless it be founded on the sacrifice of our Lord Jesus Christ, who was 'once offered' (Heb. 9:28) in order to dedicate us to himself, so that everything which proceeds from us will be accepted in him. For we are poor creatures, full of filth and infection, and thus we cannot open our mouths to pray to God to make any request of him. nor ever proclaim his praises, unless we are consecrated to him. Well, that has been accomplished, since we have been reconciled, and thus the blood of our Lord Jesus Christ today purifies all the prayers and praises which we offer to God, for otherwise they would be nothing but filth.

Now that is why under the Law when the faithful had to pray to God or to recognise his benefits, it was necessary for them to offer burnt offerings or sacrifices of prosperity to show that they were not worthy to present their praises and thanks to God themselves, except insofar as he would accept them by virtue of the sacrifice which had not yet been made. But today we must be content with the truth, and although the ancient types are no longer in use, still when we pray to God, we must always return to the death and passion of our Lord Jesus Christ when we want God to receive our praises and approve them. We must begin with this principle, knowing that we are totally polluted and that if we were not consecrated – in that our Lord Jesus Christ has reconciled us to God his Father – then all that we could say and do would be only an abomination. So much, then, for this point.

Well, it adds afterwards that 'David danced before the Ark with all his might being clad with an ephod of linen' (2 Sam. 6:14). Now the type of dress described here means that a man undressed himself and put on nothing but a linen cloth for cover (inasmuch as decency required it). In fact, this will be mentioned again later when Michal his wife reproached him for being undressed like a tramp (2 Sam. 6:20), and was ashamed of him. Well, here David took off his royal garments and all the pompous accessories to which he was accustomed, and was covered with nothing but a linen cloth. So he was there like a poor man, one of the simple and common populace. That is what we have to note.

Now one could raise the question whether today it would be legitimate for us to follow the standard of David both in the linen ephod and in all the rest. My first response is this: We must always go back to the difference which our Lord has put between us and the ancient people. For otherwise, we would create terrible confusion, which would serve to corrupt and divert the worship of God. Now that depends on an even higher principle, namely, that it is not for us to invent things which may occur to our fancy as a mode of worshipping God. Rather, we should seek to worship him by observing what he has ordained, as has been declared previously. Therefore, it is up to God to give us the rule for worshipping him properly, and his authority is that which distinguishes between the good and the bad. If we wanted to imitate the ancient fathers indiscriminately, we would create an illegitimate confusion which would corrupt everything.

That is why the poor world is so addicted to superstition that it has not discerned between the types and the truth. For what one calls worship of God in the papacy is only a mass of ceremonies of the Law, however much they may have been adjusted to the times. Also their worship is full of empty trash and pagan superstition. But be that as it may, the way that they pattern their worship on the example of the ancient fathers is an apish trick. All through these ceremonies, they have forged rituals for themselves based on the assumption that there are still sacrifices. They have concluded that these must be retained – and that is the origin of the mass. There used to be washings, so they must exist today – and that is where holy water comes from. There used to be luminaries – thus they want torches and lamps. We see, therefore, how the poor people were tricked in this foolish idea of following the ancient fathers. For though they only 'turned the pot in the other direction', yet they let out what was legitimate. That is why we must note this difference which St Paul mentions, namely, that the ancient fathers were governed like little children, and God gave them a rule like little children (Gal. 3:24). And if we today wished to pattern ourselves totally on the ancient fathers, we would cause injury to our Lord Jesus Christ, and would in effect be burying him. For we know that in the death and passion of our Lord Jesus Christ the veil has been rent in twain (Matt. 27:51; Heb. 9:3, 6ff.; 10:20) to show that the time of types has passed, and that henceforth we must worship God in another way – not as to substance, but as to form. God has always wanted to be worshipped in purity. He does not change his nature. He is spiritual. Hence, let us note that when the ancient fathers used many things under the Law, it was not that the substance of their worship was less effective than it is today, since his worship is spiritual, but the form was different. Why? Because it pleased God for it to be so. When we have no other reason, that one should surely be sufficient for us.

It is true that the Gospel also shows us that, today, God extends the favours of his Spirit with more precise design, so that the ceremonies of that time are no longer necessary for us. Indeed, they would be superfluous for us, and would even prevent our Lord Jesus Christ from being recognised with the perfection of grace which he has brought. Still, let us be aware that we were as crude as the Jews. Nevertheless, God has fully made up for our immaturity, and we need pay no attention at all to the ancient ceremonies of the Law, as far as saying that we have need of them. For God knows what is proper for us, and has held back nothing from us. Since God knew our immaturity, it is certain that he wanted to abolish all these observations to which he had subjected the Jews. He left us types – few in number – in which there is such a simplicity that we may thus contemplate our Lord Jesus Christ, as it were, face to face. For baptism is not an obscure shadow, neither is the Lord's Supper. This is not to represent to us our Lord Jesus Christ as far off, but we have in it a certain testimony that he has once manifested himself, so that he will ever remain with us, and that he even lives in us. Well now, that is one point.

But now it says that David leaped before the ark 'with all his might' (2 Sam. 6:14), which is to say that he danced. Well, we may find this very strange indeed, but let us note in the first place that God permitted his people to have many things in common with the pagans. Now it was customary for the pagans to dance and leap while worshipping their idols. God guided his people in that matter, indeed, so that they would not give themselves to wicked superstitions, nor say: 'We lack this; we must have it like the others'. Although dancing before the ark may not seem to be an action that we would really approve, nevertheless God could have granted such permission to his people. But there was also another reason, for it is certain that he wanted to withdraw his own people from all sacrilegious and dissolute joys so that they might learn to rejoice in him. It is our nature to rejoice; there is no-one who is not that way. Well, since God sees that we are disorderly – setting no limits on our joy, but instead letting our lusts run wild – he holds an appropriate remedy for us, namely, that we may learn to rejoice in him. Therefore, when we are told that David danced before the ark, let us note that it was in order that he and all the faithful at that time, instead of rejoicing in dissolute and lascivious dances, might exercise themselves in the praises of God and place all their joy in that. Be that as it may, it was done in accordance with the times, which we must always remember.

It is also true that in those times there were many hypocrites who leaped and danced with great devotion, showing signs of great ardour, and yet had nothing but falsehood in their hearts, mimicking true devotion like apes! For we know that those who are not touched to the quick with the fear of God often give the appearance and make pretence of serving him in order to show that they have great zeal for the honour of God. There were many such besides David but they did not have what he had. For he did not lack the principal thing, which was to dedicate himself to the worship of God and to know that he ought to avoid all sacrilegious and dissolute joy, so that God might accept the praises which he offered him with such gladness.

Well, we must not find it strange if he leaped and danced like that, for let us carefully consider what we are. Here is why we make rash judgements, too quickly rejecting this or that: we do not know our own frailty. Thus, as we have already said, we are inclined by nature to rejoice too much. Here is a convenient remedy to correct all our profane joy. On the other hand, we are cold when it comes to rejoicing in God! For if we do not fully taste his goodness, it will escape us and soon vanish, leaving us unmoved. Hence, we need to exercise ourselves in it and employ all our senses in it – our feet, our hands, our arms and all the rest – that they all might serve in the worship of God and so magnify him. Let us learn, therefore, that when God has desired such worship, it has been due to the frailty of men. And let us realise that it was expedient, that is, appropriate for that time, for we must always remember the difference which there is between us and them. In fact, when it says: 'The Lord will ascend with a shout and the sound of the trumpet' (Psa. 47:5), that was certainly true in the time of the Law. This refers to the ark, and in fact refers specifically to the triumphant ceremony which is described here. Now if we want to do the same (as I have said), we will create nothing but confusion! God certainly wants to be exalted in our midst. But how? We have no box which is a testimony and pledge of his presence, and in which his Law is enclosed. Also, we have no trumpets or similar things. Here we differ from the ancient fathers. Therefore, we see that when the poor world has given itself over to imitating indiscriminately what was done by David, nothing but corruption comes of it. Why? Because they were not armed with the spirit of David. We must carefully observe the rule which is shown to us so often in Scripture, namely, that since our Lord

Jesus Christ has appeared, the types have been abolished, and we must worship God without such ceremonies.

Nevertheless, the example of David should profit us a great deal. For in the first place, we are admonished to restrain ourselves and be moderate in all our joys. It is indeed a pity that even though we are impetuous, we can still find such attractive excuses and subterfuges to demonstrate that our joys are not reckless, although in actuality we may be so full of vanity that we go far astray in all our joys unless God holds us back on a short rein. Therefore, let us learn to rejoice in such a way that God will always be our aim, and let us recognise that this is testimony of his goodness and fatherly love, that in all his good gifts he gives us opportunity, he gives us the wherewithal to rejoice. That, then, is one point.

Now as for the ephod, it was not the priestly garment which was mentioned here, for the High Priest had his ephod with its exquisite adornments (Exod. 28:4). The Levites also wore the ephod, what they call 'surplice' in the papacy. For we have already said that the papists have been 'apes' in that they have wanted to take for themselves everything that was used in the time of the Law. Yes indeed, and it is because they have had no discernment and have attempted to bury our Lord Jesus Christ, as far as they could. But there was also the common ephod, which should be understood in this passage. Nevertheless, we must note that David also testified his humility before God, for he was king and could have stood there in great pomp in order not to be included in the rank and file. But since he came down from his high position in order to humble himself in the worship of God as a member of his Church, what excuse can we have when we are kept back by our laziness from worshipping God as he deserves? It is true that we will not use the ephod of David, for it would be superfluous and even a hindrance which would turn us away from our Lord Jesus Christ. Nevertheless, his example is useful for us; that is, since he who was king clearly wanted to blot himself out, we who are nothing in comparison should not be ashamed to be totally abased. Thus, when we come before God, may it be to give him all homage, and may we no longer be anything in ourselves.

We should also carefully observe that David stripped himself. Although today when we are assembled, as we are here, to testify to our faith, we do not remove either our garment or coat or doublet when we begin praying to God. Nevertheless, we must come totally naked before him, with the specific testimony that we want to be clothed in his grace so that we may have nothing but purity within us. That, therefore, is how we must follow David. Let us leave the ancient types aside, since they do not pertain to us, because they were temporary and ceased at the coming of our Lord Jesus Christ. Then let us learn to emulate the same good attitude as David, and relate all our joys to God's glory, stating that we are nothing, and that all our joy is in recognising all the favours which he has given us. Let us receive all our contentment from him alone. So much, then, for this point.

Next it is added that David 'put the ark in its place, that is, in the midst of the tabernacle which he had raised' (2 Sam. 6:17). At this point, one might doubt whether it was legitimate for David, in his position, to make a tabernacle, granted that God had ordained one made with a more than ordinary human craftsmanship. Certainly the reason that God had forgotten nothing, even down to the last thread, concerning what was required for the building of his tabernacle (Exod. 25–26) was to keep men from bringing anything of themselves. He wanted (I say) to show that every invention displeases him when it comes to worshipping him. Now granted this, did not David do wrong in building a new tabernacle? We remember that the tabernacle was for a while in Gibeon (1 Chron. 21:29). But it is more likely that after David recognised his fault in having the ark carried on a cart (2 Sam. 6:3ff.), he then followed what was ordained in the Law, not only in one or two points, but totally.

Well, the Scripture does not express every point in detail. What we must understand is what we are told here, that David offered burnt offerings and peace offerings (2 Sam. 6:17). Well, that was not legitimate for him. The priest had to fulfil that function, and it would be a serious matter to usurp the priest's position. We know what happened to his successor who wanted to burn incense alone (2 Chron. 26:16–17). He also was king, yet God did not spare him, but smote him with leprosy and left him in perpetual shame. But David did not sacrifice with his own hand, for often the Scripture will use expressions such as 'the saints have sacrificed', which means that they have followed the means which were ordained by the Law. Hence, we may say concerning the tabernacle that David attempted nothing, but followed what was ordained by God, and placed his ark there, since he knew that this was God's inviolable requirement. This is the solution of this difficulty, when it seems that one could take these words recorded here – that David made a new tabernacle – to mean the opposite of that which had been built by the express commandment of God. Be that as it may, let us note that when we start following our desires to worship God in our own way, our fantasies always become sacrileges. If we fall away from his Word, irreverence will increase to the point of sacrilege.

Moreover, it says that David prepared 'sacrifice' (2 Sam. 6:17) when the ark was put in its place, which is to show how he valued this testimony and pledge that God had given him, that he wanted to dwell in the midst of his people. Now David did not sacrifice to the ark – that would have been an abomination. Here was a casket of wood, gilded and covered with gold. Even so, it was still a dead and insensible creature. If David had actually offered his oblation to it, it would certainly have been idolatry. But he offered 'before the ark' that which he was presenting to God. Nevertheless, his heart was lifted far above the ark. Even so, he did not have to despise the ark, which is why the ark was called here by the name of God: 'David danced before God' (2 Sam. 6:14). Was God there 'in person', as one says? No, he was not visibly there, but it was enough for David to have the promise of his help signified by it. Therefore, when offerings are spoken of, let us note that they were addressed to the living God and that David, elevated by faith above the world, was not so fascinated by this visible sign that he made an idol of it.

We must carefully remember this, for there are two extremes to which men are subject. Either they will fall into superstition or they will be irreverent and pay no attention to the worship of

God. There are many today who think that baptism and the Lord's Supper are nothing, and that they could easily bypass them, as though they were angels. Well, we see a more modest spirit in David. Although he was a prophet of God, he did not in the least disdain using the means ordained for him. And though he was leader of this people, he humbled himself before God, knowing that he needed him. While recognising the first extreme, let us be careful on the other hand not to fall into superstition, which we are too inclined to do by nature. We see how those who want to be devout always go too far: some have, for instance, attached the salvation of men to baptism, and have thought that the blood of Christ was now nothing, so to speak. They say that without the water of baptism, nothing happens, and have even added charism, spittle, and all these empty rites. By their foolish fantasies, men have invented this and that in order to avoid the firm and solid determination to hold to the will of God declared to us in his Word. Hence, let us note carefully that David was not so fascinated with this ark that he made an idol of it or offered to it the sacrifices spoken of here. Rather, since he knew that God wanted to dwell in the midst of his people and had given the kind pledge of his presence that was required by their immaturity, David thus conformed himself to these circumstances, and that is why the sacrifices were approved.

It says afterwards that 'having offered such sacrifices, he blessed the people in the name of God' and sent them all away, 'giving to each of them a piece of bread, a piece of flesh, and a measure of wine' (2 Sam. 6:18–19). This has been explained in different ways, but still it is likely that there was some little measure of wine to make the meal whole. Well, it often says in the Law that when the people come on solemn days to offer sacrifices, they are to rejoice in the presence of God (Deut. 12:7, 12, 18). David followed this rule, and that is why he distributed a portion to each one of the people.

Now there are two things to note: first, the multitude which assembled, so that it says that 'the whole house of Israel' (2 Sam. 6:15) brought the ark. Of course, it was not all the people, but there was such a great number that it was like an army, for we saw earlier that 30,000 chosen men assembled (2 Sam. 6:1). And we have it in the other passage in the First Book of Chronicles, where it says that all the people were assembled (1 Chron. 13:5). For these 30,000 men were there in the name of all, and each took part in it. All the towns and villages had sent people, so this could be considered to be the whole house of Israel.

We also see an excellent zeal in this people, for they had spared no pain, even leaving their houses, their family affairs, their wives and children, and although they came at their own expense, still it was with joy. We see therefore that this people had an affection which was not superficial when they came forward to worship God and restore his worship, which had become an illegitimate mixture. Now if that was done in the period of types, how greatly is our negligence to be condemned today if we spare ourselves from offering to God the sacrifices which he asks and requires of us in truth? It is not a question of a new rule, nor of all these past shadows. But since God has represented himself to us in his living image (Heb. 1:1–3), namely, in the person of his only Son, he wants us to worship him there in such a way that what is spoken by the apostle will certainly be true of us – that we render him 'a sweet-smelling savour' (Phil. 4:18; 2 Cor. 2:15) when we embrace our Lord Jesus Christ. Everyone must employ himself and all his goods in the service of God and his Church according to the measure he has received. If we are negligent in magnifying the name of God and preaching his praises, and also if we fail to consider applying ourselves to his service, and instead use the very gifts and favours which he has put in us, as on deposit, to serve our own ambition and pride, rather than employing them for the welfare of our neighbour, it is certain that we will not need any other judge to condemn us than the story which is recorded here!

We may very well bring forward our excuses and present our subterfuges: 'Yes, I would certainly like to serve God in this place, but it would cost me my life'. Or: 'I have some wealth and thus cannot take part too openly, for I would lose so much'. When men weave these elaborate excuses, it is certain that God knows full well how to break down our laziness and can put his finger on our ingratitude and make us ashamed of it. Therefore, let us learn to follow the example of David, who let himself dance before the ark of God. Let us not be held back by worldly considerations, nor let there be any laziness in us when it comes to worshipping God purely. Rather, let us learn to overcome all of these hindrances and fight valiantly against our temptations, so that the zeal of God may conquer all. This is what we have to remember when it says that the whole house of Israel thus came together.

Well, afterwards 'David blessed the people in the name of the Lord' (2 Sam. 6:18). This word 'to bless' signifies prayers. Thus, when we pray to God for someone, it means that we bless them in the name of the Lord. Now it is true that this office was proper to the priest, as it says in the sixth chapter of the book of Numbers. But there was also another general benediction, which Solomon used and thus did not usurp the priestly dignity when he blessed the people (1 Kings 8:14), as it is recorded in its place. Let us carefully note, therefore, that when David prayed for all the people, he was not claiming any dignity for himself beyond that which God had given him, for he always acted so that the authority of God might remain fully intact. But he had a special concern, since he was king. We know that he who is head of the people has the responsibility to guide and govern them. Well, it is true that David was very aware of the charge which God had given him over the people. However, he recognised that it was nothing unless God guided it all. He did not forget the main thing, which was that God should guide him along with the people.

Well, if one should say to kings and princes today that they should pray to God for the salvation of their subjects, they would take it as an insult! They would think that they were being degraded, for they do not recognise to what God has called them, and what their responsibility implies. They would not be ashamed to recommend themselves to the prayers of their people, but to pray for their subjects would seem to them unreasonable. But as I have said, they consider it inappropriate to think of the charge which is committed to them. They have their eyes fixed so intensely on the high position in which they are placed and on their level of honour that they would like to be exempt from the rule which is universal for the worship of God. In fact, pride blinds them so totally that they think they ought to be put in the rank of God! Well, we must note all the more this passage that says that David blessed all the people there, for in that way he recognised and demonstrated how much he endeavoured to carry out his duty, and that all his virtues would be nothing unless God showed himself gracious to his people and helped in unaccustomed ways.

Moreover, the fact that David generously distributed to all the people the portions which are mentioned here is still a testimony of his zeal for the service of God. It is true that princes indeed build temples and spare nothing to produce marvellous sumptuousness, but nevertheless, that is nothing but ambition and vainglory. Furthermore, they treat the poor harshly, and eat the substance of their subjects. They distribute their goods as they please, and even build these magnificent temples on the blood of the poor, in order to be famous, as though wanting to gain paradise at the expense of others. Well, David offered to God neither stolen goods nor booty. Nor did he act recklessly, but in conformity to the Law of the Lord. That is what we must remember. In brief, all princes and all the great of this world are shown here that everything that they have ought to be used in the service of God, and that in their position they ought not to be miserly and tight-fisted. That is one point. Nevertheless, we must use discretion and prudence in order not to waste what we are offering to God, but rather let our offerings be founded in his Word and regulated by his will.

Nevertheless, there is an incident here about Michal, the wife of David, who was the daughter of King Saul. It says that she 'looked' at David through the window and saw that he danced, practically forgetting himself, and stripping off all royal pomp, so that she 'despised him in her heart' (2 Sam. 6:16). Well, her reproach against him will be discussed tomorrow, for she did not show her venom at first. Here it only mentions that she began to disdain her husband because he humbled himself before God, and was not out in royal pomp showing his magnificence, but was like a poor ordinary citizen, who wanted to be as nothing before the Lord – as he would state afterwards (2 Sam. 6:22). Well, no-one yet perceived the pride of Michal. It only says that she despised him in her heart, and only God can examine hearts.

This sentence is given against her to show that even though no word against God's honour comes out of our mouth (which could openly set a bad example), still, if we conceive some evil in our secret thoughts, that is enough to condemn us before God, even though it does not appear to men and is not noticed by them. This word that Michal despised David in her heart merits serious consideration. As we have already said, no-one could judge it at all, but here is the Holy Spirit putting her on a scaffold to uncover her impiety, so that she will be detested by everyone to the end of the world. That is the reason, then, that it says she detested her husband, David, in her heart. Well, since it is this way, let us learn to keep our affections so pure and whole that we conceive nothing in private which derogates from the honour of God, since we cannot escape his just judgement, no matter how much we put on, since (as I have already said) it is his prerogative to examine the hearts of mortal creatures. That is one point.

Nevertheless, we see how one evil produces another. It is particularly speaking about the people who had come to bring the ark of God, and it is certain that there were many of them who had left their houses, their wives and children, and everything that they possessed in this world, to glorify God. But here was Michal vaunting herself and not deigning to walk three paces, so to speak, to go to the ark, and to show the zeal and devotion that she had for the worship of God. That is sufficient to show that this glorious and detestable, evil woman felt contempt for God and had no religion. Why was she this way? First, she was the daughter of a king, indeed of a king who was condemned by God, who held him in abomination and who had even cursed him; a king whom God had forsaken, who was addicted to witchcraft (1 Sam. 28:7ff.), who was full of cruelty, of tyranny and of all wickedness; a king whom God smote with his severe vengeance for his most enormous crimes.

Well, did she not have reason to humble herself, considering not only the deeds of her father, but that she had also been a depraved whore? For she had had another husband who was by no means legitimate. She could by no means excuse herself by saying she had been forced to do it. She should rather have died a hundred thousand times than consent that such shame be done both to her and to David, who had been a faithful husband to her. Moroever, she should have recognised that such action would bring contempt on the honour of God, whom she should have held in greater esteem than all the husbands in the world.

However, we see here that this wretch had nothing in her but pride, under the excuse that she was the daughter of the king. And (as I have already said) one evil thus produces another. While she saw her husband humbled with all the people, out of pride she began dishonouring and despising God and him whom she ought to have honoured. For what could she have done to carry out her duty to David? At the least, she should have accompanied him, and even if she had no reverence for him, she should still have shown the honour that she owed to God. Instead, this diseased carcass was there at the window, to find fault in others, and make fun of those who were faithfully employing themselves in the service of God – who desired not only that he be adored by them, but by all the people. This was the source of David's motivation and devotion. The very reason why this envenomed tongue and 'sack full of poison' despised her husband in her heart and disdained him was precisely that he wanted to worship God in purity. Indeed, that is how everyone acts who is contemptuous of his majesty. They grit their teeth when they see his glory advance, and their own pomp and fame, which they maintain at his expense, diminish! But after they apply their brakes for a time, they cannot contain themselves, and they have to vomit out the plague which they have in their stomach, as this whore did. Well, that will be explained later.

Now let us prostrate ourselves before the majesty of our good God, in recognition of our faults, praying him that it may please him so to touch us to the quick as to make us groan continually, so that we will run for his help and obtain mercy. And yet may we also be touched with such repentance that we will take pains to strip ourselves of all our carnal affections and lusts, so we might be renewed to the obedience of him who created us, and work in total holiness and truth all our life. And may he not only bestow this grace upon us, but on all people and nations of the earth . . .

19

*'Before the Lord'**

Then David returned to bless his house, and Michal, daughter of Saul, came to meet him and said: How glorious was the King of Israel today, who uncovered himself today in the eyes of the chambermaids of his servants, as one of the tramps uncovers himself . . . (2 Sam. 6:20–23).

We began to see yesterday how Michal's pride caused her to treat the worship of God with contempt. For even though the king and all the people had gone to bring home this container of the covenant with God, which was a testimony that he wanted to dwell in the midst of his people, she still remained in the house. And then she only looked out of the window, and did not go back with the others, as if she were separated from the Church. Soon we see how this same pride made her despise her husband, looking upon him as a common man. It is true that her pride was hidden in her heart, but the Holy Spirit condemned this wicked attitude, even though it was unknown to men. So that is how Michal had already condemned herself, in that she had begun to disdain David because he had humbled himself before the ark. Well, it says that she spat out her venom, so that her pride, previously hidden and known only to God, was now manifested before men.

In the first place, it says that David 'came to bless his house'. We have explained this word when it was mentioned above that he blessed the people. The text also says that he came to pray to God in private that his family would prosper. This is what we

*Tuesday, July 14, 1562.

are accustomed to call in our language 'to save'. But this word 'to save' relates to what we are saying, that God has us and our lives in his hands, and that he keeps those for whom we pray. Therefore, since David had already publicly declared that all the good and prosperity of the people depended on the pure grace of God, he now gave the same testimony to his family in private: namely, that they needed God to watch over them and be their protector. This is a point which is well worth noting. It is certainly true that fathers of families (as one says) and heads of houses ought to be careful to do their duty in governing those who are placed under their authority. But the main thing that parents should do is to take refuge in God. Those who have children should recognise that they will never reach their goal, and their pain can produce no good fruit unless God takes the whole matter in hand and controls it. Those who have servants and handmaids must recognise that if God does not preside in their house, everything will go badly and there will be much confusion. Even when a man has only his wife, he must know that when his house is not blessed by God, there will be nothing but poverty. So much, then, for one matter. It is true that this dependence was demonstrated by means of a public ceremony. But there is no doubt here that David was praised by the Holy Spirit for clearly recognising that in all things he had his refuge in God.

Now it says that Michal reproached him for 'having acted like a tramp' (2 Sam. 6:20). The word implies someone vile, as they say: a good-for-nothing. She compares him (I say) to a tramp, since he stripped himself before the ark of God. Now he was not alone, but it seemed to her that he should not put himself in the rank of the common people but retain his royal gravity. She put the worst possible construction on David's self-abasement, and claimed that he had made himself like a tramp. This showed how deeply infected her heart was with pride because of her royal blood. How often we see this in those who have some noble ancestry. Even though God has abased them and removed every opportunity to be proud of themselves, yet they never fail to flatter themselves with that pride rooted in them by nature. We see many of them who cannot bow their neck, even when God has conquered them, but always remain haughty, even when they have their heads nearly cracked and broken! That is how Michal was. Her father had been condemned by God. His end was wretched. She saw his house totally broken down, and ruined so thoroughly that no-one even dared to claim to belong to this family or to their friends. So many shameful things happened to him that it was amazing. Nevertheless, she could not bow down, because she was hardened in her presumption.

Now here we see what a plague pride is. For anyone infected with it will not only despise his neighbours, but will even be contemptuous of God. For the foundation of true piety – that is, of the fear of God and of his worship – is humility. Yet while men lift themselves up and are inflated with pride, it is impossible for them to submit themselves to God. With this in mind, if we want to prepare ourselves to worship God properly, let us learn to forget all haughtiness, and not make ourselves believe this or that in order to elevate ourselves. Instead, let us be as nothing. That is how we must begin our worship of God. At the same time, we must converse with our neighbours in all modesty and kindness towards others. Nevertheless, if we tolerate a little pride in ourselves, it will most certainly engender all sorts of trouble, envy and vexation. Furthermore, let us not seek to stamp underfoot those whom we cannot tolerate as brothers and companions. For it is certain that he who is driven by haughtiness and ambition would like to see everybody put a hundred feet underground and kept under the dirt!

Let us pay careful attention to what we learn from Michal's behaviour: namely, that since she was so proud and haughty, not only did she despise her husband, but also she could not tolerate even God being honoured. Even if she did have a high regard for herself, even if she had possessed all the dignities that one can imagine in the world, still she should have remembered that the greatest kings are dust and ashes. When we compare such a frail creature as man to the living God, should not his celestial majesty abase everything that can be opposed to it? Now that is how pride blinds all those who are addicted to it.

They so forget who they are that they no longer think of their condition, and also have no regard for God. A man who no longer knows himself has certainly become senseless. How much greater idiocy when a creature holds such a high view of himself that he thinks that God is nothing in comparison with himself! Therefore, we must take even greater pains to purge ourselves of this plague which can stupefy our senses.

Now let us carefully ponder these words of Michal: 'The king was very glorious today' (2 Sam. 6:20). Here she brought up the dignity which belonged to David. By these words, she wanted to make him believe that he was exempt and privileged and did not have to submit himself to God. That is how pride brings ingratitude along with it. On the contrary, the truth is that whenever we taste the goodness of God, any occasion to elevate ourselves will be removed. That is where St Paul leads us when he wants to exhort us to humility and modesty, by saying: 'What do you have that you have not received? And why do you boast over what is given to you?' (1 Cor. 4:7). In brief, if we have the prudence to recognise that we hold everything by the pure liberality of God, it will certainly cause us always to behave as small and humble persons in subjection to him. On the other hand, when we are puffed up with presumption, it follows that we must be ungrateful to God, and endeavour to bury his benefits and abolish the very memory of them. The behaviour of Michal demonstrates this once again, for under the excuse that her husband was king of Israel, she wanted God to give up the worship which he deserved. Well, that is another evil.

In fact, she really cared nothing about the honour of her husband, but instead wanted to inflate her own importance, as though David held the crown because of her, so to speak. One sees many women like that in the world. They are very content for their husbands to be men of reputation and fame and for them to be honoured, but only in order to be more esteemed themselves! For if ambition reigns in the whole human race, it is certain that women are engrossed with it, as so many experiences prove. It is good for them to recognise it so that they might fight against this vice. There is no doubt, I say, that women are led by vainglory to be pompous over the reputation of their husbands and to trumpet their triumphs! And if their husbands are not honoured, they will become much more arrogant than they were. When a man has not advanced and is no longer greatly honoured, he will simply die. But a woman will be a hundred times more angry. She will not admit that the real reason for her anger is her own vanity – who would expect her to do so! But be that as it may, all things considered, one will find that women always think of elevating themselves, and are inflated with vainglory – so strongly that one can neither subdue nor by any means conquer them. That is another lesson we must note from these words of Michal.

Indeed, she says even more, and utters proud words like someone who is trying to convince the world of his bravery: 'Now here', she says, 'is the king of Israel who has been very glorious today. He has stripped himself like a tramp in the presence of his chambermaids and servants' (2 Sam. 6:20). As if she were saying: 'You do not know yourself!' These proud words were intended to reproach David for being unaware of his high social standing. 'For all those who were in your company', she says, 'were your subjects, and indeed your servants and chambermaids have been more honoured than you! Therefore, when you lowered yourself before your subjects and before your chambermaids and servants, it showed that you had absolutely no regard for the honour and dignity that God gave you as king.' In brief, it is the same as if she were saying that her husband had acted in an utterly foolish way, that he did not know how to maintain his dignity, and did not know what he was and to what God had ordained hm. This undoubtedly shows that she preferred the dignity of earthly kings to that celestial grandeur by which they ought to be governed. We see here how the profane would like to manipulate the favours of God so as to abase his honour. Well, the more we have received from God, the more we are obligated to him. This means that kings and princes whom God has wanted to approach him are all the more bound to serve him in humility, according as he bestows the riches of his bounty to them – as well as to everyone else in his own place. Why should the gifts of

God cause us to elevate ourselves? On the contrary, we must realise that when he has shown himself to be so kind to us, he intends to reserve what belongs to him, namely, that he alone be glorified, and that we admit that we depend on him for everything, and have nothing that is our own, but that everything comes from his liberality. That is what God intends to happen when he distributes his goods.

Well, quite to the contrary, those who have forgotten to humble themselves in this way before God wilfully blind themselves and lose as much touch with reality as those who think that they can control the clouds. That was how Michal proceeded in this matter. Since David was king of Israel, she wanted him to have nothing but pomp and worldly show. Yes, but for what reason and goal was the kingdom given to him except that God might be served, honoured and recognised as he deserved? Then when she spoke of servants and chamber-maids, she did it in a demeaning way, as though she were saying that David had not only caused himself to be despised by the people in general, but even by those who were of the lowest and most contemptible ranks.

Nevertheless, David was severely tested by this harshness from his wife. But as it happened, he continually resisted it, though not without a battle. Let us pay close attention to this, for we will frequently see that husbands are corrupted by wives. The more affectionate they were, the easier it was to pervert them. We know where the perdition of men came from: it was from the woman. We have an absolute overflow of examples of how men who were otherwise inclined to live virtuously have become debauched and turned from the right path by women. All the more should we esteem the constancy and noble spirit of David when he was not moved by the shame and mockery which his wife heaped upon him. For he could have been hurt, since he had been so despised in his own house, and certainly that could have made him bend. But he simply replied: 'Before the Lord who has chosen me' instead of you and 'the whole house of your father' (2 Sam. 6:21).

Now here is a phrase which seems to be of little substance, but it bears much meaning: 'Before the Lord'. This means that when it comes to worshipping God, one cannot do too much. Now that one phrase has more power than if David had explained word for word, and said: 'I wanted to honour God, and in fact, that is what I have done, and that is why I did not spare myself'. So if he had given this rather long remonstrance, we would have respected him less than when he pronounced this simple phrase 'Before the Lord'. These words were like throwing 'fat into the fire', and indicate that his heart was inflamed, as though he were saying: 'Alas, you wretched person, who are you to reproach me?' It is, therefore, the name of God which he puts first. He does not say: 'I have stripped myself; I have danced; I have played a musical instrument'. None of that. Rather, 'Before the Lord', as if he were saying: 'Alas, who are we? When it comes to magnifying God, must we water it down; must we maintain our dignity out of fear that we will abase ourselves too much?'

Let us draw from these words a good general principle: namely, in order to worship God, we do not need to look around either here or there to figure out how much we owe him. For we owe him a hundred thousand times more than we can ever pay, and though we try as much as possible, still we must confess that we are unprofitable servants (Luke 17:10). Even if we were able to carry out our duty in such a way that no-one could find anything lacking – for Jesus Christ presupposed this when he said that if we had done all that he had commanded us – still we would have to confess that we are unprofitable servants, and that God is not in the least indebted to us. Of course, it is impossible that we should accomplish what God commands us, for when account is taken, it is certain that we are always guilty of a hundred thousand faults for every single point that we claim we have faithfully carried out. Therefore, since we can scarcely reach the tenth part of what we are obliged to do only by taking great pains to apply all our virtues and faculties, what is necessary then, except to apply all our senses, our thoughts and our affections in the service of God? Therefore, let everything that we know and are able to do be totally dedicated to him. So that is what we have to remember in the first place when it says, 'Before the Lord'.

When we apprehend this incomprehensible majesty, we do well, on the other hand, to see what we are: we are totally frail, and as weak as water; in brief, we are only wind (Psa. 62:9), as the Psalm says. Therefore, if someone put us in the scales and then put in vanity as our counterweight, they would still find that vanity itself would weigh more than we do! Once we recognise this, then we may well be able to conclude that everything belongs to God, and that we are so much his that even if we could do a hundred times more than we are able, still we would need to force ourselves to dedicate all to him; to attribute to him all that we have done, and confess ourselves unprofitable servants. Now that is one point.

Moreover, let us also learn that the greatest should not spare themselves when it comes to serving God. Why? Because everything that is excellent according to the world must pass away when the glory of God appears before our eyes. For if the sun obscures the stars which glitter in the sky, as it shows its strength at midday, so that they no longer appear, what will it be when God decides to come forth? Will we need to be anything before him? In him we are enough. But what blindness, or rather what madness, if we desire to be opposed to him and to prevail against him! Therefore, let us carefully note the words of the prophet that when the glory of God shines forth, there will be neither sun nor stars nor high places of the world that will not be blotted out (Isa. 24:23). Let us gather from this that in all that is given to us, we must seek this goal, namely, that God may be honoured. Now when this is our desire, it is certain that (however much we may be elevated) we will always be small in our own estimation, that is, insofar as we walk before the Lord.

Moreover, David added immediately that he was 'chosen instead of all the house of Saul' (2 Sam. 6:21). By this, he signified that even if he was king, it certainly did not mean that he would fail to show where this blessing came from. We have already exposed the ingratitude of Michal, who under the excuse that she was of the royal blood and that she had seen her husband constituted king over the people, would have liked to think that God had done nothing. But David, on the contrary, argued: 'Inasmuch as God has chosen me, I must give myself to him as his. I must give him homage both from my own person and from the public honour to which he has appointed me.'

Now that is a good lesson which we must remember throughout all our lives. Namely, when we are too cold and lazy to serve God, we must begin to examine ourselves so that we might recognise the things which we have received from him, and thus conclude that since he was pleased to be so kind to us, he has greatly obligated us to himself. This consideration should motivate us to honour and serve him with a much more ardent zeal. Thus, even the very smallest should have sufficient reason to glorify God if they will only remember that he has created them and placed them in the world, and that he has actually made them in his image, and has called them to the hope of salvation. Now if he has called them to the knowledge of his truth, there again is another blessing joined to the first. And then, how many obligations will we discover when each one thinks particularly of the things which God has given him, and in how many ways he has experienced his grace? Indeed, if the small should be stirred up to magnify God, what will it be with those whom God has been pleased to honour and place in a position of dignity? For as I have said, far from the gifts which God bestows upon us giving us an occasion of pride and vainglory, they should, instead, cause us all the more to walk in his fear, knowing that we shall have to give an account for everything. Also, we must put to good use the gifts which he has given to us out of his pure grace, so that the honour will be rendered to him. Now that is what David teaches us: 'God has commanded me to be king of his people. Therefore, I must certainly be humble before him, and employ myself totally in honouring him.'

Well, when he added that God had chosen him 'rather than the whole house of Saul' (2 Sam. 6:21), it did not mean that he was entering into contention or was striking back. Rather, David added this to correct the pride of his wife. For this warned her from above that it was fighting against nature to entertain her vain imaginations. She should have thought that even if her father had been elevated to royal dignity for a time, still it was not of long duration and did not last. And then she should have remembered why her father had been deposed from the kingdom. She should have remembered that all his majesty had been covered with shame. In brief, David showed her that she was lifting up her horns like a wild beast against God, not realising that he must defeat her.

We must gather from this that if men do not lower their eyes and think of their faults when God sends them some chastisement to remove their haughtiness, it is the same as if they were so enraged as to throw themselves down into a well or into a fire. For all the corrections which God sends us are to lead us to humility. If we have been afflicted by being forgotten, our Saviour wants to use it as a means of drawing us back to himself. Because we have been damaged by it, he strips us of all the honours of this world. We see some people who cannot tolerate it when God lowers them after having lifted them up. Well, he must abase them, and if they are not totally abased, he will keep them in check; and if they do not profit from it (as I have said), they are nothing but enraged beasts. Here even is St Paul, who recognised that when God sent him afflictions or when he made him contemptible in the eyes of the world, it was a way of sifting him so that he would not trust in his greatness (2 Cor. 12:7). And if that was necessary for such an apostle, what will it be with us? Hence, let us learn that when God draws us back, it is because we would become savage beasts if we were too advanced and too much at our ease. When he takes back from us what he has given us, it is because he does not want the abundance to kill us, and because he wants to keep us sober, just as one does not give little children so much to eat and drink that they are glutted, for that would kill them. In the same way, our Saviour knows what is expedient for us. Nevertheless, let us learn, as I have said, to abase ourselves voluntarily when God gives us occasion. And may we not resemble this wretched woman spoken of here, who despised God and nature, inasmuch as she still remained arrogant, even when God himself had given her much sifting. Now that, in sum, is what these words teach.

Well, David then added: 'Indeed I shall become more vile. I

shall humble my eyes before the Lord' (2 Sam. 6:22). Here David shows that although he had not humbled himself in an absolutely perfect manner, still he had done the main thing: namely, he had recognised his smallness and made himself nothing, counting his life worth nothing unless lived for the glory of God. David's attitude deserves the most serious consideration. Now you often see kings and princes of the earth go through great ceremonies, as people in the papacy sometimes go through such impressive ceremonies and gestures that you would say they are the most humble souls in the world. They will drag themselves on the ground in order to go and kiss the cross once a year. They will go to kiss relics; they will go to gain pardons and bring from afar valuable presents to some priest or monk (who bears the cross on his back) so as to be permitted to kiss the border of their garments! They will go to such lengths, but what are they in their own eyes, that is, in their own imaginations? It is certain that they are so full of vainglory and pride that they are ruined by it. Moreover, they want to pay God by this means, and they think that they have actually done so when they go through all these ceremonies! They humble themselves so as to keep the people well under control (they say). Thus, since they think that it is God who rules in their hearts, if he abases them, they think that he is too severe, for they would like to make believe that what they are doing proves that they are paying God without owing him anything. That is how great is the arrogance of princes when they go through many ceremonies as a testimony of humility, which in fact amounts to nothing but fiction and hypocrisy.

Let us remember well what we are told here. For David testified not only in the presence of men that he had humbled himself in order to worship God and was doing all that one could wish to show his piety and religion, but rather he said: 'I will be even more abased and humbled in my own eyes'. Now this manner of speaking is fairly common in Scripture. When it says that a man is humbled in his own eyes, it means he is not inflated with vainglory, that he attributes nothing to himself, and knows that he has everything from God, having nothing that was not given him. That is what Solomon also exhorts us to do – 'not to be wise in our own eyes' (Prov. 3:7). That is, not to have a foolish opinion of our prudence so as to govern ourselves by our own brain, but that we should ask God to guide us by his Spirit.

In sum, we see how we must offer to God worship that counts. For as the prophet Jeremiah says, God regards the truth (Jer. 5:3); he is not interested in what is external, and has a lovely appearance and bright reflection before men. Rather, he wants us to have a pure and right affection. Therefore, when it comes to honouring God, let us begin in the same way that David was touched, that is, to be nothing in ourselves, to recognise that until we are blotted out, God will not have the glory which belongs to him. For every mouth must be shut when it comes to honouring God. And what does it mean – the 'mouth shut'? It means that we cannot find any reason to exalt ourselves, but that we are confounded. Now this is precisely what the true worship of God involves, that we be small in our own eyes.

Let us study this word once more: 'I shall become even more lowly, and shall humble myself all the more' (2 Sam. 6:22). This expression teaches us not only to abase ourselves willingly, but always to live in a lowly manner, if need be. Whenever we need to make ourselves reject any occasion which could turn us away from honouring God, we are always to be ready to allow him to abase us as people of no esteem, and yet at the same time let us be aware that it is his will to care for our salvation. Let us always be willing to go down lower when it pleases him, and especially when it is a necessary way of showing how zealous we are to glorify him. So that is the main thing that these words of David show us. Well, if he who was king and represented the person of our Lord Jesus Christ as a living image so humbly abased himself, what will it be with us, and what excuse will there be for us to glorify ourselves, since we cannot control ourselves in a way that brings God the honour that he deserves? Let us watch ourselves carefully, and let us practise what we are shown here, for in comparison to God we must be less than the worms of the earth.

Moreover, David added that 'he would be honoured by the chambermaids of whom Michal had spoken'. Well, here he signified two things: one is that he would be honoured by those who faithfully worshipped God; and secondly, that he preferred the respect which the good people had for him far more than all the adulation of the worldly crowd. By this, he showed that his cry in the Psalm was not an empty one, that he would rather be small 'in the house of God' than be mighty among unbelievers: that he preferred to be a 'doorkeeper' and in some corner of the temple of God 'than to be in the midst of the pavilions of the wicked' (Psa. 84:10). Now this attitude certainly proved that, in the final analysis, all that he really wanted was to be recognised and advanced to the rank of the children of God. He showed that all the rest did not matter to him, and that he sought no high position because he considered that God's acceptance of him as one of his household servants was the greatest honour that he could ever have.

But we must note these two points which we have mentioned. One is that David prized the reputation which he had among the children of God far more than all the goods of this world. Well, by that we are taught that if the despisers of God and profane people take no account of us, and even stamp us under their feet and spit in our faces – yes, if they despise us and would like to have us blotted out – we should pay no attention to any of it, and not even desire to be thought well of or have influence with them. For being loved and favoured by those who hate God can be a very bad temptation which can bewitch us. Let us determine, hence, to follow David in the example which he set for us. That is, if it is a question of reputation, let us prefer to have it among the faithful and the servants of God. Not that it is legitimate for us to seek to be honoured, for that sort of thing ought to be cut out. But instead, when there is neither ambition nor haughtiness in us, we should still be content that the children of God love us and approve of us. Then, if the unbelievers reject and despise us, let it not matter to us, and let us bear patiently their shameful criticism, as the prophet Jeremiah exhorts us to do (Jer. 20:8ff.).

Now there is still another point. It is that we ought to value the children of God more than the finest people in this world and more than those who have all but made themselves into idols. For he also said in the Psalm that he wanted to honour those who honoured God and disdained all those who despised God's majesty (Psa. 15:4) – as if it were nothing but filth and rottenness. Thus, when even the kings of this world are enemies of God, we ought to consider them as devils incarnate. It is true that we ought always to honour their office, inasmuch as it is of God. However, we should detest their resistance to God as an infection and as villainy. Now this brings us to another good reason for valuing the children of God: since it is the wisest judgement that conforms us to God, it is very reasonable that we detest that which is opposite to him.

Well, he said that he valued his Church – however small it was – more than all the princes of the earth. When, therefore, the Church is considered scum and as a little handful of misfits, yet God holds it more dear and precious than all the pomp and crowns of the great kings who are magnificent only in this life. Therefore, since it is true that God so esteems his own in this way, why is it that we are so lax to follow the instruction which David gives us here? That is, if the children of God are rejected and the world takes no account of them, we should still prefer to be in their rank and company rather than to be elevated on the shoulders of the wicked and to be even adored by them! That is what we must remember, and then we can declare with him that we prefer to rely upon the hand of God and to be in his house – indeed, in a low condition – rather than to have the greatest honours of this world.

Whenever we arrive at that position, we shall derive great profit from it for all the rest of our life. For how many are there who, instead of profiting by this example, seek to push themselves ahead, and not only take themselves far from God, but also draw back from his Church? There are many who will confess that the doctrine which we hold is true, but yet they will not even consider standing with us. Why? Because they would have to give up their position in this world; they would be disdained; they want to be able to maintain their great reputation. When they think about declaring themselves to be our brethren, it is as if they are trying to swim between two currents, and are being blown with the wind of this world. Well, since we see that this vice is widespread, let us learn to withdraw from all the allurements which could cause us to seek worldly position and greatness, and so to control ourselves that we will thus always be under the protection of our God. Now this, again, is what we must remember.

Well, in conclusion it says that God condemned the pride of Michal when he rendered her sterile for the rest of her life. It is true that the Jews, who always seek to invent dreams and reveries, make a gloss on the text here. Where it says that 'from the day of her trespass, she had no children' (2 Sam. 6:23), they claim that she had some, but that they were born dead, inasmuch as they could not gain the crown! Now that is a mockery, for it is understood that she was made sterile. If she had had children, if she had had a son, he would have had to be king. It is true that the decree which God had pronounced ought to have been inviolable. Yet according to the general judgement of men, the children who were descended from the family of Saul would have been preferred. Well, God made her sterile and it was to show that he wanted to cut off her family, and that he wanted the royal dignity to be transferred elsewhere.

We have to remember from these words what is fairly common in Scripture: that is, that to have descendants is a blessing of God, a sign of his grace and favour. Also on the contrary, when it pleases him for men to have no offspring, it shows that he is humbling them to that degree, and that he wants them to realise that they are not worthy to have this favour of being called fathers. Now that is one point.

It is true, however, that often the servants of God will not have children. But be that as it may, still it is always an earthly chastisement from which they should profit so as to lower their eyes because of it. By contrast, those who have offspring ought to realise that God has honoured them in that he has given them children, and they should be all the more careful to instruct them in his fear and service. So that is one matter.

But the main thing that we have to note here is that God wanted to approve and ratify, in effect, the sentence of David, and also that he wanted Michal to feel that because she had so filled herself with pride, she was receiving the wages that she deserved. Let us remember that not only was she chastised by the mouth of David as a prophet of God and messenger of his will, but also that God raised his hand and strength and made her feel by experience what the Scripture frequently says – that God abases the pride of the great of this world who draw back from him, and humbles those who band together against him. At the same time, he well knows how to uphold those who take refuge in him, who have nothing in themselves, who openly confess that they hold their life and all that depends on it from his pure goodness, so that the praise and thanksgiving might be given to him.

Now let us prostrate ourselves before the majesty of our good God in recognition of all our faults, praying him to make us feel them more and more, so as to make us displeased with them and hence to ask pardon for them. And so may it make us also draw back from them with such repentance that more and more we might endeavour and strive to give ourselves fully to him. May we do so in truth and without pretence, and may all our feelings and all our thoughts agree in that. And so may our life hereafter prove how sincere our zeal has been. And may he grant this grace not only to us, but to all peoples and nations of the earth . . .

20

*On Being Dead to this World**

After the king was seated in his house, and the Lord had given him rest from all his enemies around about, he said to Nathan, the prophet: See, now, I dwell in a house of cedar and the Ark of God dwells within curtains. And Nathan said to the king: Go, do all that is in your heart, for the Lord is with you . . . (2 Sam. 7:1–13).

We have here an act of David which was highly praiseworthy, and yet it was utterly condemned by God. This is to show that all our devotion must be properly directed and that we are being thoughtless and presumptuous when we fail to recognise what is right, but instead imagine in our head that things are a certain way. It is true that David's basic motive was good and holy – that is, to build a temple for God. For however much 'he dwells not in a house made by human hands' (Acts 17:24), still he wanted to be worshipped in this manner during the time of the figures of the Law. But David was too hasty in not waiting for God to order him to do this, and so he took upon himself more than was appropriate for him. And yet it was not that he failed to handle himself with modesty, or that he failed to leave himself open to submitting to God. For he did not call in his counsellors so that he could tell them: 'Here is what I have concluded – it must be carried out!' The pride of earthly kings is such that they want people to agree with them, and they want all that they have said to come into effect. Well, David did not proceed to act so presumptuously. Rather, he

*Wednesday, July 15, 1562.

called Nathan, the prophet. Indeed, although God had given him the spirit of prophecy to teach others, yet still he submitted himself to seek out the will of God. Nevertheless, he was still at fault, because in addition to addressing the prophet, he ought to have waited patiently for a fuller revelation to be given him. Be that as it may, God undoubtedly approved his fervent zeal. And yet he kept him in check to show him what we saw above, that 'obedience is better than sacrifice' (1 Sam. 15:22).

Therefore, in the first place, David is to be greatly praised for this worthy desire because 'he was at rest in his house' (2 Sam. 7:1). He did not forget this blessing that God had given him, nor lose himself in his pleasures, disregard God and become dissolute. Rather, he saw to it that God was served and adored as he deserved. Such discretion is rarely seen in the lives of the prosperous. Instead, they are intoxicated with the easy life and thus become proud and despise God, and give themselves completely to evil. In fact, David confessed that this, at times, happened to him: 'I said in my peace and prosperity: I shall never be moved' (Psa. 30:6). He assumed that he would always be in that condition. Well, God chastised him for such folly and for allowing himself to go too far. And he brought him down in such a way that he clearly recognised that if he had not been guided from on high, so that he did not carry out his original intention, everything would have been totally ruined.

It is all the more praiseworthy, therefore, that he did not forget who he was, in spite of his personal peace, especially when we consider his position and high degree of honour. In contrast, we see little 'hangers-on', who despise God and burst with arrogance as soon as they are prosperous enough to have something to eat and drink, or perhaps receive some little promotion or other! In other words, it takes very little to make men proud – and then, instead of being warmed to the worship of God, it is pushed from their minds. Our respect for David increases when we consider that he was seated on the royal throne; elevated not only above all the people of Israel, but above his enemies; that God had set a mark on him in that he had chosen him from among all the other kings. And yet in this high position, David remembered that God ought to be worshipped in the first place, and was ashamed for God to dwell in a beautiful canvas pavilion, without having a permanent temple erected in which sacrifices might be offered and in which the majesty and glory of God might shine. This attitude demonstrates what we saw yesterday, that David was like a man humbled before the Lord, that he considered himself to be nothing, and that he only sought to exalt him from whom he held all things.

Now here is where we should emulate David. If God gives us rest and prosperity, let us not be so ill advised as to throw caution to the winds and act like wild stallions, giving ourselves licence to abuse the liberality which he bestows upon us. Rather, let us realise that more than ever we must commit ourselves to his service, and seriously consider how he can be honoured in purity as he deserves, thus showing that we are not ungrateful for so many benefits that we have received from his hand.

We are also admonished always to carry out our devotion according to the rule which he has given us. For while we should be aflame with an ardent zeal to dedicate ourselves to God, we must also be prudent enough to find out the right way to do it, so that we will not do everything that comes into our head, like men who give themselves liberty to do what they have dreamed up, claiming that 'their *intentions* are good'! When they use that word, they think that God should approve everything that they do, no matter how much they cut across [forbidden] fields and do not keep themselves in the right way and on the narrow path. Thus, we know that zeal cannot be considered good unless it is properly directed. The rule is not dependent upon our opinion. Let us take care not to relax our guard to do this or that, thinking that it is a way to serve God. When you have carefully studied all the examples of devotion that exist in this world, you will find none which has a more beautiful appearance or more glorious lustre than the one which is spoken of here. For what did David want? Nothing but what was in conformity to the Word of God. He wanted to build a temple, and he gave the reason why. He did not bring in superstition or idolatry. So he did not corrupt the worship of

God. He did not introduce something for his own particular profit. What was wrong, then? Simply that he did not wait for God to declare his will to him, and say: 'It is you who ought to build me a temple'. Well, it was not supposed to be. God wanted to reserve that for the time of Solomon. All in all, though we find only good motives in David, nevertheless he did make a mistake, since God, who is the only competent judge, reproved him.

Therefore, let us consider ourselves. If that happened to such an excellent prophet, what might it be with us who are not nearly so advanced in the knowledge of the truth of God? Let us remember what I have already mentioned, namely, whenever we are strongly motivated to honour God, let us not be guided by our own imagination. Let us not attempt anything beyond his Word, but rather be so in line with it that we allow him to govern us and guide us by the path that he knows to be right. So much, then, for the second point.

Next, it says that the prophet Nathan replied to him: 'Go, and do all that you think, for God is with you' (2 Sam. 7:3). Here the prophet Nathan is much more to blame than David, for since David came to him seeking counsel, he should not have been so very hasty. Rather, he should have prayed God for revelation. Anyway, he gave a response which he had to take back later.

We see here how God has always deliberately distributed the gifts of his Spirit in limited measure to those whom he has truly established as [teaching] doctors in his Church. It is true that what he wanted to do he revealed to his prophets, as he testifies by Amos: 'Will God do anything that he does not reveal to his servants?' (Amos 3:7). But that is not to say that the prophets had perfect knowledge about everything, for this passage refers to what is appropriate for the edification of the Church. God therefore declares that he will make his counsel known so that the faithful cannot be in dire need of what is useful for their salvation. In fact, God has never shown himself to be miserly, but has always taught his own everything that they have needed. This is what Isaiah says: 'Have I spoken in secret? Have I told you to seek me in vain?' (Isa. 45:19). He declares by these words that he has taught loudly and clearly, not in a whisper, those who desired to serve him, and that his will has not been obscure but, instead, absolutely good and expedient. But be that as it may, God always kept his prophets humble. He declared to them, within limits, everything that their charge involved, and what was required so that, not knowing many things, they would recognise that they were not angels. It is true that, in their office, they were elevated to a dignity similar to the angels', for they were vessels of the Holy Spirit who spoke by their mouth. Yet they had to know that they were mortal men and frail creatures, even when they had duly discharged their responsibilities. But here Nathan did not keep himself in proper bounds. For it is said that the prophets should never undertake to pronounce a word which was not spoken to them – and this solemn warning is found on practically every page and leaf of Scripture. In other words, everything which they pronounce is to have had the express charge and commission of God.

Let us carefully observe, therefore, what it says here about Nathan, so that all those who have received the excellent gifts of the Spirit to govern the Church as [teaching] doctors and superintendents may remember that they are to walk with such extreme care and not to open their mouths to offer anything that they have contrived or dreamed. Instead, as St Peter exhorts us: 'Whoever speaks in the church, let him speak as with authority of God and make his statement on that basis' (1 Pet. 4:11). Now this is what we have to remember. Those to whom God has given rich gifts for their vocation of governing his people must be all the more careful to walk in such sobriety that they will not go beyond their limits. Rather, let them produce the fruit of the Spirit according to the amount given them by God as a deposit, and let them show that they are truly ordained by him, bringing nothing from themselves. For it is certain that all the inventions of men are so full of corruption that they turn the simple Word of God into a confused, bastard production. So much, then, for another matter.

Nevertheless, one must not say that Nathan was demoted from his position. God forgave him this fault – although he had actually departed from the truth and acted presumptuously.

But God still kept giving him his graces. That is why he sent him to David to announce to him what is related here. Well, because we cannot explain the whole story at present, we will summarise the response which God gave, and then we will work out each point, little by little, as time permits.

Here, therefore, is the summary: God wanted to magnify his mercy to David insofar as he had preferred him above all men. This is why he said that ever since he had brought back the people from captivity in Egypt, although he had raised up judges and governors, and had done wonderful deeds by their hands, giving them the victory over their enemies, still he had never given them this privilege of building him a temple. For instance, Othniel and Gideon and Jephthah and the like were ministers called to maintain the worship of God and to testify to it, for this was how God effectively saw to it that his people knew that he had really chosen them. But nevertheless, he allowed the ark of his covenant (with the altar and table and censer with which he spread fragrance) to be kept in tents and pavilions. Indeed, even Samuel, who had lived such a holy life and upon whom God had poured out marvellous gifts, still did not have this commission. But God wanted to show how special David was to him in that he preferred him above all others. This is the first point.

Nevertheless, God still pushed him back, because he had gone too far, and told him that it would not be he who would build his temple, but his son. However, God still granted him much more than he could have wished. And this is what he says in the Psalm: that God will multiply blessings on his children and outdo all that they could imagine (Psa. 40:5). Thus, although David was kept from building the temple in person during his own lifetime, and construction was delayed to the time of his son, still the promise included here is much greater and fuller than the privilege of building the temple. And why? Because instead of building the temple, it says that God would give rest to his people in a different way from what he had done, and that they would no longer be afflicted by their enemies as they had been. It even says that God would build the house of David, as if he were saying: 'He wants to build me a temple, and on my part, I want to build him a house and a firm and permanent estate'.

Then he declared that he would honour his descendants, even saying: 'Your son will call me his father, and I will call him my son' (2 Sam. 7:14). That is why the children of David are called children of God, especially in regard to our Lord Jesus Christ. For it is not without cause that the apostle uses the passage which is contained here to show that our Lord Jesus Christ is above all the angels of paradise (Heb. 1:5). And this very thing is said of David and of Solomon! Hence, let us conclude that Solomon was elevated to a dignity more noble than the angels', because of his relation to our Lord Jesus Christ, for he was like a pledge of Christ, while awaiting his coming. So we see how God established his type in David, even though he drew him back from the presumptuous construction that his uncontrolled and excessive zeal almost led him to undertake.

Well, now that we have this summary, let us proceed to what we should observe here. Let us remember, in the first place, what I have just mentioned – that God upheld Nathan and that he buried deep the fault that he had committed. For he deserved to be removed from the prophetic office, since he had acted seriously out of accordance with it. Although it was motivated by sincere zeal, still there was no excuse for it. Since God wanted to speak by his mouth, he should not have attempted to give a response according to his own mind and opinion, but should have waited for certainty and not have moved a finger without God's permission. On the contrary, he should have been well aware that God knew exactly how to declare his good pleasure at the opportune time. David also had access to the ephod which we have mentioned, by means of which, through the High Priest, God would have bestowed his grace and would always have explained what David was to do. For as we have explained, the High Priest represented our Lord Jesus Christ, in whom 'all the treasures of wisdom and knowledge are enclosed and hidden' (Col. 2:3). Well, since Nathan did not use the ephod, he was without excuse. Yet God did not reject him, but continued to bestow his grace on him, as he had from the beginning. Hence, let us learn that God upholds his own in many things. That is not to say, however, that they should flatter themselves, but rather that they should recognise the faults which God has buried deep so that they may not come into account before his judgement seat. Indeed, let us all be judges [of our own sins] and come to hate them and beg pardon for them. So much, then, for the first matter.

Moreover, God shows in this passage that in order to reveal his will, he has chosen to be served by men offering willing obedience. It is true that he could certainly thunder from the sky. He could also send his angels, who have an appropriate name for that, for 'angel' means 'messenger' or 'ambassador', so that God could make them exercise this office towards us, and we would be taught without inferior earthly means. But he has not so willed and in that way he has shown his overflowing paternal goodness to us, for if he spoke according to his greatness, it is certain that we would be totally lost. Since we cannot stand the brightness of the sun because our eyes are frail, how could we comprehend the wisdom of God if it were manifested to us as it is? Even the simple people clearly recognised this when the Law was published, saying: 'Let the Lord not speak to us, for we would be totally consumed and would perish' (Exod. 20:19). God declared that this was a good and useful request, which is why he said to them that they would always be taught not only by the Law and by its school, but he promised to raise them up doctors and expositors of his will (Deut. 5:25ff.).

Therefore, here is a rule which God has given in the Church: he wants to teach us by means of men, to the degree that it is useful for us. Furthermore, he is manifesting his infinite goodness when he graciously deigns to teach us intimately by those who are like us. For the preachers of the Word of God – who are they if not his mouthpieces? Therefore, when we see that those who are like us and are taken from the midst of us teach us in the name and by the authority of God, we have more reason to approach boldly to hear and receive his doctrine. When we see that those who are 'vessels of clay' (2 Cor. 4:7) – indeed, fragile and of nothing – are nevertheless organs of the

Holy Spirit, we ought to magnify his incomprehensible grace all the more. Therefore, let us remember this, that from all time God has willed his Word to be heard when it is carried by the mouth of men, and that he has authorised this situation in order that all the faithful might learn to walk in humility.

Moreover, as we have declared from the prophet, some were called to teach others. So today, although God is using men to teach us, as he always has, and although he wants us to be guided by their doctrine in the hope of life eternal, all the more must teachers recognise themselves to be disciples and come to his school, just as God ordained it from all time. We see the same thing in St Paul. The more he was elevated as an exquisite vessel (Acts 9:15) and had revelation of secret things – indeed, even to be caught up to the third heaven (2 Cor. 12:2, 4) – all the more God wanted him to go to the school of a man who was not held in high esteem, that is, Ananias, who taught him what he had to do (Acts 9:10). Therefore, God sent St Paul back to be taught as the disciple of one who was not of the company nor of the rank of the apostles, but of a lesser condition. This teaches us that God wants his Word, when it is preached, to be received with all reverence. He wants none to be ashamed to submit himself to it, and none of us to claim, as have some of the wild men, that if God wanted to declare his will, he could easily do it without human means. We are not to argue against what he has ordained. It is not open to question that we must be guided by the mouth of men whom God raises up for us and ordains as pastors.

Now if that were done in the time of the Law, it should be continued even more in this time of the Gospel. For now we have the liberty to participate in the fullness of the Scriptures by means of those whom God has given us to teach his Word (Eph. 4:11–12). And so St Paul, in order to break down all curiosity and to deter men from much extravagant imagination and thus to keep them in line, says that our Lord Jesus Christ is Head of his Church in such a way that he has all pre-eminence and rule. Nevertheless, he has ordained pastors and ministers so that we might be guided in the knowledge of the truth of God his Father, and be confirmed more and more in the faith, and so be received into his kingdom. Now this is the way that we must follow if we want to be approved children of God. We must strip ourselves of all presumption and receive with a meek spirit the Word of life (Jas. 1:21), as it is brought to us by means of men. So much, therefore, for this point, where it says that Nathan was sent to David, and that David submitted to this God-ordained means of maintaining the general order of the Church of which he was a member.

However, we also see a modesty in Nathan which should also be present in all the servants of God. He had too readily put himself forward, no matter how good his motive was, for he said: 'The Lord is with you and thus you shall do all that you have thought' (2 Sam. 7:3). We have already said that he was guilty in this matter. But he was not obstinate, and showed that if he was inconsiderate and ill advised, it was not because of malice or ambition, for he immediately retracted it. Therefore, when Nathan received the revelation which God gave him, and came to David and told what he had heard, he showed that he was not motivated by vainglory, nor seeking to be seen above others or be considered an angel – as if to say: 'See, I am a prophet, and so this secret is not hidden from me'. Now that is how men reveal their inconsistencies when they show that they are led by a spirit of haughtiness and pride, and always want a great reputation. However, we see the complete contrary in Nathan. That is, when God revealed his will to him, he did not argue but immediately committed himself to it, declaring that he had failed through ignorance, that God must now be heard, and that David, though his zeal was good, must restrain himself. Hence, Nathan did not stubbornly insist on his own way. He recognised that he had not behaved as circumspectly as he should have done. Now that is what we have to remember.

Well, this admonishes us that when from time to time we happen rashly to attempt this or that in word or deed, and afterwards are made aware of our fault, we should immediately change course and recognise that we must submit to God. Furthermore, being condemned ought not to grieve or vex us. For we recognise that we are but men, and will show that even though we are weak, we are not so arrogant as to speak against

God, and above all that we are not so stubborn as to continue in something that we should not have begun. Now that is the main thing that we should remember from this passage.

Well, let us come now to what God asked. He said that 'Since he had led back his people from Egypt, he had never asked them to build him a house' but that he had been content to dwell 'in the curtains of the tabernacle' (2 Sam. 7:6–7) – which was made in the desert, according to the fuller information given in the Book of Moses (Exod. 25ff.). Well, the intention of God and his counsel was to magnify the grace which he bestowed upon David, by making a comparison – as if to say: 'I have desired to show myself gracious to my people until this day. I have been their Protector, and they have experienced my paternal goodness in so many ways. And yet the grace which I have bestowed on you goes beyond all of that.' Hence, we can clearly see what God was doing here.

Now in order to apply this doctrine for our own benefit, we must note that God gently guides his Church by definite degrees, so that he does not employ all of his treasures immediately, but just as it seems good to him. And we should pay careful attention to this, especially since we are greedy and want God to give us immediately everything that comes into our imagination. In brief, we cannot stand him keeping us in a low condition – which comes in part from our arrogance, for we would like to do more than is legitimate for us. That is why we are so full of covetous and extravagant follies, and yet at the same time want God to fulfil us and gratify us in everything everywhere, with such intense desire that we never cease being angry and vexed when it pleases God to keep us in a lowly state. Even if we do not cry out openly, yet we have much chagrin in our hearts. Seeing, therefore, that it is so difficult by nature for us to be content, let us all the more learn to remember this doctrine and to practise it. That is, to be governed as God knows best. And if, at first sight, he does not elevate us above the clouds, but makes us crawl upon the earth, keeping us in weakness, and generally teaching us to be humble and small, let us walk patiently and bow our necks to receive the yoke that he puts on them. Let us even learn to exert ourselves in all the afflictions to which the Church is subject, and to allow God to do his work, which will turn to our good, since he knows what is best for us.

Today, God clearly shows what is said in the Psalm, that he wants 'to reign over his enemies' (Psa. 110:2). That is, in the position and circumstances of the kingdom of Jesus Christ, there will be many fights and much resistance (Job 16:12f.). Yet as the other passage says (Lam. 3:12f.), our Lord Jesus Christ is the end and the goal to which we hold, although there will be so much resistance that it will be amazing. Well, all of this must be accomplished. That is, many fight furiously against the Gospel, and persecute the poor faithful in one place, torment them in another, and people machinate and attempt all that you can possibly imagine in order to blot out the memory of the truth of God. Well, when we see that Jesus Christ has thus been driven from all parts, and that there are so many fires burning against the Church, there is no doubt that we are perplexed – for we are not without feeling. But nevertheless, let us keep our balance. For after we have groaned and mourned over the way in which wicked men have grieved the poor Church of God, and indeed have tyrannically opposed it, nevertheless let us draw our conclusion that, since this pleases God, we must accept it and make no reply. We can certainly pray that God will be pleased to remedy it and relieve his children, and we can also pray that he will strengthen them. But nevertheless, let us be patient when we see that he is beginning his work, and let us be resolved that he will accomplish it, little by little and by definite degrees.

This story expounds this principle to us in the flesh. For because God had brought back his people from captivity in Egypt, people had recognised his marvels in several ways, especially in their remarkable deliverance – which ought to be remembered for all time – in which the very elements of nature were moved. There was no part of creation which did not give testimony to the inestimable power of God when he chose to place his hand on his people. This is why it says that the sea drew back and that the mountains trembled and flowed down like snow (Psa. 18:7; 78:13ff.; 97:5; 114). God, therefore, gave outstanding grace to his Church; especially on the day that he led them out of Egypt as well as during the whole time that he led his people through the desert, leading them by the hand to give them possession of the promised land. Now these were amazing events. But be that as it may, we are not disadvantaged today, because we have the king whom God promised us, in whom consists all the well-being of his people. But what is more, he has also permitted the wicked to ravage, grieve, and ransack his people, as the evils of history clearly prove. It is true that the children of Israel provoked God to anger and received the wages of their iniquity when they were thus bitterly persecuted by their enemies. But even so, God helped them in time of need, for he raised them up saviours, as the book of Judges says (Judges 3:9, 15) – that is, ministers who were responsible to encourage them, which they did. Yet there was plenty of trouble, for even before the kingdom was set up, the people insisted on electing a king. Well, although God did have Saul anointed, he showed at the end that he reproved him. For the reign of Saul was cursed, since he was not the legitimate king whom God had promised.

Here is what we are to learn from this passage: we are to allow God so to govern his Church that when he does not make it fully happy, but allows many miseries and temptations to test it, and lets us see scandals, troubles and battles every way we turn, we should not fail to be patient, but rather learn that we are no better than our fathers. And although we are today in the kingdom of our Lord Jesus Christ (as we will explain more fully later), still there is no difference between us and those of olden times when it comes to battles and afflictions in the Church. Therefore, we must not allow ourselves to think that our experience here below should be like an earthly paradise, full of luxury and ease. We realise that although God has made himself known to us more freely than to the ancient fathers, since our Lord Jesus Christ has appeared for our salvation, still our life must be carried on amid various temptations. So let us realise that we are called to this condition, where we will be stamped underfoot and have our faces spat upon. May we respond: 'Amen, O Lord'.

Therefore, when we see that today the wicked are in power, and that God does not send us what we desire, let us realise that it pleases God to test our patience and so humble us, and that he wants to receive the fruits of our faith, which otherwise would have been nothing but rotten pulp! He wants to dedicate us fully to his service as if we were sacrifices (Rom. 12:1–2) – that is, that we be dead to all our thoughts and all our feelings, so that we might give way to the control of his Spirit. Hence, let us carefully remember this lesson both night and day, as we certainly need to do, given that our Lord does not want to examine us merely for one day, but to the end of our life. Also, let us be careful on the other hand, when we think that we have all of this under control, and be aware that it takes nothing to make us totally forget it. Now that is why we ought to persevere in this 'school', and always recognise that God so bestows his favours on his Church that he wants us to be as though we were dead to this world. That is what St Paul means when he says to the Colossians that our life is hidden in our Lord Jesus Christ (Col. 3:3). Thus, since our salvation is bound up in hope (Rom. 8:24), we will not walk arrogantly, presuming anything of ourselves, but will wait for our final happiness to be revealed to us on the last day.

Now let us prostrate ourselves before the majesty of our good God, in recognition of the infinite faults of which we are guilty, praying that it may please him so to guide us by his Spirit that we will not go beyond the limits of his will; and that he may kindle in us such a zeal and desire to serve him that we will never fail to recognise what his will is, for it is good. And so may we follow that will, and conform ourselves to it and be totally subject to it, in all our senses and our thoughts. And may he strengthen us today with such patience that we will not wander about, but will persevere even to the end in the vocation to which he calls us by his infinite goodness. Hence, we shall all say: Almighty God, heavenly Father . . .

21

*Christ is the True Temple of God**

And it came to pass that night that the word of the Lord spoke to Nathan saying: Go and speak to my servant David thus: Will you build me a house for my dwelling? For I have not dwelt in a house since the day I made the children of Israel go up out of Egypt until this day . . . (2 Sam. 7:4–13).

We saw yesterday how David had to be turned away from the undertaking that he had proposed of building a temple to God, without having been commanded to do so. Well, since he wilfully put himself forward, God drew him back by saying that this was not for him. When God says that he is like a guest who changes lodgings, 'who has not dwelt in a palace, but only in a tent', he is using a rather crude manner of speech. Yet Scripture does not use these words without reason, for the people had to be persuaded that God would preside over what had been given to him as a heritage on this earth. Well, we find it difficult to realise that God is near us, for we always imagine that he is far away. Above all, since we so highly value our earthly senses, if we do not see some apparent sign, it seems to us that there is a long distance between God and us, and that we have no way of approaching him. Now that is why it was necessary for God to conform himself to the rudeness of men, and why there had to be a tabernacle, so as to say: 'Here I am; do not fear that I will not watch over you, and that I will not be prepared to help you in time of need'.

For that reason, Scripture declares that God was in a tent,

*Thursday, July 16, 1562.

that he was walking among the people, and when they carried it from one place to another, it was as though he had changed lodging. We have explained how it was necessary for the people immediately to be assembled when he made a change, or when he caused the place where he was lodged to prosper. Nevertheless, let us note that when God makes himself known to us in this kind of familiar manner, taking our weakness into consideration, we must carefully keep ourselves from imagining anything about him which would contravene his majesty and his glory. For from all times, men have abused the visible signs which God gave them, so as to envelop themselves in superstitions and errors. And in fact, we see how the Jews presumed that God was attached to the tabernacle and to the temple, and that they often invoked him from an earthly point of view, as if his majesty were not celestial. In these kinds of texts, we must keep in mind how greatly the Scripture conforms itself to our weak capacities, and thus we must learn to elevate our senses when it comes to invoking God and worshipping him (as we have already explained above).

In sum, although God declares here that he had dwelt in a tent, and that he had walked here and there on the earth, still the people of Israel ought not to have conceived a carnal presence, as if God had changed nature. Nor should they have worshipped him in an earthly and gross fashion, as if he had been enclosed in a temple. Hence, let us now note that God uses such language and descends, as it were, to our level in order that we might not have the pain of wandering far to seek him – not to lead us into superstition, so that we want him to be down here with us, but rather to induce us to worship him 'in spirit and in truth' (John 4:24) by the sacraments and testimonies which he has given us. We must always keep in mind that his mightiness reaches above all the heavens, as Solomon declared when he built the temple: 'Lord, the heaven of heavens cannot contain you, and how much less this temple which I have built?' (1 Kings 8:27). 'Yet though that is true, this is so that your name will be invoked here.' That is another reason why God declared that he dwells in a tent, that he changes lodging, that he is there to accompany his people.

Finally, he used this word 'to build a temple in his name' (2 Sam. 7:13).

Well, when he speaks of his name, it is to show us that his essence is celestial and that it is not enclosed in this material temple. Nevertheless, it was a way of drawing the people to himself, because men, as I have said, are in shock at the suggestion of coming to God. They wander about in despair because they think that they have no way of reaching him. That is why God wanted to condescend to the infirmity of his people. Anyway, this temple was built in his name to signify that he would not dwell there in the manner of men, and that his glory would not be enclosed by it, but that it would be a means by which man could invoke him in trust, and not doubt that he would have mercy upon them and that he would answer their requests.

Therefore, that is how we have to join together these two modes of speaking. One is rude, simply because God clearly wanted to condescend to the infirmity of men – to their opinions and capacity. Thus, when he said: 'I dwell in a tent', he meant to reveal himself to them in a familiar way so that men could communicate with him. When he said: 'The temple will be built in my name', it was to signify that we must worship him above the skies with such reverence that we do not imagine that he is here in a creaturely fashion, but realise that he surpasses and goes beyond all things. Thus, when we clearly know how to join the two, we will have no difficulty in invoking God, knowing that he is truly with us, since he gives us the visible testimony of his presence in the sacraments. It is true that today we do not have this material temple, as in the time of the Law. But beyond the fact that God has manifested himself in the person of his Son, we also have baptism and the Lord's Supper – in which God declares that our Lord Jesus Christ has power to wash us so as to cleanse all our uncleanness, and that his blood never fails or dries up, but that it still flows today by the virtue of his Spirit, so as to flood and cleanse our souls. That is one point.

In the Lord's Supper we have testimony that the Lord Jesus Christ is our nourishment, our meat and our drink, that we have our spiritual life in him. Let us therefore learn so to trust in his promises that we will not doubt that he truly dwells in us. Now may we always keep this truth in our memory, that all visible signs are meant to represent the name of God to us, so that we will not think that Jesus Christ comes down from the skies and leaves that glory into which he was once for all received. Rather, let us lift our spirits up where he is, by faith, so that we might be joined together with him. This, in sum, is what we are to remember.

However, we also see the infinite goodness of God when it says that he 'travelled with his people' (2 Sam. 7:7), and that he changed lodgings. Indeed, it is not only in this passage that the Scripture speaks in this way, but when mention is made of the desert, it says that God marched before his people, as if he were their guide. There was also a visible sign of it, for by day there was the cloud which covered the people, and then by night a pillar of fire (Exod. 13:20ff.). Well, the Lord used this to show that he was marching in front of his people so as to take care of them. Today, these signs have passed away from us, but what we have ought to satisfy us. Let us recognise, therefore, that we are here below as poor wandering sheep; that we must roam about here and there, and that we need God not only to guide our feet, but also to suffer with us, so to speak. Not that he suffers anything in his person, but this meant to express that he has genuine compassion on our miseries, which is the same as if he were suffering because he was our Companion and were subject to suffering, as we are. So here again is what we have to remember from this figure of speech, where it says that God walked and made several trips with his people.

Now we come to what we mentioned yesterday, namely, that he raised up judges several times and, nevertheless, that 'he did not say to any tribe that they should build him a house of cedar' (2 Sam. 7:7) – that is to say, a temple, which was like a palace. He declared how from all times his mercy had been known to guard and maintain his people. For these many judges were all testimonies to the goodness of God, who did not want his people to perish. It is true that he did not keep them in good circumstances, but that was the fault of the people. There had been great invasions by which the poor people had been afflicted, now by one nation, now by another. They were oppressed by horrible torments, but it was because of their offences. They could not bear the yoke of God, and they had to be subjected to defeat in which people treated them most cruelly. Anyway, after having afflicted them, God always upheld them in their troubles. That is one point.

However, he showed here that although he raised up the judges, now from one tribe, now from another, still he had never given any tribe the honour of saying that they had built him a temple. So here is the great difference between the earlier favours which God had bestowed and those which he reserved to David and his house. This is what the Psalm says: 'I was glad with those who said, let us go into the house of the Lord. My feet shall stand within your gates' (Psa. 122:1–2). The Lord signified that he gave a singular privilege to David when he showed him the place where he wanted to build his temple. Hence, the feet of the faithful were stopped when God no longer changed location, and had a definite and permanent place. Hence, they always had to be held in suspense until God had chosen a specific place where he wanted his name to be invoked. This decision is magnified with good reason, because it was the fulfilment of the promise which was made: 'When God has chosen a place, where his name will be invoked, then you shall come there' (Deut. 12:5ff.) – in order to show the memory of his goodness, to sing his praises, and to give him thanks. The fact is that up until then, the people were constrained to sacrifice wherever the ark was.

However, we are shown that the kingdom of David possessed an exclusive blessing, which is spoken of here, and is more fully declared in the other passage from the Psalm, which says that 'God has not established Ephraim and has reproved also the other tribes, except Judah and Mount Zion, in which he has taken pleasure' (Psa. 78:67–68). Well, that signifies that God had, as it were, rejected all the rest of the people, and had taken no account of the other tribes, although he wanted them all to be joined in one body. This statement meant that God gave the tribe of Judah a special favour from which he excluded the others. For although Samuel was a man of excellent dignity, still the Lord did not choose him as he did David, and during that period he had not chosen a place where he would have a permanent station. Afterwards, Saul came in, and his kingdom was not approved by God. Therefore, Ephraim and Benjamin were sent back. There were still the tribes of Dan, of Naphtali, and all the rest. Well, God did not show them such a favour either, and say that they were perpetual heads of his people. Hence, we see how God wanted to exalt the grace which he gave to David. Therefore, although he took people now from one tribe, now from another, to be ministers of the salvation which he wanted to give to his people, still he had not said to anyone: 'You will build me a temple for my habitation'. But he left them in a middle position.

Well, this admonishes us to remain content when God distributes his favours to us in small measure, and does not lift us into a position of supreme honour. And it ought to satisfy us completely that he is our Father, even though we are lower in comparison to those who may have more noble and excellent gifts than we do. But be that as it may, still this promise is above all given to the Christian Church, for that which was reserved for the time of David was ultimately for our salvation, since David was only a type of our Lord Jesus Christ. Therefore, let us learn that our condition today is much better and more desirable than that of the ancient fathers (Heb. 11:40) in that God has chosen our Lord Jesus Christ, not to build him a house but that he is the very temple of his divinity. That is why our Lord Jesus Christ also says: 'Destroy this temple, and in three days I will raise it up' (John 2:19). For in calling his body a temple, he shows what St Paul says, that 'all the fullness of divinity dwells in it' (Col. 2:9). That is, not in mere shadow only, but in truth and 'in substance', which means that he is with us today. Now this is what we have to remember from this passage.

That is why he says: 'You shall say to my servant David' (2 Sam. 7:8): 'he who will come after you, will be the one who will build my temple'. Things are not arranged in order here but he shows us that what is interwoven ought to be both joined together and distinguished. For after God had shown that up to that point he had not given his people a definite place where his name would be invoked, he again magnifies this grace which he gave to David in that he 'took him' and drew him from the flock of sheep and from 'the sheepfolds' (2 Sam. 7:8). This is what the Psalm says, that he marked 'Mount Zion which he loved' (Psa. 78:68). For when the Scripture offers this word on the love of God, it signifies a gratuitous goodness of God – so that man may receive no part of the praise, but may recognise that everything proceeds from the utter and pure mercy of God. When it says 'Jacob whom God loved' (Psa. 47:4), it is to show that the salvation of Jacob and the grace which he received depended on the free election of God. Therefore, the same is shown now in David. For when a man is elevated to some degree of honour, he will certainly think that he has reason to be esteemed before God, but this misconception is because we do not go to the true source and origin. Even if the kings of the earth were a hundred times greater than they are, still they are of the tribe of Adam, and hence their dignity should not make them self-important, but the grace of God ought to shine forth in them and be appreciated. However, we fail to see it in this way because our eyes have been dazzled.

Well, so that David would always walk in humility, it says that 'God took him out of the sheepfolds'. For who was he? A poor shepherd, as he confessed himself and gloried over it, so that he would not be enveloped by an earthly pride which would seduce him and make him ungrateful. That is why he plainly says: 'Yes, I was with the cattle; I was a poor shepherd and cattleman, and God took me from that, and made me the guide of his people'. Hence, let us note that God will never be honoured as he deserves unless we are confused in ourselves and are aware that we have nothing of ourselves, but that we have received everything from him. For if men retain even one single drop of reputation and think that they are acquiring either this or that by their own industry, they are still stealing it from God and are despoiling him of his right. How, then, can we honour God? Let us be totally blotted out, and confess that we have received everything from him.

Well, let us study carefully this word which says: 'I have taken you from the sheepfolds', where you followed the lambs and sheep, 'to make you head of my people' (2 Sam. 7:8). Well, if that were urged upon David, how much more do we need the same warning! For we see our ingratitude, and how we seek only to obscure the grace of God. Now if David, who had a docile spirit, needed to be reminded not to lift himself up presumptuously, how much more is this doctrine and admonition useful to us. Let us remember, therefore, what we used to be, and what we were like when God took us, so that we may properly humble ourselves. After all, he draws us all together out of the depths of hell. That is one truth. We are of the cursed race of Adam. There is nothing but damnation in us. We are called children of wrath and of sin (Eph. 2:3). Well, after we have thus recognised what our origin is, we will surely have occasion to value all the more the grace of God, and to preach it – indeed, with all humility. Now this is one point which we have to remember in regard to honouring God properly.

Then it adds that God 'had been with him everywhere that he went, and had exterminated his enemies' (2 Sam. 7:9). Here God shows, in effect, that it was by his virtue and by his help that David reached royal dignity, and was kept in it. For was it possible for him to have had such notable victories if the Lord had not given him his hand and helped him? Therefore, by experience it was apparent that God had chosen him and had done so out of his pure grace. Well, this admonishes us that whenever we do not glorify God as he deserves, we should be more aware of the graces which we receive from him, and take account of them. For though we are like people in shock, still we ought to testify to (or at least mark) the blessings that he has given us which we do not even think of. Now that is why we ought to remember all the more the lesson which is shown here. That is, that we should not allow ourselves to forget the goodness of God to us. Let us give him thanks as he deserves, and take account of our misdeeds so as to ask pardon for them, and to confess that we would be the most miserable creatures in the world if he left us as we were by nature. That is how we ought to remember the blessings of God, so that we will not distort them by our ingratitude and laziness but, as I have said, be touched to the depths of our hearts by them in order to give him the thanks which he deserves. Well, that is what it says here.

Moreover, let us also note that this same process ought to assure us of the original election of God. It is true that we receive the principal assurance of our election when it pleases God to manifest it in Jesus Christ and to make us his children by faith and the Gospel. But still, when God adds other blessings out of his superabundance, there are so many signs which he gives us to make us all the more certain that he is truly our Father, that he holds us dear, and that his mercy will always be evermore engraved in our hearts, so that we may all the more place our trust in it. Now that is what we have to remember.

It says that 'God had given him a name more excellent than any of the most famous men on the earth' (2 Sam. 7:9). God now amplifies what he just said; namely, that he gave David his own assistance and help. For although he was king, yet he could have remained in mediocre circumstances. But God elevated him so high that he clearly saw that it was not a human act. In sum, we are shown here that the blessings which David had received were visible testimonies that God had shown himself to be a Father to him, indeed in an exceptional and unusual manner previously unknown.

He adds that he 'will establish a place for his people' and that 'his enemies and the iniquitous will not trouble them as formerly' (2 Sam. 7:10). Well, this is a relative form of speech, for the earth which had been given to the people as a heritage was already an inestimable blessing. In fact, it was called the 'rest' of God and the heritage of his people. Therefore, when the children of Israel entered into the possession of the land, God 'planted' them (Psa. 44:3). But now it seems that the contrary is being presented here; that is, that the people had not been planted there and had not possessed a permanent place. Yes, but he is speaking relatively here. For when God actually reached out his hand to cause this people to possess the land, then he planted them, as it says in the Psalm which we have mentioned. God had brought back his people out of Egypt, and 'they did not gain the land by their arms nor by their swords, but by the favour' which he gave them. And then: 'You have planted there your people and have extended their limits from one sea to the other' (Psa. 80:9 paraphrase). Now that is how he planted his people who entered into their rest at that time. But the ingratitude of his people caused this rest to be cut short. Therefore, this is why the poor people were restlessly tossed about by their enemies and apparently were on the verge of being uprooted from day to day. For they were continually assailed; they could not farm their fields, nor do their business. They were, in brief, 'like lambs among wolves' (Matt. 10:16).

Well now, God says that he shall have pity on his people so as to save them in another way, and that is precisely what happened. From the time of David, the country in fact did remain in peace, for no-one dared to rise up against it. It is true that David fought great wars, but after the Lord announced what is included here, the results were that he subjugated many countries, now one people, now another, according to what is said in Psalm 60:8 – 'I shall cast my shoe over Edom; Moab shall be my washpot; hence I shall place my feet on my enemies. I shall walk over the Moabites and the Philistines.' David spoke in this way to show the fulfilment of what he had been promised, namely, that God would give a permanent place to all his people. That began in the time of Solomon, who did not even have wars with foreigners, for in fact they all paid him tribute, and were his subjects. So that is how Solomon's day was different from the time of David, if we consider what the circumstances were like after the people came out of Egypt.

Well, be that as it may, this was not merely for the time of David and Solomon. Hence, we must go further if we want to find the fulfilment of the promise and its effect. There is no doubt (as will be stated more fully tomorrow) that this pertains to our Lord Jesus Christ. Therefore, let us recognise that it was for us that David received this promise, that it was put 'on deposit' with him so that he might be the guardian of it. But today, the fruit of it ought to be gathered in the Church, and hence let us be aware that God establishes us so solidly that we are attached to him, and he preserves us from our enemies.

Well, if we ask how it happens, it is certainly not a matter of external appearance. For it says here that the people shall be planted under David, that is to say, that they will have roots so as to be assured of their rest. But what is the condition of Christians? We see it, but as St Paul clearly declares, we must be pilgrims (1 Cor. 4:11). He uses a word which implies much more. We are (he says) without home and station. We are not only like a bird who is on the branch, but like the dust which is blown by the wind. Now that is what our condition is. Now how does this fit in with our being established so that our enemies no longer trouble us, since in actual fact we are always poor pilgrims and cannot have a definite place? Are we not persecuted and continually afflicted by the wicked and enemies of the truth of God?

Now the whole matter will fit together very well when we realise that even though we wander and tramp here and there, we are always sustained by the hand of God, and even though we are persecuted, we shall have victory in the midst of our conflict. Moreover, in order to understand this, we must remember that the kingdom of our Lord Jesus Christ is spiritual. Under the guidance of David, it was necessary for the people to have a visible rest in human terms, especially because they had not reached this perfection to which the Son of God has brought us. But now we must not seek our rest here below. We do not have to win our triumphs here so as to reign in an earthly paradise below, but let us realise that we must die with the Lord Jesus Christ in order to take part in his life; we must suffer shame and injuries in order to be companions of his glory. But be that as it may, when we realise that his kingdom is spiritual, then amidst the afflictions that we endure, we will know the deliverance which God gives us, and his victory. And whatever unrest and torment they may cause us, still we also shall recognise that God holds us firmly so that we are established in him, and are not cast about here and there.

Therefore, here is how we can profit from this doctrine and

apply it to our benefit: when we take time to feast our eyes on the nature and quality of the kingdom of our Lord Jesus Christ, and remember that it is spiritual and that its glory goes above the heavens. Nevertheless, we should hold this firm conclusion: since God is so strongly the defence of his Church, his enemies cannot torment it, for he will always save it. Well, if God thus afflicts it, let us note also that he blames it on our sins. For when he 'loosens the reins' on the wicked to do all the extortion and violence that they can to us, let us realise that it is for our sins, since we have annoyed him and are incapable of perceiving his benefits and fully enjoying them. Hence, let us blame our own evil and vice for all such vexations and anguish as we endure today, and let us realise that we are preventing God from continuing this grace, which would shine out much more in us if we did not prevent it by our rebellion.

It says afterwards that 'God promised he would build a house for David', and then that 'after his death, he would raise him up seed, and that he who would come from his loins, would build the temple' (2 Sam. 7:11–12) – which David had inconsiderately presumed to build. Well, in the first place, where it says that God would build a house for David, it is using a figure of speech which is fairly frequently found in Scripture. 'To build a house' is to give an estate to someone. That, therefore, does not mean persons or multitudes of goods, but it means that God will make David prosper not only in his person, but in his offspring, as we see by the flow of the text. Well, this shows us what was already mentioned yesterday, that is, that although God drew David back and rejected the idea which he had conceived, still he granted him much more than he could have wished, as he clearly recognises in the confession that he made concerning it (2 Sam. 7:18–19). Still, this word shows us that if God did not answer David in one way, he did in another.

This is very useful for us, for we would like God universally to fulfil all our desires in everything! Not only would we like him to have mercy on us, but we would like to give him instructions so that he would help us in the way which we have conceived – and then we ask why he has not done it in such and such a way. Now that is how we would like to subject God to our appetite. Well, he refuses many of our requests because they are excessive. But be that as it may, there are different ways which are strange to us, and yet he does much more for us than we could ever hope. Now here is a man who is sick. He would like God immediately to give him health. There is another who is poor. He would like to have his cellar full of wine and his granary full of wheat, and to have great rents and revenues. Well, God reserves such things to himself, for he knows what is best for us. However, to him who wishes to have health, a grace more appropriate to his salvation is granted. As for the one who is afflicted with poverty, while God does not give him riches by which he may cut his throat, still he will sustain him in a way that will be much better for him. Therefore, judging by external appearance, God refuses what we ask him. But he gives us much more – indeed, in unknown ways, as we have said.

Let us be careful, therefore, to place ourselves within his will, which is always good, and when we see that he does not want to please us in all that we desire, it does not mean that he does not fulfil the will of 'those who fear him' (Psa. 34:10), as the Psalm says. In this way, he demonstrates the singular goodness of his love to us, as if he were totally prepared to gratify us in all that we could ask of him. God will thus grant the will of those who fear him; but what will? It will be when they conform themselves to his will, as it says in the other passage, that 'all that we ask him in accordance with his will, he will grant us' (1 John 5:14). Let us be careful, therefore, to conform ourselves to it. And then when he has spoken the word, let us acquiesce in it, and let ourselves be led like poor blind folk, inasmuch as he is in 'inaccessible light' (1 Tim. 6:16) which we cannot comprehend with our carnal senses. Let us also recognise that it is not for us to put ourselves forward in this or in that, or to make imperious demands of him. That, in sum, is what we have to remember from this passage where it says that God will build a house for David – especially, even after his transgressions, it is stated that God will bestow his mercy on his seed.

Well, finally it says that 'Solomon will build a temple for God' (2 Sam. 7:13). We have already mentioned how Solomon had built a material temple, yet this was not the main thing noted here but only a small illustration which God uses – a mere shadow of the reality. Therefore, we must come to our Lord Jesus Christ. For in fact, this temple which Solomon built would have been nothing in itself if it had not been founded on the person of the Redeemer, and if it had not been a type of this spiritual temple of which we have spoken, and thus it was that the temple of Solomon was totally ruined (2 Kings 25:9). That which was rebuilt afterwards was only a lodging (Ezra 3ff.), so to speak, in comparison with this very sumptuous building described in the First Book of Kings (1 Kings 6). But when Herod built the second, he made it much smaller than the temple of Solomon. Indeed, it was a marvellous and almost unbelievable thing, built in the same place still and even called the Temple of Solomon. But what was it? Nothing, for it was nothing more than a cloud of smoke and a puff of wind, inasmuch as our Lord Jesus Christ had to come and put an end to all types – and, also, Herod was not approved. Being a profane man, he did it only to buy favour and credit with the people so as to control them more easily, finally subjugating them by his tyranny.

Therefore, when it comes to building this temple of God, let us note that it ought to correspond to its reality, which is our Lord Jesus Christ, in whose person God's majesty has been perceived, and his glory has clearly shone forth. That is why he is called the living image of God his Father (Col. 1:15), which otherwise is invisible to us. For in him we have all his wisdom, all his goodness, and all his justice to such a degree that we no longer need to have a sign to appear before our eyes, since God has now revealed his majesty in Christ in total perfection (Heb. 1; 1 Cor. 1:30).

Be that as it may, still in the time of types, it was a great prize for God to have chosen a place in which he wanted a temple to be built, which he would inhabit in the midst of his people. Hence, this promise was not useless when it said that 'this one will build a temple in my name', but was an inestimable gift which God gave to David. Well, if this type was worthy of being valued, what will it be with the truth and substance which is in our Lord Jesus Christ? Let us embrace, therefore, this infinite goodness of God, which he shows us when it pleases him to inhabit not only alongside us, but inside us. Furthermore, he wants us to be temples of his body, and to live from the substance of his Son – to the point that we are participants in his nature.

Now let us prostrate ourselves before the majesty of our good God, in recognition of the many faults of which we are guilty, praying him to make us feel them so and become more and more displeased with them. And may we learn so to yield ourselves to him that we only seek to walk wherever he calls us, and may he so multiply and increase his grace to us that our life may respond to his holy will. And may we glorify him not only with our lips, but also with our deeds, since it has pleased him to pull us out of the pit of death in order to enrich us in the hope of eternal life. And also may we be more and more confirmed in this adoption, whereby we are made children and heirs of the heavenly kingdom. And may he bestow this grace not only upon us, but also upon all peoples and nations of the earth . . .

22

*Mercy and Judgement**

And when your days are fulfilled, and you sleep with your fathers, I will raise up your seed after you, who will come from your loins, and I will establish his kingdom. He shall build a house in my name, and I will establish the throne of his kingdom for ever . . . (2 Sam. 7:12–15).

We saw yesterday how what is contained here was fulfilled in Solomon; at least partially, for he built the material temple in the name of God. But we can easily gather that the fulfilment and perfection of this promise was not found in him and in his successors. One must go much further, that is, not only to our Lord Jesus Christ, who is called 'Son of David' because of a greater excellence than Solomon, but also to all those who are descended from his race. Hence, the text clearly says that 'God will establish the royal throne to eternity' (2 Sam. 7:13), that is, that the empire will remain permanently in the house of David. The Psalm expresses this even more fully when it adds that God calls on the sun and moon to testify to his will that as long as people see them shining in the heavens, the race of David will never fail to have the sceptre (Psa. 89:36–37).

Well now, we see what happened: Solomon reigned peaceably and without opposition, but the third descendant retained only a very small portion of what David has acquired (1 Kings 12). There was a rebellion not only of foreign peoples who had been under obedience to David and had paid him tribute, but even those who were of the body of the Church rebelled, so that

*Friday, July 17, 1562.

nothing else remained to him but the tribe of Judah and part of Benjamin. Since ten and a half tribes broke off from obedience to him, he did not have the perfect fulfilment that this text speaks of. But then, what about the promise which God not only spoke, but also backed up with a solemn oath, as the other passage says (Psa. 89:36)? Well, we have always seen the sun and moon; there has been no change in the sky, so why did this revolt happen so quickly? If two or three generations – or even twenty or thirty – had already reigned, that would not have begun to fulfil the promise. But when we see that there was no-one but Solomon and his son – who was supposed to succeed him, but who in fact lost the greatest part of his subjects and of his country, and was rejected by the majority – then we realise that God did not have Solomon in mind nor those who came after him, except insofar as the Redeemer should finally be raised up from the tribe of David, whose kingdom was perpetual.

In fact, the faithful did not understand it otherwise. For the prophecy of Jacob (Gen. 49:10), which served them as an exposition of this promise, explained that this is how it would have to be. Long before the people were given possession of their heritage, and even before they had been brought out of captivity in Egypt, listen to Jacob, who declared that 'the sceptre would remain in the house of Judah, and the law-giver would be in his loins'. That is to say that he would remain there in this house and in this tribe, indeed, 'until he who ought to be sent, comes'. It is certain that he was speaking of our Lord Jesus Christ. It is true that the word implies more than being sent. But be that as it may, there is no doubt that the Redeemer of the world is spoken of in this prophecy. Therefore, the faithful have had a key with which to open this prophecy so as to comprehend what this promise is worth, and to what end it tends. The temporal kingdom, therefore, which involved the house of David, was only a type, so that the substance and ultimate reality of what is contained in this prophecy cannot be found in it.

The prophets also clearly showed that the house of David itself held this interpretation, for even though his whole house seemed to have been ruined and abolished, yet because God would not fail to be faithful, they could in the mean time await with patience the coming of the Redeemer. That is why the prophet Isaiah says that he 'will come forth a little rod from the trunk of Jesse' (Isa. 11:1). For in the time of which the prophet spoke, one would have considered that David had been mocked and the promise which he had made to David had been frustrated. First, one saw the kingdom ruined and torn in pieces, and then that enemies had pillaged and torn up everything, so that nothing was left but desolation. What could one have said except that what God promised was a lie or a dream? For the very testimonies which he brought forward – the sun and the moon – would show that the country of Judah was totally disfigured. The tribe of Abraham was in miserable extremity, under worldly shame, and it was generally held that this entire race was cursed.

Yet Isaiah does not fail to give good hope, and says: 'Although there be no more royal dignity in the house of David, and it decline to the status of its father Isaiah, who is called Jesse (that is to say, a man of the fields), so that it no longer possesses the excellence and dignity of which we have spoken, still (he says), God will cause a small rod to come from this trunk'. Well, he calls it a trunk: when one has cut the whole tree down to the ground, it does not even show. But little by little, a small new branch comes out of it. We see, therefore, how the prophet confirmed the faithful and led them to our Lord Jesus Christ, so that they could enjoy what had been promised them. That is why it says that God will cause 'his sure mercies towards David' (Isa. 55:3) to appear, and then in the other passage, that he will cause his light to shine again upon him (Isa. 60:20). He mentioned this perpetual kingdom as a clear way of showing that God considered this thing to be far higher and more excellent than all the empires of the world. In sum, when God promised to raise up seed to David, we clearly see that he did not have in mind Solomon alone, nor those who are descended from his race, but above all he had in mind our Lord Jesus Christ.

If one asks, however, if this was not understood of Solomon, we have already responded 'yes, in part', as the First Book of Chronicles, chapter 22 sufficiently explains. For David, speaking to Solomon, his son, said that it was of him that God had spoken, and he even added that he would have the means to build his house, because he would be peaceable, and would not shed blood in his time. But he had to have his type and shadow, and then the true reality would appear in all perfection. Now here, therefore, is how the whole matter fits together clearly: God certainly promised that Solomon would build him a material temple – but nevertheless, he had more in mind.

Even the apostle uses another argument to confirm this. For he says that this verse cannot be understood of any angel (Heb. 1:5): 'He will be a son to me, and I will be a father to him' (2 Sam. 7:14); nor what is said in the second Psalm either: 'Behold, I have today begotten you, ask of me and I will give you the ends of the earth for your heritage'. Now here in the second Psalm, David was actually spoken of, insofar as he was a type of our Lord Jesus Christ. But if we notice what this title implies, that he is the Son of God, that cannot be said of any of the angels. The angels are certainly called children of God, as are men who are earthly creatures. This is certainly as common to men as to angels. But when there is a unique Son, without competition, as it says, he must be in a class all by himself. Now people certainly talk of 'Mister so-and-so'; and many others are lords. But when there is one who is sovereign Lord among all others, it is certain that he is separated out from the number and rank of all the rest.

Hence, when God declares that he has a Son, that means that he is unique. From this, we can grasp what the apostle says, namely, that Christ was above the angelic estate, which cannot be imputed to David or to Solomon. Thus, everything points to him who surpasses every creature in glory. It is he who is the living image of the heavenly Father; he who had all glory in himself with [the Father] before the creation of the world (John 17:5). It is he to whom pertains all authority as an emperor, both above men and above angels; he who is named the Lord of Hosts – as shown by St John, who says that the vision which Isaiah had of the infinite majesty of God was only to manifest what the coming of our Lord Jesus Christ would be (John 12:40–41; Isa. 6:1ff.).

Since these are the facts, we have certainly made the point sufficiently clear that when God promised the kingdom to Solomon, it was not for himself nor for all of his race, but was meant for our Lord Jesus Christ. Well, Solomon (as we have stated) certainly built the temple in which God was served and worshipped. However, our Lord Jesus Christ, being the true temple, also built a house for God his Father, especially since he reconciled us to him (Eph. 2:14–18). For by this means, we are consecrated to the service of God in such a way that he inhabits us by his Holy Spirit. And we have this honour and this privilege, even though we are nothing but vessels of clay (2 Cor. 4:7) – indeed, rotten and infected – yet God receives us and wants to have his dwelling and sanctuary not only in our souls, which are more precious to him, but also in our bodies, which are poor carcasses, as the Scripture describes them! Therefore, we see how our Lord Jesus Christ built the spiritual temple in a manner much more worthy and more noble than Solomon did. There was stone and wood in that temple. It was exquisitely sumptuous. Its workmanship was very great and excellent. But here is a kind of house which is far more perfect than the building which was on the mountain of Zion. It is a temple in which so many men and women who have been converted to the faith of the Gospel are like numerous stones which have been assembled so that God might dwell throughout all the earth, so that his name might be honoured and worshipped by all, and so that everyone might offer him a free-will sacrifice.

In fact, as we said yesterday, when the house of God is spoken of, we have to pay attention to its beautiful colour, to its pomp and lovely appearance. But let us come to the foundation, which is the promise of God. Of course, we know that God was not worshipped except through types in this temple of Solomon. Hence, let us conclude that, as God is spirit and truth (John 4:24), there must also be a temple which corresponds to his nature. Thus, we are bound to glorify God, because his promise has finally been fulfilled in us, who only deserved to be built into a pigsty, since we were so full of infection and rot! Yet our Lord Jesus Christ has purified us and willed that we be built into a house set apart for him. Furthermore, we see that this promise was not restricted to the Jews, but that it had its extension in all nations of the earth when it pleased God to manifest his mercy everywhere.

Well, when it says that 'God will be a Father' to him who is spoken of here, and that he will hold him to be 'a son' (2 Sam. 7:14), that means, as we have already said, that our Lord Jesus Christ had to be the only Son, as he is by nature. Now let us see how this is the case. It is certain that since he is the eternal Word of God (John 1:1–14), he has been begotten by God and has been called his Son in the truest meaning of that word, not metaphorically, using shadowy types of the Old Testament. Now in fact, the generation of his Word is spoken of not directly, but by similitude, for the psalm which we have mentioned (Psalm 2) does not (literally) express it, yet we must borrow ways of speaking which are familiar to us. Be that as it may, our Lord Jesus Christ is the unique, eternal Son of God. But when he came into the world, then he was declared to be the Son of God. And that is why St Luke also specifically uses the expression: 'He who will be born of you will be called the Son of God' (Luke 1:32). The angel, speaking to the Virgin Mary, did not say that Jesus Christ had come of men, or that having put on our body, he had become the Son of God, but he said that he would be announced everywhere and would be known everywhere.

Well, although our Lord Jesus Christ was the unique Son in his birth, his resurrection manifested and approved his sonship all the more, as the first chapter of Romans says: 'He was declared and determined the Son of God' (Rom. 1:4). That is, by means of this mighty power which became known at that time. For Christ had lived in great weakness in this world, while his glory was still hidden. Of course, the statement in the first chapter of St John that we have 'beheld a glory' (John 1:14) which pertained to the Son of God, in all the works and miracles which Jesus Christ did, as well as in all his life, is not made without cause. But nevertheless, it was obscure because he was in the person of a servant, and even at the end 'he humbled himself even to this death' (Phil. 2:7–8) – a death so ignominious and cursed before God. But then consider the resurrection, which is a testimony that our Lord Jesus Christ is the true Son of God, as Psalm 2 also states: 'Today have I begotten you'. This is related to the fact that David was anointed king for the second time (2 Sam. 5:3), and that he ruled everywhere without contradiction. Also, this victory which our Lord Jesus Christ acquired over sin and over death was like a lowering of himself, but then he took possession of his royal crown and his majesty was known. In sum, this is how our Lord Jesus Christ was the Son of God before the creation of the world, but appeared to us when he took human flesh, and then he was approved for having done so when he was raised from the dead (1 Tim. 3:16).

Be that as it may, that is why we have liberty to call on God as our Father today. For although in a certain sense men, by virtue of their first creation, may be called children of God, since he has formed them in his image, still, since the fall of Adam we have been banished from the heavenly kingdom and hence have been dispossessed of this title. So instead of being children of God, we are called children of his wrath and vengeance (Eph. 2:3), and thus he disclaims us. He rejects us and considers us an abomination. Hence, although we may claim God as our Father, we could never think of him, except with horror, were it not for this promise. For although our Lord Jesus Christ is by nature the unique Son of God, still as members of his body, as united to him by faith, we have this privilege and honour, as the first chapter of St John says, of God recognising us as his children. Thus, we can claim him as Father; indeed, we can proclaim it aloud (Rom. 8:15). St Paul is not content merely to assert that since we have been received into union with the body of Christ, we can call on God as our Father, and make our requests known to him, but he goes on to say that we can cry out loud and clear. Indeed, we can do so in all languages, for as we have said, this promise was not understood solely of Solomon, but in general of everyone, since the wall has been broken down (Eph. 2:14) and God has willed to accomplish what he said previously – that in the seed of Abraham all nations should be blessed (Gen. 22:18).

Hence, we see how we must apply this passage for our own instruction. That is, in the first place our Lord Jesus Christ is to be exalted in this sovereign degree so that people will know that he is above all the angels, as the Son of God (Heb. 1). And then let us not doubt that in him and through him, we are made children of God, since it has pleased him to accept us as such.

However, it certainly seems that God is not literally accomplishing today what he declared to David when he added that if the Son (of whom he was speaking) should misbehave and fail, then his sins would be visited by chastisements, but they would be chastisements of men. And yet he 'would never remove his mercy from him' (2 Sam. 7:14–15). Well, in the first place, since we have applied this promise to the person of our Lord Jesus Christ, you could ask how these things could fit together: provision in case he should fail and behave badly; and unjustly – since he was the Lamb of God without spot. We know that he is the fountain of all purity. There is nothing but total perfection of justice in him; he is the mirror of all obedience; he is the living image of God. In brief, nothing is lacking in him. It is he who has fulfilled the Law. Hence, why does it say that if he should happen to fall away, then he would be punished with stripes of rods and corrections for men?

Well, we can gather from this what I have already mentioned – that it is a point which deserves being carefully noted, that since this cannot apply to the person of our Lord Jesus Christ, we can thus conclude that it was not for himself alone that God had spoken, but for us who are members of his body. We see with our eyes and can touch with our hands when God pronounces that he will be a Father to Solomon, and thus can clearly know that it is not in another sense that he will be Father to all those whom Jesus Christ receives to himself, and who have entered into him by faith. In other words, what he says in the seventeenth chapter of St John is fulfilled: 'Holy Father, I ask you, as we are one, that these might be one with us' (v. 21). Here is our Lord Jesus Christ, who is one with his Father, for he is of the same essence. But beyond that, still he is one – in that in his humanity he is called, on the one hand, God; and on the other hand, man. But in one single person he is God manifest in the flesh (1 John 4:2). It is also the case that he has an eternal divinity in himself. Scripture says that our Lord Jesus Christ joins us to himself, so that we are one body. And that is why St

Paul in the twelfth chapter of 1 Corinthians says that the Church is Christ (v. 12). He uses this illustration of a body to show that each member has its function; that the eye is not the leg and the hand is not the foot, but they are so joined together that one of them cannot replace the other so as to say: 'I will fulfil my function and will bypass the others'. Well, it is certain that there is an equally large diversity in the Church of Jesus Christ, but still the head is so joined to the body that the whole body is only one, and they are participants in the good and bad of one another. Not that Jesus Christ, who is the Head of this body, could endure evil any more in his own person, but it relates as much to the love that he has for us as to the zeal that we ought to have in his service.

Hence, when this passage says that God will be called Father, although it may only pertain to our Lord Jesus Christ, still it is so thoroughly communicated to us by grace that we can boldly rejoice in our hearts that when we come to God in purity of heart in the name of his Son, he will claim us as his children. Not indeed that we should come to him presumptuously, but in all humility. Yet we should be fully assured and determined that he will receive us and not be ashamed to call us his children (Heb. 2:11) and to consider us such, insofar as we are joined with his Son, coming to him under his shadow.

Well, this shows us that all our faith exists by virtue of the Gospel. For if we are separated from our Lord Jesus Christ, there will be no accord between the head and the members, and consequently we will be stripped of his presence, in which the salvation of men consists. Be that as it may, to call on the name of God without always basing our approach on the name of his Son will surely throw us into the abyss of death. As I have said, we cannot participate in the remarkable favours which are promised us by the mouth of our Lord and by the message of his prophets until our Lord Jesus Christ accepts us in his body, which is done by the faith of the Gospel. Well, now we see that all those who think that they are praying to God – but do not think that our Lord Jesus Christ is their Advocate (1 John 2:1) to introduce them to God his Father – are doing nothing but beating the air and even abusing the name of God and profaning it. Let us learn, therefore, that if we want to pray to God, if we want to taste his goodness and want him to answer our requests, we must begin in this way; that is, recognise that all the good gifts of our Lord Jesus Christ are given to us and that we are made participants in them. That is why St Paul says that 'he impoverished himself to enrich us' (2 Cor. 8:9) with his blessings. For he took all our wants on him in order that all that belonged to him might be communicated to us, insofar as it would be expedient for our salvation. Now that is what we have to remember from this passage.

Moreover, we must notice the order of words here. It states: 'I will be a Father to him, and he will be my son' (2 Sam. 7:14). Well, this shows us that our Lord Jesus Christ was chosen to be the Son of God in order to reconcile men with God. For that dignity did not pertain to him in his human nature, since the Son of God was higher than the angelic estate. Hence, we must come to the first source, which is that God by his infinite goodness chose to honour him whom he had ordained mediator, and to exalt him to the position of calling him Son. And this also explains why our Lord Jesus Christ has less power than his Father; that is, in regard to his human nature. Well now, let us note that we are not children of God except insofar as it pleases him to draw us to himself. For we cannot say that any of us by his industry or by his virtue has earned such an excellent right. Therefore, it comes only because God has blessed us with his infinite goodness. Hence, it is his to initiate. And when he is our Father, then we are his sons; that is, we can be fully persuaded that in calling on him, we will not be frustrated, but that he will treat us as a good father is accustomed to treating his children. So much, then, for this point.

Well, let us come to the second part of the promise where it says that 'when he behaves badly, I will visit his iniquities with the stripes of men' (2 Sam. 7:14). We have already shown that since this does not refer to the person of our Lord Jesus Christ, it must refer to us who are members of him; and it is spoken in common of him and of us, because it pleases him for us to be his body. Well, this promise was more than necessary for us, and still is. For even after God has claimed us as his children, still we do not fail to be subject to many vices, so that we offend him every day, and hence the covenant which God made with us would be broken from morning to evening and every minute, unless we rested on his goodness. Therefore, God certainly had to add this grace that 'he would not remove his mercy' from us, although we are poor sinners. This is what he plainly said when he showed how he would be the Saviour of his Church, especially by the prophet Jeremiah in the thirtieth chapter, as in all the other similar passages. He said that he would forget the iniquities of those who called on him in truth, and would blot out their iniquities, without which it is impossible for him to be our Father or for us to be his children. For even if he has adopted us a hundred times, still we deserve being cut off and banished from his house and totally disowned by him. Hence, without the remission of our sins, all that the Scripture says will be useless to us. Thus, the perseverance and firmness of the adoption by which he has received us consists in his upholding us so that our sins do not come into account before him.

Well, that is not to say that when God pardons our sins, he does not chastise us to keep us always in line. This is what we ought to keep in mind so that we will not find his correction strange. In fact, if he only said: 'I will be gracious to them, and will blot out all their faults', we could dispute and enter into battle when God punishes us and chastises us. That would only make us despair. Hence, we must have these two sentences joined together; that is, that God will never fail to be gracious to us while we are poor sinners, and yet that he will chastise us with stripes.

But this concession is added, that he will moderate them, so that they are the 'stripes of men and the wounds of the sons of men' (2 Sam. 7:14). Well, it is as if he were saying that the chastisements which he will use on his faithful ones will be paternal and humane, so that he will soften them. For if God chastised us according to the greatness of his majesty, would we not remain broken down and confounded a hundred thousand times? Hence, he must chastise us humanely, as a father does his children. This is the spring of all our consolation, and this is how our sadnesses are sweetened, so that we might not be broken down in despair when he smites us with heavy blows; so that we will know that although he is smiting us with the stripes of the sons of men, he is not doing so in his dreadful strength. For we would be broken down a hundred thousand times if he wanted to touch us with a little finger. But he chastises us with the stripes of men, as the Psalm declares more fully (Psa. 89:31ff.). We can now see why this was added, and can also gather from it that God wanted to manifest his mercy in such a clear way that men would bow down in obedience to it, in order to recognise themselves for what they are, so that they would not glorify themselves, nor become rebellious, nor become self-flattering hypocrites.

In summary, we have to conclude that while God declared that if the children of David turned away from his covenant, he would reduce them through chastisement, still he assured them that he would not forget his mercy, as we explained above. And that is why the other passage says that he will chastise them in the fashion of men, and yet that his mercy will not depart from them (2 Sam. 7:14–15). Hence, let us carefully remember what it says here, that the reign of our Lord Jesus Christ was established on the condition that when we are made children of God, we must be subjected to his chastisements, as we dealt with before. When Scripture says that God promised seed to David, it adds immediately: 'if men decline from my Law, so that they do not obey my commandments, I will punish them with the stripes of men'. By these words, God certainly demonstrates his strictness, and yet moderately. For all the chastisements which he sends upon the faithful are paternal. But in not exempting them from his corrections, he keeps them by these very means in hope of his mercy and of the salvation which he has offered.

Now therefore, after God had spoken of the position of David, he showed that his mercy would remain perpetually; and consequently, we see how we can now be reconciled to God. It is true that what is referred to here cannot be carried out all at one time. Even so, it ought to be enough for us when it says that 'God will not remove his mercy from us' (2 Sam.

7:15), however much he chastises us with the stripes of men (as we have already mentioned) and in the manner of the sons of men. For this shows that when God chastises us, it is not a sign that he hates us. It is true that, at first glance, such corrections are very bitter. Indeed, it is not without cause that the Scripture calls his chastisements signs of his anger, but when he gives us some sign of his anger, we must all the more readily embrace this promise – that he will moderate his severity, so that we will not be broken down. In other words, he will always be a Father to us and will chastise us with the stripes of men, as we have mentioned above. Hence, let us remember this promise, and know how to profit from it. For it is no small thing when God actually tells us that we will be children to him and he will be a Father to us, and that we will never lose this privilege. So if he visits our iniquities, it will not be with severity, but in order to shape us, and he will uphold us in such a way that we will never be broken down in despair.

However, since we see that Solomon is not spoken of here, let us come to our Lord Jesus Christ. And since we know the text that he has broken down the wall which was between the Jews and the unbelievers and pagans, so that all have been joined together, let us conclude that he is the unique Son of God, that we can go to God through him, and that we have this privilege of crying aloud, as St Paul says: 'Abba, Father' (Rom. 8:15; Gal. 4:6). Well, by these two words he teaches that it is not only the Jewish nation to which this promise pertains, but that it is also common to us, since our Lord Jesus Christ has broken down the wall which was between us and the Jews, by which we were banned from his mercy, so that today we are members of his household, and can freely call on him.

Moreover, if God chastises us, let us learn to humble ourselves, and not be disconcerted by it. For we hear what it says, that he will chastise us with the hand of men. That is a way of distinguishing between his majesty, which would terrify us, and the gentleness and goodness which he manifests towards us when he moderates his severity. For if God chastised us with a heavy hand, according to the grandeur of his majesty, alas, who could endure it? As the Psalm says: 'who can bear the greatness of thy majesty?' (Psa. 130:3). That would drive all men to despair. Hence, no-one can bear the grandeur of God, and if there were a hundred thousand worlds, they would be destroyed with one blow, so to speak. We must, therefore, come to this promise – that God chastises us with the hand of men, and not according to his grandeur. For who could bear the blows? The mountains (they say) flow down before him like snow; and how could we who are so fragile bear the blows of his hand? How could we endure his terrible majesty? He must, therefore, treat us with the stripes of men. That is, God must so moderate himself that he will temper his blows according to our frailty, in such a way that we can bear the chastisements which he sends us. Now that is the main point that we have to remember here.

We must reserve for another occasion a matter which we cannot handle at present; namely, that although God accepts us as his children, it does not mean that we will be exempt from his chastisements. But on the contrary, since he is our Father, he must care for us, and correct us when we have failed. But in what way and manner? With the stripes of men. For if he wanted to chastise us in his majesty, alas, who could bear it? What would it be with us who are so fragile? But this is what gives us consolation: he tempers his blows to our condition. Well, it is certain that we are so fragile that we would be thoroughly undone otherwise. Therefore, although he sometimes shows us signs of his severity when he chastises us, still he does not fail to show himself a Father towards his faithful in his chastisements, which are so gentle. For who is it that could bear the greatness of his wrath? How terribly frail we are! We are less than nothing. He must therefore moderate himself, which is why he compares himself to men; for who could bear the greatness of his wrath? If he should chastise us in his majesty, and in his glory, and should employ his power to be our judge, alas, since the mountains (as I have said) melt away, would not we, who are so weak, be a hundred thousand times blotted out? But he chastises us with the hand of men – that is to say, as a father towards his children. And he regards not what we have deserved, but in our condition, and according to our frailty, he so tempers the blows that the whole matter redounds to our salvation.

Well, we must conclude that if we want to be chastised with such corrections in order always to be upheld by the hand of God, we must be members of our Lord Jesus Christ. For we know that God always calls his chastisements, which he sends on men, the signs of his wrath; he calls them his vengeance and judgements. How should we bear them when the mountains melt before them? And when we are utterly frail, how should we be able to endure? In spite of all this, we ought to be quite satisfied that he is not angry with us when it pleases him to chastise us and that he is not going to destroy us, but to correct us as a Father does his children – all because we are members of our Lord Jesus Christ. The rest will be dealt with tomorrow.

Now let us prostrate ourselves before the majesty of our good God in recognition of the infinite offences of which we are guilty. Let us pray to him that although we are unworthy of the rank even of a worm of the earth, and are totally full of rottenness and infection, yet may he not fail to accept us as his children in the name of our Lord Jesus Christ, as he has promised us. And although we are poor sinners, may he sustain us in the frailty of our nature until we are stripped of it; and may he so reform us by his Spirit that we are truly confirmed in this promise of being his inheritance and of bearing his image and his glory in ourselves; and may he bestow this grace not only upon us, but upon all peoples and nations of the earth . . .

23

*Great David's Greater Son**

And when your days are fulfilled, and you sleep with your fathers, I will raise up your seed after you, who will come from your loins, and I will establish his kingdom. He shall build a house in my name, and I will establish the throne of his kingdom for ever . . . (2 Sam. 7:12–17).

Yesterday we saw how this passage cannot be understood of Solomon, nor of all those who succeeded David as far as the temporal kingdom is concerned. Yet at that time, God did begin fulfilling this promise which is mentioned here. We must, therefore, harmonise the two things. That is, that God was considering Solomon and the situation concerning the country of Judaea when he said that there would be a king who would reign, and yet he wanted to bring David further, that is, to expect the Redeemer of the world. And that is why this king, who was given as a type of our Lord Jesus Christ, had to be ruined, so that he finally fell away very shamefully, so that indeed not a trace would remain of him. That (I say) was necessary. For otherwise, we would have stopped short too quickly, since men always seek their happiness here below. For although God lifts up our heads and holds us up, as it were, by force to make us consider the eternal kingdom, we continue to be poor beasts with our snouts stuck down in a decaying pasture! Since men cannot aspire to the heavenly kingdom of God, it was necessary for the type of the kingdom of our Lord

*Saturday, July 18, 1562.

Jesus Christ to be removed, in order to draw upwards those whose hearts are here below. Nevertheless, there had to be some figure in the absence of our Lord Jesus Christ, that is, in the time before he was made manifest. For if the Jews had not had some previous taste of this promise, they would have been unable to draw the definite conclusion that they should hope for the coming of the Redeemer to receive full salvation. Thus, they had to have some sign and testimony before their eyes. However, God had to warn them that it was not their goal, and that they must look beyond it.

Now here is how the two matters fit together. David was, therefore, truly the son of God in that he was a type of our Lord Jesus Christ. The same thing is said here of Solomon and of all those who succeeded in his kingdom. In this sense, they were more perfect and more excellent than the angels of paradise, as has been stated. However, if we have our view solely fixed on David, we will not discover what he really represents. For the text presupposes that he who is named here is alone and set apart from the ranks of all other mortals, which will not be found true of David. Therefore, it is our Lord Jesus Christ who must be represented here, as though in a painting or a mirror.

Moreover, let us carefully note what is added to this passage, and what we began to deal with yesterday. That is, that when he who is spoken of here 'has sinned, God will visit his iniquities with the stripes of men, but that he will not remove his mercy from him, as he removed it from Saul' (2 Sam. 7:14). Well, it is certain that this does not refer to our Lord Jesus Christ in regard to his own person, for we have shown he is the spotless Lamb of God. Let us, therefore, conclude that God covenanted with him for the benefit of all the faithful who are members of his body. This is well expressed in Psalm 89:31–32, for in the place of what is said here: 'if he commits iniquity', there it says: 'if his children act iniquitously, if they forsake my law, if they profane my statutes'. It is not spoken of David who is the head, with whom God chose to covenant, but it refers to all his children and to all those who belong to him. Hence, let us realise that this promise is for the benefit of the whole Church, that is, that God will continue his mercy to all those joined together with David, as though in his race.

Well, it is an inestimable privilege that God will not remove his mercy, granted that our nature is utterly miserable. But what would it be like if God wanted to deal with us severely? Let us even imagine the case that he did not act as Judge, but that he abandoned us and left us as we are! It is certain that it would be much better for us never to have been born into the world than to be in such a miserable position. Hence, all our good comes from God's having pitied us and therefore having bestowed mercy upon us.

Well, it is not that he receives us graciously just once, for we never cease to turn away from him. He must, therefore, continually bestow his mercy upon us. We must carefully note this fact – that the first entrance of our salvation, its foundation and root, is the inestimable goodness of God, without which we would always be damned and lost. How will God, then, recognise us as his children? How shall we have any association with him? It can only be by his pure mercy. Now that is the foundation upon which all our trust should be based. That is also the root from which the water of life flows to us, with which we must be filled.

When God has shown himself to be so merciful, as I have already mentioned, he would still be justified if he did not persevere to the end with us. For hourly we give him reasons to withdraw from us! When he does draw near to us and embraces us, we take no account of his caresses and admonitions. We are so rude that it is dreadful; we never stop provoking his anger against us. Therefore, his mercy must intervene here in a continuous stream. For even if the goodness of God did not remain till the end, we see from experience that we would be all the more guilty for having experienced it in the first place, and then rejecting it.

Now that is why it says that 'God will not remove his mercy', as he 'took it away from Saul' (2 Sam. 7:15). This word is added to give all the greater lustre to the promise of God. Now if God distributed to all men equally the benefits which he has reserved for his faithful, his goodness would be more obscured, for we attribute to fortune what we see in general among us. But then we could not contemplate the essential matter, which is to know the fatherly love of God for his children. Now here David is compared to Saul: both were kings and received the anointing by the hand of the prophet. Saul, indeed, was first, and seemed to be well worthy of it. Still, one of them was cut off, and God removed his mercy from him, but it is said here that it would never be taken from David, nor from his successors. By this, therefore, God wanted to magnify this mercy which he bestows on us who are his children, for when we consider the unbelievers, we see that they are of the same mass as we. So why is our condition not the same? Nevertheless, we do not find it strange that God still separates us from them, even though there is no good in us to make us more acceptable to God. We must realise, therefore, that God has chosen us, and that it pleases him to accept us as his children – which is the only reason why he pursues his goodness to us, and why after having 'begun his work, he will perfect it' (Phil. 1:6). Now that, in sum, is what we must consider.

Nevertheless, the mercy of God must not be an allurement for us to sin, so that we take greater licence and daring under the excuse that he will pardon us (Rom. 6:1). That is why it clearly says that God will 'chastise' the children of David when they have sinned, but indeed 'with the stripes of men and with the blows of the sons of men' (2 Sam. 7:14). This is a way of saying that God will moderate all his chastisement of the Church, and will not deal with them in a severe manner. In fact, what would happen if God called us to account before his majesty in order to punish us in his way and as his judgement required? The mountains melt before him, so how could we then endure it? We see what is said in the ninetieth Psalm, that each one should know the greatness of God in order to be confounded by it, and 'who shall endure before your anger?' (Nah. 1:6). That is why Isaiah, waking up the hypocrites who were asleep in their vain self-flattery, says: 'How shall you resist a devouring fire?' (Isa. 33:14). Now therefore, if we see on the one hand what the power of God is, and we then begin to examine our frailty, we will certainly conclude that if God raised his finger, we would then perish and be destroyed. If (I say) he were to chastise us in a divine fashion and in his strength, a hundred thousand worlds would certainly have to perish, if they existed. That is why he says that he will chastise us with the hand of men, and will always moderate his blows, so that the correction which we receive from his hand will be according to our frame and feebleness. This is as the Scripture says, 'he is faithful and will not tempt his own above that which they are able to bear' (1 Cor. 10:13).

But again, God wants to go further. For when he speaks 'of men' and 'of the sons of men', there is no doubt that he has in mind fathers who chastise their children. Therefore, it is as if he were saying that when all fathers take the rod in their hand, they do not want to be executioners of their children so as to put them to death. But rather, they correct them in this way because of their love for them, so that the blows which they give them serve as medicine and purging. Therefore, in the same way, God has to afflict us with his chastisements when we have offended him, as a way of showing us his paternal love for us to keep us from perishing. Indeed, although we may feel (as we will soon explain more fully) that it is going to kill us and that we are going to be consumed, still he remembers his mercy in the midst of his wrath (Hab. 3:2), and in the very process we have the testimony of his love and of his care for our salvation when it pleases him to take the pains to correct us. For if he should allow us to wander in our fantasy, we would be ruined and lost. But we are 'chastised so we might not perish' (1 Cor. 11:32). And what is more, just as a father does not strike his son except with regret, God also shows that if he were not, so to speak, forced by our actions, he would not always continue dealing with us in this way. Of course, we cannot properly speak of forcing God, but what we mean is (as I said) that when he chastises us, he would certainly wish to spare us if it were useful for us, but he has our salvation in mind. Hence, he must use the means which he knows are good and expedient for us. For we would act like wild horses, and in the end be such a distance from him that not only would we stumble, but we would hurt ourselves and be totally broken in pieces if we were not corrected by his chastisements which he sends to us.

Now then, we see why it adds that God will visit the seed of David with the stripes of men and with gentle corrections. It is added, on the one hand, so that we might not take occasion to sin – as we would if God were to leave us unpunished – but on the other hand, it is added so that we might learn to rejoice in the midst of the afflictions which he sends on us, knowing that he is showing himself to be our Father.

Well, the fact is that he also wants us to understand that these punishments are temporal. If someone replies that this is the general situation anyway, inasmuch as the unbelievers are struck with sickness, famine, plague, and wars, just as the faithful are, the answer is that although God exerts his judgements, which on the surface appear random, and although he strikes 'as many good as wicked' (Eccles. 9:2), as Solomon says – still his manner [of judgement] is very different. For when God punishes unbelievers, it is the same as if he were submitting them to torture. In no sense does he acquit them of the very last payment, but indeed holds them to it. On the contrary, although he punishes and chastises us with stripes similar to the wicked; although he does it indifferently and we seem to be like those who are rejected, yet God punishes us in order to draw us back to himself. The chastisements, therefore, of the wicked are perpetual, for the afflictions that we see them experience here below are only the beginning of their condemnation. But the chastisements of the faithful are the complete opposite, for God punishes them, not rigorously, nor according to their infirmity, for then they would be consumed, as it says in Isaiah 33:14. Instead, God corrects and purges his own and renews them by the chastisements which he sends them. That is how the mercy of God is never removed from us, however much we may feel his apparent strictness. His purpose for us is, in fact, always good and profitable and by doing this, God shows us that we are his children, although at times he does demonstrate such severity that it makes us quite confused.

Here again we must practise what is said in the Psalm which I have mentioned (Psa. 89). For when God turns his back on us and we feel nothing but fear towards him, and it seems that he has decreed to ruin and abolish us, it tempts us severely to doubt the truth. In brief, whatever way we look, all creatures are armed to exercise his vengeance against us. Now that can surely cause all our trust to vanish, and cause us to be unable to taste one drop of his goodness. Yet we must battle on until we have concluded that God is not so offended that he does not love us, nor that his promise has no place, but rather that it overcomes all the objects which can cause us to despair.

When we carefully consider what is said there, we will find that the ancient fathers have sufficiently armed us by their example to battle constantly against all mistrust, since it has pleased God to adopt us as his children once for all. It says in Psalm 89:20ff., 'Lord, you have spoken to your saints, you have said that David was after your heart, you have sworn in your truth that his seed would never perish, and that from age to age your grace would continue towards him. You have adopted him as your son, you have said that he would be preferred above all the kings of the earth, and that he would fight against his enemies in such a way that he would always be victorious. These are your decreed sentences, and you have even ratified them with a solemn oath, and have declared that you will never die, but that your truth will be found infallible. Well now here, Lord, you have your hand upraised in order to break us down and cast us into the depths.' And the faithful are speaking from the human viewpoint. For it is as if God had broken this inviolable contract which he previously made. 'Lord, you have cast away the diadem of your king, you have so thoroughly wrecked his sceptre and his crown that your enemies despise him. He is like something left to wild beasts. It seems that you have totally abandoned him, so as to make him the most miserable creature in the world. We are nothing but trash and the offscouring of the world before our adversaries (1 Cor. 4:13). In brief, your favour no longer appears to us, and you seem to take pleasure in seeing your honour and glory trampled underfoot, when your power no longer appears towards those whom you have deigned to call into your service and to receive as your children.'

The faithful were making terrible complaints in that situation, and there is no doubt that if God had not taken care, all faith would have been abolished from the world. Be that as it may, still they did have their refuge in God, and although they complained and lamented in this way, yet they did say: 'Blessed be the eternal God' – in order to show that they had not failed to apprehend his goodness in the midst of those confusions which were almost like being in the depths of hell. Nevertheless, they proclaimed that they would embrace the grace which he had promised them so abundantly, that although the world tempted them to despair, their foundation and support would be sufficient to stand against and throw back all the assaults which the devil could make upon them. We must do the same thing. So when God scatters his Church and everything seems to be going to pieces, let us learn not to fail to say, 'You have promised it, Lord, and you will hold to it'.

Therefore, this is what we have to remember, that although God has promised to smite us with the rods of men, it does not always correspond to what we imagine or feel to be appropriate. On the contrary, it will seem that God is showing himself to be terrible, and that he not only wants to make us tremble, but to drive us to total grief. Well, even then he does not fail to continue to support us with his mercy – but it is like hidden treasure, and by humbling us to recognise our sin, he causes us to exercise our faith and prove our patience, teaching us to take refuge in him. Just as he afflicts us, he also fortifies us. So we are not to cease calling on him with sincerity, for by and by we may be assured that he will lift us up as his children. Now that is how we are to practise this doctrine, which says that God will visit us with the stripes of men.

Be that as it may, let us always return to this distinction which Scripture makes, that while all chastisements of God are definite signs of his anger with the human race, yet in relation to our Lord Jesus Christ, they testify of his fatherly love. Therefore, since it pleases God for us to be members of his household, and his adopted children, we must separate from the rank of unbelievers and reproved persons. Thus, let us not doubt that in the end he will make us feel by experience that he has always supported us, even though he surely seemed to have rejected us and trampled us underfoot.

Well, everything flows from the free remission of our sins. Hence, let us learn that our very life, not only in this world, but our being lifted up in hope of eternal life, is because God does not consider our iniquities so as to bring them into account before him, and to punish us for them, as we deserve. Well, on what does it depend? On our Lord Jesus Christ, in that through him we are reconciled to God his Father, and that is what is expressed in the Psalm where it says that if 'his children turn away from my law', if they abandon themselves to iniquity, if they behave wrongfully towards me, 'I will chastise them with the rods of men, and will not remove my mercy from them' (Psa. 89:31–34). Now here is a discrepancy of language, and this seems to be a broken sentence, where he is 'putting the cart before the horse',[1] so to speak. He should have said: 'I shall chastise them and remove my mercy from them'. Now there he was speaking of the whole Church, and of all the faithful who have been included in this promise. Why is there so much difference in these Scriptures, that on the one hand it says: 'if they have offended, I will chastise them', and next: 'I will be gracious to them'? Well, it is to show us that when God pardons us and buries our offences, it is done in the name of the Mediator.

That is why I have said from the beginning that the covenant has been contracted with one who was the unique Son of God, but that it was for the common profit of the whole body, with the result that since our Lord Jesus Christ is the unique Son of God, we can call God 'our Father' with confidence. Inasmuch as it says that God will be gracious in our Lord Jesus Christ, we should conclude that we will obtain pardon for all our offences in his name, and that God will not punish us for them severely. Now that is one matter and, hence, when we recognise what we deserve, and thus we are seeking to take refuge in the mercy of God, let us keep on the right path. That is, let us come to our Lord Jesus Christ, without whom we must not presume to

[1]Lit. 'jumping from the cock to the donkey'.

obtain the favours of God. It is certain that without him our hope will be in vain. For otherwise our coming will only be presumptuous, and will cause us to be frustrated in the end. But when we come to our Lord Jesus Christ, we cannot fail to rejoice that God has received us in his mercy. So much, then, for this point.

It is not without cause that the Psalm expressly states: 'Even if the faithful break the Law of God, and profane his statutes, if they treat his Laws contemptuously . . .' (Psa. 89:31–32). This is to demonstrate that God will not only have mercy on their minor faults, which are committed out of ignorance and error, but also on their enormous transgressions. Hence, let us note that, as under the Law, there were sacrifices and oblations for sins of ignorance (Lev. 4ff.; Num. 15:22–23), and others for transgressions which were more grievous, so the truth of this distinction remains with us today. That is, not only does God uphold us in our small infirmities, which seem to be venial before men, but he receives us in mercy, even when we are so careless as to have contravened his will – indeed, when we have wilfully broken it. Now this is not said to encourage us to loosen our control, so that we might have more audacity to sin, but it is said so that we might not fail to hope in God, even if we have stumbled very seriously in some offence.

This is to be carefully noted, for there are deluded souls who make themselves believe that there is no pardon when one has sinned unless it was a sin of ignorance or inadvertency. Well, such people show clearly that they have no fear of God, and are enveloped and wrapped up in their ignorance! They are quite wrong, for let us watch ourselves more closely, and even though we could come up with some excuse and say: 'Alas, I was surprised and did not think of coming to that point', we will find that we do nothing but stumble. And when the sins which we presumed to be very minor are weighed in the balance of God and not by our own opinions, they will be found worthy of grievous punishment. Hence, let us apply what is demonstrated here to ourselves: although we are worthy of condemnation for having been transgressors of the Law of God, for having fought against him; though we have provoked him to wrath;

though we have redoubled our sins by returning to our first vices; no matter (I say) how miserable we have been and still are – still God promises that in chastising us he will procure our good and salvation, and that his mercy will never depart from us, as has been shown above. For this sentence corresponds to the other one which we have seen: 'If your children break my statutes, I will chastise them' (Psa. 89:31–32).

Hence, let us learn in the midst of all our adversities and afflictions to begin to recognise our sins. Now that is the way we must begin, knowing that we have provoked God's wrath. And then let us be touched to the quick with true repentance so that we shall not be stunned beyond measure, but so that our grief will be softened by what we hear, for we are told here that his chastisements are temporary – and not only that, but also that they will be profitable to us, and that God will advance our salvation when it pleases him to lay his hand upon us in order to correct us for our offences. Moreover, if we have seriously stumbled, let us not doubt that we still have an entrance to obtain pardon in the name of our Lord Jesus Christ. This is explained in Scripture so that poor sinners will never be discouraged, but on the contrary, even if they are almost ready to enter into the depths of hell, they may still aspire to reach our Lord Jesus Christ, knowing that by this means God will be gracious to them. That is what we have to remember, then.

Then it says that 'the House of David and his kingdom will remain perpetually and that his throne will be established' (2 Sam. 7:16). We have explained above that this promise was not vain or frustrated in David's own experience. We have shown that there also had to be some type to engage the Jews, who were ignorant and infirm, until the coming of our Lord Jesus Christ. Moreover, we can judge by the effect and by what happened, and can see that this promise extended further, and that there was another seed of David beyond all the kings who lived up to Hezekiah, and also that the diadem, the sceptre and the throne were for someone other than those who only lived for a time. For what happened to the line of David in the time of Solomon? Now here, first, was a king of Israel who was so peaceable that none could have been more so. All the foreign princes paid him tribute. There were no Philistines, or Moabites, or Idumeans, or any others (indeed, even including the Sidonians and Ziphites) who did not have to give homage to Solomon and to pay him tribute. Thus, we clearly see that God so magnified his kingdom that this promise was indeed fulfilled in it; that he was the first-born king whom God established in excellence.

But what a poor situation soon arose, indeed so poor that it was only a cloud of smoke compared with this grandeur of the reign of Solomon. For as we have said, his son had only one tribe, and ten were taken away from him, and far from those who used to pay him tribute giving him obedience, they actually came to trouble him. They came to pillage and to sack, almost to the point of digging out his eyes: these were shameful reversals beyond comparison. We even see that Hezekiah ransomed himself like a poor captive (2 Kings 18:14ff.). He had been superior, but now with shame and mockery was finally subjugated. We see the destruction which followed and that this kingdom was in perpetual shame. Yet the Jews still prided themselves under the shadow of this promise that the house of David would be permanent. It did not last – of course not – but it is necessary to keep in mind that on the one hand, there had to be a type to lead the poor Jews further. I speak of the faithful Jews, and yet this type was not to amuse and put them to sleep in this world, but rather so that they should know that there was a truth in this promise which went beyond this world, so that by faith they might see the invisible things (Heb. 11:1).

The prophets exhorted them about this matter also, assuring them that God would restore this kingdom after its captivity, and although the diadem, the sceptre and the throne and all of that would be out of sight for a long time, nevertheless the diadem would be placed on the head of him to whom it belonged (Hos. 3:4–5). As the prophet Ezekiel said: 'Return, return the diadems' (Ezek. 21:26), in order to show that not only did this kingdom flourish in David, but that it would be disfigured and nearly totally annihilated – that the memory of it would be abolished. Yet in spite of that, this majesty would still remain above; 'for he to whom it belongs will be manifested', he says, in order to show that David and his successors were nothing in comparison with our Lord Jesus Christ. So much, then, for this perfection of the house of David, which we see could only occur when our Lord Jesus Christ appeared.

This is also expressed in Daniel, for it is clearly shown that all the promises which had been given were nothing but shadows. In fact, there was no king in the time of Daniel, for they had gouged out the eyes of Manasseh (2 Kings 25:7), and did all the shameful things that they could.[1] They had cut his children's throats, and although the word was given to the people to return to their country, they had no liberty. They were all like poor slaves there, and their hopes seemed to be frustrated. Daniel lived during that time. He saw this horrible confusion. Still, he showed that God would not fail to be faithful and vindicate the poor people who were grieved and broken down, seeing themselves thus stripped and apparently disdained by God. Therefore, he says that the king will come and will be seated on the throne of David in order to remain there for ever (Dan. 2:44; 7:27). The angel was also a good expositor of this[2] when he announced the birth of our Lord Jesus Christ to the Virgin (Luke 1:32). That is how the house of David was raised up when our Lord Jesus Christ appeared.

Let us note that all of this is for our profit, for the Son of God had no need to have a kingdom other than the one he had before the foundation of the world: he was always the Lord of Glory. But it says that he will maintain his own, and that is why all virtue and power is given to him so that we might be maintained under his hand and protection, as Scripture says.

But in order to enjoy the benefits which are mentioned here, let us be aware that we are of the house of David. We are not part of it according to the flesh. We are not descendants of his race. But yet by faith we are united to him (Rom. 4:11, 16). We are to belong to the household of God in the same way. Therefore, although we were totally cut off from the household of God, and had no acquaintance with him, still we have been made citizens of heaven, as the first canonical letter of St Peter

[1]There is a confusion of Manasseh and Zedekiah.
[2]i.e. of 2 Sam. 7:15.

says, and we are 'no longer strangers, but members of his household' (1 Pet. 2:10; Eph. 2:19). Well, since God has adopted us as his children, we must persevere so that our ingratitude will not obscure this gracious action. When we have entered his household, and are maintained in it, let us not doubt that the throne of our Lord Jesus Christ was established in order to defend us. Without that, where would we be? For the devil is seeking only to ruin us. All the powers of the world are banded against us, and what is our strength to resist them? We shall perish in one blow, we shall wither as a leaf when the wind blows on it, or we shall suddenly be brought down like cut grass. But when we have on our side him who has all force and power in himself, he needs only to blow upon the enterprises of the wicked to ruin them. Then (as I have said) the wicked will direct all their efforts to ruin us. What would happen, therefore, if we were not kept safe from elsewhere?

It says, however, that the kingdom of our Lord Jesus Christ 'will be for ever' (2 Sam. 7:16). Let us note that his throne is not here below today. Under the moon, there is nothing but what is changeable, but the seat of our Lord Jesus Christ is above the heavens. It is true that his power is certainly here, and we have need of it, for we wander like pilgrims. His hand must be extended to us in order to help us, and we would be in total torment and perpetual anguish if this privilege which we have, of help from the Son of God, were not available. That is how we are raised up and sustained, for he is full of all grace to perfection. When we see this, why should we fear? And yet when there are great troubles and confusions in his Church, let us remember that our Lord Jesus Christ reigns, and thus let us raise our eyes up to heaven in order to keep ourselves under his protection, so that we might never perish when we place our trust in him.

Finally, it says that 'Nathan reported to David according to all these works and this vision' (2 Sam. 7:17). Here again is something well worthy of being noted. If God had spoken in secret, and it had not been published, what would it be like for us today? Here then was Nathan, sent to David. But afterwards, David was like the herald of God, publishing what had been done, knowing that it was not for him, nor his race only, but for the salvation of the world that God thus raised him up. Yet let us remember that what is contained here has been announced, so that the message might come even to us, and that we might be participants in all the benefits which are brought forward here, and have the fruit and enjoyment of them.

Nevertheless, let us also note that God is the Author of all these promises. That is why the word 'vision' is used, for if a hundred thousand men had spoken like Nathan and David, it would have amounted to nothing as far as truly proving it to us. We have to know that this promise has come from God, and that we hold it as from his mouth, although it was announced by means of men. Hence, let us know how to profit from it, so that we may always consider him, who not only has been promised to us, but who finally has been given to us and manifested in the flesh. Let us realise that since our Lord Jesus Christ has appeared in the world, it is not enough for us to be participants in all that is said here, and enjoy the benefits which have been communicated to us in his person. What, therefore, shall we say? We must remember that he who has given himself has spared us nothing (Rom. 8:32), that we must follow him everywhere he calls us.

Now let us prostrate ourselves before the majesty of our good God, in recognition of the faults of which we are guilty before him; praying him that it may please him to make us participants in the favours which are promised here to us. And may we always be able to have recourse to our Lord Jesus Christ, and may he receive us in his name. Although we are poor sinners, may we always obtain mercy. And may the favours which are promised us in him not only be fulfilled in us, but may they serve to confirm us in the hope of the eternal kingdom until we have reached it. And may we learn to bend our neck beneath his rod, knowing that it is for our profit. And may our sadness be so moderated that what will seem bitter to us may not sicken us from savouring his goodness in the midst of our afflictions, since we know that it will all be turned to our salvation. And may he grant this grace, not only to us, but to all people and nations of the earth . . .

24

*Lord, Who am I?**

David then went in and sat before the Lord, and said: Who am I, eternal Lord, and what is my house, that you have led me thus far? And you again, esteeming it a small thing, O eternal Lord, have spoken of the house of your servant for a long time . . . (2 Sam. 7:18–23).

Since our spirits are so flighty, we should be much more careful than we are to apply ourselves to meditating on the works of God, for it is a study in which men are never sufficient in themselves. We hear what the fortieth Psalm says, that if we applied ourselves to know how God governs us and how he disposes the condition of the human race, it would utterly surpass all our intelligence (Psa. 40:5). We could more easily count the hairs of our head a hundred times than understand the admirable providence of God as it really is. Thus if, on the one hand, we would carefully consider that God bestows such remarkable riches upon us in guiding and conducting us and, on the other, we would recognise that our spirits wander and are so feeble that they fail and faint, we would certainly take pains to meditate much more on the works of God. As I have said, we would then remove every distraction, we would seek the means to help ourselves in order to elevate ourselves above the world. Then we would want to keep ourselves there, and avoid being immediately driven away, as has been our constant experience.

But there are very few who do their duty in this matter as

*Monday, July 27, 1562.

they should, so we must pay even more attention to this passage where it says that David, having heard the message which was brought to him by Nathan the prophet, 'entered in and sat down before the Lord' (2 Sam. 7:18). Well, this was a sign that he had chosen a secret place, and then that he gave himself totally over to recognising the benefits of God, as if he had been in his presence. It would certainly have been the case that he went down to the place where the ark of the covenant was placed, because the Holy Scripture calls it the face of God. But whether he went through this ceremony or not, all the same, in order to taste and savour the grace which had been promised him, he withdrew into a place apart, and then he sat down before the Lord. The word implies that he sat down, but it should express the idea that he stopped, and that he entered not merely to rush through, but that he withdrew there for some time. Therefore, we see how David, excellent man that he was, still knew the weakness of his spirit and, since he was a man, realised that he could be unstable – and, on the other hand, that he was helpless and worldly. For these two vices are in us: the one is that we are not able to understand the favours of God because we are wrapped up in our worldly fantasies. Then the second is that although we have had a good beginning, it takes nothing to divert us, so that our spirits are scattered and wander hither and thither.

David, therefore, withdrew into a secret place for this reason. Not that it is illegitimate for us to pray to God and to give him thanks everywhere. Indeed, it is not without reason that public prayers have been ordained so that we might give testimony before all, of the reverence which we have for God, and also that the faithful might stir up one another mutually by good example (Heb. 10:25). Nevertheless, this tradition of corporate prayer does not prevent secret prayer such as David prayed. For when we are in company with some others, either we let our minds wander this way or that, or often ambition enters in so that we speak more to moral creatures than to God. For this reason, it is necessary for us to pray in such a way that only God is the witness, and that we have no regard to creatures, so that we are not rejected by God – which is something that all of us could easily experience within ourselves. There are many who do not think of this. But this is because they are stupid and think that they have paid God off when they have babbled out loud. But those who would truly desire to give themselves over to praying to God, and realise what they are, may simply groan, without saying a word (Rom. 8:26) or without retiring into a secret place when they have nowhere to go. Indeed, if David used such means and benefited more than we, how much more do we need to do the same thing, especially in the light of our crude natures and instability? Well, this is one point, where it says that David went in. He was well able to magnify God before everyone, as indeed he did at the right place and time. But he had to retire, as it says here, so that he might sharpen himself and elevate his senses above the world.

Also, it was necessary that David keep persevering, in order to magnify the favours of God according to their merit. And that is why it not only says that he went in, but that 'he sat down'. That is, he remained there because this meditation required of him not only a minute, but it required his serious thought and his continuous examination of the works of God.

Well, then the text says that David marvelled that God had already shown himself so faithful to him: 'Lord, who am I, and what is the house of my father, that you have led me thus far?' (2 Sam. 7:18). First, he saw himself king, and not by inheritance or succession. It was not that he attained it by his industry. Of course, he did possess great virtues, and God had given him his hand as well, and elevated him by degrees in spite of Saul. But be that as it may, he remembered that he had not earned the royal dignity, but that it was a free gift of God. Now that is why he asked who was he, and what was the house of his father. Well, this teaches us to feel how deeply we are indebted and obligated to God, and how great is his mercy to us. It also teaches us to consider what our condition would be if God left us as we are. For until we have seriously contemplated our poverty, it is certain that our view of the goodness of God will be obscure, and we will not apprehend it as we should. Here, then, is the rule to which we must hold: in order to praise God properly, and to appreciate the favours which he gives us, let us begin to examine what we would be if he had left us in our first state. Well, then we will have reason to say that his goodness to us is inestimable.

We see how David practises this kind of meditation in a general way in Psalm 8: 'Lord, what is man that you are so mindful of him? And what are the sons of men that you visit them, and care for them?' There David, on the one hand, puts the state of man in the balance against the mercy of God. For we are poor dust of the earth. We are nothing but powder and corruption. In addition, within our souls there is nothing but filth, and we are so alienated from God that we do not merit being allowed among his creatures. Now that is what we are. On the other hand, we must recognise how God governs, nourishes, and sustains us, and how he guides our steps in such a way that he does not cease to show us that he has a more than paternal care for us. That is how God is honoured, therefore, when we recognise that we are nothing, that we are worthless, and that though God finds nothing in us but total misery, it is clear that he deigns to look at us in pity, and abases himself in order to treat us as his children. So this is how David meditates in general: 'What is man, Lord, that you are for him?'

Well, he even goes further in this passage, as we must too. For it is not enough that we recognise in general that we are nothing, so that the goodness of God to us is all the more admirable, but each one must consider himself in particular. For when we speak of the universal condition of men, it sounds cold, as though it were an irrelevant thought to us. We must, therefore, go beyond it, so that we recognise that men from the very greatest to the very smallest are nothing, that they are nothing but vanity and filth – on this basis each of us may consider what he is, and thus discover all the more reason to humble himself. For instance, let me think of myself in this way: I am not merely a man, but vermin. Here are my sins coming before my eyes. Then on the other hand, I shall feel the good things which I have experienced in my own life, not only the fact that God has bestowed grace upon the human race (in general) but that he has shown his grace to me (in particular), with the result that I am especially obligated to him. Now that is what we must remember from this passage. For David does not say, as in the Psalm which we have mentioned: 'What is man?'; but he says: 'What am I, and what is the house of my father, Lord, that you have led me thus far?' Now that is how we must derive benefit from this passage.

Well, if David so magnified the grace of God because he had elevated him in dignity and to this high honour as head of the people, we have even more reason when we remember that God has adopted us as his children, and heirs of the heavenly kingdom. For that means much more than ruling in this world, and the blessing of our eternal salvation surpasses every kingdom and every earthly principality. Hence, we are made companions of angels, even of the body of our Lord Jesus Christ. Furthermore, to what are we called? To be 'partakers of the divine nature', as St Peter says in his second canonical epistle, in the place where he mentions the divine nature and God's glory of which we are made partakers (2 Pet. 1:4). This surpasses all the principalities here below and elevates us above the heavens. Hence, let us learn to praise God in such a way that our miseries always come to mind and that we may recognise that beyond this we are nothing but dust and mud. Thus, let us remember that we were as good as in the depths of hell, that we were absolutely and totally lost and cursed by our nature, and with that let us compare the fact that God has extended his hand to us, and has opened the heavens for us, in order to give us entrance and familiar access there. The result is that we may call upon him in hope, and enjoy the inheritance which he has promised us. Now that is one point.

Well, David goes further and says: 'Again, O Lord, my God, this was a small thing, but you have moreover added that you have made promises to the house of your servant for a long time'. Now here is the law of men, he says (2 Sam. 7:19) – and the word which he uses implies law, but also signifies manner and rule. Well, when he thus gathers up the benefits of God and augments their grandeur so as to stir himself up all the more to praise and magnify God, it signifies that it is not enough to have conceived just once that he cares for us, and then have some confused idea of the benefits which we have received from his hand. Rather, we must openly declare them. Not that we can actually reach the ultimate, as we have seen in Psalm 40:5. And then it says in another passage: 'Lord, what are your deeds?' (Psa. 92:5). Nevertheless, David does not fail to apply himself to meditate on that which was too high for him and too deep. Hence, we must do the same. For although we are unable to comprehend the infinite number of the benefits which we have received from him, still we must attempt to take account of them. And thus let us think: 'Well, here I have experienced the grace of God in such a place, and then look how he has added more blessing superabundantly. And beyond that, he has brought me out of such and such a danger, not only from one sort of death, but from twenty or thirty!' When I have carefully thought and said: 'I am nothing,' and even when I have considered and closely watched and applied all my mental powers to commit to memory all that I have received – it is still nothing in comparison with this great goodness of God, which he has bestowed on me in infinite measure. Now that is what we have to remember from this passage, therefore, when we see that David, after having recognised the mercy which God bestowed on him in elevating him to the royal throne, added: 'And this is a small thing, Lord, that you have undertaken in addition to care as a father for the house of your servant, indeed to remain with it for such a long time' (2 Sam. 7:19).

For as we have seen, God was not just promising to give him Solomon, but the promise extended even to our Lord Jesus Christ. For it says that 'your house will be permanent' (2 Sam. 7:16). And when this is explained in more detail, God calls the sun and moon to witness, and says that as long as they shine in the sky, the house of David will remain firm (Psa. 89.36–37). Hence, it was not a question of an era, nor of two or three, but of a perfection which surpasses the world, going even to our Lord Jesus Christ. Hence, it is not without cause that it says that God wanted to provide for the house of David for a long time to come. What David was doing was lifting himself beyond all that is earthly. He had spoken of his reign in saying: 'Lord, you have lifted me up thus far' (2 Sam. 7:18); but now there was a blessing much more worthy and noble: namely, that God had ordained that there should be a kingdom established which, indeed, should endure for ever. Well, this kingdom was not for one man, but for the good and salvation of his subjects. When God bestowed this grace on David, leaving with him, as on deposit, the promise of the Redeemer of the world, it was a privilege which was surely worthy of being extolled. That is why David, showing that he could not be satisfied in himself, immediately extolled this grace of God, and valued it as it deserved.

Well, he added: 'This is the manner of men, Lord' (2 Sam. 7:19). Now some take this as an interrogative, as if David were saying: 'Is this the manner of men?' But there is no question mark. Hence the natural meaning is that David says that God has taken care of him in a human fashion. To say that this is like men of great estate and dignity is a forced interpretation. David wanted to show here that the goodness of God is all the more worthy of esteem because he comes down in such a way as to make himself familiar to us. For if we were to contemplate some sign of the majesty of God, we would be totally carried away, and yet we would still be far from attaining it. Hence, since God is very high up and there is such a distance between him and us, it would not seem likely that he would regard us. That is why it says in Psalm 138 that he dwells in a high place, but nevertheless does not fail to observe the lowly things of this world (Psa. 138:6). Therefore, this is what David understood. It is as if he were saying: 'Lord, what does it mean that you have made yourself so familiar and have so remarkably condescended to abase yourself? Here we are, poor creatures who are nothing but smoke, and yet you, who surpass all things, have come here to see what we need, and to provide for all our necessities. It is the same as if a man were setting his house in order and giving inheritance to his little children, taking the trouble to raise them, making them sleep, and providing for them all that they need.' Now that is what David wanted to express when he said: 'This is the law of men, O Lord'.

Hence, when we wish to be stirred to the depths of our beings by the favours of God so that we esteem them as they deserve, let us always come to this point: that is, to consider who God is.

While it is true that we cannot comprehend him as he is, and we are far from being able to do so, still we should confess it all the more. When we do confess his incomprehensible majesty, and then how it reaches us, we shall find that he humbles himself as a mortal man, as if he were holding us in his bosom, and we were little children on whom he always had his eye. For we do not understand how God watches over us, and how he has more than a fatherly care for us. Yet this is only because of our stupidity. However, if we want to prepare our thoughts to meditate properly on the inestimable blessings of God, we will certainly not only speak in the manner of David, but also have a better and more earnest zeal than he when we come to esteem God in this way, and immediately recognise how much we are indebted to him. In fact, when God wants to show us how great is his goodness to us, and what sort of kindness he bestows upon us, he not only compares himself to men, but he compares himself to a hen (Matt. 23:37). Well, that is very far from his incomprehensible glory. But he speaks in this way because of our ingratitude. For although in spite of our blindness, we may, so to speak, have some sense of and some groping after his goodness and his providence and solicitude towards us, yet we do not think about it. Now this is how he reproves our carelessness and shows that we are far too superficial, when he has to compare himself to a hen, who will cover us and keep us under his wings, as is the custom of a hen who forgets herself in order to care for her little ones and seek for their nourishment.

Well, this is how we must exert ourselves and concentrate our study to recognise the favours of God. That is, after having tasted what his majesty is, let us notice how he approaches us, which indeed cannot be done without his abasing himself mightily, as if he transfigured himself, so to speak. Not that his glory diminishes at all, but it only seems to from our perspective, for this is also meant to give us reason to entrust ourselves to him, so that we may soon call upon him with boldness. For if we only understood his majesty, it is certain that we would be terrified. When it comes to praying, if we were to say: 'What is God?', it is certain that we would be reduced to nothing and flee his presence. For what means do we have to reach him? Who is it that gives us this manner of praying, as if we were entering into familiar terms? Without asking permission, could we even have access to an earthly prince – and if so, alas, what would happen to us? We would never be able to pray to him and give him thanks if we had not tasted the great value of this doctrine, that God conforms himself to us in human fashion, as if he descended here below, so that we on our part might accept his help, and so that there might be a mutual agreement between him and us.

Well, this should not fill us with presumption, so that we come in with our 'flags flying', and like a brazen-faced whore, present ourselves before God! Even when we come to him in fear and reverence, we must not fail to trust him fully. We do not come to him as to mere mortal creatures, but as to him who holds everything in his hand, and as to our Father, who comes down here and wants to converse with us, as it says: it is all his wisdom – that is to say, his pleasure – to dwell in the midst of men (Psa. 132:13–14; 68:17). Now that is why we have reason not only to give him thanks, but also to be disposed to pray to him in true trust, when we clearly remember this word and fully digest it, namely, that God manifests himself to us in the manner of men.

Well, then it adds: 'What can David add more, Lord, in speaking to you?' (2 Sam. 7:20). Here David confesses that God has so blessed him with his grace that he no longer knows how he ought to call upon him, for God has done much more than he could have imagined. Well, this increases even more the praise which he owes to God. For if we have the leisure to think of all that we need, form our requests one after another, and then receive answers, although in this way God would show that he was very kind to us, still his goodness would not be so evident as when he goes before us and bestows on us all that he knows is good and profitable for us. Yet we sleep, as the Psalm says: 'Behold, those who love God shall have plenty of sleep' (Psa. 127:2). Well, this is not to say that we ought to be so nonchalant that we do not pray to God, or seek the favours which we need, but it is to show that if God waited for us to come to him, it would be too late, for we go to sleep in our evil. And then, are we sufficiently well advised and so wise as to be able to understand all that we need? Alas, we are far from it, so God must add to it. Hence, David shows here that God did not wait for him to come and seek him, and did not show himself kind and faithful to him on the basis of the measure of his poverty or the wishes and requests which he could have made, but that he surpassed all that – so much so that David had, as it were, his mouth closed!

Now this point here is well worthy of being noted. For often in our prayers, if we are touched as we should be when we are before him, it will be as though we are babbling or dumb, and we are silent before him, with the result that when we want to pray, we do not know how to begin (Rom. 8:26). Then, when we have understood something of the grace of God and of how it came to us, we will reason in this way: 'What do I want to say and ask? There are an infinite number of benefits which I have received, and my mind is not able to take them in. But you know what I am, Lord, what I want to say, and what my intention is.' Therefore, when we are in this situation, it glorifies God more than if we had beautiful rhetoric and a lovely murmuring. However, there are many who do not know what this condition is. Still, if we have practised what it is to pray to God, we will recognise what is shown to us here: namely, that God makes us dumb precisely in order that he may give us more than we can comprehend. When we do not know how to begin, we will be like poor blind folk whose eyes he has opened and whom he has graciously deigned to make experience his infinite wisdom – which I have shown to be his good pleasure – and to bestow also the treasures of his goodness on us. Now that is what we have to remember.

Although we must confess with David that we do not know what to say, still we must press on, even when we are at the end of our senses, and in praying to God are hanging in suspense. Sometimes when we have only one thing in mind, and yet cannot even express it, still we must press on and babble even if we cannot speak distinctly, and say: 'Here am I' – and, word by word, form our requests. If (I say) we cannot bring [our words] out, and we are down like poor people utterly destroyed, still we must not lose courage but persevere in praying to him. For he will accept our language, in the same way as we see a father listening to his children and understanding them. Why? Because he babbles with them and adds to what they are unable to bring forth from their mouths, explaining what they would like to say. Well, God, who surpasses all the fathers of this world in goodness and gentleness, and knows the secret thoughts of creatures, will certainly fully understand the intentions of men, even though they do not express them.

In fact, we see what St Paul says in Romans, that the Spirit of God stirs us 'to inexpressible groanings' (Rom. 8:26). Well, that is to show that we must conceive what cannot be expressed, for he knows his Spirit when he dwells in us. Furthermore, by that St Paul shows that our prayers will often be confused, and instead of talking, we will groan, and instead of declaring our intention, we will be tied up and unable to express it. Sometimes our language will fail us – and yet we will not fail to be answered by God. Again, this is what we have to remember from this passage.

Well, when it says: 'You have known your servant' (2 Sam. 7:20), this can be understood to refer to the grace of election, that is, that God had chosen David before the world was created. It is true that afterwards David would add: even as God has done all things according to his eternal counsel. However, there is no doubt here that he wanted to say: 'Well, Lord, although I am a poor creature here, and my mind is totally confused and I do not know what to say; still you know me. Behold, here am I, guide me as you see fit.' Thus, this is a passage which offers us good doctrine, when we see that even when we have many weaknesses, still they do not exclude us from God. But on the contrary, we are not to lose courage and not grow weary. We are to resign everything to him, and be assured that he will not fail to accept us, even though we are ashamed of ourselves and do not want him to cast his eye on us.

Although, when we do not know how we ought to approach God, or which way to turn in our desire to pray to God, when our faith is very weak, when we are distracted in one direction and another – when all of that happens, still let us be sure to overcome all objections. Then, when we are tempted to despair, what shall we say? You have received such blessings from God. He has maintained and relieved you while you were in extreme danger, and you are so obligated to him that it is impossible for you to be pleasing to him, since you have rebelled against him in so many ways, instead of truly recognising him. So now, how can you present yourself to him? What do you bring with you to pay him back? Thus, when we are tempted to distrust God in this way, let us, like David, draw this conclusion: 'Alas, Lord, you know your servant. Although we may put up a good front, it is certain that it will only serve to hide your face from us when hypocrisy is involved. But when we have no more strength to cry out with a loud voice, then you will not fail to answer us, for you know our hearts.'

Here, therefore, is that knowledge of which David spoke. It is that God received us in mercy – and having received us, does not fail to answer us. When we do not know how to formulate our requests, he supplements the feebleness of our faith, and overcomes all our slowness, our laziness, and finally our ignorance and dullness. As it says in the Psalm: 'I have been as a poor beast before you' (Psa. 73:22ff.), 'and yet you have not failed to show that you cared for me, and that you took my part when you made me still persevere in your love.' It is true that he spoke of this special temptation which he had when he was finding things so confused in this world, that he was slipping about as on ice. Well, be that as it may, though he confessed that he was like a poor beast, God stretched out his hand to him and did not abandon him. Hence, when we have realised what we are, in order to humble ourselves let us always go back to that, and let us fall on our knees, as they say, and always have ready these words: 'Lord, you know what I am'.

He then adds: 'Lord, you have done all these marvels for your servant according to your word and according to your heart' (2 Sam. 7:21). Here David expressed, more than before, that all the blessings of which he had spoken, every one which he had received, and those for which he still hopes, proceeded from a single source: that is, the pure mercy and graciousness of God. Well, he put in first place here 'the Word'. Not that it precedes the intention of God. For there is his definite counsel, which he declares to us by his Word. But David did not have in mind the order which is between the counsel and the Word of God, but rather he had himself in mind: his own capacity and measure, so as to meditate on one and then the other. If we want to begin with the counsel of God, what will happen to us? But he began with the Word, so as to cause us to go up by a ladder. There are many fanatics who will not fail to speak of God, and would like to argue about his election. They enter into tortured and obscure speculations. Well, such people seek to destroy themselves voluntarily. On the contrary, David shows here that the Word of God should guide us so that we might attain his counsel.

It is true that the two ought to be joined together, but he holds to this order – especially because of our crudeness. There are many who so confuse their own ideas with the Word that they would like the election of God to be buried, and never to be spoken of! Well, that causes too great a confusion, and yet what they claim – that it is enough for us to be saved by faith – is nothing. For faith shows us that God calls us to himself because he has elected us before all time, and ordained us to be his heirs. Therefore, here are two things in which our salvation consists: it is first of all the free will of God and the mercy which he bestowed upon us when it pleased him to choose us before the creation of the world. Now that is the principal foundation and the sovereign cause. After that, there is the Word by which he gives us this mercy, which (mercy) would be otherwise unknown and totally hidden. Well, it is true that the election of God (as I have said) proceeds from his counsel. For what is the election of God? It is the fact that before the constitution of the world, he chose us to be his children in our Lord Jesus Christ (Eph. 1:4). Well now, that is what precedes the Word. For it is the 'heart of God', as David calls it here. Not that God has a heart, but by this word he means the secret of God. We have, therefore, been elected before the creation of the world, and he has retained that in himself from all time. The first fact is that God has had pity on us and has granted us mercy, drawing us to know him, so that we might call on him as our Father and Saviour. Well, did he thus determine that in himself? That would not be sufficient. It is true that God could easily save us at any minute. Yet he does not want to deal with us as with blocks of wood, but wants his will to be manifested to us. How? By his Word, that is to say, by the preaching of the Gospel, in which he says: 'Knock on the door, and it will be opened to you; seek and you shall find, ask and it shall be given to you' (Matt. 7:7).

Now here, therefore, are two inseparable things. First, the will of God which is founded in his free mercy, in that it pleases him to have chosen us for his children. Then, there is the testimony which he gives us of this grace, of that mercy, when it pleases God to invite us to himself by the Gospel, and to offer us the promises of our salvation (2 Pet. 1:4), so that in receiving them we might be made members of our Lord Jesus Christ, who is our life (Col. 3:4).

I have already said that because of our crudeness, we must begin by the Word. Why? Because there are those who say to themselves that even if they have been elected by God before the foundation of the world, how and by what means will they know it? Hence, we must not be surprised if all those who vault into such speculations break their neck by their recklessness. Let us learn, therefore, to begin with the Word which is clear to us, and when we want to know if we are children of God, remember that it says that whoever believes in the Son of God will never die (John 11:26). Let us realise that God grants this privilege to all creatures, that he will accept them as his own children in the name of our Lord Jesus Christ. Let us realise that in believing in the Gospel, we are made participants in all the blessings of the Son of God, who is represented there as our righteousness, so that he truly justifies us. Now when we have realised all that is proper and expedient for our salvation, we are to accept it for ourselves. Hence, it is not without reason that David put the Word of God before his counsel. Not (as I have said) that the order was that way in God, but rather it was stated from our viewpoint, so that we might be given this specific and necessary guidance. In fact, if a man were not content to have authentic letters, well sealed and signed, but wanted to take over and possess for himself the registers which belong to the prince, would one not say that he was enraged or crazy? For there must be order. Each man shall be sufficiently assured of God's grace when he has authentic testimonies of it. So it is with those who are not content with the preaching of the Gospel, but they want to fly without wings above the clouds and want to hear the secret counsel of God! They would like God to leave his account room and his books open, and yet they despise this grace which should be sufficient for them. That is why he teaches us to apply ourselves to his Word when we would like to be assured and resolute about God's love for us, and when we would like to know the cause of his goodness: Lord, it is according to thy Word.

Nevertheless, there is no doubt that David opposed this Word to any merit which man could imagine in himself. It is as if he were saying: 'Lord, why is it that you grant me so many blessings? Because you have promised it to me.' For this reason, let us not seek the foundation of our salvation in our own dignity, or try to believe that it is our wages or reward. Indeed, no! But God promises us what we do not imagine, what we do not wish, and that of which we would never have thought (1 Cor. 2:9). That is how, in speaking of the promises of God, we must exclude any idea that we could conceive of our own dignity, knowing that there is nothing in us to merit his grace, but only that it pleases him to manifest it to us. That is one point.

Yet again, it is not enough merely to have known that God by his promises wanted to declare himself to be our Father, and has received us in mercy so that we might not hesitate to call on him. But we must come to him with the belief which is spoken of here; that is, in his secret counsel. This is to break down all the more the arguments that men are accustomed to persuading themselves with about their works meriting salvation! For if the promises of God are opposed to our merits, how much more his intention and counsel? For when did he take this counsel to do good to us? Was it after he found us to be capable? Far from it: rather, it was before the creation of the world. Therefore, since it does not depend on us, the cause must surely be found in himself. For if he had waited for our capacity, alas, what would happen to us? Hence, the whole cause of the promises of our salvation consists in his good pleasure. That is why we have even more reason to magnify his goodness – indeed, by humbling and utterly abasing ourselves. This is what St Paul says in the first chapter of Ephesians, that God calls us when he makes us preach his mercies and riches – indeed, he calls us in our Lord Jesus Christ, according as he has elected us before the creation of the world. St Paul, as a faithful expositor, clearly shows what is contained here. That is, when God calls us to himself, he does not consider our condition which is so unstable, but he calls us because he has chosen us from all time, and reveals to us that which was incomprehensible to us.

Now let us prostrate ourselves before the majesty of our good God in recognition of so many sins and offences, praying him that he will be pleased to employ such mercy towards us that we may not fail to find grace with him, so that we are ever led by his hand. And may we recognise his benefits more and more, so that conforming ourselves to his will, we might also place our trust in it. And may we walk in such humility that all pride may be annihilated in us, and may we learn so to embrace his promises that we will place our whole assurance in them. May he grant this grace not only to us, but to all people and nations of the earth . . .

25

*The Only God and his Chosen People**

And moreover, you are magnified, Lord God, and you are greatly esteemed, in that there is none like unto you, and there is no God beside you, according to all that we have heard with our ears. Where is a single nation in the earth which is like your people, even like Israel, whom God went to redeem for a people to himself, and to put his name on them; and to do great and terrible things in the earth because of your people, whom you redeemed from Egypt from its people and its gods? For you have confirmed your people Israel, to be your own people for ever . . . (2 Sam. 7:22–24).

After David had recognised the goodness of God, as we explained yesterday, he cried out that God must surely be 'glorified', so that people might indeed acknowledge him alone, and so that everything which would prevent his glory from being known might be broken down and destroyed. We must draw the same conclusion when we think of all the blessings which we have received from the hand of God. For he asks nothing of us but this recognition. In fact, he needs nothing; indeed, he is far from needing to be glorified by us, so that it brings him neither profit nor advantage. Be that as it may, all that he does require from us, when he has been very generous and has given us all the blessings that we could possibly desire, is only that we should confess that we receive everything from him, and then that we should endeavour, as far as we are able, to magnify his greatness, his majesty, and his glory.

*Tuesday, July 28, 1562.

David says with good reason 'that there is none like him and that there is no God beside him'. Many people will praise God in part and yet cheat him out of his rights, attributing to creatures what he reserves to himself alone. So let us carefully note that we do not exalt God in accordance with his dignity until we lower everything else and realise that he is so gracious to us, so that nothing will keep us from looking to him, from addressing ourselves to him, and cleaving to him in all things. This is a very useful doctrine for us whose spirits are so flighty that we stumble one way and another, always confusing some human companion with God. It helps us recognise that there is only one sovereign God whom we must approach. Now we see how this error has won out and has been in vogue from all time, both in the world and in the papacy, so that although the name of God glibly flows from the mouths of many, yet at the same time they make idols of the saints and their cults. The result is that God is mixed in among these saints, as they admit themselves in their popular proverb – that one could not pick out God among the apostles. That is how they condemn themselves, since God has willed to make them inexcusable.

We must consider this sentence ever more seriously as often as Scripture propounds it to us, because men cannot keep sufficient control of themselves to avoid making some corrupt mixture which diminishes the glory of God and departs from it, as if it were cheap merchandise. At first glance this seems to be a cold proposition: 'There is none like God, and who does not confess it?' There is no-one who does not know it. Hence, it seems far too elementary, and even little children know it. Who would contradict it? In brief, this sentence seems superfluous, especially if we do not recognise the vice to which we are inclined and addicted. For although we have been taught and retaught, only with the greatest difficulty will you find one out of ten who is content to have one single God. It is true that we do not actually profane his name. Even the papists will not say that they want to diminish his authority in order to advance other gods. But God is not a sophist, so he cuts right through to the truth, and does not stop at all the cavils that men bring up in order to disguise and cover up evil. Therefore, when we hear this name of God, let us realise that we must attribute to him all that is his. Let us notice very carefully how men steal part of God's honour from him. Experience all too often proves that they do, and also that we cannot maintain God's right, but hold back part of it for ourselves in bits and pieces. That is to distribute his glory according to our fantasy. Since (I say) this evil tendency is rooted in the nature of men, we will richly profit our whole life long by learning this lesson – remember that there is none like God, and no other God beside him.

Moreover, let us note that we have not known God as we should, until we have learned to depend upon him and to submit to him so that we find our peace and contentment in him. Yet we falter and spcculations enter our heads which divert us at some particular point, so that we do not know whether these things are from him, which clearly shows that we do not have a proper knowledge of God. The Psalm speaks of this: The Lord reigns that all the princes be brought to nought (Psa. 2). When God has his empire amongst us and we learn to adore him and to subject ourselves to him, it is certain that we will be stripped of all false opinions and will no longer wander here and there, saying: 'Now this is still good, and should be very appropriate'. All of that (I say) will be far from us when we learn that there is only one God.

Well, this teaching shows us how the poor world has always tricked itself into its own perdition. For we see how each one wanders in his foolish devotions and how men invent several gods in their own heads – not stopping with only one. That is why God complains by his prophet that people are 'forsaking him', since he is the 'fountain of living waters' who never fails, but that men 'make themselves broken cisterns which can hold no water' (Jer. 2:13). Even if someone puts some water in, it cannot remain there. Above all, those who have been taught by the Holy Scripture are justly accused when they turn away from a single God and wander about in their imaginations. Hence, let us be very clear about this point, namely, that the goal of all the blessings that God has granted us (when we become aware of them) is to magnify him. Let us realise that God is not properly honoured until people contemplate him, and both small and great call on him and recognise that they can find complete rest in him alone, and not in any companion. When we come to know God alone, let us place all our trust so fully in him that we will give him homage for all the blessings which he pours out upon us. That, in sum, is what we have to remember.

David then adds: 'According to all the things that I have heard with my ears' – which shows that he had greatly profited in the Law. Now this is what I have already mentioned: although all people in general should know God, nevertheless those to whom he has revealed himself by his Word ought specifically to depend on him for all things. This is the same as if God had personally approached them, to say: 'Here am I: follow me'. David shows that his knowledge of God was not confused – like many who have some taste and apprehension of him – but that he had learned him from the Law and knew that the world had abused itself in foolish fantasies, making themselves gods, even though there is none but the one God of Israel. Although heaven and earth leave us without excuse if we do not worship God, still we cannot know him until he declares himself to us personally. Even after we are convinced of the principle that there is one God – knowing that the world did not make itself, and that we do not live from ourselves, and have no means [of life] but his goodness and power – even when we accept this principle of one God, which nature itself teaches us, still everyone tends to allow himself to invent some peculiar opinion by which God is disguised and his virtue turned into a lie. For everything that we can bring forth from within ourselves is nothing but vanity. If we wish to imagine, on the basis of our own thinking, that it is good to worship God according to the means that we invent, we shall certainly transfigure him according to our own desires. This has been known throughout history.

Hence, it was not enough for David to have known that there was only one God, but he had to be instructed by the Law what the will of God was, so that he would not err along with the pagans. For besides, the unbelievers and profane people were not so stupid as to deny that there was a main God, but they had their idols, as does the papacy today. Therefore, although the world admitted this principle that there had to be one God alone, nevertheless it was corrupted in superstitions and idolatry and in nearly every way. That is why David, in order to remember clearly and not to be in doubt, addressed the Law and said: 'According as he had heard with his ears'. He also spoke of this in Psalm 44: 'Lord, we have heard with our ears, and our fathers have told us your infinite power which you showed to them in Egypt. For it was not by their arms nor by their strength that they conquered, but you, Lord, who governed them and stretched out your hand over them' (Psa. 44:2–3). In this way, David was dealing with this matter of hearing.

Of course, when we are willing to listen, all sorts of things can be said to us. But a certain kind of hearing is meant here: not the lies which men invent and pretend to believe, but the hearing of the doctrine which is preached to us, by which God has manifested himself to his people. St Paul means this when he says, 'faith is by hearing' (Rom. 10:17). But he goes on to add, as though it were a correction, that 'hearing is by the Word'. Yet (as I have said) if we want to believe in men, we will be carried away with many follies. Therefore, our hearing must be dedicated to God, so as to obey him and add faith to his truth. That is what David presupposes now, when he says: 'This is what we have heard'. They had much to say about God among the other nations, and yet it was nothing but lies. So David returned to this doctrine which is certain and infallible, for he knew that God was the author of his Law and not men, and that everything contained in it had the same authority as if God had opened his mouth and had personally expressed himself. Therefore, that is what he had in mind.

Now we must derive a good principle from this: the only result of following our own opinion is vanity, which causes us to misrepresent the majesty of God. The more that we claim to be wise, the more our folly will overflow, so that we end up like people who are crazy. That is precisely what men are when they want to seek God according to their own sense and reason – they will bury and totally ruin themselves. Hence, when we seek God in order to know him well, let us hold to the path which he has shown us – that we should hear his Word and receive it immediately with all assurance. Well, if David, who was an excellent prophet and teacher of the Church, placed himself here in the rank of men, and confessed that he would not know what God was unless he had been instructed by the Word, what will it be with us? How presumptuous are we for wanting God to make himself known, and yet not deigning to cast our eye on the Holy Scripture or come to the assembly where it is expounded? Hence, let us be careful to put this doctrine into practice: that is, not to despise the means which God has given us so that we might have a definite way to come to him, that we might be taught (I say) by his Word. Let us also deign to hear it, and make ourselves submissive to receive it. Moreover, since it is easy for us to hear the Word, let us be very careful to exercise discretion and prudence, so that we do not accept everything which is said to us. Faith is joined to discretion, not that men should be wise and subtle in order to dispute against God, but on the contrary, discretion means, as I see it, an absence of contradiction and opposition to what God has once for all declared. We will never be well taught except by his Word. So much, then, for this Word which says: 'According to all things which we have heard with our ears'.

Moreover, when David speaks here of 'all things', he shows that he did not take any word lightly, as many do. For if they have heard God spoken of, they will certainly accept what is said, but it will only 'go in one ear and out the other',[1] and it will seem to them a waste of time to continue listening. Many of them have great difficulty. They know that it is of the will of God, and yet it seems that they do not know very much about it. That is why they are surprised at all the blows from many temptations. At the very time when they would like to be highly advanced and have profited marvellously, the devil tries to uncover them; he finds access to them, and enters by some breach which he made, precisely because they were scarcely prepared to resist him seriously. Therefore, we should consider

[1] 'Secouer l'oreille'.

carefully what David says about not hearing in passing that it was God. This is not some broken-off sentence which implies: 'Very well, I have heard it spoken of', but rather it means that David was taught by the Law. He says 'According to all things' in order to show that we must study arduously to profit in the Word of God, and that we are never to be weary or vexed. When we are reproved, let it increase our appetite for more. We keep eating in this corporeal life in order to sustain ourselves. After we have eaten dinner, we still go on to eat supper. But our souls do not so readily seek spiritual nourishment. However, the more good things our souls take in, the more should our appetite increase for God continually to fill us. This should cause us to withdraw from this world in order to be fully devoted to him.

At this point David adds: 'What people is there on earth like your people Israel?' (2 Sam. 7:23). Here David uses what was intended for him personally as an opportunity to speak to the whole Church of God. That, in fact, is what we must do. When each one of us carefully considers how many specific ways we are obligated to God, and when we seriously meditate on the favours that we have received, we must then join our blessings to the whole body of Christ. For if everyone should remain in the corner by himself, as the saying goes, what would become of the Church? But (as I have said) when each one of us thinks in particular of all the blessings which we have received from God, it should therefore serve to bring us into the union which all the faithful should have. This, then, is the rule which David shows us here. For up to this point, he has recognised and confessed that God has bestowed the riches of his goodness upon him so greatly that he should have been completely carried away, and his spirit confused – had he magnified God as he should have done. Well, now he adds: 'Who are the people like those whom you have chosen, O Lord?' Why did he add this? For he had been speaking above of what concerned himself alone. That is so, but he knew that what had been bestowed upon one of us ought to extend to all – especially so that it might bring us into this fraternal union; that we might all be united together, and that with one mouth we might give him thanks, since we are all members of one single head.

This is why it says in the other passage: 'Lord, remember me in your assembly and visit me with your salvation' (Psa. 106:4). By that, he signified that though he should have all the goods of this world, it would mean nothing to him unless he were joined to the Church and remained in the midst of it. For in saying 'the land of your people', he meant not the land which the people possessed, but the good pleasure which God had for his people. Here is the summary of what David meant: 'Lord, may you not only bestow upon me your blessings as upon many profane people – for "you make your sun shine on the good and on the wicked" (Matt. 5:45), and want them to enjoy it equally – but may you remember me, to make me a part of your household, and one of the inhabitants of your Church. Only in the company of your good children, whom you have been pleased to adopt, can I ever find total contentment and peace. Here I shall be visited with your salvation.'

So we must remember from this passage that when we consider privately how dependent we are upon God, we must always conclude by saying: 'Lord, may I be of the number and company of your children!' Then let us also recognise that all the blessings which God has granted in particular belong in general to the whole Church. For it is not without cause that we confess in our creed, after having spoken of the universal Church, that there is the communion of saints – that is, the faithful, who are so joined together and united that all their blessings are common. These common blessings do not refer to their worldly realm, but rather it means that when God advances the salvation of his Church, we are included in it, and God cannot do good to one without all being participants in the blessing.

David, as we have already seen, wanted people to recognise who God was. Thus, he called him by the name 'God of Israel', which showed that he was the Saviour. Then he asked: 'Lord who is like your people?' It was not a question here of elevating the people in order to say that they had been glorified in themselves, but rather to show that it was God's glory which was reflected from his chosen people, as the fourth chapter of Deuteronomy says. It is very likely that David took this sentence from there, since all the prophets have derived their doctrine from the Law of Moses. Now Deuteronomy 4:7 says: 'Who is a people so noble, and so excellent, to whom God has revealed himself so familiarly? Go (he says) and see, if there is a nation so great and so noble, who is so close to their gods as you, to whom the Lord had declared and manifested himself.' It is true that the pagans boasted themselves more and more of their idols, but it was nothing but vanity and illusion. Hence, Moses remonstrated that God had given such a privilege to his people that he had ennobled them above all nations. Well, that was not to make the people proud, but to make them accept such an honourable condition and seek no other felicity except in God, as the Psalm says: 'Blessed is the people whose God is the Eternal One' (Psa. 33:12). That is why the other passage of the Psalm says that God had not declared himself to the nations and had not manifested to them his judgements and statutes (Psa. 147:20).

In sum, as David formerly protested that God alone ought to be known, without having anyone beside him, similarly he now separated the Church from all profane assemblies. So these are things joined together: just as God wants to be separated from idols, so also he wants his Church to have a mark, so that it can be discerned from all those who associate with unbelievers. This stands against any fanatics, who would like all the world to gather together so that there would only be confusion, and people would not know who had won or lost. Now here is how many profane people who cause trouble in the world, talk: 'To be separated like this is going entirely too far, and is excessively strict'. They say this simply because they care nothing about the honour and the holiness of God. Let us note well, therefore, how God wants his glory to shine out, so that there will be nothing to obscure it. Also he wants his Church to be enriched, and people to know what his flock is, so that we may learn to join ourselves to his flock.

It is nothing to say: 'Behold the people of God', unless we are among them. Hence, when David said that 'there is no people like your people', it was to show that God wanted to be known in his Church, so that we would be attentive to him. This is also the correct way to know how to separate wicked and rotten members from the Church. Otherwise, we would not be able to judge what people God has chosen for his heritage. We will be drawn above the heavens when we realise how God has wanted to draw out his own and make them one body, and has given them a head, who is our Lord Jesus Christ, to hold them in union. Then, although we live in a corrupt world, we will not fail to be lifted on high by faith. Indeed, we are the flock of this great Shepherd, to whom we have been given to keep. Scripture tells us: 'None will perish of that which has been given to him by God his Father' (John 6:39).

Next, in order to express his thought better, David said that 'God went to redeem them'. He used a mode of speech which is rather crude, but it contains a good doctrine. We know that God, who fills all, is not in a place. He is not like us, for when we would like to do something or other, we have to stretch our arms, and only with the greatest difficulty can we do something without having to move our legs. Why? Because when someone is in one place, he cannot help but move his whole body when he lifts his arm to do a task. Now that is why mortal creatures move themselves and change position, and go from one place to another when necessary. But God, who is infinite, does not change at all. Yet this passage says that he marched in order to deliver his people. But it said this simply to express God's power more clearly than men would otherwise have apprehended. Therefore, although God did not move, and did not depart from his place, still it was as though he had descended and made an appearance. That is why the Scripture uses this mode of talking: The heavens are opened, and God has come to take his seat here below.

All of that does not describe God, properly speaking, as far as his essence is concerned, but it is needed because we do not conceive that God is close to us unless he gives us some sign. That is why it says that he descends here below. It says not only in this place that God has walked, but the Psalm says that he walked through the desert with his people (Psa. 78:52–53). Did he have to walk? Quite certainly not! Even when he appeared in the person of his Son, who was the main angel for the guidance of the people, he did not actually march, though he acted like a pilgrim and traveller. Here, then, was this pillar, which gave testimony that he was in the midst of his people, not there merely to guard them, but wanting to go with them, as if he had taken as many steps as they had (Exod. 14:19). Therefore, this is what David expressed in this passage, when he said that God went to redeem his people.

Then, he added: 'to win a name and to do wondrous and terrible things because of his people, in order to redeem them' (2 Sam. 7:23). Well, all of this speaks of the redemption which was accomplished when he brought his people back 'out of Egypt'. The prophets, in fact, always used this phrase when they wanted to make the people recognise who the God of Israel was. They brought this story up, recounted it and committed it to memory, for it was linked to the Law which God gave. If God had simply redeemed his people, left them hanging in suspense, and had not given them any doctrine or foundation of Law, he would have made a mockery of them. But as I have said, these things are inseparable: God brought back his people from their miserable captivity and then proclaimed his Law to them, in order to say: 'Now here is wisdom and prudence' – as Moses explains in the fourth chapter of Deuteronomy which we have mentioned. 'Now here', he says, 'is wisdom, that you hear your God speak and follow him, according to what is contained in his Law.' Hence, the prophets spoke in this way with good reason when they wished to emphasise God's own action in having brought back his people. For in those circumstances, he dealt with a particular state of the Church and showed how he wanted his people to be governed. How? By having published his Law.

Following that, David then mentioned redemption, and said of God that 'he had won a name', in order to show that he ought to be known by all the world. Indeed, if he had not won great glory, it would have caused everyone to fall away from obeying the Law, for if men had not been bewitched by the devil, would they not have been convinced that God had chosen Israel for his heritage? Would not that knowledge have been extended all over the world? Therefore, this redemption was surely sufficient to win a name for God, so that he might be worshipped everywhere, and so that people would withdraw from the idols and superstitions to which they had previously adhered. The main reason that David spoke so clearly about the faithful and about those of Abraham's race when he said, 'God won a name', was because the poor unbelievers were addicted to their idolatries and had buried his name by their ingratitude. It is true (as I have said) that he surely merited being glorified by all without exception, as the Psalm says: 'Lord, according to the greatness of your name, your praise will be over the earth' (Psa. 148:13). His justice, his goodness, his mercy and virtue ought to be known, so that people might esteem him as he deserves. Nevertheless, God has acquired a special name towards his people.

Well, this is addressed to us, for although we are not descended from the race of Abraham, though God has not brought us back from the land of Egypt, still we have been associated with these people who were elected and chosen. Indeed, the Jews, who were little 'branches of the tree, have been cut off, and we have been grafted in' in their place (Rom. 11:17). For God has banished them from his Church, and we have entered it. Hence, let us learn to magnify God. Let us realise that if the greatest part of men are blind and do not know what it is to honour God's name, then they do not know how he deserves to be exalted. Therefore, how much more attentive we should be, and how much more each one of us should endeavour and press forward to honour the name of God.

Now today, we have the actual fulfilment of this shadow. It was a more than miraculous deed when God stretched out his hand to bring back his people out of Egypt, but we have been redeemed in a manner even more excellent and noble. This happened when he drew us from where we were in the depths of hell, under the curse, and presented himself to us in the person of our Lord Jesus Christ. Thus, the heavens were opened to us so as to put us in possession not of the land of Canaan, but of eternal felicity. When God brought his people out of Egypt, he put them in possession of this land. Well, the land of Canaan was only an earnest or pledge of this heavenly country which has been acquired for us. Since God has thus drawn us out of the depths of hell so as to call us to his kingdom, let us magnify him, knowing that this second redemption has surpassed the first.

When David stated that God had exalted his glory, he was referring to the glory of God's people: 'You have done wondrous deeds, O Lord, and terrible – because of your people Israel'. Here again is a point worthy of being noted. It is that God loves us in such a way that when he glorifies himself, wanting to be known in his grandeur and majesty, at the same time he procures and advances all the more the salvation of his people. It is as if he were making a link there, and saying: 'I want your salvation to be joined to my glory'. How? He so accompanies and accommodates himself to us that he wants his glory to be joined to our salvation. At the same time, he wants our life to depend on him – which shows how greatly he must love us. It is certain that he is concerned for his glory, which is a very precious thing. Now if we should have heaven and earth and all the elements, and even all the angels against us, that would be nothing in comparison with having God as an enemy! When we know that he loves us, what should we dread? Hence, when we see that God puts his glory in hostage to us, as a testimony to us of his love, and that he wants our salvation to be joined to it with an inseparable link, why should we ever fear any more?

Hence, let us consider these words well, that 'God has won a name' when he did wondrous things, and employed his infinite virtue 'because of his people Israel' (2 Sam. 7:23). God's mercy does not proceed from the worthiness of his people, but from his free love. God loves us now just as he has from all eternity. Not that we have deserved it, not that we are better than those whom he rejects, but it has pleased him to do this. This is what is so often recounted: that he chose that people, not because they were better than other nations, but for his pleasure. Hence, let us recognise that this love which God has for us is free.

Be that as it may, he does not want us to be separated from his glory. Therefore, if heaven and earth should be reversed, and it should seem that we must be destroyed a hundred thousand times by storms and tempests which we often see; if the whole world had conspired with all creatures against us, and they were assembled to plan our trial and ruin us, let it satisfy us that God has a concern for his glory, and that we are joined to it.

Then David added these words: 'The people with their judges' (2 Sam. 7:23; Psa. 82:6). It is true that he uses the word 'gods' here, as the other passage of Scripture says, which speaks of the king and of his successors. They are called gods in that they are his lieutenants and put his will into execution. Well, by this word David meant Moses and Aaron, and others who succeeded them, whom he appointed out of pity for his people – indeed, even to Samuel, and down to himself, as head of the people of Israel, as we have seen, and as we will explain again. In sum, David wanted to show here that when God redeemed his people, both great and small were participants in his goodness. Here he showed that although Moses and Aaron were excellent, still God redeemed them like the others, and they would not have had the slightest dignity if God had not bestowed his mercy upon them. Now this is one point.

Secondly, David wanted to amplify the grace of God here to his people. For if he had redeemed them and then left them without guidance (as I have said), what good would it have done – a body without a head? In fact, we see that without Moses and Aaron, as the Psalms say, the people would have become totally apostate (Psa. 77:20; 99:6; 106:23). Indeed, they had reached that point. We know how this people rebelled and gave themselves over to idolatry, and were not able to keep from banding together against God. Be that as it may, this would have happened even a hundred times more without the guidance of Moses and Aaron. On the other hand, they were perverse in their malice, and God would have destroyed them a hundred thousand times if he had not raised up judges for them, who served as his lieutenants and officers to correct them. So David intended to show that God not only brought his people out of Egypt in order to remove them from their slavery and captivity, but also that he immediately gave them leaders and guides. This shows that he cared for them and did not want to keep them like brute beasts and reject them. Rather, he wanted to draw them to himself when he placed them under guidance, so that they could be governed by his hand. Well, that is the second point which we have to remember.

In conclusion, he says that 'God has established a people for himself, so tht they might remain for ever'. This shows that God did not suddenly cease his care when he redeemed his people from Egypt, but he brought them to himself in order to guard them. And this is important to note. For what good would it have done if God had set his people free all at once, and then left them? Redemption, therefore, had to be the foundation upon which to build. God did build when he declared his Law and then, when he chastised his people in the desert, he did not fail to be their Saviour also. Then he gave them possession of the promised land. Later, when there was only confusion and everything seemed to have been ruined, he gave them judges and saviours. He finally established David on the royal throne, which was supposed to have been perpetual. So, when these things are added, we see that the redemption which God accomplished was not merely partial.

Let us learn to use our minds to remember well what it tells us here for our instruction. That is, when it pleases God to call us to know him, he does not mean to deceive us, as if he were saying, 'Here am I', and then immediately drawing away from us. Rather, he intends to persevere in his goodness and make us feel the fruit of his mercy. St Paul thoroughly experienced this truth, and speaks of it in Philippians 1:6 – 'he who has begun to do his work in us, will complete it'. Hence, let this encourage us to trust in God, not doubting that he will continue his grace to us more and more until he has achieved our ultimate salvation.

Now let us prostrate ourselves before his majesty, in recognition of our faults, praying him to be pleased not to prevent us, on account of our crudeness, from confessing ourselves to be his children in the name of our Lord Jesus Christ. We pray that he might so increase his favour to us that we may have our mouths open to preach his unspeakable virtues all our life, and that we may continue, both in life and in death, to glorify him in such a way that we may finally attain that life which we await, which he has acquired for our possession, as our fathers possessed the land of Canaan. And may he not only bestow this grace upon us, but upon all people . . .

26

*The Nature of True Prayer**

Now, therefore, Lord God, let the word which you have propounded concerning your servant and his house be confirmed for ever. And may they say: the Lord of Hosts is God over Israel, and the house of your servant David is established before you. For you, O Lord of Hosts, God of Israel, you have revealed in the ear of your servant saying: I shall build you a house . . . (2 Sam. 7:25–29).

After David recognised the proofs which he had been given of the goodness of God, not only to himself, but to the whole body of the Church, he returned to pray to God. And in this we see that the promises which God has given us are not to make us lazy and nonchalant, but rather to encourage us to come to him. This ought to be carefully noted, for there are many fanatics who ignore praying to God, under the excuse that they are assured by his word: 'Since God has declared that he cares for us, why should we worry? God has promised not to leave us in necessity and in need. Let us wait, therefore, until he fulfils his Word. But what need is there to go and ask him for it? That would be as if he did not see what is proper for us, or were asleep in heaven and could not uphold us whenever necessary.' Now that is how profane people abuse the Word of God, under the false pretext that they are quite certain that without seeking for it, he will always manifest himself at the opportune time. Well, as I have said, when our Lord offers us his promises, that he will be a Father to us, and that we are his children, and that he draws us to come to him, it does not mean that our faith

*Wednesday, July 29, 1562.

should be buried. But on the contrary, if in fact we are resolute and have the certainty which we ought to have that God has spoken, it will cause us to seek him and encourage us to pray to him. In sum, faith is the source of all requests and prayers, as will soon be explained to us in more detail.

However, let us carefully note these words, where it says: 'Lord, since it is thus, let the house therefore of your servant be established for ever' (2 Sam. 7:26). God had declared that he would do this. David was relying upon this promise so as to rest on it. And why, then, does he add this prayer? It seems that it would be superfluous. But on the contrary, these are inseparable things, as I have said: the prayer itself and the desire which we have to pray for God to accomplish it all and make us feel it in reality. When, therefore, we pray to God, it is not that we are doubting whether he is already inclined to do us good; or whether he watches out to support us in all our necessities; or whether he knows them well; or that when he has spoken, he does not want to carry out his Word. Rather, the fact is that our faith ought to be exercised, and that God, in offering us his mercy and grace, invites us to have the boldness to call upon him (Eph. 2:18). Without this, he cannot give us free access. So much, then, for this point.

Next, he says: 'Lord, establish your word for ever' (2 Sam. 7:25). Well, by that David is not teaching that God changes his mind, as if it were mutable, or that when he has some desire to help us, it vanishes away just like the passing fancies of mortal men. Rather, he has in mind the frailty which he knew was in himself, as in all creatures. Let us note carefully, therefore, how firm the Word of God is, and how it can never vary, and how it has an infallible truth – especially since, on our part, we are so weak that we could not of ourselves cause the Word of God to prove that its promises are true for us. Hence, let us recognise our inconsistency, and that it takes nothing to make us stagger. When we are blown by every wind, let us pray God to confirm and so establish his Word that he will perform it to us. In doing this, we will not be considering God to be inconsistent, nor detracting from his honour, but we will rather be confessing, as far as we can, that we are so liable to negate his truth that it would not exercise its power in our lives unless God carried it through.

Well, the way to establish the firm truth of this Word is for God to fortify our faith in it. For whenever we act in unbelief, it is the same as if we were pushing back the hand of God so that it might not help us, and were casting his Word so far away from us that it could not produce its fruit. Therefore, when God wants to establish his Word, he must grant us invincible constancy, so that we may persevere in it, and embrace him with an affection that we will never lose. Now that is what we have to remember in this passage.

Therefore, when we pray for him to fulfil his promises, let us note that it ought not to be for one day, but for our whole lifetime and even after our death. Let us not doubt that we are easily confused, and that our faith is so weak that it seems that the Word of God falls down like water (rather than remaining a solid rock). Let us not doubt (I say) that as we need it, he will support us and continue the grace of his Spirit to us, so that his Word might find space and take root in us, and we might recognise that as he has begun, he wants to finish the work of our salvation (Phil. 1:6). Now that, in sum, is what we have to remember from this passage.

Then he adds that by this means 'the name of God will be glorified and that it will be said: the Lord of hosts is God over Israel, and the house of your servant David will be blessed' (2 Sam. 7:26). We see here the principal good for which we must ever seek and aspire in praying to God: it is that his name be sanctified. For it is not without cause that our Lord Jesus Christ, in giving us the rule of good prayer, began this way: 'Hallowed be your name' (Matt. 6:9), so that we might always refer the requests and wishes which we ask of God to this goal. If we separate our own profit from the glory of God, we will destroy the principal blessing he has for us by our own ingratitude. For (as was dealt with yesterday) it is a testimony of the singular goodness of God, which is incomprehensible, whenever it pleases him to join together and unite his glory to our salvation. Hence, if we only care about ourselves, looking only for our own profit and for what is useful to us, and yet do not think of his name being exalted or of all praise being rendered to him – that (I say) is just as destructive as if we ruined the form of proper prayer. Well, for this reason, let us remember what is shown to us here by David. Although he was concerned for himself, nevertheless he did not forget the main thing: namely, that God be glorified as he deserves. 'Your name,' he says, 'O Lord, will be glorified.' He is placing the name of God in the sovereign position, so that our salvation might be hidden under it.

Then he adds: 'Let people know that the Lord of hosts is God over Israel'. By this he shows his affection for the whole Church, as he has already testified. Someone who separates himself from the body certainly alienates himself from God and from our Lord Jesus Christ. For when God declares to us that he will be our Father, and our Lord Jesus Christ presents himself as Mediator, so as to cause us to find grace before God his Father – it is on this condition that we become members of his body. So when someone thinks only of his personal blessing, and forgets his neighbours, then he is drawn away both from God and from our Lord Jesus Christ.

Let us carefully remember, therefore, when we have to pray to God, that we must not be 'addicted' to ourselves in such a way that we despise those whom God has joined to us. In fact, that is why our Lord Jesus Christ has also taught us to pray together. When we pray to him, although we do so individually, we say: 'Give us this day *our* daily bread, and forgive us *our* debts' (Matt. 6:11–12). This does not teach us to say: 'Lord, provide for me, and let me be sustained'. But rather we pray in common with others, for we must have pity and compassion on those who are in need. After that, inasmuch as all are sinners and debtors to God, we must also help them obtain pardon, even as we would like to be helped by them. Now this is what David shows, when, in dealing with the promise which God has made to him personally, he nevertheless comprehended the whole Church and said that he knew that God was over Israel.

However, David shows here how much God bestows his bounty on all men, as the Scripture says that he 'makes his sun shine on the good and on the evil' (Matt. 5:45), yet nevertheless he does not fail to have hidden treasure for his children. In fact, a man who is very rich, or a prince, will be very liberal to those who are not worthy of it, but still will not fail to keep the inheritance for his children. Well, God, who is not like a mortal creature since he does not diminish, and his goods cannot run out, does indeed show himself liberal, as I have said, and distributes his benefits to the good and to the wicked. Nevertheless, what the Psalm says is unfailingly true: 'Lord, how excellent is the greatness of your goodness, which you have indeed stored up for those who fear you' (Psa. 31:19)! The prophet clearly shows that if he has been generous to the whole human race, it does not mean that he has not reserved for his children, and for those to whom he wants to be Father and Saviour, more than the world can perceive. And hence David now separates the Church from all other nations of the earth, as if he were saying: 'Lord, if you dealt with us as you do with the world in general, what would be our hope? For the pigs will be fed in their sty, and the cattle will be fattened in their stable, but Lord, what is your bounty to all men, when you show that you have reserved bread for the use of your children?' Well, when God shows his bounty to those who fear him, Scripture says that it is hidden from others. And why? So that all who despise his majesty are kept from it.

Let us note, also, that this hidden bounty of God in regard to those who fear him is not merely for their lower life, but it goes much further. The goods for which we must hope from God are spiritual. It is true that we surely have his promises for this earthly life just as much as for the eternal kingdom. But be that as it may, the main thing must always be first, and the secondary thing must follow. In other words, all the temporal goods which God bestows upon us are like a foretaste of the principal thing, which is for us to know that he has created and formed us in his image, and then that he has redeemed us by the death of his only Son. Then he has finally called us to the knowledge of his Gospel so that we might be pilgrims in this world, and know that there is a better life prepared for us, to which we are called daily. Now that is why it says that God will be known as God over Israel.

However, David wants to say here that God is glorified in doing good to his faithful ones, because this shows that he is the true living God. It shows that he knew that the Eternal, the Creator, who only has essential being, and who rules the heavens and earth, is God over Israel. Even though the poor Church is oppressed, or the favours of God do not appear in it, and the wicked are at ease, and prosper, it is only our human viewpoint which keeps us from distinguishing between the true God and idols. So David prays here that when God has bestowed his riches on his Church, it will cause men to realise that there is neither glory, nor majesty, nor power, nor highness, nor divine essence except in God alone, so that all human imaginations of superstition or idolatry must be brought down. Therefore, this is what we have to remember as the main point of this passage.

He adds after that: 'Lord, God of hosts, God of Israel, you have revealed in the ear of your servant that you wanted to build him a house, and hence your servant has found it in his heart to pray to you' (2 Sam. 7:27). Here again is a very noteworthy sentence. Formerly, David has prayed that the Eternal be known as God over his people. Now he puts the two together. By this word and title, 'You, God of Hosts', he expresses the infinite power of God, and then calls him 'God of Israel' in regard to the fact that he has gathered his people and addressed his covenant to them. This was in order to say that he wanted to inhabit the country of Israel and be worshipped in his temple, and that the people might be assured that it was not a frivolous divine service like the numerous follies which men have continually invented to please God. Here was David, who on the one hand recognised that there was only one God who has created all things, and on the other, since mere power would not be enough, added that God has made himself known to his people and to his Church.

This teaches us to recognise the high majesty of God when we come to him, so that it will serve to humble us in such reverence that we will truly give him the homage that he deserves. Why, indeed, do we pray to God so carelessly, and even coldly, and do nothing but move our mouths? It is because we pray by acquired habit and by ritual, and then we are bold to run through it, as if he were subject to our desires. And what is the cause of all that? It is because we do not taste this majesty of God, which ought to abase us so that we humble ourselves before him. That is how David began. Nevertheless, let us note that if we apprehended something other than the glory of God and his grandeur, it would serve to take us away from him, and we would never be able to approach him. For who are we? And where are the wings to make us fly so high? Thus, when we know that God is all-powerful, let us be touched with such fear that we will render him the glory of which he is worthy. Then we must add the second thing which is mentioned here. That is, that since God comes down to us by his Word and makes himself familiar to us and opens the door for us, we must exercise faith – which is the key to giving us access and liberty to pray, since God, by this means, approaches us and gives us grace by which we can come to him. This is why David says: 'God almighty, you are altogether King of Israel'. By this word, he included the promise of God by which he adopted this people.

Now let us come to the main thing. He says: 'You have revealed in the ear of your servant that you would build his house, and so your servant has found it in his heart to pray to you' (2 Sam. 7:27). Well, here David shows us even more clearly what we have mentioned briefly, that is, that we cannot pray to God without faith. It is true that certainly everyone is involved in praying. The pagans made it a trade and custom, just as today in the papacy they clearly admit that it is necessary to pray to God. But yet, what foundations do they have? Papist devotions are completely fortuitous, like those of the pagans who were incited by their natural feelings to pray to God, and yet had no certainty. Thus the papists pray to God with a foolish and confused devotion, and yet they have no access to him. God also pays them the wages which they deserve. For we realise that they do not know what saint to make their vows to, as their common proverb attests: 'Each one has his own patron saint'. But they are not content with that. They want to have two or three of them, and finally an abundance and an infinite number! And now they are in doubt and trembling on every side. When they add on St Claude and St Godegrin, there will be another saint like that, and the whole troop will not be enough. And why? Because they have never tasted what it is to present oneself to God in the name of the Mediator, and have even rejected his promises, which are nothing to them when it comes to praying. All the more, therefore, must we carefully consider the words of David, for they contain important instruction. That is, we cannot find the courage to pray to God, which means we will not be able to have the properly regulated form of prayer which we need, until God has spoken to us.

Well, this word 'to reveal to the ear' (2 Sam. 7:27) – or, properly, 'to open the ear' – is to explain that when we hear God speak concerning himself and concerning things in general, it will not be sufficient to give us the necessary desire to pray. Certainly, there are those who will clearly hear the Lord speak. That is to say, when someone preaches the goodness of God to them, they will have some idea of it, but it will soon melt away. And why? Because they cannot apply what they are told for their own benefit. It is not enough, therefore, for God to speak in general, for this would only be confused. But we must hear him personally, and each one must conclude that although God may speak to all, nevertheless whether we are great or small, we should be encouraged to know that he speaks to all those who seek him with all their strength. Now that is how God will open our ears, in other words, when we know not only that he wants to be prayed to, but that he gives this privilege to me, and to this person here and that person there.

Now concerning 'the building of the house' (2 Sam. 7:27), it is a figure of speech to express: to give a certain estate to a man. It is often said that God builds a house, when he makes it prosper. In sum, therefore, David uses building as a figure of speech here in order to show that God has chosen him so as to bless him in his posterity.

Well, we see that the point of these words is that we cannot pray to God with affection, and even that we are mute, until God opens our ears. For that opening of the ears opens our mouths as well. When we have heard God speak, then we respond mutually to him, so that there is harmony and accord between his promises by which he draws us to himself, and these prayers through which we come to him. That is why it is said several times to the prophets: 'I will say to them, you are my people, and they will reply to me: you are our God' (Hos. 2:23). It is impossible for us to be able to speak so openly, and it would even be presumptuous, if we intended to thrust ourselves forward by our own power so as to say: 'God will be my Saviour'. On the contrary, he must speak first. For we are not worthy of being among his creatures, not even with the most vile and contemptible. Nevertheless, he has adopted us as his children, but only because of his inestimable goodness and his free grace. Moreover, when he has thus spoken: 'You are my people', we may boldly reply: 'And you are our Father, O Lord'.

That is what St Paul says in the tenth chapter of Romans: 'How will one call on him upon whom one has not believed? And how will one believe, without having been taught, and without his promises having been preached?' (Rom. 10:14). It seems that this principle that St Paul lays down is in vain, for one could reply that the pagans have never had a right knowledge of God, and yet they have not failed to pray, for all religion involves that. And then, there are many idolaters. What foundation will they have to pray in their ignorance? One could, therefore, make that objection to St Paul. However, he rightly presupposes that all prayers which are made haphazardly are like wind, and vanish away, and have no substance in themselves. Indeed, we only profane the name of God when we pray to him in this manner without the certainty of faith. We imagine we are doing well, like the papists who mumble and then go into their temples and run from chapel to chapel and altar to altar, crying to St Barbara, St Agatha, St Catherine, and St Gertrude. But nevertheless, what they are doing is nothing but pollution and filth. And why? Because when it comes to praying to God, we must have assurance, as I have said, and must come to God in order to reply to him when he calls us, so that we have our mouth open and are attentive when he has opened our ears to receive his promises. Thus, we know that this is a 'sweet-smelling sacrifice' to him when we call on him and have our refuge in him alone in our time of need.

This, in summary, is what we have to remember from this passage, where it says: 'Lord, you have opened the ears of your servant, and yet he has found it in his heart to pray to you'. We can certainly pray to God, which our nature leads us to do, as I have said, for we will always be convinced that without God, we are more than miserable. Even the unbelievers have experienced enough of that to remove every excuse of ignorance. However, this is not sufficient to give us courage, for we see how the papists wander and float from one side to the other, as I have said. They tremble when they pray, and do not know what they have gained or obtained. Far from knowing how to state their requests, they totally withdraw themselves from the truth, and thus cannot address the majesty of God as he has given it to us in his Son. They will make plenty of lamentations, but does that encourage them in prayer? Indeed, no! But they are like a desperate man, who when he has been unable to find water, will throw himself in the fire, or like the wild beasts who get themselves entangled. This is how the papists and all idolaters are who tremble before their idols, some offering candles, others holding 'Our Fathers' and moving their lips like apes. Is this not a pure mockery of God, who wants to be worshipped in spirit and in truth (John 4:24)? But what is the reason for this? It is because they do not have definite assurance and have not felt what the presence of God means and involves, so as to rest upon it. But they come with their ears closed, not knowing why they are there.

Would we, therefore, like to be encouraged in our prayers? We must remove everything that we imagine and all that our mind thinks up for itself, and pay attention to the Word of God when it is preached to us in order to humble ourselves under it. And yet we must realise that it is addressed to us. That is, when we hear God spoken of, who calls us his children, then we have true liberty to pray to him. In sum, this doctrine which we have drawn from St Paul is most necessary for us. The preaching of the Gospel must, therefore, be first when it comes to calling on God. Hence the faith, as I have said, is the source of all prayers; it is the mother of every sacrifice of every sort which God requires, and thus we are enabled to call upon his name.

Well then, David adds: 'Now, Lord God, you are God, and your words are true' (2 Sam. 7:28). Here David is strengthening himself again in the power of God, so that he may not waver and vary, but may remain fully persuaded that God has sufficient strength and power to accomplish what he has said. However, he also adds that these words are truth. He has already dealt with the power of God, but he is not content with that. And why? Because it is a confession of his own crudeness and infirmity for him to repeat this kind of sentence. Repeating these words is like our hammering down a nail with heavy blows so that it will be driven in and will hold firm. Thus, we must do the same thing with the power of God and its virtue. For when we have understood that God is God, that will quickly remove confidence in ourselves. Let us note what our constancy is like! Alas, it is less than a broken reed. Therefore, even when we have apprehended the power of God, we still need love and assurance quickly to enter into our hearts. And how? By continual meditation, so that we know not only in passing what God declares to us, but commit it to memory, so that when we pray to him, we might seek to call on him in such a way that he will never be far from us.

This is, therefore, the approach which David takes here, which ought to serve as instruction for us: 'Lord God, you are God' (2 Sam. 7:28). Well, at first glance, it would appear that this is nothing. That seems to be the case, but it is still a great deal when we come to know how we are obscuring the infallible truth of God, and his justice and goodness. We may, indeed, use this Word of God which will pass the lips of many. However, what is it that we are attributing to him? And when we speak of it, is it to praise him for all his glory in the way he deserves? Very far from it. Therefore, since this Word of God only rolls off the tip of the tongue, and we do not know what it contains, this is why David now brings it forward, to encourage and urge himself to realise that when God is our Father, nothing can fail us, as the prophet Habakkuk says: 'You are our God, and we will not perish' (Hab. 1:12). In this way, the faithful assure themselves that since God is on their side, he is strong enough to take care of them. So, when David uses this word about God, it is to contrast him to all creatures, as if he were saying: 'Lord, you are not a man to retract your word' (Num. 23:19). Even Balaam, that false prophet and trickster, is constrained to speak in this way. Indeed, God is not like mortal creatures who change their minds. Hence, when it says that God is God, it is to show that he is not like men who wish but are unable, nor like creatures who care only for themselves and despise others.

Therefore, in order to understand clearly what David shows us here, let us make this comparison between God and all creatures. For among the creatures, what do we find? If one has the will, he will lack the power; and then often he will not have the will when he ought to have it. And if he has it, it will soon grow cold – for there are changes and variations, which mean that if a man has openly promised something for less than nothing, he will change his mind. And then, if today he has the means in hand, tomorrow they will be removed from him so that nothing is certain. When we, therefore, attribute God's title to him, we must immediately conclude that since his power is infinite, it is sufficient that he loves us, and then since his goodness is incomprehensible, it will extend even to us as far as we need. We must conclude that since he is faithful, we need not fear that we shall fail or go lacking when we desire to take refuge in him, since it has pleased him to accept us as his children and household members. That, in brief, sums up this word.

Then he adds: 'Your word is truth' (2 Sam. 7:28). For even when we have known the power of God, as has been shown, it will still be very cold until we add this second article to it. That is, God is powerful, and will make us glad in our welfare and salvation when we receive his promises, which put his virtue into operation. By this, David arms himself against all distrust and temptation. However excellent he was in faith, still he had not extracted all corruption from his flesh. He had, therefore, many battles to go through. That is why he takes this shield: 'The Word of God is truth'.

In Psalm 19, we see David make a similar statement, which really seems superfluous: the Word of God 'is like gold and silver tried in the furnace'. Of course, we know what these words actually mean, but our main concern is the intention and purpose for which they are used here. They are used because our faith is twisted out of shape, and we are practically plunged into the mire when it comes to approaching God. We cannot immediately free ourselves from our earthly stupidity and slowness. That is why David shows us that when God has spoken, we ought to be so persuaded of his faithfulness that even if the devil brings every kind of small and great creature across our path, in order to turn us away from the trust which we ought to have in God, still this Word will be sufficient for us – the Word which is purified like gold and silver, and which will never be found to have a trace of false metal mingled with it. This means that the Word of God is so separated from all corruption that its purity must be recognised and prized for all eternity.

Here, therefore, is the conclusion of this matter, which we must observe when the Gospel manifests the truth of God in all its promises to us. For each one of us, by our personal experience, knows exactly how much we need to be fortified when it comes to keeping ourselves in the Word of God and adhering to it constantly. We need to be fortified because, in the first place, it takes nothing to knock us down – as our experience proves only too well. Then on the other hand, we see how the devil has spread his traps everywhere and how this world is full of ambushes to catch us and bring us utterly down. Not a day goes by without bad thoughts passing through our minds or, on top of that, without our being motivated by lack of trust, so that we feel that God has left us and does not care about us any more. This is not only a personal problem, but it is a problem that affects the whole Church in common. Thus, let us learn to fortify ourselves and to hold up this shield – that when we know the promises of God, and when doubt and questionings come upon us and we are almost broken down, in this very situation the infallible virtue and incomprehensible goodness of God will never fail us.

Well, today we have more reason than ever to meditate on this doctrine, for when we consider all the confusing situations which are in this world, who among us would be able to endure or stand against them? Indeed, it seems that God wants totally to devastate everything. That is the situation not only in this place, but everywhere – as I say, the whole Church is being ruined. But how are people going to call on God, and how will his name be proclaimed? He wants people to give him continual thanks, and promises that he will make those who call on him feel his goodness. But how is this going to happen, since we are still going through troubles, and everywhere we turn we see nothing but vexation and harm, and furthermore, we are so terribly fragile that the least little thing can turn us aside and drive us to despair? We must all the more, then, impress upon our memory what it says here, that God is just as faithful as he is powerful, and that he will accomplish in us what he has begun (Phil. 1:6). And although he delays for a while, he has still not forgotten us, and we cannot be frustrated when we wait on him.

Moreover, David then draws this conclusion: 'Lord, do this and bless the house of your servant, so it might last for ever' (2 Sam. 7:29). Here David is returning to the matter that we dealt with above, namely, that the church could never prosper unless it were founded in Jesus Christ, for there is not the slightest hope of salvation otherwise. For this building of the house of David did not at all consist of stone or wood or other material. And furthermore, it did not refer to this kingdom which endured for a time and then finally fell – indeed, with shame and infamy. Rather, it refers to God's will to bring salvation to the world from the race of David. Thus, after having spoken of the welfare and happiness of the Church, and even having declared the goodness of God in general, it is not without cause that he returns to this promise given to him concerning his seed, that God will establish the royal throne in his house, which will remain for ever – indeed, for as long as there is a sun and moon in heaven (Psa. 89:36–37).

This shows us that we can never be convinced and assured of the promises of God without looking to our Lord Jesus, who, in the words of St Paul, is 'the yes and amen' (2 Cor. 1:20). Paul shows us by this verse that we cannot be assured of the promises of God except by this means: our faith must be founded in Jesus Christ. While the truth of God is certainly infallible in itself, still it is impossible for us to feel the fruit and virtue of it in our own lives except in our Lord Jesus Christ. And why? Because even if someone has preached to us a hundred times about the power of God and we have conceived what it really is so far as we dull and frail creatures are able, and even if someone has also spoken to us about his goodness and all his virtues, still we could never be assured that he is our Father and that he accepts us as his children, unless we go to the source of our adoption – which is that he has elected us in our Lord Jesus Christ, and thus we may find grace in and through him. This is the case because Christ alone is the beloved Son of God, while we are all detestable creatures in the sight of God, who thoroughly deserve being cut off from the rest of his creatures. Now this is precisely why we can only be hated and enemies of God, since it is what we merit. But God says: 'This is my beloved Son, hear him' (Matt. 17:5), in order that we may find his love. Seeing that our Lord Jesus Christ is given this description, we must always keep it before our eyes, for otherwise God will not show us his paternal affection. That is why Scripture also says that 'he has made us accepted in his beloved' (Eph. 1:6). Instead of having to hate us for our sins, he is so reconciled to us that we are his beloved children – that is, insofar as we are members of our Head. Now that is why David returns to this promise of the blessing of his house.

He mentions this word 'perpetuity' (2 Sam. 7:29) so that we might know that God governs his Church to the end. This does not mean that the Church always remains in a thoroughly healthy condition and that it bears fruit, and its condition triumphs more and more. But be that as it may, he knows how to raise it from the dead when it is in the sepulchre, and how to build it up when it is broken down, and how to re-establish it when it is ruined. Yet let us hold to this point, fully assured that God, having called us to himself, has not brought us a mere earthly grace, but he wants us to enjoy this blessing just as much in death as in life.

Now this is how we must apply this doctrine and this is its purpose: namely, when we see troubles and confusion all over the world, when we see fires burning and swords unsheathed, let us firmly hold to this truth, that God will be the protector of his Church – not for a year nor for twenty or thirty, but for ever. That is one point.

And then, there are times when each one of us thinks of his special condition: 'Alas, what about me? I see I have been tricked. The devil has seduced me in this way, and I am so weak, and where is the zeal which I ought to have to serve God in all purity? Oh, I am so corrupt, and I am ashamed of myself, and do not know how to present myself to God since I am so filthy.' Now when we think like this, let us turn our minds in the following direction: since God wants us to take refuge in him by the means he has given us, therefore he will not only deliver us from such snares, but he will preserve us and maintain us to the end, just as he promised. This is because our salvation rests not in ourselves, but in our Lord Jesus Christ, who is given to us as a perpetual King – not only for this life, but for ages to come (Isa. 9:6–7).

Now let us prostrate ourselves before the majesty of our good God in recognition of the infinite faults of which we are guilty. Let us pray to him that, more and more, he will look upon us, and yet that he will receive us in mercy and grant us grace that his name might be glorified in us. And may this be a genuine proof to us that he accepts us and keeps us as his people. Hence, we shall all say: Almighty God, heavenly Father . . .

27

*The Temple – Then and Now**

After this it came to pass that David smote the Philistines and subdued them, and David took the bridle of Amnah from the hand of the Philistines. And he smote Moab, and measured them with a line, casting them down to the ground. He measured them with two lines to put them to death, and with one full line to save them alive. And so Moab was made subject to David and brought him gifts. Also David smote Hadadezer, son of Rehob . . . (2 Sam. 8:1–12).

We have seen how God returned the kingdom peaceably into the hands of David after many difficulties. But the promise which was given to him concerning the vanquishing of all his enemies around was not yet accomplished. It was not enough for David to rule over all the people of God, but his rule had to be extended to that which was promised to Abraham (Gen. 15:7; Psa. 72:8–9). For Scripture not only said that the line of Abraham would possess what the children of Israel had, after they had entered into possession of the country, but it describes four borders from one sea to the other, and from the great river to the desert. Now that is the heritage which was supposed to come to the line of Abraham: namely, from the Red Sea to the opposite sea, which leads towards . . . ,[1] which one also calls the Sea of [Syria]. And then there is the Euphrates River, and over against it, the deserts which were on the coast of Arabia.

Well, when the children of Israel arrived in the land, they did not enjoy all of that: far from it. Hence, God wanted to reserve

*Thursday, July 30, 1562.
[1]Lacking in the text.

for the time of David what he had promised to his servant, Abraham, so that the faithful might know that it was truly of the line of David through which the seed of Abraham should come, to whom this land had been promised. Well, this was only a figure of our Lord Jesus Christ, for his kingdom was not limited in any way, but Scripture says that from one end of the world to the other he shall have dominion (Psa. 2:8; 72:8). Anyway, it was necessary for the faithful to recognise that God put off fulfilling his promise until the time of David, so that from his kingdom they might be led much further. This is what is now described to us.

There are, moreover, the Idumaeans, who had always dominated – indeed, in such a way that they had often hurt the poor people of God (Num. 20:14ff.). We see that they refused the Israelites passage, although they had earnestly requested it and had promised them to pass through without violence, and so the people of God had to go round and had an arduous and very difficult time in making it. But yet it says that 'the greatest would serve the least' (Gen. 25:23). Now here is Esau, who is subjected to Jacob. That is not meant of the two persons, but of their posterity. Well, thus it is that the Idumaeans, who are the children of Esau, were peaceful in their country without any bother, and yet the poor children of Israel were terribly abused by them and by others of their neighbours. God, therefore, had to use his hand and his strength in the time of David, so that people might know that this prophecy had not been given in vain. Now this, in sum, is what we have to consider.

Well, coming to the story which is told here, it says that 'David vanquished the Philistines and subdued them'. What is then added, some take for the proper name of a town – for in the sacred history in the book which is called First Chronicles, it says that 'David took Gath with its suburbs' (1 Chron. 18:1). Hence, one presumes that this is a proper name. But be that as it may, still it comes from persons (and also signifies origin). Others take it for 'bridle', and others . . .[1], which signifies 'servants' or 'chambermaids' or 'subjection', and others take it

[1]Lacking in text.

for 'to pay tribute'. Well, be that as it may, it is to signify that this people of the Philistines were so conquered by David that instead of being in charge, they were subdued.

We have seen before now how the poor children of Israel were oppressed by this nation, and indeed it even seemed that everything was going to be lost in the death of Saul. And there is no doubt that God had miraculously preserved his people when he held back the Philistines, who could have wandered all over the country. For David did not yet have authority and was a fugitive, and hence the country was without a leader; there was nothing but breakdown. Everything was nearly stolen. The king and all his troops were inflated with this victory. If, therefore, God had not held the Philistines back with a secret bridle, it is certain that they could have acquired it all, and that there would have been horrible desolation and the people of Israel would be destroyed. But God broke off their purpose and enterprise, so that they were unable to use their victory. Be that as it may, still they were always superior to the children of Israel. Therefore, it is a notable change when they were defeated by David. Now there was an ancient covenant between Abraham, Isaac and Jacob and the Philistines (Gen. 21:22–26). But that had ceased and David was legitimately able to defeat them – because they had, indeed, committed many outrages against the people of Israel, and had not ceased to be their enemies. This was the reason why they were repaid with so many injuries and violence, murders and pillage. The time (I say) was fulfilled for the Philistines to be vanquished.

Well, the promise of this victory had been given to David, and hence God had to give him such victories in order to extend his limits and confines, as we have explained. In fact, he clearly recognised that it comes from God, for he praised him in saying that 'Moab would be his washpot and he would cast his shoes over Edom for shame, and he would get victory over the Philistines' (Psa. 60:8), and that the country also would tremble before him. Therefore, this is what it means when he speaks of the Philistines here.

Now it also clearly says that David conquered the Moabites, who had been spared inasmuch as they were descendants of

Lot, and were related to the children of Israel (Deut. 2:9, 19). And however iniquitously they behaved to the end, and even though they had conspired with their neighbours to exterminate the people of God and to abolish their memory, still their punishment was deferred. For the time had not yet come for God to chastise them, and this was to allow their iniquities to reach the point of fullness.

It says that 'David measured them with a line', metaphorically speaking, as if he had had time in his hands to dispose of at his pleasure. For it adds that 'he made two lines in order to kill and one cord only in order to save a life'. Thus, just as if a man were measuring trees and land with a line, it says that David measured men. It is a sign that a man has his possessions peacefully, when he surveys his lands and is actually in full enjoyment of them. When that happens, everyone knows what is his. Hence, to indicate that David had taken over the Moabites, it says that he measured them, and that he made some of them die by the sword – indeed, two-thirds of them, and the other third he reserved alive. In brief, that is to show that he put to death all he wanted to, that those who survived had obtained pardon, and that he certainly had the power to kill every one of them down to the last person.

Here one could ask why he treated the Moabites so cruelly. For whatever the case, it certainly seems that he should have regarded their origin. They were descendants of Lot, the nephew of Abraham, and even God had taken this relationship into consideration, so that the Moabites were exempted as by privilege. How is it, therefore, that David thus went out of bounds? Well, in the first place we have to note that the mercy which God gave to the Moabites was only for a time, and was to render them all the more inexcusable. If they had had a drop of sense, they would have thought: 'Now here is the God of Israel who was worshipped by Lot, our father, who was nourished and taught in the house of Abraham. Well, we now see how he employs his infinite virtue.' This should have reunited them with Israel so that they could be members of the Church. But far from taking this into consideration, they hardened themselves and puffed themselves up against the children of Israel, just as Moses fully explains. And then they never ceased to keep causing as many injuries as they could to this poor people. Hence, the temporary grace which God had bestowed on them served for their greater condemnation. For if God had given them no sign of his goodness, they could, like the others, have behaved in ignorance against the people. Or if the children of Israel had unsheathed their swords against them, they could have had reason to act villainously. And when a war begins, the enemy is not easily appeased. That could have excused them in some sense. But they were convinced that the children of Israel were abstaining from hurting them and were holding themselves back; not because they were not the strongest, but because they were forbidden to attempt anything. Since, therefore, our Lord gave them so many occasions to moderate themselves and yet they grew worse and inflamed themselves in all cruelty, it was quite fair for them to be punished in good measure, once for all, and for their arrogance to be broken. Now that is why, therefore, the stringency which David exercised against the Moabites ought not to be considered cruelty, but to be the just judgement of God, since they had abused his long patience and had mocked him.

Now first, this warns us not to harden ourselves in self-flattery, if God defers the punishments with which he has threatened us. We have already related how Esau had to be subjected to Jacob. Now here is a long period which passed: indeed, God's people were held captive in Egypt for more than two hundred years. The Idumaeans, however, had things their way. No-one kept them from being in charge, from holding a rather large region. Well, afterwards the children of Israel came and possessed the land with great difficulty. Yet the Idumaeans had charge of their whole possession. Who would have hoped that the promise of God should ever be carried out? Indeed, it ought to have been buried more than thirtyfold.

We must contemplate this story, as in a mirror, that if the judgements of God are kept hidden, especially for a long space of time, it is only at the end that they will have their effect. And hence, let us learn not to flatter ourselves, but when we have heard a threat from God, to tremble. And on the other hand, if we see that God does not immediately carry out all his judgements on the despisers of his majesty, and that they persecute his poor Church, let it not astonish us, as though they had escaped and would remain unpunished. Let us wait (I say) not just for a year or for some short time. And should we not see God punishing them during our lifetime, still at the end their time will come, and they will be called to account. If we did not have these testimonies which are recited here, how agitated we would be with temptation, since we would not perceive that God wants to remedy such great confusions which are in the world today. Much blood has already been poured out and horrible torments have been used against the poor faithful. Fires have been started over and over again. Then, when it seemed that God ought to have had pity on his Church, all of it has started over again more than ever, and then the devil has been unchained and the rage of the iniquitous more than inflamed. Now things are confused and no-one knows what will be the issue. And humanly speaking, one could only think that there will be infinite miseries.

Well, let us learn to consider what has been placed before us here, casting our eyes on Edom, which lived peacefully – and yet God never failed to keep in his counsel what he had once pronounced, that 'the greater would serve the lesser' (Gen. 25:23). Let us note what is said of the Moabites, that God did not want them to receive any damage from the entrance of the children of Israel and their neighbours; yet they were divided into pieces and totally ruined, and were not spared. What was the cause of such a distinction or diversity? It was that God was waiting for them. Not that he did not fully know that they would be obstinate to the very end in their malice, but he wanted to leave them inexcusable. The same thing was said about the Amorites, who in the time of Abraham were tolerated because their iniquities had not yet come to the full (Gen. 15:16).

Hence, let us learn to keep ourselves under control, whenever we see that God will not punish the offences of those who would like to ruin his Church and are his mortal enemies, since it is his to know the opportune time. Moreover, when we see such things happen to the wicked, let us learn to fear lest we too fall into such enormous abuse of the patience of God that we provoke him to wrath – which would lead to our utter destruction in the depths of hell. For our condemnation gets all the worse when God postpones chastising us, unless we recognise his goodness and are converted at an opportune time (see Rom. 2:4b). Hence, we are not envious of the wicked when we see them prospering and at their ease (see Pss. 37 and 73). For at a moment when they presume they are secure, the storm will fall, and it will not be a light or general chastisement, but God will act with double and triple rigour. Far, therefore, from our needing to suppose that what is cited here of David is cruelty, we should (instead) recognise that God teaches us all the more not to persist in our sins, but rather that God calls us to repentance and gives us opportunity to return to him, and that in contemplating his judgements, we might be taught to fear him in all reverence, and not to tempt him. So much, then, for this article, where it says that David measured the Moabites with the line, that at their defeat there was a great killing of two-thirds of them, and that he left only one-third.

Well, it adds immediately that what was left paid tribute to him. The word is that they 'brought him presents'. But this manner of speech, properly understood, means that they paid him tribute, as when the Psalm says: 'The kings of Tarshish and of Seba shall come and bring presents to you, which is to say that they will give you homage and be your subjects' (Psa. 72:10–11), in paying you tribute. Hence, that is the case in this passage.

Well, the Syrians are spoken of in the next place, starting with Hadadezer, the son of Rehob, king of Ziba. The country was his, and this quite ample country of Syria was a kingdom divided into many regions, for it extended all the way to Babylon from the land of Judah. And on the other side, it extended just as far, as one of the ends reached out towards . . . and . . . which were still large areas and thickly populated because of their fertility.[1] Now here is this Hadadezer, who was

[1]Lacking in text.

one of the kings. But afterwards, 'Syria of Damascus' is spoken of, and that is because the city of Damascus was the capital. It was situated in the region of . . .[1] Well, all of that territory had to be subjected to David according to the promise of God which we have mentioned from Psalm 72, that he must rule even to the great river Euphrates. And it was not only one region which he conquered, but several; certainly strong people and countries difficult to take. But it happened, and God by this means showed himself faithful and liberal to him, and people recognised that his kingdom was founded in the infallible truth of God, and that it had to be perpetual.

It is true that this did not last for a long time. Solomon enjoyed the victories of his father, but soon afterwards the Syrians revolted, and finally they were the cause of the desolation of the kingdom of Israel and the confusion of the country of Judah. But that was done by the admirable counsel of God, so that they would not be too taken up with this temporal kingdom, and so that the faithful might await another kingdom far more excellent. Two things were necessary. On the one hand, God needed to show, as in a figure and shadow, what ought to be accomplished by our Lord Jesus Christ. For if the Jews had not had any visible testimony, it is certain that they could have stumbled and their faith would have been cold. It therefore greatly helped them when they contemplated, as in a figure, that God had promised to bless a certain house, as they had been persuaded from all times that the sceptre would be in the line of Judah. The promise applies to David. The Jews knew that, and God showed them that it was not in vain that he had spoken in this way. Now this is what helped them so much – in order to strengthen themselves in the hope of the Redeemer and to be convinced that God would bring to perfection what he had begun (Phil. 1:6).

However, they could have swung to the other extreme. That is, they could have found their assurance in this temporal kingdom and have gone to sleep in it if it had always remained as a state. God therefore kept them from that situation in order

[1] Lacking in text.

to make them walk on the other side, as if he were turning them with reins, and had given the Jews occasion to think that what they had seen in David and in the time of Solomon was only a foretaste of the promise of God. We see how necessary this was, for today they are still attached to their foolish speculations. It seems to them that they ought to be in charge, that they ought totally to fill the throne, and to rule over all – as they are insatiable. We even see how the disciples of our Lord Jesus Christ were so confused by this foolish fantasy that no-one could divert them from it. He had said to them so many times that they must suffer with him. And even after his resurrection, they were thinking of being at their ease and in repose and becoming rich and triumphant. We see, therefore, how the Jews would have been totally taken in and bewitched if God had left the house of David in a permanent and unchanging state. But this kingdom was broken down and became decadent, and finally totally perished. This was meant to make them lift up their eyes so that they might learn not to be too fascinated by this world. And they were often exhorted by the prophets to wait for God to repair the ruins of the house of David (Amos 9:11; Acts 15:16).

It is the same way with the sacrifices. This illustration will help us to comprehend better what I have said, that the Jews had to have some sign to assure them that they would find pardon with God. Well, for this reason they also had the types of the Law. When an animal was killed and the blood shed, it was a sign of how their sins were forgiven them, and it was the means of reconciling God with men. However, we see how they were fascinated with a foolish and ridiculous superstition by which they desired to appease God in killing cattle and sheep, and did not regard the Mediator, who was typified in the sacrifices. Hence, we do not find it strange that God, having accomplished what he had promised from the time of David, immediately withdrew his hand, and this kingdom was unable to maintain its prosperity for any length of time. Now this happened so that they would pay attention to our Lord Jesus Christ.

This whole story will serve to confirm us in the right attitude today. We see how, from all times, our Lord Jesus Christ has been represented as in a mirror. But this was only a painting, compared to the substance and truth which is in him – indeed, in total perfection. Hence, we see that he was not sent quickly by God his Father, but at the time for which he had been ordained (Gal. 4:4). And then we are taught not to seek a worldly happiness in him, but as his kingdom is spiritual, let us learn to bear many miseries in this world and to be in frequent combats until we have reached this eternal rest. If the Jews were given this example, how much more has it been given to us. For this gives us something to develop our patience, since it is explained to us that the kingdom of God 'is not of this world' (John 18:36), and that we must be conformed to him by bearing much poverty, so that our life is like a shadow of death. Hence, it is said that we are like 'sheep for the slaughter' and that our life is buried until Jesus Christ appears (Psa. 44:22; Col. 3:3). So much, then, for this point which speaks of the victory that David won against Hadadezer, king of Zobah, and against the Syrians, who were sent from Damascus.

Now there is some [textual] variation here concerning the number of people, because a much larger multitude is spoken of in Second Samuel than in the First Book of Chronicles (cf. 2 Sam. 8:4 and 1 Chron. 18:4). But this is only a summary here, and in Chronicles the battles are distinctly divided. For Chronicles says Abishai conquered the Edomites, and yet afterwards it speaks of Joab, whereas Samuel speaks of David – for, after all, everything was done in his name (1 Chron. 18:12). And Abishai only killed 18,000 but David killed 22,000 Syrians. Now that is how such variations between texts are not real contradictions, because one gives only a summary of the story, whereas the other gives a more detailed distinction, as I have said.

The booty that David 'brought to Jerusalem' is specifically mentioned. Well, if there were nothing but this word, one would think that he had used all of it for his own benefit, or to enrich himself in order to triumph. But soon after, it explains why David took the spoil of his enemies into Jerusalem. It was to prepare material from which the temple could be built, although it was not to be done in his time. This is explained when it says that 'the son of Toi', the mortal enemy of Hadadezer, came and 'brought great gifts to David, of gold, of silver and of brass'. And there it says that 'David dedicated all of it to the Lord', which is the same thing that he had done with the spoil which had come from the other nations, such as the Moabites, Edomites and their other neighbours. We see, then, in sum that David made homage of his victories, not only verbally in preaching the praises of God (and we still have the testimonies of his preaching today), but also that he backed up his preaching with action, that is, in gold and silver. He dedicated these things along with his most precious treasures, and did not keep them for himself. This is very rare among men: the greater part of them will be driven by ambition and attached to their own profit. Well, here is David, who is filled with riches. Yet nevertheless, he was not so given to pompousness that he ever failed to prefer God and give him the first degree of honour. And although he did not build the temple, yet he made the first preparations so that Solomon would find everything ready.

Furthermore, we have to note in passing that God is not served by gold or silver, but that this was how it was in the time of the Law. And David did not do it without thinking, or from foolish devotion as do the idolaters, zealously blowing their fanfare. But David knew that God had commanded by his Law that the sanctuary be built of gold, silver and precious things, and this was due to the crudeness of the people (Exod. 26–27).

Today, everything is changed, not in regard to the purpose of God, which is immutable, but in regard to men. For we differ from the ancient people, as men who are come of age differ from little children. We no longer have the rudiments which were for that time, so as to want to set up a worship of God through vessels of gold and silver and brass and similar things. That would be nothing but a silly performance now, which would obscure the spiritual worship spoken of in the fourth chapter of St John. For there our Lord Jesus Christ declares to us how we must no longer govern ourselves by the Law. 'The time', he says, 'has come, when God will no longer be worshipped either in Gerizim or in Zion, for the faithful will worship God in spirit and in truth' (John 4:21–23). Now it is certain that the ancients clearly knew that God did not delight in these external things, but yet they had them because of the infirmity of the times. But today (as I have shown) those who would like to worship God pompously in this manner confuse everything – so it serves, in effect, to efface the memory of our Lord Jesus Christ. Thus, the ornaments of the papacy are just so many veils to keep our Lord Jesus Christ from being known. These ornaments are so many sepulchres to bury him, for the papists have so many flatteries and follies and false coverings that they actually remove the pure knowledge of the truth, which is how we ought to apprehend him. Yet there is no more veil in the Gospel (2 Cor. 3:12–18), but instead we ought to contemplate God in the Gospel in the person of our Lord Jesus Christ, face to face, in order to be transfigured into his glory and so to profit more and more until we reach our perfection. Be that as it may, here we have the example of David to follow, who cared for the temple of God more than for his own life.

However, let us note that the temple today is spiritual and that we do not need to bring to it such ornaments as those for which we see the Jews reproached. For after they returned from Babylon, they had such an obsession with building their houses that the temple of God was forgotten (Hag. 1:2–4). Well, for that particular time they were reproached with laxness, inasmuch as they did not apply themselves to all that God had commanded them in order to build his temple. Today, we are surely reproached for our laxness, but it is not for having failed to build great and magnificent temples. How, therefore, should we apply this to ourselves? We should apply it to the edification of the spiritual temple and the growth of the kingdom of our Lord Jesus Christ. Now his temple is being built when the stones are being gathered together (Eph. 2:20). That is, that the faithful are joined to him and that he dwells in the midst of us, and then we are truly temples of his Spirit. And similarly, when we do not make an offering to him of all that is placed in our hand, and when someone who has the means to help his neighbour and to relieve the poor in their need does not do so, that is the same as ruining the temple of God. Now that is how our laxness will be condemned before him – not for having failed to build a material temple, for as I have said, that is not to be done now. Well, this is the main thing that we have to remember.

Then it says that 'God saved' his servant David 'everywhere he went'. This is so that we will know that God has shown before our very eyes that David was chosen by him, that the royal unction was not given to him in vain, and that God was working towards this end for people to know that he had prepared another king, both more worthy and more noble. However, we see how the sacred history is not like all the chronicles and profane histories which have been compiled by unbelievers. For in those, a great deal will be said about the braveries and virtues of men, and then by and by about their good fortune. The pagans certainly knew that if fate were not in their favour, then there would be no use in industry, in force, in virtue and in everything else that man can do. Therefore, they clearly confessed that it was necessary for God to bless and for victories to come from on high. But this was known only in a confused manner. For they still held on to this good fortune, which seemed to be a goddess to them, and they thought that they could keep her up their sleeve. While they were enjoying some prosperity, they certainly made their solemn processions. But this was nothing but a false and contrived ceremony, since they wanted to be worshipped as idols and their virtues to be renowned. But here we see how this is not merely a completely cold and useless recitation which allows the braveries of David to be known. Rather, it immediately gives instruction so as to make us follow it. The point is that we, knowing that he was guided by the hand of God, will desire the same thing.

In fact, it was very necessary for God to be the sovereign head of these wars. For we see what a multitude of people came to fight against David – and we will go into this in more detail later. And then, David was not dealing with little children, but he battled against bellicose people, who could, humanly speaking, devour him with one bite. In brief, he could never have made it if God had not fortified him. Even when the

Philistines are spoken of, are not their movements a testimony that God made David prosper? In what state did he find the people? We have already shown that they were like a poor flock of lambs among wolves without guidance or command, and that they were already trembling, as it were, because of this great defeat. Well, he went ahead and attacked those who had caused such a scandal, as though a deluge had passed over them – and yet, he succeeded. Afterwards, there were these Moabites whom he went to seek over the mountains. It was a very difficult country to take, because these mountains are very high, and they are very difficult to climb. We know that in such places one man is worth more than ten. And then, they were well supplied with weapons. In all that (I say) we can understand what is said here. But insofar as our unbelief prevents us from glorifying God, that is why we are admonished that it was God who saved David – indeed, in all the affairs that he was in. And this is to signify that he not only was helped for one victory, but that God continued to do him good.

Well, what is said of David without doubt applies to all the faithful. Hence, we must gather from this passage that if we do not prevent God from helping us, not only will he assist us once, but there will be such perseverance (in his help) that when we have been brought out of one danger, he will be ready to bring us out of another. Indeed, even when we are surrounded and assailed by an infinite number of deaths, still we shall always escape when we are in the keeping of our God. Although it was a singular goodness which was shown in the person of David, still, since he was a type of our Lord Jesus Christ, what is recited of him extends to all the members of the Church. But what is the reason that God often withdraws his hand, so that we are tormented and trodden underfoot by our enemies, and receive great blows with their weapons, and that often it seems we must perish? It is because we do not give glory to his virtue. On the one hand, it seems to us that we are able to do everything by our industry and prudence, and on the other hand, we attempt many things which are not allowed us, and our spirits are so flighty that we think we ought to lift ourselves above the clouds. Hence, it is because we undertake frivolous and crooked enterprises, and whenever we have a good cause, we go about it in a perverse way and do not call on God, that we are not helped by him. But in following this rule, let us learn fully to submit ourselves to his will, and yet to walk in such a careful way that we shall always have our refuge in his goodness. And let us learn to recognise the benefits which he has bestowed on us in order to protect us, and when we do this, it is certain that we will experience what is said here about David.

Now let us prostrate ourselves before the majesty of our good God in recognition of the faults and offences of which we are guilty. Let us pray to him so to make us feel them that they will displease us, and we will ask pardon for them, and that we may learn so to dedicate ourselves to him, both in our persons and in all that we receive from him, that we will seek only for his name to be glorified, and to use his liberality in such a way that it will be appropriately distributed. And above all, let us take pains to build him a temple so that he may be worshipped both by small and great, and even that those who are still far removed from his Word might be reduced to obedience to him. And may he bestow his grace not only upon us, but on all peoples and nations of the earth . . .

28

*Justice and Judgement**

When Toi, king of Hamath, saw that David had smitten the whole army of Hadadezer, he sent Joram his son to King David, to ask him how he fared, and to congratulate him for having fought against Hadadezer . . . (2 Sam. 8:9–18).

We saw yesterday the remarkable and memorable victories which God gave to David against all his surrounding enemies, who had been giving the people of Israel so much trouble. God's causing David to prosper against all his enemies was a confirmation of his divine call as king. More was involved here than the mere fulfilment of the promise which God made to Abraham. This was also intended to lift up the hearts of the faithful so that they might know that the promise which God gave them of a king, under whom they should hope for total happiness and perfection, was not empty.

The text says that 'Toi, king of Hamath', protector of Syria, 'sent to David to greet him and to congratulate him on the victory which he had won against Hadadezer'. This, undoubtedly, is told us to show that God, in everything and everywhere, showered his favours upon David. We know that God holds the hearts of men in his hand and bends them as he pleases (Prov. 21:1). When this king thus declared himself the friend of David, and even 'gave him presents by the hand of his son', there is no doubt that God had arranged this to confirm David all the more. It is true that King Toi gladly did this 'because he was

*Friday, July 31, 1562.

the enemy of Hadadezer', and rejoiced to see his enemy beaten. But still God used this means to declare eternally and ever more fully his benediction on his servant David. That is why it is repeated here that 'God has saved him' in all his affairs. We saw this sentence yesterday, but it is not empty repetition, for when God gives us an experience of his grace, we do not understand it as we should unless he then explains to us that it is he who is Governor of all, and is addressing us. This is true whether he turns the courage and affection of men to love us, or turns them bitterly against us, giving us the means to overcome them. Whatever may happen, let us realise that our salvation is only in him, which means that we can only be preserved by his strength and protection.

After stating that God fortified David all around, the text goes on to say that he 'reigned over Israel doing justice and judgement'. This should be carefully noted, for even if a man wins amazing victories over his enemies, yet treats his own people cruelly or tyrannically, what good are his victories? These victories will not benefit or give his people relief. We have seen many warlike and extremely brave princes who even succeeded in all their undertakings, but yet were so addicted to pillage and murder that they gave their subjects the same treatment. We still see a great deal of this today. For princes assume that since God gives them their position, they have total licence to gobble up their poor subjects – to pillage, to loot, to sack everything. Therefore, when we are told here that David exercised justice and judgement in Israel, this demonstrates that his bravery was not used as an occasion to act cruelly towards his people. Although he was victorious over his enemies, he still governed himself in a totally fair and equitable manner, for he knew what his calling was. This is meant to instruct all those who are in superior positions and are divinely placed in the seat of justice.

These words 'justice' and 'judgement' are joined together in order to convey a total righteousness which is characterised by a constancy and magnanimity which resists all evil. Now there are many people who will exercise justice, but not judgement. For while they will be able to keep themselves from doing wrong, from evil, from trouble-making (and thus avoid both fraud and violence), still, when they see some poor man in trouble, they will not come to his rescue. Those who thus accommodate themselves (to evil) are upholding righteousness only half-way, even though they do no harm or injury to anyone. Hence, let us note that Scripture joins these two words to indicate that it is not enough to keep ourselves from injuring anyone, but that we ought to take as strong a stand against evil as we can. This command is given to everyone – not only to princes, magistrates, and officers of justice, but to all private persons as well. For instance, the eighteenth chapter of Genesis states that although Abraham was responsible only to govern his own family, still he said that he would carry out justice to those whom God had given into his charge and placed under his protection, and that he would teach them what was appropriate and essential so that they could exercise justice and judgement (Gen. 18:19). We see, therefore, that exercising justice and judgement is a universal rule which applies to everyone. It means governing oneself so as to treat everyone fairly and properly, and it means standing against and resisting evil whenever it is necessary to relieve poor, afflicted people, and also giving them all needed help.

And yet those who are in positions of justice have a double obligation which is far stricter. Hence, it is not enough for them merely to abstain from looting and cruelty and from taking personal advantage of their position – but they must also protect the good and innocent, and must reprimand anyone they see breaking the law. In sum, these words tell us that David knew what his duty involved as a divinely constituted king. All who are in authority ought to understand this principle, which requires them so to govern themselves that they might render a good and loyal account to God, who allowed them to be like shepherds to their subjects. In other words, they were supposed to care for their subjects.

David shows vividly how he felt when he promised in Psalm 101 that when he gained the crown, he would act in this way. This Psalm was composed before he was in possession of the kingdom. When I obtain my kingdom, he says, then I will drive the wicked from my house and will see to it that all learn to know God. I will keep my house pure and clean. As far as possible, I will destroy all wicked and flattering persons from among the people of God. So David promised this while he was waiting upon God to fulfil what he had promised in his anointment as king.

These words show us that David, unlike the hypocrites, actually fulfilled his vow. When hypocrites are in trouble, they will make wonderful promises, but when they get what they want, they merely shrug their shoulders and stick up their noses, as the old saying goes. But on the contrary, during the whole distressing time that David was waiting until the Lord stretched out his hand and made him king, he was keenly aware of his sacred promise to the Lord. We see here that when he was brought to the royal throne, he faithfully carried out his vow.

Moreover, we must gather from this that God will always prosper people who sincerely uphold true justice, for this is the best defence that we can have against our enemies. Many times it will surprise us how it is our own fault that God gives our enemies opportunities to injure us. Our trouble is that we are totally confused inside: everything is out of order, nothing is right, and iniquity is in charge. This is the same thing as if we broke down all our walls so as to expose ourselves as prey and allow our enemies to come in.

Instead, let us learn how to place ourselves in God's care so that he can keep us safe. We do this by getting control of ourselves so that we are well regulated on the inside. Then it is certain that God is well able to keep us safe from all danger and to prosper us so that we will lack nothing. Our text, then, has emphasised the importance of self-control in the life of David.

But we must go beyond David to the truth as it is in our Lord Jesus Christ; as Psalm 72 says, 'Lord, give judgement to your king, and he will govern your people in justice and judgement'. This shows that David was a type which had its perfect fulfilment only in our Lord Jesus Christ. Hence, let us carefully note that God gave only a small taste of what good government was to his people, and that he reserved the full reality until the coming of his Son. Let us recognise that our Lord Jesus Christ has been given to us so that we might be governed in justice and righteousness under his hand – not only in outward matters, but that we might be reformed within our hearts so as to walk with pure integrity in godly fear.

Earthly kings can do no more than merely keep their subjects in check so that evil-doers are punished and the good and innocent are upheld by the sword which God gave to these rulers. But our Lord Jesus Christ goes still further, for by the power of his Spirit he always watches over the hearts of men, which he reforms and renews. Thus, it is said that we are brought to justice when it pleases God to call us into his Church. That is how Isaiah the prophet speaks of it when he says that all the faithful whom God will call under his guidance will be governed in justice (Isa. 11:4). Thus, our Lord Jesus Christ not only uses human means to guide his Church in virtue and equity, but he also reforms hearts on the inside by his Spirit, since his kingdom is spiritual.

Let us also notice carefully that Isaiah says that God will have pity on the poor, he will relieve the afflicted. This teaches us that the Son of God will never fail us, that we will be sustained by his help as long as we have our refuge in him – but only insofar as we allow him to rule over our hearts. Now I said 'allow', to show that we can hinder him, in certain respects, from governing us. For when we act like wild beasts and cannot bear the yoke of our Lord Jesus Christ, there is nothing in us but pride and rebellion. The fact is that we drive him far away and do not want him to rule over us. Instead, we prefer to remain in our pleasures and to rest in our vices without being disturbed. What is that but seeking our own ruin? However, when we become docile with an accommodating spirit that submits to his control, then he will certainly be the sort of king over us that this Psalm describes (Psa. 72:13).

The Psalm says, in particular, that he will have pity and compassion on the poor, that he will relieve the afflicted. This teaches us that while we are under the guidance of the Son of God and while he claims us as his people, we are not automatically sheltered from many troubles and oppressions – because, in fact, God will let our enemies take over in order to test our patience and humble us. Even when we are afflicted and poor, we can still rejoice, for this Psalm says that this king whom God has established will take care of us in our time of need.

Let us learn, then, in the first place, to seek for justice where we can find it. That is, let us pray that God will be pleased to make us experience the virtue which he has given to his only Son, so that everything might be well governed around us, that we might walk in integrity, and that he will regulate not only external matters, but all our inward affections. And then let us learn constantly to return to our Lord Jesus Christ, and to keep ourselves hidden under the shadow of his wings when we are tormented unjustly. Let us not give up in times of severe testing, but let us take courage and not doubt that the Son of God will finally accomplish what he has promised. His promise will not disappoint us if we give him room to work in our lives. Thus, let each one of us bear our poverty patiently in our own way. When we are tormented by the wicked, instead of quarrelling, let us learn to glorify the king who watches over us, and pray that he will want to help us in our need. It is certain that he will make us experience what this Psalm promises: that he will support his poor ones, provide for their needs, and have compassion on them (Psa. 72:13). That, in sum, is what we should remember about David giving justice and judgement to all Israel.

This passage then speaks of the conduct of those who were in charge and were David's officers, such as 'Joab, who was captain general of the army'. This shows us that if a king wants to carry out his duty properly, he must be aided by those whom he calls into public office – this applies even to those in the lowest positions. Now even if a prince is personally honourable, but trusts and promotes wicked persons who are either greedy, or adulterous, or thieves, then his entire government will become degenerate. So when a prince is careless in his position, he is surely worse than a tyrant without meaning to be so, for his laxness causes more evil than tyranny. This passage therefore teaches us that princes ought above all to be careful to seek reliable and substantial persons to help them govern their people.

There are, as I have said, different degrees of authority. If magistrates, for instance, want everything to go well and to be properly governed, and yet have wicked aides who are addicted to corruption and are even degenerate and dissolute, it is certain that all their good desires will amount to nothing and will be snuffed out. We see this by experience.

Thus, the officers of David are spoken of here with good reason, in order to show that he was endeavouring to bring just treatment to his people not merely in his own person, but also by appointing subordinates who were men of virtue and even excellence. It is true that there were very serious faults in Joab, as we have seen, but all things considered, you will find that he was a man whom God had endowed with remarkable qualities. And all these others – such as the secretary or chief of staff, who was in charge of reporting all business – are named here, not out of criticism, but rather to show that David was prudent enough to call people who could help him, since he could not do everything.

David actually carried out what he promised in Psalm 101: that he would choose officers in his house, that he would teach the fear of God, and that he would drive out the wicked. How greatly this is needed today: we would see an almost angelic reformation in the world if this were done. But on the contrary, there is such widespread degeneration because authorities are often careless in putting people into office. Sometimes those are appointed who actually know what it is to govern and have some zeal for it, but most often, people who lack self-control are put into office. It takes only one wild horse to break up a team of twelve, and it is the same way when there are people in public positions who do not behave properly. They certainly throw everything into confusion. Thus, we must pay very close attention to this passage.

Since we do not always find people who are endowed with these particular virtues, we are urgently admonished to pray God to provide them for us. When the passage says that God gave these fine ministers to maintain his judgements and righteousness among the people, it is showing that God stretched out his hand to David to shower his goodness upon him. Let us realise that it is a special gift from God whenever there are people available whom we can appoint and put to work to help us maintain civil justice. And it is a sign of the vengeance of God if we are stripped of prudent men. This very thing is threatened by the prophet Isaiah when he says that little children will reign (Isa. 3:1ff.). In other words, there will be no sense or prudence in those who are in charge of the people. This is the greatest poverty that can possibly happen, for famine will not be nearly so dangerous and troublesome to the people as when they are stripped of good ministers, leaving nothing but total breakdown and disorder. Thus, let us be keenly aware that since God has blessed his servant David in this way, if we are in the kingdom of Jesus Christ, he will always give us people to maintain fairness and justice for us. Whenever we are in trouble in this matter, he admonishes us to take refuge in him – there is no other hope. This is the point we must remember from this passage.

But on the other hand, since we have mentioned that Joab had several serious failings, we must recognise that although God wants to give us good officials, yet they will always be imperfect and liable to fall often. Now the grace of God clearly shines out from the kingdom of David, who is a type of Jesus Christ, which is why those in full authority are named. This teaches us that God did not restrict his grace in those days to people who were utterly perfect and spotless. Hence, when we find vices in people who are otherwise very virtuous, let us realise that our Lord wants to use this to humble us, and so let us put up with the evil. But at the same time, let us try to correct this evil, for we must never wallow in our filth. Thus whenever we perceive some vice in an official, we ought not only to condemn it, but also to try to remove it as far as we can. At any rate, let us not be surprised if the people whom God places in the centre of the stage in order to make us experience his paternal care, have weaknesses. This, in sum, is what we must remember.

Some have considered that 'the Cherethites and the Pelethites' who were mentioned in this passage were . . . whom David had chosen for office.[1] Others even say that this implies

[1]Words lacking in text.

separation, as if he had not said that 'Benaiah the son of Jehoiada' was their leader. But by looking at the seventeenth chapter of First Chronicles,[1] we can understand this passage as well as the following passage (in 2 Sam. 8), which says that 'the sons of David were priests'. It is plainly said in 1 Chronicles 17 that these Cherethites and Pelethites were under the authority of Benaiah. Some say that some of them were archers and that the others used the sling. This was a fairly common thing in those times, as we see for instance in David (1 Sam. 17:40ff.). Be that as it may, it is very likely that they were the bodyguard of the king. So much, then, for these words, which are not of great importance.

Finally, the passage says that the 'sons of David were priests'. This expression is commonly used in Scripture. At first glance, it could almost seem that David was instructing his children in the worship of God so that they could be in the priesthood. That is why some think that David had his sons educated by the doctors of the Law as their disciples, so that they could later be in charge of the Church. Scripture says that the priests at that time were like the messengers of God to instruct the people (Deut. 17:9ff.).

When we have an obscure passage, our only action should be to clarify it by comparison with another passage of Scripture. Thus, we compare the obscure statement in 2 Sam. 8 with 1 Chronicles 18:17, which says that 'the children of David were pre-eminent'. So this word in the latter passage certainly cannot mean priest. Indeed, David would have committed sacrilege if he had wanted to introduce his sons into the priesthood. We know what happened to Uzziah for merely wishing to attempt to offer the incense to God (2 Chron. 26:16f.). 'He was not content with being king', but also wanted to usurp the priesthood, and so he was stricken with leprosy, and was separated in shame from the people. Uzziah certainly wanted to stand apart from the common rank of men, but this was far more than he bargained for – to be cut off as an unclean creature. This proves that David could not have made his sons priests.

[1]Actually chapter 18.

Even when Psalm 110 says that our Lord Jesus Christ will be 'a priest after the order of Melchizedek', it attributes this priesthood to him as a unique honour and privilege. The apostle to the Hebrews says that Christ needed no companion (in his priestly work) and that he 'did not take this priestly honour upon himself' (Heb. 5:4). Since Christ was not a priest who was subject to change, the word 'priest' in this passage cannot therefore refer to the order of Aaron. Furthermore, 'priest' does not refer to David, because David himself testifies in Psalm 110, which he composed, that it refers to Melchizedek, who was both king and priest, as Genesis 14 says. Now Melchizedek, by virtue of his kingship, also held the office of priest. Similarly, the priesthood was reserved for the Lord Jesus Christ, because it was intended for him. Now kings were also priests (because of their personal pre-eminence) among the early pagans, as we see in their books. But this is quite different from what God established, which was to portray, as in a painting and a mirror, what our Lord Jesus Christ would be. We know that kingship and priesthood are inseparable in Christ, and that he was anointed at the same time both Messiah and Christ. Thus, his anointing served for these two things – priesthood and kingship – in addition to his divine ordination as prophet.

Thus, David's children could never have been priests, because that would have been an abomination to God. What this expression really means is that David took pains to have them instructed and taught the requirements of the Law. So we must conclude that they were considered excellent persons who were eminent among the people. But this passage extended their excellent reputation in one area by analogy to another area, as though it were saying that they were sacred persons. Still, these words show us that David attempted to make his children worthy, so that he might have good and faithful successors who could train the people in righteousness and maintain them in integrity. That is why he did not bring up his children only in pompous show, but gave them personal excellence so that they might know what it is to govern and might be trained in it for the future. This shows us that he was not merely content with doing his duty during his life, but that he wanted a well-governed state to continue even after his death. He took great pains to carry this out, but was frustrated in his attempt. It is true that God raised up Solomon to succeed him, as he had promised, but what about Absalom and all the others? Why were they so disorderly?

Although kings may seriously attempt to have their children trained to govern themselves properly, yet they will not always be successful. This principle applies to everyone. Fathers, for instance, often try to train their children properly, and yet they do not get the fruit that they hoped for. This is not meant to make them lose courage, as if to say: 'Why worry ourselves so much about this matter, since those who are so concerned to guide their children properly are only wasting their time? In fact, we should just leave them alone, since God has promised to take care of them.'

On the contrary, this is the conclusion that we should draw: 'Since those who take such pains and spend so much to have their children properly taught are still frustrated in their hopes, what terrible things will happen if I care nothing about it, and put the reins in their hands so that they have freedom to become degenerate?' The sad experience of David teaches fathers to strive even harder to instruct their children.

Fathers are further instructed by this principle to commend their children to God, asking him to instruct them by his Spirit. They must realise that all their labour, industry, and vigilance will be useless unless it is blessed by his Spirit. Even when fathers spare neither gold nor silver, even when they send their children to school, and give them good examples and keep them under a firm hand of leadership – still their whole duty has not been discharged. They can do all of that, and still miss the main thing, which is to call upon God and recognise their dependence upon him to prosper the instruction of their children.

This passage, however, warns us that it is a very rare thing for the children of princes to bear good fruit, even though they have been instructed in their childhood and youth. If ever a prince was concerned to keep his family in the fear of God and to guide and form them according to good rules, it was David –

yet some of his children were wicked and perverse. Absalom wanted to drive out his father and put him to death. Others caused great trouble and sedition in seeking to usurp the royal crown. In addition to that, many other problems arose. In the light of that, let us not be surprised today if the children of rulers are so disorderly, and are more like savage beasts than reasonable creatures.

How are they instructed? People simply make idols of them, and they think that the world is created for them. Far from training them in the fear and truth of God, people 'stuff cruelty down their throat' – as the saying goes – and when they are grown, they will not be considered sufficiently important unless they are inflated with so much pride that they could burst. Their best service may be to become a pimp in order to please them and then all the others follow him, being considered idiots and fools if they are not lawless and given over to all kinds of villainy and cruelty. We must not be surprised, then, if corruption is widespread in the world, since those who ought to show a good example to others are full of wickedness and delight in it (Rom. 1:32).

This warns all those whom God keeps in a low condition in society to realise that it is to their advantage when they can govern their families peacefully, and help their children to live in a modest way, and can earn their living honestly by their labour. We see, in fact, how those who have more status or money, even though they are neither princes nor kings, cannot get along with their own children when they grow up. Their children unconsciously become presumptuous and proud. They think: 'My father is rich; why should I not be treated as my rank demands?' Then they want to act brazenly and cannot be kept in line. They even despise work and want to live off their rents. Moreover, they spend everything without even thinking. Yet as I have said, those to whom our Lord has given nothing of official authority, or lordships, or great riches, should recognise that he does this for their good and profit. Hence, they ought to be content with their estate and stay in their small position. At the same time, they should rejoice as they teach their family to live properly and see their children trained in the fear of God and kept in modesty, as they faithfully earn their living. Thus, they can rejoice because their children are not inflated with pride and presumption, and are not rude, as many are who would like to be on top and climb over others.

So this is what we should finally remember about King David, whose just and righteous actions proved his concern for the welfare of his people. Let us remember that he took pains to instruct his children and also sought officials to help him govern. Furthermore, he asked God to make him prosper by granting his rich blessing to the people. This should cause us to realise that today he continues this same grace in us, and makes us aware of it even more at the right time. Let us realise, in conclusion, that since we are in the kingdom of our Lord Jesus Christ, from which flows our salvation, he is the one who naturally causes us to experience his favours, since he is the true substance of the things which were illustrated by figures in those olden times.

Now let us prostrate ourselves before the majesty of our good God, in recognition of the infinite faults of which we are guilty. Let us pray that he will make us so to feel them that this may make us displeased with them and make us always take refuge in his mercy. May we learn to govern ourselves in his obedience so that we will show, in effect, that we are truly the people of our Lord Jesus Christ, and that we hold him as our King. And may we be so reformed by his Spirit that our trust in him and confession of faith in him will cause us to renounce all iniquities and everything that is reprehensible. May he not only shower this grace upon us, but on all peoples and nations of the earth . . .

29

*David's Magnanimity to Mephibosheth**

And David said: Is there anyone who remains of the house of Saul, so that I may show him kindness on behalf of Jonathan? Now there was a servant of the house of Saul named Ziba, whom one called to come to David. The king said to him: Are you Ziba? He replied: It is I, your servant. And the king said: Is there anyone who remains of the house of Saul, so that I may show him the kindness of God? Ziba said to the king: There is still one of the sons of Jonathan, who is lame in his feet . . . (2 Sam. 9:1–13).

The deed of David which is recounted here is surely worthy of being praised as a great virtue. And yet, it was not without an element of vice, so that on the one hand David was worthy of praise for what he did, but at the same time he was not without blame. The fact that he remembered the house of Saul shows that he had forgotten all vengeance – which is a very rare thing to do, especially if we consider the terribly cruel persecutions which have been spoken of before. David, therefore, could have been a mortal enemy of the whole race of Saul, and the fact that now he was inclined to kindness is a very rare virtue which one scarcely ever finds among men. But the fact that he waited so long and did not carry out the oath made with Jonathan shows that he forgot it, as though prosperity had intoxicated him (1 Sam. 20:11ff.). Moreover, there is no doubt that God wanted to show here the virtue of David, and it ought to serve as instruction for us. This is a lesson very difficult to practise – to render good for evil – since it is repugnant to our

*Saturday, August 1, 1562.

nature. We have to battle in order to overcome the bitterness to which we are so prone. Moreover, although David was under obligation by solemn oath to the prosperity of Jonathan, still he could have been persuaded to hate the whole race of Saul. This could have totally obscured his obligation, in the same subtle way that men always have of seeking attractive means to excuse themselves from doing their duty.

Let us come to the text, and then we will gather the fruit from it. It says that David 'asked if there were anyone else of the house of Saul'. Well, this was done extremely late, for he certainly should have remembered the house of Jonathan immediately after he was given possession of the kingdom, or at the very least after the death of Ishbosheth, but he did not do so. Now this is why he is to be blamed. However, it is better late than never. This, therefore, is said in his praise – that he asked, without anyone urging him, to do good to those who might be survivors of the house of Saul.

Now we have already explained that God had removed what remained of the house of Saul so that there need be no more contention or debate, and so that David would be in peace. In addition, the people would no longer have the problem of bad leaders inciting them to keep themselves banded together against David, as they had done earlier, and as we have shown. God therefore wanted to show his grace to David and, on the other hand, he procured the rest and salvation of all the people when the race of Saul was thus blotted out, and there was no-one who remained but Mephibosheth. But even he was rendered useless by the admirable counsel of God, as Scripture shows us (2 Sam. 4:4). For his nurse had dropped him and he had broken his feet, so that he could not walk, and to make a king of such a mutilated body did not make good sense. Therefore, it was God who wanted this child to be spoiled in his body in this way. Then people would not abuse him in order to keep the people in trouble and contention as before. But still Mephibosheth remained alive.

Well, let us note that David did not merely ask if there were any child of Jonathan, but because of Jonathan, he was ready to do good to anyone of the house of Saul. This was going very far, for he had made no promise to keep this alliance with all his relatives; rather, he had simply sworn: 'When I have won the crown, I shall remember you and your children' (1 Sam. 20:15). Now that was how David's oath and promise was worded. Well, now he says, 'Is there no-one of the house of Saul?' – which had been his mortal enemy. Indeed, it had been like a savage beast, and had persecuted him for a long period without reason. Still, David was nevertheless prepared to do good to anyone at all.

When he heard it said that Mephibosheth had survived, he called him and said that it was 'in order to show him the mercy of God' (2 Sam. 9:3). Some explain this simply as mercy. For this expression 'of God' is also taken several times in Scripture for 'high and elevated by God', and 'what is exquisite' (Psa. 82:6). If that be the case, then whatever is rare and ought to be held in great esteem is called divine in Scripture. But there is no doubt that what David called the mercy of God is the grace which he wanted to bestow then and there, and that he was calling God as his witness, as if he wanted to be discharged from any fraud or disloyalty by saying: 'Before God, in case someone of his lineage can be found, I will attempt to do them good, and that is why I call on him'. And in fact, David needed to remove all question, since no-one would ever have thought that he had good will towards that house, because it had been his enemy.

In fact, we see that as Mephibosheth presented himself before him, he trembled, and there is no doubt that when David made him come out of the house where he had been raised, he was forced to come by royal authority. He was there like a poor man, half condemned, and was more prepared to die than to live until David assured him: 'Fear not' (2 Sam. 9:7). These words were not spoken without reason. For he saw that this poor soul did not know what to do. Now we can gather the time that had passed between the death of Jonathan and the time at which David called Mephibosheth, for it is said that Jonathan already had a son, and that at the death of his father his nurse dropped him as she fled, as we have seen (2 Sam. 4:4). Thus, a long space of time had elapsed. Hence, the fact that David did not remember this promise sooner was the vice which I have already mentioned, and which will be dealt with in more detail later.

Be that as it may, David showed here that he was acting in integrity when he assured Mephibosheth, and also concretely demonstrated his good will. For he said that he was 'leaving him the possessions of Saul' which he had already seized (2 Sam. 9:7). Now such liberality should be greatly praised. Let us assume, for instance, that there had been no change; that David had seized nothing of the house of Saul. Yet he could have said: 'Even though Ishbosheth, your uncle, who usurped the kingdom and was against me, had no children, still you cannot take part of the inheritance which belongs to him'. Thus, when everything which belonged to Saul was given to him, this was not only restitution, but an even fuller liberality. This is where the virtue of David showed itself. But he was not content with that, for he took in Mephibosheth, in order 'to feed him at his table' because of the love which he had 'for Jonathan'. Further, David said that Mephibosheth would be like one of 'the sons of the king', and that he would keep him, as if he were of his own blood and parentage, and that his master's son would rejoice in all his goods. That is what he commanded Ziba.

One assumes that Ziba was not of Israel, because he was a servant from generation to generation. But he could have been a servant who was retained by this house because he was so valuable – although he could have been set free. In fact, we see that he was not a common servant, because he had 'twenty servants' under him (2 Sam. 9:10). One could say that he was chief, since he had the responsibility and charge over these, but when it is plainly stated that he had 'fifteen children and twenty servants', one gathers from this that he was in the service of Saul in the ordinary capacity – that is to say, that he was like a slave. But because slavery was not lifelong among the people of God, and there was the jubilee in which everyone was returned to his (original) estate (Lev. 25:35ff.), he could have been so attached to this house that he remained there, continuing to work and attend to the business of Saul and his offspring. Well, be that as it may, Ziba had responsibility for Mephibosheth, on condition that he would have to give account for it, and that everything would be used to take care of Jonathan's son.

When it is again plainly stated that 'Mephibosheth would remain in Jerusalem and that he was eating at the table of the king, and that he was lame in his two feet', that is still to praise David's kindness. For we know how princes disdain those who cannot put on a good appearance before men – yet here is a poor body who cannot take care of himself and nevertheless he is at the table of the king. That shows in what esteem David kept the memory of Jonathan. That is what is to be said about these events.

Let us come now to the fruit which we should gather from it, and to the instruction contained in it. We have said that David remembered rather late the promise which he had made to Jonathan, and by that we are admonished to think of our duty when God makes us prosper. We know that wealth intoxicates us so much that we only think of personal luxuries, and other concerns are, as it were, buried. And if that happened to David, let us fear for ourselves, and be on guard. For it is certain that it was not the case that he held any ill feeling or bitterness in his heart against the line of Saul. The fact was that he was occupied in setting his kingdom in order and then in carrying out enterprises, and even in giving himself a good time, for he had suffered so much all the way.

Now it is true that he is to be excused if he rejoiced when it pleased God to give him some relief. But still, he should have thought of Jonathan sacrificing his own life for him (1 Sam. 20:15ff.). It was not a small thing for Jonathan to relinquish the hope of the crown. Indeed, his father Saul reproached him for it (1 Sam. 20:30ff.). Yet then he made himself the enemy of his father (1 Sam. 23:16ff.) and, according to worldly judgement, reduced his reputation even further by voluntarily subjecting himself to David. That did not seem to be appropriate for a great nobleman. Even his father had wanted to put him to death, but that did not prevent him from continuing to the end – even to his own death. Should David have had anything more precious than the memory of such a friend? Even if an inferior man had saved my life, people would still consider me to be ungrateful if I ever forgot him. Well, David should have thought: 'Now here is Jonathan, who was the eldest son of the king, and who, according to the opinion of men, should have succeeded him. But he, of his own will, has left everything to me, and has renounced everything that he was waiting for, and everything that he expected. And not only that, but in order to save my life, he exposed himself to death. He did not act selfishly, even when his father once attempted to kill him, but he persevered and never lost courage so that he always showed to me, in effect, the love which he had for me.' And then should he not have remembered the tears and groans of their separation (1 Sam. 20:41), and even of the last goodbye which they said to each other (1 Sam. 23:18)?

Now it was extremely ungrateful on David's part that he went for such a long space of time without carrying out his duty, for even beyond the promise there was the solemn oath. Even if there were to be no promise, we are always more obliged if a man who has done us some good deed is not able to repay himself. When a man has saved my life, and especially if he did not spare himself on my behalf, even if I have promised him nothing, shall I have discharged my obligation, and will people not spit in my face, if I do not make an effort to show him the affection that I owe him? Well, beyond the word, there was the name of God which was invoked. If even David did not think of it, then we whom our Saviour raises up should all the more take care that we do not reject those to whom we are bound. Indeed, in general, we must take care that the honours, the riches and luxuries of this world do not make us forget our duty. We should not be like runaway horses, as they say, but rather should be stirred up to carry out our duty. Now that is one point.

Next, we can consider how among all the virtues of the servants of God, one will still find vices. This shows us what blindness it is to imagine merits, as people often do. For when men are so stupid as to want to chart up their account before God, as if they were able to extrapolate their good motives and say: 'We have earned this and that' – one can see how it is a diabolical folly to imagine such a thing! Now if people do not pay attention to what we have mentioned here, and what will now be explained in more detail, they could say: 'Now here is an excellent virtue in David!' Yes, but look at the counterweight in the balance: namely, that for such a long space of time he refrained from showing his affection to the house of Jonathan. He did not know that Mephibosheth had not died of famine, that people were caring for him there in secret, and that he actually feared offending the king, because David had not declared his will. That is what so marred David's kindness that it merits no praise. Thus, let us realise that when God gives grace to his servants to dedicate themselves to the good, there always remains some infirmity in what they do, so that they have no reason to glorify themselves. All the circumstances should be carefully noted, for one could simply have sung the praise of David, that he remembered Mephibosheth and that he invited him and made him sit at his table. But the time is mentioned in order to show that, in fact, he buried the good which he owed to Jonathan – and for that he is to be condemned.

Nevertheless, now he did return to his duty when he spoke of the 'mercy of God' (2 Sam. 9:3). We have already expounded this word, but it can still give us some good and useful instruction. That is, when we are tempted to evil, let us always return to God, and present ourselves before him, to realise that he is Witness and Judge not only of all our external actions, but also of our thoughts. Now that (I say) is what will keep us under strict control. For how is it that men wander and give themselves such licence and are addicted to their wicked lusts? It is because they keep themselves, as it were, hidden from God and are, so to speak, fugitives. Not that when one asks even the most wicked in the world if they can escape from the hand of God, they do not reply 'No', and admit that they will have to present themselves before him! Nevertheless, they still turn their back on him and deliberately blind their eyes or cover them up. After that, their senses become dulled, so that one can truly call them fugitives, for it is as if they had hidden themselves from God and would never find themselves before his face. Well, therefore, let us carefully note that when we are tempted to evil, here is the true remedy by which we may overcome our evil desires and get ourselves on the right path from which we have been diverted. It is that we think of God and that we seek to bring ourselves before his majesty in order to say: 'Alas, what shall we do? For will God not see everything? And is it all not written down before him? And will he not call us to account?' Now that is another point.

Moreover, when we have made some promise in the name of God, and have called upon him, let that restrain us. For example, when a man is married, let him think: 'When we promised faith and loyalty to one another, was this not done before God, in his name?' Now that is how the husband will carry out his duty to live chastely with his wife, and even to govern her with all kindness, to support her and foster peace and harmony in his household. The wife also, when she remembers that she is joined in the name of God and that marriage is a sacred thing [will thus carry out her duty]. Further, the fathers promised clearly to nurture their children, because they have made solemn protestation in baptism to instruct them in the fear of God. A magistrate who has taken the oath of duty to carry out his office will carefully think of this when he remembers God. The people, by and by, will take delight in keeping his laws, and so everything else will then fall into place. Also, when people make contracts with one another, that is how the agreements will be faithfully observed. And why? Because they will think: 'We have called on the name of God'. But, in fact, all we see is men using the courts to rescind all their promises, so that nothing prevents their reversing their contracts and they spend their time working out ways to be relieved of their promises! They bring forward excuses such as: 'I have been defrauded in a certain situation which would cause me too much loss'. In the end, this remedy will not be applied and equity and fairness will not be maintained unless people think: 'God was witness when I promised a certain thing. Therefore, I must not seek to be absolved before men. The main thing is that I look to God, bring myself before his judgement seat, and examine my conscience in order to keep the obligation to which I once committed myself.' Now that is what we have to remember from this passage.

Well, when it says that Mephibosheth thus 'bowed down before David and fell on the ground', seized as he was by great fear and imagining that he might be put to death, we are observing a spectacle which should clearly show us how the world changes. For Mephibosheth was of the royal lineage, and we have seen that the ten tribes of Israel were associated with Saul, and that only the tribe of Judah was with David until after the death of Ishbosheth. But here was this poor man, waiting as if someone wanted to cut his throat, and for no reason other than that he was descended from the house of the king. And that is often what the splendours of this world bring – that, in fact, the humblest people are able to keep themselves hidden in their little holes where no-one troubles them, or seeks for them, so that they are not subject to many dangers! Even when there are great storms and tempests, they are more secure and not such easy prey precisely because they are small. However, it is necessary that the great respond to difficulties, and be called into action first. Hence, seeing such examples, let us bear it patiently if it pleases God to put us in a low condition, and let us not seek to be in a high position, since the falls are all the greater when God causes those who are lifted up high to be thrown down.

Moreover, we see how necessity humbles people. Here was this poor man, who 'cast himself down before David', and when he was summoned, said: 'Here am I, your servant' (2 Sam. 9:6). It is true that his grandfather had been a poor countryman before his election. But still, if we consider the pride of people whose position has been lowered from their former estate, we find that it is very difficult for them to bend. They say: 'I am descended from such and such a family', and to them it seems that people should always hold them in high esteem. It is quite certain that this must have grieved Mephibosheth greatly. Well, necessity became his master in order to humble him. Be that as it may, let us learn not to speak against God when it pleases him to remove from us any grounds or opportunity for pride and haughtiness. Let us learn to abase ourselves voluntarily, to submit ourselves to whatever pleases him. And when he wants to exercise towards us the judgements which are spoken of in the Psalm – that 'he will raise the poor up from the dung heap, and make them princes in the midst of his people' (Psa. 113:7–8), and he will abase those who have been the greatest and most pre-eminent – let us accept it, even those who could say: 'I am descended from such and such a house, I still have such and such relatives who are people of honour and reputation'. Let them learn from the example of Mephibosheth not to deceive themselves in their foolish imagination. For it is like despising nature when those whom God desires to impoverish remain hard-hearted and puffed up with wind, though without reason. Now that is what we must remember from this passage.

Let us now come to David. We have shown that if he had desired to do good to the line of Jonathan, we would not be too surprised. But when he wanted to show kindness to the whole house of Saul, that clearly demonstrated that his heart was not poisoned with desire for vengeance. Well, in regard to the house of Jonathan, it is true that he should not have been his enemy, but we know how men (as I have already mentioned) are subtle in inventing and forging lovely excuses when it comes to keeping their desire for vengeance under control! As David could have said: 'It is true that I have been kept back from vengeance to some degree by Jonathan, but still he was of the race of Saul, my enemy. And then there was also Ishbosheth, who usurped the kingdom and held it by force. With violence and rage, he troubled the people of God, and kept them banded together against me, and that is reason enough for dropping the love which I owed to him.' That was how David could have made excuses, like princes seeking some subterfuge in order to renounce the service which someone has done for them. But it was a much greater virtue when he said that he would do good to all those of the house of Saul, and that he would forget the persecutions which he had suffered.

Now let us compare the injuries which people have done to us with those which David suffered. It takes nothing to puff us up so that we are never appeased and our hatred becomes irreconcilable. Yet we have not experienced one-hundredth part of what David endured, and are not able to say that we have stumbled along for so long in pain and in torment. We cannot claim that we have pardoned our enemies, indeed, even to the extent of saving them from death, as David did Saul (1 Sam. 24:10). But we give place to our hatred and are inflated with disdain. Indeed, even as I have said, we are like savage beasts, and there is no way to keep us in a kindly state. Thus, David showed great virtue by not considering that Saul had persecuted him for so long, that Saul's people shamed him so by ravishing his wife (1 Sam. 25:44), that they had conspired to cut his throat so many times (1 Sam. 23:10ff.), that the people themselves had been against him, even seeking every way possible to put him to death in order to gratify the king (1 Sam. 23:19ff.), that he could not find a little corner to keep himself hidden and secret (1 Sam. 22:5), but that he was a fugitive (1 Sam. 21:1), now in the woods, now in the caves, now among his mortal enemies (1 Sam. 24:4) and always in danger of dying. Hence, we see immense strength of character in David for overcoming and putting underfoot all of these painful thoughts which could have caused him to take vengeance and act unkindly.

There is still more, for he could have been influenced by fear of the future, for we know that the princes of this world are distrustful and so eager to control their affairs that, although they have no reason for doubt, yet they protect themselves by rationalising: 'Well, this could happen, and I would be in such and such a danger'. In brief, they always wonder if the sky will fall on their head, and they want to prevent others from doing them evil, as I said. Hence, David could have thought: 'Should someone be raised up from the lineage of Saul, some sort of mutiny could arise, and people might return to Saul's house in order to remove the crown from me'. David could have thought that. The fact that he was prepared to reject the influence of all such passions shows the integrity of his life.

Now that, in fact, is the point that we should reach. That is, to walk on bravely when we are tossed about by some worry which could deflect us from the right path. Accordingly, the devil always presents us with objects of fear and doubt: 'If you do that, it is true that it will be a work that pleases God, but yet it will cause you trouble'. When, therefore, we think of such things, let us look in the other direction and see that by following God's commands we will be protected, the angels will guide us in our ways, and that we will be upheld when tortuous paths are ahead of us. For who is it who prevents men from walking straighter? For instance, the magistrates, whose responsibility it is to rebuke everything evil, often cover it up. And why? Because they do not want to be hated: 'Now I know that a certain man is so angry that if I once annoy him, he will not cease to pursue me – all these considerations will make me completely turn away from what I ought to do'. And that is not the case in only one place, but everywhere. The ministers of the Word of God should have their mouths open to rebuke the faults which they see. But they cover things up and pretend not to see. And the reason? It is because they might be disdained by some, and they do not want to lose their friendship. More often is it the case even with private persons, where we see no-one going straight and people only half carrying out their duty. We are cold when it comes to carrying out our duty. And why? Because fear prevents us. Well, we must resist these fears by letting faith be our guard, knowing that when we follow the path which God proposes for us, then he will make all our enterprises prosper, so as to make them turn out well. He will certainly know how to find the means to deliver us, whenever we are oppressed or tossed about with many doubts. So much, then, for this point, where we see that David was not concerned that if he elevated someone from the line of Saul, it could possibly cause trouble for him, prevent him from reigning peaceably, and cause greater treachery than ever.

Moreover, we see how God gave him opportunity to do good to Jonathan's son. For even if no-one had been found of that house, it is still true that David would not have failed to do good to the whole house of Saul. But since there was a legitimate son of his friend to whom he was indebted, there was no more cause for hesitation. We see, therefore, how God reserved Jonathan's son for him, so that he would be all the more stirred up to do his duty towards him, for this poor creature would move anyone to compassion. There is no doubt that it was of great value to

David to consider the abasement of the house of Saul mirrored through this person. Saul was the first king of the people, and he was indeed elevated by God, as has been shown. When David saw that poor disfigured creature, a body lame and broken, and then considered that it was only through his father that he had been kept alive, he had reason to think: 'Alas, what a change has occurred' – and even apply that lesson to himself, and learn to walk in the fear of God, realising that there is nothing secure in this world and that even the strongest kingdoms would always be in turmoil if they were not upheld by God through his providence.

Nevertheless, as we have argued, David had reason to recognise God's grace to him once again, since it was Jonathan's son alone who survived. David should also have been even more encouraged, seeing that God had delivered him from everything that could have destroyed him, and that because of this he was accepted not only by him, but by the people in general. This is another point which should certainly be remembered. It is certain that David had clearly recognised earlier that God had seen to it that the people were reunited in one body, and that the kingdom was at peace. But this would serve all the more to refresh his memory and represent to him, over again, the grace of God – which we should never forget, for it would have been possible never to think of it, had not such an example been kept before his eyes.

Well, as for the fact that he gave Mephibosheth what belonged to him and beyond that, that he gave him all the possessions of Saul, we see that he did not do it for gain and to win praise, but out of true affection before God, as we said above. The result shows that he was absolutely sincere when he assured them that the mercy which he wanted to show to the line of Saul was as true as if he had called God there as judge and witness. For he could easily have been excused even if he had given to Mephibosheth merely his portion. Indeed, among men (as I have said), that would have been considered quite fair. He could have said: 'Now your grandfather Saul had certain possessions. Well, this particular part could have come down to your father Jonathan. But there was your uncle

Ishbosheth and the others. I am under no obligation concerning their part. Indeed, by the rebellion and sedition which they caused among the people, they certainly deserve to have their goods confiscated. Still, this part which belonged to your father will be reserved for you.' If he had spoken thus, he could not have been reproached for ingratitude or cruelty. But he went even beyond that, for he gave him all Saul's possessions. We see, therefore, as I have said, that David did not desire to discharge his duty half-heartedly in the manner of men, but that he went about it with such determination that it was as if God were shown to him there in visible form, and had dictated to him what he had to do.

Therefore, we must remember not to be miserly and restrained when it comes to doing good. For while we may be generous to some extent, there will always be 'shops in our back alley' which engage our attention, and thus we may attempt to retain some portion for ourselves! We will never be real when it comes to doing good unless God has thoroughly mastered us. Therefore, let us carefully note this example of David, lest when some illusion comes to us of tricking another person by an attractively false pretext, we say: 'It is true that I owe you such and such a thing, but you clearly see that it could be lost, if I wanted it to be – and anyway, you will be satisfied with half of it!' Now that is how men usually do it. But we must watch ourselves very carefully and reject the use of any petty objection which could absolve us before men. We should always remember that, before God, we must not go in two different directions, wandering lamely here and there. Rather, we must move ahead with determination and integrity, and be open to what our Lord shows us is pleasing to him. Let us remember this.

Now, far from this being faithfully observed, people have to be forced to do even their required duty. Do we not find that we cannot get those who are in debt to pay as much as they ought to pay? They always turn a deaf ear, and then try to hold back part of the sum, and defraud those to whom they are in debt. This is very far from following the rule which God has left, that men ought to show love to one another (John 15:12).

Now concerning the honour which David showed to Mephibosheth (2 Sam. 9:13), this is something else for which he should be much praised. For he could easily have left him in his house, after restoring him. Since he was there broken and mutilated in body, and could not walk, he could certainly have used this as an excuse, saying that he kept himself hidden because if he were seen in that condition, he would only have been ridiculed. But still he loved this poor creature for the love of his father, Jonathan. Furthermore, he showed that he was not being led by the kind of ambition followed by the princes of this world, who are always wanting to parade their triumphs – and who, if their lives are not full of pomp, feel dishonoured. That is why princes only seek out people who will build their reputation and give them credit. But God rightly punishes them, for when they seek the honour and esteem of men in this way, they nurture the scum of the earth in their houses! A prince would be terribly ashamed of honouring someone who did not have an attractive appearance or look impressive.

Well, what does it all amount to? The majority will be whoremongers, while others will be nothing but thieves, their sole aim being to cheat and ruin the poor in order to enrich themselves. Others will be drunks, others blasphemers. In brief, this is the plague of royal courts, so that by comparison whore-houses are often less detestable! God punishes them because of their pompousness, and because their only desire is self-aggrandisement. Indeed, when one looks at them, it seems that everything ought to tremble, since they put on such an imposing appearance! But nevertheless, they do not have the main thing: namely, the fear of God and the kindness due to their subjects. Thus, we should particularly observe what is told us here about David, who was not ashamed to have a poor lame man at his table. Indeed, although Mephibosheth had been brought up secretly, so to speak, in a house in the country, Scripture says that he will be like one of the sons of the king. And why? Because David considered his promise to have been made before God, as we have already shown.

Now let us prostrate ourselves before the majesty of our good God, in recognition of all our faults and offences. Let us pray him that more and more he will make us feel them, and that this will cause us to humble ourselves before God. And although we be lifted up with some measure of honour, let us not fail always to submit ourselves to him and to our neighbour. And let us remember the bond of charity between us, praying that it might remain inviolable, and let each one endeavour so to behave towards his neighbour that God will be glorified in the midst of us, and that we will be careful to do and follow the example of David as it is described here. And may he not only bestow his grace upon us, but upon all people and nations of the earth . . .

30

*The Two Bases for a Just War**

After this the king of the sons of Ammon died; Hanun his son reigned in his place. And David said: I will show kindness unto Hanun, the son of Nahash, as his father showed kindness to me . . . (2 Sam. 10:1–12).

Scripture explains here how David was compelled to go to war again, although it had seemed that God had conquered all his enemies, so that none should have been able to bother him any more. This teaches us that however much things which we wish do happen, and however much it seems that God desires to exempt us from all annoyances, yet there is nothing certain in this world and it only takes a turn of the hand to make some change happen. That is the reason why those to whom God gives the grace of enjoying rest will not go to sleep in it, but will always have an eye wide open, as they say. They will use the prosperity which God gives them, but nevertheless will not fail to be prepared for the time when it pleases God to test them through new temptations. Now that is what we have to consider in the first place in the example which we have quoted. Indeed, when it seems that all our enemies are conquered, they will not fail to raise their horns from one day to the next. For the devil who pushes them will never allow them to make peace or a truce, insofar as he is able to prevent it.

Nevertheless, the occasion of this war is to be noted, namely, that David wanted to build up friendship with the Ammonites,

*Monday, August 10, 1562.

and he even tried to bury all the hard feelings which had previously existed so that those memories would no longer endure. Now his motive was good and holy. Yet he was compelled to wage war against the king of the Ammonites. There is no doubt that this event, which was quoted immediately above, forced him to do so. It is true that it did not happen without the secret counsel of God. So here was David's situation. He did not fight against the king of Ammon and his people except when he was forced to, as was the case at this time. It is certain that he would have recognised the good which he had received from Nahash, the king of Ammon, if he had been able, and had been allowed to do so. One must, therefore, conclude that the Ammonites came to assail him. And although he only sought to be their friend, still they had irritated him in such a way that he could not avoid waging war with them. Anyway, he said that 'he would show kindness towards Hanun, even as he had been treated kindly by his father' (2 Sam. 10:2). Well, when he recognised in Nahash's son the benefit which he had received from his father, it was a sign that he had not forgotten his original obligation to Nahash. Thus we can now see what I have said.

If one asks what the text means by the kindness of the king of Ammon to David, the Jews – who are talented in inventing lies – say that after the father and mother of David had their throats cut by the king of Moab, and the rest of his relatives had fled, then the king of Ammon received them and treated them kindly. But these are just fantasies. However, we can clearly discern that David in his weariness, afflictions and adversities needed to be relieved, and that he sought help here and there, and that the king of Ammon was able to receive him when he could bear no more. The fact that this is somehow the case is shown to us by Scripture, in that David in his afflictions still found much more mercy with this pagan king than with all the people of Judah. Well, we know that those who have to suffer, and are troubled and persecuted, will be dependent on many people, because there is no way to escape unless they ask for help here and there. Now that is how it was with David.

Yet, because it did not work out well in that Hanun mocked and despised David's friendship, some think that God wanted to chastise him for having thus sought fellowship with unbelievers. It is true that the Ammonites are kept back and banned from the Church by the Law (Deut. 23:4). But nevertheless, it is not said that David could not act kindly towards them, for he is not rebuked for having had an alliance with King Hiram (2 Sam. 5:11), and yet he was an idolater. We see also that Abraham had an alliance with those who had nothing in common with him as far as religion is concerned (Gen. 21:22ff.). It is not said that one should seek such alliances, but as God presents occasions for them, sometimes it is necessary to form these alliances. For when Abraham was dwelling in the midst of unbelievers, what could he have done, especially when he saw that he could not achieve peace unless he had a mutual agreement? And when the king of the Philistines came to him, he was certainly obliged to swear and promise to be loyal to him.

As regards David, it is not said that he made a practice of allying himself with the Ammonites, nor that he wanted to go any further than showing them that he would be a good neighbour to them. He accepted them for what they were. But be that as it may, still he wanted to reassure them so that they would have no occasion to start a needless war. Well, we have said enough about these details, and yet we must not conclude that this deed of David was reproved by God, since the son did not do what David thought he would do. For our own good intentions will often be frustrated, and yet God will not fail to approve what we tried to do. We even see that what Solomon later says was fulfilled in David – that is, when he exhorts us to do good to our enemies and to render them good for evil, adding that we 'heap coals of fire upon their head' (Prov. 25:22). Thus it happened to David. For although Hanun was ungrateful and treated David with treachery and cruelty, still everything turned out to David's advantage so that this miserable Hanun remained confounded when the coals of fire were heaped on his head. So much, therefore, for the deed of David, for which he can in no way be condemned.

The story of how David did not want to leave the king of the Ammonites in doubt or suspense is recounted as a praiseworthy virtue that should be remembered. David regularly made war and we know that warfare is passed down from father to son. David, therefore, wanted to prevent every possibility of trouble when he sent messengers to Hanun. It is true that the text speaks of 'comfort over the death of his father' (2 Sam. 10:2), yet there is no doubt that by this action David was only testifying to Hanun that henceforth he would be his friend, as David's preface indicates. He said: 'Now as his father has shown mercy towards me, I will show mercy to him also' (2 Sam. 10:2). Well, according to our translation, David meant by this word that he would show kindness, that is to say, he would show that he was a friend and good neighbour and peaceable to the Ammonites, that he would abstain from doing them any injury or trouble, and thus that he wanted them to realise his desire to show them nothing but kindness. Now this was David's intention.

This teaches us to follow his example when it comes to recognising the benefits which we have received. And indeed, we are to attempt to return the same kindness not only to our benefactors but also to those who shall be descended from their line. For a kindness should never be trampled underfoot, and when we are not able to repay the good which we have received to the persons to whom we are obliged, let us do like David and let us realise that God wants the memory of it to continue for ever. Now that is one point. For although ingratitude is far too widespread a vice, if we have good common sense, we must not fail to hate it. Hence, let us be careful to keep in mind what we are shown here. That is, when we are obligated to people who have helped us in time of need, let us try to do the same for them as far as we can. At the very least, let us have a mutual affection for those who have shown us friendship, granted that we are obligated even to return good for evil to our enemies and to those who persecute us. Now that is one matter.

Moreover, when we have done our duty, let us not be too clever in figuring out what shall come of it. Let us take refuge in God, who knows exactly how to work it all out. However, let us keep to the path that he shows us. For there is nothing which prevents men more from doing the duty of their vocation than when they imagine things such as: 'It is true that people must honour God, and therefore I ought to do so, but I shall be the loser for it, and God will not recognise the good which I want from him. It is a waste of time to ask God to do anything good for me.' The result of such argumentation is evil, and the devil is only seeking a way to divert us from the simplicity with which we should serve God and our neighbour. Hence, when it comes to doing good, let us not be too concerned about our own profit; let us not speculate in order to know what the outcome will be. Let us put it all back in the hands of God, since the outcome depends on him, and yet let us do what he commands us. Hence, since we must render good for evil, if it pleases him for someone to render us evil for good, and it seems that we have wasted our time, let us realise that he is still pleased with our service when we act in this way.

It certainly seems that David had stirred up war against himself when he sent ambassadors to Hanun, and one could say that we ought to leave alone those who are incapable of kindness. But be that as it may, it was enough that God had approved what was done by David, although everything had turned back upon him in confusion. Yet under the shadow of this war, David was actually granted a marvellous victory. For although at first glance, David's failure to come to terms with Hanun seemed an ill-advised attempt in the light of the terrible treatment that his enemies gave him, yet at last God showed that he knew how to take care of his own by bringing them to a successful and happy outcome when they walked in simplicity, as David did.

Now that is what we have to remember. When many objects which could corrupt us come across our path and act like nets which are spread out to keep us from walking in the path which God has pointed out to us, let us maintain the simple trust which says: 'Still, we must obey what we are commanded by God. He wants me to fulfil my office and duty, and that is the way that I must go. It is sufficient that God accept the obedience which I render him. As for the outcome, he will know how to take care of it in such a way that although we must endure some trouble and annoyance, still all of it will be converted to our good and to our salvation. Now we must rest upon this.'

Next, it says that the counsellors of Hanun said to him: 'And do you think that David wants to honour your father? Instead, he is sending these people in order to spy and search and destroy the country' (2 Sam. 10:3), as if they came to seek, in a roundabout way, an occasion for making war. The messengers were then punished for it; for 'he shaved off part of their beard' (2 Sam. 10:4), so that they would be exposed to the mockery of everyone, and 'he cut off their clothes so that their shameful parts were uncovered'. Now if he had killed them, he would not have committed a greater outrage, and without doubt this action was contrary to universal common law. For from time immemorial, people have considered ambassadors to be sacred and privileged, even in time of war. If anyone is sent as an ambassador with a message which displeases the enemy, people still protect his right to return, for an ambassador is like a passport. And in fact, an ambassador ought to be favoured because he tends to maintain peace among men, or to remove troubles which have already started. That is why God impressed on all men, by nature, the rule and law that ambassadors ought to be sacred.

Now here we see, above all, what distrust is. That is why it is not good for us to be consumed by a distrustful spirit – like many people who, thinking they are wise, consider everything doubtful and accept nothing without suspicion. We see some who are so wicked that they actually cultivate this distrustful attitude out of ambition and vanity: 'I must distrust everything and know how to disguise my feelings'. What is the outcome? Their attitude causes wars and quarrels. Well, when we are consumed by this sort of distrust, it is certain that we will start fires to which there will be neither end nor measure, and we will not be able to put them out once they have been started. Experience demonstrated this only too clearly. Let us not go as far as kings and princes, but let us take common people. If a man distrusts his wife, the master his servant, one neighbour the other, it spreads a venom which corrupts the heart. And instead of winning peace, people lose it. Because of this suspicion, people carry such 'a chip on the shoulder' that the smallest object which darts before their eyes causes them to become irritated and annoyed. Then the evil grows worse on both sides so that most of the trouble proceeds from this evil source. That is, men are too inclined to distrust and remain suspicious so that they actually lose control of the situation, although they thought they were manifesting the greatest possible prudence.

Well, this story should serve as an instructive, exemplary warning against this thoroughly perverse vice. For the counsellors of King Hanun distrusted David, and thereby they were the cause of ruining both their master and the whole country. Hence, let us learn not to be influenced by our own malice to put a bad interpretation on what could be taken as good, and if something is done which we could doubt, still let us not do so. When we have to deal with people who are full of disloyalty and treason, it is true that we must stay on our guard and carefully watch so as not to be corrupted. When we conclude out of mere suspicion that 'Here is someone who only thinks of hurting me, and I do not know what he means', God will certainly punish us at once for such an attitude. For when our useless manipulation of circumstances inevitably brings us down, God will pay us the wages which we deserve. What, therefore, happened to the people of Ammon reminds us to take things in good part, and not to let our spirits be poisoned with suspicion and distrust when it is not necessary. Now here again is a matter which we should carefully observe.

Well, we see how when men once grow angry, they hold nothing back and lose all moderation. The counsellors of Hanun thought that David had wanted to spy out their land. Now on the basis of this sheer imagination, they concluded that they ought to consider him an enemy. They decided, 'We must therefore do the worst that we can'. Let us learn by what is placed here before our eyes to resist our passions early so that we do not voluntarily lose control of ourselves. For as soon as some passion takes control of us, reason loses its influence.

Now, that reason and sense of fairness which God has placed in us have to wage a strenuous battle against our passions. Our passions come from foolish and extravagant thoughts. For when we have cast our eyes here and there, and have lent our ears to everything that people wish to say to us, we lose our sense of moderation. Hence, thoughts and frivolous imaginations influence us so that reason is chased off with no more place to stay. Then our passions act like the waves which beat in a tempest, and we are tossed about more and more until we lose our self-control like confused, lost people.

We can observe this with our own eyes in the story which is told here. For the Ammonites went from one extreme to another, even to falling into this extremity of provoking David to anger – and, indeed, of giving him just occasion for war by this shameful thing that they did to him, which was as bad as if they had cut the throats of his ambassadors. For those whom he had sent represented his person. Hence, the shameful thing that they did was aimed at David. Well, that vengeance is worse to a man of sensitive feeling than death would be – that someone despises him to the point of disfiguring him, just as if he had been put on a scaffold, and then had his clothes cut off in shame and disgrace. And all of this was to spite David. We see, therefore, how the Ammonites maintained no moderation, and it was because they let down their guard on their own passions. This teaches us to keep control of ourselves all the more, and to fight against these stormy passions whenever we see that they are influencing us. We must fight for our reason to be in control of our passions so that we may maintain self-mastery. So much, therefore, for one point.

Well, after that Scripture adds that 'the Ammonites seeing that they stank' – for the word means that, or that they were hated by him – 'went to hire the Syrians' (2 Sam. 10:6). In the First Book of Chronicles it says that they made themselves odious (1 Chron. 19:6), or that they had committed a disgusting thing. For although the verb is not from the same root, still it has that meaning. Thus, we see that the Ammonites, after such excess, recognised their fault – not in order to be displeased with it, but rather in order to make it worse.

Well, their 'repentance' was too late. And in this we see that those who follow their tempers and the impetuosity of their passions always have leisure to repent when in fact there is no more time left to do so. For however we carry out our cruelty, whatever meanness or injury we do to our enemies, the more we 'soak in our evil to bathe in it' (as the proverb says), the more pleased we feel. We do not see a speck, therefore, of all that can result from evil when we are preoccupied by this lust which drives us on, telling ourselves it is good to avenge oneself, and that at least we shall have got the best of our enemies, and they will have to die of spite when they receive such a blow! Now that is what we really think, no matter how we act on the outside. But soon afterwards, when the heat of our anger has passed, then God shows us, as in a mirror, what we have done, and forces us, whether we like it or not, to feel and face up to our evil.

It is true that when we have committed some folly, we would like to enjoy ourselves continually in it, just as when we first started doing it – but God does not allow it to be that way. Instead, it seems as though he were keeping us locked into it. We are like a criminal who would very much like to harden himself when he has committed some crime, but if justice is to lay hold on him, he will have to remember his evil and feel a remorse which will torment him. For God has sergeants and secret officers when he sends us pricks in our consciences and when we have to feel within the evil that we have done. So it happened to the people of Ammon, as we see. For although they had shamefully treated the ambassadors of David, there is no doubt that they glorified themselves over it and acted boastfully, so as to say: 'Now we are certain that this fellow was only spying on us. We have shown that he had better not play with us.' So here they are, like poor drunkards who have escaped a fever or a headache which they deserved by their intemperance: they no longer think of it. So it is with those who are called to account, or rather dragged by force to recognise it, who when they do evil, never have the time to think of it.

In other words, we see that when those who have done evil come to themselves, it is not always in order to repent but rather to redouble their evil. It is true that the sadness which we feel for having done evil will be for our salvation (as St Paul shows in the Second Epistle to the Corinthians, chapter 7, verse 10), under the condition that we endeavour to repair the evil and to bring ourselves back to the right path. But this is not given to all. For when it pleases God to send remorse to his children, it is in order to make them displeased with their vices so that they may obtain grace and pardon, and then may be fully converted. Well, unbelievers will certainly experience remorse, but this will only serve to put them in a rage and fury, or to gnash their teeth against God, or to add one evil to another.

Now here are the Ammonites, who see that they have made themselves odious to David. It is their conscience which rebukes them. It is not necessary, therefore, for David to press them to confess this shameful thing which they have done. It is only necessary for their conscience to be their judge. Well, that is a beginning. For the faithful must apprehend their misdeed before they come to repentance. The Ammonites, however, instead of appeasing David, thought that they must play double or quit! They acted, therefore, in desperation and did not consider how this evil could be corrected. Rather, they did the worst that they could and sent to Syria to hire people – and thus wasted their resources with these great expenses, since they certainly thought that they would never be able to obtain pardon from David. So it is with all the wicked whom God clearly forces (as I have said) to feel their evil. Yet he does not give them the grace of arriving at the remedy. Instead, they jump beyond restraint, like a drunkard who has become fevered by his intemperance, and rather than abstaining, as he should, in order to get rid of his evil habit, greatly increases his drinking until he is totally ruined. So it is with those who undoubtedly have some remorse, but nevertheless remain obstinate in their evil ways. For they will not cease to add evil to evil until they are totally destroyed.

Now there are here 'different parts of Syria' (2 Sam. 10:6), and the names do not all agree with those which are listed in the First Book of Chronicles (1 Chron. 19:6). For the first Syria, which is called here 'Bethrehob', is called there 'Syria of

Rivers', and that is what some have called Mesopotamia, because it is situated between two rivers. Well, in other words, one sees that the Ammonites hired many nations in their service. Not that all had the name Syria in common, but one can see that Syria had various names in its outlying territory, as today one will say High and Low Germany. It is the same with Hungary. And when a country has various provinces, one will call their names according to this same principle. So it was with the country of Syria.

Well, be that as it may, we see that this people, who could have lived peaceably, started a war by their recklessness and presumption. And this is the wages of those who undertake this kind of thing in their presumption. They will soon have to pay a very dear price. Hence, let us be careful to attempt nothing which is illegitimate. For we shall suddenly have to pay a painful price afterwards. And above all, let us keep from being reckless, and whenever we are tempted to undertake drastic action, let us immediately beat down the temptation so that God will not render to us what we see he rendered to the Ammonites: that we wind up destroying ourselves and losing everything. For David had not intended war against them, had it not been for what they did. They even undertook it before they were really faced with it, and they thought it a better strategy to start it themselves. That is an example of how we do not cease adding evil to evil until we learn to restrain ourselves. And indeed, the devil takes possession and uncontested control of us and then carries us in every direction. Hence, let us be on our guard that we may be poised and settled so as not to attempt more than God permits.

Well, then it says that 'David sent his army' under the leadership and direction of Joab (2 Sam. 10:7) and that 'the Ammonites camped before the gate' (2 Sam. 10:8) of the city, and that the Syrians readied their troops over on the opposite side, so that Joab was surrounded on all sides. Seeing that he had his enemies 'in front and behind', he left his army and 'took the strongest with him in order to go against the Syrians' (2 Sam. 10:9) – for they were an entire army. He put himself there as the most valiant and the most expert. 'The rest of his army, he entrusted to his brother Abishai, and said to him: If the Syrians are stronger than I, you will come to help me, and if you are weaker than the Ammonites, I will come to help you' (2 Sam. 10:10–11). He made these arrangements, therefore, as best he could. Then he exhorted Abishai further to strengthen himself: 'Let us take courage,' he says, 'for our people and for the cities of God. Let us fight bravely, and indeed the Lord will do what seems good to him' (2 Sam. 10:12).

We see here how God guided Joab to anticipate and prevent the evil which was set for him. It is true that men of war usually do this. Yet histories show that the most clever have often been surprised by fright, so that they have been conquered without a blow being struck, by failing to have considered something which ought not to have been left neglected. Only after it was too late did they discover the problem. But on the other hand, we gather from history that those who have acquired the science of war by long practice, who are brave in trouble and who know how to give expert advice on what is expedient, for all their practice and expertise, can still have their eyes blinded by God when he pleases, since he reserves the means of victory in his counsel. Yet at the same time, he gives prudence and discretion to those to whom he wants to give the victory. Let us recognise, therefore, that this is a special blessing of God, not just once for all, but that we need to be blessed by the Spirit every hour and every minute. Now that is what we have to remember, therefore, when this text talks about the virtue of Joab. He is praised for his action. Nevertheless, there is no doubt that God holds up this mirror before our eyes so that we might know that prudence is worth more than all the forces of the world, so that we might learn to take refuge in him, and so that he may guide us and authorise and show what will be good and useful for us in all our affairs.

Let us come to the exhortation which is included here. Joab tells his brother Abishai 'to fight for their people and for the cities of God' (2 Sam. 10:12). Now here are the only two just causes of war: the good and common safety of the people, and the honour of God, which is included here in the second place. Not that God's honour should be considered of least value, but the main thing is often placed at the end and at the tail, as being of the most value. Be that as it may, men will never have a just cause for waging war except for the common good and conservation of the public condition, or for the honour of God. These should take precedence over all that men can conceive. However, if we consider, on the other hand, the reasons which have always caused wars, we will find that the majority stem from avarice and ambition.

Now here is a prince who undertakes war. And why? Because he wants to be great! Either he has no other goal or he is as insatiable as the pit of hell. He wants to get everything for himself, and he thinks his income will not be sufficient for him. Now that is the source of wars. Distrust is also mixed in with these motives. For when a prince has a strong enemy, he says, 'If I advance myself, I will be first'. Then he concludes, 'It is necessary therefore to wage war, and when I have some advantage, I will profit all the more from it'. And this is what I have said: 'When we are wrapped up in suspicion, it is impossible for us to be kept back from evil'. And yet, how does this affect the common good? A prince will have some poor subjects, yet he will have to raise his taxes and assessments endlessly and unfairly. And then he will shed human blood. It will not bother him to make many widows and orphans, nor for many houses to be burned, and for all their goods to be taken as lost, and all those other things that usually happen in wartime. That is one point.

Well, as for the honour of God, men never even consider it, but instead seem to want to stamp it underfoot when war is coming. For then they issue themselves a licence to do all kinds of evil, seeming to join together deliberately against his majesty, unconcerned that he might deal with them. It is true that when unbelievers make war, they always pray to God and engage in their [religious] processions. They are amazingly devout when they are waging war. But in spite of that, they commit excessive sin and act as though war gives them the privilege of abolishing the authority of God. Even when the Philistines made war, it is certain that it was only 'for the common good'. Today, the Venetians say that it is 'for the civil good' when they trouble the world with their enterprises. But it is certain that it is simply avarice and ambition to be great and famous which drive them to make war, coupled with a distrust of different people, because, in fact, we see that they have destroyed what they have gained by looting and plundering. That is how one evil leads to another. It was the same with the Romans. For the reason that they whipped and stirred up the whole world was simply for their aggrandisement and to acquire more and more fame and renown. But soon they became inflamed by the desire for riches. And yet when they had acquired one country, it was clear that if a certain neighbouring country was not conquered, it could harass them. Thus, they found occasion to make war without any just foundation. All these are the attractive excuses and practices which such people have utilised, giving no warning to those whom they have needlessly molested.

Well, we should carefully consider this passage to learn that we should never attempt war without its first being for the common good. In this way, the war may be a means of seeking peace when the evil of our enemies utterly forces us to such a necessity. Also, there is the honour of God, which is the principal cause (as I have said) when it comes to his being worshipped and honoured. It is true that it is not for everyone to take the sword in his hand. The authority of our princes must, therefore, guide us. This is to be kept in mind by all private citizens who are concerned for the honour of God. But whenever the war is undertaken by a just authority, let us realise that it is good and legitimate. Now it follows that if the honour of God is involved in it, we must not undertake it with false pretexts, but rather for the right reason. We must be able to protest both before him and before men that we seek only that his majesty be maintained and that he reign over us, and that we live together under his obedience with common accord. The rest will be explained tomorrow.

Now let us prostrate ourselves before the majesty of our good God in recognition of the infinite faults of which we are guilty. Let us pray that he will make us so to feel them that this will not serve to harden us in despair, but rather to humble us so as to obtain pardon and to bring us back to the right path; and to renounce all our offences so that we seek only to give ourselves to his service and to profit in it more and more; so that we fight above all against ourselves and our own vices, and then that we give back to him the threats and cruelties of our enemies, knowing that our help rests in him and that he will defend us. And may he not only bestow this grace upon us, but on all peoples and nations of the earth . . .

31

*God on our Side**

Joab delivered the rest of the people into the hands of Abishai his brother, and ordered them to go before the sons of Ammon. And he said: If the Syrians are stronger than I, you will come to help me, and if the sons of Ammon are stronger than you, I will come to help you. Be valiant and let us do valiantly for our people and for the cities of our God . . . (2 Sam. 10:10–19).

Yesterday we began to discuss the two bases for a just war among men, which are: for the honour and worship of God and for the safety of all the people. Here are the two considerations which all those who rule and whom God has chosen to bear his sword should have: firstly, that the honour of God be maintained, and religion kept in its purity and, secondly, that the people be maintained in peace. Those who are seated on the tribunal of justice and have superiority are ordained as officers of God for the protection of his subjects. However, they must not forget the main thing – namely, that God is to have his sovereign empire and all people are to give homage to him. That is how wars can be legitimate, namely, if the honour of God is procured and if the rulers have regard for the peace and welfare of the people.

Now it could certainly be the case that a war is undertaken with a just cause, and yet the one directing the war actually offends, because he is only using the honour of God as a pretext for his war-making. We see many people who argue for a good cause and, indeed, seem to be motivated by nothing but zeal.

*Tuesday, August 11, 1562.

Yet when we look at their motives more closely, we discover that under the pretext of the honour of God and the public good, they are actually seeking an occasion to enrich themselves. For instance, in these troubled times, how many are there who are fighting under the very shadow of the banner of Jesus Christ, making profession of the Gospel, and yet in actuality are addicted to pillaging and plundering, and sing of nothing but their wealth and grab money wherever they can get their hands on it? Why? Now if it really is only a matter of marching and doing their duty, and of procuring the honour and service of God without any profit in it, very soon their zeal will become as cold as ice! But if it is simply a question of gathering into the treasury and banks, suddenly they become the greatest zealots in the world. So zeal is not the only thing that counts, but we must also have pure motives in order to honour God.

Well, when we are fully determined to worship God and to maintain the common peace and welfare, then we will be able to practise effectively what Joab says here, namely, to strengthen ourselves and have an invincible constancy (2 Sam. 10:12). For a good cause which is right will always make us brave. It is true that the wicked will be brave enough in their audacity – and too much so! But if a good conscience is leading us to walk honestly before God, to do what he approves, and to serve the common good of the people, it is certain that it will strengthen us much more than if we had all the weapons in the world on our side and the means in hand to defeat a great number of our enemies. Let us carefully note, therefore, that in the first place we should have the foundation of a good conscience, so that we attempt nothing which is not part of our calling and in God's good will. Thus, we will not gnaw our bridle with our teeth, nor carelessly roam somewhere which is questionable, but be determined to stay within the will of God.

However, Joab added that the 'Lord will do whatever will seem good to him' (2 Sam. 10:12). Well, it certainly seems that Joab was thinking like all those poor unbelievers who have always risked their lives on chance when they had a good cause to fight for. Well, that would not be appropriate for a man of faith who would be taught in the Word of God. For this is precisely where we should differ from profane people, that is, when we have a good cause, we are to learn to take refuge in God and to assure ourselves that he will be on our side to help us in time of need. For we have certainly seen pagans who have not spared their own life when it came to the public good and to the liberty of a country. We have the testimony in all the histories, where many magnanimous people are found, who forget both wives and children and their own lives when it came to opposing some tyranny, or the ambition or cruelty of those who would have liked to dominate against reason. Yet God abandoned them in need, and they were confounded, although their cause was good and just. Why? Because they trusted in their own selves and did not consider that the victory came from on high. Rather, they wanted to do their duty no matter what, in order to gain a reputation among men. We must not, therefore, be surprised if God made them confused. For although they had a good cause, they carried it out badly. Since we know that the issues cannot turn out successfully except by his goodness alone, and that he must make us prosper in all our deeds, we must always come back to this point of calling on God in all our affairs. Otherwise, we shall always be living as though chance determines our situation.

Well, it certainly seems that Joab resembles these unbelievers here, for instead of praying to God, trusting that he would give victory to those who have a good cause, he said: 'The Lord will do what will seem good to him'. He talks like someone confused, who does not know what it is to rest on the promises of God. But however brief the words are, there is no doubt that Joab looked further. In the first place, he confessed that it was up to God to govern, which the pagans did not do. For although, with their natural sense, they may have understood and even said that God controlled battles, yet they were never very persuaded of it in their heart. If their mouth was speaking, their thoughts were elsewhere. In brief, we see that when they declared what they actually thought about the honour of God, they had nothing but their good fortune in mind. God, therefore, was cast down from his position. Well, Joab shows here that God keeps everything so much in control that when men have battled and bravely persisted, it is still up to him to give the victory. When the pagans made conquests, they certainly said that it was God who had favoured them, but it was all for their own glory. For instance, when they dedicated temples and similar things, it was only to pull God down from heaven in order to maintain their standing, and they were always concerned about their own glory. In brief, they were far from approaching what Joab states here, namely, that he clearly understood that no matter how bravely he behaved, all his forces could still do nothing unless God gave the victory. Now that is what this sentence means, where Joab exhorted his brother Abishai to be valiant, and then he was immediately encouraged to do the same. But after having spoken thus, he added: 'The Lord is over us. It is up to him either to make all that we have done useless, or to make us prosper according to his good will.' Now that is one point.

But if someone replies that he did not call on God – still, although his words are brief, they do imply invocation, as if Joab were declaring: 'We must have recourse to God, and put everything that belongs to him back in his hands'. He glorifies him in these words, as if he were saying: 'Even if we have done marvellously, still the whole thing will amount to nothing unless God blesses it'. Now that is how the sense of Joab's prayer – although it is not formulated here – is still essentially seeking the help of God, so that it might please him to have pity on his people.

Well, if someone still claims that Joab did not show that he trusted in God, that he was not thoroughly assured of the promises of the Law, the reply to that is that God does not give particular promises about this or that to his children. We certainly have this point which should firmly persuade us that God will never abandon us, and that in the end he will show that our hope in him was not in vain, so that our faith will not be frustrated when it rests upon his mercy and his truth. Nevertheless, we must remain in suspense about many things. For instance, when we ask God for our daily bread, it is not that we are assured that he will send us a good harvest or a great vintage. We should leave that in his hands, and patiently await what pleases him. When we have any illness, we must rest well assured that he has not forgotten us, and that we have such access to him that, in the end, we will feel that he has looked on us in pity. The promise of God should be fully sufficient in regard to that. However, when we would like to have the word that today or tomorrow he will restore our health, we do not know – we are even in doubt of living or dying.

Therefore, when Joab said that the Lord would do what seemed good to him, it was not that he was failing to wait upon God to uphold his people in the end, and maintain this good cause of which he had spoken. But he did not know whether God would like to humble him for a time, and if he would like him to be defeated by his enemies; to lose instead of winning. He could not be certain about that, for he had no special promise about it. We see, therefore, that Joab's uncertainty was not lack of faith, for we can certainly doubt, although we embrace the promises of God and hold them as absolutely certain and infallible. What we doubt are the things which are not clear to us. That is how he wants us to remain in suspense about many things and to leave it all to his secret counsel and his providence.

Now that, in sum, is what we have to remember in this passage. In the first place, let us learn to strengthen ourselves in God when we see the wicked acting like people in a frenzy, throwing themselves about haphazardly with reckless blindness. Let us be ashamed not to be at least as brave as they are when we are doing our duty, and we shall be able in good conscience to declare before God and men that what we are doing is because of our duty, not out of temper, and that we shall persevere to the very end in our duty. Above all, let us have this attitude so that our undertakings will be for the common good of the people. On the other hand, let us see to it that God is honoured and served and that religion is retained in its pure simplicity. When we see to that, let us not doubt that God wants to maintain his cause, as much for his service as also for the common good. For we know that it is he who has ordained the forces of authority in this world, and that all order depends on his providence. When we ask to be maintained and kept in the state where he has placed us, let us bravely uphold this position against all doubts and objections and obstacles which could hinder us. And also, when it comes to battling for the name of God and for his honour, let us never be dismayed when we see that all the world is against us; on the contrary, let us be strengthened.

Moreover, the main thing is that we have our refuge in him, for here is what the victory depends on, namely, that he be on our side, for we have no other glory except to say: 'If God be for us who can be against us?' (Rom. 8:31). We see how David shows us an example of this: 'I shall not fear when all the armies of the world have besieged me, as long as God be for me' (Psa. 3:6). 'The staff of my God,' he says, 'will comfort me in the dark shadow of death' (Psa. 23:4). When I know that he is my shepherd, and that he will take my side, then shall there be 'anyone who can make me afraid'? Now that is what we should have in mind when we have carefully considered if the cause we are maintaining is good and just, granted that we are not so presumptuous as to say: 'By my prudence and by my virtue I shall successfully reach the goal'. Let us be careful of such a sacrilege, because God well knows how to repay us the wages we have merited, and we will remain confused, even in a good cause, if we have not honoured him and rendered him the right which belongs to him.

Moreover, when we do attribute this praise to him, that it is his to govern and not ours, let us afterwards pray to him, for faith is not slothful speculation. Many will confess with the tongue that God will govern and be for us, but yet they will never address themselves to him. Those kinds of words vanish in the air and wander aimlessly! But when we are convinced that it is up to God to govern, and that all that we can do amounts to nothing unless he chooses to bless it, then let us also learn to pray to him and to worship him, confessing that we hold everything from him, and then let us wait on him also for the victory. Moreover, although we are not assured that we will live today or tomorrow, whether we will win a victory, whether we will overcome our enemies, whether we will prosper in all our affairs but, instead, are in doubt and perplexity concerning what God wants to do for one day or one month – still let us not fail to carry on, no matter what. Let us say: 'Let the Lord do what will seem good to him' (2 Sam. 10:12). For this means that Joab was disposed to die as well as to live.

Therefore, when we have a good cause, let us be ready to march forward and to lose our life in it if it pleases God. If we decide in our hearts that we have absolute certainty concerning the outcome, we will be acting presumptuously if we do not have a completely clear and distinct promise. As I have said, there is no special promise either in this place or in any other. Well, what then? We must await whatever outcome is pleasing to God. If we were thoroughly assured of gaining everything, and things would come to us as we wished, it would be no great virtue in us to gain the victory. But when it comes to risking ourselves so that we must hold our life in our hands in order to offer it to God as a sacrifice, when death shows itself over against us, and yet we do not swerve and do not use our frailty as an excuse – now it is there that virtue is displayed. Let us carefully note that when we have taken on a good cause in the service of God, even if we have many hindrances, we must not, for all that, fail and lose courage, but persevere with unconquerable faithfulness.

This doctrine should be carefully practised today, for if we did not follow it, we would already have been confounded a thousand times, seeing that our Lord has chosen to afflict his own in many places. For example, here are some poor folk who have had their throats cut; so many horrible and bloody butcheries are happening, and many outrages are carried out – because of tyranny and cruelty. Afterwards, poor believers are driven from their houses. Again, there are many who have escaped with their life, yet nevertheless have their possessions stolen. Their wives and children become poor vagabonds, fleeing here and there, always in danger, like birds hidden under the branch. Thus, when we see such changes, it is certain that because of our weakness, we could drop everything and despise God, and think that it would be foolish to carry on further. For instance, we have seen even among the pagans someone who was esteemed more heroic than anyone else. However, when he came face to face with death, because he had upheld the liberty of the people, but had had nothing further in mind, suddenly he trampled his great virtue underfoot when he saw that things were not turning out as he wished. His heroism was nothing but a mockery; it was only an illusion, and all those who were deceived by it have nothing but wasted time for their pains. Because of this, he was very angry and vomited out blasphemy. Now this was the fruit of his unbelief, for when he did not consider anything higher than human wisdom, God put a stop to his chatter and confounded him. Well, on our part, as I have said, let us learn to trust in God, and although we must face many adversities and troublesome things, let us continue, nevertheless, and wait for what will please God.

It is true that our conclusion should certainly be that he will guide his Church. But this is not to say that he will guard it in the way that we might imagine. It is often necessary that he raise the dead; it is necessary that he 'create a new people' (Psa. 102:18), as the Psalm says. That is, he must maintain his Church in such a way that it seems that it must become a new creation (2 Cor. 5:17). When it appears that all is lost and in despair, what he can do is like a restoration and when he puts things back in good order, it is as if he had created a world in order to reshape it. Hence, let us learn to strengthen ourselves in such a way that when God does not want to please us in all our wishes, but permits us to receive blows from the rod, and we seem to be poor people, scattered and totally abused – even when this happens, let us not fail to hope in him. May this hope console us, so that we may ever continue our journey, even when we are unable to move either our arms or legs; may our heart show its vigour, enabling us to carry out our duty in such extremities. Now that is how we must practise today this doctrine that our Lord will do what seems good to him.

We see that even when David was driven from his kingdom, he returned to this when he had terrible troubles: 'The Lord will do concerning me what will seem good to him' (2 Sam. 15:26). 'And if it pleases him for me to be king, he certainly knows how to maintain my position. Let him deal with me as with one of his creatures.' When he spoke in this way, he was not like a man in despair, but on the contrary he was clearly trusting in God, although his human circumstances had been severely disturbed. Hence, no matter what our external conditions may be, let us always keep our minds on this conclusion, that God in the end will have pity on us as on the whole body of his Church. Nevertheless, let us allow him to dispose events differently from what we think should happen, and let us not be so heated in our feelings that we are angered when things happen contrary to our desires. Or let us not be lazy, and let us not lose control, as many people do when they fail to see the progress that they had imagined. They know how to withdraw themselves easily and to pucker their lips, pretending that they do not know what is the matter. Well, so as not to be so fickle, we must practise in every circumstance what is said here – that the Lord will do what seems good to him. Now that is the content of this passage.

Well, next it says that 'the Syrians fled before Joab' and that the Amorites, seeing their soldiers (who were costing them dearly) fleeing, 'they retreated to the city' (2 Sam. 10:13–14). Joab and Abishai did not pursue the Syrians, but it says that they returned to Jerusalem. Now this is a testimony that God was merciful to David, and since he justly took up arms, God also assisted him. Yet his enemies were vanquished in such a way that, soon after, the Syrians returned with an even greater force (2 Sam. 10:15ff.). Hence, one could say that it was Joab's fault, in that he should have pursued his victory and not have returned so soon to Jerusalem. But if we consider the outcome, Joab's moderation was blessed by God. For it became an occasion of even greater victory to David, and God made the whole affair profitable. It is the same when he desires us to endure a hard situation for a time, but in the end makes us feel that it was good and useful for us, so much so that we would not desire to have had the whole matter go according to our wishes, inasmuch as God has given us far more than we had been able to think (Eph. 3:20). Now that is how he takes care of us.

Nevertheless, we are warned that when God has helped us once, it does not mean that we can remain in perpetual repose! What is said here about a people must be applied to each one personally. When God has extended his hand to us in order to help us in need – although there was no defeated army involved, but rather, in one way or another, he has shown that he cares for our salvation – still let us not believe that we are relieved for ever. Let us not foolishly think that from here on it is only a question of our rejoicing and winning triumphs – for that kind of thinking will deceive us. When men promise themselves this and that, one must not be surprised if they do not get what they wanted. Why? Because when we boast to ourselves about reaching some goal by our wisdom, since we have invented some method in our head, we will be cast down and frustrated in our attempt, and rightly so. Now that is how we must think of ourselves, so that we are prepared to return to battle anew when God once delivers us from this or that conflict. Let us realise that it is only a delay, so that we might have the leisure to refresh ourselves, so to speak, and take courage to enable us always to march on forward. Here again is what we have to observe concerning the statement here, that the Syrians fled.

Now afterwards, there was fear in Jerusalem because 'the enemies re-assembled' in greater power than before (2 Sam. 10:15). The constancy of David was the cause of an even greater victory, as we have said. Yet we must learn not to be annoyed when it pleases God to spare enemies and those who trouble us. Why? It is nothing new. Let us notice what has happened to all children of God since the beginning.

Moreover, when it says that 'Hadarezer brought into his hire the Syrians who were beyond the River' (2 Sam. 10:16), it seems at first sight to be a contradiction. As we said yesterday, the Ammonites had hired those who were between the rivers, that is, the Tigris and the Euphrates. So how is it now said that Hadarezer hired people from Syria? Well, this word used here means many regions, so much so that often this province of Syria includes even a part of Cilicia, and then goes beyond the Tigris. Now without going into a long disputation, the question can be readily solved: although formerly there were Syrians in Mesopotamia, as we call it, yet there was no great quantity of them, but several came out from among the neighbouring Syrians. In fact, Hadarezer, who is spoken of here, was the one who had already been vanquished by David – or his son, who had the same name. He had hired that nation, which was not beyond the Euphrates but near the country of Judaea. Hence, one must not be surprised that he had drawn in people from beyond the river.

What is more, when it says that he had hired people, they must not be understood as his subjects, for that would not have been necessary. For when the Scripture says 'to hire people', it means that they are foreigners. It does not say that David had hired any besides his subjects, but here Hadarezer went overboard. Although there were many kingdoms under his authority and control, yet it did not include this country mentioned here. We see, therefore, the solution quite clearly. That is, formerly only the subjects of Hadarezer had fought for the Ammonites. But now having seen his own weakness, he went further and massed together people from every side – indeed, from places that were not under his hand or empire.

'Then when David had assembled all Israel, and having passed over Jordan, he came' against Hadarezer and against Shobech, his captain, 'and defeated them; indeed he even defeated seven hundred chariots and forty thousand' men. It says: 'forty thousand horsemen' (2 Sam. 10:17–18). Now there seems to be a great contradiction here, because in the First Book of Chronicles, it says that he defeated 7,000 chariots – in other words, thousands instead of hundreds, and then instead of horsemen, it says footmen (1 Chron. 19:18).

Well, for one thing, when chariots are spoken of, we must note that the ancient mode of fighting was in chariots. It would be very strange to us today for a man to be mounted on a chariot in order to fight his enemies! But still that was the custom as we see in the histories. Indeed, they had chariots with great blades attached, which would turn so powerfully that they were as effective as artillery. For a man in his chariot was like a thunderbolt, and then there were these blades which cut whatever they could touch. Therefore, such chariots could rout an army. Similarly today, we do not have elephants with which to wage battles, but they were a great strength in olden times. That is one point.

But the difficulty is still not solved, for it is far from being seven hundred or 7,000. Seven thousand chariots is an extravagant number for those times. We must therefore accept this, that in reality there were seven hundred chariots, but that they were in such array that it was like 7,000, which were the most excellent means of attack in battle, since they had the prowess to throw themselves forward, like a thunderbolt, to defeat their enemies.

As far as 'horsemen' or footmen are concerned, one assumes that what is said in one place refers to the other. Therefore, when horsemen are spoken of on the one hand here, and footmen on the other, one accepts that in reality there were 40,000 footmen defeated, and 40,000 horsemen. Now this is a very large multitude of horses and it would be extremely difficult to assemble such a number today or to find food enough to feed so many horses. But we must discern between the people of that country and ourselves, and even between the animals. For the Turks could certainly bring 30,000 or 40,000 horses in their army – which all the princes of Europe would have the greatest difficulty knowing how to do. Why? Because men need much food and so do horses. Well, one does not have to have either hay or oats for the horses of those countries. Their men are content to sleep on a hard place with little food. Stables are not necessary for their horses, but the horses of our countries are more delicate than the men! Hence, there could certainly have been 40,000 horsemen, and as many footmen. Be that as it may, if there was such a defeat, and there were so many horsemen and so many footmen, even if we are allowed to reduce the numbers by shifting some words, still the defeat was great. We cannot resolve the question. But that is not where we should stop – with the number of people and the diversity of certain words.

To what, therefore, must we pay attention? This is what the Holy Spirit wanted here: on the one hand, to show the affliction of David, and what a multitude of enemies had besieged him, and then what cause he had to magnify the goodness of God for giving him such an excellent victory. Even if David had defeated only seven hundred chariots – which, in fact, were like

7,000 with their equipment and all the accessories of the horsemen who were around – it was a great deal. If he had defeated even 40,000 men, whether on foot or horse, it was a great number. If we do not double the number in order to make 40,000 men on horse and 40,000 men on foot, but only take 40,000 men on foot, then we take a part for the whole, as if it were said: as many men as horses; or: 40,000 horsemen, but that includes as many horses as footmen. Now this is the most likely and if we take it this way, we can learn valuable lessons. For on the one hand, we see how viciously David was assailed. Certainly it would have frightened him to see that there was such a great multitude of chariots and footmen and horsemen. On the other hand, when we see how wonderfully God helped David, we must deeply contemplate his invincible force, so that we might trust in it when we are in such anguish as David experienced.

There is no doubt that he practised then what the Psalm says: 'Some trust in their chariots and horses' but I call upon God in my tribulation (Psa. 20:7). Since he once said that, there is no doubt that he exercised himself in such meditation. And when he saw the chariots and horses ready to swallow up everything, he was well aware that he always had recourse to God and recognised that all his power lay in God. That is why, in the other passage, he says (based on what he had experienced) that the king will not be saved in war by his horses or by his force, but salvation must come from God (Psa. 33:16–17).

Hence, when we are assailed with great temptations, when we are seized by death, let us realise that God is powerful enough for our salvation, and if it pleases him to employ his own power, he will preserve us, as he did his servant David. He will do it insofar as we do not hinder it from our coming to our side, as Isaiah says: for there is no doubt that we hinder the arm of God and stop his ears by our iniquities (Isa. 59:1–2). And we put, as it were, a bar between him and us when instead of walking where he has told us, we behave like wandering animals, turning our backs on him and going far from him. Therefore, as long as our rebellion does not prevent God's goodness and mercy from flowing down, we will feel that what is recounted here belongs to us, and is a personal testimony to us that there is no force so terrible in this world, which God cannot break and destroy when it pleases him to save his children. Now that is the main thing which we have to remember from this passage.

Although we cannot at all resolve how these 'forty thousand horses' and 40,000 footmen ought to be taken, still we must follow what is most likely, namely, that when footmen are spoken of, the whole army is included. It is as if it were said: As many footmen have been defeated as horsemen. For when the defeat of horsemen is spoken of, it must be understood that there were that many footmen, and when footmen are named, they imply as many horsemen.

Well, it says that the Syrians were so weakened that since that time 'they have not dared give aid to the Ammonites', but 'became tributaries of David' (2 Sam. 10:19). Also we see that David was content to have won peace and repose in his country. For he well knew that God wanted him to remain within his borders, and since God had assigned him his borders, which on that side were to be extended from the Euphrates to the Red Sea, he was content with it. It is true that he could surely have exterminated all the Syrians, but it was enough for him to render them tributary. Yet we see that God not only gave him victory against his enemies, but gave him peace more and more. When we do happen to win a battle – and a second and a third – nevertheless, our enemies will not cease to lift up their weapons. But it is a special blessing from God when he conquers them in such a way that they dare not take action any longer.

Well now, this is what David gained from having sent [the embassy] to King Hanun at the beginning (2 Sam. 10:2). Although he plotted against David and viciously insulted him and then sought occasion to ruin him, still God turned the evil to good and to his advantage. In giving him victory, he made him more and more secure, on the one hand, against the Syrians. For they restrained themselves, and if that had not been so, they might have been able to engineer another new war. Now see how they were abased – so much so that David remained in peace. He had occasion to hope more and more in the goodness of God and to strengthen himself in him, after God had thus tested him in so many battles – for the whole affair had turned out to his profit. Then on the other hand, by this victory he also conquered the Ammonites. For because of this, they were forced to keep themselves quietly at home, because they needed foreign help and could not obtain it. Now that is how God took care of David.

This is written for us so that we might know that God is able to break enemies' heads and put them in confusion when it pleases him. However, in order to humble us, he often wants us to realise that we are nothing but cowards, and instead of encouraging us, he will terrify us before our enemies. Even so, when we are conquered, our reaction is not the same as unbelievers' reactions when it pleases God to render us victorious over them. For he will astonish them in such a way that they will tremble before we even touch them, and they will remain so humbled that they will be without any strength. That is how he often protects us, and although it seems that our enemies are able to do wonders and carry out all their undertakings, nevertheless they will remain confounded. Moreover, when God removes our strength, let us realise that when he does this occasionally, it is so that we might remain constant and adore his counsel. So although we see so many revolutions today, let us go back to this, that just as he has upheld his own in all ages, we must conclude that he will do so to the end.

Now let us prostrate ourselves before the majesty of our good God in recognition of all our faults; praying him that more and more he will give us the grace to be stripped of all our carnal affections so that we might be reclothed in his justice and fight – both within and without – against the devil and against his deputies, and against our own evil desires, so that the praise of all our victories might be given to him. And recognising that he is the Protector of his Church, let us wait upon him all the more in true trust and give him thanks throughout our whole life. And may he not only bestow this grace upon us, but upon all people and nations of the earth . . .

32

*David's Adultery with Bathsheba**

> *When the year was over, at the time when kings go out to battle, David sent Joab and his servants with him and all Israel, and destroyed the children of Ammon, and besieged Rabbah, and David remained in Jerusalem. It happened that during the evening David rose from off his bed . . .* (2 Sam. 11:1–5a).

Now here is a story which should make our hair stand straight up on end whenever we think of it – that a servant of God as excellent as David should fall into such a serious and enormous sin that he could be judged as the most morally lax and promiscuous person in the world. For it would be extremely difficult to find anyone anywhere among the tyrants, or among those who have been the most desperate of all, committing such an excessive crime as David, who thus put himself in the class of monster! For here was David, who was the king, and consequently ought to have been the soul of the Law in order to give it force. He should have maintained control so that each person could enjoy his own possessions. He should have been the protector of chastity in order to preserve marriages. He should have maintained the life of his subjects. He should have prevented anyone from committing any violence or extortion. That is one point.

Nevertheless, did he have an excuse for desiring the wife of someone else? Well, he had more than a dozen excuses, indicating how much he had forgotten himself! For we know the order which God has established, which should be inviolable:

*Wednesday, August 12, 1562.

'It is not good for the man to be alone; let us make a help suitable for him' (Gen. 2:18). He did not say: 'Let us make him two or three'! Indeed, David was not content with a dozen wives, but took up to eighteen and then, in addition to that, he showed himself worse than brutal when he ravished the wife of someone else, polluted holy marriage, and even engaged in the act of thievery – he who (as I have already mentioned) should have preserved the Law in its integrity. Yet all of that happened to him.

But this was still not all. For David sought to cover up his adultery out of shame before men, without any scruples, or untouched by any remorse. He paid no attention to God. He considered neither him nor his angels. He was acting like a sheer brute; however, he sought to cover his corruption before men by his hypocrisy. Well, not being able to do so, he had the poor husband killed – the very man who was so faithful. For who kept the whoredom of David and his stinking filth from being covered up? None other than Uriah, who was so faithful to him that he even abstained from his own wife when it came to risking his life for the king. That should have made David's heart bow and break, even if it were harder than a stone. Well, still he went on to commit this sin, which was far more wicked and detestable; that is, he procured the death of this man to whom he was indebted all the way. And not only that, but he placed the whole people of God in danger – so much so that it caused a horrible defeat, as events turned out. However, God did soften his wrath and vengeance a little. Be that as it may, there were a multitude of poor men who perished because David ordered Uriah to be put in the front line.

Well, having done all of that, he merely wiped his mouth – so hardened had he become in his evil, as though he was possessed by the devil. Even when the prophet came to him and set before him, in parable form, the deed which he had done, he was quite able to pronounce the sentence of condemnation against others. Yet he spared himself, and felt that he had done nothing. He considered himself completely innocent. That is how blind he was. Is it possible to see a more dishonest cruelty?

When we see that this happened to such an excellent man, how will it be with us? Hence, we surely have reason to tremble and be stirred up to pray to God not to lead us into temptation (Matt. 6:13). For the most competent among us will very soon find himself surprised by temptation, and we have only to make one false step to draw down as many troubles on ourselves – just like when a poor sinner becomes thoroughly immersed in the very depths of hell, by taking up one vice which he becomes pleased with and then another, so much so that he becomes utterly stupid, and his conscience is deadened, so that he acts as if he had no more intelligence or reason, but had been transformed into a brute beast! Well, all of these things will be more clearly brought out in due course, but we had to give this as a preface, so that we might be prepared from the start to watch for instruction.

Now the repentance will come later. For if there had only been David's fall, it would certainly only serve to confuse us. For who in the world would be able to rely upon the grace of God if David, after having been elevated to such a degree of honour, had stumbled and God had never raised him back up? But we find that God still bestowed mercy upon him, not wanting him to perish, and that he brought him to repentance, accepting the confession that he made in all humility and with a true heart. Now in this (I say) we must recognise that although God for a time abandons his elect, indeed even to the extent of giving them the marks and sores of the reprobate, still he always has his eye upon them so as to draw them back. When he has humbled and abased them and made them feel their wretchedness, then he will show his mercy and overcome all their miseries. That will be the second part of the story, which will come in its proper place.

Let us begin with what is dealt with here: it says that 'it happened at the time when kings go forth to battle, that David sent' his captain-general 'Joab with his other troops' and officers 'and all Israel' (2 Sam. 11:1) – that is, chosen people and men of war. Thus, he made a great army. It does not mean that all the people went but that, as we have seen above, he recruited enough men from all the cities of Israel to make a great host. Hence, this was a very large number of people going forth. Yet David remained in his house at rest.

Now it is not without cause that this expression is used, that 'kings used to go forth then'. It is not said merely of war, and indeed may very well imply even more. For kings were accustomed to travelling here and there as governors of their countries, to render justice to everyone so that subjects would not always have to be bothered with going to a certain place – or making long journeys at great cost and expense. Indeed, if anyone looks into what they used to do in those days, they will find that it was not more than three or four hundred years ago that kings and princes corrupted this duty and used it as an occasion to come and go from one region to another. And what was the reason for this? In order to devour the poor, instead of visiting and remedying the needs of the country, as they had done in the past. For although the country's needs are reported to an officer of the king, still the king himself cannot feel personally the ills which he should remedy, without being there on the spot. Besides, the subjects must always come to air their grievances and quarrels. But when the prince does not budge, sitting there like a great block of wood, is that not making a pure mockery of and detracting from the honour of God and their subjects? Must everyone in that case leave his house at great expense and trouble in order to come to seek the peace and justice which belong to them? Is it not contrary to all reason and sense of equity? For princes are not made for themselves, neither to lull themselves to sleep in their luxuries and lusts, but for the common good of the people. It is, therefore, an honourable service when it is carried out according to the institution of God.

Hence, this circumstance was put here in order to show that David did not carry out his duty. By thus sparing himself and staying in his house in order to be at his ease, he threw himself into the net of Satan, and one evil fed on another. Therefore, since David was condemned here by the Holy Spirit, bringing shame both on himself and on his people, let us learn to apply it to ourselves – each one in his own particular calling of God. Let us not seek ease and luxury for ourselves, nor seek to soak it up and surround ourselves with it, but let each one apply himself to working faithfully (I say) and putting his hand to the task. David was king, but on what condition? Did he not have to recognise his obligations towards the people?

Nevertheless, he sent his people to war. If one says that a king or a prince is bound always to go to war in person, it is true. But let us carefully consider the words which are included here: 'Kings go forth, and David remained in his house' (2 Sam. 11:1). By that we are shown that since he was neither sick nor hindered by other affairs, he did not carry out the charge which was committed to him, thus giving an opening to the devil. The temptation which came to him, then, was like a payment for his moral laxness. And because of his wanting too much relaxation, he did not think of what God had called him to, and of how much need there was in the country, which should have called him here and there – least of all did he think that the war which he was waging against the Ammonites certainly merited his being there. It was certainly legitimate for him to have sent his people there but nevertheless temptation overcame him so that he put his own people in danger. Now we know that a noble king will do much in his army, for everyone will apply themselves more when they see the head doing his duty. But here he was like a man relaxed and without any care. We see, therefore, how inexcusable it was, and that this expression is not redundant but shows that he remained lazily in his house, instead of superintending the country and valiantly fighting for the common good, and that he kept himself in the shadows, seeking only to enjoy his royal dignity without labour.

Now that, in sum, admonishes us to be prepared against the attacks of Satan, and not to give him access to us, for he knows only too well how to come in. We know how many means he has of engineering our ruin. Hence, even when we are on our guard, he will always make some brush to gain access to us. Thus, we must meditate all the more on this doctrine, in order to ward off his blows, and especially to avoid situations where we might throw ourselves into the net of Satan.

Next, it says that David arose during the evening, and seeing a woman who was bathing, enquired who she was. He finds that she is the wife of Uriah. Thereupon, he sends and makes her come to him and commits shame and adultery (2 Sam. 11:2–4), which was then the cause of much greater and more horrible confusion. Well, concerning his sleeping, he is not to be condemned as much as it would seem – though several who have not experienced the style of living as it was at that time have wanted to reprove David here for the great intemperance of sleeping after dinner. Well, they did not eat dinner. But such criticism is inappropriate, for the ancients only had one meal, and were accustomed to sleeping during the middle of the day, and then staying awake most of the night. Hence, we must not spend much time on that. So when it says that 'he arose in the evening', it was in accordance with the general custom, even of those who were very sober – and who were not like many people today who do not know what it is to live without eating and drinking and sleeping.

Now it says that he was walking on the roof in the manner of that country, for there were platforms on the housetops, and their houses were not like ours. This custom remains there even today. Roofs are like towers, and even in the Law of God, it is expressly commanded that there be barriers, so that no-one will fall off (Deut. 22:8). Now that is why there is no difficulty with this walking on the roof.

Then David 'gazes on this woman whom he sees bathing'. We do not know whether it was by necessity or otherwise. For the manner of bathing then was fairly general, and if one condemns Bathsheba for bathing, what will it be with Susannah, of whom we read the same (Sus. 5:15, Apocrypha)? We must not, therefore, invent vices in order to condemn someone else. But let us weigh what is good or bad in the scales of God, and not of our own fantasy. Now in regard to Bathsheba, she is not to be condemned because she bathed. But she should have exercised discretion, so as not to be seen. For a chaste and upright woman will not show herself in such a way as to allure men, nor be like a net of the devil to 'start a fire'. Bathsheba, therefore, was immodest in that regard. This can certainly happen to those who are otherwise on their guard, as we read of Isaac (Gen. 26:8), who would never have thought that the king of the Philistines had observed him with Rebecca. Nevertheless, when he was privately with his wife, the king looked at him. Hence, we see that the most modest and temperate can often be surprised. Again, this ought to instruct us to remain on our guard. For if those who do not undress, and neither act nor look immodestly, sometimes fall by being off their guard, what will it be with those who act licentiously? Now that is what we have to note about this point.

Well, it says that David enquired who this woman was, and when they replied that she was the wife of Uriah, he sent to fetch her. Here we see that the sin of David was aggravated by his sending for her, after enquiring who she was, as if he were nourishing this wicked desire which had come to him, instead of resisting it, as he should have done. If David had encountered this woman and had been surprised into committing this act of wickedness and villainy, he would have had some excuse. But since he was far from her, and it was not a question of his talking in order to induce and solicit her to adultery, and he had to do it by an intermediary, there were plenty of reasons to have mortified that wicked desire which he had conceived. Even though he had immodestly gazed upon her, still he could have immediately rebuked himself and prayed to God. Even if all that he felt was shame, David could have thought: 'What? If I do this, I will show myself to be wicked and insolent for wanting to abuse another man's wife.' Therefore, both the time and the other hindrances should have hindered him from accomplishing this evil desire. All of that (I say) ought to have served as a remedy for him. Hence, his enquiring who she was made this crime all the more enormous. For he had already cast his eye on this woman, and had been touched by a wicked desire. Therefore, this sin is already 'conceived' in him, as St James describes it (Jas. 1:15). If he had done nothing more than feel this wicked desire to enjoy that woman, he still did too much. But not content with having offended God in one way, he went on to light the fire in order to arouse himself all the more, and thus doubled his evil.

Well, this warns us that when we feel tempted and inclined to some vice, we must immediately control ourselves and keep Satan from entering any further to take possession of us. Let us, therefore, be careful not to kindle an evil fire, but rather let us listen to the admonition of St Paul to Timothy: 'Kindle the grace of God' (2 Tim. 1:6). He used this picture, which means: to make the favours which he has received prevail. He calls that 'to kindle the fire'. Why? Because when God plants in us some little drop of his grace, if we are too lazy and negligent to make it prevail, it is just as if we were totally extinguishing this drop of purity. We must, therefore, put it into operation. It is like a fire which is ready to go out being rekindled, so that it may once more burst into flame and keep burning. Indeed, this is sufficiently often referred to in the Scriptures – that to extinguish the grace of God is like putting out the fire. But when we possess one single spark of the grace of God, we must immediately be filled with a true zeal and ardour so that this fire will not go out. Let us be careful, therefore, not to put it out by our carelessness, but let us protect it by prayers and petitions, and also seek to kindle it. That is, when we have some evil thought, let us not nourish it until our heart is finally set on fire, so that we go on to carry it out as well as merely thinking it. Nor let us encourage ourselves in a perverse desire and mix it in with another vicious thought that we already have. So this is what we must consider when we see that David enquired who this woman was.

With that in mind, let us remember that if we are in the process of doing evil, we must immediately break it off and turn our back on it and remove ourselves from every opportunity that we may have to conceive and carry out the evil which we have premeditated. This is our all too frequent experience every day. To go beyond David, what causes men to abandon themselves to evil like this? Well, it is because they do not resist evil when it initially approaches them, but excuse and flatter themselves, as though they wanted to draw Satan to themselves and to plot together with him, saying in effect: 'I have made a breach for you. Enter boldly and fear not.' They will actually extend him their hand to help him overcome them! In fact, if we were not so perverted that we willingly desire to be led into evil, and to try to make a larger opening for the devil, we would certainly be preserved, and would be completely victorious against all the assaults that Satan makes on us, for he never ceases trying to enter our lives to take possession of us. But we are too much like David in this matter – so if the devil has, as it were, perverted our ears to evil, we seek to go even further. We seek these occasions ourselves, and put the rope around our necks in order to hang ourselves in the end.

When it says that they told him it was the wife of Uriah (2 Sam. 11:3), he should certainly have been touched at the very least. Although the devil had seduced him, still this information should have served as a restraint to rebuke him, and even to cause him to hate, from the bottom of his heart, this wicked desire in which he was already entangled. For Uriah was not unknown to him, as we can gather. He definitely knew that he was a man who was working in his service. Well, mere humanity (even if he had had no regard for God) ought to have led him to this conclusion. We see many people who are adulterous and dissolute, yet who still have enough honesty left in them not to want to do wrong to a friend whom they respect. But David did wrong to Uriah, who was his friend. And indeed, he should have considered: 'Here is a man who is risking his life for me. Should I now go and ravish his wife, and dishonour her; should I plan such a vicious deed; should I be a traitor to him who is so faithful to me; and should I rob him of his honour?' If David had had a drop of kindness in him, it is certain that these considerations would have held him back. But we see how, for a time, the fear of God was blotted out in him, and eventually all other virtues – so he acted like a man with no sense. He continued to carry out the government of the kingdom, but even so, brute beasts would have behaved better than this poor wretched creature!

Concerning this matter, we must realise how great are the illusions of the devil. For though there may be every reason in the world to keep us from doing evil, still in spite of them all, our eyes are covered over by our wicked desires. We may go through rivers, mountains, and forests, but all along the way we will find the devil's net spread out to catch us – absolutely nothing will prevent him from corrupting us more and more. Hence, we need to pray to God that he might not permit us to be entangled in wicked desires, and might speedily relieve us, give us some sparkle of purity, and eyes to see the ambushes and ditches which are around us, and that he might not permit us to be blind when the sun is shining. For (as I have already mentioned) it is certain that if (as nature itself teaches us) kindness were rooted in us, we would put underfoot many of the wicked desires and appetites which overtake us. It would only take a simple rebuke to make us view with horror not only what we have actually undertaken and what we have pushed ourselves into, but even what we have conceived in our secret thought. Yet when we see that our weakness invites us to do evil, let us come to recognise those things which in the past have corrupted us, so that we will hate them and seek the remedy in the sheer mercy of God. Hence, let us learn to be very careful to let reason rule and have our eyes open to every warning, so that we will pray to God not to permit us to have our eyes bandaged over so that nothing profits us – which is what we see happening to David. For the very name of Uriah should have broken up all these evil desires, although he was already too enmeshed in it. But it made no difference to him – he sent for her.

Now here David went a step deeper into evil, for he not only offended God, but drew his own servants into the same guilt, so that he was guilty not only for his own sin, but also for the sin of those whom he used as pimps. Nevertheless, we see how the courts of princes are always full of this filth and infection, as if they were public whore-houses. There are always plenty of whoremongers who are so utterly licentious that they make a trade and business of it, as they say. For if the servants of David had been what they ought to have been, it is certain that they would have resisted their master, and immediately told him how terribly pernicious this thing was, and that he was losing control of himself. But here they were, quite prepared for what he commanded them – that is, to seduce the wife of someone else, and to draw her into such perdition that she would have been finally lost if God had not ultimately had mercy on her.

Although David protested in the Psalm that he would purge his house of all filth (Psa. 101), yet what a terrible cheat he became, even to being the leader of a pack of villains! But notice, as always, how it happens that when a prince is not very careful to preserve his house in integrity, the devil will soon completely take over every part of it. It is true that even when the prince attempts to regulate his household, and tries with all his might to run it properly, he will never be able to prevent the existence of all kinds of corruption. Be that as it may, even though David would have claimed that he was trying hard to do so, he did not completely carry it out, and was not able to prevent vice from being present. Well, even if he had not spoken hypocritically, and had actually had a firm will and sincere desire to keep his house pure, we still see that men try hard, with all their strength, to avoid any opportunity for wickedness, even though they cannot manage to do so. That is one point.

Nevertheless, let us carefully note that when – in order to carry out our wicked desires – we invent this or that to help us, iniquity is always being doubled and reaching its fullness, for with all of that in us, we will draw souls into perdition. If one man cuts another one's throat, does he not deserve a great punishment? But when he corrupts another person by his wicked greed, and offends God by his behaviour, is he not placing in perdition his own soul, which ought to be more precious than his body? Yet that is what happened to David! Hence, we see that if God had dealt with him severely, he would have had to render account not only for himself, but for those whom he had used, by whom his house was soiled. It was exactly the same as if he had made it a den of thieves and a nasty, filthy, bawdy house which would drive God entirely away. Now that is what else we have to remember from this passage.

Well, it happened that when Bathsheba was brought to David, 'he slept with her' (2 Sam. 11:4), as the Scripture simply says, in order to hide what is wicked. For in fact, we should consider adultery to be such an abomination that we would actually be so honourable as not even to pronounce what ought not to enter our minds. When the relationship of man and woman is spoken of, the Scripture says 'they have slept'. It is certain that the Scripture means to specify something else. But this is also to show us what St Paul says, so that we would imitate him: 'Brethren, let adultery and all other uncleanness not even be named among you' (Eph. 5:3). Not that this term does not have its place, and must certainly be used at the right time and place, but (as I have said) St Paul wants to draw us to this kind of modesty and sobriety, so that we will not allow ourselves to become shameless. For instance, when people speak of the relationship of a man and woman (as I have said), and discuss it publicly (just like many people who go too far in this matter), they are taking licence in what they say – which means that people will cease to feel shame, and will easily excuse themselves at every turn. Therefore, we must surely maintain this manner of speech, and be aware that God wants to keep a bridle on our tongue, to accustom us to complete chastity, with the result that we are not shameless and dissolute when it comes to speaking of something or other.

Finally, it says that 'the woman was cleansed from her impurity and returned to her house' (2 Sam. 11:4). Well, these words show us that men have always had some discretion between good and evil engraved in their hearts. That (I say) is found even among the Jews and, indeed, among the pagans, who have not been able to ignore the fact that they have a natural ability to judge that fornication, thievery, murder, and all other vices are contrary to good, and yet have had enough of these things within themselves to be condemned. This is what St Paul is saying, that no-one should be surprised if everyone is subject to condemnation. For those who do not have the written Law will not fail (he says) to be their own judges (Rom. 2:14–15). Why? Because though they want to sleep in their self-flattery, their conscience summons them before God. Then if they have done evil, they must come to account for it, and they will feel inner pricks and remorse over it. However, if they have done well, they will live in peace. Therefore, since the pagans, who have never heard a word of the Law, experience such remorse, we do not find it strange if Bathsheba was convicted of her evil after she had committed adultery with David.

Nevertheless, how did she get rid of her guilt? 'She purged herself from her impurity.' There is no doubt that this was meant to be understood of the sprinkling which was done after someone had been soiled by some sin which they had committed. God ordained this ceremony, not to enable people to acquit themselves by a simple ritual and then consider themselves absolved, but rather to lead them to repentance. For when a person had some blemish in himself, he needed to seek to be purified and he needed to know how, why, and to what end. That was why he was then, as it were, taught by God to recognise his own poverty so as to say: 'Here am I, a poor dirty creature, and now I am seeking the remedy, as God has been pleased to show me'.

Now that is what should have come into the minds of all who were purging themselves of every blemish. For when they were coming to appear in the temple to cleanse themselves, they were confessing their sins as if they had appeared before God. Nevertheless, could water wash and purge souls? We know very well that such is not the case. Hence it was given, as I have said, to 'prod' men so that in true repentance they would have recourse to the mercy of God, and thus ask his forgiveness for their sins. Now that is what this ceremony was leading to, though when it says that Bathsheba purified herself, in what sense was her purification real? It was nothing but a shadow, full of hypocrisy. The very fact that she felt that she was guilty before God was in itself a good beginning. But she did not continue, she remained in mid-stream. She thought that she had been properly absolved when she sprinkled herself as required by the Law, but she only considered the external appearance.

Well, from all that, we must remember that when we have offended God, we are to begin examining ourselves, and feel that we are really polluted before both him and his angels, and hence we are to seek to purify ourselves – but not in a hypocritical fashion. We shall gain nothing if we wish to deceive God in this way. Instead, let us be displeased with ourselves – even to the point of hating the evil which we have committed – and then, in all humility, let us come and present ourselves as guilty before God, as wretched malefactors. Let us ask him to be pleased to cast his eye upon us – not to chastise us severely, as we deserve, but rather to deal with us as his children. May he bury the offences which we have committed, and may we keep him as our Father. Now this process shows us that the mercy of God is not intended to give us more boldness to do evil, but rather to keep us from it. Those who think that they are dealing with God, and yet indulge themselves in their transgressions, are casting themselves down willingly. For this is a clear mockery of God and shows contempt of his goodness, as though someone were wanting to have him for a companion and make him a participant in their iniquity. Let us, therefore, be humbled and groan over our sins, and let our evil be purged insofar as we have been touched to the quick with a true repentance. Furthermore, let us confess that we are worthy of being punished with such severity that the very depths of hell would be too good for us. Yet, being our own judges, and able to condemn ourselves (1 Cor. 11:31), let us not fail to hope that he will be kind and gentle to us, and let us not doubt that he will turn away his anger and fury from us in order to embrace us as his children.

Now let us prostrate ourselves before the majesty of our good God in recognition of the infinite faults of which we are guilty, and which we should keenly feel within ourselves. Let us pray to him that he will be pleased to bestow on us the treasures of his goodness, and that he will not permit us to perish in our poverty, but that he will keep us back from it. And may this serve to force us to glorify his holy name, just as we formerly caused it to be blasphemed. Hence, we shall all say: God Almighty, heavenly Father . . .

33

*Uriah, a Man who Feared God**

The woman, having conceived, sent a messenger to David, saying: I am with child. Then David sent to Joab, saying: Send to me Uriah the Hittite. And Joab sent Uriah to David. So Uriah came to David and David questioned him, how Joab fared, how the people fared, as also how the battle was proceeding. . . .(2 Sam. 11:5–13).

We saw yesterday how David was corrupted, through a single look, into desiring the wife of someone else – which clearly shows us how we need to pray that God would turn our eyes from vanity (Psa. 119:37), for there is no doubt that it was this experience that taught David to make such a request. We saw, furthermore, how he added fuel to the fire of his own lust by enquiring who the woman was. Well, that has always served to kindle the flame. This again warns us to cut the cord very quickly when the devil tempts us to evil, and to get away, and not seek opportunities to fall into his nets. For since we are so fragile, and are unaware of our weakness, we can be suddenly taken by surprise.

Now we read that Bathsheba sent word to David, to tell him that she was pregnant, and then that David attempted to cover his corruption and his shame. But he merely 'covered himself with a wet sack', as they say. He sent word to Joab, his captain, for Uriah to come. Now he was counting on Uriah going down to his house and sleeping with his wife, and then thinking that she was pregnant by him. 'Well, the sin is safely buried', David

*Thursday, August 13, 1562.

thought. But God mocked such hypocrisy, and did not permit Uriah to go and sleep with his wife.

Here in the first place, we must note that we pay more attention to men than to God. When it comes to covering our wrong-doings, we deliberately turn away from the judgement of God, to keep from being terrified by it when we have offended him, rather than coming to account before him, in order to receive our condemnation. But it should make us tremble to know what the wrath of God is. If a king or a great prince is angry with his subjects, will they have any rest? By contrast, God barely pursues us, and we simply push back all our feelings and attempt to put our consciences to sleep when he wants to wake them up. And yet there is no other way of salvation but that. For until we have recognised our offences, with all humility, we must not hope to obtain pardon from God. Otherwise, he would have to renounce himself and his justice, and change his nature. Hence, a sinner cannot obtain pardon and be absolved before God until he has condemned himself (1 Cor. 11:31–32). We do the same thing as a terrified sick person who flees medicine, although it is good for him. For we like to put all suffering aside, and give ourselves a good time, so that when God calls us to repentance, we always seek some subterfuge.

Now if we are unable to avoid his judgement, in the end we attempt to make an escape, and flee like poor debtors, as they say. We may contemplate this reaction in David. For since he saw that God was calling him to repentance, he should immediately have been affected and have wished to appease the wrath of the eternal Judge. But it made no difference to him, and instead he applied his whole mind to covering up his shame before men. It is amazing how we are so dominated by ambition that we not only want to be valued by appearing virtuous, but also like to be publicly honoured. Thus, when we bring dishonour and shame upon ourselves by our own misbehaviour, we still want to cover it up, just as if we were fighting against God himself. So on the one hand, we have hypocrisy and on the other, ambition – both of which are vices and deadly plagues. The hypocrisy was that David was concerned about men but turned his back on God, and despised his majesty. How incredibly stupid he must have been to have done that. On the other hand, he always wanted to be highly esteemed and to maintain his reputation with men. But if that was the case, why did he lower himself to such vicious misbehaviour? Who but himself had ravished his honour, and yet he wanted to maintain it in spite of what he now was.

Well, we see that this attitude is commonly held by everyone. For (as I have said) instead of our trembling as we should when we have provoked God, it does not bother us nearly enough. It is true that we are affected for a time, but not to the very depths of our being. Besides, we quench, as much as we can, all the remorse that we feel and which could lead us to repentance. Now that is one point. But yet we fight to seem honourable at all times, to keep our reputation unblemished and unembarrassed before men. Yet it is our own misdeeds which accuse us; our trial is conducted by ourselves. Therefore, since we see how desperately inclined we are to these two vices, let us learn from David's example to go in the opposite direction. That is, let us lift our eyes above (as soon as we have done something wrong), not in pride and presumption, but so that we will be brought low, which is what God requires.

Further, let us learn to bear our shame before all the world, since we have merited it. And let us realise that we have gained nothing from all the many tricks and stratagems used to keep our will from being known, for God will always show it to us. Now here was David, who thought that he had found a good plan when he called Uriah, to make him sleep with his wife; but David was frustrated in his expectation. And who caused this? God, who was pursuing him. It is true that it was for his salvation. Now there are some illnesses in which sleep brings death. In those cases, the physician will annoy the poor patient terribly by pulling his nose and ears and pushing him on every side. Then the patient will be very angry and distressed over this, for he wants nothing but sleep. But to let him sleep (as I have said) would be to lose him. So it is with sinners who just try to flatter themselves and to put their conscience to sleep. For if God awakens them, not allowing them to be like animals, they become angry about it, even though it is for their own good.

Since God had procured the salvation of David, he wanted his shame to be known by everyone, and this was why he did not permit Uriah to go to sleep with his wife, and thus provide David's adultery with a cloak or covering. The same thing can happen to us, which is why David's experience should serve as an instructive example. We see by experience that those who seek to disguise or bury their evil deeds simply wear a hypocritical face. They double the evil, and thus make themselves all the more ridiculous by thinking that they have invented this or that in order to provide such hiding places where they will not be perceived by men. God, on the contrary, causes their actions to be even better known and to be held in greater mockery and shame than if, at first sight, they had frankly confessed their first transgression.

Well, from that we must note that God holds the hearts of men (Prov. 21:1) – for if Uriah had not been prevented by the secret counsel of God, one could not have presumed that a man would abstain from his wife. Indeed, he had been away from his house for a long time and had suffered much hardship in the war. And when he finally had the means to sleep at ease, and to be no longer on the hard ground, and in fact could visit his household and rejoice with his wife – knowing that he must return to the war – it does seem completely against nature for Uriah not to have wished to enter his house. In fact, it would not have happened, nor is it likely that he would have had such courage, if God had not provided it for him. Therefore, let us note carefully that at the very time when anyone would like to please us, God will so control their feelings that the opposite of what we thought will happen to us, and those whom we desired to have in our hands will resist us and take the contrary view. In sum, it is certain that when Uriah refused to go into his house, it was a just judgement of God on David, to lead him to recognise his sin. In the end, this served as medicine for him, as we shall see.

When David says: 'Enter your house and wash your feet' (2 Sam. 11:8), that was the common mode of speech at that time. For they walked around barefoot, so that after they had gone down the road, they used to wash their feet. This was normal, as we see in the example of Abraham (Gen. 18:4), and then also where St Paul speaks of women who 'have washed the saints' feet' (1 Tim. 5:10). That is to say, they have taken them in, given them kind treatment and have relieved them. Now that is one point.

When David saw that he was frustrated, because Uriah did not want to sleep with his wife, he racked his brain, seeking time to accomplish what he had failed to obtain by his first suggestion. He tried him again and called him. Previously, 'he had sent him a present to his house' (2 Sam. 11:8). Now 'he called him to his table' (2 Sam. 11:13). This already showed that God had unquestionably cast him down. By his own actions, David would show himself to be guilty, although he was trying to do the opposite. For sending a royal present would have seemed rather strange, and could have caused Uriah to feel some suspicion. In this, we see how God removes every vestige of prudence and discretion from those who live with a bad conscience.

Nevertheless, David's great perplexity shows us that even kings cannot flee the torment with which God pursues all those who have offended him. It is true that the princes of this world would certainly like everything to be legitimate for them. Indeed, tyrants have a proverb: 'Why should I not be permitted everything that enters my imagination?' Their royal dignity implies it, and such people think that other people's desire to subject them to justice and reason detracts from their dignity. They certainly manifest this kind of pride. Nevertheless, God knows exactly how to bring down their thoughts when he constrains them – whether they want to or not – to feel their offences, and to have no rest in their conscience, but rather to be in continual turmoil. No-one had accused David, but even while his sin was still unknown, he felt under pressure. Although he did not know exactly where he was in this matter, he began running in strange directions; first he would seek one way out, then another.

We see that when men are as blinded by hypocrisy as David, God does not fail to leave them, as it were, in fires of torment, and shows them that he is their Judge. When we despise the judgement of God, and when we want to conserve our good reputation before men, it is our just reward that God draws us, pulling us as with a rope, in the very opposite direction from where we want to go, and brings us by force into his judgement. Let us carefully note, therefore, that a bad conscience will always be accompanied by torment, anxiety and anguish – as it says, the wicked 'will flee when no man pursues him' (Lev. 26:17, 36). One of the curses which God has proclaimed in his Law is that the life of transgressors will be hanging like a thread, their eyes will be made hollow, and they will tremble day and night, not knowing whether they will live for another minute. Somewhere else it says, 'there is no peace to the wicked' (Isa. 48:22; 57:21). For although they harden themselves as much as they can, and put themselves to sleep like brute beasts, so stupid that they have no remorse which could draw them to God, in the end, God frightens them, so that wherever they look, they do not know where they are. Thus, if we wish to have true peace, let us have a good conscience, for that is where we should seek it. Furthermore, let us not hope to have peace when we flee the presence of God, and especially when we attempt to abolish his justice. Instead, let us practise the doctrine of St Paul, to 'have peace with God' (Rom. 5:1). Now the wicked, at times, certainly experience a deadness to the disturbing pain of guilt, because they are not thinking about themselves, but this 'peace' is not lasting, as we have shown. And the reason? Because instead of presenting themselves before God, they go further from him. Therefore, to have permanent peace, let us be careful to present ourselves before him, and deeply examine our conscience. When we feel guilty, let us groan and sigh over our sins, and ask pardon of him who is ready to give us mercy when we come to him in sincerity of heart. This summarises what we have to note in this passage, when it says that David was extremely anxious when he saw that Uriah did not want to go into his house.

Well, the rest that Uriah did take is certainly worth considering when he says: 'The ark and Israel are in tents, Joab, who is our captain, is in company with all the people, and shall I enter my house, in order to drink and eat and to sleep with my wife? I will not do it' (2 Sam. 11:11). It is true that one cannot make a general law from this. For several had remained in their houses, to drink and eat and sleep with their wives, and that did not make them worse before God. It would be unfair and unreasonable to condemn all those who had not gone to war. Hence Uriah did not wish to make a law stating that while an army is prepared and in camp, it is not legitimate to drink and eat in one's home. But (as I have said) God led him to refrain.

Moreover, Uriah considered the special obligation which he had. For he was not in the same condition as the others who had remained at home. When a man goes to war, he must forget his house, as St Paul quotes to illustrate how ministers of the Word of God must not waver when it comes to the duty of their office. Rather, they must forget all the business of this world (2 Tim. 2:3–4). He says that he who fights must have his shop closed, must hand over his possessions to someone else, and discharge himself from all the duties of his house. Thus Uriah, having been chosen to march to war with the others, being a member of the army, and knowing his duty, did not depart from it without permission. It was the express command of the king which caused him to leave his duty. It was not because of his weakness. Hence, Uriah spoke in a manner worthy of his vocation.

This should teach us to think of our calling, and the charge that God has committed to us, and the position in which he has placed us. For there is one consideration for a man who has a wife and children, and another for him who is not married. Then again, he who is called into the judicial system must not want to remain at his ease, as if to say: 'I only want to do as much as this person', and thereby neglect his duty. Instead, he ought to think: 'God has given me the honour of employing me in such a capacity; I must carry it out'. It is just as true of a prince in his high position as of all others. And when a minister of the Word of God brings up this problem and that problem as a shield to excuse his indolence, will it do him any good? Hence, Uriah teaches all of us, in this passage, to consider to what task God calls us, so that we may faithfully carry out our duty in our particular situation. Now that is one point.

In addition, we see what great reverence he had for God when he mentioned, in the first place 'the ark of God', and then added 'all the people'. Also on the one hand, he showed to Joab, his captain and chief, the honour of which he was worthy and, on the other, he especially honoured King David. Above all, he put God first – which, indeed, he deserved. Therefore, we see clearly in this sentence how Uriah was a man who feared God, and had his heart in religion. For he would not have spoken of the ark unless, through it, he had been mastered by the honour of God, and eager to give him the honour that he deserved. The ark is mentioned here as if God were the head of the army, and the ark were their greatest shield, given to show the people that they were fighting under the guidance of the living God. It is true that we do not have that kind of external sign today, but still it should serve us. Let us see what this symbol which existed under the Law actually meant. When they were carrying the ark, it was to show that the war was supposed to be conducted by God. But it would not have worked unless the war was just, and they were waging it properly – which is why God commanded silver trumpets to be kept in the sanctuary. Now they did not take trumpets from the royal palace or from any private place, but from the sanctuary. And they had to be blown by the Levites, as messengers of God, who were expositors of the Law.

All of these details had one point in view: that wars were not undertakings plotted by men according to their own imaginations, but the people were to act in the fear of God, and conduct themselves in such a way that God would not be offended with them. Today (as I have said) these symbols belong to us, not that the use ought to be the same as under the Law, but rather that we should consider what they actually meant. That is, if we claim that we follow God, he must always preside, he must always be our head, and must always be before the eyes of those who are waging war, so that they will recognise that, without him, everything that they undertake will be confused. People make a very poor job of practising this today, so that we have all the more reason to be on our guard. Those who boast of battling for the honour of God nevertheless have their eyes on pillaging and stealing, and thus go astray through their wicked desires. In short, they go beyond the limit, as though there were neither law nor rule. Thus, we must note most carefully what is mentioned to us here.

Furthermore, one sees very few soldiers like Uriah, who are so constrained by obedience to God that they prefer his honour and service above everything else. Uriah was a valiant man, as one can see, when he did not spare his life, but threw himself forward where they ordered him to go. He did not act the coward. See how he was thus approved as a valiant man and was famous for it. Now today, those who want to make themselves into heroes think that they will never gain renown for being brave and valiant unless they behave like giants, and thus despise God, and battle against him. For we have seen this vile and corrupt attitude which will not even consider men as soldiers unless they deny God, and blaspheme him shamelessly with their lips. Thus, we should note even more closely what we are shown here, that a man who was so widely respected for his bravery, nevertheless did not fail to proclaim that God meant more to him than any ease, any luxuries and any physical pleasure. 'The ark', he said, 'will be under the tent, and shall I leave it to sleep with my wife, in order to be at my ease? I shall not do it.'

After that, he manifested concern 'for his people and his captain'. In this, he showed that he totally honoured God, but still wanted to carry out his duty to those who were in charge, such as the king and Joab, and consequently all his companions in the army. Now that is one point.

All in all, let us learn to honour God in his sovereign position, and yet also to do what is inseparable from his honour, that is, to carry out our duty to those to whom we have obligations; to render obedience to our superiors with all humility; to share willingly in the same condition with those with whom God has assembled us, and to act in such a way there that no-one will desire what is his own, but that we will all seek to serve one another. So that is one point.

Well now, it is certain that God placed these words in the mouth of Uriah in order to keep David more than convicted, so that when he heard such rebukes, it felt to him just like several blows of Uriah's fist, wounding to the depths of the heart. Even though Uriah had no intention of burdening David, nor of giving him such a reproach, still he fully prosecuted his case. For when Uriah spoke of the ark, David should have thought: 'Alas, I should be in front of this testimony which God has given us so that we may call on him'. Certainly, David knew how to state this matter clearly when he was not blinded by this cursed lust, when he said that he only desired the presence of God (Psa. 42:2; 84:2), and also wrote, 'When shall I appear in your tabernacle, and in the assembly of the faithful?' (Psa. 27:4; 84:10). He should have cared nothing for being king in comparison with being able to call on God in the sanctuary which he had ordained. Well, David now heard from the mouth of Uriah: 'Look at the ark which is in the field, as if God were fighting for us'. (That box was the pledge of his presence.) David, therefore, should have considered: 'Since it has pleased God to elect me as head, I must be careful to apply myself diligently to do what my position calls for, if I want God to have his eye upon me, to care for the country which he has placed in my hand, and for the people whom he has received as his children. And since my subjects are so zealous in this matter, and are not sparing themselves, what will it be like if I am careless? It will bring eternal reproach upon me.' Now that is what should have wounded the heart of David.

Then Uriah said: 'And by consequence, Israel'. David (as I said) was head of the people, and all the people were like his body. Therefore, when David was not moved in the slightest by seeing these poor people enduring so many hardships for the honour of God and for the maintenance of his crown, but remained lazily in his house, and went on to violate and ravish the wife of his subject, thus reversing all right order – must one not clearly say that he had totally forgotten himself?

Indeed, when he heard the officers of the king spoken of, should he not have been touched? When Uriah said: 'I will not be in a better condition than the servants of my lord' (for he was referring in the third person to David), should David not have thought about it? 'Now here is one of my subjects, who not only honours me as he should, but also all of my officers, so much so that when he is permitted to give himself a little bit of legitimate pleasure, he refuses it all, preferring to sleep before my door, subject to the wind and the rain rather than in his own house and with his wife in complete comfort. Indeed, his heart is so disposed to fight for me, out of the reverence that he has for me, that he only desires to return to battle with his companions. And yet, wretch that I am, I have dishonoured his wife; I have been so morally lax and so wicked as to have ravished his companion; it is as if I had torn her in pieces.' David, therefore, should have been touched, and have been instructed by these words which God put in the mouth of Uriah. Without a doubt, Uriah was not saying these things by his own will so as to give David the strong reproof which he needed. Yet what he said profited nothing.

Then, besides that, he added the oath: 'By your soul and by the life of your soul, I shall not do such a thing' (2 Sam. 11:11). Well, it is true that we must swear by the name of God, and that it is idolatry to use any other. But this form of speech was not meant to diminish anything from the honour of God, or transfer it to the creature. For when we swear by the soul of a king, it means we are proclaiming how dear his life is to us, and we are treasuring it as the most precious thing that we could have, just as everyone swears by his own soul. This is more than a merely perfunctory statement, it is also a testimony that we are drawing what is clear to us out of our treasury, as it were, in order to confirm our faith.

To sum up, we see how the tongue of Uriah was governed by the secret counsel of God, so that he taught David in such a way that he received greater condemnation. As I said, these words were like so many blows with the fist and with darts to break and pierce his heart. But yet, did it lead him to repentance? Indeed, no. Rather, he continued wanting to seek avenues of escape: 'he made Uriah remain another day, and the next day he called him to the banquet and made him drunk' (2 Sam. 11:12–13). Uriah was not literally drunk, but this word 'drunk' is used figuratively in Scripture to describe all banquets where men have drunk more than usual, although they have eaten soberly. Now in a banquet, one certainly drinks much more than ordinary, and yet one is still sober. Indeed, when David speaks of the favours of God and of his infinite liberality in Psalm 104, he says that 'wine is to rejoice the heart of man' (v. 15). Well, it would surely be enough to have bread and water for our nourishment, but he wants to show that God is so generous that he wants to give us – out of his superabundance, and beyond natural necessity – wine, in order to make us rejoice. Now this does not mean that we are to let down our guard, for we see that when people allow themselves to drink more than nourishment requires, drunkenness eventually gets the best of them. A man must surely restrain himself. But that is not to say that when he is at a banquet, he cannot rejoice in such a way that he will drink a few more glasses of wine than usual, without bothering either his body or mind.

Now it would seem, at first sight, that this would serve to give us licence to drink beyond measure, but it is the contrary. Actually, we must be aware of all those things which are legitimate for us. For 'everything that is done without faith', says St Paul, 'is always sin' (Rom. 14:23). Therefore, when we do not know whether God has permitted something, we dare not budge a finger, lest our conscience becomes seared as with a hot iron. Consequently, we would not know whether to eat a piece of bread or not until we had the kind of certitude that St Paul requires in this passage. That is, we must know that God has given us permission to do it, and that it is according to his good will. Hence, a man should not dare drink a drop of wine unless he knows that he is receiving it from the hand of God. Therefore, when one rejoices, granted that it is with true moderation and without excess, it is a legitimate thing. So this is what should be understood when it says that Uriah became 'drunk'.

It is true that David intended to make Uriah drink until he was too merry, as they say, and that, hence, he would go and sleep with his wife. But what was the drunkenness of Uriah really like? He stayed away from his wife, as he did the previous night. If he had been literally drunk, it is certain that he would not have done that, and would not have been able to abstain from going to his wife. Therefore, when he was content to be at the king's door and soberly to maintain his chastity, it was a sign that when he came away from the table, his mind was not confused. Now that is a good type of drunkenness – that is, a man should be permitted to relax and to rejoice, under the condition that he is always disposed to honour God and to apply himself to carry out his duty. For we must keep these two considerations in mind when we drink and eat: that is, to keep from hurting either our body or mind, so that we may always be free to employ ourselves in the service of God and in whatever way he calls us. Now that is how it was with Uriah.

Well, David should have been again all the more confused when he saw that all the subterfuges which he invented in his head got him nowhere. It should have moved him to pray to God and to be displeased with himself over his sin. But nevertheless, he gave it no more thought than a brute beast, and thereby reached the height of all iniquity when he wrote to Joab: 'Put Uriah in the most dangerous place, and cause him to die' (2 Sam. 11:14–15), and let the enemy come on him. It is hard to believe that David had so lost control of himself that he could stoop to commit such a horrible, depraved crime. How much more should this exhort us to pray to God to 'lead us not into temptation' (Matt. 6:13), and to keep us in fear and trembling under the shadow of his wings. Now who thinks that he is strong enough to make himself stand, when David stumbled? It is not a question of flattering ourselves, no matter how many favours God has bestowed upon us. Instead, let us be even more careful to cling to the good and to be content with it. Even this will not come from our own virtue, but we must be fortified from elsewhere. All our strength, therefore, lies in recognising our weakness, and in having our refuge in God, so that we might rely upon his help.

David (as we have already said) had, since his childhood, manifested such a fear of God that you would have thought that he was a little angel and a paragon of all virtue. He had endured to the end so many afflictions, one after another; he had demonstrated an invincible patience. He had exemplified such righteousness that one would be at a loss to ask for anything more perfect. He seemed to have been so totally renewed that all corruption seemed to have been removed from his flesh. When he began to reign, we also clearly saw his virtues. But when it came to women, that was where he showed his imperfection and an inexcusable vice. For he had already corrupted marriage by assembling such a crowd of women. Anyway, David had an absolutely terrible fall, which should make us tremble when we think of it. Imagine such a king and prophet of God, a man clothed with such great and excellent virtues, turning into a traitor and the murderer of a man who had been so loyal to him. If David had ordered a thousand others to be murdered, still he should have spared this man. Yet he so totally lost control of himself that he became possessed by a furious and diabolical rage, so that he not only consented to the death of his own faithful servant, but he even plotted it. Where would all this lead? Moreover, what had happened to his sense of shame? He wanted to hide his crime from men, but now he had to go on to uncover it to Joab, and thus people would know that he was a murderer, since Joab could not have managed it by himself, but had to have many accomplices.

We see, therefore, how David was cast down, and how God extracted his confession here, as if to say: 'You, by your own actions, must place yourself in a shameful position and be a spectacle to the whole world'. Hence, let us learn to strengthen ourselves and (while leaving the rest to another time) keep ourselves in such a way that the devil may not have possession of us, so that one evil may not follow another until we come to the very height of all iniquity. Rather, let us so honestly recognise our guilt before God that we may immediately seek the remedy which is shown to us: to be displeased with ourselves and to pray God to pardon us, so that not only may our past sins be buried, but that we may be returned by the Spirit of God to the right path, in order to continue in it for the rest of our life. May we thus serve as good examples to our neighbours.

Now let us prostrate ourselves before the majesty of our good God, in recognition of the infinite faults of which we are guilty, praying to him that he may be pleased to make us so feel them that it will cause us to groan continually and to be so upset that we may seek to conform ourselves totally to his good will. And thus may we be purged from all hypocrisy, so that we will not have our eyes or our senses attached to this world, nor to the consideration of men. Rather, may we only think of walking as though we were in the presence of God and his angels; so we will remain so obedient that we will glorify his name. Hence, may we not be blinded in the way we take, and may we not be called to account before him for him to have to judge us according to our iniquities. And may he not only bestow this grace upon us, but upon all peoples and nations of the earth . . .

34

*The Mark and Seal of David's Shame**

On the next morning, David wrote a letter to Joab, which he sent by the hand of Uriah. Now he wrote in the letter saying: Place Uriah in the hottest part of the battle, and draw back from him, so he may be smitten and die . . . (2 Sam. 11:14–27).

Now here (as I explained yesterday) David reached the height of iniquity when he added to adultery the murder of an innocent man, and not just one, but many. Indeed, he put the whole army in danger, just as if he were bringing down the curse of God on all the people. Now that (I say) was such an enormous crime that even if he had been nothing but virtuous all the rest of his life, this single act would have made him despicable. This instructs us, as we have argued already, not to let down our guard when we begin to do evil. For the devil will surely know how to make us plunge deeper and deeper until we are completely swallowed up. As I say, let us be fearful and not even think of covering one evil with another, and hardening ourselves. When we are guilty before God, let us be prepared to admit it before men, rather than to abandon ourselves to our sin, as David did.

Nevertheless, we see how God blinded him. For Joab must have known his villainy. It is true that David certainly wanted to colour what he was doing, and without a doubt, he pretended that Uriah fully merited being treated in this way, for he did not explain to Joab the reason why he wanted him to die. But he

*Friday, August 14, 1562.

was to presume that Uriah had behaved badly and that the king had found him disloyal, because people always judge another's decision according to that person's level of authority. But be that as it may, this was not sufficient to hide David's corruption. Hence, God permitted him to be found guilty, by one person after another. He became indebted to his domestic servants when he made them his pimps. Thus, the story had already become public knowledge. But for the present, David took refuge in Joab.

Further, we see how David was hardened in his evil. For when he had seen that Joab had killed Abner, he had gravely protested: 'May this return on his own head and on his descendants, and may this murder not be imputed to me, but may I be found innocent' (2 Sam. 3:28–29). Well now, what should he say concerning the death of Uriah? He strongly felt that it was a most wicked crime for Joab to kill Abner, and in protesting his innocence, he said that the judgement of God and his vengeance would be unleashed on him who was guilty. Well now, this time it is David who is the murderer, indeed, a traitor, but not towards an enemy – unlike Joab, whose reason for killing Abner was to avenge the death of his brother. But here is David, treacherously sending his own servant to death, to whom he was morally bound to the uttermost. Why was it, then, that he did not consider what he was doing? Here we see that when sinners are hardened, they lose their sensitivity to good or evil, like someone stupid. When someone puts a question to us (as will be explained more fully later), we give our opinion according to common sense, and our reason is in charge. However, when we are carried away by evil desires, we lose our moral discernment, and our spirits become completely foolish. If this happened to David, who was such an excellent man, what will it be with us? Here is something else we have to remember: on the one hand, David was so concerned about losing his honour before men that he forgot God more and more. But on the other hand, it gained him nothing, for God mocked him, and sent him even more confusion, so that he ended up having a great multitude of witnesses who would judge his crime and enormous guilt.

Moreover, when it says that Joab ordered the assault on the city, and that he put Uriah in a place where he could not escape without great difficulty, we are once more reminded of the fidelity of Uriah, who spared not his own life when it came to fighting. These factors keep adding to the greater condemnation of David. For even if the men had been worthless, having them killed was an utterly reprehensible deed. But far from that, David's crime was aggravated even more for failing to spare innocent blood – particularly the blood of one who was so loyal. Here we see how David had lost every ounce of human decency. His incredible ingratitude to Uriah showed that he had become shameless.

Nevertheless, one might find it strange that God permitted Uriah to die like this, given that he was innocent. For we have seen the reverence which he manifested in the service of God, and that the ark was so precious to him that he was even conscientious about entering his house to rest or take his ease while the ark of God was in the field. Why, then, did God not help him in time of need? Where were the promises by which God testified that he would never forsake his own (Psa. 37:28); that their blood would be precious to him (Psa. 72:14; Heb. 12:24); that even a hair of their head would not fall, and that they were numbered by him (Matt. 10:30); that he would guide their steps, and that he would cause them to be guided by his angels (Psa. 91:11); and that they would be fortified with a double rampart; that he would be their strength and their shield (Psa. 28:7); that he would hold them dear as the apple of his eye (Deut. 32:10; Psa. 17:8); and everything else that it is possible to say? It seems, therefore, that these promises failed for Uriah; it seems that he was frustrated for having carefully served God.

But from this we can gather the exact opposite: the faithful have no stopping place in this world as their final goal. Otherwise, one would have to conclude that God is an idol or a phantom. When we accept the principle that God is the Judge of the world, and that we must all pass before his bar and render account of our works; when we thoroughly accept this truth, the death of Uriah, as well as that of Abel and the like, will serve to confirm our belief in eternal life. Indeed, there must be a better life than this one, for otherwise we would have to say that God was asleep in the heavens when Uriah was put to death, and when Abel was killed. Hence, we see that this death, instead of horrifying us, is useful to us, because it is like a mirror which represents eternal life before our eyes. Although it could have caused unbelievers who hastily judge the works of God to quit his service, those who use it as an excuse to reject God's service are motivated by nothing but their own presumption.

Hence, since God permitted Uriah to be killed in such a way, let us recognise that the wages of the good and faithful are not received in this world. And when they are afflicted, everything is turned to their good and is for their salvation, as it says in the eighth chapter of Romans. For St Paul gives us there a definite rule which teaches us how to benefit from all the afflictions which God sends us. If we endure (he says) heat and cold and hunger and thirst, or if we must pass under the sword, and if we are put through as many miseries as can possibly be imagined, still it does not keep God from loving us for ever, or keep us from being in his good grace. For 'all things are turned to good' (as I said) and redound to the salvation of 'those who love God'. Hence, when we read these promises, that God never forgets us, that our life will be hidden under the shadow of his wing, that we are dear to him as the apple of his eye, that we will never be stripped of his help, let us recognise that this does not exempt us from having to suffer many terrible things, and finally death – when the right moment for us arrives; that is to say, when God wills it. Nevertheless, let us be content to know that even death will be our entrance into a better life, so that this consideration will serve to strengthen our patience and make us even more certain that God will never forget us.

This is how we must practise the other doctrine which is in the fifth chapter of Romans – that is, when we pass through much anguish, trouble and torment, let us always consider the outcome (vv. 3–4). For that will produce patience, and we know that this is how we are sustained by the will of God. Otherwise, we would immediately fail, for we are nothing but smoke and wind. Hence, God must surely help us when we feel temptations coming upon us. God's help then gives us a reason to hope in him even more, for our hope cannot fail to extend even to death itself, since we must look far beyond this world. Therefore, after we have deeply experienced the strong hand of God upholding us, nd keeping us from being completely beaten down by temptation, we have the means to strengthen ourselves all the more and call upon him, right up to the very hour of death. Thus, we ask him to let us fully enjoy that which we can never completely take in while we are in this world. For it is enough for us to have some taste of his goodness here below, in order not to expect any permanent rest here, but instead, always to aspire to this eternal rest. This is how we should judge the death of Uriah, and recognise that we most certainly have not been forsaken by God when he takes us to himself, for we must always go home that way. So let us not be surprised or think that God has mocked us in his promises that he wants to be our Saviour.

Then it says that 'Joab sent to David to give him a report', and ordered the messenger to say at the end (in case David became too angry): 'Your servant Uriah is also dead'. This happened, and then David was content – so stripped of his senses that he was not even sorry for the others who were dead (2 Sam. 11:18–25). He was as guilty before God as if he were actually carried away by the devil. We see that, for a time, he was totally corrupted, indeed to the point of being like a man who was reprobate and utterly incorrigible.

Now as to this story which Joab told the messenger to repeat: it says that 'David could have argued that they should not have come so near the city' (2 Sam. 11:20–21), because he knew that they would expose themselves to death, and the example of Abimelech, son of Gideon, is mentioned here (Judg. 9:50–51). (It is true that Gideon is here called Jerubbesheth, and in the book of Judges he is Jerubbaal (Judg. 6:32), either because his father had taken the vengeance of Baal on himself, or because he had taken sides in the debate about Baal. Actually, the name Jerubbesheth is the exact opposite, because it is said in mockery. Jerubbaal means 'he who took up the quarrel with Baal' – when he threw down and shattered the idol. But instead, he is called here Jerubbesheth; and the name means exactly the opposite! Well, it all comes down to the same thing.) Be that as it may, Joab anticipated what David might say; he could have accused him of recklessness for having risked the army by making them draw near the wall. For in those times, people used to fight with pieces of stone, and they even had instruments to throw these stones with lances and darts, because they had no artillery. Abimelech would not have been killed, if the woman had not taken a stone and thrown it on his head. Joab simply wanted to show that he did not make this move through lack of consideration, but that he did it for a reason, and thus he added, in conclusion, that Uriah died immediately.

Now let us come to David. It says that as soon as he heard of the death of Uriah, he pretended 'to console Joab', exhorting him to take courage, to keep the city continuously encircled and that, finally, 'he would overthrow it', and be successful (2 Sam. 11:25). We see (as I have already mentioned) how his conscience was dead, and his mind was as dulled as if he were totally out of his senses. Even though he had desired the death of Uriah, he should have been deeply touched after hearing of such a defeat, for it would further discourage his whole army, and the Ammonites would be encouraged against him. Now that is one matter.

He also heard of the death of several men in his service. He saw that the name of God was blasphemed, which was even worse. When we consider such stupidity, will we not decide that David was no longer the same person who is mentioned above, and of whom the text will be speaking later, but that he had become a senseless beast? Yet all the more should we be on our guard. For how did this happen to him? It was because he forgave himself for the deed which he had committed, and in so doing went far beyond the limits of self-flattery and hardened himself in order to cover his shame. The devil had taken such possession of him that it no longer mattered to him whether the name of God were blasphemed; or if he had suffered such a loss before his enemies; or if many of his people were put to death. Let us learn (I say) by this, to pray to God not to permit us to wander so far astray that we can no longer discern between black and white. We must not become like savages who, hearing of the death of many people, are not touched by it but have lost every ounce of human kindness. We must pray to God that he would not permit us to be hardened like this.

And on the other hand, we saw the presumption of David, who seemed to want to despise God. For he exhorted Joab to take courage, and promised him that he would defeat the city. Very well, but who was it who would have to give him victory, and from whom did he expect it? If he had had an ounce of sense left, and had not been totally beside himself, he would still have said: 'If God does not guide us, we are cursed and will come to confusion'. David clearly knew how to speak glibly; yes, as if he were holding God 'up his sleeve', he said: 'You shall take the city; fight boldly'. Yet not only was he a murderer, but now he was committing despicable treason. Of course, he did not think of it in that way, but it was the same as if he were wrenching God's power and glory from him, making an idol of them, and making fun of God. Now that is how low he had sunk.

Furthermore, when he said that 'the sword consumes this one as well as the other one' (2 Sam. 11:25), we see how he was drunk with innocent blood. It is true that princes often speak in this way when someone comes to tell them of some defeat, and they furiously scratch their ears, vexed over the loss that they have sustained, which has weakened them, driven them backwards, and advanced their enemies. But afterwards, they only twist their mouth with disdain, and do not consider these tragic facts or say to themselves: 'Now here are as many widows as slain men; what a shame to see so many orphans, and all of this for me'. They never pay attention to those considerations. But rather: 'Courage! courage! we have other subjects, etc., we always get more men'. It is true that if a prince is dead, it is an incomparable blessing. But when large numbers of people are dead, it is the same thing for the prince as being freed from entanglements. We see, therefore, that princes do not worry much about the death of their subjects, and it scarcely affects them, as long as it does not cause them to lose any revenue or authority.

But David was even more detestable. For it was not the case that the people spoken of here died in the war, in his service in and of itself, but it was he who caused them to be butchered, as if he had cut their throats, like poor sheep. Then, when he said: 'Oh, the sword consumes this one as well as that one' (2 Sam. 11:25), he was speaking of fortune, like an unbeliever who had never heard God mentioned. In this, we see how he was abandoned for a time, which was why (as we will show more fully later) he asked God for his free spirit to be restored to him (Psa. 51:12). By doing so, he confessed that he had been stripped of all grace; that what he had previously possessed of intelligence, of integrity, and of uprightness had all been taken away from him, so that he had become utterly deprived of them. Hence, in these events expounded here, we see him without an ounce of the fear of God in him, or of human honesty, or compassion, or anything else worth while. This is what we must remember from this passage.

But above all, each one of us should carefully consider himself when we see how God unleashed his vengeance on someone who was 'after his own heart' (Acts 13:22), as he is spoken of in the Psalm.[1] May we all think more carefully about ourselves than we have been accustomed to doing, and may we do so thoroughly. For we should not say that we will all be restored like David. We shall see how God granted him mercy, but insofar as this present account is concerned, we see him as a damned man, and one who was possessed by the devil and alienated from God and all his favours. In brief, there is nothing in this passage but despair.

Indeed, what is added here – that he 'took the woman' with whom he had committed sin, and 'married her', even before she had borne the child, taking the mother with the child still in her womb – constitutes another shameless action. Previously, he had tried to cover his shame, which is what caused the death of Uriah. Indeed, if Uriah had been willing to be a pimp with his wife, and to go along with the deception, it is certain that his life would have been spared. We, on the one hand, see that Uriah

[1]Not in the Psalm but in the citation above.

abstained from her company, but that it was David's utter lack of honour which pushed him to commit the second sin. Well, now he wanted all the people to be witness to it, and took the wife of him whom he had had killed! And then he also kept the child for himself. Even little children themselves could have stood in judgement. This is how it is with those who try to guard their reputation with the world and be well thought of, avoiding blame and dishonour. Eventually, they so clearly show themselves for what they are by their own actions that if someone actually attempted to ruin their name in all circles, he would not be able to do so nearly as effectively as they do themselves by their own foolishness! In this, God is also mocking them, when he uncovers the corruption that they thought they had carefully hidden.

Well, altogether we see here how David was paralysed, like someone who has been covered with dung and is reeking with its odour and does not even care! For where other people would die of this kind of infection, some suck it up, like a fish sucking water. So it was with David. But as we shall see, this sin, though asleep, still did not fail to keep watch, and what is said in Genesis was fulfilled by it: 'Sin will be near the door' (Gen. 4:7). Well, by this illustration, we have shown that when we once let down our guard on our wicked desires, and blindfold our eyes to keep from making judgements any longer, we then become so hardened in our obstinacy that our situation seems like a beautiful park where we can take walks! Well, in this park we will play many tricks, thinking that we are free for ever. But what next? The truth must finally come out. When princes with their followers are in a beautiful hall, they have a good time, showing off to one another there. But yet, where is sin? At the door. Oh, it is a dreadful doorman! Imagine a man who has been very much at his ease, who has had all his desires, and has drunk and eaten delightful food. If he were always able to remain in that condition, he would be pleased with his circumstances and never think of the outcome. But in the end, he must yet find this doorman, and leave the house where he is making merry. However, when people are at their ease like this, the doorman is still there, making no show whatsoever and not always perceived. But he is a good watchman, and they are appalled when they have to render account to such an enemy. So it was with the sin of David, for we find him straying and despising God and men. Now it seemed as though he had broken all restraining ties and cords, and had put every Law under his feet, with the result that there was no more shame left in him. But nevertheless, sin remained at the door – spying on him, waiting for him. He would finally have to come out and face judgement to which we see God drawing him by Nathan, his prophet. So much, therefore, for this hardening which took place in David, and for the unyielding malice which he demonstrated.

Moreover, let us learn that even when we have been able to put on a good appearance for a time and men have perceived nothing of our vices, still God thoroughly knows how to bring it out. Even if we are hidden by a mountain, he will make the whole thing fall down and our corruption will appear, so that everyone will spit in our face, and the shame which we have fled will be doubled and keep increasing even more. Now if David had not tried so hard to exempt himself from shame before men, but had returned to God, it would surely have been hard, and his faults would certainly have been discovered, as eventually did happen. Many people would have spoken of it and murmured, but God would have hidden it much more than David could have done himself. But when he plotted all that he could, even to the extent of causing innocent blood to be shed, we can see that he had been hardened to such a degree that he cared about nothing else but covering up his villainy so that he could continue in it, instead of seeking the true means of blotting it out.

Who was it that moved David to marry this woman? It was not she who solicited it, for we must carefully note that he ordered her to be fetched back into his palace, and celebrated the wedding while she was pregnant (2 Sam. 11:27). Now that is absolutely clear. No-one needs to discuss this any longer or offer any further conjecture. Even a small child could know: Here is this woman, who is pregnant; her husband is dead; he has not lived with her for a long time. We therefore conclude that the king is the father. For as soon as her husband is killed, he rejoices and triumphs with this woman. Thus, we see how David declared, by this marriage, the sin which he had committed in secret, and was like a beast. It is necessary to speak of it in this way, and one can only judge that he had been bewitched.

Hence, let us be very careful to pay more attention to God when we have fallen, so that we may groan over and finally confess our offences, so that they may be covered and buried – rather than trying to cover them by our own industry to keep them from appearing before men. For even when we have done much bargaining here below, in the end God will permit us to be much more deformed, and in exchange for the little shame that we would have received, we will have so much as to be totally weighed down! David had a terrible fall, and then exerted all his powers to cover up the enormous crime which he had committed with this woman. Well now, he had to take her for his wife.

This also served to condemn him. For it was with good reason that it was forbidden, in ancient times and by the Church councils, for those who had committed adultery together to be married. Now we are referring to a man who has committed adultery, that is, with an adulteress. It is different if a man who has raped a girl is touched with repentance. If, in that case, he takes her in marriage, it is a fruit of his repentance that he will not allow this girl to be condemned. Rather, he is displeased with what he has done, and says: 'We are two poor creatures and miserable sinners. Very well, we have been ill advised. But now let us endeavour to serve God, and to repair the ill already committed.' Therefore, when a man has committed fornication with a girl or with a woman who is not married, he may very well take her as wife. But in adultery, there are many special reasons to prevent it, for that would be opening the door to any wicked person or anyone who wanted to poison their spouse. If a man who had committed adultery with a married woman were permitted to take her, after the woman had attempted to kill her husband, it is certain that any parity would be immediately perverted, and the strongest would take over. In brief, such a thing should be considered contrary to nature. Thus, it aggravated David's crime all the more when he took Bathsheba for his wife, after he had abused her; indeed, while she was still married to Uriah.

Well, it says next that 'she mourned for her husband' (2 Sam. 11:26). But again we see her hypocritically going through another farce, just as she had done when she cleansed herself from her uncleanness. She certainly knew that she was detestable to God because she had committed adultery. Yet she used the sprinkling which God had commanded in his Law in order to wash herself (Lev. 14:7; Num. 8:7). Still, the pollution continued to cling to her, and she paid no attention to what Jeremiah says, that God is not interested in the external appearance, but seeks integrity of heart (Jer. 4:14; 1 Sam. 16:7). Hence, she now returned to a similar fiction; for she went through a time of mourning for her husband. Perhaps she was touched by it. For she would surely have had to be utterly insensitive not to show some love to a man whom she had married, who indeed was so virtuous, as we have seen. But still, she exposed herself to shame when she returned to the house of her adulterous partner. This shows us that it was not a true affection, but rather feigned, when she mourned over her husband.

Moreover, we also see how she personally profited from the situation. For she should have hidden herself, but instead, she went on to place herself in an eminent position, so that she could be seen from afar. And what could one have seen? Here was an adulteress, who was the cause of the death of her husband, going around brazen-faced, and giving herself a good time with her adulterous partner, with a murderous and disloyal individual. Well, when she consented and willingly agreed with such a villain, what could one judge but that both had conspired in the death of this poor man? That is what people could have said. For even if a woman is debauched and has lived imprudently, still if she keeps herself hidden at home, the evil could drain away. But she readily went with David to live in his house, forgot the death of her husband, and paid no attention to the villainous and detestable outrage which had been done to him. Without argument, she joined herself to him who put the sword in the hand of the enemies of God in order to put Uriah to death. All of this clearly shows that she had utterly lost control of herself.

Nevertheless, we see how God uncovered their villainy when he gave them a child of this adultery. It is true that having children is a blessing from God. In fact, he honours men and women when he places them in the rank of father and mother, for in a sense he is comparing them to himself. This shows that the name of Father, properly speaking, belongs only to God himself (Eph. 3:14–15). Hence, it is a testimony of his favour when he gives offspring to men and women. Yet we see that, often, when God gives this blessing to the wicked, afterwards they turn it into evil. When the child who is spoken of here was given to David, he rejoiced because of him, but afterwards he was removed from him to cause him more anguish. David would have much preferred that he had never been born, since in that case he would not have been in bitterness close to death. Hence, God undoubtedly showed that this blessing would serve to confound David. This would be like what he says in the sixty-ninth Psalm, speaking of the state of the wicked: 'Lord, may their tables be turned into a snare and a net, may their prosperity be in ruins' (v. 22). This means: the favours of God, which the wicked receive, are turned to their evil. Well, because David was God's enemy for a time, this is precisely what had to happen to him.

Hence, when God gave David a child, it was a mark and seal of his shame, and the child was a witness who cried out even louder than if all the trumpets in the world had been sounded, that David was an adulterer and a murderer. As we shall see very often, fornicators will cover up their sin, and people will never be able to draw them out into the light, except by their children. But God makes them speak, even before they have come out of the womb of their mother. When the fornicators have gone around smirking and mouthing their innocence and have protested that people are doing them a great injury in accusing them, God finally makes their belly swell up, and those who have been so arrogant are confounded. The little child in their womb will speak as a witness of the judgement of God and of the iniquity of those who would like to cover up their shame. This is what happened to David. If the child had been born in her house and in secret, in that case people would have known her corruption. But he had to be born in the palace of the king, as if all by himself he were erecting a scaffold and proclaiming a public announcement of David's adultery upon it, the very thing David had taken such pains to find a way to hide.

Hence, we see all in all how God carefully executed his judgement upon David. We see, on the other hand, how David was paralysed and stripped of his senses. Since he had rejected the clear insight which God had given him, he of necessity acted like a blind man, stumbling here and there, walking in the midst of darkness because he did not follow the light of God. When we see these things, let us learn to walk wherever God may call us, and to profit from his Word and from the favours of his Spirit, by whom he illumines us. Yet while he is executing his judgements upon others, let us fear these judgements, too, so that we humble ourselves and tremble because we too are afraid of being plunged into the depth of the abyss, as we see being done to David.

Now let us prostrate ourselves before the majesty of our good God in recognition of the infinite faults of which we are guilty, praying him that more and more he may make us feel them, and that this will serve, not to make us cover them up, but to cause us to confess them openly. Thus may it be, that even if we are condemned by the world, we are yet assured of being absolved before God by his infinite goodness. And may he not permit us to go on in such blindness and hardness that his name is blasphemed because of us. But since he has received us as his children, and as his Church, let us dedicate our whole life to glorify his holy name. And may he not only bestow this grace upon us, but upon all peoples of the earth . . .

35

*You are the Man!**

Now the Lord sent Nathan to David, who when he came to him said: There were two men in a city, one was rich and the other poor. The rich man had flocks and herds in great abundance, but the poor man had nothing except a small lamb, which he had brought up and nourished, and had grown up with him and his children . . . (2 Sam. 12:1–6).

We have seen how David was asleep in his wretchedness, and how his conscience was totally deadened. In brief, he was like a brute beast. Now David himself would certainly have liked to have remained in this condition. But yesterday we heard a word which was precisely aimed against this numbing repose that he was taking – that 'his action, nevertheless, was displeasing to God' (2 Sam. 11:27). Here was David, pleasing himself and wallowing in his own evil. But nevertheless, he had God as his adversary, who cannot bear so wicked a deed with such wide effects. At first sight, one would say that this word is unnecessary – that a crime displeased God – but it implies much when we consider the position that David was in. He had ravished somebody's wife, and was peacefully enjoying her, without any opposition. They were even applauding him, for the great of this world always have flatterers to bury them in their vices.

Now this was David's position. Hence, it is not without reason that this word is included, that even though men do not sound forth a word, and though David was completely asleep,

*Saturday, August 15, 1562.

and though it certainly seemed that what he had done was legitimate for him, since he had not been punished – still, it was not true that David would be let off that easily, since *God* was against him: indeed not, even though God had not yet pronounced his sentence. For here was David, not apprehending the wrath of God. It seemed to him that he had escaped, and that he would never have to render an account. And why? Because he was not urged to repentance, he had no message of the anger and of the vengeance of God. Now that is how it could be that God, on the one hand, is furious, and yet David felt nothing of it, no more than a poor beast.

Well now, Scripture tells us that 'Nathan the prophet was sent to him' (2 Sam. 12:1). If one had given David what he desired, it is certain that he would not have wanted his 'mange scraped away', but rather he would have preferred to have been spared! Instead, God, procuring his salvation, sent something far from pleasant to David (2 Sam. 12:12f.), that could not flatter his ears. He was condemned to death and God told him that not only would he be punished in his person, but in his whole house. As he had shed innocent blood, so also detestable murders would be committed among his own children; one would kill the other. That is how it turned out, and we will see this in its place: that two brothers killed two other brothers, for Absalom killed Amnon (2 Sam. 13:28–29); and then there was Solomon, who killed Adonijah (1 Kings 2:25). David was persecuted by his own son (2 Sam. 15ff.). Then he experienced great defeats. The child who was begotten in adultery was snatched from him. Indeed, it caused him such anguish that he put on sackcloth and wept and groaned over it bitterly (2 Sam. 12:15ff.). Now therefore, here God was awakening him. Not that it was not hard for him, but it was for his good and his profit. Just as doctors will not always be gentle, or pleasant, though they are concerned for our well-being – this was the way that God rebuked David by his prophet, Nathan.

Well, in order to understand this better, let us pay attention to our own condition, whenever we are like escaped animals, or when we wilfully despise God, when we have offended him, and when we are hardened as if there were no more authority over us, and we wished to strip him of his office, so that he should no longer be Judge of the world. Nevertheless, if he is angry with us, and if we are guilty of similar stubbornness towards him, let us notice our condition. For those who flatter themselves in their vices and give free rein to them have God as their adversary. And yet, they feel nothing of it; the sword is over their neck, but they think that they are very secure. Let us learn, therefore, all the more to subject ourselves voluntarily to all correction. For it is the sole means by which we may seek a meeting with God, when we are wounded to the quick, and when such sadness and anguish are produced that we no longer know where we are, until God has made us feel his grace and his mercy.

It is true (as I said) that the natural desire of men is to want to be flattered, wanting people to support them, and never to plead with them. When they have failed, they want people to leave them alone just as they are, or even to attempt to cover up their shame. Now that is what we seek, and yet this is nothing but our perdition. It is as if a sick person wanted to be left alone in his condition, with nobody to help him: what more could happen except that he would miserably perish? Well, we must fight against this wretched desire. Thus, let us learn once more that we are inclined to hypocrisy, and also that we have such pride that we would like our vices to be recognised and considered virtues. However much, therefore, we may already be stripped of this desire, let us fight against ourselves, and let us seek to be saddened instead of rejoicing. Let us seek to have our vices actually pointed out and prefer to be pricked in the very place where, because of our wicked lusts, we only ask to be flattered.

This was sufficiently shown to us in the example of David, when yesterday it was said that 'the deed committed by him was displeasing to God'. What did that involve? 'The wrath of a king', says Solomon, 'is a messenger of death' (Prov. 16:14). And when we have against us the Creator of the world – he who sustains all by his virtue; he before whom the mountains tremble and flow down (Psa. 18:7; 97:5), as the Scripture speaks of him; he whose wrath and vengeance is a devouring fire which consumes all (Isa. 33:14); he before whom the angels are afraid – when he is against us, with his hand uplifted in order to exterminate us, and yet we are at our ease, making ourselves believe that all is well, would it not be better for us never to have been born, and for us to have been aborted from the wombs of our mothers? Therefore, since in fact the condition of David was so terrible from the time that he was enjoying someone else's wife, and all the while no-one uttered a word to him, and God was furious with him, let us note that there is nothing better than when God sends us messengers of his wrath. For then he can make us feel his mercy and cease to enjoy our sins, so that we may apprehend his vengeance and our conscience may torment us, to the extent of humbling us to seek pardon and remission in him, until he has accepted us.

In fact, that is how we are led back to the right path, as St Paul says in 2 Corinthians (chapter 7, verse 10). For if sorrow does not come first, it is impossible for us ever to be touched with repentance. Well, we will never be accepted otherwise. For when men pardon themselves, God must condemn them. How, therefore, can we be pardoned by him? When we judge ourselves, as St Paul says (1 Cor. 11:31). For he shows that it only inflames the wrath of God more and more against us when we are not concerned about our own offences, and try to bury them. 'If we learn to judge ourselves carefully,' says St Paul, 'we will not be condemned' by God. For our presumption and recklessness only provoke his wrath against us all the more, and we are despising hm and proverbially 'spitting in his face' when we try to make our own case good before him. That is why he exerts his force against us. Hence, when God has taken pity upon poor sinners who are alienated from him and are in the process of perdition, in order to bring them back he begins in this way – by giving them 'occasion for sorrow', as St Paul describes it.

It is true that we would much prefer to flee this sorrow. But we ought to seek it, and St Paul exhorts us to receive it peaceably. Insofar as it brings us repentance, we must not find it bad, for indeed it is finally intended to lead us to salvation – rather than to shut the door to the kingdom of God on us, and abandoning us to Satan. Now it is God who is calling us back. Well, that cannot be done except by force! For men, on their own initiative, will never be displeased with themselves over their own sins, and though they feel them, still they go on further, and cannot be properly humbled. It is therefore necessary, as I have already said, for sorrow to come first, and for us to feel it, so that we may be appalled when we realise that God is opposed to our position. Then we must recognise how dreadful is his wrath, and then humble ourselves in such dismay that it is as if we were already destroyed. Through all this, may we learn to hate the evil which had formerly pleased us, and which had put us to sleep. Now that is what we have to remember, in the first place, from the story which is given here of God sending his prophet, Nathan.

The fact that God was very angry was naturally expected of him. For all iniquity must be an abomination to him who is the fountain of justice. He will be angry, therefore, about the transgressions of men. But when it says that God sent Nathan to David, this is not common to all; it is a special benefit and a singular privilege which he grants to his children. Hence, let us note carefully that from the very greatest to the smallest, no-one, when he has offended, can escape the hand of the Judge: I mean the heavenly Judge. But when God grants us this grace, let us be our own judges, and after we are condemned, we may obtain pardon and acquittal before him. Now that is an inestimable benefit. That is what has been shown to us here, when God sent his prophet to David.

Well, it is true that sinners will often be drawn to repentance and God will lift his hand, as he speaks, so as to bring them back. He says to them: 'Come, come, return now' – and yet all the reproofs which he gives profit nothing. It is not enough for someone to batter our ears with the word of the prophets and their doctrine, but it is a question of God touching our heart, as we see that he touched the heart of David. Be that as it may, here again is a certain and infallible testimony of our salvation, that God calls us to repentance.

Well, it states that Nathan came, and did not at first openly accuse David, but employed an illustration in order to reach him gradually. Indeed, he wanted to draw from him this confession, that whoever had done such a deed deserved death (2 Sam. 12:1–4). Nathan, therefore, brought forward an example of what one calls a parable, and said that there was a rich man who had a poor neighbour. The neighbour had only one little lamb which he had brought up and nourished on the crumbs of his own bread, which had drunk out of his cup or goblet. If he had spoken of a husband and wife, David would immediately have known what that meant; but he disguised the matter by this illustration, so that at first David did not apprehend what direction Nathan wanted to go. Next, he said that the rich man, who had some traveller to whom he wanted to give hospitality, did not want to touch his own animals. Although his stable was very full and well supplied with sheep and cattle, he did not want to diminish his own supply in the least. So he went to ravish this poor lamb, his neighbour's only possession, and served it to his guest.

Well, upon hearing this, David became angry, so we see that he still had some seed of the fear of God. It is true that if we judge by external appearances, he was numbed. It seemed that the devil was possessing him, and had removed all sound reasoning from him. But this shows that his faith was like a dying fire under the ashes. For when Nathan came to set forth his case to him, he was immediately moved with fury and said: 'As the Lord lives, the man who has done this will not escape punishment, and for one lamb, he shall restore fourfold' (2 Sam. 12:5–6). We see, therefore, that he was touched by this means, and even condemned himself: 'I have sinned'. But the fruit of his repentance will be dealt with in its place. That is why Nathan used an illustration – so that David would be led, little by little, to repentance.

Next, moreover, Nathan wanted to extract this sentence of condemnation from his own lips. It is not that he was sparing him as king, nor that he dared not take the liberty. For in saying, 'You are the man!' (2 Sam. 12:7), he spoke very openly. He did not use the 'sweet water of the court', as they say, when he condemned David to death, and said that he had ravished what belonged to his neighbour. Indeed, there is no doubt that there were many other words. It is true that the speech is quoted here in brief. But we know the custom of Scripture to touch on a word which ought to be expounded extensively. When Nathan openly accused David of ingratitude, he reproached him with the possessions that he had received from God, and thereby he showed him that he had committed such a wicked act that he had compelled God to be his adversary. He added, on the other hand, the threats that God would not spare him; that blood would always be on his house; even that the child which he had had would be removed from him; and finally that someone would cause him such shame that, in contrast to his having committed this adultery in secret, the sun would be witness to a wicked deed done to him, more abominable than had ever been seen. That is, his own son would have the trumpet sounded and erect a platform to commit the same crime, ravishing David's wives, and proclaiming himself there a reprobate for all to see. We must approve of Nathan's instruction when he spoke in this way, for he did not speak to David as to a king, or have any regard for his person, which might have made him tone it down. But, as I have said, this is how David had to be brought back. On the other hand, he had to pronounce his own sentence, as if it were a horror to him to hear such a deed related, so that this gave Nathan an even greater opening, and he simply quoted what David had already pronounced from his own lips.

Even so, we have to note that, in general, we always recognise good and evil well enough. But we are totally witless when the case applies to us; so much so that our eyes are dulled, all our senses are lost and, in short, we do not apply it fairly to ourselves. For instance, when someone speaks to us of thievery, there is no-one who does not confess that it is a crime worthy of punishment, and cannot be tolerated among men. Fornication is detestable, but none are so unashamed as to say that it is not wicked. It is the same with murders. In short, when someone asks us a question, we always know how to answer it. I speak even of idiots who have never known books and have never been to school, when someone questions them about a general fact. Yet the most able, when someone points out to them the condition in which they are caught up, are confused and do not know how to discern between black and white! And what is the cause of this if not hypocrisy blinding us? As a result, our eyes are bandaged through self-love, so that we never manage to recognise a fact accusing us. For we always regard our honour and our profit, rather than equity and justice, so that our senses are corrupted and perverted when it comes to our own condition. And this is what is said in the common proverb, that 'no-one is a competent judge in his own affairs' – as experience demonstrates far too often.

Nevertheless, this is not to say that we are excused when self-love or ambition or avarice blinds us, so that we do not know whether something is good or bad. For when one vice draws on another, the condemnation doubles. Therefore, since this ignorance among men proceeds from avarice or pride, one must conclude that this is good reason for us to be punished doubly before God. We must all the more thoroughly endeavour to tear out this wicked affection, which is far too deeply rooted in us – that is, of loving ourselves even to the point of so burying ourselves in flattery that we lose our sense, reason and intelligence. For it would be very bitter to us for people to call us beasts, and we see men, even the crudest and most ignorant, not wanting to have this reputation of being like beasts. Yet we see that everyone makes himself a beast voluntarily! For when we bandage our eyes with self-love, to whom will we attribute that evil?

We must, therefore (as I have said), work and take pains all the more to put underfoot this wicked lust (of self-love), and learn to judge ourselves, so that our reason may never be stifled. And when we have failed, let us always begin to censure ourselves before coming to others. For we are so arrogant and hasty in reproving the sins of others that we attribute everything to evil [motives]. Hence, what does it all amount to? On the one hand, we condemn this and that person, so that no-one can escape our tongue but, on the other, we would not like to enter into an examination to recognise our own faults, unless someone places them before our very eyes! For as I have said, we always know how to judge the faults of others, but we cast our own behind our backs. Now therefore, when we see that David has thus condemned the one who had done such a wicked deed, let us note that he saw very clearly into someone else's business. Nevertheless, he was, in regard to himself, so blinded, so stupid and witless, that it seemed to him that God was asleep. Now that is one matter.

However, it is a frivolous exercise to seek for subtle expositions in order to conform absolutely everything in this parable to some particular thing in David's experience. It is true that it is not without cause that it speaks here of 'a traveller' (2 Sam. 12:4), to whom the rich man gave lodgings. But to devise an allegory, for example, that lusts are like strangers who wander about with no fixed place, is to move rather too far from the simplicity of the text. Hence, let us be careful, instead, to be content with the natural sense. Why is it that a traveller is spoken of here? It is to show that David did not ravish the wife of someone else, as though he was deprived of wives and had done it out of necessity! For he should have contented himself with a single wife, as had been ordained by the institution of God. Instead, he had more than a dozen of them! When he had eighteen of them, was that not exceeding all measure? When he wanted to add Bathsheba, was it not as if he wanted to ask of someone else, when in fact he had enough? Nor was it a question of having experienced either hunger or thirst – resulting in taking the goods of someone else. It is true that a thief is not excused when he has picked open a lock and stolen something. If he claims that he was not able to do anything else, that he was not able to earn his living, that he did not know which way to turn, and that necessity drove him to it, still these words are worthless. Even so, one will have pity on a poor man who has thus been carried away by this dire poverty. But if someone who has plenty, and more than he needs, ravishes the goods of someone else, is he not far more guilty? Let us note, therefore, that Nathan simply wanted to magnify the crime of David here, since he did not ravish someone else's wife out of ordinary need, but because there was no end to his greed. It was as if he had wanted to spend liberally out of another man's purse at the very time when he had too much himself. This, in sum, is what we must remember.

Now we see how God not only sent his prophet to David, but that he made his message prevail, and we see this when he received the correction so patiently. It is true that Nathan's illustration should have already mortified all David's resistance. For he could do nothing but admit the truth, since he had already pronounced the sentence. What else could he have said when Nathan was speaking, except lower his eyes and be silent? God certainly must have been in charge of this, for the Word will be useless, even if we have it hammered in our ears, until our Lord makes us hear it, that is, that he change the hardness of our hearts, and convert the stone into flesh, as the prophet Ezekiel describes it (Ezek. 11:19). Therefore, although God sends his Word to us in order to exhort us to repentance, it will be nothing but wasted effort unless he speaks within by his Spirit. For we are deaf and blind. In fact, David was like a poor brute beast! All his senses were preoccupied; the devil had taken such possession of him that he was like someone bewitched. What, therefore, would Nathan have gained if God had not had pity on David, and prepared him to receive the doctrine of reproof which was brought to him? But that will be expounded again in more detail later.

Now it is sufficient in dealing with what is related here that we realise that God has shown that he did not want David to perish – as if after he sent his prophet to him, David simply rotted in his crime! But after that, he added the second thing, which gave power to his Word so that it bore fruit, and so David was touched by the very means that is shown to us here.

Now, although Nathan did not want to flatter David, as if he feared and dreaded him, nonetheless he dealt with him gently and drew him out little by little, as we have seen. And often God will do the same thing. It is true that he can unleash fury like thunder when it comes to dealing with us. Indeed, if we have been flattering ourselves in our sins for a long time, it will not be sufficient for God simply to speak; he will have to shout! If it is not sufficient for him to shout, he must raise his hand and pull our ears, and even pick us up by the hair of our heads by sheer force! God, therefore, will certainly use such violence. But be that as it may, still we see him conforming himself to our weakness and employing the most appropriate methods to bring us back. In fact, if we pay attention to so many exhortations in Scripture, by which God encourages poor sinners to return to the way of salvation, we will realise that he employs a similar kindness to us as he did to David.

For example, he says by his prophet: 'And he who is fallen, shall he not arise? And he who has wandered from the good path, shall he not return?' (Jer. 8:4). Thus, when he sends his prophet in order to warn them, and say: 'Here am I' – this picture is like the one which is given here. For if God had said: 'Now what are you doing? You are just seeking to ruin yourselves, and started doing evil a long time ago.' If God had spoken in this manner, as he often does, that would not have had such influence as the example set forth. It is the same as if God were saying: 'If a poor man has stumbled, will he not look in front of his feet? If he has fallen in the mud, will he not use both his arms and hands to get himself out? And those who have fallen in a much harder way – that is, from my grace – should they not seek to bring themselves back? Indeed, when a man making a trip sees that he has wandered from his way, and finds himself enveloped by woods and forests, will he remain there without the least pain or worry about finding his route, and want to perish voluntarily? No, on the contrary, as soon as a man realises that he has made a mistake and strayed from the path, he will take pains to come back to the right way, and finally arrive at his lodgings. Well now, you are wandering; you have turned your back on me and you are far from me,' says the Lord, 'and why do you not therefore return to seek me?'

We see, thus, that God did not deal in this way with David alone, but in general he calls every poor sinner in the path of perdition by this parable. They ought to be convinced by their common sense, unless they are totally taken over by the devil, in which case there is no more hope that anyone can bring them back by any correction at all. Now this is still another point that we must carefully note.

Well, when it adds that Nathan said: 'You are the man!' (2 Sam. 12:7ff.), clearly exposing David's ingratitude to him, and then adding threats – in the first place, we have to note that when the prophets and all those who have charge of teaching, see that a man is not intractable, it 'opens their mouth' and gives them reason to continue, until they see that he has been completely won. By contrast, secondly, when a man behaves like a ferocious beast, and is totally closed so that one does not know how to approach him, and instead of humbling himself, grits his teeth and kicks this way and that – one must leave him as a lost man. That is how God assesses the situation, seeing men so disfigured with rage that he said that he would not strive as formerly, pleading and sending his prophets to call back the wretched, but would let them go to ruin. It is the same as if God were pleading against those who resist his Word when he strongly rebukes them. Now he says that he will no longer strive, and his vengeance must be executed, his offers have been too long rejected, and he is compelled to apply his hand to them.

Hence, if we would desire to give God an opening to draw us to repentance, let us not have this spirit of bitterness of which Scripture speaks (Rom. 3:14), full of venom and pride, and thus rejecting any correction. As one sees in those who cannot stand someone pricking them even with the gentlest touch; for venom will immediately come out. Let us avoid (I say) having this spirit of rebellion and bitterness but, as St James says, let us 'receive the word, when it is sown in us, with a meek spirit and in gentle and kind affection' (Jas. 1:21). Now that is one point.

Nathan, therefore, had the door open, as it were, when David, at first hearing, declared that this man was not to be tolerated (2 Sam. 12:5). It is true that he was not thinking of himself, for hypocrisy was still holding him in this ignorance, as we have seen. But still he showed us a good principle. Nathan went further when he saw that David was already disposed to receive the correction. For it was a sign that he was already making himself meek when he judged in favour of equity and uprightness, and when he even had such zeal that he did not want the evil to be tolerated, but wanted to rebuke it with his royal authority. Now that is one thing.

Nevertheless, we should note that if God treats us sharply at the first encounter before making us feel his mercy, we should not find it strange, but subject ourselves willingly to it. It is true that we certainly like him to begin gently, and indeed, we would like him to bow down before us in order to please us. Indeed, we would like to strike him in the face, as if he were a common lodger in our house. Now this impudence will come out in nearly everyone when God does not restore them as they would like. Let us learn, therefore, when God comes to us in such force, to bow our heads and recognise that we need chastisement. For it is certain that it would be done gently if he saw that we could bear it, and that we were capable of it. But St Paul explains to us, in his own person, why God employs such hard and sharp remedies, more than we would like. For if he gave in to everyone in the way that they would like, we would be like brute beasts, for our nature tends to go in the opposite direction from equity and reason! It must, therefore, be the way that he desires.

Now consider where St Paul offers a choice to the Corinthians as to how he will come: 'Do you want this (he says) to be with gentleness or with a rod?' (1 Cor. 4:21). Now it is certain that St Paul did not give harsh punishments. We have seen his patience. What did he mean? In the first place, he had a charge from God to rebuke the Corinthians. But he saw them full of pride, although he had given them so many admonitions. And so he says: 'It seems that I am very extreme, but it is up to you to choose whether you want me to come to you with kindness or with a rod. I am getting nowhere with you, it is making no sense. You want people to flatter you, and to allure you, and to pamper you. Nevertheless, you are rude, and full of pride and haughtiness, and in sum, are incorrigible. Therefore, if I want to serve God and carry out the charge which he has committed to me, I must have the rod in my hand – not a material rod, but the spiritual sword which pierces through hearts and examines them to the very depths' (Heb. 4:12). Thus, he had to proceed in this manner.

Now let us think of ourselves, and be careful that – according to St Paul – we are of so humble a spirit that we may be ready to return to God at all times, whenever we have offended him. Let us not find it strange when we see that after he has given us his Word with gentleness, he strikes us with heavy blows. For otherwise, we will reach the point of which Ezekiel speaks (Ezek. 33:32) – and our Lord Jesus Christ uses this example and illustration of the prophet (Matt. 11:17). When someone preaches gently to us, without enough severity to prick us in our sins, it is as though someone had played the harp to us and we were saying: 'Oh, how beautiful is this song!' Now that is where we are. Hence, let us note that when God deals strictly at the beginning, and not only astonishes us but seems to want to strike us down totally, let us note that he does this because we are so lazy and slow. This is especially so when we abuse his kindness and take the opportunity to plunge ourselves even more deeply into our sins, unless he unleashes his violence in this way to force us, so to speak, to return to him.

It is true that a servile fear will amount to nothing, but he often corrects us in such a way that we are forced to recognise our bankruptcy in order to be displeased with it. And this correction is more than necessary for us. But it must gradually create a willing heart in us. For we see that when a sword is highly polished, it cuts like a razor. Yet why is it that one must scrape it in order to sharpen it before it can cut? We are, therefore, like a badly furbished sword when our Lord calls us to himself! He must smite us with great blows, and when he has thoroughly sharpened us, then we will be ready to be used. We will, I say, have true courage, and God can then use us and handle us at his pleasure. Now we must not be surprised if he uses such means. For we are always crude until he catches us in our flight and drags us by the hair of our head and says: 'Be still!' So here is one point.

Now let us note, also, that it is not enough for our misdeeds to be brought forward in general, but corrections must be joined to them. For it is not without cause that the Word of God is called 'a two-edged sword cutting both ways, in order to divide thoughts and affections, and to examine the secrets which are in us' (Heb. 4:12). For if God suddenly gives us a blow – just as a surgeon wanting to remove a tumour makes cuts with his scalpel, so that the tumour opens and the infection comes out –

similarly, it is not enough for God to use severity merely in order to convince us. For there are so many hidden things in us, there are twisted thoughts, there are haughty affections, and God must uncover all of that. Hence, it is not enough, in general, for him to set forth our faults, but corrections must be added in order to prune, so to speak, our thoughts and desires, and thoroughly to exercise us. Then beyond that, there are these threats which are linked to them. But these things cannot be discussed at present in detail. We will reserve them for another time.

Now let us prostrate ourselves before the majesty of our good God, in recognition of so many offences of which we are guilty. Let us pray that, more and more, he may make us feel them, so that we might seek his mercy without any hypocrisy; but instead, be so wounded with sadness and displeasure that we may groan at having thus provoked him to wrath. And may we profit more and more in his fear, so that our life may be truly reformed in his obedience, and instead of straying far off from him, may we be ready to follow him, step by step, on the path which he shows us, in order to attain salvation. And may he not only bestow this grace upon us, but upon all peoples and nations of the earth . . .

36

*God is Not the Author of Sin**

Nathan said to David: You are the man! Thus says the Lord God of Israel: I have anointed you to be king over Israel, and I have delivered you out of the hand of Saul. I have given to you the house of your master, and the wives of your master into your bosom, and I have given you the house of Israel and Judah. And if that is too little, I shall add many other similar things . . . (2 Sam. 12:7–12).

We have already seen how the prophet Nathan, in order to magnify the crime of David, reproached him with the benefits which he had received from the hand of God. Certainly, ingratitude should always be detested. Here is a point that we have to note carefully – namely, the more generously God deals with us, the more he commits us to serve and honour him in all purity, and it will be inexcusable if we are negligent in doing so. Therefore, let us value the benefits that he bestows upon us; otherwise, it will cost us very dearly. For God cannot – and indeed, should not – allow his goodness to be despised nor people to trample underfoot the favours which should be precious to us.

We see how he reproaches the whole people of Israel in general, whom he has freely chosen from among all other nations of the earth, and to whom he has not ceased to do good, nor give them help in all their need, without receiving much in return from them. He compares them to a vine (Isa. 5:1ff.). 'My vine,' he says, 'what have I done with you? I have planted you,

*Monday, August 24, 1562.

and carefully cultivated you and have done everything possible in order to make you fruitful; waiting for you to bear me good grapes, but you have repaid me with anguish and bitterness. Is that how to recompense me for the pains that I have taken? Do you want to strangle your master?' Well, what was said to that ancient people is addressed to us today.

As a general principle, therefore, let us learn to consider carefully the many ways in which we are indebted to God, since he has ransomed us by the blood of his only Son (1 Pet. 1:18–19). Not content with that alone, he has made us participants in the salvation which has been acquired for us by the knowledge of the Gospel. He wanted his testimony of paternal love to be ratified in us. He entertains us as though in his own house, and wants us to be part of his flock, not in the capacity of servants but as his children (Jn. 15:15). Since we have received his benefits, if we do not learn to dedicate ourselves fully to him with integrity, we are sacrilegious and ungrateful.

Well, from this, each one of us must become aware of our own particular condition. So I would say, let us voluntarily enter into account before God if we do not want to be dragged there by force to face accusation, and immediately receive a sentence of condemnation. To avoid this, let each one consider how many of God's blessings he has received since birth (Rom. 2:4), and in how many ways he has been delivered and kept safe by him. Then we will have to be our own judges and not wait for God to open his mouth to reproach us for our ingratitude, which we see he did with David.

Moreover, it is good to explain in detail what is said here, because there are several difficulties. It states: 'God had constituted you king over Israel, after having delivered you from the hand of Saul'. Now in regard to that, we know how God took David from a stable, where he tended the animals of his father. No-one expected him to gain the crown. Thus, when he was taken from such a place, where he had neither dignity nor nobility, it showed God's goodness shining with even greater lustre. In fact, David certainly knew that the grace of God was to be magnified even more because he was called to the kingdom from being a poor shepherd – indeed, from being left behind in the house of his father, as we have seen, where he was considered the last and the least of all. Thus, Nathan had every reason to remind him of this.

Now he adds that 'God had delivered him out of the hand of Saul'. For it certainly seemed that it would have been much better for David if he had always remained in his first situation, rather than being called to a charge which brought him so many troubles and enemies and so often put him in danger of death. Though, as we have seen, Saul then made him hated by the people and alienated from them, he was content with his insignificance. But insofar as he endured much trouble and torment, and was greatly and grievously persecuted, God, 'in giving him the house of his master', showed all the more how much he loved him. Now that is why Nathan specifically mentioned here that David had been delivered out of the hand of Saul.

Tht should have affected him so much that he would have walked with greater care, for if he had been afflicted with poverty for a time and, as it were, raised from the dead into life, should it not have kept him in line? Therefore, when God lifts us up into some position of dignity or degree of honour, let us be even more aware of what we were beforehand. This first condition ought to hold us down, so that we are not blinded by the prosperity which might come upon us later. So this is further added to evidence given of David's ingratitude – that he did not recognise that God had protected him from the hand of Saul, as a lamb snatched from the wolf's mouth. He was so very often a step from death, but kept his life, as though God resurrected him thirty and forty times! Thus, he should have renounced the world and his own desires even more.

Next, it says that 'God gave him the house of his master; indeed even with his wives'. Now when he succeeded Saul, it was by the judgement of God. For although Saul had been ordained king, he had to be shamefully degraded because he failed to recognise who he was, and rebelling against God, went from bad to worse. But be that as it may, still the grace of God showed itself more generously towards David, who turned from being a subject to reigning as king; from being in the hands of

Saul to keeping the descendants of Saul under his feet, so to speak. That change was again very remarkable and it should clearly have instructed David to humble himself. This confirms what I mentioned just now; that is, that if God has taken us from an obscure place, and has put us in an excellent position, far from it needing to make us proud, it should make us compare the state that we were in with the one where we are now, so that we might learn to confess and preach how indebted we are to God. Then, in giving him praise for what we have received, we should remember to walk in fear of him, and not forget who we are. For 'what do we have that we have not received?' (1 Cor. 4:7). We should, therefore, return to this exhortation of St Paul. It is very reasonable that God should receive our confession of all his benefits (Psa. 103); not that it should merely roll superficially off our tongue, but that [inner] reality should be joined to [outward] praise, so that in all our life we would show how truly we are indebted to him, holding everything from him.

There is now a question concerning Nathan's statement that 'God had given the wives of Saul to David' (2 Sam. 12:8). We have shown above that although God tolerated the ancient fathers having had several wives, he never approved of it. For when he instituted marriage, he said: 'Let us make a helper for the man who will be like him' (Gen. 2:18). By saying this, he showed that one man should not have two or three wives. This pronouncement was not for one period only, but given as an inviolable rule. Having several wives, therefore, is to reverse what God once established, in wanting the man to have a sole helper. Indeed, since the fall of Adam, we know that marriage helps men handle the weakness and corruption into which they have fallen, as St Paul says in First Corinthians: in order to avoid fornication, let each man have his own wife (1 Cor. 7:2). He does not say: two wives! Then, there is also the reciprocal truth: let every woman have her own husband. Having several wives, therefore, breaks down this first rule, that there is a definite principle which should control men – they must not seek to have several wives. So why did God contradict himself when he gave Saul's wives to David? Now we ought to consider, as an important principle, that we may legitimately enjoy all the goods which God gives us. But there is not a single time that God, in his patience, tolerates what in itself is not legitimate. Therefore, even if God tolerates something, he still does not approve of it, even though he seems to do so. Yet God may pardon something that has been done which is bad and ought to be condemned, so that it passes away and runs its course.

We shall understand even better what St Paul says when he wants the pastors of the Church to be married to only one woman (1 Tim. 3:2). This passage has been misunderstood by people who have twisted it all around. For the words, almost obscured by these misinterpretations, mean that he who is established as pastor of the Church should not have two wives. Well now, it would be strange if other Christians, who have not mounted the pulpit and who do not have the office of teaching, should have several wives!

We see what I have just mentioned, that although this corruption and abuse was not in the least approved of by God, still for some time he endured it when there was no other swift remedy available. For it was far too common a custom among the Jews for a man to take two wives. That is why our Lord Jesus Christ brought his disciples back to the pure institution of marriage (Matt. 5:27ff.; 19:3ff.). It is true that God had declared it by his prophets, and indeed, actually preferred a man to reject his wife totally rather than mistreat her by adding another one. Yet divorce was said to be bad, yes – but that was because of the hardness of man. The Jews were duly admonished concerning this matter, but it was like speaking to the dead, for they were hardened in their wicked desires when they made this perverse custom into a law. Therefore, when our Lord Jesus Christ showed that marriage ought to be honoured in such a way that each one is content with one wife only, what could those men have done who were already chained in these bonds? To have cast away their second wife would have been a cruel and hard thing, for the women would have been frustrated and abused. It was better, therefore, for the poor women to have continued on and been content to bear the pain and the vice of their husbands, since it was an incorrigible evil.

Hence, although this was tolerated among the people, St Paul did not want the pastors to take such a liberty.

Well now, we see how God permitted things to run their course, bad as they were. So this is what we must remember from this passage: God did not approve of David having several wives, as has been dealt with above. However, in handing over to him the succession of Saul, he gave him his house, and hence his wives. It was certainly not legitimate for him and, in fact, kings were expressly forbidden to have a number of wives, according to what has been said. For although the rule applied to everyone in general, God expressly forbade polygamy to kings, for he was so well aware that princes always usurp what does not belong to them, because no-one calls them to account, and they think that they are not subject to the law. Hence, David was doubly wrong. Be that as it may, God still put up with this evil. Thus, David's ingratitude to God was even greater, since God had permitted him more than was legitimate for him, and did not impute to him an offence for which, otherwise, he deserved rejection. Thus, when God showed himself kind to him in this way, pardoning him so mercifully for the evil that he had done to him, and then David was inflamed again by his wicked lusts to ravish another man's wife – that is what made his sin so much worse. This is what we have to remember.

Next, he is accused of 'having despised the Word of God' (2 Sam. 12:9). Let us keep in mind here the instruction which David received, as he confessed it in Psalm 7. This instruction was the same for him, it seems to me, as a figure in his account book, designed to render him all the more guilty. For a man who knows the will of his master and takes no account of it will be doubly chastised; hence, 'Those who have transgressed under the Law, shall be condemned by the Law' (Rom. 2:12). If David had been a poor pagan, he would still have been inexcusable. For nature and his own common sense should have taught him enough to know that it was a wicked deed to ravish someone else's wife. We even know that this was a conviction among the pagans, as well as among ourselves, who have the Law. We see this, for instance, in the case of

Abimelech (Gen. 20:9). David, therefore, was quite clearly a criminal before God, even if he had never been in the school of the prophets. But he was very experienced in the Law, and was a prophet himself. Yet the fact that he was thus blinded by his brutal lust is the reason why it is stated, loud and clear, that he despised the Word of God.

Hence, since God has bestowed on us the grace of manifesting his will to us, let us note that we ought to walk even more carefully and be on guard. For if poor ignorant people do not escape condemnation, what will it be like for us to whom God has given the benefit of showing us the way, if we do not follow, and each of us wanders off after our own evil lusts? Therefore, his is a point to be carefully considered.

The purpose of saying that 'David killed Uriah' (2 Sam. 12:9) is to show that God does not merely regard the act, but rather the motivation, for David was actually absent when Uriah was killed. He was at home and the others were fighting against the enemy. Yet he is unfailingly considered to be a murderer, and based on their common sense, men agree with this judgement. But there is an even more powerful reason for us to learn that when it comes to concocting all these pretexts which we can bring up before the judicial seat of God, such as not having put our hand on him (for instance) – that, nevertheless, the deed will always be expressly attributed to us, and therefore we cannot be absolved. David could easily have protested that he had not killed Uriah. But he had no reply, since he was the cause of the deed.

This is why the prophet Isaiah cries against the Jews: You have bloody hands, and yet you come in my temple to offer sacrifice, thinking to please me (Isa. 1:10–15). Well, to whom did he address himself? To all the counsellors of the king, and to those who had authority over the people, and who would certainly have liked to have their reputation upheld! Nevertheless, the prophet did not fail to call them murderers, since they had violated others' possessions and by their avarice and inhumanity had caused the poor to die. Hence, it is not enough for us to claim that we did not actually use the sword to kill someone. For if we are guilty of the death of someone, although we may quibble over the means that we used to do it, all our quibbling will be trifling and not accepted or received before God. Let us, therefore, learn not only to keep our hands unpolluted before God, but also all our senses, and not to consent to evil, to avoid being considered accomplices of those who do so.

Then it says: 'David killed him by the sword of the enemy' (2 Sam. 12:9). Far from the guilt being lessened by the fact that the Ammonites killed Uriah, it actually aggravated the crime of David even more. Next, it adds that the name of God was exposed to shame and blasphemed by the unbelievers. Therefore, when it says that David delivered Uriah into the hands of the Ammonites, it is more dreadful than if he had killed him with his own hand. Thus, all these attractive excuses which he was making were far from useful for him. So let us note that when we attempt to absolve ourselves before men, we not only 'cover ourselves with a wet sack', as the popular proverb says, but we provoke God more, actually uncovering our offences and evil deeds, so that what was once a simple fault reappears in a more aggravated form because we wanted to 'beat around the bush'. To summarise, this is what we have to remember – that although we may be able to escape the judgement of men, it does not mean that we have been absolved before God. For he has another measure and another scale which we do not have.

After these rebukes, Nathan added these threats. For it was not enough for David to be condemned, but his sentence had to be declared to him: Inasmuch as you have thus 'despised' me, blood 'will not depart from your house' (2 Sam. 12:10). This is the first threat. Now we have already mentioned this, and have briefly shown how it was accomplished. David's own sons killed each other. There was Absalom killing Amnon. And what was the reason? The other had violated his sister. Now here was incest, wickedly committed in the house of David. And as if this was not enough, murder had to result – indeed, between actual brothers. After the trespass of David, Solomon had Adonijah, his brother, killed. When all that happened, would one not have said that it was a wicked and unhappy household? David had to suffer this punishment and receive his wages. Now this is the first thing that we should note.

If God did not pardon David without punishing him so severely, what will it be like for us? It is certainly true that God preserved him, and that this was a special grace. But still, the grace which God bestowed on him did not prevent judgement from being mixed with it. On the one hand, note carefully that David was a transgressor of the commandment: 'You shall not kill' (Exod. 20:13). On the other hand, God had to give him such a blow that he would feel it for the rest of his life. Nor was it a simple blow; rather, it was the same as cutting off an arm or a leg, and saying: 'You shall not die, but you shall lose one of your members'. Thus it was with David. The child which he had begotten was soon taken away; then his own children killed one another, and his house was like a den of thieves. It was not a question merely of shedding human blood; acts of incest were committed, so the most filthy and rotten things in the world happened there. When we see how David was dealt with, alas, what will it be like for us? Therefore, let us consider walking much more in the fear of God, in the future, not provoking him to anger, so that after he has pardoned us and bestowed his fatherly goodness on us, he will not have to be so severe that there is nothing for us to do but gnash our teeth.

Well, after saying that, Nathan added: 'I shall raise up evil against you out of your own house, for I shall violate your wives and give them to your neighbour' (2 Sam. 12:11) – that is to say, to his own son. Now here is how your wives, therefore, will be ravished and violated in the presence of all the people; that is, 'in the presence of this sun which shines. You have wanted to do it in secret, but I shall have it done in the presence of all Israel', and 'the sun' (2 Sam. 12:12) shall be a witness of it, in order to show that I am a just Judge, and that nothing can keep me from dealing with secret things – indeed, the most hidden things.

Here was a punishment which surpassed all the others. If one had allowed David to choose, it is certain that he would much rather have died than bear such shame. For a man would rather have his throat cut or have the most cruel tortures inflicted upon him than see his own wife raped. Now what happens when the son himself comes to take his father's wife in order to sleep with her and pollute himself with her? That is against nature. It was not even a question here of only one woman, but since David had several of them, he had to bear a greater punishment (2 Sam. 16:22). Moreover, there was this circumstance: Absalom was not content with committing fornication with the wives of his father and wickedly abusing them, but he had a public platform constructed, so that all the people could see. Then he had the trumpet sounded everywhere, as if someone wanted to mete out justice by condemning a poor criminal, announcing: 'Let everyone come to see the justice which I want to mete out to my father, and let everyone recognise how much shame I am bringing upon him. This will not merely turn his house into a bawdy house, but will create such shameful confusion that everyone will be appalled, and will speak of it for ever.' Now if David had been allowed to choose (since he had a most courageous spirit), it is certain that he would a thousand times rather have chosen to die than suffer such humiliation. But he still had to go through all this, even though God found him so much to his liking, and he had testimony of this in the Psalm:[1] 'I have found a man after my own heart' – still God dealt with him in this severe manner.

We have here to remember most carefully another instruction which should touch us to the quick. Let us compare ourselves to David. Have we been elevated to such an excellent position? When a king and prophet, a man who was even a type and image of our Lord Jesus Christ, was treated so roughly, what will it be like for us, who are neither kings nor princes nor prophets nor types of Jesus Christ, although we are members of his body?

Moreover, this word is to be seriously considered, where it says that although David wanted to hide his sin, God would still uncover his corruption before the 'whole people of Israel' (2 Sam. 12:12). This was to show that the more we try to bury our offences, the more certain it is that God will bring them into the open. For it seems that we are wanting him to despise us completely, or at least ignore us in his judgement, but instead we

[1]Not the Psalm, but 1 Sam. 13:14.

worry about the approval of other men. This shows, as we have already argued, how utterly perverse we are: 'I will be afraid that men might have a bad opinion of me, and yet I do not care what God and his angels think', we seem to be saying. Are we not out of our minds when we come to such a position as this? What a notorious contempt of God! But there is still more. It seems that we are wanting to fight against him by showing ourselves up as villains entering a den of thieves. On the one hand, here is God wanting us to walk before him and our life to be a lamp which shines (Matt. 5:15–16), giving a good example to everyone. Instead, on the other hand, we are digging a cave, so to speak, underground to hide our corruption. However, it is uncovered even more effectively, as we see in the prophet Isaiah: 'Woe unto you who seek deep [hiding] places' (Isa. 29:15). For the Jews thought that they could deceive God with their finesse, which is what hypocrites have always thought.

It was not without good reason that Nathan said to David: 'You have wanted to do it in secret'. It is true to say that David hid himself like a partridge (as they say). For in fact, his wickedness was published widely and well known. Whatever excuse he might make, still the finger had to be pointed at him and he had to have everyone as his judge, from the greatest down to the smallest. Yet he provoked God even more in that he was acting hypocritically. His hypocrisy caused murder. The reason why it is said 'I shall do it in public' was because he despised God and only showed concern for his reputation with the world; because he wanted his sin to be abolished by his tricks and pretexts, as though he wanted to put God to sleep, which was an utterly ridiculous sort of mockery. In other words, the vengeance of God would appear before the world.

Therefore, the more we desire to flee into the earth and cover ourselves, the more certainly will God drag us out by force, and lift us up on a scaffold, so that everyone will see the very wickedness which we wanted to cover with leaves and cloaks and whatever we were able to gather together. In short, if we want God to make our innocence shine out, as we have been promised; let us walk before him with sincere integrity. When we offend him, let us not cloak ourselves in trickery; let us not travel on twisted and meandering paths, but let us return completely to him, denuded of any thought of deception, determined instead to groan and sigh for having offended him. When it pleases him for our sins to be known by men, let us humble ourselves and accept this kind of correction voluntarily. In fact, we will not always display all the sins of which we are guilty before God; that, in fact, would be impossible. But be that as it may, if God wants to chastise us sometimes by such means, let us allow it. Furthermore, if we want God to preserve our good reputation, let us attempt to maintain simplicity and steadfastness before him and before his angels, so that when we do well, we can testify that it does not come from a false or feigned courage, but because we want to be pliable before him. So much, then, for this point.

Nevertheless, a question arises here concerning God's declaration that he would do what he said in the uncovering of this matter. And what was it? That he would violate the wives of David and give them over to the hands of Absalom, and corrupt them through him. But is it appropriate for God to strip a man of his wives, and give them over not to a mere fornicator, but to someone who commits incest? If one speaks of the deed of Absalom, it should certainly make our hair stand on end, for a son to come and take his father's wife and pollute her, especially in these public circumstances which we have described. Now here was such a base crime that we should all be horrified by it. We know that God hates iniquity (Heb. 1:9). Why, therefore, did he attribute this to himself? He said here that he would put the wives of David on a scaffold and would have them corrupted by his own son, so we see how God presides in an admirable fashion in that he always remains just and beyond reproach, however much he uses the wicked as his instruments. It was Absalom who was the rod that God used to punish David. And in what way? By the incest that we have already mentioned. But how could God not be soiled? After all, it does seem that he involved himself with Absalom to be his partner in crime.

Well, I have already said that God has an admirable way when he executes his judgement, a way which surpasses all human intelligence, so that it only remains for us to humble ourselves before him and to confess that everything that he does is just. If his judgements are a profound abyss, let us not fail to submit to them, in order to put a stop to the babble of these fanatics who would like to tell God what to do. For when someone tells them that nothing happens here below unless God ordains it, and that he disposes the whole thing according to his good will, then what will they say? They will reply that God commits sin and is the Author of it. Indeed, that seems to be so, but the Scripture does not explain it in that way. In fact, when we say that God disposes the whole, we must come to the end result, and ask why he does it. It is that it is up to him to assess judgement. A judge will not be guilty when he sends a criminal to the gallows, but rather held criminal before God, if he does not do so. For he who spares the wicked is just as guilty as he who punishes the innocent, says Solomon (Prov. 17:15). The judge must do his duty, therefore. And what is that? To kill men; though, in fact, the authority is given to him by God (1 Pet. 2:13–14). So one must consider his ultimate purpose. Now if a mortal man, having this charge from God, is valued when he puts men to death, why should God himself be brought to account? How can we dare accuse him on the basis of our own imagination, by saying: 'Well now, this is strange. I do not know how this is done.' That is what these fanatics conclude out of their own presumption when they decide that God is the Author of sin if he controls everything by his providence.

When Job confessed that it was God who had snatched away his assets, he immediately understood fully that human thieves were like the hands of God, like rods which he was guiding by his providence (Job 1:21). He certainly knew that the devil was the instrument by which God was executing his sentence, in order to prove his patience. So he did not fail to say: 'God has done it'. And how were his assets stolen, his houses ruined, and all his possessions taken as prey? God did it by the hand of thieves. Will this make us say that God is contaminated? Indeed not, for he does it by his counsel, which is quite other than human. This is why Psalm 39 says: 'I have made myself silent, and have not opened my mouth, for you have done it' (v. 9). The psalmist wanted to despise himself, unable to bear his affliction, in utter anguish and great distress. But since he knew that it was God who was pursuing him, he quieted himself and kept silent, confessing that this was reason enough for him to submit himself to all that God would give him. What was it that David endured? Persecution, violence, and cruelty at the hands of his enemies; he suffered it all. It is true that he asked vengeance for it, but yet he attributed it to God. When he thus spoke, it was not to make God an accomplice in his murders, but to show that when we are afflicted by men, God is in charge of it, secretly ordaining everything that they do, so that he should be considered just in all his deeds, and men should be condemned.

Now that is how God presided by the hand of Absalom when he violated his father's wives. God planned it, yet without Absalom knowing that God was doing it. And why? Because although Absalom was wicked, it still did not all happen by chance, but was just punishment, which David should have recognised with complete humility. We cannot confess that God is just without also attributing to him all equity and uprightness, which is how we should put this doctrine into practice.

In fact, what would happen if the wicked – and even the devil, who is their father – could do something by themselves without the express permission of God? What would our condition be like? Here we are surrounded by so many thieves and all sorts of people just seeking to devour us. Now 'the devil is a roaring lion, who roams here and there, only seeking prey' (1 Pet. 5:8). And would he not soon have swallowed us up? If, therefore, the devil were not held in control, and all the wicked were not governed by the counsel and the secret and incomprehensible power of God, where would we be? Thus, let us realise that whenever the wicked are in control over us, and trouble us, although they do it unjustly, God is still in charge of it, and we must return to that fact. For we will never know how to profit from it, although we endure it, unless we hold to this principle. That is, though the wicked are pursuing their disordered lusts, yet God is guiding them nevertheless.

Well, it is true to say that they do not think that this is happening – which is also why they are never credited with serving God. For they did not want to do so, as is said of

Sennacherib, king of the Assyrians, who chastised the people of God by his command (2 Kings 18:17ff.). He was not thinking of doing this at all, but since he was a tyrant of the highest degree, God compared him to an axe (Isa. 10:15), saying: I hold him in my hand like an instrument for cutting off bad branches (Isa. 10:33–34). Now he was not at all thinking of it in that way. Furthermore, God showed that while Sennacherib would be condemned for his actions, God would not fail to be a just Judge.

Let us learn, therefore, to discern the fact that however much men fail to understand the meaning of their iniquities, and however much we must always detest the evil that they commit against the Law, God does not fail to exercise his justice in such a way that the evil is turned into good. That is to say, as far as he is concerned, he knows how to use evil beyond our thoughts, so that he converts it into good – that is, to a good end – in such a way that he will not only always remain just, but we shall have occasion, all the time of our life, to glorify him everywhere, in every way.

Now let us bow down before his majesty, recognising so many faults which we have committed, praying him to make us feel them more and more. And may this make us displeased with them and repudiate ourselves, in order to obtain pardon and mercy for them. And may he make us walk in such obedience to him that in giving a good example to men, we may not be trapped in our sins and flatteries, but may learn to dedicate ourselves fully to him in body and soul. And may he not only bestow this grace upon us, but on all peoples . . .

37

*David's Humble Confession of Sin**

David said to Nathan: I have sinned against the Lord. And Nathan said to David: The Lord has also removed your sin from you, and you shall not die (2 Sam. 12:13).

We have here a very brief confession, which would seem very meagre if we had not been given the fuller description of his repentance which David shows us in Psalm 51. Also, we have the response which the prophet, acting as his very mouth, gave on behalf of God, showing that David had been willing to be touched and had admitted his offences, not as a legal formality, but from the very depths of his heart, as they say. Hence we must not always stop with the text but can sometimes go beyond it, as it were, when Scripture shows us sinners who have recognised their condition, and been humbled. We see an example of practically the same thing in what our Lord Jesus Christ recounted of the poor publican who, lowering his eyes to the ground, did not use flowery rhetoric towards God but simply said: 'Lord, be merciful to me, a poor sinner' (Luke 18:3).

Now here are three or four words seemingly expressed at random, but in spite of their brevity our Lord Jesus Christ pronounces that he 'returned to his house justified' (Luke 18:14), meaning that he had been absolved and approved by God. Therefore, when it is a question of our coming before God, let us note that we do not obtain grace by flowery language. Our heart should be pure, and our mouth simply trying to

*Tuesday, August 25, 1562.

generate a deeper response, so that God may be glorified both inwardly and outwardly. That is not, of course, to say that sinners may not use long statements. But those who have really felt what the judgement of God is, and daily enter into account to condemn themselves for their sins, often use broken language to God. They may utter only three and a half words, and then remain in this kind of confused condition. Anyone who is faithful may experience for himself what we see here.

Nevertheless, we are given more details of David's example, which we can follow in the Psalm already mentioned. For in Psalm 51, he does not simply say, in a word, that he has done wrong, but wants the whole world to know about his uncleanness. Thus he uncovers himself, almost publishing his shame, seeming to be quite willing to show his infamy to everyone, not only during his lifetime, but to the end of the world. He even shows how dull-witted he had been, by using the following preface when he composed this Psalm: 'After Nathan the prophet came to him, after he had gone in to Bathsheba' – as if he were saying that after being far from God, and imprisoned in an abyss of confusion, God nevertheless did not fail to scold him. Now by saying this, he is showing that he was dead to his own condition, that he was reeking, so to speak, stuck in his own filth, until God brought him back by sending the prophet to him. These words make it clear that David did not confess his offences out of mere ceremony, but with a willing heart.

Then when he asks God for pardon: 'Lord, have mercy upon me, according to your clemency and goodness' (Psa. 51:1), he is going far beyond the word recorded here. He continues: 'According to the multitude of your pity and mercy'. There he calls not on the mercy of God alone, but is wanting to gather an infinite amount of mercy, pity, and compassion, knowing how great his need is. When he asks for pardon again, he is not satisfied with one single request, but he says: 'Lord, take away my iniquity' (Psa. 51:9) and then: 'Remove my sin, Lord, wash me and be sure to purge and wash away the uncleanness with which I am contaminated before your face'. Then, again he says: 'Lord, wash me with sprinkling of hyssop' (Psa. 51:7), to carry out the sacrifice of the Law (Lev. 14:6–7), as if to say:

'Lord, may you give me complete certainty that I am purged by your goodness, so that I will not feel damnation in myself'. An earlier statement in the Psalm confirms David's attitude even more when he says that his sin 'is ever before him'; that his iniquity accuses him ceaselessly. Now that is what David meant by this word: 'I have sinned' (2 Sam. 12:13).

Therefore, we see that when David humbled himself before God, he was not satisfied with the standard kind of confession that hypocrites make. So that we may really benefit from this example, let us pay attention, in the first place, to who David was, and the characteristics that he demonstrated. Here was the king, accused firmly and pointedly by the prophet. Not only was his offence placed before his eyes, but he called himself a criminal and an evil-doer precisely because he himself had declared that the one who did wrong to his neighbour – that is, the rich man to the poor man – was a man of blood (2 Sam. 12:5–6). 'That is you', says the prophet. This is something that could have bitterly wounded him, for it did not spare him or use flattery. On the contrary, Nathan called him a murderer, and reproached him for having plotted with the enemies of the Law – with unbelievers – to shed blood. He also added the following promises of trouble: that evil would be raised up for him from his own son, that his house would have bloody murders committed in it, and that this royal line would be dishonoured.

Now when a king can listen to such condemnation, it is a sign that he is humbled. We see great pride in the great people of this world. In the papacy, for instance, although they may start to beat on their breasts, and though they may go and see a priest to make a pretence of mortifying themselves and 'bearing the cross on their back', still they do not want to be rebuked. Instead, they want people, as it were, to overlook any fault, and prefer others just to 'tickle their ears', rather than cutting through their pretence. That is how great men of this world would like to be exempt from the common law; so in the same way, David could have behaved rudely. However, he showed he had voluntarily humbled himself and kept his mouth shut, which meant more than if he had talked a great deal. For in saying: 'I have sinned against the Lord', he accepted and received the condemnation placed upon him by Nathan; as if to say: 'Alas, I have no reply, I want to be my own judge in this matter, and however it pleases God to proceed against me, I will accept his will. I simply reply, Amen.'

Thus, the confession of David had more virtue by its silence than it would have had in impressive words. For usually what we see is that when hypocrites confess their sin, they do it in such a way that no-one can add a word afterwards! When a man says: 'Look, I have been caught out – but anyway, I do not want to be excused, because this is a serious fault', it is so that no-one can add anything! For you see how touchy such people are and how quickly they will spit out venom if anyone says a single word to them. It is true that they do speak rather candidly, but if anyone comes along to examine them more closely, and considers the matter equally candidly, they cannot stand someone else repeating what they themselves have said. Clearly, their confession was simply fraudulent. However, it was the contrary with David. By keeping quiet, he gave the prophet liberty to condemn him as freely as he wished, and remained in this humble attitude, willing to suffer the consequent confusion and shame. Even if everyone had spat in his face, he knew how much he deserved it. So let us carefully note this fact that, in David's disgrace, silence meant more than the language which he uttered.

Now, when a king is humbled like this, whatever should happen to his little companions? Yet among them, we often see such pride that none of them can bear to be rebuked! It is true that people who have committed such grave and atrocious offences often do not deny that they thoroughly merit being censured. However, they would prefer it to be done very gently, and if anyone probes them to the quick, like a surgeon putting his knife in a wound, or cauterising it, it is so painful to them that they gnash their teeth in torment! Therefore, when people who are quite insignificant in the world's eyes are yet so delicate, wanting to be flattered, let us clearly note that it was a particular virtue for David to be humbled in this way and forget his royal dignity – knowing that he was worthy of rebuke, however great he was. And he knew that even though God had elevated him to such a high degree, he still had to come to account. Nor had he forgotten what is said in Psalm 82:6, that although kings are lieutenants of God in their position, they will still die, just like the lowest in their kingdom, and thus it will be necessary for them to prepare to give account for their life, just as much as those who have no reputation. David, therefore, realised all that. So just as the prophet Nathan showed laudable nobility of character for having come there in the person and authority of God, to rebuke the king without being a respecter of persons, so also David showed admirable virtue in having submitted himself to what Nathan said, and for not having replied. What is more, he even approved the condemnation by Nathan and was, as it were, dumbfounded over his shame and corruption.

Well, we must keep this lesson in mind all the more and learn that whenever God is so gracious as to call us, and as we are appearing before him to be rebuked, we must be touched at his very first call, and carefully refrain from excuse-making, for all our hiding places will do us no good. Afterwards, if we in fact turn ourselves into rebels, we will only be kicking against the pricks (Acts 26:14). We also know what Psalm 32 says, that the hardened man will be treated like a wild horse or a mule (v. 9). When those animals do not want to obey, one cuts their belly with harsh blows of the rod, first on one side, then on the other. Therefore, God will do this, says David, with all those who think that they can defeat him by their stubborn hardness against him. What else ought we to do but to humble ourselves as soon as God calls us to judgement? It is true that if we were very wise, we would not need to wait until we were called, and until he sent us prophets to pronounce judgement on us. Everyone certainly ought to take measures ahead of time, but because we are so wrapped up in our hypocrisy, the least we can do when God awakens us is to hear his voice; and after he has set our sins before us, we should acquiesce in his judgement without protest. This is the least we should do. Particularly since we are nothing in the eyes of the world, do we have any excuse at all for wanting to be prouder than a king, or liking to be played up to or flattered as well?

Moreover, we can gather from this that David was not so alienated from God that he no longer had any seeds of right feeling in himself, even though it was like a dying fire under the ashes. Of course, as has been shown, it is a horrible thing that he, a prophet and doctor in the church, did not consider what he was doing, but instead, after committing fornication and this adultery, he added the sin of murder, involving treason and disloyalty. And in addition to that, even after what had happened, he still remained in that dreadful condition – not like a drunkard, but like someone bewitched, or a totally wild beast. In spite of all that, we can still clearly perceive that he was not so stupefied that some small spark did not remain in him, although it seemed all but buried. For when he did recognise his offence, it was with tremendous grief, as we have already pointed out from Psalm 51, which we will look at again. That reaction shows us that God still kept him retained for himself, although he seemed to be a wild beast, totally lost.

It will often also happen that, for a period, the elect can seem devoid of the Spirit, and you would think that the Spirit given to them has been totally quenched, for they no longer seem to know what religion is, or feel the fear of God. But in a single moment, God can make them feel their offences, clearly showing that they have been asleep, so to speak, and not dead at all. Thus, if they have been insensible, it is because the grace of God has been stifled by their ingratitude. Be that as it may, still this life is never totally dead within us. We see evidence of this in David when he so suddenly recognised himself for what he was, and not turning away in the least, honestly and openly declared that the prophet Nathan had every right to accuse him.

Further, let us note the fruit borne by this message of Nathan. Here is the beginning of that sadness which brings repentance after it, as St Paul describes in the Second Epistle to the Corinthians (chapter 7, verse 10). It is quite true that we become angry when someone comes to urge us to recognise our sins; we are especially stunned when someone speaks with great force and penetration. That is because we just want someone to sing to us peacefully and gently tickle our ears! In short, we flee as far as we possibly can from melancholy. This doctrine of repentance is an odious one to us, and we would prefer it practically never to be brought up. Moreover, if someone expresses disgust at our sins, when someone shows us what we have deserved, once it has become public knowledge, we would prefer to push all such matters far away.

Still, it is impossible for us to grasp or benefit from the grace of God, or his will, without experiencing sorrow. How can we be reconciled to God unless we have first felt our offences? We will never be touched with the judgement of God so that we condemn ourselves unless we have first felt his judgement. All those, therefore, who will not be their own judges must experience the fact that God will deal with them (1 Cor. 11:31). Now, we cannot judge ourselves willingly and without pretence unless we have entered into self-examination of our iniquities, and have specifically felt horror at ourselves, hating the evil within us, and confessing our corruption. This sorrow should lead us to repentance, as St Paul proposes there, which is why he says that although he has made the Corinthians sad, he is not sorry for it (2 Cor. 7:9). He would have liked to please them in every possible way, but they could not handle that. Why? Because they had not understood that this sorrow, calling them to repentance, was ultimately to lead them to experience salvation (2 Cor. 7:10).

In that passage, he showed two kinds of sorrow: one worldly, the other godly. Now worldly sadness is the one which I have just mentioned, when sinners prefer to remain in their filth, fleeing as far as they can from the presence of God, wishing to avoid any sense of guilt. Then, if someone comes along to prick their conscience and disturb them, they will be in torment; and after God has chastised them and put his hand upon them, they will be quite unable to bear his rod. They will argue violently: 'And what is this? Must we be so rudely treated? How is it that God is so harsh with us? Who could bear such a thing?' In other words, when those who have offended God hate themselves while humans indict them, but then are tormented when God has smitten them, and find his rod so harsh and severe – now that is the worldly kind of sorrow. For where does it lead except death? The poor sinners just plunge themselves more deeply into their abyss.

But there is also a godly sorrow. It is the kind which voluntarily flows out of us when we experience the bitterness of which King Hezekiah speaks in his song (Isa. 38:15–16), and we have it not just for one day, but for the whole of our lives. When we feel regret for having violated the justice of God, so that we hate the evil which is in us, we would like, if we could, to take vengeance for it, as St Paul also mentions in that passage. He says that sinners must be furious and indignant with themselves, and that having in this way hated themselves, they should simply seek to be reconciled to God (2 Cor. 7:11). Because they recognise that they are far from him for having transgressed his Law, they should assume the person of the prosecutor for God, and make themselves their own adversary, and take vengeance on themselves. And then they might say: 'And who are you, prosecuting me? Alas, what have I done? Oh, poor wretch that I am, how can I dare present myself so soiled before God?' Therefore, when we hate ourselves in this way, we have reached the kind of sorrow which must be ours in order to have true repentance, and reconcile ourselves to God.

For this reason, let us note that it is more than necessary for us to be directly accused and summoned before God, as though drawn by force, so that our case may be formulated, and the items brought forward. If it pleases God for us to be there as poor convicted evil-doers, let us bow our head. For if David needed to hear such threats, what will it be like for us who are not nearly so excellent? We would never come to repentance unless we were drawn to it, as it were by force – just as David confessed in the Psalm that we have mentioned, when he said that he did not recognise his fault until the prophet Nathan had come to him. It is as if he were asserting that, beforehand, he was like a poor dumb animal; insensible, with no more remorse in him, or intelligence, or discretion. Hence, if God cause our accuser, by his rebukes, to seem to cut us with a knife or cauterise and burn us, let us recognise that it is useful for us; let us learn to profit from it and not to be hardened. For we will gain nothing by arguing against God. However long we deeply desire to prevaricate, and proudly stand against him, still he will have to overcome us in the end, just as the psalmist says (as we have already mentioned). Here again is a point which we must remember.

Well, let us return to what is briefly mentioned, that is, that David, by this word 'sinned', did not at all confess carelessly, nor merely make a face to signify that he was guilty. Rather, he was in such confusion that it would have been like being plunged into despair if God had not held his hand, and if he had not hoped in the mercy which he implored in the Psalm already mentioned (Psa. 51:1), knowing clearly that God condemned him precisely in order to get him to that position. Then once again, let us not use any other style or form of speech before God than that which we see here: the heart is still speaking while the tongue does not utter a sound. We shall certainly be able to say: 'Alas, Lord, we will perish unless you display your goodness and mercy to us, which alone can overcome our infirmities'. For as we have shown, our silence means much when we acquiesce in the Word of God by which we are vividly rebuked. Even when our conscience reproves us, let us realise that it is God who is teaching us to condemn ourselves. Although not uttering a word with our lips, may we always have everything that David included in this Psalm. That is, that he was rebuked in his heart, and his sin was ever before him; that he groaned over it and sought nothing less than a proper restoration with God – even though people did not know these things.

Therefore in the first place, let us learn that when we have offended him, we must not merely say, in one word, that we are guilty, in order to acquit ourselves, but that we must feel it willingly. Depending on what the case demands, we must be severe judges against ourselves if we desire our actions to be blotted out from the account of the wrath of God. It is true that all the sins which we commit are not like that of David. But when there is a great host of them, some more grievous than others, we always have occasion to humble ourselves after David's example if we are not totally hypocritical. Hence, let us begin to examine our many sins. For anyone subject to some particular vice will find himself in arrears every day and almost every minute, and then again, when we have been preserved from one ill, we will fall into another. If we consider carefully the importance of the reference to being purged from all covetousness (Psa. 51:5–6), alas, we will discover in how many ways we are guilty before God for wicked thoughts passing through our spirits and our senses. One of us will be given to fornication, another subject to self-indulgence and lust, another full of ambition, and how many thoughts come before us and circulate in our heads! Where do these things come from, if not from this wicked root of covetousness? Also, even in our very dreams, we must recognise our offences before God! For most often when we have dreamed something, it is certain that it comes from the fact that we were entwined in evil, and so when we fell asleep, our spirits were stopped at the point where we had been meditating.

Hence, let us carefully consider the great number of our offences, and weigh them – not on our scales, but according to the dreadful judgement of God shown us in Scripture. Then we shall have very good reason to say: 'Lord, please pardon me according to your goodness; Lord, withdraw your anger from me' (Psa. 85:4); 'Lord, regard not my iniquity; Lord, who shall be able to withstand the fury of your wrath?' (Psa. 130:3). We will use this language, and yet let us not have so glib a tongue that we speak too proudly and distinctly. Even the most idiotic and the hardest will certainly be held inexcusable, since they ought to know enough to humble themselves properly and to give glory to God in his justice.

Now this is the reason why David cried out that he had 'sinned against God; indeed against God alone' (Psa. 51:4). It was not that he had not offended men, but was to show that it was because he was king that he had not been accused and no-one cried against him. Indeed, they only wanted to please him and applaud him – in the same way as we know that great men of this world are always supported. That is why he said: 'Lord, it is against you, you only', signifying that even if he had all mankind on his side, applauding him and making him believe that it was nothing; even if they piled up excuses for him, that he must no longer torment himself; that though he had made one mistake, still no-one should pursue such a matter against a king, and after all, his dignity certainly merited more privilege than any others – even if they said all that, he was far from wanting to authorise himself by this kind of thing. Instead, he humbled himself further in saying, 'Lord, it is you alone who accuse me', that is, 'Your judgement means more to me than if heaven and earth were against me, trying to seek vengeance as my adversaries. Lord, you alone are more to me than all of that.' So let us carefully watch ourselves, to learn how to say: 'Lord, I have sinned'. Let us pay attention to how David said it, with his underlying feelings expressed in this Psalm. For this was not for him alone, but for the general instruction of the whole Church. Therefore, we should contemplate his feelings as though looking in a mirror in this Psalm, for they are honestly represented to us.

Now David did not merely mention 'sin' alone, but he added the words 'crime' and 'iniquity', and then another description, that it was a crime where blood was shed, deserving death (Psa. 51:1, 2, 3, 9, 14). By contrast, we see that Daniel, when he made a confession of sin, applied his iniquities to all the rest of the people, for he said: 'Lord, *we* have sinned' (Dan. 9:5ff.). But because he was there as a doctor (of the Law), he was not like David speaking to Nathan, for David had to cease speaking as a prophet, and to be like a trembling dog, so to speak. Now Daniel, who was a doctor in the Church, and who was supposed to dictate the form of proper prayer, did not say: '*I* have sinned'. But there is a similarity. When David, needing to be restored to his dignity as prophet, called on God in honest confession, he did not just say: 'I have sinned', but 'I have committed a crime, shedding blood and deserving death'. So when Daniel said: '. . . our transgressions; we have sinned, O Lord; we have turned away from your commandments; we have committed iniquity', he was gathering up a great mass of words designed to put men into the depths of hell. Hence, David also used them in this Psalm, when it came to showing us how we must come to God. Not, as I have said, that we should have all these precise words on our tongue, but still our heart should resound, although our tongue does not speak a word, to truly confess our shame before God.

David was still not content with that, but he moved on to the very womb of his mother (Psa. 51:5) – not, however, like a hypocrite, for there are many who will attempt to lessen their offences in this way, and say: 'Now look, we are all sinners'. When they have used this excuse to include themselves among everyone else, they think that they ought to be absolved. This is nothing but thoroughly wicked impudence. When a man says: 'Now I am a sinner, but so are the others', this is only to 'ward off the blows', and to prevent God from executing justice. People who have argued in this way will discover, in the end, that they have only made their debt even heavier. However, David spoke differently from this. For after he saw that he had so grievously fallen, he remembered that from his birth and the womb of his mother, he had not ceased to commit sin upon sin, and that since then he had been guilty. 'When my mother conceived me', he says, 'I was already a miserable creature full of iniquity.' In other words, this was the realisation that he was accursed, and that he would be cut off from all hope of salvation unless the Lord granted him mercy.

Therefore, let us learn from his example, whenever we have committed some huge and dreadful offence, that we too should take stock of ourselves and wonder: 'Alas, am I now beginning to provoke the wrath of God against myself? This has been the case since my birth, and indeed I keep on starting again every day. It is not just a question of one sin, but as soon as I have set to and committed one, I have embraced another, and piled up a heap of them, so that they are like a mountain. So now, O soul, may you find pardon, and take refuge only in him who has so kindly waited for you.' Now that is how every fault that we commit ought to provide the occasion for us to enter into self-examination, and to go even as far back as our mother's womb, confessing that from there on we have been part of this corrupt mass of Adam's race, conceived in corruption and filth.

Nevertheless, David magnified his sin even more because of the additional circumstance that God had illuminated him with his Holy Spirit more than others. It was far from the case that he was flattered himself, under the excuse that he was more excellent than all the rest of the people! Yet this is the procedure that the hypocrites follow, for if they have a good reputation and some authority, and then someone rebukes them, they snap: 'To whom do you think you are speaking?' In order to keep God at arm's length, they make a shield of some quality of theirs, and then also of their reputed knowledge of it, declaiming: 'Indeed, yes, I am a beast! I know that at least as well as you!' That is how men will try to protect themselves against God when they have the reputation of possessing either knowledge or dignity. But David made no excuse out of the fact that God had revealed to him knowledge of his mind. On the contrary, David meant: 'Alas, it was my office to teach others; I was to show them the way, and yet I did all that I could to corrupt them. And then again, I know that he who has received more is more responsible.' Now since God had granted him the special grace of being a doctor and a prophet in his Church, he knew that it was like a deposit committed to his charge, for which he must render account. Now God must be glorified for all the benefits which we have received. So when a man who is outstanding in knowledge and deportment, and is in a position to teach others, transgresses, he should certainly be far more distraught in his mind, as we see was the case with David. So this is what we have to remember.

Nevertheless, there is still something else which is very interesting, for in asking pardon, in recognising his uncleanness, he said: 'My iniquity is ever before me' (Psa. 51:3) – my sin gives me no rest. Now by that, he clearly showed that in fact he had not fled the judgement of God, as the hypocrites do, by trampling down any anxiety, not wanting to 'nurse melancholy', as they say, but rather to give themselves a good time. David did not act in this way. For when the judgement of God was presented to him, and his offences were placed before him, he did not cast them behind his back, but allowed God to condemn him in every way. Then he showed immediately that he had been willing to be touched. Hence, as we wish God to pardon our offences, let us learn to condemn them. He definitely promises to 'put them in the depths of the sea'

(Mic. 7:19), so that they may no longer be seen, but blotted out and totally forgotten. But when he puts them in the depths of the sea, it is then that they are before our eyes. And he blots them out when they are engraved within our hearts, and we feel them, leading us to humble ourselves and be displeased with them. There again is what we have to remember when we read that David declared that his offences were in his memory, before his eyes.

When he went on to recognise that God would be justified in condemning him, and then when he asked to be 'washed with hyssop', we see a further confirmation of what I have just mentioned – that God relieves sinners just when they are feeling even more humbled. David could have been greatly tempted when he saw himself cast so far away from God. He could have judged that the promise which had been given to him was totally annulled. This could have made him say: 'Oh, God must not condemn me, or I would be so rebuked and cut off that everything which I have previously hoped for would be cast down and I would be excluded from it'. On the contrary, David agreed with the judgement of God, wanting him always to be glorified and praying: 'Lord, condemn me, and then you will always be recognised as a just Judge. In spite of everything, you never cease to be immutable. Although we may be condemned a hundred thousand times, yet you certainly know how to provide the remedy for our sins.' That is how he reacted.

Then, after that, came the matter which we have mentioned, concerning the ceremony of the Law, when he asked to be cleansed with hyssop (Lev. 14:6–7; Psa. 51:7), by this sprinkling which had been commanded. Not that he was fascinated by this external ceremony, but it was as if he were saying: 'Lord, ratify the assurance which I need, that you have pardoned my sins by the very sacraments which you have instituted'. For as baptism today is a pledge of our cleansing, so it was with this sprinkling in the time of the Law. Therefore, when we too have committed an offence, let us turn back to our baptism, and pray that God would be pleased to confirm what was given there figuratively: that is, that our uncleanness has been purged by the blood of Jesus Christ. For water could not wash us by itself, nor by its nature. But though that is true, putting water on us is still not an empty figure, but it shows that we must plunge ourselves in the blood of Jesus Christ, absolutely every time that we are soiled with our own pollution. Let us be encouraged to plunge into his blood, since the promise [of cleansing] has been sealed in our baptism.

To keep our 'plunging in the blood' from being a one-time action, let us be careful to hold on to this word 'redouble', which David uses. Although he wanted to express the great number of his wrong-doings by this word, he still needed to experience daily remorse, that is, to find his rest in the goodness of God, and to obtain pardon for his sins – not once, but on and on without ceasing. Certainly, when we have actually felt our evil and have tasted the goodness of God, reconciling us to him and giving remission of our sins, we ought to be assured that, for his part, he has buried them all. However, we must not expunge these sins from our memory, but rather, we should practise what is mentioned in the song of Hezekiah, where he says that he will remember the bitterness of his soul that he experienced when God had humbled and subdued him (Isa. 38:15).

Moreover, let us not be ashamed [to do that], for it will glorify God. We see how David wanted to show that God would indeed be just in condemning men (Psa. 51:4). In composing this Psalm, he wanted to erect a memorial, like raising a pillar which would be seen from afar, with engraving on it, where the crime which he had committed would be written. This was his way of showing that God was justified in condemning him. Thus, when we feel tempted and strongly inclined to defend ourselves, or when the devil allures us to keep us from making a full confession of our faults, let us deliberately think of these two things: should we not further the glory of God, and especially, should we not recognise how he has spared us, even though we have offended him? It is quite true that he will clearly be glorified in the condemnation of the reprobate (Rom. 9:17). But in our case, we have this privilege, that when he humbles us on the one hand, he relieves us on the other. In showing us his wrath on one side, he leads us to his mercy on the other. Thus, when we see that this is the way that God wants to be justified, when we see that he is rushing towards us, and yet that he spares the wicked, let us be deeply distressed, and as it were, steeped in shame. How could we ever envy the reprobate? Once more, this is the main thing to remember.

Furthermore, if on some occasion we seem to have been abandoned by God, let us be especially aware of his inestimable goodness, in that he has given us his hand to draw us out of the depths of the hell into which we have plunged (Psa. 40:2). Let us go on to do what David did in that situation, and recognise that we will never be completely restored without something bad being left in us. Something that I cannot define will always remain in us, making us like a man who has come through a sickness, but still has within himself some remainder of his illness which is not thoroughly purged, and which needs new medicine. Hence, we must be attentive and careful to pray to God to be pleased to purge us with whatever it takes for those things in which we have offended him to be blotted out, and to ask him to continue his grace in us, so that we may walk in his fear until we have run our course, so that we may serve him with purity and honour and be totally his.

Now let us prostrate ourselves before his majesty, recognising all our faults, praying that he may be pleased to make us feel them so that we can be displeased with them, and recognise that he has just reason to destroy us without the least mercy. By this means, may we experience such sorrow that there will be no other remedy except our taking refuge in his goodness. May he also be pleased to show himself full of pity for us, so that we may taste more of his grace. In order to receive pardon for our sins, let us learn to be our own judges (1 Cor. 11:31), touched by his Spirit in such a way that all the rebukes which are given to us will serve to prosecute our case – not to drive us to despair, but so that we may be humbled so much that we experience his salvation. And may all our afflictions and griefs be as agreeable to him as a sweet-smelling sacrifice (Num. 28:2; Phil. 4:18), and may we be increasingly guided by his hand, so that our whole life may be dedicated to his obedience. And may he not only bestow this grace upon us, but upon all peoples and nations of the earth . . .

38

*God Chastises his Children for their Profit**

Then David said to Nathan: I have sinned against the Lord. And Nathan said to David: The Lord has also removed your sin, and you shall not die. Nevertheless since by this deed you have given occasion to the enemies of the Lord to blaspheme, your son also who is born of you, will die (2 Sam. 12:13–14).

We looked yesterday at the confession that David made after he had been rebuked through the mouth of the prophet Nathan. Basically, we have seen that he humbled himself immediately. He made no reply. He was not in the least obstinate, though his royal splendour could have prevented him from condemning himself and recognising his fault so freely. On the contrary, he realised that, before God, 'every mouth must be shut' (Rom. 3:19), and that every creature must be silent – that this is how we must glorify him. Moreover, we have just seen that although his confession was brief, it proceeded from such strong feelings that it has been set forth for the instruction of the whole Church, for he spoke as a criminal, content to admit condemnation in a word, and thoroughly ashamed of himself as he did so. But then, after that, God opened his mouth so that he might show us what our repentance ought to be like, and that his example might serve as general instruction to the end of the world.

Here we must note how God receives poor sinners, and accomplishes what he says by his prophet, that 'he desires not the death' of his own, nor to lose them, but that 'they be

*Wednesday, August 26, 1562.

converted and live' (Ezek. 18:23). We see this portrayed in a living portrait when God pronounced by the mouth of his prophet that David's sin was pardoned. As he was quick to make himself docile and bow his head, indeed making himself nothing at all before God, we see that God responded by readily receiving him in mercy. And that is how he will act towards all sinners, for it is not a story which applies just to one man. On the contrary, God tells us that he is always ready and prepared to grant us mercy when we come to him – if it is without hypocrisy, and if we feel the way that David did. This passage should certainly be carefully noted, where we see these two things joined together, flowing from a common thread: the poor sinner saying: 'I have offended', and God saying: 'I have also pardoned you'. Now here David was acting as his own judge, and then God declared that he would not call him to account any more, and that his faults had been buried under this word that God had removed his sin. In other words, it had been put out of memory, and God no longer wanted it ever to be spoken of, for it was a thing of the past which no-one should think about any longer.

This ought to give us courage, absolutely every time that we offend God, to return boldly to him, knowing for sure that we shall find him ready to grant us mercy. It says that he is 'patient' and long-suffering (Psa. 103:8), and even that he is so good that as soon as he sees poor creatures degraded by their offences, his only desire is to grant them pardon and have communion with them. Since it is this way, he does not wait for us to come to him, but he takes the pains of coming to seek us, that we may be near his grace. What a shame if we disdain to meet with him, when on his part, that is all that he seeks! Not that he needs it, but it is for our salvation; it is for us that he suspends his rights; for he well knows that if we had to make payment, we would continue to be overwhelmed. Now when God thus exhorts poor sinners to repentance, it shows us that he always keeps the door open, to make us find favour with him and to obtain pardon.

Certainly, in calling us to himself, he does not want to frustrate us. So when he wants us to be touched with the realisation of our sins, it is a sign that he is bringing about our salvation. In fact, when he touches us with repentance, it is a definite pledge of his favour to us. For although we are urged to come to him, we would remain obstinate, and never take the right steps unless we were touched by his Holy Spirit. Therefore, repentance is already a gift of God, assuring us that God will have pity on us, and that he does not want us to perish, but rather return to his grace so that we will be known and acknowledged as his children. That is why the Psalm says that 'in his mercy is life', and that 'his anger endures only for a moment' (Psa. 30:5). If he is actually furious with his own children (for we are now speaking only of the elect), he is immediately appeased, for his mercy continues from day to day and is permanent – indeed, for life. Now David uses this type of speech to signify that God will guide us in life as well as in death, and that we shall never be abandoned.

Let us carefully remember what has been clearly mentioned. Whenever God is offended with us, or we have caused him to become our adversary, giving him a reason to arm himself against us and seek vengeance, even then he still beseeches us to return to him. St Paul, in fact, uses that word 'beseech' when he shows us what a treasure the Church has, which God has placed as a deposit in the hands of his ministers and messengers; that is, when the Gospel is preached to us, our Lord Jesus Christ is set forth in it as payment and satisfaction for our offences (2 Cor. 5:18–21). So, not content with just offering Christ, he even beseeches us by the mouth of his servants to be reconciled to him. What a shameful thing that is for him to humble himself like this and conform himself to us, even though we are so unworthy of it. Yet we turn our backs on him and make ourselves deaf! Let us learn, therefore, to make use of this inestimable benefit, so that it does not become useless through our ingratitude.

Next, let us carefully note the order shown here. That is, because of our pride, God cannot deal gently with us until he has touched us to the quick, even mortally wounding us, so that we sense his wrath, are frightened, and completely humbled. For Nathan was not sent to David in order to extract a simple confession of one word, or simply to say that his sin was pardoned, but he began in another way: 'What have you done, you murderous criminal!' He set forth the judgement of God to him with such force that it would have totally destroyed him if he had not been lifted up by the hope which was now given to him. Therefore, let us not find it strange if God, for a time, shows himself to be terrible, sharply rebuking us and judging us in a way that shows us his fury. We need it. Because of our slowness, that is what we need; otherwise we would just grimace each time we stumble badly, and despise his grace whenever we fall into some sin. Certainly, we would hope for him to show himself merciful, since we know that he is prepared to receive us graciously. Even so, we would not know what it means to obtain pardon if we had not previously known what it was to draw down his wrath. What Psalm 90 says must be duplicated in the faithful: to the extent that we know the majesty of God, those of us who fear him must also be amazed at his anger (Psa. 90:7). The papists do not really know God's nature or the strength of his arm, though perhaps they may be forced to entertain some notion of it, albeit involuntarily. Thus, whenever it is necessary to humble us, God must strike with great hammer blows to prepare us to receive his grace. So now we come to the opening for the remission of sins: namely, sorrow – which we dealt with more fully yesterday.

That is also why David, in the longer confession which he made to provide doctrine for the whole Church, said that 'the sacrifice which God requires, and which will always be accepted by him, is a broken spirit' (Psa. 51:7) – that is, a poor desolate soul in anxiety and torment. We know that, in ancient times under the Law, sacrifices were offered for two reasons: first, to warn sinners what they really deserved when they saw the poor animal having its throat cut. This was to show their condemnation in physical terms, and draw them to repentance. After that, they were to exercise faith as the blood was sprinkled on the altar, promising that God would be appeased and their offence forgotten. Now David, in leading us from the figures of the Law to the pure truth, is saying that we cannot be participants in the purging which our Lord Jesus Christ has accomplished, nor can we be delivered from our misdeeds, or our sins be remitted, even though he has made the payment for them, unless we come to offer a sacrifice. But it is the sacrifice of anguish and distress. In our confusion, we realise that we do not know which way to turn, because the wrath of God has seized us with such terror, and that we will have no respite until we find it in him and in his promise.

Thus, what is related about David in this passage belongs to us, and we can gather a general principle from it. In other words, as soon as we are wounded by a true apprehension of the judgement of God, then we are prepared to receive his grace; the way has been opened for us to call on him. But that is not all, for in his infinite goodness he goes ahead of us, assuring us that our sins are past, that is to say that they are no longer taken into account. Without this, there could be no repentance, for as the Psalm says, we must find mercy in God before we will fear him (Psa. 130:4). Now true fear, involving reverence of God, is what is spoken of there, bringing us to submit ourselves to him. Of course, even the wicked experience a certain amount of fear and astonishment, but it does not prevent them from continuing in rebellion and despising God. But in order to become obedient and find peace, we must have tasted that God is gracious, and that we can find mercy with him absolutely every time we seek him. If we are not persuaded of this, then surely we are puffed up with rebellion, poisoned against him. Our spitefulness and chagrin will make him turn his back on us.

Since we cannot place ourselves under obedience to God with the reverence and proper subjection that children ought to show towards their fathers, until we know that he will be gracious to us, we must surely study this passage very diligently. For it shows an inseparable link between the repentance of poor sinners and the goodness of God (Rom. 2:4), which comes forward so swiftly to receive them and say: 'Behold, all of your offences have been buried'. This is what we must remember.

This is why we should value the pure doctrine of the Gospel. For without it, we would not be able to have any rest, but would always be in a hell on earth. In the papacy, for instance, they are good at crying out 'Repentance! Repentance!' – and even include some words about the remission of sins. But they have no assurance – far from it – for their poor consciences are always in suspense. They must earn merits, so that they never find a true remedy to give them rest. Someone will tell them that if they have not confessed everything, they will be damned and unable to obtain pardon. Then those poor people will go and whisper in the ear of a priest, like a drunkard who has drunk too much, and begins to heave and vomit what he has taken in excess, and then feels unburdened! But it is far from true that a man should simply recognise all his faults once a year, as they say they do. Even if we confess our sins morning and evening, we must still agree with what David says: 'Who can understand the multitude of his sins?' (Psa. 19:12). For we offend God a hundred times without even thinking of it, so that when we name one sin, there are thirty or forty others.

Well, the papists are always in confusion, doubting whether they have confessed half their sins, for only one [failure] is needed to send them to perdition. Besides, when they have disgorged their blasphemies in the ear of a priest, they hope to have satisfied and recompensed God. Yet, what repentance do they have? 'Oh,' they feel, 'it is enough that we have gone through some ceremony and have made a lovely performance!' They are sent from one altar to another, and from chapel to chapel, visiting those base flatterers, singing masses, going over prayer beads, and mumbling some prayer to I do not know what saint. They do all that, trotting about, or going in a cart, or on a pilgrimage to some lovely saint, all in order to keep punishing their bodies. The poor folk go to great pains in fighting against God to win some merit of their own.

We see, therefore, in the papacy, that the devil has won at that point, so that poor sinners cannot agree with what St Paul says in the fifth chapter of Romans, which teaches us that 'we cannot have access to God except by faith in our Lord Jesus Christ, through whom we have peace with God' (vv. 1–2). Now it is impossible for us to realise what this peace is, that is, a rest and certainty which is given to us, unless we realise that our sins have been blotted out by the sheer goodness of God. Here we see that the promise which is given to us in the Gospel is that our Lord Jesus Christ is, for us, the pledge and substance of our redemption. Therefore, we ought to be very attentive to this doctrine, and apply ourselves to study it, knowing that it is the main point of our salvation, as Zechariah calls it in St Luke when he says: 'The remission of sins is the knowledge of salvation' (Luke 1:77). Thus, he shows that until we are assured and convicted that God is favourable to us, and that we are accepted as his children, we do not actually know what salvation is. Without that understanding, we will always be surrounded by inescapable confusion. Here, then, is another point that we have to remember from this passage, where David is promised that his sin has been pardoned.

Next, let us immediately note that this was announced to David by the prophet. This is to help us learn to receive what the Gospel tells us about the remission of sins, with all the authority that it bears. It is true that we would very much like God himself to descend from heaven, or send his angels, to bring us this message. However, he wants us to accept it when it is announced to us by someone mortal. This is what St Paul says, that we are like 'vessels of clay' (2 Cor. 4:7), for we possess nothing but frailty; yet it is precisely in us who bear the Gospel that men find the assurance of salvation. Even though we are only worthless vessels of clay, God has placed 'treasure in us' of inestimable value. Even though we are defiled and soiled with infection and filth, this is the means that God uses to reconcile us to himself by his goodness, once we are assured of the message announced to us.

David was a great prophet, who still teaches us today, yet he had to be reduced to the level of a commoner and hear the voice of a mortal man. Thus, let us clearly remember that if we are to have assurance of the goodness of God, we must hear the message that he sends with all humility, instead of listening to perverse theories spun from the brains of fanatics! Whenever the Gospel is preached to us, let us be aware that it is the solemn embassy spoken of by St Paul in the place mentioned earlier (2 Cor. 5:20). Let us not doubt that God wants to meet with us, and that if, in all obedience of faith, we receive the promise given and addressed to us, then we are joined to him as if we had never been separated, and he had never divorced us because of our iniquities. Well, that is one point.

Now Nathan added, as a signature to confirm his promise, that David 'would not die'. This passage was clearly understood to refer to temporal death, but it was also like a sign to David that God had pardoned his offence. If someone replies that this means that all the wicked will perish as soon as they have offended, and that if they do not, it is evidence that their sins must have been pardoned, the reply is easy. The truth is that God does not execute his judgements immediately, but he waits patiently on the wicked, so that at the end they will be even more inexcusable – which only increases their condemnation. However, God never fails to make his grace felt to the faithful by special privileges. When the life of the wicked is prolonged, is it a sign that he pardons them? Not at all. Rather, he is waiting for them, wanting to lead them to repentance. Then, after they have abused it, they should feel utterly distraught. But the faithful have grace given to them immediately, so that when God supports them, it is because he wants to draw them more closely to himself, and give them courage to come to him, by assuring them that they will obtain mercy.

Now here you find the great difference between profane people – all those who despise God and are reprobate – and those whom God reserves to himself as his children. For unbelievers prosper in this world when they despise God, and when they are indescribably wicked; they eat, drink and make merry, saying that God is asleep. Pride abounds more and more, until they become utterly vicious, wild animals, which is why the wicked do not profit at all from the fact that God upholds them and deals kindly with them. However, when it pleases him to spare his own, he makes them aware of it, so that they will have a good taste of where his kindness leads, and convinced that he is dealing with them just like a real father, may have the boldness to call on him and to take refuge in him. On the other hand, we see unbelievers getting into a frenzy, and instead of embracing the pleadings and threats addressed to them, throw themselves into the depths of hell, not valuing salvation at all. Thus, they receive none of the substance of the spiritual benefits offered to them. They are greedy little people who swallow down their meat without tasting it – insatiable, fathomless pits, who get none of the substance of what they eat and drink, but instead burst wide open when everything turns out to have poisoned them! This is how all unbelievers react. On the other hand, those who do not take their food like that receive good nourishment and give thanks to God. Thus the faithful benefit from the blessings that God sends them, and even if he gave them only a drop of wine and a piece of bread, they would savour it, whereas the profane and unbelievers, as I have said, would not be able to feel a single drop of his goodness.

Therefore, let us note that when David was told: 'You shall not die', it was as if the prophet were saying: 'You deserve to be exterminated a hundred thousand times over, but God has preserved you and let you remain in your royal dignity. God's granting of mercy is thus an earnest of his unconditional goodness to you.' We could, indeed, compare this sign to a down payment, for if someone buys some possession or merchandise, they will give a shilling or a penny as a deposit, to show that the transaction is made and completed. So, by this sign, our Lord assured David that he would not die. Thus, every time he gives us the opportunity to repent, let us learn that he wants us to think of our sins, and then having thought of them, not fail to bow our heads in utter humility, completely persuaded that he is always ready to receive us if we seek him without hypocrisy. This is what we must note, when David is told in the above passage: 'You shall not die'.

Altogether, we must gather from this passage that when God sends chastisements to us, they are medicine – if, in fact, we are his children. Thus, his chastisements should benefit our salvation. This point has been mentioned above. However, it ought to be fully discussed, since the opportunity presents itself. Here is what David said: 'The Lord has chastised me, but he has not delivered me over to death' (Psa. 118:18). Now he also shows us how much he valued this message which he had received, and how well he knew the purpose for which it came; that is, that God thoroughly chastises his own, that though they have to feel the blows of his rods very heavily, the wounds will not be fatal. Now what has been mentioned is a privilege for the elect, those who are the children of God – for every affliction and malady is the fruit of our sins and, consequently, a curse of God. Therefore, when we see the unfortunate children of God enduring heat and cold, hunger, thirst, and such things, let us realise that these are curses coming from God – that is, as long as we are not judging chastisements on a merely human level.

But we must come to the promise which exempts us from the general curse on the whole line of Adam. This is what we have already seen in the Psalm (Psa. 89:31ff.), that God will chastise his children, that is, all those who are members of his Church; that he will chastise them in order to reform them when they transgress his commands. Nevetheless, he 'will chastise them with stripes of men' (2 Sam. 7:14), that is, he will not utilise his divine power and strength to chastise them severely, because that would destroy more than a hundred thousand worlds! For who could survive before him if he employed his wrath? The very mountains would melt and flow down like snow, and whatever would become of us? We are less than powder! If we had to bear his anger and fury, the very depths would be insufficient to hide us. However, he says that he will correct us with the 'stripes of a man'. He will not forget his mercy: this fact is the true salt which gives savour to all the correction that he sends us, that we know that he is not removing his mercy from us. It is to this truth, therefore, that we must return when we are told that David has this sign that he will not die (2 Sam. 12:13). Its purpose was to enable him to experience relief within himself, and to know that God did not want to punish him as he deserved, but was receiving him as a poor, lost and desperate soul, wanting to preserve him for the kingdom in which he was established.

Now we see this even more clearly in what follows: 'Yet, because you have caused the enemies of the Lord to blaspheme his name, the child which is born to you' as a result of this fornication 'will die'. We are shown here how God had spared David, showing such swiftness in declaring his mercy to him that David did not need to seek any other relief, yet he did not fail to point him to the fault which he had committed. Now we could find it rather strange that God pronounces the sin of David to be past, and yet punishes it. It certainly seems that this does not fit together. For if our sins are forgiven us, why does he still judge them? If a criminal is pardoned, is he told: 'You shall go to prison, and from there to the gallows'? Or, 'Your sin is pardoned, but you will be punished for it anyway'? However, if we notice what this punishment was, it is clear that it was not given to chastise David for this offence, which had been forgiven, but rather to humble him even more in the future – and so that what was done in his person might serve to instruct us.

It is true that the papists make heavy weather of this passage, just as they so often twist all of Scripture to prove the necessity of the penitential system that they have imagined. They say that when God pardons sins, he only deals with the guilt, but excludes [from pardon] the pain which we have merited. Now, as I have said, this is to pervert the whole foundation of Scripture, for after they say that those who have offended must be chastised in order to recompense God, they then conclude that they can redeem themselves! They admit that when we do what is ordained by the Law, we cannot make satisfaction for our sins. But they have discovered works of supererogation as a method of payment, just as though a man were repaying in silver what he borrowed in gold! That is the absurdity of their fancy imaginations! But then, because they find that we cannot really make satisfaction for all our offences, but must constantly repeat it, that is why they have invented their purgatory – the place where they must pay to the very last farthing (Matt. 5:26). Then, since the poor souls of the trespassers (as they say) cannot earn merits, we who are on earth must help them by providing masses, and funeral rites, and such things.

Well, from that example we can see how one sin draws on another! However, when it says that our Lord Jesus Christ has borne the payment of our sins; that the chastisement of our peace was laid upon him, does it not blot out all the frivolous imaginations which the devil has invented to obscure, and even destroy, the glory of God? That is why it says that our Lord

Jesus Christ 'bore our sins on the tree' (1 Pet. 2:24). And how much of our sins? Does it mean only the guilt? Not at all, for the satisfaction is also included. That is why, also, it is so often said in the Gospel to be 'the ransom' (Rom. 3:24; 1 Cor. 1:30; Eph. 1:7; Col. 1:14). What is a ransom if not setting a man at liberty? Suppose I owe this much money. Very well, here is the payment, and in doing this, it is discharged. So, as it says in the Psalm, our Lord Jesus Christ has paid the debts of all sinners. This is what I have mentioned from Isaiah: that all the chastisements were laid upon him (Isa. 53:4). What is this chastisement, if not satisfaction for all the sins that we have committed? This truth is witnessed to over and over again in Scripture, which would not be the case if we wanted to insist on what the papists believe. Let us, therefore, be satisfied that when God receives us in his mercy, it is to purge us entirely and not half-way. In regard to satisfaction, it has been made in our Lord Jesus Christ, so that the pardon granted today may be free, and so that we may not presume to bring in anything of our own in order to appease his wrath.

Now that is what happens, even though God does in fact chastise us just as he did David. Why? Is it that he wants to have payment? On the contrary, it is for our profit, so that we may be humbled. While it is true that David was humbled enough to say that he felt nothing but anguish towards God, and that he hated his offences, nevertheless, he had to be subdued even more. For even when we wish to be cleansed, we are still so full of dishonesty, of refuse and of wickedness that it is horrible. God knows what we need to chastise us, even though he has pardoned us. But this chastisement is not for the past, for he does not say: 'You must pay for your sin'; but on the contrary, it is for the future. He informs us that we must be on our guard, and learn to hate the sin, and to understand what it means in such a way as to make us walk much more carefully. That is why David was told that his child would die. It was not that God had avenged himself on David, and had sought payment or recompense, like a creditor who says: 'If you do not pay me in gold, you must give me your vine, or else bring me back the merchandise'. How ridiculous it would be to imagine that! But when God chastised his servant David, after having forgiven him his fault, it was to make him more watchful, and make him feel his evil more keenly, and think of it, instead of forgetting it. Like all of us who so easily pardon ourselves, David would not have remembered so well the lesson which Nathan showed him if it had not been sealed by this correction, given to subdue him.

What is said here of David as an individual should be relevant to all of us in general. Although God receives us in mercy, and buries all our faults after it pleases him to adopt us as his children, will we be exempt from all affliction? Will not the poor faithful be tormented with illness; will they not find that they suffer many wants and adversities; will they not enter into many dangers; will they not be in great anguish of body and soul, as though God were keeping them as slaves, so to speak? It is certainly true that we do, indeed, see that God makes his own pass through many miseries. Nevertheless, it is not that he hates them, but as I have said, he is actually encouraging them by these things to return to himself. Poor unbelievers will stick out their tongues at us, for when God smites his enemies once, he smites his own two and three and four times, in order, indeed, to lead them to repentance. We see that today. But should we be shocked by it? It is meant to lead us into self-examination, and keep us from being proud of our blessings, so that we will keep in mind our past transgressions. Moreover, it is to help us recognise our frailty, and remain even more on our guard in the future; and then, so that we will groan at having offended the divine majesty, and be encouraged to pray to him and ask him please to control us so that we may not wander as in the past. This is the kind of medicine that God is giving his children, when he strikes them with his stripes to correct the offences which they have committed. Hence, when it plainly states here that David was afflicted in the person of his child, we are to understand simply that God wanted to make him realise more deeply the enormity of his offence.

The judgement of God must be carried out in the person of his son. Now here was a little child who had just been born. Must he be punished for the sin of his father? How can the passage be true which shows that the child will not bear the iniquity of the father and that the father will not suffer for the child (Ezek. 18:20)? It seems that God is contradicting himself. Now let us note that when the prophet Ezekiel says that the son will not bear the iniquity of the father, he meant to put limits on the poisoned thinking which existed among those people. For the Jews had this proverb: 'Our fathers have eaten sour grapes, and our teeth are set on edge' (Ezek. 18:2). That is to say, our fathers have offended, and we are punished for it. Thus, they were accusing God of being cruel. So, speaking to them, he says that the son will not bear the iniquity of the father, for God will be quite able to deal with all men individually. Thus, while it may be that a one-year-old child will not be found guilty, as far as we can tell, nevertheless, from the womb of our mothers we are nothing but filth (Psa. 51:5), and as we said yesterday, we have nothing but corruption within ourselves. We must, therefore, be 'children of wrath', as Scripture calls us (Eph. 2:3); that is to say, heirs of eternal damnation.

In fact, why is it that little children are baptised, unless they are guilty before God? If this were not the case, it would be like a game! Has this little child offended God? There is no evident reason for anyone to condemn him. But what we have here is a 'child of wrath', as I have already said. So what is it that saves him? The pure grace of God. Now it is true that God does, indeed, save the little children of his faithful people without baptism. But the sign is still to show us and provide proof that little children are cursed by God, until he has received them in mercy, and according to his promise, which says: I will be your children's God (Gen. 17:7).

We see, therefore, that when the little child of David was punished, it was certainly right, for God holds all creatures in his hand to do with them what seems good to him. Consequently, the child did not suffer an unjust judgement – but, also, we must return to the root cause which we have already explained, that it was to humble David more deeply, and draw him to true repentance. Let us learn, therefore, to give glory to God, recognising that his counsel is so admirable that we cannot reach such heights, and when he punishes the father in the person of the child, let us recognise that there is nothing more to say. The will of God is the rule of all perfection, and his righteousness of all righteousness. That is the conclusion that we must reach.

To conclude the matter, let us notice carefully what is mentioned here; that is, when David's child died, the result was that David felt how much God detested the sin that he had committed. For offspring are a sign of the blessing of God on men, and when he makes them fathers, it is like communicating to them the title which belongs to him alone (Eph. 3:14–15). So, also, when he removes children, he is certainly afflicting the fathers. In this way, God wanted to cause David to feel his evil, for what he had already felt was not enough. For even if we remembered this lesson every day and humbled ourselves before God, and even if we really exerted ourselves to do so, we would still not go as far as we could.

But above all, let us note the reason given here: 'Inasmuch as you have made the enemies of the Lord blaspheme' (2 Sam. 12:14) – they had their mouths at the ready to curse God and his Church. Now we see here that although God hates fornication and every other crime, he values his honour so much that when we expose his name to shame before unbelievers, that is a much more dreadful sin than any other that we could commit – for unbelievers are just waiting for an opportunity to make fun of true religion, and spit out blasphemies against God, and so crude remarks are on the tip of their tongues, like torches ready to set their rage aflame. This is an example of an offence that is so serious that it takes from us any hope of life and salvation. Even so, God did not refuse to pardon David, though he wanted him to realise the seriousness of that sin.

Let us take stock of our own situation, therefore, and since God sets before us how we should obey him each day, let us remember that we do obtain pardon for our iniquities, and that since God shows that he is willing and able to receive us, it is quite reasonable for us to experience blows from his hand. Let us begin to examine our lives, and we will come to confess openly God's power and good will, through which we are received to salvation and renewed by his justice. Now that is our true goal.

If we ever speak of our impurities in the ear of a ravening wolf, who would like to break up and dissipate the authority of our Lord Jesus Christ and turn a holy place into a pigsty, where will it end? When something like that happens, is it not the case that people who are fairly respectable, and who apparently have some fear of God, decide that they are as genuinely renewed as they should be, according to their own definition of righteousness? Their life ought to show them up as liars. For we observe deceit and stealing, dissoluteness, pride and wicked desires. In other words, all we can see is sinful excess – just as if people are deliberately wanting to despise God. Alas, when will we provide an opportunity ourselves for the Gospel to bear fruit in our midst by our doing these things? Do we not give the wicked an excuse to make fun of the true religion?

Therefore, since it is this way, let us not find it strange if God's hand presses down on us. For when he did not spare his servant David, what right do we have to expect to be exempted? Indeed, let us also recognise that it is all for our own good. For everyone tends to take the opportunity to flatter himself when God causes us to prosper, and instead of being humbled as we should, we just do evil. It is simply a question of our going astray, and putting ourselves out of bounds, instead of being kept in his fear. Yet God does not lose the right to deal with us when we abuse his patience and goodness like this! When everything goes according to our wishes, we make ourselves believe that our sins are surely covered. Indeed, prosperity itself is like a bandage which keeps us from seeing, so that even at midday we see absolutely nothing and thus stumble all over the place – since we cannot use the benefits which God gives us, but rather convert them, by our malice, not only into poison, but actually make them kindle the fury and wrath of God upon us even more.

That is why it is always necessary for God to have his rod in his hand, ready to strike us with heavy blows – indeed, with harsh and vexatious scourges – to conform us now on this side, now on the other. For we are like donkeys, who need someone to shout: 'Get up, get up!', and then need to be beaten with heavy blows with the rod to make them walk – and yet forget it so soon that it must be frequently repeated! Now that is what we are like when God gently invites us to himself; yet he must – to his regret – torment us and frequently touch us with his stripes. Let us benefit from this because of the example of David. And as we shall see later, when God has his hand raised, let us keep our mouths closed; let us bow our heads and humble ourselves before him, to ask him for pardon, patiently awaiting the outcome of his righteous will. This is not to say that when he smites us with heavy blows, it is to make us go away from him, and to make us throw ourselves away, without his wanting to care for us any longer. On the contrary, he wants to fulfil in us the promise that because our sins are blotted out, he wants to keep us under his control for the future, so that, at the end of our days, he may receive us into his glory.

Now let us prostrate ourselves before the majesty of our perfect God, recognising the infinite faults of which we are guilty. Let us pray that he may be pleased to draw us to the kind of repentance that means that we do not become depressed over any affliction that we have to receive and experience, but that, as we are willingly humbled under him, he might relieve us, and give us the will to go back to him. May we then call on him in such a way that we may be capable of feeling that if he ever decides to give us a reason for human sorrow, we may have greater reason to rejoice because of what he pronounced by his prophet Nathan. Hence, we shall all say: God Almighty, heavenly Father . . .

39

*On Facing Affliction and Bereavement**

Now Nathan returned to his house, and the Lord smote the child which the wife of Uriah had borne to David, and he was afflicted. So David asked God for the child, and fasted, and came out and remained all night stretched out on the earth. The elders of his house got up in order to come to him, to make him arise from the ground! But he did not want to, and did not eat bread with them . . . (2 Sam. 12:15–23).

The first thing that we have to note about this story is that the threat made through Nathan was not in vain, and that David was punished for his sin by the death of his child. We have already explained how such a judgement of God seems strange to our fancy. However, we should still adore him, by confessing that he is just in everything he does, even though he does not show us the reason but keeps it incomprehensible. We see how David was chastised, remembering what we saw yesterday: that the faithful, although they may have been granted forgiveness, still need to be humbled, and need God to make them increasingly aware of the evil that they have committed, so that in the future they will be more on their guard.

Nevertheless, it says that David, seeing the child sick, began 'to fast', and 'to pray' to God with tears, which shows us the strength of feeling in his prayer. It is true that it is not required that, absolutely every time we pray, tears should flow from our eyes. It is also not necessary for us to change our clothes, put on

*Thursday, August 27, 1562.

sackcloth, and lie down on the ground. But when God touches us to the quick so that we actually apprehend his wrath, there is every reason for our prayers to be filled with the strongest feeling: in other words, unchecked by our normal reserve. For we should pray to God every day, morning and evening. Now in praying to him, we make some sign of reverence, depending on where we are, but it is not required of us to follow David's example everywhere and in every detail. But when God afflicts us as he did David, we cannot help but apprehend how seriously we have irritated him – unless we are stupid! Thus, if we experience such an extraordinary affliction, we should wake up, and not simply go through our ordinary routine. Rather, we should force ourselves to pray to God and humble ourselves before him, as David's example instructs us to do.

This passage is not the only place where the Scripture teaches us to pray to God very vehemently and passionately when we have been beaten with his stripes, but rather, it is a common teaching all the way through. So let us learn not to be inattentive when God shows us that we are to come to him in humility, and with repentance. Let us be very careful to make ourselves so tender that we may learn to come to him wretched, lost and in anguish. Although we may not change our clothes to put on sackcloth, yet our body must respond to our inner feelings.

As for fasting, it is still available for us today, for preparing ourselves when we decide to pray to God. Fasting also is a warning to us, for when we drink and eat, we are not as attentive as we should be in thinking of our sins. But a man who abstains from his ordinary food thus has the opportunity to recognise that he ought to apply himself wholly to God, behaving as though he were out of the world, so to speak. Otherwise, the fast would be frivolous, and indeed simply hypocritical; just as in the papacy, where they hope to win merits with God and to do him some acceptable service. As regards fasting, I will leave out all the rest of their games and ceremonies. For what is the point of abstaining from meat, and then swallowing other types of food? Now let us ignore this vice which, in other words, is a superstition. But let us simply deal with David's kind of fasting. They think that God ought to be very happy with them for fasting, and that it constitutes a type of satisfaction. But this is to want to transform God. For what does it matter to him if we are fasting, or if we have drunk and eaten? As St Paul says: The kingdom of God does not consist in those things (Rom. 14:17), and there is no more holiness in a man who has not drunk or eaten than in someone who has taken his meal. The whole point is (he says) that we relate the fast to its proper goal, that is, for it to make us apply ourselves better in praying to God. For after we have drunk and eaten, we are not as active, and then we are not as attentive to recognising and groaning over our faults until we ask pardon for them. So this is what the fast should do: stir us up to greater vehemence, and then, along with that, act as a warning. Just as a man who has something impressed on his memory will care about it much more deeply, so the fast serves to make us aware that we are poor sinners, and move us to direct our thoughts much more towards his mercy.

Fasting is also at the same time an exterior testimony, for someone who desires to move a judge to compassion will not take out his beautiful clothing; he will not primp or have his hair fixed to win favour. On the contrary, he will lower his head. He will act like a man already half-condemned by himself. That is how fasting acts as a reminder to us, so that God is glorified in every way, while we are humbled and reduced to confusion, and so that when it pleases him to receive us mercifully, his goodness may have greater lustre. This is what we should understand from this passage, where it says that David fasted and laid himself on the ground, wanting to pray to God for his child.

A question might arise here which is (it seems) difficult to resolve. Our prayers should be founded in faith, or they will fall down, for it even profanes the name of God to pray to him unthinkingly. That is why St James says that we must trust that we shall obtain the content of our requests when we come to God, for a man in doubt is like the waves of the sea when there is a tempest, and that person ought not to think that he will obtain grace (Jas. 1:6ff.). It will be quite useless for him to call upon

God. Our Lord Jesus Christ does not require us to pray to him in faith without giving us good reason (Matt. 9:22), to which St Paul responds that we cannot call on God at all without having known about him (Rom. 10:14). Now calling on God like this does not refer to a simple knowledge of his existence but rather that we must be thoroughly convinced that our requests will not fall to the ground, but be received by him. This assurance that he will receive us is another reason why we call on him, for without it we would never come to him. Surely, it would be presumptuous to open our mouth to come to him and lay all our cares in his bosom without permission. How shocking it would be if the very clods of dirt wanted to lift themselves up above the skies and say: 'I shall speak to my God, so that he may uphold me!' If we anticipate him, that is to say, if we wish to present ourselves to him by our own momentum, such a presumptuous attitude will certainly not be an appropriate way to pray for salvation. So God needs to encourage us, and that cannot be done unless we have the assurance that our requests are not spurious or useless.

Now since our prayers should thus be founded in faith, how is it that David prayed without the assurance that he would be heard? What is worse, it seems that he wanted to despise God, by disdaining the threat that he had been given, in that he wanted it to turn out otherwise. One could say, therefore, that the prayer of David was out of order, and that he had quite forgotten himself, because though Nathan had pronounced the death sentence against his child, he still wanted God to retract his word and not execute it. However, let us note that the faithful, after hearing God's threats, have often considered that it was intended to stir them up to pray more ardently, so they have not taken them as closed and absolute, as they say, but have thought that they might still obtain mercy.

In fact, very often God simply threatens when he does not want to smite us, just as a father may threaten his children to make them change, so that it will not be necessary to put his hand on them. So God uses that kind of language when he wants to keep from being too severe with those who repent and turn themselves around with straightforward courage. Now that is how God's threats do not always come into effect. Nevertheless, it is not that they are meaningless, for we must always pay attention to their purpose. If God threatens us with punishment, I have already shown that the threat is not useless when someone turns around and returns to the right path.

Nevertheless, I am saying that God's threats are always as firm as his promises. The promises of God are infallible to all those who receive them, for when the Gospel is preached, God is giving a general offer of remission of sins to those to whom you are speaking. Now there are many who are not in the least interested in accepting such a benefit – which, as the apostle says to the Hebrews, is how the Word of God can be useless to us (Heb. 4:2). Well, even if they are ignored, the promises of God are not to be taken lightly by people who do not believe them. It is the same with the threats, for they are always guaranteed. People who are incorrigible will despise what was said to them; they will assume that God cannot cause terrible vengeance, and direct their contempt at God alone. But even then, the threats are never without effect, for they are either for the condemnation of those whom God wants to terrify, or for even greater vengeance on the obstinate. Still, the faithful, recognising that God often threatens his own to avoid punishing them, have carried on praying to him, even though they had been told: 'You certainly cannot escape'. We have seen that Samuel mourned over Saul, although God had demoted him (1 Sam. 15:11). This was to see if there might be some means of obtaining pardon. Yet there was less reason for Samuel, because he well knew that it was a definite sentence which had been given against Saul. But still, he battled on by faith, in that he wanted God to bring Saul back to the right path.

Indeed, it often seems that the faithful are fighting and lifting their horns against the will of God, even though they are faithful to obey and submit to him. For as I have said, they do not take a message which God sends them as meaning that prayer is ruled out, but rather, as if God were stirring them up – and this was a particularly sharp pin to prick them! That is how it was with David. Although he had heard, by the mouth of Nathan, that the child had to die, he still hoped in God, and though he was assured of the fact that he would yet be punished for his fall, he never stopped praying to God for the little child.

Still, the problem is not really solved, for someone might say that something happened by chance, whereas we need to have assurance, when it comes to praying to God, since there is no other way to give ourselves entrance to him but through faith. Now this is easily resolved: namely, when Scripture speaks of certainty (Heb. 11), upon which prayer ought to be founded, it means a certainty that God hears us because he knows how to be good. But that is not to say that we should always have assurance about a particular thing. Let us take an example. If I am ever sick, I shall pray to God to look on me in pity, give me relief when the pain presses me, and raise me up healed. Still, I will not be certain that God wants to deliver me from that illness; perhaps he wants to take me out of this world. However, in spite of that, I will not give up praying but I will await the outcome, however it pleases him, and I shall even be sure that I should ask.

This is not to say that as soon as I ask him, he immediately makes me well. For the illness could be long, and instead of relieving my pain, he could increase it. Now if someone says that we are praying without faith when we do not have assurance in particular instances, they are speaking improperly. The point is that God does give us access to come to him, and in giving it to us, he in effect shows us that our desire for supplication has not been frustrated. Furthermore, he wants to keep us in suspense about many things. This is also why, when there are no special promises, we ought to add a condition to all our requests, although it may not always be expressed. And what might that be? We must pray to God to give us relief from our pain, but acknowledge that he is still the one who is to have control over our lives. That is, insofar as God has not revealed to us what he wants to do, we must submit ourselves to him, and desire that he dispose of our life as he pleases. We must rest content, whether the pain increases, or whether it passes, so as not to do wrong. When it does please him to take us out of this world, let us be ready to leave it. In other words, may his will rule over us, so that we will overcome every affliction and subject ourselves completely to it. Now that is how, in praying to God, we must not say that we have assurance concerning any particular matter for which we are asking. But it is enough for us to be persuaded that our supplication will be welcome when we address our requests to him, since his grace has opened the way. Moreover, prayer always bears fruit. But we do not know exactly how, and since it is beyond our senses, we must wait with patience, and yet always persevering in our prayers. That is why David was not like a shaken reed in praying to God, for he was sure that God would give him mercy in the end. He placed everything back in God's hands, but then, as long as the child lived, expected that God would grant him mercy.

So that is how he acted, and is also where we should follow his example. Thus, let us learn to pray to God in all our extremity, and even when it seems that nothing else can be done, let us keep on, nevertheless. Now we sometimes find fanatics who simply seek to confuse everything and remove this true hope from us by saying: 'You see that here is a narrow place that you cannot get through. You have no hope in such a terrible predicament; there is no way that you can get out.' When these things are thrown up at us, to turn us away from that right determination to pray to God, let us discount them and say that although we do not know what it will please God to do – and according to our human reason and intelligence, there seems no possible solution – this is not to say that God does not have secret means which are incomprehensible to us (Rom. 8:26). Hence, let us consider what he has commanded us to do: that is, to wait in patience and humility for whatever the outcome will be. Although we are like poor blind men – certainly so – we ought to be satisfied by this clear teaching given to us; namely, that God does care for us, even when he seems to have turned his back on us. This, in sum, is what we have to remember.

In fact, the prayers of the saints will clearly show us how they had faith, and it is certain that God did not forget them. Yet they were still not so sure that they said: 'I shall obtain this or that'. For they cried out and used blunt language: 'Oh, God has forgotten us, and how long will your wrath be burning against us?' (Psa. 79:5; 80:4). 'And how long will you sleep?' (Psa. 44:23). Now here are the saints complaining against God! They make themselves believe that he is asleep, and no longer thinking of their salvation; that is, they feel that he is asleep because they do not understand that he is watching over them. Nevertheless, there is no doubt that even when they speak in this way, they continue to hold to the principle that God does not want to deceive them, and that their requests will not be frustrated. Now we see this even in the complaint made in the person of our Lord Jesus Christ: 'My God, my God, why have you forsaken me?' (Psa. 22:1; Matt. 27:46). When he questions whether God has forsaken him, it is as if he were a poor lost man. But still, this anguish which gripped him did not lessen his faith, for when he affirms that he holds God always before him, he is persuaded that he is his Father and his Saviour.

Thus, let us always hold on to these principles: on the one hand, that when God has adopted us as his children, he will perform the office of Father; and on the other hand, when he invites us to pray, we must be assured that it is not in vain, and that we may pray boldly to him. For we cannot fail to be acceptable to him because we have the promise that our prayers will not fall to earth, and that he will always go beyond our thoughts and do everything better for us than we can conceive. However, if we are perplexed over this or that, let us still persevere in praying to him and waiting patiently on whatever he will be pleased to do. Now this is what it really means to pray effectively.

Well, let us come now to what the text says. That is, that the servants of David came to him and wanted to exhort him to drink and eat, and asked why he was lying there on the ground, since he was king. This illustrates what has already been explained earlier, namely, that his grandeur or elevated position did not fill him with so much pride that he did not humble himself as he should. He saw a poor little baby suffering. Now God was showing him, as though in a mirror, what he deserved himself, for the child had not offended in this area. Still, he lingered for the space of seven days, and his illness was so distressing that it moved even the most distant people to compassion. When David saw his own flesh and blood there, and since he knew that God had smitten the child for the sin which he had committed, there is no doubt that he was in terrible distress. Therefore, when he prayed to God for the child, there is no doubt that he was still considering himself, and was also praying to God to obtain pardon for the crime that he had committed. It is true that we may just pray to God for a child, without knowing why he afflicts him. But David was not ignorant, because he had heard from the mouth of the prophet that the child would have to die; that God would 'beat the dog in front of the lion', as they say, and that in this small creature, God would show David what he had deserved. Let us carefully note, therefore, that David prayed not only out of parental affection, and because of his grief for his child, but because he was still keeping himself and his fall in mind. This led him to humble himself before God, as if, in requesting God to heal the little child, he was saying: 'Alas, Lord, here am I. May you receive me in mercy, and may it be felt on my behalf by this little creature who is suffering because of me!'

Therefore, this in sum is what David attempted in praying to God for the healing of the child. Otherwise, we would not know how to accept what follows: that is, that when the child was gone, he rejoiced. At least he changed his clothes and 'got up and went to the temple and returned to his house and drank and ate' as normal (2 Sam. 12:20). Now if it were not for the consideration that I have mentioned, we would find such a sudden change very strange. It is natural to weep over those who are close to us, as we have seen earlier in the mourning of David over Saul and Jonathan (2 Sam. 1:1ff., 17f.). He will be seen later weeping over Absalom – indeed, even to the extent of crying: 'Absalom my son, Absalom my son; would that my life could redeem Absalom my son' (2 Sam. 19:1–2). In that situation, he acted like a man who had totally lost control of himself. Yet he says here: 'Since the child is dead, I must no longer be grieved' (2 Sam. 12:23).

Now here is a contradiction which is extremely peculiar. It seems that David has completely stripped off any human affection when he says: 'The child is dead, he will no longer return to me'. That is of course true, but it does not keep us from mourning somewhat, even though we know that we will not bring the dead back by our tears. Still, it is only with great difficulty that a father can keep the death of his son from bringing him some sadness. But as I have said, we must note that David always had his sin in mind, and although he had compassion on this poor creature, he did not forget himself or the sin which he had committed. In other words, this was the reason for his tears and fasting; that is, he recognised that it was the hand of God which was armed against him, and that it was this which stunned him and made him humble and caused him so much sorrow that he refused to rejoice or eat and drink as usual. Thus, this is the first thing to note about the fact mentioned here, that David, having heard of the death of the little child, got up.

However, in what his servants said to one another, we can see that they recognised what is natural for all men to do: that is, to mourn the passing of those who are close to us. This is engrained in us; so that if a father pays no attention to the death of his son but just nods his head, he must be some kind of monster! It is not that our crying has any value as far as making them return to us, and indeed, this is not why they do it. When we weep for the passing of those who were close to us, it is not intended to make them return. For when it is plainly said that the faithful have wept and mourned deeply over the passing of those who were in charge of the Church, did they do this to bring them back to the world (2 Sam. 1:12)? Certainly not. So why did they weep? Does it discredit them? Certainly not, but it rather deserves praise, and shows the affection which they felt for the Church of God. Indeed, Isaiah reproaches the Jews for the brutal way in which they were untouched with pity when God intended to take back his own (Isa. 11:12f.).

Hence, it is a natural human emotion to mourn when someone of ours has passed away, and indeed, our sorrow is a testimony of how strongly we feel that God's hand is against us. When he has deprived us of those who were to teach us, we ought to be sorrowful over it, just because they were important people. But we should be moved with greater emotion when we see that the Church of God is similarly stripped, and then feel remorse for our sins and ask pardon for them. Hence, we are not to make a general rule out of this word: 'He shall not return to me', for we already believe this. We do not have to take it literally, as though we should rejoice when someone has passed away and not feel any vexation at all. Rather, let us always distinguish between what was particular to David and what is common to nature. For David was in the particular situation of weeping for his son during the life of the child. But when he saw that God had carried out what he had ordained, he no longer argued, since he saw that the matter was closed. So the sentence was executed, and he no longer tormented himself, but accepted the judgement of God, receiving it with thanks, as we shall see later. This is the main thing to remember from this passage.

Moreover, when he said: 'He shall not return to me' but rather 'I must go to him', he was showing here the hope that he had of life after death. For people will not say that dumb animals go away to their fathers and mothers or to their children! Why? Because these are creatures who have only a temporal life. It is quite true that we only live in this world for a limited time, and to all outward appearances, one could say, as does Solomon, that it is the same thing that happens with the death of a man as with the death of a horse (Eccles. 3:19). However, let us take into consideration the fact that we are created in the image of God, and that there is a better life for our souls. Thus, David is assuming here that men are not to be like dumb animals.

But when we possess the infallible assurance that according to the Law of God, we must all be gathered after this temporal life, and that there is another life prepared for us, we ought to pay careful attention to it. The fathers did not have as much clarity as we have today in the Gospel. They did not have such clear and evident testimonies as we do, for our Lord Jesus Christ, being risen, has shown us that we are participants in his resurrection. He is the first-born from the dead, as St Paul says, so that we will be gathered to him (Col. 1:18). However, we can still see that David clearly knew that although he had life in this world, he had to await another life, even more certain than this one. Through this knowledge, he preached a strong sermon to us, for we can see that he was always aware that after his death he would without doubt contemplate the glory of God. Let us learn, therefore, that though we are in this world, we should live in it in such a way that we realise that we are invited to another life, which will be permanent, and that God has chosen to separate us from dumb animals by imprinting the mark of his image in us. Let us not be like the profane, who think everything is extinguished at death, but let us realise that it is the passage through which we go to those who have preceded us.

Furthermore, it is not enough to have heard in a general sense that we shall pass into another life, but let us learn to be joined with the faithful who have gone on before us by faith and with a true obedience and holiness, so that we may be received into their ranks and into their company. Thus, when we see Abel cruelly killed by Cain, let us realise that God wants us to endure in this world, but not if it means letting our condition become worse. Let us be content to be gathered with Abel. Now we know how precious God considered his life to be when he said that the blood of the deceased cried out before him (Gen. 4:10). Well, here Abel was gathered in to a better life than all the ideas of immortality which we could invent in the world! And when we see the life of Abraham, let us learn to follow the example of his faith, and imitate him as he is set before us, and then there is no doubt that we will be gathered with him and the other patriarchs, and thus with the apostles and our Lord Jesus Christ, who is the head of all the members of the Church. So this is what we have to remember when it speaks of following those who have preceded us in death.

Moreover, when it says here that David went 'to the house of the Lord' before taking his food, we must note how he was in total subjection to the will of God, even to the extent of giving him praise for the passing of his son. That is how we must do it, for to pray to God, and yet to resent it if things do not go according to our wishes, is not true prayer. We would like to summon him when we go to him, by saying: 'O my God, hear me in this'. But if he does not want to and we become chagrined over it, is this praying? No, this is rather wishing to constrain him, as if it were for us to give rules to him and impose law on him! For this reason, let us carefully remember what is shown us here by David. For David had groaned and wept; he lay down on the ground and fasted, in praying to God, until his son had passed away. Hence, when he heard of his death, he realised that he might become tainted with murmuring against God, and with being resentful. So what did he do? He sought the remedy – which was to go to the temple and 'worship' there, and make solemn confession that even though God had punished his child, he did not want to harbour any resentment.

In order to be able to practise this effectively, let us carefully learn the lesson of St Paul to the Philippians, where he says that our prayers are to be known by God, and that we can lay down our feelings and worries in his bosom, in fact with thanksgiving (Phil. 4:6). St Paul is not without justification in joining these things together, trying to show that our requests ought not to be made with bitterness, which will result in our becoming angry and depressed if God does not want to content us in everything, in every way. Instead, when we pray to him, we are to add thanksgiving. Then, even when it seems that we are apparently refused, let us not fail to bless his holy name, following the example of what is recounted here of David. For although the death of his child was grievous to him, it did not make him angry with God, but rather, he submitted himself with appropriate humility. He was not hypocritical in coming to the temple, and when it says that it was to worship God, there is no doubt that it was to attribute to him the honour belonging to him. Now what does this say, if not that he is the master of our life and disposes of us as seems good to him and that we find all that he does to be good. This is how David maintained the worship of God. It was not an empty ceremony, as if he were wearing a mask and acting in a farce, but he came there in truth and sincerity. In this way, there is no doubt that he praised and blessed God, even though things did not turn out as he had hoped.

However, we should also distinguish carefully between this joy of David, and that of merry-makers who are just trying to make a mockery of serious matters. We may see people who are so barbarous that a man who has lost his wife, for example, may just try to go out by himself, to forget all his sorrow. Now that is to be denuded of any trace of humanity. There will be others who will be troubled far more deeply than they should, so that it will not be a question of thinking about God, his judgement or his mercy, but they will remain unresponsive, sullen and bowed down. David did the contrary. Although he mourned over the death of his child, yet seeing that he had been delivered from the miseries of this world, he no longer mourned as he had before, but in spite of it all, went on to seek God. And for what reason? It was in order to worship him; in other words, to humble himself before God in recognition of the enormity of his sin, and then to bless his name, by attributing to him total control over his creatures. That is what we should do. We must rejoice fully in the midst of all our afflictions, since we can go directly to God; for if we rejoice in any other way, it will be accursed. In fact, our rejoicing can only be crude and disgusting if it has no reference to God. But after we have experienced a time of sorrow, and then realise that God has not forsaken us, and we find that our bitter experiences are sweetened by hoping in him – now that is true rejoicing which will be blessed.

After all that, David did, indeed, return to his house and rejoiced there, eating and drinking in his usual way. Indeed, when God uses affliction to call us to groan and weep and be touched with repentance, I believe that he does not want us to be swallowed up in sorrow. There certainly have to be limits, depending on the level of our infirmity. Therefore, let us not become cold towards God, like some people who relax their self-control, and even spin themselves on and puff themselves up in their sorrow, in an attempt to refuse all consolation.

This is not what God requires. Instead, while on the one hand when he gives us some sign of his anger, we ought to be wounded by grief in that we have offended him, so on the other hand, we must consider the fact that he does uphold us. Since we could be totally weighed down by our sorrow, he wants us to retain a balance, and never fail to rejoice over the good things that he gives us. Moreover, he wants us to know the reason for which he has created us. Since he is pleased for us to be in this world, it is not for us to completely abstain from eating and drinking because we feel under pressure. That would be deliberately making war on him. In other words, our fasting should be within limits.

It is knowing that God wants us to rejoice in the good things that he gives us for our nourishment which will make it possible for us to return to our ordinary life. In addition, when we use every opportunity that he gives us, we can legitimately do so for as long as he wants to keep us in this world. But all that does not prevent us from always recognising our faults. Even though the papists dissolve in grief and display their sadness, going into uncontrolled despair and then throwing their fury up against God, and even though others are stupid and go to all imaginable extremes, still let us maintain a proper balance – that is, let us fast at the right time and place and then let us groan and pray to God and ask him to relieve our sorrows, so that our own grief may be within limits. Let us be careful to realise that our emotions will be disordered and excessive if they are not held down. Let us always return to this fact: since it does please him to keep us in this world, we must use the opportunities that he gives us, as we wait for him to receive us to himself. Also, may we follow the saints who have preceded us out of this world, so that at our passing away, we may be exempted from any misery or torment.

Now let us prostrate ourselves before the majesty of our good God, recognising so many faults of which we are guilty; praying him that more and more he may wish to touch us by his Spirit, in such a way that our only desire is to renounce ourselves and be displeased with ourselves for all our vices and infirmities. And yet let us learn to be so patient in all our adversities that his name may be blessed by us, both in what we feel and in what we say. And even if he does not deal with us according to our wishes, let us not fail to force ourselves to render obedience to him. May we be a sacrifice for him, both in life and death (Rom. 12:1). And may he not only bestow this grace upon us, but upon all peoples and nations of the earth . . .

40

*Solomon, whom God Loved**

David consoled Bathsheba, and went in to her and slept with her. After that she bore a son, whom she named Solomon, and the Lord loved him. David placed him in the hands of Nathan, the prophet, who called his name Jedidiah, because of the Lord . . . (2 Sam. 12:24–31).

We have seen how David, having lost his son, recognised not only that God was a just Judge in punishing him, but also that he should be deeply aware of his paternal goodness. If he had not felt this, he would not have come before God to worship him and give him thanks. In this passage, David's grief was over; not that he would not always be aware of his sin, but he had returned to his ordinary way of life.

Now it also says that he 'consoled Bathsheba his wife'. There are many fun-lovers who, when they have committed fornication and some evil has happened to them because of it, are quite well able to come together with another partner in fornication. But this cannot be understood of David, as the text certainly makes clear. It says that God sent his prophet Nathan, so we can see that the consolation which is spoken of here was accepted only because it came from God. Indeed, there is no doubt that David carried out what he professed in Psalm 51, where he speaks of all this. He says that he obtained mercy from God, and far from abusing it, as do profane people, he 'will teach transgressors' and be like the Master, desiring to direct

*Friday, August 28, 1562.

and bring them back to the right path from which their corruptions had caused them to stray. If David taught, at a general level, anyone who was contemptuous of God, or who had led a dissolute life, and brought them back to the right path with him, insofar as God had granted him mercy – there is much less reason to doubt that he did the same thing with regard to his wife. Because both of them had grievously sinned, he undoubtedly exhorted her to repentance, so that there was a mutual accord between them.

Then, he also considered (as we have shown) that God did not want his severity to humble his people excessively, for he knows our frailty and sustains it (Psa. 103:14). That is why he does not want us to be 'swallowed up in sorrow' (2 Cor. 2:7). In other words, this is what we have to remember; namely, that David received the message sent to him by Nathan as meaning that it was not only for him, but at the same time for his wife Bathsheba, so that they rejoiced in the grace that God bestowed on them – not only, indeed, for having buried the great offence that they had committed, but also for blessing their marriage.

In this, we see how God presides far above the opinion of men; indeed, his actions may be against all human sense. For how was this marriage begun? It was an unspeakably wicked transgression for David to have seduced the wife of another who was spending his life in his service. Indeed, the marriage was sealed with innocent blood. Here was poor Uriah faithfully obeying him, and on the other hand, David committing an awful murder against the people of God (2 Sam. 11:17). Hence, if God had wanted to be a severe Judge, everything should have been cursed. We see, instead, that this marriage was singularly favoured by God (2 Sam. 12:24): for Solomon came out of it – the very one who was supposed to be the image of our Lord Jesus Christ, to succeed to the crown on earth as God had ordained. In all this, we can see how God made the fact that he had removed from him the child who was born in adultery turn out for good and for David's salvation (2 Sam. 12:15). For that child would have been older than Solomon, which would have caused a further battle. Thus, God removed him, so that the inheritance came to Solomon with less opposition. It is quite true that Adonijah strongly wanted to oppose him (1 Kings 1:5ff.), but in spite of that, here is Solomon with the ascendancy, since God chose him to be king, just as he had previously exalted his father, David. This is what is shown to us, therefore, in this statement that David consoled his wife, and then that he had a son, who was called Solomon by his mother, and indeed, that the prophet Nathan had been sent with approval.

Then in particular, it says that 'he was loved by God' and for this reason David gave him the surname 'Jedidiah', which means the same as 'loved by God'. Let us remember, therefore, in the first place, not to do ourselves harm with worthless consolations when God makes us sad, or rejoice in this or that. Instead, let us return to him, so that he who has made the wound might heal us, for we shall find no other medicine. We must particularly remember this lesson when we see that our Lord turns us on our heads. Whenever we are beaten by the hand of God, we will just be numb and seek out entertainment as seduction away from pain. In other words, the only way that we will be able to feel happy is if our conscience becomes deadened, and we find distractions all around and no longer think about God or ourselves. Now that is a disastrous way to cheer one's spirits – just like a man wanting to go to sleep and throwing himself into the water in order to sleep softly and relax there! Thus, when we have begun to flee from God out of a desire to relieve our sorrow, let us learn, instead, to pray. Whenever he humbles us, let us pray that *he* may relieve us, and when he wounds us, that *he himself* may heal the wound, as there is no other who can do it. Now that is one point.

Moreover, when we pray to God, let us not doubt that he can console us, because this is his office, and this title is attributed to him by St Paul himself (Rom. 5:15; 2 Cor. 1:3), all of which exhorts us not to doubt that, for his part, he is ready to dry all our tears and turn them into laughter. This is to give us reasons not only to reduce our mourning and anguish, but to laugh out loud, so to speak, and rejoice as we see the inestimable goodness which he demonstrates to us. What is recounted here about David and Bathsheba belongs to us. We see in them two poor creatures more miserable than anything else. Here is David, who was like someone with no principles for a time, and Bathsheba, a miserable fornicator who abandoned her principles, breaking faith with her husband, and then seeing her husband killed because of her. Therefore, here were two desperate creatures – yet God visited them. He consoled one and then the other. He even sent his prophet Nathan to show again that although they fully deserved his pursuing his vengeance on them to the uttermost, nevertheless he wanted to pass by and abstain from wrath. And from that time forward, said Nathan, God would receive them in mercy, so that the marriage which ought to have been an abomination would prosper, and that the marks of his own mercy would be upon it. This is a particular testimony of how God does not forget poor sinners: that is, insofar as they return to him and are not hardened in their crime, nor despise his grace by which they are called back to the right path from the place where they were wandering, wretched and confused. Here is another point to remember.

Moreover, let us also learn that when God offers us the promises of salvation, we must apply them to our situation, as David did; not only for ourselves, but also for those who were involved in the same condemnation as us. For it says that Nathan had been sent, or that 'God had sent by the hand of Nathan' (2 Sam. 12:25). Through this, we are shown that the promise of God was not useless, and that it was taken by David and Bathsheba to mean that they could hope that God would still be gracious to them. In fact, God even went as far as bestowing a singular mercy upon them, which no-one would ever have conceived, as though he had converted the darkness of death into the brightness of life. Therefore, whenever our consciences rebuke us for having offended God, and then if we come to the temple and someone there shows us how great is his goodness to all those who seek him and take refuge in him, let us embrace it immediately with true assurance of faith, so that we may discover that such statements are made for us, as if God were extending his hand to us. Also, when we read such things and remember what we have heard and understood, may we always place confidence in the blessing that God offers us. That is, let us rest in his mercy, not doubting that all our offences are wiped out. So this, again, is what we are to remember from this passage.

Now when it says that 'God loved Solomon', it is to show us here, as in a living picture, that the love of God rests on those who seem good to him. It depends on nothing outside himself and his free goodness. If you carefully seek the reason why God loved Solomon above all the other children of David, what will you find? He was not the oldest son. Indeed, those who had primogeniture were cast down, as happened to Esau (Gen. 25:23). So all human dignity is excluded here. If someone says that it was for the love of his mother, the fact is that she was the wife of a common army man. If someone says that God guided the marriage, how could that be the case? It began with an adultery much more villainous and detestable than anything else; then murder was added to it – not only one, but several. Yet from this filth and this rottenness, God drew out Solomon, whom God did, indeed, love. Now if you compare him with others, you will find that the love spoken of here was not based on the dignity or the nobility of Solomon, but rather that God received him in love, as Scripture says.

There is no doubt that what is said here about Solomon pertains to all the members of the Church, since he represented our Lord Jesus Christ. Thus, let us be careful to note that just as God bestowed his grace upon our Lord Jesus Christ, so our being in communion with him does not proceed from us, nor do we bring anything from our side. But we must come to the source from which all our good proceeds and upon which it depends: that is, the fact that God loves us. As Moses very often pointed out to the people before David was born: 'The Lord loved your fathers' (Deut. 4:37; 10:15). What is recorded here about Solomon is at the same time asserted in the Law about Abraham and the holy patriarchs: that God loved them. If we ask why, it is certain that we will not find the answer when we consider who they were. Abraham was, indeed, the mirror of every virtue and perfection, but when God first called him, what was he? A wretched idolater! Where did he come from? From among those who had no knowledge of salvation. So here he was, drawn away from the depths of hell, also well aware that he had been freely loved by God, that is, absolutely unconditionally. But it pleased God always to continue this liberality. The precise reason for this is expressed by Moses, for it was not (he says) that you were a greater number or had a greater dignity than others, but because God willed it to be so (Deut. 7:7–8). This is what we should remember from this passage.

Now the prophet Nathan is specifically spoken of, because the love of God would be useless for our salvation unless we were aware of it. It is true that God could make it of great value if he wanted to, but we are speaking of the means which he wants to use. In other words, when he loves us in himself, he then wants us to be participants in this great blessing. So he tells us about his good will. This is why the message of the prophet is linked to the love of God. This is the substance of what St Paul shows us in the first chapter of Ephesians, that God has called us, he says, to the knowledge of his only Son, based on the fact that he had loved us beforehand in him (vv. 3ff.). So here is the love of God which not only preceded our birth, but was also 'before the foundation of the world', as he puts it. But after that, God has to make us experience that love which would otherwise be hidden from us, for if he did not, we would always be wretched, damned and cursed creatures. But because God has loved us, next he draws us to himself, and then, when we have felt and known a Father being so kind towards us, from our side also we may be joined to him, and give ourselves to his service.

The reason that particular mention is made here of sin is so that we may not be like those fanatics who, when someone speaks of the predestination of God, say: 'Now it's all the same to me. It doesn't matter to me what happens, because God has determined everything beforehand, and his plans will always be accomplished.' Let us not separate what God has joined together, for here are two inseparable things. On the one hand, God ordains what pleases him concerning us, and when it pleases him to love us, it will be known to us afterwards, and the doctrine of the Gospel will bear witness to it. Yet on the other hand, if we want to be sure of our election and of this free goodness of God by which he has chosen and adopted us as his children, let us add faith to what is shown us in the Gospel, and follow the rule given to us in the first chapter of St John: that is, whoever believes in the Son of God shall be considered a child of God (John 1:12). Let us, therefore, believe in Jesus Christ in order to have the ratification of this promise. Let us have so much confidence in it that we may always be able to persevere with certainty in calling on the name of God, until we arrive in his glory, and take possession of the inheritance which he has promised us.

Well, what is said here about Solomon's second name does not mean that David wanted to add anything to the first, and far less that he wanted to impose a name which would cancel the other. For it is stated in the First Book of Chronicles that God announced to David that he would call his son's name Solomon (1 Chron. 22:9): Behold a son will be born to you, and his name will be Solomon, because the state will be peaceful under him. For this name, Solomon, is taken from the word 'peace'. So that is why the name was imposed on the son of David, as though he were called 'peaceful', not only with regard to his own person, but also since God would give peace to the whole kingdom of Israel in the time during which he would reign. Now since God had spoken in this way, David would never have had the audacity to want to blot out a name which was sacred and which God had given by his authority. Well, there it is. Yet David greatly desired this benediction – signified by the name of Solomon – to be so known that people might realise that its origin and source was the love of God of which we have been speaking. Therefore, far from the name of Jedidiah being intended to obscure what came from the mouth of God, it was a confirmation of it, just as if David were saying: 'Now here is my son with the title of peace, because God has wanted to exercise his grace to his people, and so that Solomon might be at rest, not worried or molested by enemies. Now here is a favour which should be highly valued in itself, but people still need to know where it comes from, so that if God has imposed a name on the one born to me, I want people to know that the name which I am now giving him is only confirmation of the wonderful goodness of God to me, and that the reason why he is my son proceeds from God himself.'

Therefore, this all tends to show us that the basis for our salvation consists in the pure goodness of God and in his free election. When we say that we are saved by faith, and yet that our salvation has no other cause than the election of God, these do not contradict each other. But when it is stated like this, it is to indicate that there cannot be faith without the election of God. When we speak of the eternal election of God or this doctrine is preached to us, then we take it in by faith, so as to come to salvation. Why? Because if the love which God has for us were not confirmed in us, he would seem to be only half a Saviour to us. But when we say that we have embraced this love and election by true faith, then we have all that is required for our salvation. And to that is added the fact that God illuminates us and makes us participants in this faith, precisely because he has loved us before the foundation of the world. Now here are two things which agree so well that the one helps the other. So this is what should be understood by this passage: the son of David was called Solomon by the mouth of God, but also the father wanted people to know why God bestowed such grace on him. This was, of course, because he loved him – out of his free and generous goodness, as we have seen.

Then we are told another story, and the Scripture ceases speaking of Solomon here until it returns to him later on. It says that God bestowed yet another mercy on the marriage, in that God gave victory to David over his enemies, against whom Joab was fighting (2 Sam. 12:26–29). Now this should be carefully noted, for the action that David had committed strongly deserved his army being routed in total confusion (2 Sam. 11:17). He had exposed it to the enemies of God, and those who were fighting against him, particularly when his wicked lust had blinded him, and because he wanted to take a man's life. Well, that was a very good reason for God to have justly proceeded against him as a Judge, and for his army to have been defeated and the Ammonites to have overrun his country and to commit many outrages – which he certainly deserved. But far from God using such severity, he gave him victory over his enemies.

We see here, therefore, that when it pleases God to grant us mercy, he continues doing us good, adding mercy to mercy in infinite numbers. In this, we have ample opportunity to magnify him, whereas in fact many fanatics want to call him to account and argue with him. Why? Because he exercises such patience towards some, and towards others is severe. Well, instead of following these poor wretched souls who arrogantly come to God unaware of their own confusion, let us learn to worship God with great sobriety and reverence, just as much during the judgements which he strictly exercises against some, as when he bestows his goodness on those whom he receives in mercy. In the very place where they have deserved utter confusion and disaster, he enriches them with his benefits – as we can see in this example here.

So here are the Ammonites defeated by Joab. Let us note here that God has reserved this honour for David to have the victory. Joab, in his duty as a good and loyal servant, had called for David, and declared that he did not want to have the title of having defeated the Ammonites; that he did not want his name to be proclaimed throughout the royal city, by which he meant that it would be extremely wicked disloyalty to usurp to himself the title and authority which belonged to his lord. Yet the origin of Joab's wish came from elsewhere. And who was it that moved him to do it? Let us realise that God induced him. This means that there is nothing here of fortune or human virtue in this passage, but that it was God who wanted to continue and increase his goodness to David that went far beyond fatherly kindness, by granting him this honour of winning the victory, even though he deserved to be ruined at the enemy's hands. Now here is even stronger confirmation than we have seen so far. It is that God not only pardoned the enormous sin which David had committed, but instead of applying the punishment that he deserved, he exalted him, as though he deserved to be advanced in every way.

It says here that David, having conquered his enemies, 'took the crown from the head of the king, and someone placed it on his head' (2 Sam. 12:30). Immediately following that statement, the weight of the crown is given as being a talent, in addition to the precious stones on it. Now people have seriously misinterpreted this, because when you speak of 'a talent', you are talking about sixty pounds weight, that is to say, sixty marks. The ignorant have claimed that to carry sixty marks of gold would have been too heavy a burden. So they have imagined that this crown was suspended over the head of David, because otherwise it would have broken his neck! But they have not realised that it was actually measured in silver marks, so in fact, the whole thing was only worth around twelve hundred pounds, to take the monetary value assessed by people who have experience in evaluating that kind of thing. Here was something worth around twelve hundred pounds, therefore, excluding the precious stones. Now it is quite different if you go back to a silver mark which was valued appropriately, and remember that gold in those times did not have as high a value as today – anyway, if you compute it all, these sixty silver marks made the same as a talent of gold in ancient times. It was approximately the weight of five hundred and twenty pence – and then, including the precious stones, it would not have been heavy enough to break a man's neck!

It is very likely that David had been crowned earlier with a diadem. In fact, when he thanked God for the benefits which he had received from him, he said: 'The king shall rejoice in you, for you have placed a crown of fine gold upon his head' (Psa. 12:1, 3). Some understand this to have been the crown of the king of Ammon, but it is quite certain that he already had a crown or a royal diadem. This can also be gathered from Ezekiel. When he says that the king will be humbled, he uses a word which implies the same as a diadem or a very expensive crown and says that this crown will be overthrown (Ezek. 21:26). Now he did not understand that to refer to the crown of the Ammonites, but rather to the proper diadem of the kings of Judah, since they were figures of our Lord Jesus Christ. For he says that the crown or the diadem will return to the head of the one to whom it belonged, that is, to our Lord Jesus Christ. So David certainly had a royal diadem, as indeed one can gather from other passages. Even so, he was crowned again, because this diadem of the king of Ammon was more precious.

Well, the whole matter leads to this point: that we are here contemplating the remarkable goodness of God in ornamenting David in this way, in the very place where the blood of Uriah must have cried out for vengeance, for that was where it had been shed! Yet far from holding it in his memory, God wanted him to be crowned there. Thus we can see how God not only pardons our transgressions, but crowns us with his benefits, as if we were quite worthy of receiving wages from him (Psa. 103:2–4). In the very place where we might deserve to be exterminated from the world a hundred thousand times, he lifts us up to the heavens. Therefore, we have a mirror, so to speak, of the infinite goodness which God bestows on all of his children, so that what we ought to feel in ourselves and actually experience is shown to us here in the person of David, so that we can recognise it even better. For we despise the benefits which we receive from him, and put them under our feet, but when Scripture sets David before us, we are more likely to recognise from his experience the great liberality with which God has upheld us. Hence, we can apply all of this to ourselves, so that by humbling ourselves, we magnify the mercy of this good heavenly Father, as he deserves. All in all, this is what we should remember.

Now it says next that David condemned all the Ammonites to be grievously tortured (2 Sam. 12:31). He had them cut in pieces; he made them pass through the fiery furnace or his men used shards; he made them draw iron harrows across their backs and their stomachs, and drove them under the axe. We see extreme treatment here. Not that the same people who had been smitten with axes were drawn under iron harrows and then after that were cast into the fire, but that there were different sorts of punishments for different people. Some were cast into the fiery furnace, others were put under the iron harrow, which had been broken in pieces. Others were under the axe, that is to say, were massacred right there and cut in pieces. Others were sawn in two. Now this does seem to be barbarous treatment, and you could say that David went much too far in this area, yet we know that he was of a gracious nature. How on earth did he come to use such cruelty against his enemies? Now we can see by this that after displaying patience for a long time, God shows those who have been obstinate that even though he has waited for them, he has not forgotten their iniquity. For the judgement recorded here, which David gave to the people of Ammon, was not an act of vituperation, but rather he was treating them as they deserved. This is what this whole story amounts to.

Well, let us consider now who the Ammonites were. They were descendants of Lot (Gen. 19:38), and ought to have had some memory of the relationship which they had to the children of Abraham. Well, far from recognising it, they molested the people of Israel as much as they could (Num. 21:21–23). They never wanted to allow them passage,[1] nor even a drop of water. Although they certainly knew that these people did not want to do them any injury or damage, they still prevented them, as far as they could, from possessing the inheritance which God had given them, and shut out the grace of God. They plotted with the mortal enemies of the people of God to ruin them, and caused so many murders that they fully deserved to be beaten down a hundred thousand times (Judg. 10:7–8). In spite of all this, how did God deal with them? From the time that the children of Israel were prevented from passing into the land which was promised to them, God still said: 'Do not touch the children of Ammon, for they are your relatives (Deut. 2:19): I remember Lot and do not want you to be harsh to them'. Now here God is returning good for evil; he showed patience towards them, that is, while he waited for them. But since they stubbornly continued going from bad to worse, they had to see his arm suddenly stretched out in severity to exterminate them.

Thus, when the Ammonites are spoken of, let us realise that the Holy Spirit wishes to show us here, as though in a picture, that if God spares the wicked, it does not mean that he has forgotten to carry out his office of Judge. Yet this is precisely why the wicked abandon themselves to all kinds of licentious

[1]Is this a confusion of Edom and Moab? Cf. Num. 20:14–21.

behaviour. It seems to them that God must no longer be seeing anything when he puts off punishing them for a year or a month, so they rejoice and triumph! In short, everything is legitimate for them, as though God had given up his rights over them. That is how they make use of the respite, and indeed, we are all far too inclined to indulge in that vice. For who is there who does not abuse the goodness of God when he does not visit us as our demerits deserve? Yes, if we have offended him and he leaves us in peace, do we not take the opportunity of going to sleep in our evil, as though, since God continues to uphold us, we had licence to do wrong! That is where we behave like horses who have escaped from their master! Thus, we are warned by all this to keep ourselves in check, and be diligent in thinking how we stand, not waiting for God to come out against us, or for him to come with his arms reaching out to chastise us. Instead, let us be willing to recognise our faults and then grieve over them and view them with horror, and realise that we would fully merit the most terrible punishment if he had not looked on us with pity. Even if he does spare us and we do not have to suffer anything, let us not fail to be on our guard, and humbly keep ourselves under his yoke, just as if we were already feeling his blows. That is one point.

Now there is another application of this doctrine. When God does not seem to see the iniquities committed in this world and punish them, we are incited to murmur: 'Now how can God leave these wretched people in peace? How can he give them such eminence? Here are the wicked doing as much evil as they possibly can, and he even seems to regard them with favour, while we are exposed like prey.' This is how our impatience can tempt us to murmur against God. Now when such temptation comes into our spirit, let us benefit from this historical example, and recognise that God's continuing to uphold the Ammonites returned on them an even more dreadful punishment when they refused to consider repenting. Ought not our hair to stand on end when we hear that the entire people of a country were exterminated like this, some drawn under those iron harrows, others sawn apart, others driven under the axe, and others thrown into the fiery furnace? These are all terrible things to hear. All the same, the Ammonites had injured and continually molested the Church of God, despising both the abominations given to them, as well as the gentleness and kindness displayed to them.

Hence, let us not doubt that after God exercises long patience with those who persecute his poor children, his judgement will be awful enough to make heaven and earth tremble. Therefore, in the first place, let us learn not to mock God, nor play with him, as though with a small child, when he does not punish us. Then on the other hand, when he is slow in punishing the wicked, let us not consider him to be like men who after having a sleep, as they say, forget the shame which was done to them. Above all, when we see his poor Church being persecuted and afflicted in every part, let us not doubt that God also sees it all, and that in the end he will call them to account before him, and then will reveal his sternness and punish them in his fury. Whatever he does to them, let us be careful not to resemble them or be ensnared by them, either out of fear or spite. Rather, let us live very prudently, patiently waiting for God to show his hand, to defend and keep us secure, showing how much he cares about the salvation of his people.

In order to apply this story to our advantage, let us recognise that all the benefits which David received belong to us. For he was a type of our Lord Jesus Christ, and if he was in need of his grace, which he had received by faith, how much more ought we to be assured of the same salvation when we remember that the Son of God has appeared to us, and is daily set forth to us in his Word! And since we know that God is always the same, this truth is what ought to make us overcome, again, any illusion from Satan.

Now we have said that those who were tormenting the children of Israel, that is, the Ammonites, were their relatives, and thus under obligation to look out for them to the very end. Hence, let us not be surprised when we see that people who ought to have the same kind of connection with us are the very ones who persecute us most cruelly. Let us not fail to wait for our salvation from on high. In fact, we see that the Philistines, who were the enemies of the Church, were not as barbarous to

Israel as the Ammonites, who (as I have said) were supposed to be united to their brethren. But all this is to show us that we need to watch people who are called our kinsmen more carefully than those who would be considered strangers. In the same way, we see that those who call themselves Christians today and claim to be in the Church of God, are, in fact, like bastards, and making themselves worse than savage animals, are mortal enemies of God's majesty, and all those who desire to offer him pure worship. Yet let us not doubt that God can reverse their enterprises, and that he is on our side and will keep us safe in every danger, wanting to show us how much he cares for our salvation. Nevertheless, when we see so many troubles able to turn us from the right path, let us pray God to strengthen us, safeguard and keep us under his protection. Above all, let us always wait on his perfect will, until we see the fulfilment of what is shown to us here.

Now let us prostrate ourselves before the majesty of our good God, recognising the infinite faults of which we are guilty, praying to him to be pleased to make us more and more aware of them, so that in this way we may prevent him from unleashing his severity upon us. Instead, may we see it unleashed upon both his and our enemies, which will confirm to us more and more the testimony which he gives us of being our Father, and of governing and guiding us in life and in death, in such a way that we may always be his beloved, and claim his holy name to take refuge in his goodness alone. And may he not only bestow this grace upon us, but on all peoples and nations of the earth . . .

41

*The Rape of Tamar**

It happened after this, that Absalom, the son of David, had a sister who was beautiful, who was called Tamar, whom Amnon, the son of David loved. And he was in such anguish that he fell sick for the love of Tamar, his sister; because she was a virgin, and it seemed difficult to Amnon to have a relationship with her. Now Amnon had a friend named Jonadab, son of Shimeah, brother of David. And Jonadab was a very prudent man, and said to him: Son of the king, why are you so discouraged every morning? . . . (2 Sam. 13:1–14).

Although David was granted peace by the consoling promise given him by the prophet, he did not escape the punishments with which he had been threatened (2 Sam. 12:10). Here in his house, an act of incest was committed which was far worse than fornication. It would already have been a tragic heart-break for a king to see his daughter raped by anyone but it was a far more enormous crime when her own brother abused her. Now this was the judgement of God which David was bearing, and it was as if God had condemned him to be shamefully exposed to the whole world. Nor was this the end, for as we shall see later, this act of incest brought on a murder when Absalom killed Amnon (2 Sam. 13:28–29). So David was doubly afflicted in that his daughter was raped, and then his son's blood was shed. Nor was this done by some foreign enemy but by someone whom he had begotten – Absalom – with the result that he had to drive him away and

*Saturday, August 29, 1562.

banish him from his kingdom for a long time, as will be explained in its place (2 Sam. 13:34ff.).

We should always remember the threat which the prophet made. Hence, let us note the reason why God punished David in this way, even though he had pardoned him for his offence. In the first place, when we see that such an excellent man as David was not spared, but that God used great severity with him, even though he did grant him mercy, we must also recognise ourselves that although God does not want to treat us with extreme severity as our Judge, he must nevertheless take his rod in hand in order to chastise us. He does this so that we may be subdued, and feel even more compelled to confess our guilt before him and obtain pardon for our sins. So then we will become increasingly assured of what we have heard in his Word, that he is ready to be reconciled with us. This is the goal of all his dealings, as we have already pointed out above. It is an utterly ridiculous folly to imagine that God took vengeance on David in the same way that we humans wish to be avenged when someone wishes to harm or injure us in some way. God is not motivated by such passions. Besides, we must note what has been said, that the sin of David was already buried; God had put it away. Hence it is quite certain that David's punishment was not a type of satisfaction, but it had regard to the future, and to the fact that God wanted to subdue him increasingly and make him feel the gravity of his offence, as well as the fact that he wanted it to serve as an instruction for everyone.

Thus, we must profit from this instruction today. Now here (I say) was a jewel in the Church. Here was a man who had been chosen by God and had an incomparable testimony, but nevertheless he had to be corrected by the very offence which he committed. However, let us learn not to be too feeble or fussy or find it strange when God acts severely towards us. Rather, let us recognise our great need for such medicine. Although we may not feel the seriousness of our evil, we must leave it to the judgement of God. When he is no longer seized with pain, a sick person may believe that he is fully healed; but he may still be nourishing a secret illness, which could lead to a greater evil if no-one can see ahead. The doctor will know all about this, so the sick person must submit himself to his counsel and take medicine. When medicine seems quite unnecessary to us, at the very least let us give God credit for knowing our secret maladies, so when it pleases him to remedy them, let us not shrink from taking the purgatives which he knows are good and expedient for us.

It is true that we can always beg him to spare us, since we are weak, but though that is true, we must still come to the place where we confess with David that we need to pass under God's hand. There were very good reasons for him to admit this, for much as he felt it himself, his example would also be profitable for all. He said, therefore, that it was good for him to have been humbled and chastised by the hand of God (Psa. 119:71), and in this way he thanked him for not delivering him over to death, as we have seen earlier. So for this same reason, let us learn to receive patiently every correction that God sends us. After we have recognised our offences, and been touched with repentance, then if God pursues us still further, as though wanting to start the trial over again after granting pardon and absolution, let it not trouble us unduly. Rather, let us recognise that there is nothing better for us to do than submit ourselves to God, because we do not know what is profitable for us and he has to make up for our ignorance!

We are told here that 'Amnon loved his sister Tamar', although she was the daughter of a different wife of his father's. This warns us that even those who have been taught in the Law of God, and ought to be living committed, God-fearing lives, have not failed by forgetting themselves so completely that, far from their having profited in the school of God and therefore giving themselves to him in integrity and sincerity, they seem never to have tasted what human honesty is. For instance, take Amnon, who was nourished in the house of David. Now we know that the man who was in the position of being a prophet and doctor of the whole Church did not neglect the instruction of his family. Because of David, therefore, Amnon would certainly have realised that fornication was detestable. Yet here is a case of incest: it was not legitimate for Amnon to cast an impure eye on his sister Tamar. He ought to have held her in honour, so that such a thought should never have entered his heart.

When we see this, let us realise that even though God has favoured us by declaring his will to us, since we know what his Law commands us, and what it forbids us, we must not consider ourselves to be exempt from every temptation. Rather, let us be vigilant and take heed to ourselves, for we see that our having knowledge to discern between good and evil does not amount to much after all. Our disposition dominates instead! If it is wicked, it throws off any trace of reason in such a way that we act like absolute villains. Although it seems that we used to have the whole will of God at our fingertips, yet we will be lost, for our lust and passions are terrible beasts and very difficult to keep under control.

Hence, we have to pray to God, as we are instructed in the Psalm, to guard our eyes that they may not follow after vanity (Psa. 119:37). For they are like torches ready to set our hearts alight, with the result that we experience, as I have said, neither honesty, nor self-control, nor moderation. Hence, seeing that we cannot cast our eyes here or there without finding some object to mislead us, we have even more need to pray for God's control so that we may not be tempted by impure gazing. In fact, we have to pray to God not only in this area, but in everything. For some people will be ruined when they see a beautiful field or a lovely piece of property; others when they see a beautiful house which pleases them. In short, the devil has infinite ways of seducing us. He will allure us and trap us unless God preserves us. Now that is one point.

There is also a second warning; namely, that Amnon nurtured this evil within himself. Although wicked lust had tempted him to commit fornication with his sister, he should have quickly come to himself and considered how grossly immoral that act was, against nature, and even in the eyes of men, such a disgrace that he should immediately have ceased from it. For these reasons, Amnon ought to have broken the hold of his lust, but he wallowed in it. It is true that some would say that this poor man was pitiful, for he became weak, wore a sad face, and in short, just dragged along (2 Sam. 13:2)! But what was the reason? It does not say that he was displeased with himself over his evil, nor that he was fighting against it. On the contrary, it was simply because he could not enjoy his sister Tamar. Thus, the only reason that Amnon was so sad was simply because he nurtured this raging lust in his heart. Yet this passion was like a vicious animal, which has to be tied up in chains, and kept behind iron bars.

Now it does not speak well for us when we have to be restrained in this way, by force. We are not at all virtuous when we longingly consider evil, but are simply unable to carry out our wicked desires. Rather, the point is that we should be subdued willingly, and renounce ourselves and our lusts in such a way that the fear of God may rule over us and gain the victory. It is true that when we have wicked passions, it is not so easy for us to vanquish them. But even so, we must still make them captive so that God may be master over us, and that little by little we may reach the point of hating what we used to love, and detesting the sin which we used to nurture. We do not see this at all in Amnon, but instead, as I have said, his lust continued burning brightly. Still, he was unable to do what he desired so strongly, and for that reason he grew ill. Hence, let us note that when we are prevented from doing the evil that we have conceived, it is no indication of virtue. Instead, we must give our hearts to God so that we valiantly fight on until our wicked passions are mortified.

Here again, we have to note the evidence of honesty in the house of David when it says that his daughter 'Tamar was a virgin', and that Amnon could not approach her. This was a sign, therefore, that she had been raised in such a way that there had been no occasion for her to be raped, and also that those who would have wanted to corrupt her did not have access to her. It showed virtue on David's part for having been diligent, like this, in keeping his daughter chaste, but we can see, on the other hand, how subtle the devil is, for in the end David let his daughter be corrupted under the pretext of going to prepare food for Amnon. Hence, let us learn to be so diligent that whenever any opportunity to break our rules comes up, we may think carefully two or three times lest we ever turn back from the disciplined way of life which we have decided to pursue. It often happens that when we are following a good set of rules, one little slip causes our determination to come crashing down, and it takes only a minute to reverse it totally. Now this is what we need to remember from this word, where it says: Tamar was so carefully guarded that one could not approach her.

Let us return to Amnon. It says that he had a cousin, Jonadab, who was his familiar friend, and indeed, was a prudent man. He asked him why he was in such distress and why he did not tell him his trouble, so that he could remedy it. Then Amnon confessed to him that he had fallen in love with Tamar. Now he came to this confession circuitously because he was ashamed, for nature itself would have shown him that it was a wicked thing. 'I have fallen in love with Tamar, sister of Absalom, my brother'. He could easily have said: 'My sister, Tamar'. Well, as I have said, a natural sense of shame showed him that he ought to have been embarrassed by such wickedness, so he said: 'I love my brother Absalom's sister', as though she were not his sister, and not at all related to him! Now here was Absalom, who was his brother; so would not Tamar also have been his sister? Thus, we can see how people who are motivated by evil will follow devious paths, as though they were able to avoid facing the issues of good and evil or could prevent the judgement of God. But even if God's judgements are held back, however many dodges those kinds of people attempt, they will finally be trapped.

We have to note here in connection with Jonadab that his prudence was actually a wicked cunning. What it says here is that he was a 'very prudent man'. Very well, Scripture values any virtue given by God, for we know that the reason and intelligence which we have are like a glimmer of the Spirit of God. For it is not for nothing that he is called the Father of lights (Jas. 1:17). There is, therefore, nothing but darkness outside him. When God made us reasonable creatures, as they call us, he certainly imprinted his image and likeness upon us. If, therefore, God has imprinted his image in men, if he has given them sense and discretion, if they are prudent – and indeed, many of them are very sharp, possessing wise and able counsel – it is certain that God has shown himself to have been most generous to them in having bestowed such a wonderful gift upon them. Hence, when prudence is spoken of, it is always a gift of God from which his glory should shine forth.

Nevertheless, it was not to Jonadab's credit that this virtue was attributed to him, for he was all the more condemned by God for having profaned a gift which he ought to have used properly. Therefore, when we see that the Spirit of God stated here, as a reproach, that Jonadab was a prudent man, and that he so forgot himself as to be a pimp for his male cousin, disgrace his female cousin, and be disloyal to his uncle, the king – it all warns us to pray that if God has given us some prudence, he would also add integrity and sincerity so that we may keep ourselves from craftiness. For as I have said, people who are understanding and have more excellent gifts than others are all the more obliged to make the glory of God shine forth from the gift which has been deposited with them.

Now it is a kind of sacrilege when we use the intelligence which he has given us for trickery. Altogether, let us learn from the figure of Jonadab that it is not without good reason that the Scripture says that the head and 'beginning of wisdom is the fear of God' (Psa. 111:10), and that without it, all human prudence would not only be useless, but provide the opportunity for greater evil. If a man who is sharp-witted and has good judgement and swiftness of spirit gives himself over to evil, then he is like some despicable wretch in a fury, who has got his sword in his hand, and he will be able to do far more damage. Now a man who becomes utterly frantic may well strike other people, scratch them with his nails, and bite with his teeth! But if he has a sword, he will then be able to kill everyone that he runs into! So it is with those who have more intelligence than others. Yet let us learn to pray to God that when he increases the gifts of his Spirit within us, it may please him to guide us in such a way that we may apply and refer them to the end for which he intended them: that is, that our prudence (as I have said) may be united with integrity, so that we will not act craftily nor engage in evil trickery. Now that is one matter.

Next, however, we can see how the wisest are sometimes blinded by God, and commit such enormously wicked deeds that it seems that they are totally devoid of intelligence. For Jonadab ought to have considered, in the first place, that it would be a mortal offence if it came to the ears of the king that he had given counsel for his daughter to be violated. So where was his wisdom? He was prudent and not given this title without justification. However, he went on to gratify the carnal lust of his cousin and friend, and put a fellow human in a bad situation. For it was an unforgivable sin to be a pimp and cause the daughter of the king to be violated. Well, that is how God converted his prudence into barbarity. After that, he should have thought: 'Now it is my duty to rebuke my cousin'. Even a man of low condition is ashamed when one of his relatives has committed fornication. He would like to redeem it with his own blood if that were possible, but here was Jonadab advising him to rape his cousin! So once again, he utterly forgot himself. Now this shows us how God blinds those who do not live a God-fearing life. Yet let us not presume on any agility of spirit that we may possess. Even if we are considered to be the wisest in the world, unless we are kept in obedience to God, it is quite certain that he will abandon us, with the result that our very wisdom will serve to cast us down into such dreadful licentiousness and wickedness that we would be better off dead. In short, we will be utterly swept away, as it were. Here again is instruction which should help us.

However, we see that this kind of worldly friendship does not involve a commitment to obeying God. Instead, each one wants to gratify his companion, and that is what causes so many vices to be fostered in the world today, and so many people to be hardened in their vices. This kind of behaviour so often hinders the justice of God and keeps it from running its course. For if two men are friends, one might be given to avarice, the other to fornication. Each one will want to gratify the other in such a way that the one who is a fornicator will bandage his eyes so as to see nothing wrong when his companion gives himself over to fraud and thievery! He will pretend to see nothing, and even try to disguise his evil with an attractive smile! Similarly, the one who involves himself in extortion and stealing like this will want to gratify his fornicating friend. He will attempt to give him his pleasures, and cover his corruption – whatever shame may come out of it – and thus they will work hard to hatch plots in secret, to reverse completely all the rules of fair play in favour of whoever they want to gratify. Now this is what man-centred human prudence amounts to. What it does, as I have said, is to maintain vice, as experience proves only too often.

Hence, let us learn to love one another in such a way that we remember that God has joined us together, and that we must refer to him the true affection which we have for one another. When that is so, what will then happen is that instead of friends flattering one another so that they abet one another in their vice and entertain each other with it, they will admonish one another to withdraw from it, and follow the good. That is how we are to show friendship: namely, we should try to reform someone who is going to perdition, if ever we see him indulging in some terrible vice. Of course, it is true that 'love covers a multitude of sins' (1 Pet. 4:8). That is to say, we are to put up with one another's weaknesses, and not to be too severe, as though some people can be superhuman! Solomon also says that it is hatred which uncovers sins (Prov. 17:9). That is to say, you are not to reprove those who have fallen in a spirit of hatred, but with the kind of affection required in all faithful God-fearing people.

It is quite true, as I have said, that when we have a Christian friendship, we will have to put up with the vices and infirmities of our neighbours. But this will not be to abet them in it by flattery. For if I see a friend of mine stumble in some vice, I will not be so mean as to let it pass from my sight without pointing out to him how it will cause him shame. Now if I ever see that his honour might be, as it were, abandoned, and that he is going rapidly down the path of perdition, if I do not say a word about it, am I not a double traitor, inasmuch as he is my friend, and he trusts in me? Well, however true that may be, this teaching is implemented very poorly in the world, for (as I have said) most friendships are nurtured by flattery. Seeing, therefore, that this corruption has existed throughout history, let us learn to conduct our friendships in a godly way. Also, let us not look for people to love us in order to gratify our evil desires, because this will cause our perdition. In fact, we see that Jonadab, with his trickery and his desire to gratify his cousin, put the noose around his neck. First, he ruined him in relation to God, and then put him into perpetual disgrace, and finally, he caused his throat to be cut. This is the fruit of human ambition between friends to gratify one another's vices.

Moreover, when it says that Amnon 'pretended to be ill' (2 Sam. 13:6), it was not that he had not already been languishing, pulling a sad face and acting depressed enough to 'drag his wings'! But in spite of all this, he was still walking around, just like people that we often see who claim that they are dying on their feet! However, they do not lie down, and they flee the bed as long as they can drag along their limbs! So it was with Amnon. Now he lay down, pretending to be ill. Actually, he was quite able to come and go as usual, but he pretended to be completely broken down. And 'when his father came to see him', he ought to have immediately been moved by his kindness. His father cared for him so much that he came to discover the state of his health, yet Amnon went on treasonably to ask him for his daughter, saying: 'Send my sister to me that I may eat from her hand'. Hence, we see how totally blinded he was. Not only were his eyes blinded by that wicked passion which had seized him, but the devil was possessing him in such a way that he was totally out of his senses. Indeed, he employed even more tricks than we have yet seen. He no longer says: 'Tamar, the sister of Absalom, my brother', but: 'Send me Tamar, my sister, that she may make me two cakes, so that I may eat from her hand'.

We ought to remember what I have recently been pointing out, that those who are given over to evil would like to hide themselves and disguise the fact. To keep their corruption from being known, they will run around all over the place, but what will their subterfuges and evil tricks finally gain them? They are caught red-handed. Was it not a childish quibble when Amnon said to Jonadab: 'Tamar, sister of my brother'? Why did he speak in that way? Because he thought that he was covering up his evil, or at least, greatly lessening it. Thus, we can see how God mocks the trickery of poor wretched souls who have totally abandoned themselves, but still hope to disguise their evil, and flee from paying God their fare by travelling down twisting byways and thus keeping from coming to account. Now Amnon thought that he had hidden his wicked intent very cleverly by saying: 'Tamar, the sister of my brother, Absalom'. But later, he had to uncover himself entirely by saying to David: 'My sister, Tamar'. In this way, we can see how God mocks such people. There is no alternative to walking always in integrity. Even though Amnon's plans had been carefully laid, this word 'sister' should have broken up this wicked passion hiding in his heart, like a tumour which ought to have been cut out so that he could be cleansed and purged of its infection. If (I believe) he had carefully thought of the word 'sister', he would have been so deeply touched by remorse that it would have stopped him from going any further. He ought to have said: 'O my sister, O my sister, I who am your brother' – if he had thought of that, it is certain that God would have given him grace, that he could have conquered this dreadfully wicked corruption. But what happened? He forgot himself, and pushed away, as far as he could, any consideration which could have held him in check.

This warns us to fight against all such temptations. If we begin thinking about something which could cause us to consider the moral consequences of our actions, do we profit from it? In what way? When we are tempted to fornication, and God sends us a good thought, how will we use it? We can say the same thing about theft, and every other vice. Let us bear in mind that 'this is accursed', and conclude: 'If I do this, am I an abomination to God?' For this is the goal to which the Law leads us, to flee evil and to pursue good. If that thought enters our memory, we should immediately make a shield out of the will of God (Eph. 6), and arm ourselves with prayer in order to break down the cursed temptation, which is doing its uttermost to drag us down. But in fact, we use it in a totally opposite way. For when some good thought comes into our mind, instead of using it as a true and constant desire to resist evil, we would rather lay it aside, and hope that it will remain dead, so that the temptation can sweep over us as if there were nothing to hold it back, just like a river overflowing its banks. This is exactly how we act.

That is also how Amnon acted. He gave himself even greater licence to do evil by using this pretext: 'Tamar, sister of Amnon', so that the evil did not come directly before him to shame him into considering God. But in the end, when he wanted to cloak his fornication, then he 'cut his throat' and no longer said: 'Tamar, sister of Absalom', but: 'Tamar, my sister'. Although God constrained him to speak like this to wake him up, in fact it only resulted in hardening him, for the devil had such control of him that he did not know any more about kinship than a dumb animal. Hence, as I have said, when God gives us some good thought, let us put it to good use as soon as possible, and not wait for the devil to get the best of us while we are preoccupied. So much, then, for this point.

When it says that Tamar came and that David sent her to Amnon, although David could not be blamed for this, and even though he was certainly entirely innocent, we can see how subtle the devil is. He pops in as soon as he finds a breach, just waiting for the door to be opened. Indeed, he knows how to enter without being invited, just asking for a little crack. This is a warning to us that when we have made a good resolution, we must do all we can to keep from changing it, out of fear of giving the devil an opening. Although we are on our guard, he will still find enough leeway. For instance, here was a girl whose chastity was carefully guarded. There was no means of access to her. Her brother could not openly admit the wicked plot which he had conceived in his heart. In short, here was David, who had guarded his house prudently as a good father and as a true king. But even so, notice how he was suddenly surprised. Although he had worked so faithfully in looking after his family, his poor daughter experienced disaster, and he even gave her over with his own hands, without realising it.

Hence, let everyone pay very careful attention to their own situation. Those who wish to safeguard the honour of their house will sometimes seriously ruin it, even though they are quite vigilant in doing good, for it only takes a day, or even a minute, to reverse what they have faithfully carried out for one or two, or even ten years. Hence, the example which we are given here should instruct us, so that we may be on our guard, and may give no opportunity to Satan to find any unguarded breach to enter, but rather close the gap against him, as far as we can do so. This is (I believe) good instruction which we should carefully put into practice – if, in fact, we are wise. But in actual fact, we see that it is much more likely for people to give themselves licence. Now how many husbands are there – I am not talking about somewhere far off, but in this very city – who would like there to be dances! Now what does such a request mean, if not that they are wanting to open a bawdy house, which are seen around here only too often? That is the real reason that there are husbands who would like their wives and daughters to dance. Why? So that they can fornicate, which means that they will go to perdition, and receive perpetual shame. Even though we can see that fornication is forbidden both before God and man, how many people, in fact, are there who go to all lengths for their wives and daughters to be in style? Yet we know that this kind of thing tempts people to fornication. Thus, it is obvious to me that they are ultimately wanting to be pimps for their wives, and along with them, they must want to be covered with an awful shame that there is nothing that they could ever do to blot it out.

Hence, we really have to remember the lesson which is shown to us here; that is, that we must always maintain good self-discipline most carefully, not by fits and starts, but with enough perseverance to repel the devil all the time. Thus, after he has tried to break through, first on one side and then on the other, he will be unable to surprise us, however he tries. We have seen earlier that Bathsheba was eyed by David when she was taking a bath, and this was the cause of his seducing her, although he had not planned it. What will happen when we voluntarily cast ourselves into Satan's nets? Will God not rightly permit them to strangle us? Thus, it is even more important for us to be guarded on every side, since the devil seeks nothing else than to have us for prey. So much for this point.

Now it says that Amnon wanted to force his sister, and that she resisted; but the situation was such that she was, in fact, violated by force. Wanting to avoid this, she pointed out: 'My brother, you must not come to this, for this unworthy act ought not to be done in Israel, and you would be considered shameful in Israel' (2 Sam. 13:12–13). It is true that the word sometimes implies 'folly'; but this translation would be entirely too mild. Hence, it is taken here to mean 'unworthy act', as we have already seen. She said further that if he asked her in marriage from his father, 'he would not refuse it'.

Now there is a question here. How is it that Tamar said that she would be given to her brother? For that was not legitimate according to the Law (Lev. 18:9). When the Jews have to resolve a question which is contrary to their belief, they always immediately invent a lie, and drag in a thousand allegories; this is what they have done with this passage. They say that Tamar was conceived in fornication by David, and that he had found his mother, who was a beautiful woman, and had raped her and had this daughter by her, and then also that he had had Absalom by her! And who revealed that to them? On what sort of occasion do they drag in these kinds of dreams? It is when they cannot very easily disentangle a question that they disguise the thing which they cannot resolve, not finding it hard to devise a few ways of escape! They think that they have gained a great deal by the claim that Tamar was the outcome of an adulterous relationship, and that this will alleviate the difficulty. It is the typical custom of these forgers that after they have thoroughly gone through all their dreams and have not been able to come up with anything, they find some frivolous excuse to break the impasse, and never speak the truth.

However, in actual fact, Tamar could certainly have referred the matter to the will of her father, clearly knowing that he would not be unaware of the illegality of the incest, but she was not well enough instructed to have been able to figure this out.

In fact, what she did is far too common among men. Even when we sincerely wish to avoid an evil, we often fail at some point. On the other hand, it turns out to be extremely difficult for us to be guided by the Spirit of God so that we exercise prudence in everything and in every way. For as I have said, we may persevere well at one point or another, but when it comes to the third or fourth time, we fail; and we should all recognise this weakness in ourselves. We clearly know how to say: 'That is bad; one must be careful of it', but then we are surprised that we have fallen into another sin. In short, whatever prudence we may possess, it is only partial, unless God supplies what we lack. That is how it was with Tamar. She saw that incest was a wicked thing, and that it would be absolutely dreadful to do such a thing in her father's house against her will. She knew all these things. But then she referred the matter to the counsel of her father, as if her father were above the Law. Now that is where her counsel was only good in parts.

Be that as it may, let us carefully remember what is pointed out here and prepare ourselves so that the devil will not be able to surprise us. Let us also benefit from this chastisement given to David. He had given himself far too much liberty – that is, endlessly and unceasingly taking such a large number of wives. Thus, the appropriate salary and dividend was returned to him: God punished him. Above all, let us recognise that this threat of Nathan's did not fall to the ground (2 Sam. 12:10), and learn from that not to provoke God to wrath, but to keep ourselves under such careful control that our bodies and souls may be dedicated to him in total chastity.

Now let us prostrate ourselves before the majesty of our good God, recognising all our sins, praying that he will mercifully receive us, and strip us of every carnal lust, so that we may not be left to our own devices of hiding ourselves and turning away from him. But instead, may we be consecrated to him (Rom. 12:1), and our eyes, our ears, our feet, our hands, and all our senses be attentive to seek out and receive his perfect will, so that we submit ourselves to it and are renewed more and more by it, trusting ourselves to his justice. May we thus conform ourselves to it so that we may battle with an invincible determination against all assaults thrown against us by Satan and by our own sins. And may he bestow this grace not only upon us, but upon all peoples and nations of the earth . . .

42

*The Obligation to Punish Evil**

Now after Amnon had violated Tamar, he hated her with a greater hatred so that the hatred with which he hated her, was greater than the love with which he loved her. Hence Amnon said to her: Get up, go away. And she responded to him: This is not right; this evil of putting me out is greater than the other which you have done to me. He did not want to listen to her, but called his servants who served him, and said: Throw her out now away from me . . . (2 Sam. 13:15–25).

We have already seen the very sad story of Tamar being raped by her own brother. This brought great disgrace on the house of David. But in this, God was beginning to chastise him because of the licence which he had taken in seducing someone else's wife (2 Sam. 11:4). It is also true that this was not all, because we shall see how God later executed the sentence which he had pronounced, that David's very own wives were raped by his son (2 Sam. 12:11). But here already was part of his 'salary', that his daughter should thus have lost her honour. However, next came a much more outrageous act: Absalom revenged the outrage done to his sister by killing his brother Amnon. So on the one hand, the house of David was like a bawdy house, and then on the other, like a den of thieves, with one brother cutting the throat of the other!

Before coming to a conclusion, let us carefully note the points which are covered here. It says that Tamar, seeing that she was raped, wanted to remain with Amnon, her brother. Now in

*Monday, September 7, 1562.

that, there is no doubt that she could not see clearly, for though the evil had been committed, it was still not right for her to persist in it. Such a marriage could not be legitimate according to the Law of God (Lev. 18:6). Then the very order of nature itself would have opposed her being married to her brother, for although they had two different mothers, it was enough that they were both descended from David. Here were a half-brother and sister, so they could not be married to each other. Now if incest had been committed, it ought to have been recognised as evil, but it was necessary for each one individually to humble themselves before God. In wanting to persist, she clearly showed that she was badly taught in the Law of God, and secondly she showed that she was more concerned about her own reputation than she was about what was legitimate for her. That is how it is with the majority of those who have fallen, for they do not have great remorse, causing distress over their offences, but rather they are tormented by considering that they have fallen into public disgrace.

Hence, let us learn that if something evil happens to us, we are not to be over-concerned about our reputation, but we are to think of coming before God, and appearing there, to render account. If we are just trying to be exempted from any public disgrace, it is a sign that our eyes are blindfolded in relation to God, and that we are not concerned in the least about his judgement. The example of Tamar, therefore, instructs us that if we fall into some disgrace, we must not forget the main issue because of a secondary consequence. That is to say, our senses should be elevated above the world, so that we think about the fact that God is a just Judge and nothing is hidden from him, and that even if our evil is buried out of sight of mortal creatures, still in the end we must be called before his judgement seat, where our sins will be punished, and we will receive the precise condemnation that we deserve because of them. Now that is one point.

Thus, though she was wrong to do so, Tamar certainly felt that she would have to be justified by her brother taking her in marriage. This shows us how people actually do themselves harm with useless attempts to cover up sin. Marriage is a sacred thing, and so to abuse it is like profaning the Law of God, which is equivalent to sacrilege. Now here was Tamar, who was horrified at having been raped by her brother, but thinking that everything would be repaired, or at least hidden, as a result of the cover that this marriage would provide. But on the contrary, this would actually be twice as bad. Even so, she said that her brother was more wicked for driving her away and not wanting her than he was for violating her. Now if you compare one to the other, it is obvious that evil which continues unchecked is always greater and more excessive. If a man commits fornication but then recognises his offence, and so abstains from that evil, it is not as wicked as if he persists, and goes from bad to worse. So Tamar was blind at this point and we should not be surprised at that, because hypocrisy easily wins when we have not considered God.

In fact, that is why David, speaking of the remission of sins, advises us that we must be without guile and without fraud. He says: 'Blessed is the man whose sins are pardoned' (Psa. 32:1), for it is in this that our whole salvation consists. Now since people would like to make themselves believe that God is appeased towards them, they do nothing but make a slight frown when they have committed some misdeed, and think that they are reconciled without repentance. That is why David clearly added that 'the spirit must be purged from guile' and falsehood (Psa. 32:2). Now by that, he did not mean the kind of trickery that we use when we are fighting one another, but he was speaking of that kind of hypocrisy with which sinners put themselves to sleep, by succumbing to self-flattery, and becoming entangled in it, so that their conscience is as good as dead.

That is how it was with Tamar. As we have seen, as long as she thought that her public embarrassment could be blotted out, it was all the same to her; it did not greatly matter to her whether what God had judged in his Law was actually carried out or not. She was prepared for the whole matter to be dropped as long as she would not be blamed in public. Hence, she tried to use marriage as a false cover-up, thus making the offence which had been committed twice as bad. That is, she was motivated only by superficial appearances when she said that

Amnon was committing a greater evil in chasing her away than he had done in raping her. It was as if she were saying that it was a greater sin for him not to persist in his evil than it was when he gave himself over to offending God by that raging lust which had set him on fire.

As I have said, we must pay even closer attention to ourselves. Especially when we have fallen into some sin, let us take time for careful consideration, and even turn our senses away from this world, so that we can think of God. In this way, let each one of us learn to prosecute his own case and condemn himself, that is, according to the Law. Then, let us realise that God has not spoken unnecessarily, so that as we begin to understand how he judges, we will see that our condemnation is already written and registered, and be appalled. This summarises what we have to remember on this point.

Now it says next that she took 'dust and cast it on her head and tore her dress' – that is, a long 'gown which was of many colours'. It adds that the 'daughters of the king were dressed like this when they were virgins' (2 Sam. 13:18–19). That custom meant that virgins were more splendidly dressed; and because it could not have been a decent thing for married women, it specifically says that the daughters of kings were clothed like this 'while they were virgins'. Now when Tamar saw that her virginity had been taken from her, she tore this gown, which she had as a testimony of her chastity. She threw dust on her head, as was commonly done, for people in anguish customarily did this. People followed the custom of throwing dust on their heads in order to show their repentance and humility, especially when some calamity occurred, and they felt the wrath of God. It was a ceremony intended to humble oneself and to show that one was in extreme anguish. That is what Tamar did. It says, moreover, that 'she put her hands on her head' (2 Sam. 13:19), as people do when they wish to cry out in lamentation. This is how she did it: 'she cried out', so that everyone might know the violence which she had suffered. She thought that this would cause people to know that she had been corrupted by her brother, without having consented to it. If she had not given any sign of it, people would have judged that she had been in agreement with him.

The sum total of all this is that she wanted to declare to everyone that she had been violently taken by force, and that she had not consented to evil. We still see how she was more concerned about her honour than about her conscience. Now it is true that we ought to do good before men to avoid any scandal, just as St Paul exhorts, giving himself as an example (1 Cor. 10:32f.). For if we do not take into account how people judge us, there will be many people who will use that as an excuse to corrupt themselves. We must, therefore, walk in such a way as to be a good example to all and so that our life may shine forth in order to demonstrate the way to serve God. Nevertheless, that consideration must not dominate us in such a way that we no longer think of God. We must, therefore, balance our reputation with our conscience, so that we are always more concerned to walk with integrity before God – and have the testimony borne to the fact that we live prudently – than to be held in good repute among men. Now Tamar did it all backwards, for she kept on wanting both the mighty and the insignificant to know that her brother had raped her, and that she had not consented. Yet where was God and his justice? These were, so to speak, asleep, for she was content with squatting in her filth and being the wife of her brother! In this way, she reversed the whole order of nature. She wanted to pervert the sanctity of marriage; she wanted to persist in this evil to the very end.

This gives us all the more reason to remember the lesson which we have already shown: that is, to behave so well in public that we are not involved in scandal, but nevertheless to prefer to suffer complete ignominy, if need be, rather than have a bad conscience before God. For we cannot avoid people wrongly blaming us from time to time. We must carry on, as St Paul says, 'in good repute and in disgrace' (2 Cor. 6:8). We must be so strong that if men speak evil of us and deprecate us for having done good, we may not be corrupted by their talk, but bear it all patiently. But the main thing is that we call on God to be witness of our integrity. In time, he will surely know how to deliver us from any shame. Although men may be against us and judge us, in the end God will be our surety. We must call on him to do this, as in the example that Jeremiah gives us (Jer. 15:15ff.; 20:7ff.; 26:7ff.), when he was, as it were, torn in pieces, and people were speaking evil of him. People were calling him a deceiver, a rebel, and were charging him with every disgrace possible to think of. 'Now my surety is in heaven', he replied. 'I call upon God as witness; may he give testimony that the words which I am announcing to you contain the truth.'

That is how we must do it, so that if we are trodden underfoot; if people spit in our faces; if men vomit out every possible vituperation against us, we may call on God as our surety, as long as we have walked properly before him. Now this is the main thing. The second is that we must shut our mouths against any evil speaking, and avoid giving any opportunity to people who are seeking to criticise us. However, above all let us be careful of being so influenced by what men could think and say that we forget the judgement of God before which we must appear. So much, then, for this point. Then, when it comes to showing signs of repentance if ever some evil happens to us, let us endeavour to repent before God rather than before men. It is true that if we have done evil, we surely ought to proclaim publicly that the wrong distresses us, and ought to humble ourselves by making confession of our failure, for the example and instruction of our neighbours. But still, God should know about our tears and groans more than mortal creatures, since nothing can be hidden from him, and it is his office to search out the most hidden secrets. This is another point which we should remember from the example of Tamar.

Now it says that Absalom said to Tamar: 'Do not torment yourself, it is your brother; drop the matter!' Yet he still not only kept the offence in his heart, planning to avenge it, but he was not able to hide that he hated Amnon, although 'he said not a word, either good or evil' (2 Sam. 13:22). Here we see how Absalom consoled his sister by saying something which was hypocritical. For when he said to her: 'It is your brother', it seems that he was wanting to induce her to forgive him for that offence, because of their kinship, as though he were saying: 'Whom will you blame? It is true that Amnon has seriously wronged you but, even so, he is your blood; he is truly your brother. You must, therefore, forget all this, and make the best of it. If it were some stranger, you would have far more reason to be angry about it. What else can you do? What will you gain if you wage mortal war on him?' Now that is how Absalom gave the excuse of kinship to induce his sister to pardon the offence which Amnon had committed. But what he said was totally hypocritical, for was not Amnon just as much his brother also? So why did he continue hating him?

Now through this, we ought to learn to speak sincerely when it comes to consoling those who are sad and perplexed. It is never proper for one man to console another, unless he has true compassion. One must speak frankly and from the heart, otherwise there is no compassion or kindness. Let us, therefore, carefully remember that whenever it comes to exhorting those who are afflicted to be patient, and of diminishing the sadness of those who are mourning, we ought to speak sincerely, and not use empty rhetoric, which is what most often happens. For when someone is vexed, I fail to consider how I would like someone to treat me if I were in such a state. So it does not matter to me what I bring up, as long as I put on a good appearance of consoling the other person. In short, when it comes to exhorting one another to be patient, we go about it ritualistically, and not based on truthfulness or what is most appropriate. Hence, if we want to exercise this office properly, let us learn to begin examining ourselves and take the Word of God for our rule so that we may not go in the opposite direction and be lost. Let not only our mouth speak, but also our heart, and altogether let us act totally differently from Absalom. He should have first instructed himself, and then his sister, but for his part, he was nursing a mortal hatred, which poisoned his thinking and led him to conceive the murder which he later committed. Yet he claimed to show his sister Tamar that she must pardon everything, since she could not take vengeance on her own brother. Here is another point which is worthwhile noting.

After that, it says: 'He did not speak to Amnon either good or evil, because he hated him' (2 Sam. 12:22). Now it is quite true that he did have just cause to take vengeance – that is, humanly speaking. But even so, God still commands us to love our enemies, and return them good for evil (Matt. 5:44; Rom. 12:21). Thus, Absalom did not have to put on an act that was different from what he was thinking, but although he had been extremely provoked, God wanted to lead him to the position where he was to abstain from all vengeance, for there was no excuse for it. Therefore, when someone has injured us, we must always remember that God is the Judge over us. When he afflicts us for our sins, or on the other hand, when he simply wants to take control of us, let us conquer all our passion and submit ourselves to whatever he commands us.

Therefore, when someone has injured us in some way, if we want to be victorious at this point – by refraining from all vengeance – let us note, in the first place, that God is our Judge in this matter, and that we never receive any injury from the hand of man, without it proceeding ultimately from him as a just chastisement. When we recognise this, then we shall have occasion to lower our eyes, which will effectively serve to calm that rage which otherwise would inflame us. When someone has done us some wrong, we would immediately like to attack them. But if we consider carefully that God has moved his hand, wanting to chastise us for our own faults, then we will be beginning to pacify our violent anger. So this is the point so far.

But there is another point also: that is, that God wants to show that he is master and has total superiority over us, and that he commands us that it is our duty to fight against such passions until they are subjugated; that is to say, until they are obediently submitted to him, and until we are like obedient captives to him. Therefore, when I feel passions within myself that are excessive and violent, like boiling water which is foaming over, then I must renounce my rights and forget the injuries which have been done to me. Now in this way, God is wanting to show that I do not belong to myself, but that I am his, and that he must gently control all my emotions. So (as I have said) this gives us reason for fighting against ourselves in order to be on our guard, especially when we are tempted to avenge ourselves, and 'cast fire down their throat', as they say.

Beyond that, we must remember the admonition of St Paul that 'our battles are not against flesh and blood' but against the powers of the air, and against our spiritual enemies (Eph. 6:12). When men do us an injury, they are motivated by Satan; he is their guide and their master. Therefore, let us keep in mind our ultimate enemies, so as to be on guard against them. Suppose that a man comes up to me to kill me, and strikes me. When I become aware of the evil, after I have been wounded, I will not be angry with the sword so much as with my enemy who used it. For the sword did not have any evil desire to wound me; so therefore, I have to turn to the enemy. Here let us learn not to be like dogs, tormented by someone throwing stones at them! They pay no attention to the hand throwing the stones, but tear at the stone! Let us learn from St Paul that our fight is not with mortal creatures. It is true that we can clearly see our enemies in this battle, but let us be principally concerned with the devil who is driving them, so that we can arm ourselves with all the forces and weapons offered to us by the Word of God for gaining the victory against such a powerful enemy (Eph. 6:13ff.). Hence, when someone has given us occasion to want to claim revenge, let us learn to be patient, and not completely lose control. This, to summarise, is what we should remember.

Now we should be even more determined to follow this doctrine when we see what happened to Absalom (2 Sam. 12:13ff.). For the space of two years, he nursed the hatred which he had conceived, until he at last spat out his venom, and executed the vengeance which he had conceived in his heart. In all this, we can see what St Paul is pointing out to us: it is that 'we give place to the devil' when 'the sun goes down on our wrath' (Eph. 4:26). It is true that, according to Paul, when we become suddenly angry, we offend God. We have long been far too guilty of this kind of behaviour. But we nurse this wicked emotion; it dominates our hearts and the sun goes down on it, and then the devil takes possession of us. But we need to get rid of everything which can be used to incite us to vengeance. For there is no-one who does not have a horror of submitting himself to the devil. If someone asks the most dissolute people, 'Would you want the devil to be your master?', it is certain that they would respond 'No!' and detest the very idea. Now St Paul tells us that when we allow any hatred to lurk in our hearts, we are submitting ourselves to the devil, and casting ourselves into his bonds, so that he holds us there as captives, and as slaves under his tyranny. This is shown to us, as clearly as in a mirror, in the person of Absalom. For his hatred of his brother Amnon, because of the injury he had done to him, brought on an even greater evil; and the devil, having found his nest there, stirred him up even more until he had completed his wicked enterprise.

For when it says that 'he was not speaking to his brother Amnon either good or evil' (2 Sam. 13:22), this was to show that he did not hide his anger. It would have been a greater sin if he had put on a good appearance. However, he openly showed his hatred for him, and since he wanted everyone to know it, there is no doubt that he wanted to prove to the public how brave he was by his rude actions. Absalom was undoubtedly motivated by the same kind of ambition that often dominates men. For if someone who has been provoked acts decently towards his enemy, people will accuse him of being obsequious and having a servile spirit rather than the courage of a real man. That is how people judge those who act generously and 'swallow' injuries. We see how the great of this world put on a severe frown when someone angers them; they wear a furious expression; they just look straight ahead, and want everyone to see it. They applaud themselves over this kind of behaviour as if it were a great virtue. That is how Absalom acted. He wore a sad face; he did not want people to perceive that his sister had been raped, but to say the least, he was vexed over it in his heart, and disdained the one who had offended him in this way. But what happened next? It only kindled the fire even more, for he cast himself even more deeply into the hatred in his heart.

So let us learn not to nurse our vices, lest we give place to the devil. For he already has too much advantage over us without our relaxing control over our emotions. Thus, in this matter of vengeance, let us be careful not to gratify ourselves in it, or flatter ourselves, but rather, if someone has angered us, let us fight until our wicked desires for vengeance are put to death. It is true that merely putting on a good appearance amounts to nothing if hatred remains rooted in us. For 'he who hates his neighbour in his heart' (as St John says in his canonical letter) 'is already a murderer' (1 John 3:15). Note that it says 'in his heart'. When we regard our enemies with malice, even though we do not show any other sign that we are angry with them, we will not escape becoming murderers if there is venom inside us. Thus, while it certainly is meaningless to put on a good appearance, even so, we are always just asking people to tempt us and spur us on further, whenever we actually want them to know how offended we are at having been provoked. This serves to take away all our feeling and apprehension of the judgement of God. When we make virtues out of vices, are we not manifestly despising God? Thus those who, because of foolish ambition, would like to show that they resent (as they say) the evil which has been done to them are acting as though they wanted to be the ones who could grant themselves approval and attribute to themselves the vengeance which belongs to God alone.

To summarise, let us remember that if we have suffered some injury or disgrace, we must forget the original evil, especially so that we will not hate our enemies, although we may feel justified in doing so. On the contrary, let us break off anything that could incite us to further evil; let us not 'cut wood to build the fire higher'! Hence, let us attempt to be reconciled with our enemies, so that we may avoid that pride which will cause us to be even more embittered. Experience shows too often that it not only nurtures hatred, but that it actually increases it to the highest degree. Whenever I have an enemy, and I deliberately attempt to show how angry I am with him, then I am continually tempting myself more and more. That is how we make two devils out of one. Seeing, therefore, that the devil wins over us, let us learn to remove all his opportunities. By forgetting the injuries that people have done to us, let us endeavour to return good for evil. It is not enough that we abstain from evil-doing, but we must busy ourselves in doing good to those by whom we have been injured. Because this is difficult and repugnant to our senses, let us learn to turn over control of ourselves to God. And as I have already stated, when he brings us to this test, let us attempt to hold ourselves back, and to submit to his Word.

On the other hand, it says that 'David having heard these things was vexed over them' (2 Sam. 13:21). Here was another great scandal. For he was king, and at the very least he should not have allowed such a deed to go unpunished. If someone claims that he was sparing his son, yes, indeed that is true, but this excuse will be useless before God, and it is certain that for the king to behave like this was twice as bad. For if he had been a private man and had spared his son, it would have been somewhat excusable; but when he was king and ought to have maintained equality in justice; when he ought to have punished all corruption and every evil deed which had been committed, but yet spared his son, his house then became a testimony to the fact that he did not punish rightly or with sincerity. Afterwards, his house became a place where thieves and fornicators were nurtured, whereas it should have been the safeguard of the faithful, and provide a retreat and residence for those who were supposed to be employed in the keeping of the Law and of all justice and uprightness. But now its royal dignity served to hide such a detestable offence committed against God. Was there any equity in that?

Now there are some who would like to excuse David on another pretext, that is, that he was not able to punish his son Amnon because he clearly knew that the evil was proceeding from himself, and that he was the chief author of it, so that, instead, he was supposed to groan, knowing that the decree of God made it happen. Yes, indeed, he was involved, but since God had not demoted him from his throne, and since his sin had been blotted out, he ought to have shown signs of repentance in this area. When a man has failed, it is true that without special grace he cannot be a competent judge of the evil which others have committed. But if he is forgiven the evil, he ought to have even more ardent zeal, and show fruit of his repentance. Therefore, David should not have tolerated, in the least, Amnon's committing such a despicable crime. Instead, he should have thought: 'I happened to seduce someone else's wife, and the adultery which I committed has brought me great evil in that I have been a murderer, and a traitor, as it were, to the people of God. Now here is my son who has committed such a repugnant act, which is condemned by the Law of God. If I tolerate it, what sort of example will I give people, when they see that in the royal house there is a fornicator, and also that there is a murderer who remains unpunished? Surely I ought to fear that such a crime may come back on me.'

In other words, David ought to have foreseen the evil, and even if he had not condemned his son to death, still he ought at least to have subdued his body; he ought to have held him in prison and in stocks – either for a time or for life. It does, indeed, say that he was vexed over it (2 Sam. 13:21), but this was not sufficient to excuse him before God. Let us note this point carefully, for it is certain that David was given a sentence of condemnation here for not having punished the misdeed of his son. Now it was not that he applauded him, or that he approved him, but that he was lax and was not as severe or stringent as he should have been. Therefore, this was David's sin.

Now we are taught in this passage that it is not enough for evil to distress us, but that we should also correct it, or at least make an effort as far as we are able. We must (I say) exterminate the evil and, indeed, force ourselves to do that. We will not be let off for saying: 'I wish it had not been done; I am perplexed over it; it distresses me'. When we have made all these beautiful excuses, it is still certain that we will not avoid standing condemned before God. Above all, fathers are instructed here. When they see that their children have done wrong, it is not enough to be angry, but they should use whatever correction is necessary for the child to be brought back to the right path, and see that they have no further opportunity to let themselves go astray, by keeping them under control.

Well, this all points to the responsibility of fathers, but magistrates at the same time are given their lesson here. Since David was king and it was God who had made him sit on the seat of justice, and handed him the sword, he ought to have punished evil-doers justly, and not have spared his son. Yes, he was perplexed over it. But what of that? This was not carrying out the duty to which he was called, nor performing his office as he should have done. Hence, when a man is in a position of justice, let him try – insofar as he is able – to reprimand crimes and scandals, and let him know that it is not enough simply to be angry about them. It is, of course, true that there is some virtue in merely detesting evil. For instance, a father who is displeased with the evil which his children commit is not as wicked as one who readily accepts their wrong-doing. But even so, the courage of a man who is obliged to uphold justice must not (I say) melt away, so that when he has made some semblance of having repaid the evil-doer, he thinks that he has done enough. Now this, in summary, is what we have to remember.

In fact, what follows this story shows that David was chastised as he deserved for not punishing Amnon. If David had done his duty, he could have prevented the horrendous homicide which took place; the wrath of Absalom would have been appeased. If he had seen Amnon condemned – in prison for life, or suffering some other punishment – even though he was still wicked, Absalom's vengeance would, in fact, have been put to death. If our enemies are afflicted, however, it may be that we forget the injuries which once irritated us because we are ashamed of 'fighting against a dead dog', as they say. Now here was David, who could have appeased his son if he had carried out his duty. But when he did not perform his office, and left evil unpunished, it was the same as putting the noose around Absalom's neck, as if to say: 'Avenge yourself; since I am the king and want to enjoy myself, I shall be lazy and let you do it'. That is how he caused the murder which Absalom committed, and roused the wrath of God against himself for not having punished his son.

This will often happen to people who find it easy to grant a pardon, for they prefer to spare people with a foolish kind of mercy: 'Oh well, if he has done wrong, he will correct himself'. But the whole matter remains written down before God, and so the one who has thus been spared, and not been given the whip, will have to be led to the gallows before everyone. People like this, who do not want to punish minor faults, in fact amass even greater condemnation on their head, because they see many examples of this every day. Although it may seem that the matter has slipped away, God is still angry. Suppose, for instance, that there is some poor criminal who is going to be led to punishment and death because he has deliberately fallen into sin. He ought to have been punished for many faults for which he was pardoned instead; and since no-one corrected him, he piled up an enormous burden of guilt, so that now God wants to reveal the laxness of those who were supposed to have charge of him. Hence, many people flatter themselves for the friendship that they bear towards those who have done wrong. Thus, those people will be the cause of the others' ruin, and yet the evil will return on the head of those such as magistrates, who have been too easy in offering pardon, by sparing criminals or closing their eyes and stopping their ears in order not to see or hear, tacitly assuming: 'It is quite certain that God will perform his office effectively, without people meddling with it'. But later, they will receive their wages, for they will have to be confounded along with the delinquent whom they had desired to tolerate and spare from correction. Let us, therefore, learn this lesson, so that we will attempt to remove evil, and not cover it over, lest it grow even more. Rather, let us avoid the vengeance of God, so as not to experience what happened to David.

Now let us prostrate ourselves before the majesty of our good God, recognising the innumerable faults of which we are guilty, praying him to make us feel them so much that it will serve to make us wait patiently. And may we learn from day to day to strip ourselves of all corruption, and of our carnal lusts and the vanities of this world, so that we may be clothed in his justice, and renewed by his will. Yet may we at the same time show the kind of fruit of repentance that will serve to lead us back to the right path, which we had rejected, and by and by attract others to it. May he not only bestow this grace upon us, but upon all peoples and nations of the earth . . .

43

*The Murder of Amnon**

When Absalom had strongly pressed him, he did not want to go there, but thanked him. And Absalom said: If you do not come, I pray you let my brother, Amnon, come with me. The king replied to him: Why should he go with you? And Absalom pressed him to let Amnon and all the sons of the king go with him. Now Absalom had commanded his servants . . . (2 Sam. 13:25–39).

We have to pursue this pitiful history of the death of Amnon, which should, however, be instructive for us. For in it, as though looking in a mirror, we can contemplate the truth of God, and see that his threats never fall to the ground. This confirms us in taking his judgements seriously so that we will, day by day, live in awe of him, and keep ourselves from provoking his wrath against us.

Now it says that Absalom was begging David to go to this banquet which he was giving, and that David, excusing himself, said that it would be too expensive for him. Then he requested that at least Amnon might come. David again attempted to avert his vengeance. There is no doubt that he was afraid, because Absalom had not hidden his hatred of Amnon. He was afraid, therefore, that he might cause a disaster in such a gathering, as in fact it later turned out. Yet we can see that he had lost his liberty in that he had to pretend, instead of speaking frankly to his son Absalom, as he should have done. Since the fact that Absalom mortally hated Amnon was very

*Tuesday, September 8, 1562.

well known, David ought surely to have been able to say that he perceived that this banquet was nothing but a thinly veiled opportunity for treason. Even if he had, up till then, spared his son, he could at least have remonstrated with him to get control of himself. In fact, even if he had not been a king, he ought to have spoken in this way in his authority as father. But he covered up the whole matter and did not dare open his mouth to express what was in his heart. Hence, we can see how one evil attracted another, for he should not have allowed his daughter, Tamar, to have been ruined; then, since he had allowed that deed, and had given no punishment for it, he did not even know where he was.

This is how God punishes anyone who does not have sufficient virtue or bravery of spirit to carry out their office. When they have declined to take action and flowed with the stream, as they say, some kind of reversal will happen to them, and then they will be lost, turning hither and thither, unable to find a way out of all their affairs. It is quite true that even when we desire to serve God in utter sincerity, we will face many temptations and the devil will place obstacles before us, so that very often we will not find the way out. Yet everyone who is determined to walk uncompromisingly in their vocation, in the end will not be lacking in counsel. God will extend his hand to them in time of need, and after testing them for a time, will finally look on them in pity and guide them, so that the path will be made straight under their feet, so to speak. But if we are not straightforward in our behaviour, God must pay us the wages that we have deserved; that is, many vexations will come our way, entangling us in many worries from which we will find no means of escape. That is what we have to notice in the person of David, when we see that, although king, he made a ridiculous excuse, saying that it would be too much trouble for Absalom if such a company of people gathered at his expense.

Then again, when it came to whether Amnon should go, all he said was: 'Oh, no, there is no need for it'. He evidently did not dare to uncover the evil which he knew all about, for he could have said: 'I am suspicious of this banquet. I am already aware that for the space of two years you have been declaring vengeance against your brother. You are not reconciled with him now, so what does it mean that you want to have fellowship with him? There is some kind of evil intent here. You are covering up some kind of treason.' David (I say) could have said this, and should have done so, and yet he dared not. Why? Simply because he had not carried out the charge that was committed to him, but had allowed fornication to be committed in his house – indeed, incest – and had allowed such a scandal to remain unpunished.

Nevertheless, we can see how cruel Absalom was in telling his servants that when they saw Amnon joyful in the midst of the banquet, they were to attack and kill him. If a particular quarrel had come up, that would have provided an excuse for someone to have said: 'Absalom was upset'. But now there was nothing to provoke him to evil except this hatred which had lurked for so long in his heart. Amnon suspected nothing, and indeed he would not have joined in the eating and drinking at the banquet if he had perceived anything. When Absalom explained his plans, he certainly knew that Amnon was not thinking of any risks and did not have the least suspicion, which made Absalom's trickery all the more wicked. For what incredible inhumanity was this: to cut a man's throat under the pretext of friendship? How dreadful it was to treat his own brother like this, and then in such company – at a solemn banquet, which was a testimony of the union which ought to have existed between them. And when we consider, on the other hand, that they were born of the same father, whom God had elevated above all others, chosen to be his only king and lieutenant in the world, and officially anointed and consecrated – in the light of all these things, we cannot hear this story without feeling profoundly ashamed.

This warns us to hold down our passions, because when we begin to give ourselves any licence to do evil, the devil enters in and takes possession of us in such a way that we then become blind. Until then, we had felt some remorse; we had been thinking of turning away from the evil thing; but when we are conquered like this by the devil, all our senses are bewitched; godly sentiments no longer control us. Thus the fear of God has ceased to hold us in check and restrain us. Now this is what we must learn from the case of Absalom, when it says that with his senses taken hostage, as it were, he commanded his servants to rush upon Amnon and kill him in the middle of the banquet, at the very table which was the sign of fraternal friendship.

Even the pagans, wanting to foster kindness among one another, have said that the table of a host is sacred. Now this word 'host' can be taken in another sense. It did not apply to those who gave lodging to travellers, but rather when someone took in his friends, they said that the table was like a host. Indeed, they imagined that God was presiding at it, and have spoken of it in that sense. In fact, at all their banquets they mentioned their idols who had access to the assembled company, implying: 'We are joined and united together as members of one body'. If nature had taught this to poor blind folk, who neither knew nor understood what God was or what his Law was, what should have been the case with people who were circumcised from their infancy and nurtured not only with the people of God, but in the house of the king, who was himself such an outstanding prophet? That house should have been a school of all righteousness, and yet in this matter Absalom was forgetting everything which ought to have been engraved on the hearts of men! What we can see here, therefore, is so dreadful and shocking that it is enough to make our hair stand up on our heads! However, the point is that the whole matter is written for our instruction, to teach us to learn to hold down any hatred or bitterness, and prevent our hearts from being puffed up, and above all, that we must not allow any malice to linger in our spirits through our hardness of heart. Thus, when we face such problems, let us show that the devil has not taken possession of us through our grief. So much, then, for this point.

Now we see, on the one hand, the audacity of Absalom, and on the other, how he pretended to a zeal for righteousness and equity when he said: 'Be strong, and be valiant' (2 Sam. 13:28). In doing this, he showed that he was totally out of control. For in the first place, how should we strengthen ourselves other than by doing good? And on the other hand, this word 'valiant' ought to be reserved for virtue. From where does the strength that God gives us come? Most importantly, we do not have it of ourselves, and the word which he uses here is in the book of Solomon; it is a gift of God.[1] So then, if God gives us strength and virtue, for what purpose ought we to ask for it if not to serve him? Similarly, when we need to take courage, what is the purpose of it? Will it be to despise him, and 'lift our horns' against him, or behave like savage animals, just as though we wanted to annihilate his majesty and the power that he has over us? Not at all! But yet we see that Absalom had so completely lost any sense of shame that he abused this noble language when, in fact, he clearly despised God.

Let us learn from this to recognise the gifts of God, so that we always apply them to their proper purpose, and also be very careful not to be insolent or wear a 'face of brass' – so that we no longer discern between good and evil, but apply the gifts of God to all kinds of iniquity, deliberately contaminating them, so to speak. There is no more wicked uncleanness than for us to turn to evil what God has designed for us to put to noble use. Then again, is it not true that all the strength that he gives us is so that we may help one another? When a man runs like this against his neighbour and even against his own brother, where does it all lead? Well, this is one point.

On the other hand, we see how his servants were too feeble. It does, indeed, often happen that when it comes to servants carrying out their duty, they are lax and careless; but when they are supposed to commit some crime, they are the most eager in the world! This evil partly arises from the fact that men are vicious by nature, which is why they will take action more readily when someone wants to involve them in some misdeed! Since they are inclined to evil in themselves, no-one should be surprised by the way they act. But there is also a second reason. When a servant faithfully carries out his duty to his master, he feels that he will get no great credit for having done so. But if he commits one wicked act, he puts his master under obligation to him, and thus holds him captive, so to speak. Someone who has faithfully served according to his job description feels that he

[1]The editor of *Supplementa Calviana* (p. 375, n. 37) suggests that 1 Kings 2:2 could be meant.

has earned his wages – being fed and clothed – and so, then, when he asks for a discharge, he will be told: 'I appreciate what you have done and that will be all'. But if a servant sells his honour to his master, it is quite different. Then he may say to himself: 'My master is a fornicator, I shall be his pimp; he has already disgraced himself by doing this, so I am not bound to him in the same way. If he wants to be strict with me, then in the light of all that I have done, I will have a hold over him, and he will have to act like a cowering dog. Hence, I shall have the advantage over him, and he will not be able to say a word to me, without my having an immediate come-back. I shall keep him under such obligation to me that he will be unable to go in any direction that displeases me.'

Now we must particularly learn what is shown to us here by the Holy Spirit. That is, that people who have some authority are not to abuse it, but should know that what is given to them by God ought to keep them within the limits of the law, so that the superiority which they exercise may always be subject to God's sovereign control. We must always come to the point where every human position of superiority or dignity or degree of honour is in accordance with legal rules, and these ought to fit so harmoniously together, almost like a sweet melody, that the whole matter may cause God to be honoured, as both small and great do him homage together. That is why I have said that any superiority involves subjection, because the more God honours men, the closer he brings them to himself, with the result that they become even more aware that he is above them, and so keep themselves within the limits of the law. So much, therefore, for those who have charge over others.

Now people who are subject to others should learn to obey their masters, but in a way that will never deprive God of his rights. That is why, when St Paul exhorts children to honour their fathers and mothers, he adds this word: that it is to be 'in the Lord' and according to his truth (Eph. 6:1). Then he taught the same thing to servants, that full obedience always involves this exception: God must always be in first place, and man must not be corrupted, by getting into a position where he casts himself against God, or desires to seize his seat – as though he were not specifically indebted to God for having elevated him. Everyone, therefore, who is under someone else's authority must pay careful attention to how they behave. For instance, even a child who has a father who is wicked and contemptuous of God must be alert and vigilant so that he does not allow himself to be corrupted or seduced by paternal authority. Let him remain constantly alert not to throw off the yoke of God. Anyone with the freedom to choose should be very careful not to have a master who corrupts him, but rather who keeps him in the fear of God. Now this, in summary, is what we have to remember.

It says that 'all the sons of the king fled' (2 Sam. 13:29) when they saw the death of their brother, Amnon. I have already mentioned the circumstances of their kinship, which made the deed even more terrible. For here they all were, enjoying themselves, and it was precisely then that 'Absalom spied this opportunity: when the heart of Amnon, he said, would be gay with wine' (2 Sam. 13:28). Not that he was totally drunk, but even when men drink in moderation, their spirits are more free after enjoying a good meal. This actually increased and aggravated Absalom's treason far beyond what I said about the sacred aspect of the table. Since Amnon was invited to it, Absalom should have guaranteed his safety. A host always has responsibility to devote his life to seeing that he does no injury to those whom he has received in his house. Lot clearly referred to this principle when he said to the people in Sodom: 'Now since they have entered under my roof, how can I allow this outrage to be done to them?' It is, of course, true that they were angels of God, but he knew nothing about that. He took them in as guests and would rather have died than allow this outrage to be done to them.

Therefore, what should Absalom have been thinking about when he invited his brother? Let us assume that even if he had renounced any relationship to Amnon because of the injury and disgrace which he had done to his sister, still, consideration for all of his other brothers should have held him back, softened his heart and aborted his plot. For looking around, he could easily have said to himself: 'We are all of one blood, although there are so many children who come from different marriages; still, we have all been begotten by the same father'. Therefore, when he saw a table at the banquet surrounded by relatives, and yet still continued to nurse this malice in himself, without any compunction, until he finally carried it out, it shows us what a brute he was, for this cruelty was more than barbaric.

When it says in the Psalm that it is a pleasant thing to see brethren unified (Psa. 133:1), this is to show that when God calls us to be joined and united by some bond – whether kinship or marriage, or some other human link – it is certain that we are being exhorted to see that coming together like this is an acceptable way of serving God. That is also why two illustrations are added: that it is 'like the dew that descends from the Mount of Hermon', and 'the sacred oil that ran down the face of Aaron, and that flowed down his beard' (Psa. 133:2, 3). These two illustrations imply that, in God's eyes, union is a holy thing, and also that it is the way of holding the human race together, to keep us from being like cats and dogs, clawing one another. Nor are we to be worse than wild animals – who at least do not eat each other up, but love one another and spare one another. I am speaking here of those animals who are not of different species. For a dog will instinctively assault a wolf, and a wolf a sheep. But when animals are of the same species, they love one another, as I have said. However, they do not have any discernment. Where does their fraternity come from unless it is that God is condemning men by the behaviour of animals? We see that Absalom forgot all of this. This should always teach us to be on our guard, so that Satan may not 'dig out our eyes', leaving us so stripped of any human sentiment that we are prepared to abandon ourselves to crimes which are utterly heinous and enormous.

When it says that 'rumour came to David that all his sons were killed' (2 Sam. 13:30), it is not only to tell us of the uproar which took place, for that is quite common. Whenever something like that happens, everyone get excited, and if one man is killed it will seem as though it was a great number! If someone mentions some trouble in a city, it will seem as though it was a whole country! Now this type of confusion is a common occurrence, but the Holy Spirit had a further consideration for our instruction, which was to show us what an extreme trial this was to David, because for a time he thought that all his sons were killed. Now here was the king, sitting peacefully at home. He had children by several marriages – so many of them, in fact, that if four or five of them were dead, there would still be someone to succeed to the crown. But in a moment of time, it looked as though they were all butchered, and that not a single one remained to him, except a detestable murderer who deserved to be obliterated from the world. All this brought terrible anguish to David.

However, all of that was still nothing in the light of what David ought to have been thinking if he compared what had happened to him with the promise of God (1 Chron. 22:9–10). For when he had Solomon, it was revealed to him that he was the one who was elected, and who was supposed to hold the royal seat. That is one point. Then later, it was revealed to him that this kingdom would continue until the coming of our Lord Jesus Christ. It was revealed to him that Solomon was the image of the Redeemer of the world, and that one could not hope for salvation apart from this means. So where was this promise to David now? It was exactly as if God were showing that he wanted to mock not only him, but everyone else, and that there was nothing left for David but condemnation. Now if the truth of God is not permanent, whatever will happen in the future?

David, therefore, had an awful struggle to go through. It was not simply a question of human affection. Here was a king who had lost his large number of children, and then had seen his own son cut his brother's throat. So in addition to the act of incest which we have already mentioned, murder now took place. Thus, a horrendous infamy occurred in his house; an utterly barbaric act which had never been heard of before, that so many brothers should be killed at one blow. It was not only a question of that, but David must also have thought: 'God has mocked me; I see myself tricked here, so what have I gained by having trusted in his promises?' But this had still further ramifications, for everyone else could have been disillusioned as well. There was no hope of salvation except by the promise lodged in Solomon, and yet since his throat had been cut, what had become of the promises of God or any kind of religion now? David could have become very angry, insofar as he was given over to the devil in the first place. If God makes us a promise, and then shows us that we have waited for it to no avail, and that he has mocked us, it is quite certain that religion would have to be overthrown, and all that would remain would be anger and diabolical rage! Here, again, are some of the temptations which David faced.

This shows us that God amazingly upheld him. Even when it pleases God to test us to the limit, let us learn to keep ourselves in his fear. This is very important, for each of us magnifies the troubles which we have, in order to justify our blaspheming God, or becoming so exasperated that we no longer show any measure of self-control or personal moderation. If a father has lost a son and someone comes to console him, he will not bottle up his emotions, but bursts out: 'Yes, indeed, I have good reason for speaking this way. I had a son whom I loved. I had high hopes for him; I had planned something good . . .', and so on and so forth. In short, it seems that we want to make every effort to lift ourselves up against God when he afflicts us. It is the same with a woman who has lost a husband and the husband his wife. Besides our tears and groans, we mix in foolish opinions and cry: 'Oh, I had such prosperity and such respect because of my husband. Things were going so well for us.' On the other hand, the husband may think that God cannot raise him up a wife who can keep things in order; he will come up with so many worthless reasons that it is pathetic!

Let each of us, therefore, carefully examine ourselves, and we will find that we would like to make God believe that he is treating us too hard, and is excessively strict. So we must carefully note this passage, which says that David was being severely tested when he thought that all his children had been killed; that their throats had been cut by their own brother; that he had been bereft of the very son who was supposed to inherit the kingdom and succeed to the throne. But what was worse, he was tempted to think that God was mocking him, and that he could no longer hope for salvation; that there was nothing but confusion in all the promises which had been given to him by the prophet; that all of it was nothing but deception and illusion.

Nevertheless, we can see what he did: 'he tore his clothing and threw himself on the ground' (2 Sam. 13:31). Now this was another sign of humility. Even though those who are overcome with fury throw themselves on the ground and tear their beards and clothing, this was not what David was described as doing. Rather, he was lamenting before God. In fact, no-one could say that he did it like someone who was enraged and furious. In fact, 'his servants kept him company' and threw themselves on the ground to lament and sigh with him. We see, therefore, that David did not go overboard in excessive anger and become furious with God, but that he voluntarily humbled himself. In all this, we can see that he was like some poor broken creature. By tearing his clothes, he showed he was mourning, but yet he demonstrated that he was acting only as someone who was wretched and confused, keeping his mouth closed to keep from murmuring against God. Yet he must certainly have felt that since God had smitten him like this, there was nothing left for him but utter humiliation. Now this is the point in this passage that we need to consider, so that when we pass through the greatest temptations and extreme difficulties, we may have a reason to resist them, and stand firm through them, faithful to the last. Thus, we will not 'raise our horns' to rush against God, but will lament over our sins until it pleases him to enlighten us and relieve our sorrow.

Now it says that the very person who had advised Amnon to corrupt his sister came to console David (2 Sam. 13:32). We have said that he was a man with real perception, but he used it badly when he counselled Amnon to rape Tamar. Anyway, David remained where he was. Someone brought him a report that 'all of the children of the king had not been killed', but 'only Amnon', who had offended Absalom (2 Sam. 13:32–33). This was a quarrel which had been covered over, and had smouldered in secret, so that the fire could not be extinguished – which was why he alone was dead. So then, since Absalom was not at enmity with his other brothers, he was content with avenging himself on the one who was his enemy. David was not satisfied with this, for as I have said, it was only a report until they told him: 'Here are your children' (2 Sam. 13:35). Then he saw them coming to him, and when they were all together 'they all began to lament and weep' (2 Sam. 13:36) – and rightly so, for we are all moved when someone of our own blood is taken from this world. Furthermore, when killing is involved, we react in horror. Now here was the father seeing what had happened, and realising: 'Someone whom I have fathered has killed his brother, who is his blood and mine. Furthermore, he has committed this terrible murder in the presence of all his brothers. This brings defilement which can never be cleansed, so that my house must be held to be the most wicked in the world, because here is a stain which is to pass from father to son. This is something that will have to be known to the end of the world – and I, David, will be humiliated because of it.'

Moreover, there is no doubt that he recognised in it the conclusion of the sentence that Nathan had pronounced to him: 'Blood will not depart from your house' (2 Sam. 12:10). He saw, therefore, that God was punishing him in this for the murder which he had committed against Uriah, and that this deed proceeded from that one. Therefore, when David mourned, it was not only for the wicked deed which Absalom had committed; it was not that he was deprived of his son, but because he knew that his sin was the root of the evil which had happened. It was exactly as though God were holding him there on a scaffold, to disgrace him before the whole world, and were sounding the trumpet to engrave his condemnation permanently in our memory, by bringing before our eyes this second murder which had been committed. Indeed, all the people could have openly said: 'How did it happen that one of the king's sons should have killed another like this? Oh, of course – the father was a murderer himself. God told him that he would be his Judge, and so here now is the execution of that judgement.' So this is how David's confusion was renewed before the whole world.

That is why, also, it clearly states that he 'ever mourned over his son' (2 Sam. 13:37). Now this word 'ever' is not taken to mean his entire lifetime, for that would be a contradiction of the direct teaching of the text, which adds soon after that 'David was consoled over the death of Amnon' (2 Sam. 13:39), because nothing more could be done. Hence this word 'ever' implies that David's mourning continued for some time. This is because when someone mourns, it eventually passes. When someone is in anguish, it still takes time to make them forget the grief, or at least, moderate it. It is quite true that a man who has received some great affliction will regret it all his life. But though that is true, it does not mean that he is so extremely affected by it that he groans and constantly sheds copious tears, and makes all kinds of endless and incessant complaints! Thus, time does moderate that (2 Sam. 13:38). Hence, David's mourning over his son, Amnon, was moderated, so that by the end of three years he had come to terms with his loss. He did not completely lose his grief, but was not continually lamenting. This is the sense that the word 'ever' expresses here. And I have already explained the reason: David was not weeping merely over the death of his son and the disgrace that it had brought him before the whole world, but he lamented and wept over his own sin, and knew that this murder had to be imputed to him, because it was just judgement from God.

Hence, let us learn that whenever God chastises us with his rod, we are not to be grieved because of the evil which it causes us, but because of the root cause of that evil. This point deserves careful attention. No-one, when God strikes them with his rod, will be so unaffected that they will not at least cry out: 'Alas!' and be quite upset. However, let us consider the reason for this. Most people, when they are afflicted, will say: 'Oh, this dreadful evil!' and will not realise that everything comes from the hand of God. There are others (I mean those who have profited the most) who, although they confess that it is God who is afflicting them, do not begin to examine their sins. And yet, they are in such distress when the evil seizes them, that they can only moan. Why is this? Because the evil which they are suffering is making itself felt! But true wisdom (depending on how hard and strong the hand of God is against us) is for us, then, to consider the offences that we have committed, so that we will be displeased about them, and ask pardon from God. When we find that the evil continues, may it serve to make us feel that our offence is so great that God cannot be appeased right away. Now this is what we have to remember when it speaks of the grief that David experienced 'for so long' over the death of Amnon.

To summarise, we can see that true virtue is not in being insensible, or that a man should harden himself when God sends him some affliction, but instead he should humble himself, and after recognising his fault, lament over it in such a way that he will not do wrong in the future. For when God strikes us with his rod, what will it be like if we then act like stones or dead weights, which someone can beat with great hammer blows without their being moved? That is not a sign of constancy, but is more like fighting against God. That is to say, it is obstinate hardness, which (as I have said) implies rebellion. Even if we do not actually change our nature and go on the offensive, still our hardened condition cannot be considered virtuous. What is needed, then? We must openly confess our problem, but then we must go on to deal with our problem in such a way that it causes us to humble ourselves before God. Above all, as I have said, we must not only cry out : 'Alas' when we feel his blows, but we must consider the root cause, and realise that when he afflicts us, his judgements are just and right, and that we are fully guilty before him. Now that is how we must follow David's example.

Now after this, the text says that 'he was consoled over the death of Amnon' (2 Sam. 13:39). This passage can be taken in two ways, for when it says that he was consoled over the death of Amnon, one could say that the fact he could be consoled was evidence that his sorrow had been slight. On the other hand, whenever we lament, we know that it is natural for us to have to come to terms with our loss eventually and for there to have to be an end of our sorrow. Thus alternatively, one could simply say that David was consoled over Amnon's death. That is to say, this death had greatly saddened him, but finally he came to terms with it. Now this does not imply that he had forgotten his own fault, for if that were true, his recognition of it would, indeed, have been entirely too slight. Now Absalom was absent for the space of three years, and before that time was over, David's anger towards him was assuaged. It follows, therefore, that it was not for more than two years that David mourned and was angry with his son, Absalom. Let us note, therefore, that when he was consoled, he did not forget the fault which he had committed, but instead this phrase refers (as we shall see afterwards) to his having forgotten the vengeance which Absalom had taken.

This warns us of how our passions can change, and that although they may have raged for a time, they later calm down. This shows that David did not take seriously enough the evil which had been perpetrated, and thus did not punish it as he should have done, because he was motivated only by human feelings. However, if David had had a zeal for justice, he would have been continually motivated to do his duty. If we really do have a zeal for justice, even though we wander about and are totally lacking in stability, nevertheless, it is quite certain that ten years from now we shall still have the same zeal that we have today. But it says that David's grief over the death of Amnon was appeased. Now this is a testimony that he had no zeal for justice. We could certainly excuse his not having punished Absalom, since he was one of his children. But though that is true, when he could be appeased without Absalom even asking for forgiveness, we can see that from the very beginning he did not have a proper desire to punish evil without respect of persons. Then after that, he hardened himself once more. Why? Because he was a father.

Now it is true that, on the one hand, such fatherly reaction should be a highly esteemed virtue, but on the other hand, it also contains elements of vice. David showed virtue when he had compassion on his child, as on his own body. It is quite true that Absalom thoroughly deserved to have David detest him and never return to him. But in spite of that, because he was a father, he felt that he had to forget that injury, and the love which he had borne towards his daughter, even though that had been shattered and more or less crushed. Nevertheless, his reaction was mixed with elements of vice, as I have said. For if he had had the zeal which he should have had, he would certainly have hated Absalom's crime, not just for a year or two, but ten years later. But in fact, we can see that David received the wages due to his lack of zeal, and that God afflicted him through his own son – all because David had spared him.

This teaches us to turn ourselves over to God, seeing how exorbitant our passions are, because once they have taken us over, we completely lose any discretion. Seeing, also, that our affections are completely unstable, and that our lack of stability always entails some excess and vice; seeing that, on the one hand, we are fragile and pathetic, and on the other, when the devil possesses us, we become hard and completely without restraints, let us learn to turn ourselves over to God. We should especially do so when we see such examples set before us from the house of David, which ought to have been like heaven on earth, with God himself living there! When we also see the temptations which came on David, let us learn to humble ourselves however often God wants to humble us by trying our patience, and let us learn not to lose courage. Let us realise that since this happened to a man whom God loved so much, and who had had such a singular testimony compared to others, we should not find it strange if today we have to pass along the same route – if we (I say) have to persevere with humility through all our afflictions. That, in summary, is how we must benefit from this story, so that if we make the proper application, we will know that such experiences will not be terrible for us, but will be for our salvation.

Now let us prostrate ourselves before the majesty of our good God, recognising the infinite faults of which we are guilty, praying him to make us feel them so much that it may cause us always to call on him, and take our refuge in the grace of his Spirit. Thus, may we be guided and governed in such a way that the devil may not gain entrance to us, and that we may valiantly fight against every temptation, and that all of this may be to glorify this good God, as we submit ourselves to him, and attribute to him the praise that he deserves. May he not only bestow this grace upon us, but upon all peoples and nations of the earth . . .

GENERAL INDEX

To avoid unnecessary repetition, initial letters have been used for names appearing more than once in an entry, e.g. Joab – Abner; death of A.

SCRIPTURE INDEX

In some instances in this index, verse references have been supplied, although the text cites only the chapter.

2 SAMUEL